Marion Shoard is a writer, broadcaster and lecturer. She specialized in environmental affairs for 25 years and is the author of *The Theft of the Countryside*, *This Land is our Land* and *A Right to Roam*. She developed an interest in the care of older people in the mid-1990s when her mother, then in her mid-80s, already suffering from osteo-arthritis and fast losing her sight, fell victim to Alzheimer's disease. Miss Shoard now operates a consultancy in eldercare and campaigns against ageism. She also continues to write and broadcast on environmental affairs.

Other titles in the same series

The Daily Telegraph: Learning and Attention Disorders
Dr William Feldman

The Daily Telegraph: Prostate Disorders
Dr Yosh Taguchi

The Daily Telegraph: Alzheimer's Disease
Dr William Malloy and Dr Paul Caldwell

The Daily Telegraph: Sleep Really Well
Dr Paul Caldwell

The Daily Telegraph: Menopause
Dr Sarah Brewer

The Daily Telegraph

A SURVIVAL GUIDE TO
LATER
LIFE

Marion Shoard

ROBINSON
London

Constable & Robinson Ltd
3 The Lanchesters
162 Fulham Palace Road
London W6 9ER
www.constablerobinson.com

First published in the UK by Robinson,
an imprint of Constable & Robinson Ltd, 2004

ISBN 1-84119-372-0

Printed and bound in the EU

10 9 8 7 6 5 4 3 2

To my mother, Gladys Shoard,
with thanks and love

'The past is a foreign country, but so is old age, and as you enter it you feel you are treading unknown territory, leaving your own land behind. You've never been here before.'

Jan Morris, *Trieste and the Meaning of Nowhere*

Faber and Faber, 2001

Contents

Acknowledgements   xi
Foreword by Dr James Le Fanu   xii
How to Use This Book   xiv
Introduction   xvii

Part One: Growing Older
  1 The Ageing Body   3

  2 Changing Needs   18
       The Body   18
       The Mind   28
       The Spirit   36

Part Two: The Care Machine
  3 State Support   43
       Social Care   44
       The Health Service   55

  4 The Voluntary World   78

Part Three: Staying Independent
  5 Adapting Surroundings   91
       Gadgets and Aids   91
       Incontinence   109

  6 Moving Around   116
       Mobility   116
       Exercise   136
       Falls   145

7 Where to Live   159
    Moving House   159
    Retirement Housing   177
    At Home   201

8 Keeping in Touch   218
    Making Friends   220
    Day Centres   230
    Faith Groups   234
    Animal Magic   238

9 Professional Helpers   244
    Your GP   244
    In the Home   259

Part Four: Care Homes
10 Choosing a Home   311
    Basics   311
    The Selection Process   325

11 The Cost   363
    Fees   363
    Paying the Bills   365
    Spouses and Partners   390

12 Going In   394
    A Trial Stay   394
    Preparing for Entry   394
    The First Few Weeks   400
    Life in the Home   402
    Moving Out   407
    Respite and Intermediate Care   411
    Advice   413

Part Five: Hospitals
13 Treatment   417
    Ageism   419
    Rehabilitation and Other Care (Example: Strokes) 436

14 Your Life in Their Hands   447
    Withholding and Withdrawing Medical Treatment   448

15 Discharge   463
    Living with Continuing Care   474

Part Six: Money
16 State Benefits   481
    Fundamentals   481
    Benefits for All   484
    Benefits for the Needy   491
    Administration and Advice   499

17 Self-help   502
    Private Pensions   502
    Insurance   503
    Living off Your House   505
    Protecting Inheritance   508

Part Seven: Representation
18 Legal and Financial   515
    Granting Enduring Power of Attorney   522

19 Nursing and Other Care   532

Part Eight: Carers
20 A Vital Role   545
    A Statutory Carer   547

21 Practicalities   556
    Carers' Assessments   556
    State Benefits for Carers   568
    Other Calculations   569
    The Main Caring Relative   572

    Conclusion   575

Appendix: Complaints   577
      Complaints about Local Government   578
      Complaints about the NHS   581

References   584
Useful Contacts   606
Index   631

Acknowledgements

I am very grateful to The Authors Foundation for giving me a grant towards the research expenses incurred in this project.

I am also grateful to experts in the field as well as friends who have given me the benefit of their wisdom and experience and also checked parts of the manuscript, in particular Carolyn Adams, Professor Sam Ahmedzai, Luke Clements, Dr David Cohen, Dr Sue Davies, Downs Solicitors of Dorking, Kate Fearney, Sara Friday, Cynthia Heymanson, Di James, Alexis Jay, Margaret McIntyre, Professor Mary Marshall, Professor Peter Millard, Dr Christine Oldman, Judith Torrington, Glenda Watt, Phillip Weaver and Vi Butler, Helen Cherrill and James Player at Age Concern York. Any errors that remain are entirely of my own making.

I should like to express special thanks to my daughter, Catherine Shoard, who has provided much support, not least in visiting my mother regularly but also in helping me to deal with my mother's decline and putting our experience in context. David Cox has again offered much help with this as with my earlier books, talking through ideas as they were emerging and offering suggestions for script amendments; for this I am extremely grateful.

Many thanks to all the staff at Constable & Robinson, particularly Pete Duncan, Josephine McGurk, Sandra Rigby, Pam Dix and Elizabeth Hutchins, and to my literary agent, Charlotte Howard, for their enthusiasm, support and advice.

I am grateful to all the people I have come across on trains and in buses, in day centres, care homes and supermarkets, on street corners and in their own homes who have given me their impressions of the problems and delights of old age. I should also like to thank the many professionals in the eldercare world who have been so generous with their time over the past two years.

Foreword

Marion Shoard's *Survival Guide to Later Life* is an epic achievement: truly comprehensive in scope and radiating good sense. It is almost impossible to imagine how she has managed to so successfully encompass the diverse issues and problems confronting the older age group, and those who care for them. The authority of her knowledge and opinions is grounded in her own personal experience. When Marion Shoard realized her mother would no longer be able to look after herself, her natural reaction was to seek help and guidance from others but this proved surprisingly elusive. To be sure, the various voluntary organizations provided essential information and leaflets, but there seemed to be no one to show her the ropes and guide her through the vast and complex 'system' that is the Health and Social Services.

She discovered there were many avenues down which to travel, many corners to explore for there is no uniform solution for the needs of the elderly person. Rather they are best perceived as part of a trajectory moving from a situation of virtual independence to total dependence, with numerous shades in between. She encountered many difficulties and frustrations which, in retrospect, might have been avoided – and we are now the lucky beneficiaries of her wisdom and experience.

Marion Shoard starts, quite rightly, with the most vital attribute for survivors – their health, before providing a lucid exposition of the many types of provision that are available. This, however, is only part of the story. Just as important are the skills – or dodges – that are necessary to ensure that things happen as they should. This, if anything, is the most substantial challenge of all – as anyone who has had any dealings with social services or institutions of any sort will know only too well. Here Marion Shoard's advice is literally invaluable, brilliantly illustrated by the following telling example of 'what to look for' in choosing a care home – and the importance of the quality of the teabags.

The cook would of course be working within a budget which will be set by the home's proprietor or manager according to the relative priority given to good food and maximum profit. One sure-fire indication of this trade-off is the type of teabag used. It hardly needs saying that the quality of cups of tea or coffee can be terrifically important to residents. As you tour the home with matron you will probably pass through the kitchen. When you are there, look around. What brands of teabag and coffee are used? If you cannot see, ask. If it is a really cheap kind and the resulting beverage is served highly diluted, you can be pretty sure that costs are being kept to a minimum in other areas where the comfort and well-being of resident conflicts with profit: from the choice of lavatory paper to the amount of lighting permitted, the temperature of the communal rooms and whether residents are offered seconds at lunch.

It would be impossible not to have confidence in the opinions and judgement of someone with such a sharp eye which brings us to a further great virtue of her book – how she deals with the vexed question of money. The care of an elderly person is inescapably expensive, and who is going to pay for it, and how, can be a source of personal bitterness and acrimony. There can be no better example of the benefits of knowing the ropes in obtaining the often substantial financial support which is available. Here again Marion Shoard has original and judicious suggestions.

The measure of the significance of her book is that it is difficult to imagine how people ever manage to cope before she wrote her *Survival Guide to Later Life*.

James Le Fanu

How to Use This Book

This is not a book that has to be read from beginning to end (although I hope many people will do so). Perhaps you have grabbed this volume in the hope that it will help you with a crisis that has suddenly overwhelmed you. Maybe you are in hospital, still unwell, but told you must leave immediately because you are bed-blocking. Or an elderly relative faces this situation. If so, you can turn straight to *Chapter 15: Discharge*, which forms the final section of *Part Five: Hospitals*. You will not need to have read everything before the bit you need. Throughout the book, cross-references are provided to other sections likely to be relevant to the immediate subject matter.

Reading the introductory material in the *Introduction* and in *Part One: Growing Older* is not essential, but it is intended to provide a useful context for specific problems confronting you. It describes the differences between the bodies of older and younger people and some of the psychological as well as physical needs of older people. It is intended to provide a framework that will help you to understand problems of mind and body. For instance, the lighting in a care home you are touring may take on a new significance when you realize that older eyes need between two and three times as much light as younger eyes.

Equally, grappling with an outpost of the social services system may prove easier if you grasp the underlying logic which drives such establishments. The essentials of the machinery of support provided for older people by government and non-governmental organizations are set out in *Part Two: The Care Machine*.

The next section of the book (*Parts Three, Four* and *Five*) is organized chronologically, following the developing stages of ageing. *Part Three: Staying Independent* suggests ways in which you can continue to live independently and happily at home, rather than going into a care home, even in the face of considerable disability. This may involve not just guaranteeing warmth and safety but also fitting helpful equipment and acquiring ingenious gadgets. It may mean hiring help in the home, making new social contacts and finding out about what are often extremely generous travel concessions. There is also the question of where to live – staying put, moving in with others, or opting for retirement housing.

One in 20 people over the age of 65 lives in a care home, and the choice of such an establishment may be one of the most important decisions anyone has to make. *Part Four: Care Homes* tells you not just how to choose a home, but how to prepare for entry and how to make sure life inside is as enjoyable as possible.

Part Five: Hospitals tackles the contentious topics of ageist discrimination and withholding life-sustaining treatment, but more mundane issues like infection control and continence care, which often matter far more, are also explored. There are separate sections on strokes, a particular source of widespread misunderstanding, and on long-stay NHS care.

Part Six: Money may bring welcome as well as unwelcome surprises. Those who have made respectable provision for their old age may find unexpected non-means-tested benefits available to them, while those with modest resources of their own may be better off than they imagine.

However much or little money you have, you need to make sure that your affairs are dealt with as you would wish if you become unable to direct them yourself. *Part Seven: Representation* steers you through the world of powers of attorney and the like, and makes suggestions about finding proxies in the medical and social care worlds too.

The needs of carers have long been unrecognized, but partners, close relatives or friends who support older people living in their own or the carer's home do now have statutory rights. *Part Eight: Carers* describes what these little-known rights are and helps you decide whether to become a carer or to allow yourself to be cared for by someone else.

Throughout the book there is help to be found in making the many decisions that may confront you, but if you have already made a crucial decision on, say, the selection of a care home or retirement accommodation, you may still find the relevant sections useful. They may give you ideas for improvements you could seek and a grasp of changes afoot which could help you.

Although this book is directed primarily at older people themselves, their close relatives, partners and friends should find it equally useful. People working in one part of the eldercare world who want to improve their grasp of other areas may also find it helpful. The chapters on care homes and hospitals are addressed primarily to relatives and partners, since the reality is that the older people involved, who must of course be in ultimate control, are often not in a position to remonstrate with doctors or hospital administrators or trek round 30 care homes.

The terms 'disability' and 'disabled' are used broadly to embrace any kind of physical or mental disability, from an arthritic knee to dementia. Where I use the word 'disabled' in the sense of major incapacity, such as an amputated leg or near blindness, I make this clear.

Since the fundamentals of the health and social care system were set up before the establishment in 1999 of the Welsh Assembly and the Scottish Parliament, it is very similar throughout the United Kingdom. However, separate guidance to parts of the system, and in Scotland separate legislation, is being introduced. Where this differs fundamentally from that applying in England, I have indicated. I concentrate on guidance material provided in England, though I direct readers to equivalent documents from the Welsh, Scottish and Northern Irish authorities. The law, procedures and financial provisions described are as at 7 October 2003.

In the section called *Useful Contacts* you should find the address, telephone number, textphone number if available and the website of most of the organizations mentioned in the text, together with details of a few additional organizations which can provide useful help.

The author provides a consultancy service for individuals and organizations. If you wish to take advantage of this, you can contact her through her website or postal address, also provided in *Useful Contacts*.

Introduction

Growing old in Britain today is very different from what it was 50 years ago. One of the most far-reaching developments of the twentieth century was that for the first time in recorded history it became normal to grow old. Once you reached 60, rather than dying within a few years, as your parents probably had done, you found yourself with another 20, 30 or even more years still to live. In other words, while living to advanced years had been the experience of a small minority, it now became commonplace. This has transformed our society and generated unexpected problems that will, at some time, affect us all.

Demographic Change

It is a common misunderstanding that the ageing of the population means that people today are simply living to a greater age than their forebears. It may be true that Jeanne Calment, the Frenchwoman who died in 1997 at the age of 122, set a world record for reliably documented lifespan, but the phenomenon of people living to a great age is certainly not new. Peruse churchyard tombstones and you can find plenty of examples of a world in which men and women lived to see their seventieth, eightieth and even their ninetieth birthday, while various phenomena felled their middle-aged children. A wall memorial in the little Saxon church of St James at Avebury, Wiltshire, for example, tells of Charles Mayo, born in 1788, who worked as a doctor for 60 years and died aged 92 from natural causes. Twelve months later, in 1877, his son, also Charles and a ship's doctor, died during a voyage to Sydney; he was 40. Plato lived to be 82, John Wesley to 88, Socrates and Queen Elizabeth I to 70, but these, like Charles Mayo Senior, were the exceptions. Many more people failed to survive the hazards of childhood and then those of early and mid-adulthood such as accidents, warfare, casual fighting, disease and childbirth.

It is neither longevity nor the lifespan which one human being can attain which has gone up dramatically but life expectancy, or the average age at death of the whole population, as a much larger proportion of people live to advanced years than in times past. At the start of the nineteenth century, life expectancy was scarcely 40 years, but today it is at least 75 years for a man and 80 years for a woman.[1] During the second half of the twentieth century, life expectancy increased steadily by two years every decade[2] and it is almost certainly still continuing to do so.

The reason lies in a series of often unremarked advances in public health, water supply, air quality, town planning, wealth and nutrition – not just in medicine, as is often assumed. These developments have enabled people to survive afflictions such as typhoid, influenza and childbirth, which swept away the most vulnerable, in particular babies and young children, in earlier times.

Lengthening average lifespan in the twentieth century has been accompanied by another fundamental change – a reduction in the number of children being born. Together, these two phenomena have radically altered the proportions of the young and the old in our population. In nineteenth-century Britain, people had numerous children, at least partly to ensure that at least one or two would survive to support them in their later years, as people still do in the developing world. As the twentieth century wore on, more and more children survived, and one reason for having them disappeared as the Welfare State took on the burden of care in old age. In the second part of the century, increasingly assertive women grew readier to look outside home and family for fulfilment and became more wary of the burden of parenthood. Where the ten-child family was not unusual a century ago, three became a lot, and the norm either one or two.

Older people are therefore making up a larger and larger proportion of the population. From as far back as reliable records exist (in the 1700s) until the 1920s, the proportion of people aged 60 and over in the English population remained around 8 per cent. Then, between 1921 and the end of the twentieth century, that proportion doubled, from 10 to 21 per cent. This increase is expected to continue. In Wales, by 2020 there will be almost the same number of people in their sixties and over as there will be in their twenties and thirties.[3]

Not only older people but also very old people, that is, those aged 85 and over, are also more in evidence. In past times, the number of people over the age of 85 was small and fairly stable. Today, in the UK, over-85 year olds are the fastest growing age group in our population. They comprise only a small proportion of it, but one which has grown by leaps and bounds, and continues to do so. By 2050, the number of these 'oldest old' in the UK is expected to be three times greater than it was in 1999.[4] So octogenarians, nonagenarians and centenarians are going to be far more commonly encountered than they have been until now.

The make-up of Britain's older population is changing, as well as its relative size. At the beginning of the twentieth century, there were almost as many elderly men as elderly women. Since then, the proportion of women has steadily grown. In 1921, 9 per cent of the male population was over 60; in 1999 the figure was 18 per cent. For women, the comparable figures are 10 per cent and 23 per cent, so nearly a quarter of all women are over 60. People from ethnic minorities make up only a tiny proportion of the elderly in Britain, but this figure is of course also growing. It is estimated that the number of people of pensionable age in minority ethnic communities almost trebled between 1981 and 1991.[5]

Challenges

If lots of us are going to live to be old, and many very old, how should we treat those later years? We plan our children's lives and our working lives, yet few plan for old age in a systematic way, still less for old age with disability. There is something about preparing for old age which ranks it alongside personal finance reorganization or testicular examination: we prefer to place it on the back burner or, even better, forget all about it.

Does the media educate us? No. Television encourages us to interest ourselves, often in enormous depth, in art, football, music, how to bring up our children and the lives of the stars, but not how to choose a care home, our rights when threatened with discharge from a hospital where we need to remain, or the nutritional needs of older people.

An exception is the financial side, which the reality of National Insurance contributions combined with exhortation from pensions providers and the government makes inescapable. Those who do take action on this front may feel retirement has been taken care of, but money may well be the least of our worries in old age. Real poverty among the old has effectively been abolished by social security provision. Today, age automatically qualifies you for state help if you need it: once you are 60, you are entitled to cash from the state to top-up your own income to over £100 per week. In addition, this means-tested help for the poorest older people (the Guarantee Credit element of Pension Credit) opens the way to valuable additional entitlements such as council tax relief. This means that for those below a certain threshold, saving for old age can be a mug's game, benefiting the government rather than the saver.

If penury is not the ogre that it was, old age still holds terrors enough. These arise mainly from what may happen to our physical and mental health. Living longer means having many more years in which to develop both illness and disability: if you like, the price we pay as a society for the bounty of extra years. This does not of course mean that people need expect to contend with disabling conditions as soon as they reach 60: just as their greater wealth, better diet and living conditions allow a larger proportion of the population to live longer, so the lives they live as older people are healthier than those of their forbears. But although the period of very poor health before death has been pushed back, it nonetheless still bedevils many people. And the additional years of old age beforehand can bring conditions which, though not life-threatening, are inconvenient and awkward.

Physical

The ageing process brings changes to most systems of the body. In some cases, like the greying of hair, these do not matter much, but others create real difficulties. Nearly 40 per cent of people over the age of 75 are hard of hearing or deaf, largely as a result of atrophy of their hearing apparatus. However hard you train, your muscles weaken inevitably as you age, so you are not going to have the stamina and muscle strength and power you have known before. Your responses will be slightly slower and your immune system less robust.

These are changes to the body which are part of the ageing process, but there is also a host of diseases and conditions which, while not caused by ageing, are far more frequently encountered amongst older people. Cardiovascular disease leading to strokes and heart attacks, Alzheimer's disease, osteoporosis, osteoarthritis, Parkinson's disease and visual impairments such as cataracts and glaucoma are some of the more common of these. As many as 3 million Britons, the majority of them elderly, have to cope with urinary incontinence. In addition, diseases like diabetes and cancer become a lot more common in old age. And of course you take into old age any pre-existing long-term medical conditions, from migraine to asthma.

A survey in 2000 suggested that 70 per cent of people over 65 have a long-standing illness, and about half of those two or more such illnesses.[6] Of those living in the community (not in care homes or long-stay geriatric hospitals), a quarter suffer from arthritis or rheumatism. One in six also has a heart problem and another one in six has high blood pressure. A third sometimes have difficulty moving around; in care homes, this figure rises to four-fifths.

As we reach old age, we are unprepared for these conditions and diseases. The media do not educate us all on what it feels like to have, say, osteoarthritis; we have no idea of the sort of movement which causes pain, let alone the range of treatment available or what others can do to make movement less uncomfortable. Can you describe the changes which typically take place in the minds and the lives of people with dementia? Most probably not. Yet the condition affects more than one in five people over 85.

The exclusion of older people from the workforce has many unhelpful effects, one of which is that those still working find it difficult to understand properly the older people with whom they must deal. The general practitioners, social workers, physiotherapists, psychiatrists, nurses, town planners and road safety officials who play a key role in responding to the needs of elderly people have not been old themselves in the way that they have been teenagers or middle-aged people.

When my mother developed age-related macular degeneration, or AMD, I was amazed at how unfamiliar was the term, even to care home proprietors. Yet AMD is the most common visual impairment in people over the age of 55, with half a million sufferers in the UK. As sight is progressively lost in the centre of the field of vision until the person can see things only at the periphery, considerable adjustment is necessary for the person with the condition as well as those helping them. AMD is also typical of many of the chronic conditions of old age in that medicine can offer little in the way of cure. Progression of the 'wet', rarer form of this condition can often be slowed down through laser or other treatment, but there is no clinical treatment for the 'dry' form which affects about 85 per cent of sufferers.[7] Although the problems AMD brings may be alleviated with appropriate lighting, gadgets and technique, the condition does not go away, any more than it does for those who have fallen victim to Parkinson's or Alzheimer's disease.

In the majority of the long-term chronic diseases of old age, treatment simply blunts some of the symptoms some of the time rather than effecting a cure. That treatment may nonetheless bring unwelcome side-effects, such as constipation or thinning of the skin, with which people have to learn to cope or subject themselves to further treatment.

Mental
Another reality of old age today is the mental challenge of coping with chronic conditions and diseases, compounded by limited public understanding of what is happening to the sufferer. Half of people with AMD are affected by hallucinations as the brain adjusts to loss of vision, and these can be frightening. Yet the vast majority of people who do not have AMD are completely oblivious to all this.

Sometimes the extension of life delivered by medicine can itself pose a huge mental challenge. My father died at the age of 75 as the result of emphysema, the progressive wearing out of the lungs, caused in his case, as in that of many other men of his generation, by heavy smoking years before. However, a man in his situation could now expect to have his life prolonged for several years with the help of drugs and a ready supply of oxygen from a machine or a cylinder. Neither medication nor oxygen supply can do anything to repair the lungs, so the sufferer may find walking across a room reduces him to a breathless wreck, while even short excursions outside require a wheelchair. Pulmonary rehabilitation is a rapidly developing field and targeted exercise can improve a person's capacity, enabling him to walk 20 yards rather than 10, but even so, life is still pretty restricted.

People who would once have died from heart failure and heart attacks as well as forms of lung disease other than emphysema can also be kept alive, but though hearty they may not be hale. Heart disease, for instance, makes people breathless when they exert themselves. Some sufferers need a wheelchair, but may survive for years. Partial recovery from a major stroke can leave people mentally intact, but having difficulty co-ordinating their movements or perhaps completely immobile.

How would any of us cope with such a life? No matter how mentally resilient we might consider ourselves to be, would we survive for a month, or five years, with our spirits intact? Nonetheless, plenty of people live apparently happy lives in such circumstances. But just think about the challenge.

Environmental
Challenges of a different kind arise from the attitudes taken by society to frail older people, as demonstrated by the facilities it provides for them out of doors. Many older people do not drive or have had to stop. They find it more difficult to get to the shops than did their forbears 30 years ago, now that so many local shops and facilities have disappeared, to be replaced by out-of-town superstores. To get to these, they need to use a bus, but the service may not be frequent and the bus stop may lack seating or a shelter. Getting around towns and cities generally is much more difficult than it was 50 years ago if you have some degree of disability. Once, councils considered it part of their civic duty to lay on seating in streets and parks, along with

flowerbeds and public conveniences: all this was part of an ethos of civic pride. Railway companies followed this lead with heated, comfortable waiting rooms and plenty of seating on concourses and platforms. Today, facilities such as these are simply not being provided – and a great many have been taken away. This makes the environment far less easy to negotiate (except for severely disabled people such as blind people or those in wheelchairs, for whom special provision has often been made).

This environmental change also diminishes the dignity of the citizen, who may be driven to request the use of private facilities, like lavatories, because public ones are no longer provided. A decline of deference compounds the challenge of moving around out of doors. [8] Many of today's older generation remember a time when younger people automatically sprang to their feet to give up a seat for a grey-haired citizen, anyone with any visible disability or a woman. Today you can travel on trains and buses and see young children occupying seats, overseen by indulgent parents, while older people and pregnant women are forced to stand. For many, cars and labour-saving devices in the home make life more comfortable and easier than it was for their parents when they were old. But if there comes a time when these people are no longer cocooned in the warm comfort of their cars, or they cannot see, bend, move around or manipulate tools easily, what then?

Social Change

When in the early 1950s my grandmother became frail, my parents, brother and I moved in with her, sharing her little terraced house in Ramsgate, Kent. As my mother did not go out to work, she could look after everybody. She could also rely on a support network: three of her five siblings were still living in the town in which they had grown up. Today, things might be very different. Dr Sarah Harper, the director of the Oxford Institute of Ageing, has talked about the emergence of 'the beanpole family': as we live longer and have fewer children, the chance of being a grandparent or a great-grandparent increases, but we have fewer brothers, sisters, cousins, aunts and uncles.[9] Also, 50- and 60-somethings today were among the first working-class children to benefit from higher education, which has given them a choice of professional jobs undreamed of by their parents but which have often taken them away from their home town.

For reasons such as these, older people in Britain today are often living out the extra decades of life not in an extended family home but with one other person, such as a spouse, or alone. One third of men and two-thirds of women over the age of 75 live on their own. Of course, many have made a positive choice to do so. But what is inescapable is that if you live alone or with a partner who is frail, if you become frail or disabled in some way and can no longer bend to open the oven door or to put on your shoes, you are going to have to look for assistance.

These days people in that position can arm themselves with a quite astonishing range of sophisticated gadgets, doing anything from helping them put on their socks to swivelling them on a seat into the bath and then down into the water. Nonetheless, they may still need some form of human help.

Their instinct may be to look in the direction of their children. But quite apart from the logistical problems this could bring if your children live in another part of Britain, or indeed the world, just what support should you expect from them? In rural Senegal, when a man gets married he builds a house in his village for himself and his wife, and next-door he builds a house for his parents, because he expects to look after them too. But in Britain today, what is expected of children is far less clear, even in communities in which we assume that children still unquestioningly look after parents, such as British Asians.[10] As a result, older people can find themselves having to cope with very challenging situations essentially alone.

Attitudes

Social change of another kind during the late 20th century has brought with it a wave of toleration for some hitherto disadvantaged groups but not, on the whole, for elderly people. They still have to live with the reality that in society as a whole they are not the most valued citizens. Turn on the television and the murder of a child can dominate news bulletins for weeks. But the news that an old lady has been battered to death is handled briefly.

However wise or charming they may be, or however great the sacrifices they may have made, older people have inevitable disadvantages in the popularity stakes. The youthful body has always been considered more attractive than the ageing one. This does not seem to be purely a matter of aesthetics. White hair, lines and sagging skin have a clear association: they remind us of death and degeneration and our own mortality. Furthermore, there are features of the ageing body which can excite other negative reactions. Weakness in any form is often disdained in favour of strength, while slowness of movement can be seen as irritating as well as pathetic.

Another idea is that older people are useless – their absence from the workplace devaluing them as a group. For the individual, work provides income, interest, companionship, a routine and the feeling of making a contribution to society. Without these things, older people seem less important to younger people, and often to themselves.

The exclusion of older people from the workplace has one incidental effect which is particularly unhelpful. Because the GPs, social workers, nurses, town planners, road safety officers and so on retire by 65, none of these public service workers who have enormous potential to influence the lives of elderly people have had first-hand experience of old age in the way that they have been children and may have been parents.

Ageism

Disdain breeds outright discrimination. Policies operating in our health and social care services would be considered outrageous if they applied to younger people. When you are old and become ill, often you do not recover very quickly after an infection or an operation, and may have to cope with pre-existing chronic conditions as well. In the past many elderly people were looked after for long periods in NHS establishments tended by qualified nurses and doctors and trained health care assistants. However, successive governments in recent years have overseen the wholesale removal of such beds. Between 1987 and 2001, nearly two-thirds of long-stay geriatric NHS beds were simply taken away – 50,600 in all.[11] The people needing these beds have not of course disappeared: they have become more numerous. They have been forced to find the care they need elsewhere – either from their partners or relatives or in private care homes. Think what the outcry would be if nearly two out of three NHS maternity beds were removed and prospective patients were told to have their babies at home, to pay for private health care or fight for a small and dwindling number of free hospital beds – as older people are effectively told to.

A second aspect of health service ageism is in the way 'health' is defined. 'Health' problems, whatever the quality of the service, are treated free. Most of the care we need when we are old arises from health problems. If you have fallen victim to osteoarthritis, you may need another human being to help you move around, dress yourself, visit the loo and have a bath; if you have moderate to advanced Alzheimer's disease, you may need human help with every single task of daily living, including feeding yourself and cleaning your teeth. Yet these types of care are not defined as 'health care'. Instead, they are 'personal care' or 'social care', which means the person receiving the attention has to foot the bill. When in 2001 the government introduced to a blaze of congratulatory publicity 'free nursing care' for older people in nursing homes, its beneficence excluded all this help since it did not fall within the 'nursing care' definition it chose to adopt. The only part of the UK where the situation is different and the state does fund social care (though not housework) is Scotland (pages 389–90).

Wherever you live in the UK, if your care needs are so great that you have to go into a care home, you are expected to use all of your savings to pay care home bills until those savings (including money released from the sale of your home) have dwindled to about £20,000.[12] Some people do not have property to sell and their total savings and income are low; their costs are met by the state through local councils' social services departments, after they have contributed their pensions. But the first group, the 'self-funders', often have to pay not only for their own care but also subsidize that of fellow residents whose bills are paid by the local authority. You can find self-funders paying over £200 a week more for a place in a care home than social services pay. For example, in 2003 the London Borough of Merton was paying private care homes £363 for a residential bed for an elderly person; such a bed would cost a self-funder £540 a week.[13] It is not known precisely how widespread this practice is, but it is generally acknowledged to be common. Thus when in 2003 *Which* researchers asked 70 randomly selected care homes for their prices, more than 40 per cent quoted prices higher than the maximum level published by local authorities.[14] Many self-funding residents will have no idea that a substantial amount of the proceeds from the sale of their homes is going to save the state a financial burden it would otherwise have to bear. There is no other area of the welfare state where such a state of affairs exists.

Sometimes ageism is less obviously deliberate and more the result of a combination of ageist attitudes on the part of society as a whole and underfunding in the care of elderly people (itself a product of ageism). The idea that every citizen has certain basic rights which should not be infringed unless there is a compelling reason to do so is one of the foundations of our society. In 2003 the British Institute of Human Rights published a study on the impact of the Human Rights Act, which seeks to enshrine these rights. It singled out personal care for older people and disabled people as the area where lack of knowledge of human rights in public services was most disturbing. On older people, it said that there is 'overwhelming evidence that older people are routinely treated with the lack of dignity and respect that simply would not be accepted in relation to other social groups'. The Human Rights Act 'currently seems to have no bearing on many of the decisions that are made in relation to older people's lives'.[15]

In the face of such a bewildering array of unexpected and ill-understood problems, how are we to confront the mixed benefit of a long period of declining years? Most of us will face these problems to a greater or lesser extent in due course. Many of us will face them before our time comes as we are perhaps suddenly called upon to guide an elderly partner or relative through this labyrinth. All of us therefore need to wise up. This book attempts to provide a way into a not always appealing but ever more important world.

Part 1
Growing Older

Chapter 1
The Ageing Body

Ageing is a feature of human experience about which we are almost as reluctant to think as we are about its inevitable conclusion. Yet ageing is not merely something that waits in store for all of us; it is a process which holds us in its relentless thrall from the very moment of our conception. We like to think of ourselves as static beings, treating our first grey hair as an affront to our sense of ourselves. But just as we are ultimately mortal, so we spend every second of our lives locked into a process of physical and mental change which we may influence but cannot stop. Many of the frailties we observe in older people reflect processes which began much earlier. We think of the old as enfeebled, but we lose nerve cells in our brains from the moment we are born, while our muscles begin an inevitable decline in strength of 1.5 per cent per year from the age of 30. Exercise can help shore up declining muscle strength, but it cannot completely prevent it.

Though ageing is part of all our lives, no one understands it completely. There are 300 theories seeking to explain it. The most plausible is that ageing is the result of the accumulation of mistakes in the material (DNA) needed to reproduce and repair cells. This theory, propounded by Professor Tom Kirkwood, who gave the Reith Lectures on Ageing in 2001, argues that human beings are not programmed to die. Instead, over time random molecular damage accumulates which finally proves too much for our cells' repair systems.[1]

No two people age in precisely the same way. A few people go grey at 20; most of us will find that about 50 per cent of hair follicles are grey by the time we are 50. For some women, the menopause comes at 40, for others at 60; a few go through it in their thirties. Because of this variability, doctors find it useful to consider a person's 'physiological' or 'biological age', which is reflected in their physical condition and the state of their main body functions, separately from their chronological age. Psychologists look at 'psychological age', which is gauged by the way someone feels and acts or reacts to people and circumstances. These variations in ageing impose additional dimensions of variability on older people, who are of course already distinguished one from another by genetic differences, skills and life experiences. In addition some older people will suffer serious diseases; others will escape unscathed.

Which changes to the body are an inevitable part of the ageing process and which are caused by disease, which may or may not invade?

The Brain

In spite of the contrary stereotype, most people will see no noticeable deterioration in their mental faculties however long they live. In contrast, no matter how hard we train, athletic performance inevitably declines from when we are in our twenties and our potential physical strength peaks.

This is not to say that our brains do not alter as we grow older. They do, and the character of the alteration varies a great deal.[2]

However, these variations matter little if at all, because the brain is one of the organs of the body which possesses a large amount of spare capacity, which means it can cope even with a considerable loss of nerve cells or neurones.

Many cells shrink rather than die, and some are able to create new connections (or synapses) with others. Scientists have demonstrated that this still occurs in the brains of people in their seventies, and it almost certainly occurs in people much older too. Since learning requires the formation of new synapses, this explains why older people are perfectly capable of learning new skills and remembering new facts. The creation of new brain cell connections also explains why people who have suffered a stroke are often able to regain lost functions. A stroke kills an area of brain tissue by cutting off its blood supply. Sometimes the brain is able to compensate for the death of certain neurones, say those facilitating movement, by recircuiting synapses so that other neurones can carry out the work of the dead cells.

Dementia

Where significant permanent intellectual decline occurs in older people, it is almost always the result of a disease of the brain, such as Alzheimer's, perhaps the most feared affliction of old age and a disease which is highly age-related,[3] with its incidence shooting up during the seventh, eighth and ninth decade of life.

Alzheimer's disease involves deterioration in the infrastructure of brain cells: neurones twist themselves into a characteristic configuration of 'plaques' and 'tangles', while at the same time the brain atrophies and large neurones are lost. No one knows why this happens. The result is progressive loss of mental capacity in many areas, including memory, language and the capacity to cope with the activities of daily life, so that sufferers require help with an increasingly large number of tasks from, in the early stages, managing their financial affairs, to, later on, washing and feeding themselves. The condition may become apparent slowly over many years or in a matter of months. It is an insidious disease and the person will have been developing it before symptoms appear.

There is a danger at the beginning that relatives and professionals will want to take steps to protect the sufferer from any physical danger by placing them in a care home, but risks should be weighed carefully and people allowed to take risks if they want to. Cocooning usually results in marginalization, shrinking lives and diminishing people. Until the very last stages, Alzheimer's may not be accompanied by any comparable degeneration in the parts of the brain responsible for experiencing emotions, pleasure in anything from food to company, reassurance or sexual gratification. In the middle to late stages many sufferers are aware that they are human beings, but cannot remember or relearn who or where they are, so feel lost in time and space, in a perpetual, puzzling present. They are therefore likely to seek reassurance, to feel stressed and be endlessly searching for 'home'. At the same time, their decline in language skills – they lose the ability to summon up words – means they find it harder and harder to communicate with others, although they may still be able to understand much of what is said to them.

Alzheimer's is the main cause of dementia – a general term for a similar lasting loss of cognitive powers which is generally progressive but can vary enormously both in the rate of change and the parts of the brain affected. The other two causes (and in some patients more than one is present) are the formation of structures in the brain called 'Lewy bodies', and a large number of small strokes. Multi-infarct dementia – 'multi' means many and 'infarct' means stroke – is the second main cause of dementia after Alzheimer's disease.

Dementia may not be an inevitable result of ageing, but unfortunately it is common. Between one in four and one in five people in the UK over the age of 85 are suffering from some degree of dementia. Of course, this means that even if you are over 85 you stand a three in four chance of avoiding it. Any decline in cognitive ability in people not afflicted by conditions like Alzheimer's and multi-infarct dementia is small and is often compensated for in other ways, so in real life it probably does not matter much. Perhaps as many as 10 per cent of older people show no deterioration in their brains at all as they grow older, except perhaps in extreme old age, according to studies conducted in Britain and the United States.[4] In other people the difference shows up mainly when you compare 'fluid intelligence' and 'crystallized intelligence'. Fluid intelligence governs our ability to solve problems, put things in order, do jigsaws, break codes, all using new material we are receiving through our senses; crystallized intelligence uses culture- and person-specific knowledge which we have amassed with experience throughout life. Insofar as any trend can be discerned, it seems likely that our crystallized intelligence continues to grow as we age, while our fluid intelligence goes down after the age of 80. If you are looking for a fighter pilot, you look for someone with high fluid intelligence; if you are looking for a judge, you seek out someone with a high level of crystallized intelligence.

All this means that while unavoidable change to muscle strength means that our current Olympic athletes would be extremely unlikely to win a gold medal in their eighties, people whose work involves their intellectual abilities may carry on producing work equal to that of 50 years before. In some areas of work, older people are deliberately retained for their mental skills. In the United States, CBS's *60 Minutes* current-affairs programme makes a point of having septua- and octogenarian correspondents in its front-line team. Creative artistic endeavour too can be extremely productive in old age. Picasso was painting, exhibiting and planning future work right up to his death at the age of 92; his 88th and 89th years were among his most successful as a painter. Just as he had done throughout his life, Picasso changed his style in his later years. But while Picasso produced his most radical work in his thirties, other creative artists have done so in their seventies, eighties and nineties. Ralph Vaughan Williams wrote five of his nine symphonies between the age of 60 and his death at 86; his eighth and ninth, in particular are very different from his earlier work, with much more colourful orchestration. In our own day, Anita Brookner (born in 1928) and P. D. James (in 1920) show no sign of losing the capacity to create complex and imaginative stories. Both Catherine Cookson and Barbara Cartland, who died aged 92 and 98 respectively, were writing until the end, with Cartland penning on average 23 books a year in her eighties.

Cardiovascular Change

The development of dementia may not be a universal feature of ageing, but others unfortunately are.[5] Hardening of the arteries will affect us all. Cross-linkages form between molecules in the artery walls and calcium is deposited between them, making the arteries stiffer. This process meets all the characteristics of ageing – it is universal, progressive, irreversible and eventually harmful.

As arteries harden in this way, fatty deposits are often laid down on the insides of the blood vessels, causing them to fur up. This second process is strongly linked with diet and a reduction in cholesterol intake can affect it.

One of the effects of furred arteries is to slow down blood flow. This can be particularly significant for the brain, so it is not surprising that older people who show no decline in cognitive ability are usually free of cardiovascular disease. (Other variable factors found to correlate with a lack of mental decline are absence of other chronic diseases, an intellectually stimulating environment and the sort of personality which permits adaptation to changing circumstances during the middle years of life.)

Narrowing of arteries can have far more serious consequences. If arteries are narrowed to a considerable extent by the accumulation of deposits, then a clot will more easily form in the bloodstream. When such a clot interrupts the supply of blood to the brain and damage to brain cells occurs, a stroke has taken place. Strokes are a major killer of older people and leave many others severely disabled. As noted above, a succession of small strokes can cause dementia. The other main potentially catastrophic result of this arterial change is a heart attack. This occurs when a blood clot cuts off the supply of blood to the heart. Heart muscle cells are then damaged or die, and cannot conduct electrical impulses in the way that they should. This may mean that such heart pumping as continues is insufficient to sustain life.

Finally, arterial disease is a major cause of rising blood pressure. The length of the main artery, the aorta, increases with ageing and this, together with a decrease in the elasticity of blood vessels means that the heart has to work harder if it is to maintain normal blood flow to all the organs of the body. The additional workload imposed on the heart results in change to cardiac muscle and this in itself can eventually lead to heart failure. High blood pressure is not an inevitable result of the ageing process, and does not occur at all amongst people in some parts of the developing world, while some older people see a levelling off or even a reduction in blood pressure after a rise until their seventies. But it is a dangerous condition, since it is implicated in many serious or life-threatening afflictions, such as heart attacks, strokes, ulceration of the legs and kidney failure.

Skin and Hair

Where the ageing process affects organs and systems other than our cardiovascular system, it often does so in ways which are not in themselves life-threatening. Again we have to distinguish between changes which are the inevitable result of ageing as opposed to diseases (potentially treatable) which are more likely to occur as we grow older. Ageing predisposes us to develop, say, Alzheimer's or cancer, but it does not cause them.

Perhaps the most harmless changes of all are those of which we are most aware – those affecting the hair and skin. The greying and the thinning of the hair are a universal and inevitable feature of ageing. Some men go bald, while all find that the hairs in their ears, eyebrows and nostrils become more wiry and grow more

lustily than hitherto. Thinning and balding make us more susceptible to damage from the sun's rays, which can lead to skin cancer,
which is why it is important for balding men to protect their
faces, ears and necks with wide-brimmed sunhats.

As the hair thins, so too does the skin. One inevitable feature
of ageing is that the layer of cells under the outer surface loses 20
per cent of its thickness. This and other changes to the skin of
older people mean that wounds take longer to heal. Bleeding
occurs in layers of skin, causing bruises – a condition known as
senile purpura. At the same time, structural changes to the elastic
fibres in the skin reduce the skin's ability to smooth out and this,
together with gravity, makes wrinkles commonplace.

As we grow older, our sweat glands gradually atrophy. One
result of this is that older people are unable to sweat as much as
younger people and are therefore less able to regulate their body
temperature, so they are more liable to suffer heat exhaustion. A
decrease in sweat and oil secretions from the skin also leads to
dryness. This makes the skin more vulnerable to infection.

Sometimes there is also a reduction in the amount of fat under
the skin. The cause of this is disputed: it may be the result of diet
or disease, rather than ageing itself. Whatever the cause, it means
there is less cushioning over the bones, so while a younger person
may not care whether cushions have been provided, lack of them
can cause real discomfort to an older person.

Where people are bedridden and applying continuous pressure
on particular sections of skin covering bony prominences, loss of
subcutaneous fat padding makes them more likely to develop
pressure sores. Continuous pressure on the same area, say, part of
the hips or a heel, cuts off its blood supply, the skin and subcutaneous fat die, and a pressure ulcer forms. But it is not like having
a wound on your shoulder, which you cover up until it heals: a
pressure sore is in an area which is being rubbed or rested on all
the time, and as a result it is extremely painful. People who
develop pressure sores stay in hospital longer and take longer to
rehabilitate.

The loss of subcutaneous fat also makes older people more
susceptible to hypothermia. In younger adults the fat acts as an
insulator protecting the body temperature against heat and cold
in the world outside. Without that insulation, the body of an

older person chills more quickly if the ambient temperature is lowered and this, together with diminished blood supply to the skin, means elderly citizens need well-heated rooms.

The Digestive System

Some parts of the digestive system change little with age, or if they do, the changes pose few problems. The stomach shows no important change: indeed, it is an organ which has such a large functional reserve that even if four-fifths of it is removed, the remaining fifth can still keep the body functioning. What may be significant for some people, however, is the liver's reduced ability over time to metabolize certain drugs. Liver volume declines by about 30 per cent in people over 65 years and blood flow in the liver is 20–35 per cent lower in healthy elderly than in younger people.[6] This means that older people may react to a drug quite differently from younger people, and may indeed react differently from how they themselves did when younger.

In many parts of the digestive system, ageing brings atrophy and/or a reduction in the production of mucus, saliva and other secretions which aid digestion. These changes can lead to serious conditions. As the walls of the large intestine atrophy and become weaker, older people are more likely to develop outpockets from the large intestine wall, a condition known as diverticulosis. But there is no single age-related change in our digestive systems which poses a serious health risk.

Ageing can, however, predispose us to dental problems. Older people tend to lose bone tissue in their jaws, causing the teeth to loosen and exposing the roots. Another common problem is gum disease, which can lead to a 'pocket' between the gum and the tooth in which tiny pieces of food can become trapped and acted upon by bacteria, which can lead to infection. As a result of such factors, tooth decay is four times more common in older people. As the gums atrophy still further, false teeth may become uncomfortable and this, together with missing teeth, can make chewing difficult, with the result that people may turn to soft foods and omit the fibre and other foods they need to achieve a balanced diet. In this way, an older person can become malnourished.

Sex

The reproductive systems of both men and women show very significant and dramatic changes as the body ages. The first such change, puberty, applies to both sexes, the second, the menopause, only to women. The menopause marks the cessation of egg release by the ovaries and of the monthly cycle. As the ovaries stop releasing eggs, they cut down the production of female hormones, resulting in various degenerative changes. The vagina becomes narrower, shorter and less elastic, while the glands which produce its lubricating secretions atrophy. As glandular tissue in the breasts which produced milk is replaced with fat, they lose their firmness. But although women lose their fertility, they do not lose their capacity for sexual enjoyment.

For men, changes in later life are more gradual. There is no abrupt end to the ability to produce children which women undergo, and most men remain fertile throughout their lives. However, the reproductive organs of men do undergo some atrophy with age, which can have an effect on the efficiency of the system, although, as with so many age-related changes, there is considerable variation between individuals in the timing and the scope of change. Older men can take longer to achieve an erection and it may be less firm than a younger man's. The force of ejaculation is often diminished and the amount of seminal fluid may be less. Furthermore, it usually takes much longer for an older man to be able to repeat the sex act than for a younger man. None of this rules out sexual activity, and in practice the sexual pleasure of older women may increase, if only because the timing of the performance of older partners may be more to their taste than that of younger men in allowing them more time to become aroused. As leading American geriatrician James Birren's *Encyclopaedia of Gerontology* puts it, 'The older man: loving, lovable'.[7]

Muscles, Lungs, Joints and Bones

Irreversible changes within muscles occur as we age, involving the loss of muscle fibres and of nerve cells transmitting impulses to them. We can seek to mitigate these changes through exercise, but we can never regain the muscle capacity which we enjoyed in our younger years.

The result of these changes is a decline in muscle strength and power from around the age of 30. These changes do not really affect our day-to-day lives until we approach old age. Thus, at the age of 80, some individuals are not able to rise unaided from a low chair without arms. This means that the bench-like seating provided in bus shelters and shopping malls is often of little value to elderly people unless they can find some means of pulling themselves to their feet.

As we age, the nerve cells in our muscles which command them to act decline in number, so it will take us longer to respond to the firing of a gun or the sounding of a fire alarm. This change combined with reduced muscle power means that people over the age of 80 find it more difficult to cross a road before the lights change than when they were younger. As a result, they may try to rush, trip and fall over.

Changes to the muscles are not the only reason why athletic performance declines as we grow older. Increasing rigidity of the pipe parts of the respiratory system, reduced elasticity in the lungs themselves and deterioration in the walls of the tiny air sacs of the lungs in which the exchange of gases occurs all combine to reduce the breathing capacity of older people. We cannot avoid these changes; they can be accelerated by harmful substances such as cigarette smoke. Older people are particularly susceptible to conditions such as emphysema and chronic bronchitis which result from lengthy exposure to toxins.

Physical prowess is also reduced by a decline in the moveability of joints such as the knees and elbows. This is the result of the deterioration of the cartilage, an inevitable part of the ageing process; it can actually be worse in athletes, since some of it is thought to be the result of repeated trauma. For a great many unlucky older people, these changes in the joints are compounded by chronic inflammation of the cartilage, which can lead to its degeneration – a condition known as osteoarthritis. People with osteoarthritis frequently have trouble climbing stairs, walking, standing, dressing themselves, bending down, getting in and out of bed and cutting their toe- and fingernails.

Finally, there is a weakening of the bones themselves. As people age, their bones become less dense. This process affects both men and women, but because the bones of women are smaller to start with and they experience additional loss after the menopause, they tend to end up with weaker bones than men. Lighter bones are much more likely to fracture or break in an accident. The danger is greatest in white women and least in black men, who have heavier skeletons than white or Asian men.

Osteoporosis is a disease which is an extreme version of this process and is characterized by low bone mass and deterioration of the support structure of the bones. More than a third of women suffer at least one fracture as a result of a blow to bone weakened by osteoporosis during their lifetime; the risk among men is less, but it is still substantial.

Kidneys and Bladder

Another feature of the lives of many elderly people is a need to visit the lavatory more frequently than younger people. This is the result of changes in their kidneys and bladder. Structural changes in the kidneys reduce their ability to concentrate urine. As a result, more urine has to be passed to rid the body of waste products, so that many elderly people find that their sleep is disturbed by a need to urinate.

Some older people also experience a delay in the sensation indicating the need to urinate until the bladder is almost full. This may mean that they do not know they need to pass water until it is almost too late to get to the lavatory. In men, enlargement of the prostate gland may make passing water more difficult, with the result that the person needs to use the lavatory more frequently than normally.

These changes to our urinary systems can make going out much more of a problem as we grow older, especially as local authorities seem to have decided that many of the public lavatories the Victorians built are somehow no longer necessary and can be closed and sold off for other uses.

Urinary incontinence – the uncontrolled loss of urine – is not an inevitable part of the ageing process, but it is common among older people (page 109). It has a number of possible causes and the condition fortunately often responds well to treatment (pages 111–14).

Sleep

The amount of sleep we need changes through life, because it is associated with the release of a growth hormone. People who are growing fast, such as very young children and older teenagers, need most sleep. Later, as Winston Churchill and Margaret Thatcher have shown, it becomes possible to lead a very active life on only a few hours' sleep a night.

Generally speaking, the sleep of older people is shallow and they drift in and out of slumber. Small wonder, then, given additional problems such as an increased need to urinate at night, that if their sleep is disturbed by extraneous noise they may show more annoyance than younger people.

Sense Organs

The sense organs also change as we age. A reduction or distortion of the sense of taste frequently occurs. This may not seem to matter much, but it can affect what older citizens are prepared to eat, and if the pleasure they take from their food is significantly reduced, they may not eat enough.

Studies suggest that older people may experience an even greater reduction in their sense of smell than in taste. But apart from trying to make food and drink as tasty as possible, for instance through the imaginative choice of foods and flavours, and perhaps with judicious use of flavour enhancers such as monosodium glutamate, there does not seem to be very much that can be done.

Most of us know we are likely to become more long-sighted as we grow older (because the lens in the eye becomes harder with age and so less responsive to the attempts of eye muscles to change its shape in order to focus images). A lesser-known change is that the muscles of the iris, which controls the amount of light entering our eyes, become more sluggish. As a result, they do not contract sufficiently to allow enough light to enter the pupil. This cannot be artificially corrected with glasses, so a 60-year-old will need twice as much light as a younger person to see as well, while an 80-year-old will need four times as much. I was ignorant of this important fact when I toured care homes to try to find a place for my mother to live. Now, I would be concerned if I saw a dimmer switch controlling electric light in the main lounge and would want to know precisely why and when it was used. Why turn down the level of ambient light when older people need so much?

Low light causes even greater problems for people suffering from age-related macular degeneration, or AMD, which is not an inevitable result of ageing but is common (page xxii). While AMD should not lead to total blindness, it tends to involve the loss of the centre of the field of vision, so that sufferers have difficulty in perceiving fine detail and contrast, and end up with an ability to see only at the periphery. Particularly if you have AMD, you are going to need all the light you can get to make sense of the world. This is not the case if your problem is a cataract. Cataracts, which are common in old age, involve a loss of transparency of the lens. Images become blurred and the sufferer is disturbed by glare. Fortunately, they can be treated successfully.[8]

From the time we were babies, the tiny sensitive hairs in the inner ear which convert sound signals into electrical signals have been gradually dying off. By the age of 40, this will have affected our hearing. For some, atrophy of the hearing apparatus is exacerbated by its earlier subjection to, say, the noise of exploding shells in war or loud machines in heavy industry. Nearly 40 per cent of people over the age of 75 are hard of hearing or deaf. This can be a miserable state: you may misunderstand other people, or even feel they are conspiring behind your back, and as a result become suspicious, isolated, lonely and depressed.

Deterioration of the organs of the ear can also affect the sense of balance, making older people more like to fall over, since they cannot regain their balance quickly enough if it is disrupted.

Although the sense of touch does not seem to be much compromised by age, older people do often lose sensation in their extremities. Loss of sensation in the toes can make somebody more prone to fall over.

General Physiological Change
Our bodies have the capacity to adjust constantly in the face of external environmental change in order to maintain a complex internal environment involving, amongst other things, the amount of water, the temperature and the concentration of chemicals in

all our cells. The ability to maintain this stable internal environment (known as homeostasis) depends on many organs of the
body, including in particular the kidneys and the part of the
nervous system of which we are not conscious but which is
responsible for controlling body functions such as heartbeat. As
we grow older, our capacity to maintain these levels lessens.

This difference in homeostasis is one of the reasons why the
impact of drugs on our bodies changes as we grow older. But
other factors come into play too, such as the way the liver metabo-
lizes drugs because of the way it ages (page 10). So the use of any
drug, its precise dosage and its potentially harmful side-effects
need extra consideration when elderly people are involved.

A second physiological change involves the ability to cope with
emergencies. If you are out shopping and the supermarket suddenly catches fire, your body needs to step up your heart rate and
your respiratory rate and move you speedily. The ability to do this
is known as the body's 'functional reserve', and it gets smaller as
we grow older. The body organ systems of younger people
contain reserves far greater than will be needed; elderly people
are living at the limit of their functional reserve. When all is well,
the old manage as well as the young, but when they need extra
acceleration or stamina, they may be unable to muster it.

Diminished functional reserve in particular organ systems as a
result of ageing can exacerbate problems if the body is weakened.
Older people are less resistant to infection than younger people
and they often take longer to recover from illnesses, accidents or
surgical operations. If illness or stress to the system should undermine the body's ability to maintain a constant internal environment, many different body systems are threatened. While younger
people can function perfectly adequately while one lung recovers
from an affliction such as pneumonia, in older people both lungs
will be working at their full capacity. Therefore a similar attack of
pneumonia can push their lung system over the edge. Similarly,
the kidneys of older people do not have as much reserve capacity
as those of younger people to cope with disease or trauma: they
are under strain already. As a result, elderly people can become
dehydrated more easily. Therefore when older people become
sick, perhaps from some relatively minor affliction, they need
expert care, otherwise they can go downhill very quickly.

Finally, the symptoms shown by an ageing body are less easily related to their cause. Older people sometimes 'present', as doctors say, with symptoms apparently unconnected to the condition which has prompted them. If you are young and you get pneumonia you will have symptoms such as a fever, pain in the lungs and shortness of breath. But an older person suffering from pneumonia may have no respiratory symptoms: instead they may start falling over and become temporarily confused and incontinent. This non-specific presentation of symptoms in elderly people means that diagnosing their ailments is far more like a detective puzzle than for younger people.

All these things may sound like bad news for the elderly person and of course they are, to some degree. But they do have one advantage: they make the field of geriatric medicine extremely interesting. For one thing, symptoms may provide false clues to the nature of a malady; for another, several pre-existing conditions may well have to be taken into account in diagnosis and treatment. Someone turning up at a doctor's surgery with a chest infection may already be suffering from high blood pressure, arthritis, diabetes, hearing loss, cataracts and depression. Whereas geriatric medicine used to be a Cinderella among medical disciplines, today it is attracting more and more high-flyers, fascinated by the extra dimension ageing itself adds to the challenge of treating disease.

One further dimension making the medical treatment of older people fascinating is the tremendous variation amongst them. It is hard to exaggerate the extent to which older people differ. The ageing process itself has many facets, affecting different people at different ages in different ways. Some people will develop age-related conditions and some will not; some will develop several; those who succumb to disease will react in different ways. The ageing process and the development of diseases act not only on the different sets of genes which each of us inherits at birth: they also act on people with widely different interests, skills, likes and dislikes, levels of fitness, life experiences, patterns of marriage and divorce, children, step-grandchildren and so on. Older people may appear more similar to each other than children seem like other children, but in fact the differences between us increase with age.

Chapter 2
Changing Needs

Our needs alter as we grow older. They are also likely to be misunderstood or ignored by those younger than ourselves.

The Body

Food

One of the most pervasive and dangerous myths about older
people is that they do not need to eat very much and that they do
not require the vitamins and other nutrients that we associate with
the diet of others, such as young children. It is easy to assume that
as elderly people are not growing, they do not need to build up
new body tissue. As the replacement of muscle by fat is an inevitable part of the ageing process, flabbiness in chins and arms may
suggest that older people should be cutting back on their food
intake, even when they should be worrying that it is inadequate.

The truth is that under-nutrition and even malnutrition are
common amongst older people, and not just people who are too
poor to eat well. Studies have found that up to a startling 40 per
cent of older people admitted to hospital were suffering from
malnutrition,[1] When you are 80, an adequate intake of vitamins,
fibre and the other components of a healthy, well-balanced diet
are just as essential as when you were 20. Unless they are
extremely energetic, older people do not need quite so many calories as younger people, not just because they engage in less
physical activity, but also because their bodies consume less
energy while resting because of the reduction in muscle fibre.
This means they do need fewer carbohydrates – the sugars and
starches which generate energy. Yet the requirement for virtually
every other nutrient does not decline significantly with age. In
some cases it increases.

One reason for this is that the body's ability to fight disease
declines as we grow older. Good nutrition helps the immune

system to function efficiently. For a study in 1992, 96 elderly people living at home were given either a nutrient supplement or a placebo tablet. One year on, immunity was seen to be so much better in the group which had received the supplement that they suffered less than half the number of days of illness caused by infections as the others.[2]

The healing of wounds requires the formation of new tissue. The fragility of the skin of older people means that they suffer more cuts than younger people. Some have also to cope with pressure sores and leg ulcers. Certain nutrients such as zinc play an essential part in forming new tissue; without them, wounds heal more slowly or not at all. Protein also helps wound healing and in view of such considerations, *The Oxford Textbook of Geriatric Medicine* recommends a higher protein intake for a given body weight on the part of older people than of younger people.[3]

Older people also often need more vitamin D, 'the sunshine vitamin' essential for the absorption of calcium in the body, than younger people. Calcium counters the loss of bone density which characterizes osteoporosis. It also hardens bones; a condition known as osteomalacia, in which the bones are too soft, is also common among older people. Both osteoporosis and osteomalacia increase the risk of falling and make injury more likely in the event of a fall. Because milk-based puddings are popular sweets in care homes and because elderly people were brought up to believe that milk is at an especially nutritious food, there is probably not that much under-consumption of calcium amongst older people in the UK. However, many are not getting sufficient vitamin D to enable their bodies to use the calcium properly, particularly during the winter. We can obtain vitamin D from the oils in the livers of sardines, herring, salmon and tuna and from milk and dairy products. But diet alone does not give sufficient vitamin D. Our bodies can manufacture it themselves, in the skin, but to do so sunlight is essential, so you should try to get out in the sun, even on winter days. Housebound people and those living in institutions are at highest risk of not getting sufficient sunlight. A useful safeguard is to take vitamin D supplements: one study found that older people who did were 22 per cent less likely to break a bone and 33 per cent less likely to fracture their hip, wrist or forearm than a control group.[4]

As long as you consume slightly more protein and vitamin D than younger people you should be all right if you eat a varied, balanced diet – in other words, a large quantity and wide variety of fresh fruit and vegetables, plenty of fibre, oily fish, milk, olive oil and wholemeal rather than white bread, without too much processed sugar and salt.

However, if you suffer from or are at risk of particular medical conditions it is worth finding out whether diet can help. For example, there is evidence that a diet rich in lutein and zeaxanthin (found in deep green leafy vegetables such as spinach and chard, as well as egg yolk, broccoli and sweetcorn) can reduce the risk of developing age-related macular degeneration (page 15) by as much as 43 per cent. A high-dose supplement of certain nutrients can reduce by 25 per cent the risk of developing advanced AMD in those at high risk.[5]

In spite of the bad image of fat, our bodies need a number of essential fats, and ageing does not alter this. You can certainly reduce the risk of heart disease and stroke by avoiding too much saturated fat, just like younger people, but it is not clear that people over the age of 70 should take extreme steps to reduce cholesterol levels.[6]

Fibre is important for young and old to aid digestion and reduce the risk of colon cancer. One of the most frequent reasons for older people consulting their GPs is constipation. Taking in adequate fibre reduces the likelihood of constipation by increasing the volume of stools produced and reducing their transit time in the digestive system. Fibre-rich foods are pulse vegetables such as baked beans and lentils; fruit and vegetables (eat edible skins such as those of potatoes); dried fruit and nuts; brown rice, wholemeal bread and wholegrain cereals.

Difficulties

A combination of factors combine to make getting food, preparing it and consuming it more onerous for many older people. If you have only a few teeth, or ill-fitting dentures, biting and chewing anything from chocolate to lamb chops is arduous, if not impossible, so much of the pleasure you used to take for granted from your meals and snacks disappears.

Poor dentition is frequently related to low levels of nutrients in the bodies of older people. So if you are in a care home and your dentures get mislaid, it is very important to get them replaced as soon as possible (and label them before you go in to reduce the risk of loss). If your own dentist does not make home visits, contact a community dentist. The longer you wait, the longer you will experience difficulty with eating, while your gums may be changing in such a way that adapting to a new set of dentures when they finally arrive can become a problem.

Difficulties caused by inadequate teeth can be exacerbated by other changes which can accompany ageing, such as a reduction in the volume of saliva and atrophy of the jaw muscles (making chewing more difficult) and other changes to the digestive system as well as impairment of the senses of smell and taste. The result is that as people get older they simply may not consume sufficient food – a phenomenon sometimes called 'the anorexia of ageing'.

Elderly people living on their own may not bother to cook very often, and if they find frequent trips to the shops difficult, they may cut down on fresh produce. But tinned potatoes and carrots lack the nutrients to be found in the fresh versions of these foods, and pre-cooked food which is kept hot for a long time, as in meals-on-wheels, is likely to be short of vitamin C and folic acid. Moreover, even when older people get hold of fresh vegetables, they may prepare them in ways which fail to take account of modern nutritional practice – boiling them to mush when steaming would retain far more of the nutritional content.

One reason to get out to the shops often is that you may come across some of the new types of food with which shops constantly experiment. An American study provided evidence that regular consumption of cranberry juice can reduce urinary tract infections among older women, with 300ml or half a pint a day cutting infections by nearly a half.[7]

One other problem is that when we are older we often take far more medicines and pills than when we were younger, and some of these interfere with our metabolism in a way which increases our need for particular nutrients. For example, folic acid, found in liver, nuts and green vegetables, is essential to cell division and the formation of red blood cells, but several drugs interfere with the body's ability to metabolize it. Fifteen per cent of older people living at home and nearly 40 per cent in institutions had a folic acid deficiency, according to a study in 1998. [8]

Weight

How do you know whether you are under- or malnourished? Obviously weight is one indication. *The Oxford Textbook of Geriatric Medicine* advises that: 'Significant recent weight loss of greater than five per cent of original weight should never be ascribed to normal ageing.'[9] Unintentional weight loss of more than 3 kilograms (6.5 lbs) over three months should set alarm bells ringing. It could indicate disease, depression, infection, a side-effect of drugs – or simply not eating enough, because what is offered is unpalatable or because feeding difficulties have developed.

Older people in care homes or hospitals may not receive the help they need to consume their food. Help may be necessary because people cannot see their food, manipulate cutlery, handle foil covers, cut up food or transfer it to their mouth. Those with dementia are especially vulnerable. They may not remember whether they have had a meal; they may not realize that the food in front of them is for them.

If a relative with dementia is fast losing weight while living in a care home, do not let the manager reassure you that he or she is being well cared for and that weight loss is inevitable. The chances are that the home is not monitoring your relative's food intake and giving any help needed. To counter the suggestion that a change in the body metabolism of dementia patients may be a cause of the weight loss which they often show, in 1989 a team set about measuring the food and fluid intakes and the energy expenditure of a group of elderly dementia sufferers. They showed that the cause of their under-nutrition was without doubt inadequate food intake.[10]

Weight loss is not the only indicator of poor nutrition: indeed, some people may have the correct weight, but only because of fluid retention, for instance around the ankles and in the legs. If you suspect under-nutrition, get a referral from your GP to a dietician. Various screening tools have been devised to assess nutrition problems in older people; these should form the basis of a plan by a dietician to rectify any problems – reversing weight loss and ensuring the adequate intake of nutrients.

Of course, some people are overweight. Obesity is clearly undesirable. It is known to increase the risk of diabetes, strokes and high blood pressure, and to make conditions such as heart failure, arthritis and asthma worse. Overweight elderly people who need help with moving or bathing can be more difficult for workers to handle and because of this, they can be pressed to lose weight in ways which may cause them harm, so beware of this. If you are seriously overweight, again ask your GP to refer you to a dietician, who can draw up a plan for gradual weight loss based on realistic goals and avoiding any threat to nutrient needs.

In fact, obesity is not as widespread amongst older people as might be thought. Researchers in 1989 (admittedly some time ago) found that while 40 per cent of young men and women were overweight, the figure in those over the age of 70 was only 10 per cent.[11] Studies indicate that being underweight and poorly-nourished poses a health risk to more older people than being overweight.

Salt

There are specific conditions of old age which can be made worse by the wrong diet. In the Western world, ageing is often associated with a rise in blood pressure (page 8). Too much salt can push up blood pressure.

This does not necessarily mean that you should stop adding salt to the food on your plate – unless you swamp it with salt. The salt which is added during cooking or at the table accounts for only about 15 per cent of our total intake. Most comes in processed foods – anything from biscuits and bacon to cornflakes and ready-made meals. So scrutinize food labels rather than impounding the salt cellar.

Enjoyment

To ensure adequate dietary intake alone, it is crucially important that you take as much pleasure as possible from your food when you are older. The British are prone to regard eating as a means of fuelling up to work, rather than an important activity to be respected and enjoyed in its own right, except on special occasions.

Think of where you can best obtain nutritious food and savour the experience of eating it, ideally with other people. Day centres and luncheon clubs are one possibility (pages 230–34). You could mix and match, trying Indian and Chinese day centres and clubs as well as ones which serve traditional British food.

If you are going to eat at home but can no longer manage to prepare a full meal yourself, do not let the social services department of your local authority steamroller you into taking meals-on-wheels if you do not think they will suit your dietary requirements or cultural taste. Insist instead that your nutritional and social needs be met in some other way, such as through a homecare worker helping you prepare a meal in your own kitchen or through transport being provided to take you to a lunch club or day centre.

If you are contemplating moving to a care home, a trial stay is one key way of finding out what the food is like, especially breakfast – a meal rarely observed, let alone sampled, by visitors. If in hospital or a care home, you should be given any help you need to consume your food and time to eat, particularly if your swallowing is slow, perhaps because of Parkinson's disease or a stroke.

Water

All human beings need water, but when you are older, you may need more than when you were younger, mainly because of age-related changes to your kidneys. Without sufficient water, the cells cannot function properly. Unless something is done, death will occur. Insufficient water also makes the blood thicker, leading to an increased risk of strokes through the formation of blood clots, which cut off the supply of blood to parts of the brain. Dehydration, even fairly insignificant dehydration of which the sufferer is probably unaware, can lead to temporary confusion in older people. As many as one in six elderly patients admitted as medical emergencies was suffering from acute confusion which was related to dehydration, according to a study in 1980.[12]

How much fluid you need varies according to body weight. The more cells you have in your body, the more liquid you need. *The Oxford Textbook of Geriatric Medicine* recommends 30ml of water every day for every kilogram of body weight. Generally speaking, older people need about 1.5 litres – 3 pints, or between 8 and 10 cups of non-alcoholic fluid each day. This is in addition to the water in food. If you are exercising, or sweating as a result of stress or a fever or a cold, you will need to drink even more.

It is important that you should not rely entirely on strong tea and coffee for your intake. These contain caffeine, so act in some degree as diuretics – in other words, they make you excrete more fluid than they provide. Herbal teas and coffees do not contain caffeine, so try to vary cups of ordinary tea and coffee with these, as well as squashes, juices and milk, if you do not always want water.

As we grow older, the sensation of thirst often becomes blunted, so older people sometimes do not realize that they are not getting enough to drink. This means that by the time they feel really thirsty, they may already have become quite dehydrated. So they should drink even if they do not feel thirsty.

People who are suffering from incontinence are often tempted to cut down on their fluid intake. However, it is very important that they should maintain an overall fluid intake each day of 8–10 cups. Contrary to what you might expect, people who become dehydrated can become more prone to incontinence. (This is because the less you drink, the more irritated the bladder becomes by concentration of the urine, and the more frequently you need to pass water.)

Apart from the fear of continence problems and the decline of thirst, there are other reasons why older people often drink too little. Some people have mobility problems; others cannot communicate easily their need for a drink. Studies indicate that people living in hospitals and care homes are particularly at risk of becoming dehydrated, particularly if they drink only during scheduled meals, they cannot help themselves to a drink and the staff are negligent. [13] In their book *Healthy Ageing: Nursing Older People*, Hazel Heath and Irene Schofield recommend:

> Older adults who cannot obtain fluids by themselves should be offered hourly drinks and have sufficient fluids with their meals. Routine and regular prompts may be necessary for frail older people. Water should be situated in the most accessible place and

favourite drinks should be offered to break the monotony of drinking only water.[14]

If your elderly relative develops even a minor illness, particularly in very hot weather, do make sure he or she is drinking enough. If in hospital or a care home and there might be a problem taking in sufficient fluid, perhaps because of swallowing difficulties, make sure that your relative is encouraged to drink frequently with a light, easy-to-manipulate container if he can reach out or, if not, that somebody is delivering sufficient fluid, that a fluid chart is in place to monitor intake and that it is being filled in accurately.

Equable Temperature

Every winter about 40,000 more deaths occur in Britain than in the rest of the year, and most of these involve older people. Only a small proportion (about 800 per year) are the direct result of hypothermia; most of the remainder involve older people suffering from respiratory and circulatory diseases. Just as with food and drink, older people's need for warmth is slightly different from that of younger adults, and it is important that they (and their relatives) should understand the difference.

Our bodies maintain a constant core body temperature through a sophisticated regulatory mechanism. When it is hot, the heat taken from our bodies as sweat evaporates and cools us, while heat is also released through the dilation of blood vessels close to the skin. When it is cold, the blood vessels near the skin constrict, so that body heat is conserved. In addition, we shiver and our hairs stand on end, thus trapping a layer of insulating air.

As part of the ageing process, the efficiency of this mechanism declines, along with the reduction in homeostasis which is a key feature of the ageing process (page 16). Also, our ability to tell how cold it is and thus alert our body to take action declines. So older people are not quite as good at maintaining the constant body temperature needed for optimum health, and may not realize that the ambient temperature is as low as it really is.

Another factor is also in play. As we grow older, the proportion of the cells in our bodies which are actively functioning, and therefore generating body heat, gets smaller. One way to generate internal body heat is to use muscles in work or exercise, another is to process food. So older people who are immobile or who are not taking in enough calories are going to be particularly at risk from low temperatures.

The body's heat regulatory mechanism itself has an undesirable side-effect. When the blood vessels constrict to conserve body heat, they restrict circulation, thereby causing blood pressure to rise. This makes the blood thicker and more likely to clot, which increases the risk of heart attacks and strokes.

The World Health Organization recommends a minimum indoor temperature of 18°C (64°F) but, for rooms occupied by young children, handicapped people and sedentary older people, it recommends 20 or 21°C (69°F) day and night. When the temperature falls below 16°C (61°F), resistance to respiratory tract infections may be diminished. If the temperature drops still further, blood pressure will rise, blood will become viscous and the risk of a stroke or heart attack will increase. This is quite apart from the risk of hypothermia itself. See also page 347.

In very cold weather try to stay indoors, especially when it is windy. Wind whips away heat from our bodies: a strong wind on exposed skin has the same effect as a temperature drop of several degrees. Insulate your body as effectively as possible. Layers of clothing plus thermal underwear are better than one heavy layer. The clothing should be loose, to provide insulating layers of air and lightweight, since heavy material slows you down. Wool is a better insulator than synthetic materials such as polyester.

As half the body's heat loss occurs through the scalp, hats are extremely important. Scrooge's nightcap was extremely sensible. Try to stop heat loss through body extremities by inserting insulating insoles into boots or shoes and wearing thin pairs of gloves under woollen mittens. Cover exposed skin on legs, neck, face and ears as much as possible, ideally with two layers at least of scarves, stockings and so on.

In bed, several blankets will provide more insulation than one or two thick ones and duvets are very effective. Although electric under-blankets have to be switched off before you get into bed, you can buy over-blankets which can be kept on during sleep.

Keep active, both to generate body heat from muscular

activity and to keep the blood circulating properly. It is best to alternate physical activity with periods of rest, so spread housework over a longer period rather than doing it all at once and then resting for a long period. Even if you have difficulty moving, try to walk around the room or do exercises while sitting down. If you have to wait around outside, try to keep moving. One of the most dangerous things you can do is to sit immobile in a cold bus shelter for 20 minutes.

During cold weather you should have plenty of hot drinks and at least one hot meal every day. If you cannot move around easily at home, try to get somebody to make up a thermos for you. Keep your home as warm as possible and use a thermometer to check the temperature. If you cannot afford to heat the whole of your home to the required level, live and sleep in one well-heated room during spells of very cold weather. If you can get out, try to spend time in well-heated public buildings such as leisure centres and libraries. Take all the steps you can to insulate your home and to install effective heating systems. You may be eligible for government help to install central heating and to pay fuel bills (pages 208–9).

Elderly people are also more vulnerable than the young when the weather is very hot. In hot weather, older people should remain in air-conditioned buildings or use a fan, take plenty of rest, avoid exposure in the middle of the day and generally alternate periods in the heat with cooling periods. Out of doors they should wear a hat and loose clothing, and drink between 2 and 3 litres of water (more than 4 pints) every day.

The Mind

A twentieth-century American psychologist called Abraham Maslow proposed a hierarchical pyramid of human needs, applying to all age groups.[15] At the bottom are the most basic needs: food, air and water. If these needs go unfulfilled, whether or not other needs are met is irrelevant. But most of Maslow's other tiers were psychological. These remain less absolute than physical needs. If we do not receive enough liquid or we become too hot, we die. But if no one ever hugs us or if we have low self-regard, we may end up with a life which we feel is not worth living.

Safety

Maslow's second tier of needs concerned safety: he believed that human beings have a deep-seated need to feel secure. Falling over is a major source of physical injury and psychological trauma amongst older people, so they need environments which throw up as few trip hazards as possible. But Maslow argued that individuals need not only to be safe but also to feel safe.

Safety concerns are both objective and subjective. You may harbour a fear of going out of doors in the evening lest you be attacked and may allow this fear to confine you to the house. Yet statistics show such attacks to be unlikely. While a man runs a 19 per cent risk of encountering a violent incident between the ages of 16 and 24, the figure drops to 9 per cent for women of the same age and, for both men and women over 65, to less than 1 per cent, according to a Home Office study for England and Wales in 2002.[16] Vastly more dangerous to elderly people than muggers or yobs is traffic. Nearly half of all pedestrians killed on our roads are over 60, although they make up only one fifth of the population.[17] Yet many older people show none of the fear of crossing the road that they store up for dangerous assailants.

Some of the most troubling threats we experience involve threat of impending, massive and unwelcome changes to our way of life. The deep unease often experienced by younger people who feel that their job is at risk through some corporate takeover has something in common with the dismay older people may feel when facing a move away from what is perceived as the safe environment of their own home to a care home.

Our homes are our refuge from the outside world, the comfortable surroundings to which we long to return when we go away and the places from which we draw the strength to go out and face the world. The older we are, the more time we have had to refine this refuge, and the more entrenched we may feel in it. Our homes embody countless choices we have made over the years: they reflect our own individual values, preoccupations, hobbies and tastes. Tidy or untidy, spacious or cramped, with an extensive garden or a window box, our homes are part of who we are. Our own living space will probably have shared many events with us – Christmas family parties, attempts at decorating, illnesses, other memories of people and of family pets. Small wonder, then, that when older people find themselves suddenly placed in hospital or a care home, they can feel at best disorientated, and at worst alienated and despairing. Enabling people to find in new environments, such as care homes, pleasure and reassurance comparable to those to be found in a home of one's own is a daunting challenge. Feeling you have no choice but to leave your own home to live among strangers would be a blow to the most robust, let alone those challenged by declining faculties. Yet thousands of elderly citizens face it every year.

Affection and Acceptance

Maslow's called his third tier 'love and belongingness'. He felt that once people's basic physiological and safety needs were met, the next most important human need was to both give and receive affection, and to feel that you belong and are accepted somewhere. All of us know from our earliest memories of contact with our parents how important love and affection are to human happiness. Of course, this is no different when we are older. And yet 'You're the only person who hugs me now' is a lament heard all too frequently by those who work with elderly people – and those are the lucky ones who receive hugs from care workers.

Most of us feel happier if we avoid a hermit's existence, but few people realize that research indicates that our physical health also benefits from contact with other people. At one time psychologists maintained that a reduction in social activity in later life was natural; this was known as 'disengagement theory'. But advocates of 'activity theory' argue that it is beneficial to maintain and develop new social contacts in old age, for instance through voluntary work, seeing friends and attending clubs and meetings. Research supports the second theory: people who continue to engage with their fellow human beings live longer and have fewer health problems. A study by Kate Mary Bennett of Liverpool University found that those with significantly lower levels of social activity were more likely to die sooner than the others and to experience deteriorating physical health (see also page 218).[18]

Yet old age often brings with it removal from friends and relatives through a change of residence, and potentially even more painful losses through bereavement. Elderly citizens often have to cope not just with the loss of a spouse or partner, but with multiple bereavements – of friends, brothers, sisters, even their own children. Of course, not all people grieve when their partner dies. Some are relieved by the death because they feel freed by it – perhaps because they were trapped in an unhappy marriage by the now-abandoned taboo against divorce. But a minority of people who lose a partner in later life die very quickly afterwards, probably as a result of grief. Others may take a long time to adjust to the loss.

If a baby or a child dies, we support and sympathize with the bereaved parents. We may not even begin to imagine the magnitude of the adjustments to be made by a 90-year-old whose partner has been wrenched away by death. He or she may face a bewildering array of practical tasks previously shouldered by the deceased person, at the same time as struggling with loneliness after a lifetime of company. So just because death must be inevitable at some point if somebody reaches old age, bereavement may be no easier to cope with. Increased longevity means people have had longer to form close personal bonds.

On top of sorrow caused by loss, bereaved older people are left to remake the aspects of their life bound up in the life of the deceased. The lost person may have been an important source of identity and self-regard, a confidante, best friend, lover, the only giver of hugs and kisses. Dr Elaine Creith, a clinical psychologist specializing in older people, says a bereaved person might ask: 'What is my identity without the person who has died? How do I cope without this person? What does it mean to my functional life – for instance, if I cannot drive? What do I tell people? Will other people help me grieve? Will they think I am mad if I tell them that I see the dead person every night?'[19]

Grieving is natural when a partner dies, but for some people it becomes a pathological condition. Psychologists differ in how they distinguish normal from pathological grieving, as well as in how they think people should cope with either. During most of the twentieth century, the fashionable view was that grief should be resolved by letting go and moving on to new relationships. But studies published during the 1990s showed the importance to many people, particularly older people, of maintaining a bond with their dead partner indefinitely while forging new social ties.[20] According to this second view, if people find coping with bereavement difficult, they should be helped to look for ways in which they can create an enduring relationship with the dead person which is less painful.

Disability

Problems meeting needs of the mind can be bound up with the condition of the body. The most common type of disability for both men and women over the age of 65 involves mobility, affecting their ability to walk, stand and to use stairs, with one third finding movement sometimes difficult.[21] This alone can make it difficult to retain social contact. Making new friends, perhaps to make up for those lost through death or separation, is also difficult if you cannot hear or see very well. If you seek a new lover, varicose veins and wrinkles may be shared by those you encounter, but you yourself may also have acquired disfigurements which are not universal – a missing breast perhaps or a savage operation scar.

Addressing any mobility problems you may face may not bring instant love, affection and a sense of belonging, but it can certainly help. Keeping in touch also helps us to be easier people to be around. It can be difficult to maintain a sense of humour if you live for long periods on your own and go out rarely. Yet the more you can maintain a sense of humour, an interest in others and concern for the outside world, the easier others are likely to find it to be around you, and thus the more valued you are likely to feel.

Many people simply feel better for a change of scene. Just being in a green space can reduce stress levels, as measured by blood pressure or brain waves, within minutes, while twenty minutes in a park or the countryside can also reduce the heart rate, lower levels of stress hormones circulating in the blood, and even increase cognitive performance according to research.[22] Most of us take for granted the variety of sights, sounds and atmospheres we encounter in woods, street markets, the seaside and so on. This experience starts to recede for those who have difficulty moving around. Walking seems available to all, but it holds problems for many elderly people. So do car, bus and train travel. Yet these means of transport in themselves offer a change of scene and thus of perspective. Buses and trains offer passing contact with others and chance conversations with strangers and with young children, even if only overheard, quite apart from the stimulation of the view through the window.

Sex

The capacity for sexual enjoyment does not go away as we grow older, for men or for women, and sex can be more appealing to older women (page 11). This being so, it is a shame that many older women find it difficult to engage in heterosexual activity because of the skewed ratio of women to men – the result of the fact that at present women outlive men by about seven years, and that older widowers and single older men frequently choose younger women as partners.

Our failure to acknowledge the sexual and romantic needs of older people – the result perhaps of our association of romance with the young and the taboo aspect of sex and old age – perhaps hits hardest those who are inhibited by disability from initiating contact, while the nature of the environment in which they live seems to frown on such a notion. In care homes and long-stay NHS geriatric units the discouragement of sexual or romantic encounters seems to be the norm. But are we needlessly depriving these people of a last pleasure? Are we denying a human right as well as a human need?

Self-esteem

Maslow's fourth tier was a need for self-esteem. Whatever our circumstances, we are more likely to feel positive about life if we have a sense of our own self-worth. Studies by psychologists have shown that the higher people's self-esteem, the more likely they are to be able to survive and successfully adapt in difficult circumstances, such as a move to new housing or to a care home. Older people with high self-esteem are also more likely to be able to survive bereavement.[23]

The self-esteem of older people can be very fragile. It is not just that they are frequently denied the status, confidence and sense of value to be derived from work, parenting and much consumer activity. The circumstances of their lives often conspire to erode self-esteem. The deaths of family and friends rob people of figures who reaffirm their self-image through shared respect for past deeds and common experience. Such blows are made even worse if a move to a care home means that an elderly person is ensconced permanently in an institution in which they are surrounded by people of different persuasions, from whom there is little means of escape.

Choice and Control

One of the ways in which we can enhance self-regard is to feel in control: that we are exercising choice in our own lives. Research has shown that increasing residents' control over their own lives in care homes improves mental alertness, increases involvement in activities and speeds adjustment to surroundings.[24] As things stand, residents in many homes have little choice of food. They are usually allocated rooms, rather than choosing them; some find they have to share with other people. They are allocated individual 'key workers' – they do not choose them and may dislike them. Residents of sheltered accommodation rarely get a say in the appointment of their warden.

In care homes, residents could be given more choice, more privacy and more responsibility. Because they can no longer do everything for themselves, we need not assume that they can do nothing. It is easy to see why managements find it easier to sit people on chairs and do everything for them, but they might find that using residents' capabilities is not always counter-productive. Some residents could be made responsible for handing out newsletters, tidying the lounge or checking and arranging flowers. They could be given a role in the management of care homes, helping to decide on the menu, the destination of trips, the type of activities offered, the sort of facilities to be acquired and the recruitment of staff. Prospective employees could be asked to meet residents so that residents' comments could be fed back into the decision-making process: who is better placed to assess whether a candidate for a job would empathize with residents than the residents themselves?

There are many other ways in which professional help often robs older people of more control over their lives than it needs to. Efforts supposedly designed to enable people to go on being independent often leave the recipient of help with absolutely nothing to do save receive it. If somebody has difficulty cooking a meal, the usual response by a local authority is to arrange for meals-on-wheels to be brought in. Instead, a paid care worker could help the older person, side by side, prepare a meal, with perhaps another put in the fridge for the next day. That way, the older person would not only be more likely to have his or her nutritional needs met, but would also keep active, exercise choice over an important area of daily life, and, one hopes, enjoy companionship and pleasure in a shared task.

We also need to enable older people to find a sense of achievement in work done for them, even where they are physically unable to do very much. They need to feel that a care worker or other person who has performed a task they are no longer able to do for themselves goes away having received something from them. Weakness can be a unique bridge to forming enriching relationships. Not dependence but inter-dependence should be the watchword.

There are many ways in which close relatives and friends can help sustain the self-esteem of their loved ones. They can offer practical help in taking them to meetings – or in persuading the meetings to come to them. They can avoid unthinking prioritization of activities from which their older loved ones are usually excluded (such as work and parenting) and putting time and effort into those which remain available to them. When after a day at work an elderly relative telephones with news of a day of coffee and chat, strolls by the sea and Scrabble, we may be tempted to view such activities as trivial – indeed, we are programmed to do so. In the great scheme of things, a boardroom tussle or an exam crisis is considered more meaningful. Why, in an even greater scheme of things?

Self-fulfilment

Maslow's final need, which he believed people only came to if the four lower needs were met, is 'self-actualization'. This is a sense of personal mission, of belief in something beyond yourself. It is not static but involves a personal journey of discovery and at the same time of self-fulfilment, so that we feel our life has a meaning and that we have found a place for ourselves in the context of things. In the sense that it is a very individual quest, it is perhaps a Western idea, so people who have grown up in cultures which put more emphasis on groups than individuals may not feel a need for self-actualization quite as keenly as the people Dr Maslow had in mind.

One of the ways in which people find self-actualization is through intellectual stimulation. The joy to be gleaned from intellectual pursuits certainly does not seem to diminish with age. Many people find such delight enhanced by discussing what they are discovering with other people – and of course that also fosters a feeling of belonging to a community. Today, 85,000 people in 400 groups have formed the University of the Third Age in the UK. Outside such formal arrangements, countless older people, either individually or in groups, satisfy their craving for intellectual stimulation through French conversation, discovering local history or discussing the philosophy and politics. Those who get out to learn do, however, tend to be the 'young' elderly, not because intellectual needs diminish with age, but because mobility problems increase.

Of all the needs of elderly people it is perhaps that for self-actualization which we most often ignore. Society often sees older people as a burden and dismisses them because they are not seen to be doing things which are deemed productive – rather than as fellow travellers on a path of personal discovery. Mary Brooks, a Quaker in her late sixties, put it to me like this:

> We should emphasize the advantages of older people having time – taking time to wander, taking time for beauty, having time to stand and stare and grow inwardly. We have to find ways of growing which are not dependent on rushing around everywhere, and stop judging our own and other people's lives by how much we and they do.

The Spirit

Pursuing our spiritual needs can bring benefits other than a sense of contact with the numinous, whether through music, nature or religion. There is the physical activity involved in anything from going to a Druid dawn ritual to selling second-hand books to pay for a new church roof. There is the sense of community and belonging which comes from meeting like-minded people in chapel or meeting house, mosque or synagogue, church or temple. Sometimes the two are blended, with physical activity reinforcing a sense of shared values, as in lusty hymn singing.

In old age the spiritual quest can become more urgent, as we are reminded more starkly of our own mortality. Frequently, however, the quest becomes beset with difficulties at this stage. It is not only that you may find it more difficult to get to a place of worship or religious meeting: chronic pain and disfigurement or mental health problems can bring additional challenges to what you believe.

The Reverend Nigel Copsey, who works as a hospital chaplain in Surrey and London, told me of his mother-in-law, who had been a missionary and throughout her life had felt her good health was a sign of approval by God. In the last year of her life she was afflicted by serious mental illness. This caused her first real spiritual crisis. At the very least, chronic illness can prompt the question, 'Why me?'

Some may have been wrestling with confused spiritual needs for a long time. A friend told me of his grandfather who in 1917 left the church of which he had been an active member partly because of his experience of war. Fifty years later, months before he died, he told my friend: 'You know, I used to think that by the time I got to this stage I would have had it all worked out. But I haven't.'

No scientific survey has been carried out of the extent to which older Britons feel in some sort of spiritual limbo, but it does not seem beyond the bounds of possibility that many are in such a state. For today's elderly people have lived through a period which has seen fundamental changes in public attitudes to religion.

When today's 80 and 90 year olds learned about Christianity in the 1920s and 1930s, attitudes to the ultimate questions of life and death were an important part of individual identity which shaped their private moral and public behaviour. These young people lived at a time in which they were expected to accept what they were told; if questions surfaced in their minds, they usually kept them to themselves. Hilda Ashton, a lifelong Methodist, explained to me: 'If you started doubting whether there was a

God, you might well fear to pursue the thought, lest you be struck down on the spot.' For the past 20 or 30 years, however, these people have been living in a very different world, a world in which beliefs, ideas – even facts – are subjected to a constant barrage of questioning. Just because you are old, you are not immune to this process. Questions which may have been rumbling around in your brain for a very long time without being faced suddenly come into focus. Did the miracles really happen? Is there really anything beyond this life, and if there is, will I meet my loved ones there? Mrs Ashton again: 'Everybody these days is talking about dinosaurs, so why don't they figure in the Genesis account of creation?'

Appearances can be deceptive. It is certainly true that church congregations are often dominated by grey-haired citizens, but they may not be endowed with timeless faith. 'We assume that older people in the church have a blissful faith and an unwavering hope for the life to come. In fact, many of them wrestle with the dark night of the soul,' the Reverend Albert Jewell, then senior chaplain to Methodist Homes for the Aged and the author of a book called *Spirituality and Ageing*, told a conference on The Church and Older People in London in 2001.

So the urgency of the spiritual quest in old age, as well as the potential benefits it can bring mean that elderly people of a Christian persuasion are probably more in need of the church than any other age group.

However, a survey in 1999 found that many of the elderly people interviewed felt marginalized by their churches even though they might have given them a lifetime of service. [25] Three main areas of concern were insensitivity to the impact of changes in personal circumstances such as moving house and especially bereavement; inadequate pastoral care; exclusion from the fellowship life of the church – committees and so on; and unhelpful worship, which did not seem to be taking account of the needs of older people. So-called 'all age worship' was something these respondents felt was geared overwhelmingly to the apparent needs of young children.

The vast majority of older people in Britain have Christian roots, but obviously these issues are relevant to other religious groups in our increasingly multi-cultural society. As Hindus and

Sikhs are eclectic and all-embracing in their spiritual approach, they may not face as many challenges as Christians. For Britain's Muslims, however, the problem may be more acute than for Christians. The Enlightenment during the eighteenth century opened up the Bible to discussion and debate throughout the Western world, so that some of its stories can now be regarded as myth and metaphor rather than incontrovertible fact. In contrast, the Muslim world is more fundamentalist, countenancing only one version of the Koran, which it takes absolutely literally as the word of God taken down by the Prophet.

It is an undeniable fact, however, that all kinds of churches and other religious and spiritual organizations perform a very useful, if not central, role in the lives of many elderly Britons pages (234–36). So it is important to ensure that older people can retain and consolidate these links. Later (pages 234–38), we look at various ways in which this can be done. For instance, one type of help which people often do not exploit as much as they might is that offered by chaplaincy teams in hospitals. Whether you are in hospital for a short stay or for a lengthy period, a chaplaincy team can provide at the very least a friendly ear. They can also of course offer spiritual support, not only to those of the Anglican and Catholic faiths but to those of many others as well: they have their own paid staff but they can also bring in local imams, rabbis and so on.

Another way in which they can help which is not often widely known even among professionals is that they may minister in care homes for older people. Sometimes churches do this, holding services in the homes with ministers visiting; the practice does not always provide comprehensive coverage. One instance I have come across involves a group of trained lay people working for a chaplaincy team based in a hospital in Surrey. This team was particularly keen to respond to the spiritual needs of dementia sufferers. Ignorance about dementia may lead even church ministers to feel that religious input is wasted on people who cannot show they understand a simple talk, let alone a mini-sermon, but this ignores other aspects of a religious experience – familiar words, hymns, smells and symbols. The Surrey group's co-ordinator, Estelle Earnshaw, told me in an interview in 2001 of a recent visit to a care home for elderly mentally ill people:

The last couple of times we've had one lady who has been quite angry and withdrawn: at the end, when we go round chatting, she's been unresponsive, not wanting to know. In her working life she had a caring role, but she now has Alzheimer's. She is a Christian, with a fairly lively evangelical background. But this morning she looked as if she had been transported to heaven. She just sat as we were singing and you could see she was singing along within herself, although she wasn't able to verbalize. It was very moving, such a privilege. And other people who I would say are a little confused just enjoy the old hymns, going back to what they recognize: they will sing along very openly. Others just seem to enjoy the spiritual air and the time of quiet.

Part Two
The Care Machine

Chapter 3
State Support

The eldercare machine has three arms: the health service, the social services departments of local authorities, and a mass of voluntary organizations (to which we turn in Chapter 4). Older people make up 20 per cent of the population but occupy 60 per cent of NHS beds. This is because most of the afflictions acknowledged as medical hit us at the very end of our lives and the fact that the bodies of older people take longer to recover from operations and illnesses than do those of younger people, so they spend longer in hospital recuperating.

When the Welfare State was set up in 1948, the needs of elderly people were not foremost in the minds of its creators. At the beginning it was assumed that as the purpose of the health service was to make people better, over time the nation would become healthier and the NHS would wither away. No one foresaw the plight of those elderly people who were to live longer than anyone then realized but whose later years would be beset by chronic conditions. As this unexpected burden has increased, the NHS has sought to extricate itself from responsibility for dealing with it. Older people have increasingly either had to make provision for themselves or have had to look to local authority social services departments.

Social services departments provide or organize non-health 'care', but it is not free to users: they must pay for it, although social services departments may subsidize the cost. This may sound at odds with the idea of a cradle-to-grave Welfare State. The idea, however, is that elderly people suffer from frailty and disability affecting their capacity to carry out everyday tasks from which they can never be cured and which should not therefore be considered 'medical'. In practice, of course, the distinction is often unclear and is considered grossly unfair by many.

The origins of local authority involvement in care are quite different from those of the NHS. While the roots of the health service are in the post-war dream of a better Britain in which every citizen would have an equal right to top-class health care, social services departments' roots lie in the much earlier idea of local communities having responsibility for people in the parish who could not look after themselves, such as unmarried mothers or frail elderly people incapable of work. The parish expected relatives to look after their elderly infirm, but if they would not or could not, it reluctantly put them up in the workhouse.

There is still a lot of difference between these two arms of the eldercare machine. The health service is built on a high level of professionalism and qualifications and a well-known and respected code of ethical behaviour, including, for instance, confidentiality. The social services system, which used hardly to require professional qualifications at all, is now trying to raise itself up to a similar level of professionalism, but it still has some way to go. On the ground, the quality of staff and the service provided are highly variable, as spectacular cases involving child deaths have repeatedly shown.

The government is keen to bring health and social services together in single organizations, and this is happening to some extent with the formation of health and social care trusts. Overall, however, there is still quite a large divide between the social care and the health care machines, except in Northern Ireland, where the two have been run together for several years. This divide is reinforced by a tradition of government underfunding of social services compared with relative generosity to the health service. High-tech hospitals with dramatic treatments are glamorous; social services care is a dreary poor relation and generally treated as such.

Social Care

Of the social care machine's three main arms, closest to the ground are the social services departments of local authorities; in Scotland they are called social work departments. The tier of local government holding social care functions and responsibilities is the county, metropolitan borough and unitary authority – Buckinghamshire County Council and Wakefield Metropolitan Council, for example. In Northern Ireland health and social services boards administer both social care and health service provision.

Then there are a number of national public organizations independent of national governments but working closely with them, such as the Scottish Commission for the Regulation of Care and the General Social Care Council.

Thirdly, there are arms of government: the Department of Health in England, the Department of Health, Social Services and Public Safety in Northern Ireland, the Social Policy Department of the National Assembly of Wales and the Community Care Division of the Scottish Executive.

At the top level there are parliamentary committees and also sometimes other national structures. In Wales, for example, a new Welsh Assembly Government Cabinet Committee on the needs of older people has been set up, and a National Older People's Forum for Wales is to be convened.

Social Services Departments

Many people have no contact whatsoever with the social services department of their local authority until they are old. This is because, unlike, say, refuse disposal or highways, social services deal only with certain categories of people who need help. Apart from frail elderly people, those groups include people with learning disabilities, people with physical disabilities, people with mental health problems and children facing difficulties. So if a social worker turns up on your doorstep when you getting on, he or she may be the first you have met. Yet local authority social services departments control vast budgets which can have an enormous impact on the lives of older people. The social worker is the gateway to much publicly provided support and merits much attention.

Social workers, or care managers, as they are increasingly being called, wear no uniform and are often misunderstood and unpopular. They come to public attention mostly in their child-care role, in which they have to try and support parents while taking their children away from them if this support proves insufficient. Social workers like to emphasize their caring rather than their coercive function, but they can exercise considerable power over the old as well as the young. Through control of various budgets, social workers can largely determine whether older people whose means do not allow them to pay for the care they need because of a disabling condition remain in their own home with care workers coming in to help or have to transfer to a residential or nursing home (often now called a care home). Social workers usually seem to be the warm, caring people they would generally like to be. The problem is that tight budgets, heavy workloads and political priorities within which social services operate may mean that what they propose is not always what is best for an individual.

Over the past 20 years or so, there has been a major shift in control over state spending in eldercare from central government to local authorities. Central government influences these organizations, but they retain considerable freedom of action. As a result, some authorities give the care of older people very high priority, while others drag their feet over performing even the tasks which the law demands.

Any British social services (or social work) department is likely to be a large organization, spending perhaps £100 million per year. As well as assessing people's needs and providing services itself, it will enter into contracts with private companies and voluntary organizations to provide other services.

One important function social services departments have lost is inspecting residential care homes for older people, which has passed to new national organizations (pages 53–4). Also, in recent years, local authorities have sold off most of their own residential care homes for older people, except in Scotland. However, all local authorities play a central role in placing residents in privately-run care homes, and so are involved in the care homes world in a commissioning capacity. There are also social workers attached to hospitals who play a major part in arranging for elderly people to be discharged from hospital (pages 463–7).

Social work has only recently become a profession in which, as a condition of entry, qualifications involving specified examinations and practical work from approved training courses are required. As a result, some people working in social services departments have a postgraduate qualification, some do not. Some have a diploma in social work, which may or may not be a graduate qualification. There is much more of a mixture of experience and qualifications than in more established professions. Alongside social workers with qualifications, there are social services officers or social work assistants who may have learned what they know on the job, or have had a background in, say, care homes.

Social services departments control spending on three main areas of eldercare. The first is 'community care', that is, support for people to continue to live in their own homes through subsidizing facilities people visit, such as day centres and home care workers, who help with personal tasks like washing and dressing and/or practical chores like shopping and cleaning. The second is care homes, in which an older person goes and lives permanently. The third area is 'respite care', that is, temporary care usually so that a family member who looks after a frail elderly person (known as a 'carer', page 547) can take a break. Funding in these areas comes from three main sources: the elderly people themselves, the local authority through the council tax and business rate, and central government, with the local authority controlling disbursement.

Each year, the government works out how much it thinks a local authority should be spending in all fields, bearing in mind the character of the population and the area. It then transfers money accordingly. Most of the money that a council receives for eldercare from central government is allocated through this 'standard spending assessment',[1] but there are also specially targeted additional grants. If all this money is insufficient, a council will either have to raise more local revenue itself by putting up the council tax or transfer resources from other areas such as pavements or libraries, or provide only a restricted service for older people. If government believes a council is spending too much on eldercare, it can cut the grant it pays.

Yet councils retain considerable discretion on eldercare spending and there is much variation between them. League tables of social services departments' performance are regularly reported in the national press.[2] Some councils provide lots of day centres with free transport to get people to them; others provide very few and charge for transport. One council will set an upper limit of, say, £280 per week on the amount by which they will support senior citizens in their own homes; a neighbouring council's limit may be £360. Once people need more help than such limits allow, the council may say the only option is to move to a care home offering 24-hour support. This is a cheaper option if the older person is moderately wealthy (with savings including the value of property exceeding about £19,500[3]) since such people will have to pay the fees themselves and so they are tipped off the local authority's budget completely. In future, local authority control of such decisions may be influenced by greater involvement by people working in the NHS, such as doctors, nurses and occupational therapists, since social services departments and health bodies are being encouraged to work jointly as much as possible. In a small but growing number of places new 'care trusts' have been set up in which health and social services for older and disabled people are integrated. The introduction in 2002 of 'free nursing care' for elderly people living in care homes (which provides a contribution to fees to cover nursing costs whatever your own financial means) has also made medical people more involved in decision-making. Whatever the impact of this change, those older people and their relatives who assert their own interests most vigorously are still likely to get the best service.

Handling Social Services
Some social services departments are very easy to work with, but others are very difficult, and consumers have to exert pressure to get them to do things they are required to do by law. Later we examine in more detail the main areas in which older people can have dealings with social services, but in handling these departments a few ground rules come in handy:

- After a phone conversation with somebody in social services, it is a good idea to write to confirm anything useful which emerged, for instance that the official agreed to do certain things. If the authority does not subsequently write back and deny that these things were said, then any subsequent investigation would deem that they were said.
- If you want to make sure that correspondence is acted upon promptly, send it by recorded delivery. Some authorities will allow requests to get lost. If you have not written by

recorded delivery, you may have to phone or write in again (and again).

- Keep a copy of any correspondence you send to social services and note all phone conversations, logging the name of the person to whom you speak and the date and details of what is said. That means you know who to ask for if you telephone again. But if you cannot reach that person, you can ask for their line manager. Everybody in social services is supervised by a line manager, so that there is a tight chain of command from the bottom to the director of social services at the top, and above him or her, elected representatives. Within the department, the buck stops at the director of social services, who is responsible for and therefore could be sacked for what the lowliest social worker does.

- Do not countenance delays simply because an official from social services with whom you have been dealing is away, perhaps on holiday, even if only for a day. Ask instead to speak to the line manager.

- Line managers are also useful if you are unhappy with what somebody from social services tells you. If you are, ask (in as non-combative a way as possible if you do not wish to lose their goodwill) if you could just check that with their line manager.

- Social services should never start charging for anything without having agreed a clear contract beforehand. If it does, you ought to be entitled to refuse to pay. If the social worker says her organization does not put such things in writing, reply: 'Would you mind if I just checked that with your line manager?'

If you still have problems, consider filing a formal complaint. Social services departments tend to get quite a lot of complaints on anything from home care workers turning up late repeatedly to major questions of people being refused equipment or services costing large amounts of money. Social services' formal complaints procedures are described in the Appendix, together with other formal means of redress, such as application to the Local Government Ombudsman, as well as tips on complaining.

Most people who end up complaining do not realize at the beginning of their encounter with social services that they are going to end up wanting to make a formal complaint. This is one of the very good reasons why it is a good idea to keep a detailed record of every transaction you have with them.

Bear in mind however that the most effective means of reversing an unhelpful decision or getting a council to take action is often to alert the local media. A few TV cameras . . .

Records

In dealing with social services, bear in mind that you have a legal right to see your file. Openness of data held by public authorities about citizens is one of the extremely important but little publicized advances of the late twentieth century.

The Data Protection Act 1998 makes accessible any record of any personal information held by a health body or a social services department for the purposes of their health and social services functions. The information covered is not simply factual material, but also 'any expressions of opinion, and the intentions of the authority in relation to the individual': in other words, you ought to be handed the entire file, unsifted unless there are special circumstances, for instance that it contains material about another person.[4]

It is worth telephoning the local authority to start with to ask to whom you should write to view records, as this can save time; and you might care to post your letter by recorded delivery, otherwise the authority may claim they have never received it. The Data Protection Act says that the information should be disclosed 'promptly' and in any event within 40 days. When I asked to see my mother's social services records using my enduring power of attorney (page 518), it took six months from my initial request to my actually inspecting her file.

When you ask for records, you don't yourself have to worry about precisely where those records are kept: it is up to the local authority to assemble them and provide you with an opportunity of looking at them, although you may have to say where the information is likely to be held. If you subsequently suspect that some of the records have not been divulged, go back and specify which records you think might have been overlooked and ask to see them.

There is no need to say why you want to see the records. And don't write and say, 'Please let me know if you have still got any records', because that implies that they might not, which could lead them to say that they don't think they can find any. Assume that they have got a full and complete set of records and leave them to say, 'I'm sorry, we don't,' in which case you can come back and ask why not.

Abuse

A new and separate area of responsibility of social services departments is the prevention and handling of the abuse of older people and indeed of other vulnerable adults such as people with learning disabilities.

Essentially abuse involves the exploitation of trust between two people when one is unable to protect himself or herself and the other violates the other's human or civil rights. Sometimes abuse takes the form of a criminal offence such as theft, fraud, assault or rape. But it can take other forms, such as neglecting to provide somebody with sufficient food and heating or not giving them their medication, or intimidating, harassing or humiliating them.

The government takes the protection of vulnerable adults from abuse seriously and in 2001 published a document called *No Secrets* in which it set out an extremely useful definition of abuse:

> Abuse may consist of a single act or repeated acts. It may be physical, verbal or psychological, it may be an act of neglect or an omission to act, or it may occur when a vulnerable person is persuaded to enter into a financial or sexual transaction to which he or she has not consented, or cannot consent. Abuse can occur in any relationship and may result in significant harm to, or exploitation of, the person subjected to it.

A consensus has emerged identifying the following main different forms of abuse:

- **physical abuse**, including hitting, slapping, pushing, kicking, misuse of medication, restraint or inappropriate sanctions;
- **sexual abuse**, including rape and sexual assault or sexual acts to

which the vulnerable adult has not consented, or could not consent or was pressured into consenting;

- **psychological abuse**, including emotional abuse, threats of harm or abandonment, deprivation of contact, humiliation, blaming, controlling, intimidation, coercion, harassment, verbal abuse, isolation or withdrawal from services or supportive networks;

- **financial or material abuse**, including theft, fraud, exploitation, pressure in connection with wills, property or inheritance or financial transactions, or the misuse or misappropriation of property, possessions or benefits;

- **neglect and acts of omission**, including ignoring medical or physical care needs, failure to provide access to appropriate health, social care or educational services, the withholding of the necessities of life, such as medication, adequate nutrition and heating; and

- **discriminatory abuse**, including racist, sexist, that based on a person's disability, and other forms of harassment, slurs or similar treatment.[5]

No Secrets instructed local authorities in England to play the lead in developing policies and procedures locally for the protection from abuse of vulnerable adults involving other public authorities, in particular the police and the health service, as well as voluntary and independent organizations; similar instructions has been issued in Wales in a document called *In Safe Hands*. Each area is required to have prepared a local strategy and guidance on adult protection, which you should be able to see. Although similar national guidance has not been issued in Northern Ireland or Scotland, similar interagency strategies have been developed there.

All social services or social work departments throughout the UK have a 'duty of care' to vulnerable people. This means that if they suspect abuse has occurred or is about to occur, wherever a person is living, they have a duty to investigate. This is very important. As a result they should offer help not only at any time during office hours to a person who fears that they will be abused, has been abused or witnesses another person being abused, but also during the night and at weekends. Social services and social work departments publish the telephone number of their emergency duty team for out-of-hours help; close liaison with other public services means that you should get access to it even if you telephone, say, the police.

National Registering and Inspection Organizations

The Scottish Commission for the Regulation of Care, the Care Standards Inspectorate for Wales and, in England, the National Care Standards Commission register a wide range of organizations in the eldercare field and carry out inspections of their activities. These include care homes for older people and domiciliary care agencies (which provide care workers to go into people's own homes). Nurses' agencies, private health clinics, private hospitals and hospitals run by charities (thus taking in many hospices) are also covered. Each national organization is a quango, operating separately from government but having close links with it. The Commissions have national, regional and local offices; the National Care Standards Commission, for example, has a national office in Newcastle-upon-Tyne, together with nine regional and more than 70 local offices scattered across England.

The registration and inspection of care homes for older people used to be carried out by local authorities and health authorities, but in 2002 it was transferred to the Commissions. In the past, many residents of care homes as well as their relatives were completely unaware of the identity of the people who inspected homes, and many prospective residents and their representatives never examined inspection reports. The replacement of so many diverse organizations by one body in each country which, it is hoped, will have a significant public presence, should make people much more aware of whom to approach if they wish to raise concerns with those who are in a position not only to inspect but also to insist on improvements.

The Commissions have the power to insist on changes if they discover, perhaps through a pre-arranged inspection, perhaps through a tip-off followed up by a visit, that a care home or domiciliary care agency is flouting national regulations. They also have to have regard to the extent to which an agency or institution is complying with national minimum standards for care homes and for domiciliary care agencies on matters like staff training. The various regulations and standards, which take a similar form in the various countries of the UK, can be obtained from the Commissions. They are discussed in detail in Chapters 9 and 10.

It is expected that a Northern Ireland Commission for Care Services will be set up in 2004 and will carry out similar work to that carried out by its sister Commissions across the Irish Sea. Until that happens, the inspection of care homes for older people will be continue to be carried out by teams of inspectors from the Province's four health and social services boards.

In England, the National Care Standards Commission will probably merge with the Social Services Inspectorate to form a new Commission for Social Care Inspection in 2004. This will mean local authorities and the services they provide in social care will be regulated by the same body.

Social Care Councils

Confusingly, other entirely new quangos have been set up at the same time as the various Care Standards Commissions with functions in the same area.

The General Social Care Council (in England), the Scottish Social Services Council, the Care Council for Wales and the Northern Ireland Social Care Council are national organizations with a similar status and relationship to government as the Care Commissions. Their role is to improve the quality of all the people who work in the field of social care – social workers, the managers of domiciliary care agencies and care homes as well as care workers, of whom there are one million in England alone. These are sometimes called 'social care workers' or 'care assistants'. Sometimes such people call themselves 'personal assistants', particularly when they work privately for individual clients.

The prime impetus for the Councils' registers has come from scandals over the abuse of children in children's homes and misconduct by social workers who have failed to protect children in their care. The registers should mean that people who have been fired from a job or been successfully prosecuted or disciplined because they have mistreated or neglected to care for somebody in their charge will not get on to the registers.

However, omission from the relevant register will not necessarily tell you that much, at least in the early years. At the time of writing, registration was not compulsory for any type of worker in England, although it is likely to become so in the future. However, one would presumably expect people to submit their names for entry if they wish to be seen as committed members of a profession. In any case, registration will not come about overnight. Social workers will be the first group to be registered, followed by the managers of care homes and staff who care for children in residential homes. Registration of care workers will come later; in England, it is unlikely to begin before 2005. Clearly, registration of the hundreds of thousands of such people is likely to be a mammoth task.

The Social Care Councils are also publishing codes of conduct for the various types of worker to be covered by registration. Once people are on the register, they will be expected to abide by the relevant code and therefore keep to certain patterns of behaviour whose prime aim is to protect the interests of those for whom they are caring (page 271). In time, the Councils will interest themselves more and more in the training of these various workers. However, there are at present no plans to register people who carry out non-personal care in the homes of elderly people – such as cleaning, gardening, shopping or visiting. Nor will the wardens of retirement housing, the managers of day centres or volunteers in the eldercare field need to register. It might appear churlish to suggest that volunteers should have to be registered, but those people who deliberately set out to abuse older people, whether by inflicting harm or filching money from their purse, may be drawn to those groups which registration does not cover. It is also important to bear in mind that inclusion of somebody on the registers by no means provides a 100 per cent guarantee that someone is a caring person, or is not guilty of abusing an elderly person in the past or of some other serious misdemeanour. Just as only a small proportion of speeding motorists ever get booked, so many people who abuse older citizens are never found out, let alone formally reprimanded.

The Health Service

To a mother or father, the parts of the health service which assume greatest importance are maternity and paediatric services, and the kind of issues over which you agonize are whether you should get your child immunized against infectious diseases. But as an older person or the relative of one, you struggle with completely different ethical issues and find yourself in parts of the health service of which you may hitherto have been completely unaware.

The Department of Health, the Welsh Assembly, the Scottish Parliament and the Northern Ireland Assembly oversee state health care provision. Each of these organizations has an informative website covering the range of health and social care provision in the relevant country. The key point to remember about the NHS throughout the UK is that whatever it provides is free to the consumer – unlike provision through the social services departments of local authorities, which must usually be paid for by those who use it, unless their income and savings fall below a certain threshold. When you are in an NHS hospital you do of course receive free medical care, but it is important to be aware that if you are outside hospital you still have a right to free medical care, whether you are living in your own home or in a care home.

It is worth quoting the schedule of free health care provision which the NHS offers, because this guarantees important health care rights. One statement which refers to people who have long-term care needs, as do many elderly people, is contained in a circular which the Department of Health issued in 2001. It reads as follows:

The NHS is responsible for arranging and funding a range of services to meet the needs of people who require continuing physical or mental health care. The range of services which the NHS is expected to arrange and fund to meet the needs of their population either at home, in a nursing home or a residential home includes:

- primary health care
- assessment involving doctors and registered nurses
- rehabilitation and recovery (where this forms part of an overall package of NHS care as distinct from intermediate care)
- respite health care
- community health services

- specialist health care support
- health care equipment
- palliative care
- specialist transport services.[6]

'Primary care' means care outside hospitals, in the community. 'Palliative care' means the care of terminally ill people, and 'respite care' means provision of care as a break for somebody, such as a relative, who is caring for an unwell person. Respite care can also be arranged by social services, in which case a charge may be made to the user. This government statement has important implications for users, some of which are not well known. The guarantee of free palliative care (which can involve a substantial amount of nursing and the use of specialist equipment) means that we all have a right to die in our own home with the medical support we need provided by the NHS, if we wish to do so.

In England, health care is provided and organized on the ground by different types of organization. Health authorities are being reorganized into a system of much larger strategic health authorities; large district hospitals are run by NHS trusts. Health care outside these hospitals, in the community, is the province of primary care trusts. The system in England alone is almost mind-bogglingly complex, while different administrative systems are in place or in the process of being changed in Wales and Scotland (the equivalents of primary care trusts are health boards and local health boards respectively). To side-step this complexity, in this book I shall simply use the expressions 'health authorities' or 'health bodies' to cover whichever institution is responsible in any particular case, be it a trust, a board, a strategic authority or another organization.

Pledges

As we all know, the NHS is a massive spender of public money. Although in theory it thus belongs to us all, it is in practice quite difficult for individual consumers to stand up to it successfully, for instance when complaining about it or challenging its decisions. In England, the Department of Health influences the NHS through a number of means. There are controls on spending, circulars – some of which require health bodies to take action and others which merely exhort and advise – and, in recent years, 'national service frameworks'. These frameworks set out the services which members of the public are entitled to expect from the health service, and are issued with the objective of jacking up standards to a certain minimum level.

John Major's government issued *The Patient's Charter*, which set out a number of rights for patients as well as legitimate expectations in all spheres of the health service from GPs to the big district hospitals.[7] In 2000, Tony Blair's government launched *The NHS Plan*, which contained a number of commitments for the NHS which are embodied in *Your Guide to the NHS*[8] and replaces *The Patient's Charter*. In my view, this later document is less useful for patients than *The Patient's Charter*: it undermines the idea that patients have rights to health care by promoting instead the notion of NHS commitments, which put the emphasis on what the system chooses to provide rather than what the citizen needs. Although *The Patient's Charter* has been superseded, it would be difficult for the NHS to deny that the individual rights and patient expectations it embodies should now be set aside. I have therefore reproduced below what seem to me to be the most valuable sections for older people of both documents.

The Patient's Charter asserts as follows:

You have the right to:

- receive health care on the basis of your clinical need, not on your ability to pay, your lifestyle or any other factor
- get emergency treatment at any time through your GP, the emergency ambulance service and hospital accident and emergency departments
- be referred to a consultant acceptable to you, when your GP thinks it is necessary, and to be referred for a second opinion if you and your GP agree this is desirable
- have any proposed treatment, including any risks involved in that treatment and any alternatives, clearly explained to you before you decide whether to agree to it
- have access to your health records, and to know that everyone

working for the NHS is under a legal duty to keep records confidential

- have any complaint about NHS services (whoever provides them) investigated and get a quick, full written reply from the relevant chief executive or general manager.

The Patient's Charter also provided a number of important expectations, including:

- You can expect all the staff you meet face to face to wear name badges.
- You can expect the NHS to respect your privacy, dignity and religious and cultural beliefs at all times and in all places. For example, meals should suit your dietary and religious needs. Staff should ask you whether you want to be called by your first or last name and respect your preference.
- You can expect the NHS to make it easy for everyone to use its services, including children, elderly people or people with physical and mental disabilities.

The most valuable commitments in *Your Guide to the NHS* are:

- The NHS will provide a universal service for all based on clinical need, not ability to pay.
- The NHS will respect the confidentiality of individual patients and provide open access to information about services, treatment and performance.

Your Guide to the NHS Guide contains some useful commitments on the standards of care which patients can expect in hospitals. These are:

- All patient areas, visitors' toilets, outpatient and accident and emergency units (including chairs, linen, pillows, furniture, floor coverings and blinds) will be kept clean.
- In most cases, you should be offered treatment in single-sex hospital accommodation.
- Your nutritional needs and dietary requirements will be assessed

(for medical, religious or cultural reasons). You will be provided
with a variety of good food, and given any help that you need to
eat or order your meals.
- From 2001, there will be a 24-hour NHS catering service with a
new NHS menu operating in all NHS hospitals.

The 'national service frameworks' promulgated by Tony Blair's
government could be extremely useful for securing better health
(and social care) provision for older people since they set out basic
minimum standards in a number of areas. Separate national
service frameworks have been issued on coronary heart disease,
mental health and diabetes; there is an equivalent document on
cancer. The specially good news for readers of this book is that in
2001 the government published the *National Service Framework for
Older People*. This is a thick document, which contains separate sections on strokes, falls, depression and dementia and much other
useful material, together with a slimmer but very useful volume on
Medicines and Older People. If you do not obtain any other publication about eldercare, get hold of the *National Service Framework for
Older People*. It is available free from the Department of Health.

The Framework establishes two basic standards which the
government considers older people should expect when they
receive health (and social care) services. These are:

Standard 1: rooting out age discrimination: NHS services will be
provided, regardless of age, on the basis of clinical need alone.
Social care services will not use age in their eligibility criteria or policies, to restrict access to available services.

Standard 2: person-centred care: NHS and social care services treat
older people as individuals and enable them to make choices about
their own care. This is achieved through the single assessment
process, integrated commissioning arrangements and integrated
provision of services, including community equipment and continence services.

The first standard is clearly very useful at any hint of ageism in
the field of health or social services. The second can be called
upon when consumer choice is denied.

Although these national service frameworks do not strictly speaking apply outside England, it would be difficult for health bodies in other parts of the UK to argue that they should not apply. National strategies and policies are being developed in other parts of the UK and readers should keep a lookout for such documents as they are published. The Welsh Assembly, for example, has published national service frameworks for mental health services, diabetes and coronary heart disease; a framework for older people is to be drawn up.

Records

The Data Protection Act 1998, which gives everyone a right to see and to copy their health records, has had a lot of influence on patient care. You are now able to see whether a doctor has written a 'do not resuscitate' instruction, for example, in your notes. You do not need to explain why you wish to see your medical records. You can also require the health body to arrange for any medical terms which are unintelligible to be explained.[9]

When in hospital, it is important to ensure that important information is duplicated – for instance, it may be that any instructions on resuscitation are held in a set of records in one place, but not in another. It is also important that your medical records are accurate so that when, for example, you are discharged, your GP and his or her team know precisely why you have been in hospital and whether or not you were successfully treated. If they are not accurate, insist that they be amended before you leave hospital.

Quite separately it is a good idea to keep your own record of symptoms, treatment, the specialist medical staff you see and what they recommend. Such notes can be especially useful if you are fighting to get your health body to fund NHS Continuing Care (which can run to around £600 per week and pay care home bills for a person with challenging long-term conditions – see pages 469–78).

Patients' Organizations

Community Health Councils

Community health councils represent the public interest in the health service in their districts. They provide a very useful ally for

patients and relatives since they are independent of the health
service and, as well as providing guidance, also write critical
reports. However, the community council system is being fundamentally changed, except in Northern Ireland. In Wales and
Scotland, health councils, as they are known north of the border,
are being beefed up. In Wales, the Assembly has given community health councils an enhanced advocacy role, new powers to
inspect premises owned or controlled by health bodies of all
types (from strategic health authorities to community pharmacists) and has set up a new body called the Association of Welsh
Community Health Councils. In England, on the other hand,
community health councils were abolished in 2003 and replaced
with two new types of organization.

Patient Advice Liaison Services (PALS)
The first is Patient Advice Liaison Services, or PALS for short.
Since 2002, these have been springing up with their own desks in
the reception areas of hospitals. Their purpose is essentially customer services. They should act as a central contact point where
you can obtain a wide range of information about the hospital's
services and guidance on how to obtain access to other health
information. What many people do not realize is that PALS have
also been set up for primary care trusts, since the government
intends that PALS should be able to provide information about
the whole of the health service, not just the large district hospitals. Precisely what PALS do will turn partly on what patients and
relatives ask them to do. For example, you might not have
thought of approaching PALS to find somebody to visit a relative in hospital or to accompany them to outpatient appointments, but PALS might well be able to help, using their lists of
volunteers and people on work experience. If you have a
concern about your relative's treatment in hospital, you could
also have a word with PALS, although you may also wish to talk
to the ward manager and the matron (pages 76–77). The PALS in
your primary care trust might help you find a dentist, for
example. Talking to PALS will be different from making a formal
complaint, although PALS will be able to tell you how you can
set about lodging one.

Independent Advocacy Services

New Independent Advocacy Services are being set up for each primary care trust (but not hospital trust). Their function is to help people who may want to take issue with the NHS. They resemble the old community health councils in England. While PALS have been established in most areas, this is not yet true of Independent Advocacy Services. However, your PALS ought to be able to tell you whether one is in operation in your area.

These new organizations exist alongside the established systems for complaints about the NHS. However, before making any kind of official complaint through any institutional route, you should consider carefully.

You may achieve a more immediate result whatever your concern simply be hinting that you will file a complaint or by side-stepping the official complaints procedure and going straight to the hospital's chief executive or alerting the local press or your MP.

Sometimes you will be assured that your complaint was prompted by an untypical hiccup in the system and you will be asked to withdraw it. Do not do this unless you are convinced that long-term remedial action has been put in place. For example, a hospital may try to persuade you to withdraw a complaint about inadequate staffing by putting in additional agency nurses for a day or two, only to take them off once you withdraw your complaint.

The Commission for Health Improvement and NHS Quality Improvement Scotland

The Commission for Health Improvement, which came into operation in 2001, has the potential to improve NHS services to consumers. It works closely with the Department of Health and the Welsh Assembly, but operates independently from them and can examine the operation of any NHS institution. It has launched into a programme of investigating every hospital trust and every primary care trust every four years, through what it calls 'clinical governance reviews'. These typically involve looking at a patient's passage through the system, say, an elderly person who comes into A and E with a broken hip. In response to the CHI's review report, the hospital or primary care trust puts forward an action plan. It is then up to the strategic health authority to ensure that improvements are put in place.

When the Commission carries out such reviews, it invites public comment and may hold patients' forums. So if your relative is in, say, long-stay NHS geriatric unit, contact the Commission to find out when it is going to be examined.

You can also send suggestions to the Commission about which aspects of particular institutions you think it should examine. However, if you have serious concerns, you should contact the Commission immediately (amongst other organizations), as it can also carry out 'special investigations' where it understands some serious service failure may have occurred.

Unlike the National Care Standards Commission and its sister bodies, the CHI has no powers to enforce change itself. However, its reports often attract considerable publicity. These reports are to be found on the CHI's website, or they can be bought from The Stationery Office. It has the power to operate in Northern Ireland, but only at the request of the Northern Ireland Assembly. It is expected that the Commission will be expanded to form the Commission for Healthcare Audit and Inspection in 2004; if and when this happens, its role will also embrace health care provision by the private sector.

The equivalent body in Scotland NHS Quality Improvement Scotland. This has embarked on systematic visits and inspections by 'peer review teams', which contain lay as well as medical people. These also focus on a patient's journey through the system, but unlike the CHI's approach, they pay much attention to clinical standards which QIS draws up itself after consultation. Standards published to date include infection control, treatment of various types of cancer and older people in acute care in hospitals. These standards can be very useful wherever you live in the UK as they provide guides to what patients and their relatives can expect.

Consent

No medical treatment can be given (apart from in very restricted circumstances such as for people who are unconscious or have been detained under the Mental Health Act) unless a patient gives consent. When we go to see our GP, our implied consent is assumed and when we have an operation, a hospital will ask for our written consent. But it is important to be aware that we can withhold consent at any time. Doctors must ensure that patients who consent to treatment understand the nature, benefits and risks of the investigation or treatment being offered and of any alternatives, and the consequences of not receiving treatment. All patients can refuse to participate in research and teaching if they wish to do so. Any doctor should know that breezing up to a patient's bed with an entourage of students and saying, 'Mrs Jones, you don't mind, do you?' is bad practice. Mrs Jones should be consulted properly beforehand.

If you would like a relative to be able to act on your behalf in the medical world, you may have difficulties. Enduring power of attorney does not cover medical representation (pages 454–6). However, in Scotland a new law has provided for patients who have lost mental capacity to be represented by new 'welfare attorneys', so long as they appointed these before their mental faculties declined significantly (page 537). New legislation providing for an extension of power of attorney in England and Wales to cover proxy decision-making in the medical field is expected to be passed during 2004 (pages 539–40).

Primary Care Professionals

The most obvious division in the NHS is between care provided outside a hospital, or primary care, and care provided in a hospital. The gateway to primary care (and indeed to much hospital care as well) is the general practitioner, or GP.

GPs

There are about 38,500 GPs across the United Kingdom. A surprisingly large number operate single-handedly as a one-man or one-woman practice: 28 per cent in England and Wales in 2001, with a further 19 per cent in two-partner practices. So while multi-partner practices are becoming more common, they are far from being universal.

Within each non-single-handed practice there is usually a certain amount of specialization. However, every GP is expected to be able to take virtually any kind of patient and so to spot any of a huge number of medical or mental conditions, whether their patient is a day-old baby or a centenarian. This is expected even though paediatric and geriatric medicine are hugely complex fields in themselves.

Doctors do of course have to undergo training. A minimum of five years at university and a year in a hospital is followed by three years' practical to become a GP, of which half must be in general practice. This may sound a lot, but the 18 months in general practice in particular is not that long for the amount of expertise which needs to be acquired. (GPs in Norway have to spend four years in general practice before qualifying.) Once our GPs have qualified, they are expected to keep abreast of developments, and are paid about £3,000 every year to go on updating courses. The average income which each GP received from the NHS in 2003 was £61,618.

Older people must expect to have to call on the services of their GP much more frequently than when younger. This is reflected in payment scales from the NHS. Elderly people should not therefore feel reluctant to take up doctors' time. Also, it is a part of GPs' contracts with the NHS that patients aged 75 and over should receive a comprehensive check-up from their GP every year, quite apart from other consultations (page 249).

All doctors, including GPs, are registered with the General Medical Council, which has responsibility for protecting patients and can discipline doctors and if necessary strike them off the register. The British Medical Association, in contrast, is a professional association of doctors and represents their interests, provides services for them and lobbies on their behalf; the Royal College of General Practitioners seeks to encourage and maintain high standards in general practice, principally through education and training.

In 2002 Parliament set up the Council for the Regulation of Health Care Professionals to oversee the work of existing organizations which determine who can practise as a GP, dentist, nurse, optician, osteopath, chiropractor or pharmacist throughout the UK. It does not abolish existing organizations like the General Medical Council and the General Dental Council, but as well as introducing additional controls over existing organizations it does in theory provide a more comprehensible port of call for members of the public who consider that a health professional should not be practising.

We all have the right to change our GP. We do not have to tell our old GP, but can simply ask the new practice to register us. All patients should be offered an initial consultation within 28 days of registering with a GP. GPs can refuse to accept patients without giving a reason, and they can remove patients from their list.

Older people living in care homes have of course as much right to see their GP as anybody else. The Department of Health set out care home residents' rights in a circular to care home managers in 2003:

> Residents of care homes can expect the full range of personal medical services and the same rights of access to primary care as any other patient group. And, as for everyone else, this service is free at the point of delivery. GPs should not, for example, charge residents of care homes for flu immunisation jabs because immunisation of people with asthma, diabetes and all people over the age of 65 is provided free of charge by the NHS.[10]

If the manager of a care home tells you that you do not need to see a GP, that is just his or her opinion: the decision is still yours.

Driving

GPs are bound by strict confidentiality rules, but one important exception affects older people. Every person who holds a driving licence is required to notify the Driver and Vehicle Licensing Agency of any change in his or her health which might be relevant to the ability to drive, such as a deterioration in eyesight or syncope (page 127). When such changes occur, the GP normally asks whether the patient has informed the DVLA. If not, the doctor will explain the legal duty. If the patient refuses to accept the diagnosis or the GP's view of the effect of the condition on his ability to drive, the General Medical Council recommends a number of steps. It suggests that the GP can propose that the patient should seek a second opinion about the condition and make appropriate arrangements for the patient to do so, while advising him not to drive until that second opinion has been obtained. If the patient continues to drive, the GP should make every reasonable effort to persuade him to stop. This may

include informing the next of kin (which would normally consti-
tute a breach of the confidentiality rule). If the GP fails to persuade the patient to stop driving, or if the GP discovers that a
patient is continuing to drive contrary to advice, the GP should
disclose the relevant medical information immediately in
confidence to the medical adviser at the DVLA. Before giving
that information, the GP should inform the patient of the decision to do so. Then, once the DVLA has been informed, the GP
should write to the patient to confirm that the relevant information has been disclosed. The matter is then up to the DVLA.

Complaints

Those with a complaint about the service provided by their GP
practice, including the conduct of the GP, are supposed in the
first instance to use the complaints procedure which should be
offered by the practice itself. If they are dissatisfied with the
outcome, they can approach the primary care trust or its equivalent in other parts of the UK and, if an issue of professional misconduct is involved, there is always the General Medical Council.

It is important to decide what you want – an apology, getting
somebody struck off, or better treatment. If you want better
treatment, a formal complaint may be a mistake. Complaints
about a GP are taken personally. If you are complaining about an
individual doctor, you may be treated as somehow impugning an
individual who ought to be considered above reproach. Those
subjected to such attacks tend to stick together, and as they
provide the gateway to a great deal of help, you can live to regret
crossing them. Complaining about a GP is a step that needs to be
considered carefully, just as a parent will think twice before complaining about a teacher or headteacher.

If you are dissatisfied with your GP, probably the best immediate action is to write to him or her formally, perhaps restating
the request for a refused referral or whatever the bone of con-
tention is. If your grievance is less precise – perhaps your GP
takes so much holiday or maternity leave as to be rarely available
– then you could have a polite word with the senior partner in
the practice who might suggest you switch to another practice
member. You could of course make enquiries yourself about
other practice doctors and make future appointments with a

different one, so that in time he or she effectively becomes your GP. Get advice before you start complaining from organizations such as the Patients' Association, a Citizen's Advice Bureau or an advocacy organization (pages 82–3).

The GP is only one of a wide range of health professionals, though he or she normally controls your access to the rest of them. Some of these people will be attached to the GP practice, some will be in the community health team and others based in a hospital. A good GP ought to have easy contact with all of these people.

Nurses

Just as there is a register of all qualified doctors which indicates who has valid qualifications and who has been cautioned for professional misconduct, so there is a register for nurses. It is held by the Nursing and Midwifery Council (NMC). While the NMC safeguards the public, the Royal College of Nursing is a trade union lobbying on behalf of nurses.

The key qualification is registered nurse (RN). People can only call themselves registered nurses if they have studied, usually for three years, at university on an accredited programme. Nurses have to update their training and at any time the NMC can contact a nurse for proof of this. The three-year training includes core training which takes one year; then specialization in either adult care, child care, mental health or learning disabilities nursing. Those successful in their studies will have their name placed on whichever branch of the register they have specialized in. For example, a care home which specializes in the care of elderly mentally ill people would be expected to have a nurse who had specialized in mental health on its staff, called an RNM (registered nurse, mental health).

Although people over the age of 65 occupy 60 per cent of hospital beds, the nursing of older people is not one of the branches of nursing in which people can qualify after their three-year course. It merely figures as one component in adult nursing, in the core course and in the follow-up training for general nurses. After their three-year training, nurses may pursue further specialist training. The main specialist nurses you are likely to come across in the eldercare field are:

- community or district nurses (with training in treating people in their own homes)
- tissue viability nurses (specializing in wounds, pressure ulcers and ensuring that the often very thin skin of elderly people does not tear)
- continence nurses (very important, as incontinence affects many elderly people and much more can be done to alleviate distress than most people realize)
- gerontological nurses (specialists in the care of older people, and so far thin on the ground)
- palliative nurses (specializing in the care of terminally ill people). These include Macmillan nurses and Marie Curie nurses for those with terminal cancer and Admiral nurses for those in the later stages of dementia. Admiral nurses are provided under the auspices of the Dementia Relief Trust.

Most of these specialist nurses are spread unevenly across the UK; practice and district nurses are much more common. Practice nurses are based in GP practices. They carry out nursing tasks such as syringing ears, removing stitches and changing wound dressings and they may run clinics. Sometimes the practice nurse carries out the annual health check which every GP is required to undertake on all patients aged 75 and over. Although you are most likely to see the practice nurse in his or her office, practice nurses do visit people in their own homes.

District nurses go out to people's homes more often than practice nurses; there is some overlap. They often visit patients after they have been in hospital and advise and treat those with long-standing conditions, changing dressings and giving injections.

Some nurses work in private hospitals, hospices, nursing homes and for nurses' agencies. If you are hiring a nurse yourself, it is important to check with the NMC on his or her qualifications and also that he or she is skilled in the area in which you need expertise. A nurse who trained years ago and worked in the operating theatre is not necessarily going to know how to nurse somebody with Parkinson's disease. Agencies which supply nurses to people in their own homes have been regulated and inspected from April 2003 by the National Care Standards Commission, using regulations and national minimum standards; similar arrangements are being put in place in other parts of the UK.[11]

Mental Health Specialists

Your GP will have access to a community psychiatric team. This should contain a psychiatrist; for older people psychiatrists are often called psycho-geriatricians. Psychiatry is a branch of medicine: after training first as doctors, psychiatrists pursue a minimum of three years' post-graduate study in psychiatry. They tend to treat mainly with drugs.

While GPs often think of referring elderly people to a psychiatrist, they might not consider a clinical psychologist. Yet such people can be very useful, particularly if therapy rather than medication is called for. The professional body is the British Psychological Society, which has a register of chartered clinical psychologists; some practise privately. As clinical psychologists are not qualified medically, they cannot prescribe medication themselves, although they may make recommendations to a GP or a psychiatrist.

Community psychiatric nurses, or CPNs, provide support for patients with psychiatric problems living in their own homes or non-NHS institutions such as care homes.

Psychotherapists and Counsellors

Anybody can call himself or herself a psychotherapist, yet treatment by an unqualified practitioner could result in permanent damage. However, somebody who is a member of the United Kingdom Council for Psychotherapy will have received four years' part-time training and supervised practice, after obtaining a first degree (not necessarily in a related subject).

For counsellors, look for an accredited (not just an ordinary) member of the British Association of Counselling and Psychotherapy. Accredited counsellors will have had at least three years' training. They also agree to adhere to a code of ethics and subject themselves to the organization's complaints procedures.

If in doubt about a counsellor's qualification, ring up the British Association of Counselling and Psychotherapy, which provides details of local organizations that offer counselling and details of the qualifications and theoretical approach of individual practitioners. It also publishes useful factsheets about the differences between counsellors and psychotherapists and their various approaches.

Hospices usually have their own bereavement counsellors; the larger GP practices also often have their own counsellors.

Physiotherapists

A qualified physiotherapist probably knows as much about the skeletal and muscular systems of the human body as a doctor. He or she can help people suffering from arthritis and osteoporosis, weakness in the muscles, walking difficulties, difficulties in retaining balance and breathing problems. Treatment can be administered to relieve pain, and particular exercises and movements are encouraged.

The key qualification is not simply 'physiotherapist'– anybody with lesser or no qualifications might call themselves a qualified physiotherapist or something similar – but 'chartered physiotherapist'. Only people who have passed university exams recognized by the Chartered Society of Physiotherapists can put the initials MCSP after their names. Only members of the society are allowed to work in NHS hospitals; about one fifth of all physiotherapists operate in private practice. You can check membership of the CSP by telephoning its membership department in London.

Occupational Therapists

Occupational therapy developed after the Second World War to help injured servicemen and women to adapt to injury and disability. After a three- or four-year university course leading to a degree in occupational therapy, successful students become state-registered occupational therapists and their names are kept on a list by the College of Occupational Therapists.

The majority of occupational therapists work in the public sector, mostly in the NHS. They help people who have to cope with illness and disability to manage their day-to-day living. Someone who has lost the use of an arm after a stroke might be taught new ways of performing household chores such as meal preparation and shopping, and personal care tasks such as dressing and bathing. Occupational therapists are also trained in psychology and can help people cope with both the physical and mental challenges which ageing can present.

Occupational therapists are experts in the gadgets and home adaptations which can help people with dexterity and mobility problems. Social services departments employ OTs to advise on such matters in the homes of older people, and to assess whether somebody meets the criteria to receive adaptations and gadgets for free.

Dieticians
State-registered dieticians are usually based in large NHS hospitals. They take a four-year full-time course or a two-year post-graduate diploma, after a degree in, say, physiology or bio-chemistry. Many elderly patients in hospital are malnourished, and dieticians are called in to work out their nutritional needs and how these can be met. They can recommend particular diets both for people who can take food in the normal way and also for those who can be fed only by other means, such as tubes which pass directly into the stomach (page 457). But they can also come up with recommendations for older people in their own homes, community hospitals and care homes.

Speech and Language Therapists
This profession developed to help people disabled in the First World War. Speech and language therapists have usually taken a three-year or four-year university course and work in the NHS. Qualified practitioners are members of the Royal College of Speech and Language Therapists and can put the letters MRCSLT after their name. They provide help with eating, drinking, swallowing and communicating.

Others
There are a number of other health professionals with whom you might come into contact, such as chiropodists, aromathera-pists and orthoptists. A UK-wide body set up in 2002, the Health Professions Council, is compiling a register of all qualified prac-titioners in many specialisms. The Council can put you in touch with the relevant professional body, such as the Society of Chiropodists and Podiatrists, as well as many of those described

above, or check on a person's claimed qualifications itself; it is also able to investigate complaints. However, some health professions are not covered. Thus there is no national registration scheme for fitness or exercise instructors, for example.

Hospitals

Older people can find themselves in one of six main types of NHS establishment. The most familiar is the district general hospital, to which they might go for an operation or as the result of an emergency admission through A and E. Elderly people may stay longer than younger patients, but will not stay that long, as this is the most expensive environment in which care can be provided. Newspapers imply that district hospitals should be the focus of concerns about the NHS, but for older people, they are only part of the story.

Community or cottage hospitals can be very different from their district siblings. While the latter are usually large and controlled by a hospital trust with its consultants and doctors, community hospitals are often much smaller and very much the province of GPs. There may well be specialists from a nearby district hospital who visit frequently, but community hospitals often lack the specialist on-site medical staff and range of hi-tech equipment of a district hospital, such as laboratories for analysing blood samples and X-ray equipment. If a patient needs a doctor during the night, the hospital may well have to call the local GP practice. Cottage hospitals may be pleasant, homely, small-scale places in which to receive round-the-clock nursing and some medical care and perhaps therapy, but they are not geared up to delivering high-tech medical interventions.

Attached to a district hospital there will often be mental health wards, at least one of which will usually be dedicated to older mentally ill people. These are often assessment wards in which people with conditions such as dementia are placed so that treatment can be evaluated and improved. People do sometimes stay in these wards for quite a long time, although they will of course eventually be discharged. Sometimes an assessment ward will form part of a specialist mental hospital. An older person may also go to another type of specialist hospital, such as an orthopaedic hospital.

After discharge from a district or a community hospital, some older people will go back to their own homes, some will return to a care home in which they were living before they went into hospital, but others who need a high level of continuing support may opt to go into a care home, with or without subsidy from their local authority (pages 464–74).

Those patients who have ongoing medical needs may go on to a long-stay NHS establishment where their medical care as well as their accommodation and hotel costs will be met in full by the NHS (after deductions such as benefits). These people qualify for what is called in the eldercare world 'NHS Continuing Care' (pages 469–78). If they do not go to a long-stay NHS ward or unit, the NHS may purchase their care by footing the bill in a private nursing care home. NHS long-stay units may be attached to large hospitals or may exist as self-contained units, often rented as part of a care home, though managed separately from it. The total number of beds for older people in NHS long-stay units has been cut heavily in recent years. Since the care they provide is not only free but often better than that provided in private care homes, elderly people needing continuing care have an interest in pushing hard to secure a place in an NHS long-stay unit, but this is not easy and many fail.

Hospices, which specialize in the palliative care of people with terminal illnesses (not only cancer) are by no means all part of the NHS. There are about 20 NHS hospices in Britain; there are a number run by large national charities, such as Marie Curie and Sue Ryder; and there are about 200 independent hospices, mainly independent charities. These second two groups provide two-thirds of palliative care beds. They receive some of their funding from the NHS, but also have to find much of it elsewhere, through charity shops, running their own lotteries and so on.

Hospices may provide in-patient beds, day-care, 'hospice at home' (involving staff going out to people in the community), spiritual support and a bereavement counselling service. Health bodies buy care from hospices and a patient can be referred by an NHS doctor such as a GP. There is an annual directory of hospices available from the Hospice Information Service, while Help the Hospices works to support them and provides information about hospices in particular areas.

Sometimes when elderly people leave hospital, their health authority accepts that they need care for a further period, usually up to six weeks, for recuperation and rehabilitation. This care, provided free on the NHS, is called 'intermediate care'. It is often provided in a care home, a community hospital or sometimes in the patient's own home. Typically it involves a patient being moved from a district hospital to a nursing home for personal and nursing care, while a visiting health specialist, such as a physiotherapist, provides regular intensive therapy. Sometimes intermediate care operates to prevent hospital admission. It is discussed in detail on pages 422–6.

Personnel
Many of the health professionals in hospitals, such as speech and language therapists and clinical psychologists, are the same as those working in the community. The hierarchy of physicians in a hospital is as follows:

Consultant – the specialist in cardiology, cancer, geriatric medicine or palliative care, for example. He or she normally heads a team of junior doctors.

Specialist registrar – doctors training to work in a specialist field which will allow them to apply for consultant posts.

House officer and senior house officer – newly qualified doctors who are spending two or three years working in a variety of fields in hospitals so that they can decide in which area they would like to specialize. House officers or senior house officers are the people who staff A and E units during the evenings and at weekends.

Pre-registration house doctor – medical students who have obtained their initial degree and are spending one year in hospital as part of their training.

When people go into a district hospital they usually have a 'named nurse', someone who is responsible for overseeing and co-ordinating their nursing care. *The Patient's Charter* says patients can expect a qualified nurse to be responsible for their nursing care while in hospital and that they will be told his or her name. This concept is not always enforced, and in any case has its limi-

tations, mainly arising from the obvious problem that the particular nurse will not be on duty all of the time.

Every hospital ward has a ward manager, who may be called
the ward sister or the senior charge nurse. Above the ward
manager is the unit general manager, who may oversee a number
of wards for elderly people in an elderly services unit or perhaps
a number of medical wards in an integrated medical unit,
depending on how the hospital organizes itself. This general
manager will be responsible and accountable for what goes on in
all these wards.

Matrons are accountable for a group of wards and should be
'easily identifiable to patients, highly visible, accessible and
authoritative figures to whom patients and their families can turn
for assistance, advice and support and upon whom they can rely
to ensure that the fundamentals of care are right'.[12] A matron
ought to be able to deal with problems in areas such as hospital
food, ward cleanliness, hygiene, poor nursing and broken facilities. The managers of care homes often call themselves
'matron', but the term in that context does not imply anything
very specific, although it will probably mean that the manager
has a nursing qualification.

Chapter 4
The Voluntary World

How would elderly people manage without the ministrations of voluntary bodies? A galaxy of bodies inspired by voluntary effort, though often fielding extensive full-time professional staffs, does untold wonders in alleviating the misery that can so often attend declining years. But in spite of the goodwill that fuels the sector, elderly people and those who wish them well need to exercise care even here. All those standards and regulations bearing down on the NHS and social services are generally absent. The professionalism of voluntary organizations' paid staff and some of their volunteers can be high, but kind people who have had no training can do harm. And there is no state-backed system guaranteeing provision. A famous national organization may have a patchy network of branches. What each branch will offer may differ widely. Much may depend on fluctuating sources of funding, such as the national lottery. A lively service here today may thus be gone tomorrow.

Groups for Elderly People
Some of the main national organizations are well known, others much less so.

Age Concern
The Second World War caused special hardship for older people who could not easily get to underground shelters and had to cope with destroyed or damaged homes. Volunteers who formed themselves into a committee during the war followed up that work once peace returned by campaigning for special provision for older people and legislative change, such as reform of the workhouses. Age Concern emerged from this process and is today an impressive organization, both lobbying for a better deal for older people and providing much help and advice on the ground.

Age Concern England continues to lobby Parliament for improvements in the lives of older people, submit evidence to official committees and commissions, issue press releases and develop links in Europe. It also produces valuable information for the wider public, in particular regularly updated factsheets on a wide range of matters; variations of these factsheets are produced by Age Concern Scotland, since there are some differences north of the border. Age Concern England also publishes eldercare guidebooks, provides a national helpline and runs training days. It receives money from legacies, charitable donations and partnerships with companies. It also sells services, from travel, pet and motor insurance to funeral plans (do not assume that services will be cheaper than those of competitors).

Age Concern Scotland, Age Concern Cymru and Age Concern Northern Ireland are separate organizations which also provide advice and information and lobby their own national elected bodies and executive agencies. Age Concern Scotland, for example, has been very active in the campaigns to secure free nursing personal care, free public transport and grants for the installation of central heating in older people's homes.

Complementing the national organizations are hundreds of local groups, some large, some small, all independent, and each engaging in a range of activities. These groups receive no central funding, so they have to raise money in whatever ways they can, from the national lottery and approaches to local businesses to raffles, insurance sales and grants from local authorities, for instance to run day centres. The groups' range of activities, in particular their ability to hire staff, depends on their skill and luck in raising cash and the number of volunteers they can muster. Age Concern Sheffield is one of the most active groups. It provides advice through paid staff on anything from benefits to the location of lunch clubs; it runs a handyperson service, providing people who will go into the homes of elderly people to carry out small tasks; it runs day centres; provides a cleaning and shopping service; runs a lifelong learning project organizing courses on anything from local history to cookery for men; and campaigns on local issues which affect older people. While Age Concern Sheffield cannot run to writing letters and making telephone calls on behalf of individual people, Age Concern Bath and North-east Somerset runs a mobile advocacy service and a mobile counselling service.

Sheffield is one of the larger, wealthier groups, however: in some places there is no Age Concern; in others what they do is very limited and only a fraction of what could be done were volunteers and money available.

Help the Aged

Help the Aged is essentially a fund-raising and campaigning charity providing information to the public. Information is dispensed through useful free booklets, priced reports and helplines at national level, which include Seniorline, specializing in welfare rights and on how to obtain grants and services from local councils.

Fundraising takes place locally, but Help the Aged does not have local offices which provide advice. It gives grants and much valuable behind-the-scenes support to local and national organizations and projects. Its campaigns often attract a lot of publicity, for instance 'Dignity on the Ward' in 1999–2001.

The organization grew up in 1961 out of an appeal to help older refugees. Part of its funds still go abroad, to disaster relief and an adopt-a-granny-scheme. A sister organization, Help Age International, has branches in many parts of the world.

Counsel and Care

This organization is far smaller than Age Concern or Help the Aged, but nonetheless it provides some similarly useful services. It too publishes factsheets on a range of topics. It offers a national helpline which includes advocacy, that is, taking up individual cases. Counsel and Care runs training courses designed to impart values, principles and knowledge for care staff in care homes. To this end, it sends trainers into homes as well as offering courses in central locations. It campaigns for improvements in the care of older people, specializing in the publication of reports in important areas of care practice. Although it offers advice to people in Scotland, Wales and Northern Ireland, its expertise is slightly less for those parts of the UK and it does not publish factsheets specific to those territories.

Action on Elder Abuse

Abuse occurs when people in a position of strength, such as care workers or relatives, abuse their position of trust by doing harm (pages 51–53). Action on Elder Abuse has been successful in campaigning for recognition of the problem and government action. It provides help to people who are or might be the victims of abuse as well as those at risk of abusing, campaigns for improvements and seeks to make us all more aware of the abuse of older citizens. Perhaps its most valuable resource is its free helpline, which provides information and emotional support in English, Welsh, Urdu, Hindi and Punjabi, although the Asian languages may be temporarily unavailable. Its website has a chatroom.

Ethnic Minority Groups

Support for older people from ethnic minorities comes mainly from local community organizations which seek to look after the interests of all age groups. However, in 1998 the Policy Research Institute on Ageing and Ethnicity was formed. This UK-wide organization seeks to improve the position of older people from non-white ethnic minority groups. It carries out research, runs campaigns and seeks to educate (for instance on the care of people with dementia). It is in the process of compiling a list of local organizations.

Better Government for Older People

This is less an organization than a network. It was inspired in 1998 by a feeling that the needs of older people were not high enough on the agenda, that older people tended be seen as a burden in terms of health and social services and that their views were not adequately taken into account when services were provided. National advisory groups have been set up and there is an older people's partnership group covering the whole of the UK. These and many local groups share information, create partnerships and seek to influence policy. If you are keen to help inject a fresh look at the way in which transport, education, housing, social care or employment provision can be better geared to the needs of the older population, then Better Government for Older People could be for you.

The National Pensioners' Convention

This is also a fairly recent group, formed in 1979, with many national bodies and federations of groups associated with it. It is essentially a lobbying group, urging in particular the improvement of financial benefits for older people, from the removal of standing charges on utilities to an increase in the basic State Retirement Pension and the restoration of the link between the pension and average earnings. The Convention provides briefing papers and pamphlets on the subjects on which it campaigns.

Association of Retired and Persons Over 50

This social and campaigning membership organization tends to attract the more middle-class, active older person. It offers advice on tax, legal matters and domestic services (it can help you find a plumber) while local groups run social activities in 'friendship centres' (not buildings). It campaigns against age discrimination and is now part of a loose association of older people's groups called the Age Concern Federation. However, unlike Age Concern, it charges a modest fee for membership and access to its full range of services including a magazine and annual handbook. In this it resembles and to some extent overlaps with Saga, a purely commercial organization offering a wealth of advice (on anything from relationships in later life to tax planning), friendship (through Saga circles and of course its well-known holidays) and insurance. Saga even has its own radio station.

Advocacy

While many voluntary organizations will give you advice, only a very few will provide somebody to actually represent you – writing letters, attending meetings and so on in your place or with you, as your 'advocate'. In this context the word does not imply legal qualifications. Advocacy can be very important for three main reasons:

- Eldercare is complicated and it is often difficult for people to understand their rights and how best to go about securing them.
- Older people may be unwell and as a result not feel up to taking issue with, say, public bodies. Some will be mentally

incapable of doing so because they are suffering from dementia. People with significant visual and/or hearing impairment may also find fighting their own corner challenging. Yet these last three groups are often particularly vulnerable to having their rights infringed.

- There is the potential for conflict between the interests of older people and those of their closest relatives, including live-in carers, who might otherwise represent them.

While a few years ago advocacy for elderly people was pretty well unknown, today there about 300 groups across the United Kingdom offering it. You can track them down through the Older People's Advocacy Alliance (OPAAL). The groups differ in many ways – in their relative degree of independence, whether they concentrate on specific issues or specific groups (such as people from ethnic minorities or those suffering from dementia) and their level of expertise.

You need to be careful: the last thing you need is bad advocacy. Try to look for organizations which are truly independent. Are they receiving funding from local authorities with which they might have to take issue? They might be reluctant to bite the hand that feeds them. Bear in mind that voluntary groups themselves increasingly provide services. Also, look for a group which will offer quality. Does it really understand the world you want to take on? How much help will it give to you? Will it send out one letter on your behalf or will it pursue your case through to the bitter end? And will it truly represent you, rather than speaking for you without having a real inkling of your interests and preferences?

If you have an advocate, you want somebody who will explain clearly the pros and cons of particular courses of action and then give you 100 per cent support whatever you decide to do.

Older People's Champions

Readers in England may hear of 'older people's champions' and jump to the conclusion – understandably in view of their extremely promising title – that these are people who will act for individuals. This is not the case.

Essentially, people, usually in local government or the health service although they could be in voluntary organizations, offer themselves as older people's champions, and at the time of writing nearly 2,000 had done so. Nowhere is their task clearly defined, but it seems to be to cajole the care machine more effectively and swiftly into implementing the *National Service Framework for Older People*. Champions receive briefing reports from the Department of Health.

Securing the implementation of the Framework is also the main aim of the 'director for older people services', based in the Department of Health.

Carers' Organizations

Carers are people such as partners, close relatives, friends or neighbours who provide a significant amount of help to people living in their own homes, or in the homes of carers (pages 546–7). Organizations which have grown up in recent years specifically to help carers are described on pages 571–2.

Disability Organizations

When you see 'disabled' in the title of a group, do not imagine it helps only people with major disabilities such as people in wheel-chairs facing discrimination in the workplace or blind people. Telephone Update, for example, Scotland's national disability information service, will provide you with information on gadgets which can help you and where you can buy them if you are hampered only a little by an arthritic knee or are only slightly hard of hearing.

The oldest of the national disability organizations is RADAR, which was formed in 1977 with the amalgamation of two organizations which sprang out of the needs of people seriously disabled as a result of two world wars. RADAR provides advice through a helpline and literature to people of all ages, not necessarily with a very marked disability.

The British Council of Disabled People (an umbrella organization for several disability groups) is also keen to make it clear that it would like to help elderly people whose level of disability may be only slight. The British Council has a different approach from that of RADAR: its prime objective is to empower disabled people by promoting their equality and inclusion in society. Its ruling body has disabled people in the majority, while many of its staff are themselves disabled.

The Royal National Institute of the Blind and the Royal National Institute for Deaf People are older organizations which offer extremely valuable help, again not just to people with a very high level of sensory impairment.

But it is always worth looking around. There may well be more than one organization dealing with your own disability. You may want advice on getting the most from health and social services but might also benefit from attending meetings of self-help groups at which people with the same condition talk about their experience: this can not only provide tips on making the most of local services but also provide valuable reassurance. Suppose you have age-related macular degeneration (pages 15 and 20), for example. The RNIB covers all types of sight impairment, so can give advice; it also lobbies in Parliament for better laws and provision for visually impaired people and tries to alter public perception of sight problems. But you could also usefully seek out the Macular Disease Society, which is a hands-on support organization providing information on that condition alone, how its progression can be slowed down through diet, the low-vision aids which could help you, and tips on how to weave a path through the world of optometrists and opthamologists. This society also has local self-help groups at which people with the condition meet and share experiences.

Tripscope is another invaluable group for people with any degree of disability, whether sight, hearing or movement. It was set up in 1987 by Claudia Flanders, the widow of Michael Flanders, half of the musical duo Flanders and Swan (*Mud, Glorious Mud*) with the aim of making travel easier for people in wheelchairs than it had been for her and her husband in the 1950s and 1960s. Claudia Flanders' vision was that any disabled person contemplating a journey using any transport mode (public transport and car) should be able to ring a single number for one-to-one help. Her vision continues to be realized after her death by a committed team based in Bristol, dealing with around 30 enquirers a day.

Medical Organizations

Organizations which focus on particular diseases and afflictions common amongst older people are particularly valuable. These are usually membership organizations, but the membership fees tend to be very low and you get a lot of bang for your buck.

The Stroke Association is an example of one of the best of such national voluntary bodies. This is an impressive and well-funded organization which funds research and provides training courses for nursing home staff. Free publications, a national helpline and an impressive network of paid support workers based in 16 regional centres throughout England and Wales offer even more obvious benefits for the afflicted and their relatives. These workers advise on how to secure welfare benefits and therapy, although they do not provide strictly medical guidance. The regional centres also provide a base for trained volunteers and paid staff who help people to regain their ability to write, read or speak, and for local stroke clubs. In these, people provide mutual support, with volunteers helping new stroke victims and their families on a one-to-one basis; there are about 50 local stroke clubs within Greater London alone. A welfare grants fund makes one-off payments for individual items of equipment and towards the cost of holidays for stroke victims and their carers.

Voluntary groups exist for all the main ailments that are relatively common amongst older people, including osteoporosis, arthritis, Parkinson's disease, depression, diabetes, heart disease and Alzheimer's (the Alzheimer's Society covers all forms of dementia). From these organizations you are likely to get information sheets, at varying levels (those produced by the Parkinson's Disease Society are particularly impressive). There are likely to be national conferences, a national helpline (often very good), advice on the location of suitable holiday accommodation and recommended books. Some hold information on care homes specializing in their particular field, although they tend not to recommend particular homes.

Some of these groups are wealthy, as they have benefited from legacies from people who have suffered from the particular affliction. As a result, many of them are able to employ regional officers to support and extend the work of volunteers. There may be local facilities: many local Alzheimer's Society branches, for example, run day-care centres.

Websites
Some of the websites which can be helpful in the eldercare world are listed along with addresses, telephone and textphone numbers on pages 606–30. One organization was set up specifically to provide information over the net: Caring Matters. If you live in England and your relative lives in another part of the UK it is not that easy to find out how the eldercare system differs there. Try using this website, which is regularly updated.

Part Three
Staying Independent

Chapter 5
Adapting Surroundings

Significant loss of sight or hearing, developing incontinence and difficulty in moving without pain are all grim challenges to face, particularly when we are getting old and frail. Fortunately, help is at hand.

Gadgets and Aids

One aspect of the lives of older people which has perhaps changed more dramatically than any other is the range of gadgets and aids which enable them to stay independent and make the most of life. A host of inventors, largely unsung but offering far more benefits to humanity than more famous counterparts, have come up with ingenious practical solutions to everyday problems. These range from putting your socks on if you can't bend over, to pouring from a kettle if your hand shakes, to moving around your house, garden, neighbourhood and town if your legs are not what they were. Such aids may sound trivial, but they can be tremendously empowering.

However, this is an area in which you can spend a lot of money and, without sound impartial advice, spend it not very effectively. The walking frame on wheels which looked enticing in the shop may stand unused in your hall cupboard because you become frightened it would run away with you. Or you decide you would feel too conspicuous with it out of doors and wish you had found something which looked more like a shopping trolley – or even tried an electrically powered scooter.

An array of possibilities needs to be investigated fully before anything is bought, whether it is for inside or outside the home.

In the Home

The Living Room
You can buy armchairs with a lever which raise the support for your legs and another which lowers the back, enabling you to

Gadgets and Aids

- A pendant alarm is the number one gadget.
- The range of equipment for people with disabilities is unexpectedly vast.
- View the whole range of what is available before you buy, and seek expert advice on expensive items like mobility aids.
- Browse through catalogues before you stir, for instance those from the RNIB and RNID.
- Disabled Living Centres are the best places to view equipment.
- Be wary of buying from a door-to-door salesperson or a shop with a narrow range unless you are very well briefed.
- Expect to receive wheelchairs, Zimmers, walking sticks, special beds and mattresses free on the NHS.
- If the NHS or social services are slow to provide equipment, complain.
- If you don't want human helpers in your home, a gadget or aid may do the job instead.
- Apply for Attendance Allowance, which is non-contributory, non-taxable, non-means-tested and can be used on anything you like.

recline or even lie flat. There are electrically powered pushbutton control chairs whose seat can be made to tilt forwards to help you get out of them and to go back to help you sit down. Look for a chair which is comfortable, provides firm support for your back, which you can handle confidently and which, if it is lifting you up, will do so without making you topple over.

Phones which store your most frequently used numbers save a lot of dialling. If you are forgetful you may have difficulty remembering which button dials whom. Tiny labels may be hard to read, but you can get a phone which has space for a photograph alongside each of the memory buttons. If you cannot hear too well, you can have a phone with a flashing light instead of a ringer, and an amplifier you can tune in to your own hearing aid. If you are deaf, a textphone could enable you to communicate with another deaf person or with a hearing person, while through a system called Typetalk a hearing person can hear a message typed in by a deaf person. Mobile phones and cordless phones can of course be helpful, but for older people miniaturization is not necessarily a boon. Look for an instrument with large buttons if your hand is not too steady.

Reading stands are helpful if your hands tremble or are easily tired. If reading small letters is difficult, plenty of magnifiers can be found. Some contain an in-built light; some will hang around your neck; some are mounted on a stand; some are adjustable. Don a pair of prism glasses if you want to read while you are lying flat – the glasses will change the angle, so you can rest an open book on your stomach and still read it.

Arthritis may stop you holding a pen easily. Try a grippet, a device that slips around a finger while the pen is placed in a slot. There are large wall clocks which also show the date, and talking clocks for people who cannot see well. Changing a light bulb is exactly the kind of simple task which can become impossible for elderly people. You can, however, get a light which hangs on a long cord from the ceiling so it can be easily reached when the bulb needs changing.

You may have seen a pill dispenser with separate compartments reflecting the times each day when a pill must be taken. You can also get a device which makes a little noise at the time you are supposed to take one. And you can buy a device which crushes pills and another which cuts them in two.

The Kitchen

You can get a kitchen fitted with work surfaces which have a raised outer edge to stop liquids falling on the floor and making you more likely to slip over. You can have the edge of the work surface, and indeed the edges of cupboards and the sink and other features, picked out in a contrasting colour to help you see them. If you cannot see the divisions on your scales, you could place pieces of hard red rubber on them to emphasize the divisions, or you could buy talking scales. You can even buy a talking microwave oven. If you cannot see easily when a cup is full, you can buy a simple and cheap device that will hang over the edge and make a noise when it is covered; there is a similar product for the bath. A tip for the visually impaired: as a tin of dog food looks much like a tin of baked beans, have lots of different drawers for different things. People who cannot see well need a lot of light; you can get cupboards which light up when opened, like a fridge.

Strokes sometimes leave people unable to get much use out of one hand; arthritis can leave people without a firm grip. Fortunately, there are plenty of kitchen gadgets available to help. There is a work station consisting simply of a slab of hard plastic with spikes coming out of it on which you can place a potato which you can then peel with one hand, or a piece of meat which you can carve. You can get a wall tin-opener with a pull-down handle, and a grater which hangs on the wall with a container to catch the gratings. A simple but effective device consists of a T-shaped piece of wood with a V at the end into which you place a jar so it can be held firmly while you put all your effort into unscrewing it (with another handy device). There are scissors which need no force to be applied as they rely on a spring mechanism.

Lots of elderly people suffer from some tremor, perhaps severe if they have Parkinson's. A cup which is almost impossible to knock over, however much your hand shakes, sits on a very wide base with rubber underneath to stop it sliding. It narrows at the waist, then has two handles either side of the upper part. You can get non-slip place mats which prevent your plate from sliding, and non-slip devices for the backs of chairs, if you slide forward easily.

Filling a hot water bottle or tea or coffee pot is one of the most dangerous things you can do if you have a tremor. Funnels can help a bit, but by far the best device is a special kettle tipper. A stand with a spring allows the kettle to tilt over only one way and to bounce back. You keep the kettle on its stand so that it faces into your sink. When you pour from the hot kettle you do not need to lift it, but simply to hold its handle; it is kept firmly in place with special guides.

The Garden

A range of light gardening tools, from trowels to spades, made from carbon fibre, have been devised for people who can no longer manage heavy versions. Another range offers tools which are especially heavy, to counteract tremor. Another handy device is a stool on which you can kneel, which when turned over becomes a seat. Two firm handles on either side are there to help you push yourself up. Ideal Christmas presents!

The Bathroom

For somebody who has trouble getting on and off the lavatory seat, there are raised toilet seats which can be clamped on to the existing one, which raise the seat by six inches. You can put grab-rails either side to help pull yourself up, or bars which you push up against the wall when not in use. Most social services departments will provide at least the first two types of device. A more sophisticated aid is a lavatory seat which tilts forward to help you get off and tilts backwards and down to help you get on, operated with a press button.

The most basic device to help you get in and out of the bath is a broad board which you place across the bath, sit on and then swing your legs over into the bath. The disadvantage of this is that you never sit underwater, so you will need to ladle water over yourself or get a helper to do so. A more sophisticated and helpful variation is a removable bath lift. Battery-operated, it consists of a little plastic chair which you place in the bath (or leave there). You turn it towards you, sit on it, swivel round, then press a button and find yourself lowered down. You sit on the seat when you wash, then press another button to be raised to bath-top height.

The Bedroom

For people who find it difficult to get themselves up from bed there are lever devices which can raise them, similar to those installed in some armchairs. A simple, useful idea is a rope ladder bed-hoist: you pull yourself up by putting hand over hand up the ladder. You can buy a foot-rest to stop yourself slipping down the bed when you are seated, and adjustable back-rests and devices for raising part of the mattress. If you have difficulty getting in and out of bed, it is often a good idea to raise the bed itself, so you have less distance to move; this can be done with steel brackets on which the bed sits, which are fixed to vertical tubes on castors.

You will not see the bedroom portrayed as a theatre for sexual activity in any of the catalogues of gadgets for older people. Why not? Sex remains important in later life, and gadgets can have more of a part to play. Problems with erectile function are a notorious bugbear of old age. If you can manage to get yourself into a sex shop, you may well find the assistants extremely sensitive and pleased to guide you through the range of helpful devices available.

Stairlifts

Stairlifts can set you back several thousand pounds, but they can make the difference between using two floors of your house or having to move everything on to one level. Although social services departments will often help foot the bill (page 108), many people end up buying their own equipment rather than wait while their application is processed. Stairlifts can go up straight staircases, curved staircases and even spiral staircases. You need to have a pretty wide staircase if you want it to take the type of lift that has an especially wide base which can also carry a wheelchair. Some people even get a through-floor lift installed in their home, and social services or the housing department of local authorities will sometimes fund these for people who are wheelchair-bound, with a Disabled Facilities Grant (pages 206–7). A through-lift is like an ordinary lift, but not fully enclosed over the top, and goes up through the floor of the room above.

Alarms

Wherever you are on your property, an alarm with which you can summon help can get you out of trouble. The most useful type is simply a pendant which you wear round your neck and on which there is a button which you press if you need assistance. When you press the button, a call centre is alerted which tries to reach you and can do so anywhere in your house or in your garden, so long as it is not too large. If it cannot talk to you to ask what is the matter, it rings prearranged numbers, such as those of people living nearby who have agreed to help out and have been given door keys or, sometimes, your GP practice or the emergency services. Cords or buttons attached to the wall are less useful because you have to be able to reach them in an emergency.

It is important to have the alarm with you all the time when you are on your own property, in the garden as well as in the house, including the bathroom. Many people have falls going to the bathroom during the night and cannot summon help because they have unfortunately left their alarm by the side of the bed. When you have a bath, don't take the alarm off until the last moment and then place it on the side of the bath (although if you forget and leave it on, it should not normally be damaged).

Pendant alarms are so useful that I should not be surprised if more and more people who live alone and who are younger, say in their fifties, start to get them. Sometimes local authorities provide their own schemes and these can be cheaper than those provided by private companies. But you do not have to rent an alarm; you could buy one and then simply pay an ongoing charge to the organization providing the call centre. It is important not to wait until you have had a fall before you get one. You may never need to use it, but it could save your life. If you do nothing else as a result of reading this book, obtain a pendant alarm.

Mobility and hearing problems are very common in old age. What gadgets are available in these areas?

Walking Aids

If you are just looking for something to carry your shopping and a way of resting on the way to the shops or at the bus stop and you are not too large, have a look at a type of shopping trolley with a hardened top on which you can sit. These look much like any smart shopping trolley, but the sides are strengthened. They have four wheels, and unlike most shopping trolleys, they have a brake.

The more familiar four-wheeled shopping trolleys are not supposed to be walking aids: they are not designed to be leant on heavily, normal ones have no brakes and the height is not adjustable, so if it is not right for you, it can give you backache if you lean on it. However, a lot of elderly people prefer shopping trolleys which incidentally offer some support to walking aids which proclaim their infirmity.

If you are thinking of investing in a purpose-built walking aid, you need to try out a variety of different ones first. And you need expert advice. The best approach is to get your GP to refer you to a physiotherapist or occupational therapist who can work out exactly which of the many different models available would best suit you. He or she will ensure that the one selected fits you in terms of height, weight and type of hand grip, and will show you the correct way to use the aid and how to maintain it. Even an ordinary walking stick needs regular checking to see that the rubber ferrule on its base, which should be slip-resistant, is not worn, cracked or loose, and that the stick itself has not cracked. If you go down the NHS route, you may get the equipment free or subsidized. If you decide to buy something independently or your mobility difficulty is not sufficiently serious to prompt your GP to take action, don't just go out to the shop in your local parade. Make your first port of call a centre which can demonstrate a wide range of equipment and give you independent expert advice, such as a Disabled Living Centre (pages 105–6).

Another reason for not buying mobility equipment off the peg is that what will prove most helpful will depend on why you are finding walking difficult in the first place. Some people want a mechanism to distribute their weight and thereby lessen pain from particular joints, muscles or ligaments. Some need an aid to provide stability and balance. Some look for help to move more quickly and more efficiently. Some want to improve their posture and be helped to stand upright. Some look for an aid which will increase their confidence in their own walking ability, perhaps because they have been frightened after a fall.

There is also the environment to consider: indoors or out, in confined spaces, up and down steps, and so on. More than one type of aid may be called for. Measure significant dimensions before you choose: your doorways may be too narrow for some types of equipment. Does the aid need to be lightweight and collapsible because you want to take it with you in the boot of a car, or does it need above all to provide a stable support for movement indoors? You also need to consider hands and forearms – it is possible to find an aid with armrests which allows weight to be borne through the forearms rather than the hands; contoured hand grips spread pressure more evenly through the palms. Other physical considerations may be relevant; for example, arthritic fingers may make the manipulation of fiddly equipment difficult. If you do acquire a mobility aid, it is important that you use it safely (pages 99–103 and 215–6).

The main types of walking aid are:

Zimmer Frames

These frames provide safe support, with rubber ferrules on the bottom of their four legs which help to stop them from slipping. They are used mostly indoors and are usually provided by the NHS. The main disadvantage is you cannot get into small spaces with a Zimmer nor walk in the normal flowing manner, as you have to keep stopping and starting in order to pick up the frame, then move it forwards and step into it.

Zimmers vary – in some the height is adjustable, while in others it is fixed; some can be folded; the type of handgrip can be varied; some are wider than others.

Frames with Wheels

Some Zimmer-like frames have four wheels, but these do not suit people who are concerned that the frame will run away with them. They may need a frame in which the two back wheels are replaced with ferrules.

You can also obtain metal frames with three wheels, hinged at the front so they can be easily folded. But they are not as stable as the four-wheeled type, and the bar to secure them in the open position may be difficult to secure if you have a sight impairment or arthritic fingers.

Tripods and Quadrupods

These are walking sticks which divide at the base into three or four legs; they are more stable than a single pole and are particularly valuable for people with poor balance. Also, unlike a stick, they do not fall over when you let go of them to do something else, like opening a door. Tripods and quadrupods enable the user to get into spaces which would be too small for a Zimmer frame. However, you have to be careful that you do not trip over one of the legs.

Sticks

Sticks are easier to use than tripods and quadrupods if you are walking any distance. It is important that you get one which is the correct height. Metal sticks tend to be stronger than wooden sticks and their height can be adjusted. It is important to be aware that if you are using a stick to reduce the weight on one side of your body, perhaps because you have a painful knee, then the stick should be used in the opposite hand, with the leg with the painful knee and the stick moving forwards together.

Walking sticks have a different structure from canes for blind and partially sighted people. Canes are never used for support: you hold them across the lower part of your body to protect it and to check the existence and height of obstructions such as steps. The long canes used by people with little or no vision are held out in front and the user needs to attend a training course before acquiring one. Blind or visually impaired people who need the support of a walking stick can obtain a white walking stick. A piece of red tape around the stick indicates that the person using it is also deaf.

Rollators

These are two- or four-wheeled substantial walking aids with largish wheels which are used outdoors. There is often a shopping basket or a string bag, and perhaps even a little seat on which you can sit and rest. You can choose the type of brake and handgrip and it is important to feel confident that you can control the equipment easily so that it does not run away with you. Rollators can be enormously useful, but they tend to be heavy, so if you have steps up to your front door, you need to think about where you would leave it or who could carry it into your house.

Triangular Outdoor Frames

You can buy triangular frames with large wheels suitable for outdoor use. They have the advantage over the four-wheeled type in that they can be folded and thus stored more compactly. They are not quite as stable as rollators, but you can manoeuvre them into smaller spaces. Again, you can choose between different types of braking system, handgrips, baskets and bags. Like rollators, they tend to be heavy (in order to provide stable support).

Scooters

Many elderly people value their electrically powered scooters or buggies very much and prefer them to walking aids such as rollators or wheelchairs because they feel they have a sportier image. I heard of a husband and wife who had matching scooters and reported that the vehicles had changed their lives. But you can waste a lot of money on a scooter if you later find you cannot use it. You need to consider such matters as:

- Could I get it in and out of my house or flat?
- Would I need a ramp?
- Where could I store it? In the hall? In a garden shed?
- Who is going to charge up the batteries for me? (The recharging equipment is not large but it is heavy and recharging needs to take place close to a power source.)
- Could I operate it?
- Where will I get it serviced? (Electric scooters need servicing once a year.)
- Where will I drive it? (You are not allowed to drive a buggy in the road unless there is no pavement. It will not go down a kerb so you need to cross at points where pavements have been dropped.)
- If I take it to the supermarket, what will I do with it there? You might be able to drive it into the supermarket, but might have to keep getting out of it to take items off the shelves.

A large scooter may be roomier and have more space for shopping, but you may be unable to manoeuvre it round the angles in your house or get through your front or back door. Three-wheeled scooters are usually more manoeuvrable, but four-wheeled are more stable.

It is very important to get instruction before you take your scooter home. One woman in her nineties explained to me that although she considered herself *au fait* with vehicles generally (she had driven for 60 years and cycled until she was 80), her main reservation about her scooter was the difficulty in understanding how to operate it when she first bought it. She told me that instruction was given in the shop, but she wished she had been shown how to operate it in the environment in which she was going to use it.

Wheelchairs

Wheelchairs are something you will often find you can get for free, through referral from your GP, on long-term loan from the NHS. Some are powered; others need to be pushed. You may not need to be unable to walk to qualify – my mother, for example, was given a new, sophisticated chair at a time when she was still able to walk but found walking more than a few hundred yards painful. Friends and relatives were then able to push her in the chair when she wished to rest her legs.

Health bodies within the NHS have a wheelchair service. Some people are sent a wheelchair from a standard range; others are assessed individually by a physiotherapist for their own chair, considering their precise requirements in terms of size of wheel, height and type of cushions. The cushions are important not only for comfort but also to reduce the risk of pressure sores in vulnerable individuals; they come in many varieties, including gel cushions for people at high risk of developing sores, and one-way-slide cushions, so that the sitter does not slide out. If travelling by bus, you need to be aware that some bus companies may not take wheelchairs, on the grounds that their occupants could not easily get out in an emergency.

The person who is going to push the wheelchair should get advice on matters such as the height and weight of the chair, as pushing can damage your back. Indeed, it is a good idea if both the pusher and the person to be pushed are assessed for the most appropriate chair. Someone who is going to do lot of pushing might want to invest in a wheelchair with a motor. But you also need to bear in mind the weight of the chair if you are going to be lifting it, for instance in and out of a car boot. Chairs with a motor are heavier, and chairs without are not light. The charity Ricability can give you details of gadgets which help lift heavy items into car boots.

Wheelchairs can be borrowed from the Red Cross (as can other items, such as commodes), although they will not necessarily be very sophisticated. Shopmobility, an organization with local branches, provides wheelchairs for hire in town centres. Telephone ahead of time on your first visit to reserve one and to find out what identification you need to bring – perhaps only your pension book. There will be a small charge.

People going into a care home should take their NHS wheel-chair with them, as this may well be a much better vehicle than any which will be provided permanently in the home. In any case it should have been designed specifically for them, so other chairs will be less comfortable. It is important to sort out who is going to take responsibility for ongoing maintenance: you do not want the wheelchair sitting in the home for weeks on end with flat tyres or a foot-rest missing.

Make sure you are shown how to keep your chair or any mobility aid in working order; and if you will be pushing a wheelchair, be certain the supplier shows you how to minimize the strain on your back and ease the chair up and down kerbs smoothly.

Although an NHS chair should be of high quality, it will not necessarily be top of the range. If you want to buy a more expensive chair than your health authority will provide, it should give you a wheelchair voucher representing the value of the chair it is prepared to provide, so you can top it up. If you can pay extra, it is worth looking through catalogues. It is even possible to buy a wheelchair which climbs and descends flights of steps or enables the user to stand upright to reach high items, perhaps on supermarket shelves.

Helping Hearing

The United Kingdom has around 8.7 million people who are hard of hearing or deaf; the vast majority are elderly. Two levels of equipment are provided to help hearing. There is equipment which the National Health Service should provide, such as a personal hearing aid, and other equipment which can be useful, such as flashing alerting devices, which is the responsibility of social services departments.

Hearing aids are free on the NHS. To obtain one, you need to be referred by your GP to an audiologist in a hospital. Audiologists are not medical consultants: their expertise is in the technical aspects of hearing. They can diagnose hearing loss, recommend the most useful type of aid, show individuals how to use their aid and train people such as staff in care homes on how best to help people with hearing loss. Sometimes, as the first step, a GP refers a patient to an ear, nose and throat specialist at the local hospital, but this may not be necessary and can increase the time taken to get a hearing aid. So, if necessary, talk to your GP about a referral direct to an audiologist.

In the past, NHS patients have obtained unsophisticated analogue aids which amplify all sound, including background noise such as traffic and sirens. Far better are digital hearing aids. These can be programmed to amplify (or play down) sound at particular frequencies. If your ear has lost the ability to detect a particular frequency, nothing can be done: a hearing aid cannot create sound.[1] But a digital aid can be made to amplify particular frequencies which an individual ear is weak at picking up, for example, the frequencies at which we utter consonants, the key to understanding speech. A digital aid can also be programmed to play down particular frequencies. However, digital hearing aids are expensive, costing perhaps £2,500 each – and of course you may need two.

The Royal National Institute for Deaf People has been partly successful in its long and energetic campaign to persuade the NHS to issue digital rather than analogue hearing aids and some hospitals now issue them to NHS patients, but by no means all. This means that some people will wish to buy a digital aid privately. Before you do so, obtain the RNID's guide *Buying a Hearing Aid?* Once you have bought the aid, get it insured. The smaller types of hearing aid are easily lost. Whether you obtain your aid through the NHS or privately, make sure you understand how to work it, how to clean and maintain it and how to replace the batteries.

A personal hearing aid relies on its own in-built microphone. This is fine if you are trying to pick up sound close by in the absence of a lot of background noise. But in a church, mosque or lecture hall where the speaker is some distance away and others are shuffling and rustling in between, you may struggle to hear what is being said even with your hearing aid. You may need to campaign to get your local lecture hall or place of worship to install a hearing loop system. A loop system has a microphone which picks up the sound where it is being generated and feeds it into a loop of wire. You switch your personal hearing aid to the loop pick-up setting and, hey presto, it is as if you were standing next to the speaker.

In a care home, a loop system in the lounge enables people

with hearing aids to switch to the loop for watching TV. Other general listening devices which are useful in care homes include a free-standing device with an amplifier and earphones which can be kept around for use. (In care homes it is also helpful if there is good, even lighting so that people who are hard-of-hearing can see a speaker's face easily. Staff should also be trained to speak to such residents in a way that makes it easier to follow what they are saying.)

As well as obtaining a personal hearing aid from the NHS, you should also ask the social services department of the local authority for an assessment by its sensory support team. What equipment you receive, either for free or subsidized, will vary with the authority, as eligibility criteria differ, but you should certainly get something, might obtain a great deal, and will probably come by useful advice as well. The adaptations and equipment at home which social services departments could provide – or you could purchase yourself – include flashing-light alerting devices to indicate that somebody is at the front door, doorbells which are easier to hear, flashing lights to show that the telephone is ringing, alarm clocks which vibrate, special textphones and telephone amplifiers (page 92) and a device for listening to television other than through a personal hearing aid.

Help from voluntary bodies is also available. The RNID publishes information leaflets on gadgets and aids, and many are on display in Disabled Living Centres (see below).

Information

Because there is such a wide range of gadgets and aids available, and because you can spend a lot on them, anyone thinking of investing in something should make a trip to one of the 51 Disabled Living Centres based in major towns and cities throughout the UK. Here, items from different manufacturers are on display and impartial advice is available from trained staff. The centres are co-ordinated by the Disabled Living Centres Council, which is a charity. You will probably need to telephone ahead to make an appointment to view the equipment and/or to get the (free) advice of resident occupational therapists based at most of the centres, although there are often drop-in days. At a larger centre, such as the Manchester one, which houses 3,000 different pieces of equipment, you would have an appointment lasting perhaps 60 or 90 minutes at which you could try out the various different kinds of, say, walking aids or stairlifts; then the centre would give you information on local suppliers.

It is extremely important to buy from a reputable supplier who will also provide or arrange ongoing maintenance. The centres in places with few firms selling disability equipment sell as well as display. Many centres have information about obtaining second-hand equipment.

If you buy disability equipment from a door-to-door salesperson, not only will you lack the advice of a professional occupational therapist, but isolated in your living room, you will probably have little idea of how much you might reasonably expect to pay (pages 211–12). All the items at Disabled Living Council centres are priced, so you can easily make comparisons. If an item is not on show, the centre can tell you about it – all centres have access to a 16,000-item database, a truly enormous amount of information.

The centre in London is called the Disabled Living Foundation and it publishes advice booklets and factsheets on choosing a wide range of items, for example, a mobile hoist, pressure-relief equipment and a powered wheelchair. There are five different factsheets on footwear alone, as swollen feet call for a different approach from corns and bunions. Disabled Living Centres also exhibit invaluable gadgets for helping people get into and out of their clothes, and some of the centres have a clothing department. They provide catalogues in this field too, for example for Cosyfeet. The centres also give out free extremely useful guides by Ricability, an independent consumer research organization that produces reports and guidance on products for older and disabled people. Its publications offer help on choosing, amongst other things, a telephone or text-phone, a scooter, a pendant alarm, and domestic appliances such as irons, vacuum cleaners, toasters and electric kettles.

Behaving Sensitively

You may be a relative who has gone to great lengths to obtain gadgets, perhaps for your mother or father, only to find them refused. It is easy to forget that actually using these things often requires psychological adjustment. You may well have imagined that your father would be only too pleased to be wheeled in a wheelchair, but he may find the prospect very upsetting. Since it serves as a reminder of arriving infirmity, he may feel frightened, frustrated, helpless and think everybody would be staring at him. It may help to wheel him in an area in which he is not known until he gets used to the chair. Even pushing a mobility aid can seem to its user to be taking him or her out of mainstream society and into a victim class which he or she does not wish to inhabit. Below I give a flavour of the equipment and clothing available for people who have continence problems (pages 111–15), and clearly even if you are only helping your mother to deal with highly absorbent Kylie sheets, it is important to be aware of how she might feel about having to use them.

To make matters worse, many conditions, and therefore the equipment which can help people deal with them, attract a stigma. Unlike sight loss, hearing loss is stigmatized, perhaps because it is confused with mental frailty (pages 226–8). So unlike glasses or a white stick, hearing aids are often shunned by those who need them. Relatives have an important role to play in sensitively encouraging older people to seek help if they are hard of hearing and to encourage them to seek a referral from their GP to an audiologist to obtain a hearing aid if one is necessary.

Paying for Equipment
Much of this equipment costs a great deal of money, but you can often get help with footing the bill.

Do not expect to have to pay for anything which counts as medical equipment. Pressure-relieving mattresses, continence equipment, hoists and feeding tubes are all items which you should expect to get free, although they may be loaned rather than given. If you are living in a care home, expect free medical equipment (and services, such as those of a district nurse) just as you would in any other environment. Your right to this was asserted in a Department of Health circular issued in 2001 (page 56). The NHS also provides free mobility equipment such as wheelchairs, crutches, Zimmers and walking sticks. What the NHS will not provide for free is shopping trolleys which double as walking aids, including the extremely useful ones you can sit on, or electrically-powered outdoor buggies and scooters.

Other equipment may be provided by the social services departments of local authorities after they have assessed you as needing it. You might get equipment and gadgets like support bars beside the lavatory or a bath seat, for example. What, if anything, you pay for this varies. The vast majority of local councils in Scotland were providing gadgets and equipment free in 2003 though in England there had been much variation. Now the government has announced that in England people assessed by their local authority from June 2003 as needing gadgets or aids (or house adaptations to cope with frailty or disability up to the value of £1,000) should get them free.[2] Scottish authorities are expected to provide equipment for free for frail older people leaving hospital (page 206).

Where councils have been used to charging, watch out for attempts to continue it. Wherever you live, you may wish to challenge the eligibility criteria your council has used in allocating equipment. Similar systems of eligibility criteria apply to human help in the home (pages 278–79) and similar issues may arise. You may need to lodge a formal complaint about the application of eligibility criteria (pages 578–80).

Another possible hurdle is the assessment. Local councils do not usually provide equipment, except the most rudimentary, unless you have been assessed by one of its professional occupational therapists. These people are highly trained, fairly well paid and spread pretty thinly in most areas, with the result that it is by no means unusual to wait a year for an assessment.

In these circumstances, what can you do? If you are not trying to get financial help from your council, you could simply use the free services of a specialist occupational therapist at a Disabled Living Centre and then go and buy the equipment. If you want the council to help you out, you could commission and pay for your own assessment. The local council would hesitate to disagree with such recommendations unless it could produce its own professional occupational therapist to question them, which it would of course be hard pressed to do. Check with your local council what their response would be before you go ahead. You can get details of chartered occupational therapists in your area from the College of Occupational Therapists (pages 72–3).

The government has said that health organizations and social services departments should be operating joint equipment stores from April 2004.[3]

A different budget is available for certain types of large equipment which involves adaptations to the home. The installation of large expensive items such as stairlifts and lifts between floors which can take a wheelchair, as well as ramps to enable people to get into their own front door, can be funded with the help of a Disabled Facilities Grant (pages 206–7). House adaptations in England to cope with frailty or disability costing up to £1,000 should normally be provided free (page 205). Sometimes voluntary organizations and benevolent associations help pay for the cost of disability equipment.

Incontinence

One of the greatest of all the bugbears of elderly people is incontinence. It is not an inevitable feature of the ageing process, but it is common and its incidence increases as ageing progresses. It has been estimated that it affects about 20 per cent of older men and 30 per cent of older women living in the community.[4] When you also count in people living in care homes and hospitals, the total may be as high as 3 million.[5]

Continence problems for people who cannot move around easily to strip and remake their bed and load the washing machine (if they have one) is one of the main reasons why people stop living in their own home. It may not be the main reason for transfer to a care home, but it is frequently a contributory factor. Even if it does not erode independence in this way, it can be highly restrictive. Sufferers may feel they cannot go away on holiday or stay overnight with friends. If they are incontinent during the day, they may fear long journeys by bus or car (trains may of course contain toilets). Any trips out of doors may seem impossible, particularly now local authorities seem to have decided that public lavatories are no longer necessary. Sufferers may avoid sexual activity, with couples who have slept together for a lifetime taking to separate beds.

Incontinence

- Ask your GP whether treatment such as medication or exercise might work.
- Continence pads and much equipment should be provided free on the NHS.
- A surprisingly wide range of clothing, bedding, pads and equipment can help.
- Every health organization has continence nurse advisers offering valuable advice.
- The Continence Foundation offers a helpline and information.
- Get a Kylie sheet for your or your relative's bed.
- In a care home or hospital insist on a full discussion before any change to continence management is proposed.
- Children should be expected to sympathize, since muscle damage caused by childbirth is often to blame.

Causes

There are several different types and causes of urinary incontinence. Sometimes the sensation that the bladder is full is reduced or absent, with the result that its muscles contract unpredictably, expelling liquid; this is often associated with prostate enlargement or with damage to the nerves of the bladder. Or the bladder may become unstable, so that its muscles contract unpredictably with only small volumes of liquid.

For women, one of the most frequent causes of incontinence is a weakening through the trauma of childbirth of the pelvic floor muscles that regulate the release of urine; at the same time, diminishing levels of the female hormone oestrogen may cause the sphincter muscles, which control outflow from the bladder, to atrophy. In men the most common cause is an enlarged prostate gland.

Stress incontinence, which arises from muscle weakness, may mean you involuntarily pass urine when you sneeze or cough. Sometimes the problem is simply that the mechanisms which tell your brain that you need to go to the lavatory have become impaired, so you do not realize the need until it is almost too late.

Even those who escape actual incontinence may develop a need to urinate more frequently and immediately.

Faecal incontinence (affecting the bowels rather than the bladder) is of course a bigger problem, but far less common than its urinary equivalent. Faecal incontinence manifests itself most commonly as overflow diarrhoea caused by constipation. Faeces accumulate in the body and liquid seeps past them from higher up the bowel. This condition can be treated and prevented.

Both sexes may experience temporary incontinence as a side-effect of other illnesses or medical conditions, such as a stroke or pneumonia, a urinary tract infection or stress.

Coping

For an older person living at home, ongoing incontinence presents a considerable challenge. There may be wet sheets to deal with every day, not to mention soiled clothes, and the person affected will want to bathe or shower every morning. Nonetheless, many older people cope with the problem alone, without ever mentioning it to anybody. They buy a plastic undersheet from the chemist and wake each morning feeling very uncomfortable in sopping wet sheets, hoping that tomorrow the problem will have gone away.

The problem is best tackled head on. Those affected should first discuss the matter with their GP. It is easy to assume that because going to the lavatory is an activity treated with little respect and incontinence is not life-threatening, GPs will show little concern. Women often feel that problems in their lower regions are to be expected and accepted, and men may be reluctant to medicalize difficulties. For some people, there may be additional psychological factors in play. A study in 2001 of Pakistani Muslim women living in Yorkshire found that incontinence not only lowered self-esteem but also increased stress, because it rendered them unclean and thus unable to pray until they had repeated the act of ritual cleansing. These inhibitions, compounded by language problems, prevented their discussing their problems with nurses and doctors.[6]

Most people do not realize how much can be done. The Royal College of Physicians estimates that 70 per cent of people suffering from incontinence will respond well to treatment.[7]

Gerontological nursing specialists Hazel Heath and Irene Schofield report: 'With a comprehensive assessment leading to a correct diagnosis and the appropriate treatment, incontinence can often be cured and, if not cured, at least better managed. Simple nursing interventions can achieve cure rates of up to nearly 70 per cent.'[8] This does not mean to say that the problem will always be completely cured or eliminated, but it can often be reduced.

For ongoing incontinence, treatments include drugs which relax or stimulate the bladder, collagen injections, bladder retraining (which may be accompanied by medication) and the acquisition of gadgets like urinals and commodes which reduce the time taken to reach a lavatory-equivalent.

One lesser-known solution is exercising the pelvic floor muscles, which control the outlets from the back and front passages and in women also the womb. Just like any other muscles in the body, these get stronger with exercise. A continence nurse adviser or a physiotherapist specializing in the pelvic area can give you one-to-one instruction. Essentially, you squeeze in and lift up as if you were trying to prevent yourself passing urine or faeces and hold the contraction up to a slow count of 10, relax for a count of four, and then contract again, up to a maximum of 10. It is best to do the exercises after emptying the bladder. As these exercises are invisible, you can do them while waiting at the bus stop. Dr Joan Bassey of the University of Nottingham Medical School wrote of incontinence, 'Specifically designed exercises for the pelvic floor have been shown in a single-blind randomised controlled trial to be significantly more effective than other forms of treatment or no treatment at all.'[9]

Sometimes a cause for incontinence can be found which is temporary or treatable, such as enlargement of the prostate gland or the stress of a change of environment such as admission to hospital. Incontinence may prove to be the side-effect of certain drugs such as sedatives and tranquillizers, which can perhaps be changed.

Under exceptional conditions, an 'in-dwelling' catheter may be prescribed by your GP or a nurse for long-term use. Catheters are small-bore plastic tubes inserted direct into the bladder; urine drains through them into a plastic bag. They are mainly used in hospitals and care homes, but plenty of people living at home on their own also use them; they can be changed regularly by district nurses. Catheters do have considerable drawbacks, however, such as increased chance of urinary tract infections and potential loss of dignity and it is very important to weigh up the pros and cons before you have one fitted (pages 427–29). There are circumstances, however, in particular an inability to drain the bladder, in which there is no option but to use a catheter.

As in so many other areas of eldercare, the way to get the most out of the NHS is to gain access to one of the new types of specialist adviser. There are now more than 300 continence clinics across the United Kingdom. The area each clinic covers varies greatly, and each may have only one or two nurses, but they offer expertise in a field which turns out to be surprisingly complex. You do not need to be referred by your GP: continence clinics offer an open referral system and you can get the address of your nearest clinic from a directory held by The Continence Foundation. Other possibilities are referrals from a physiotherapist who can teach you pelvic floor muscle strengthening exercises and advise on improving your mobility, an occupational therapist who can advise on equipment to help use the lavatory, and a hospital consultant, such as a urologist, if you need more specialist treatment.

At the very least, a consultation with a GP or continence specialist will help you to understand the cause of the condition. If it cannot be cured, its severity may be reduced. Outside advice may also make you more determined to face up to the problem and to deal with it systematically, perhaps by installing a washing machine and tumble drier and replacing blankets with duvets to make bed-making less strenuous. You may find that your social services department organizes a laundry service as part of its homecare services for older people.

Clothing and Equipment

Special undersheets called Kylie sheets are a good investment. The Kylie disperses night-time urine: made of quilted, absorbent material, it soaks up fluid and spreads it, thus keeping the body comparatively dry. The principle is used in babies' nappies, which aim to keep the infant's bottom dry while absorbing urine.

A wide range of undergarments is available. What is appropriate will vary with the amount of urine being passed, capacity to manage the system, and gender: continence pads for men need to be shorter than for women and, naturally enough, differently located.

Kanga pants, based on the Kylie-sheet idea, absorb the fluid away from the body into a little plastic pouch filled with absorbent material outside the pants; the pouch can be unbuttoned and its contents removed. As long as the pad is changed regularly, the garment and the skin beneath remain dry. This is usually much more comfortable than plain plastic knickers worn outside a continence pad, since the plastic can become hot and sticky and urine close to the skin may damage it, but the type of system which will best suit any particular person will vary. Kanga pants are not suitable at night, or for double (urinary and faecal) incontinence, but they enable many people to forget about the problem during the day.

For men there is a range of penile sheaths and appliances. In one device, the urine passes down a tube into a bag attached to the inner calf, hidden under trousers; this needs careful fitting. For men who suffer only slight dribbling, there are special pouches consisting of super-absorbent material with their plastic backing kept in place by close-fitting pants.

Elderly women who suffer incontinence are often tempted simply to buy a packet of sanitary pads. However, sanitary pads are designed to cope with a far smaller volume of liquid and offer much less absorbency than continence pads, which may seem more expensive but actually offer better value.

Continence pads are sophisticated devices and if you have to use a lot, the costs can mount up. You ought to be able to get pads of some kind for free through the NHS Continence Service, though they will not necessarily be the most sophisticated. Pads come in varying degrees of strength and thus cost, so make sure you are given pads that are strong enough.

If you are in a care home and paying your own fees and are charged for continence pads or continence equipment, you should object (page 388).

Men can get devices such as sheaths and leg bags on prescription, and of course prescriptions are free for older people. However, Kanga pants and the like are not available on prescription for women. What you get will vary according to criteria set by your local health authority such as your primary care trust. Some will provide for two free Kylie sheets – though they may not be the most sophisticated type, or the ones which tuck in. You probably will not get free protection for chairs or a waterproof duvet cover.

A wide range of hand-held urinals and other equipment is also available, so do not just rely on the limited stock of your local chemist. Disabled Living Centres display a range of continence equipment and clothing (pages 105–6) and the staff are generally extremely sensitive, as well as knowledgeable. You could also ask the practice or continence nurse based at or contactable through your GP surgery to advise you. The Continence Foundation can tell you about the wide range of products available; it operates a national helpline.

Disabled Living Centres also stock clothing which can be useful if the problem is getting to the lavatory in time. If arthritic hands make manipulating ordinary underclothes tricky and time-consuming, try wide-legged or cami-knickers, which fasten with Velcro at the front of the crotch. You may be able to adjust existing clothes, for instance by replacing buttons or zips with Velcro openings or fixing an extra tab on a zip to make it easier to locate quickly.

Chapter 6
Moving Around

As we grow older, we often become increasingly apprehensive, indeed fearful, about moving around out of doors. Why not stay at home when a holiday could present all sorts of difficulties, like arriving at an unknown station to find there is no lift and no lavatory? Shouldn't I stop helping in the Oxfam shop because I have had a couple of dizzy turns, so might fall and hurt myself? What with slippery pavements and muggers, shouldn't I venture out only when someone will give me a lift? Accidents and falls and arriving home with sore feet and aching legs are serious matters, but to withdraw from the world can amount to a kind of premature death.

Mobility

If there is one single thing apart from adequate food, drink and warmth which keeps older people feeling healthy and engaged with the world, it must be maintaining mobility. But remaining mobile, whether at home or in the wider environment, is a huge challenge for many older people. Those suffering from breathing problems, perhaps caused by a chronic chest condition, need to stop to draw breath, particularly when confronted by a hill. Arthritis sufferers may find that movement of the knees and other joints is extremely painful and may fear a knee giving way under them. People with corns and bunions may long to take the weight off their feet. Waterworks problems may mean people need to reach a lavatory quickly. Yet today's older people have to cope with changes to the environment which make life more difficult than it was for their counterparts in the past. One of the reasons for this is the widespread removal of many ordinary public facilities – public lavatories, bus shelters, seating – which can make a walk to the shops or a trip on the train or bus a nightmare when it might otherwise be a delight.

Public lavatories are not easily found. There has been a massive loss of such facilities in urban areas: local authorities are under no obligation to provide them and local councils have been closing them wholesale to rid themselves of the costs of maintaining and cleaning them. Their absence may cause older people much anxiety. How does it feel to have to go into an unfamiliar garage or restaurant to ask to use the loo?

Within a town centre and its surrounding streets you are not likely to be well provided with seating. Where benches are provided, they are normally in parks, rarely along suburban streets. Seats at bus stops, where they exist, are often tiny perches. Fifty years ago, railway stations were typically provided with warm waiting rooms furnished with roomy benches with high backs and arm rests. Seats at railway stations were almost as plentiful as they are today in airports. At some stage, the comfortable wooden benches were replaced with metal seats, cold and hard and lacking the arm rests which make sitting and rising easier. These, however, are better than nothing – which is more usually what is on offer. During the 1990s, Railtrack took a policy decision to remove a great deal of seating from stations because it was thought to promote vagrancy and public disorder, just as litter bins and left-luggage lockers were swept aside wholesale lest terrorists leave bombs in them. This situation may, however, be about to improve somewhat: in 2003 the Strategic Rail Authority published a new code of practice for railway stations which includes requirements for seating.

On the streets of our towns and cities, uneven pavements, pavements strewn with slippery leaves or litter, potholed alleyways and paths with inadequate lighting can all present real hazards: you might twist an ankle or take a tumble. Equally important, they present a psychological barrier to going out. So too can other forms of surfacing which may not be dangerous but are tiring to cross, such as gravel. I once happened upon a delightful sheltered housing scheme in the middle of a little town in Wiltshire. Next door was the parish church, but the paths across were all gravel. Try pushing a wheelchair or a mobility aid through gravel.

It is important to distinguish between the needs of the elderly and the needs of disabled people. Massive strides have been made in facilitating movement for disabled people. There has been a huge investment of public money in provision for blind people who walk with a stick, notably in strips of bubble pavement to warn of impending kerbs. Large sums have also been spent on improving access for people in wheelchairs by lowering kerbs, as well as installing ramps, lifts and special lavatories. However, there has been no equivalent spending on provision for people who are simply frail; indeed they have lost facilities rather than gained them.

As if these obstacles to mobility were not enough, today's older people have to go further than their predecessors just to carry out the day-to-day business of living. The advent of widespread car ownership has driven shops out of urban neighbourhoods into venues out of town which are easily accessible by car, but not on foot or by public transport. This may be all very well for elderly people who have cars, but many have to give them up, cannot afford them or never learned to drive.

There is a popular misconception that the vast majority of older people have cars. This is wrong. In Scotland, for example, in 2001, 53 per cent of people over the age of 60 did not have a driving licence. This may not be a problem if somebody else in your household has a car, but only half of Scottish people over 65 were in this position. [1]

There is, however, much that elderly people themselves as well as their relatives and friends can do to help them move around more easily.

On Foot

Some people find that their lives are completely transformed by electrically-powered scooters or buggies. Mobility aids which carry shopping bags and shopping trolleys with a strengthened top which doubles as a seat can be invaluable (pages 87–101).

Comfortable footwear is important. Great strides have been made in this field in recent years: you do not have to make do with whatever is on offer in the high street (although trainers with their cushioned soles can provide welcome relief from traditional court shoes and lace-ups). Nowadays there are firms which specialize in footwear for older people, such as Cosyfeet. Your local Disabled Living Centre can provide guidance (pages 105–6).

Altering the Environment

As you try to get about, it makes sense to work out the problem areas. What journeys may be desirable but are difficult if not impossible at the moment, and how could they be made easier?

Mobility

- Maintaining mobility is important to maximize choice, independence and fitness.
- Cuts in public services like lavatories and the relocation of shops out of town mean older people find it harder to go about their daily lives.
- Seek out walking aids, continence aids and comfortable shoes.
- Lobby the council for safer road crossings, more dropped kerbs, better surfaced paths and more seats and toilets.
- Ask your supermarket to install shopping trolley lockers.
- Use the Disability Discrimination Act to get adjustments to services.
- There are extremely generous travel concessions in Northern Ireland, Scotland and Wales and in limited parts of England.
- The new low-floor buses are easy for frail people to use; the floor can be lowered further to help people on and off.
- Cars can be adapted to make them easier to use.
- Don't push yourself to drive: use public transport instead.

Road Crossings

Many journeys on foot require us to cross busy roads. If older people are involved in accidents as pedestrians, they are more likely to be injured or killed than younger people. Seventeen per cent of pedestrian casualties on Britain's roads in 1998 were over the age of 60, but 46 per cent of pedestrians killed were 60-plus.[2]

Speeding is the main cause of road accidents. If you think speeding is dangerous at a particular place, ask the local authority to introduce traffic-calming measures. Similarly, if you have to cross a major road and the illuminated crossing does not allow enough time, then you could write to the Road Safety Section of your local authority and ask it to increase the length of time allowed.

In both cases it is a good idea to telephone the council in advance to find out to whom you should write. Councils organize themselves differently in different areas. Stockport Council, for instance, has an Accidents Investigation Unit. You do not have to have been involved in an accident to write to such a unit, and they do not restrict themselves to accidents involving serious injury. Some councils may carry out the same activity through a different section, such as traffic management or road safety. Or you could address your letter to a general official, such as the highways officer or the transport officer.

So have a look at the places where you cross the road and think about their safety. As I write this, from a small, quiet market town in Surrey, an elderly man and his wife in their seventies out on a shopping trip were killed instantly last Saturday afternoon by a lorry at a road crossing. This incident has alerted residents to the fact that that junction would have been safer and the double fatality perhaps prevented had it included a pedestrian crossing, as opposed merely to traffic lights.

Pavements

Your council may be lowering pavements at road junctions and crossings, but their programme may not fit the journeys you want to make. Tell it. A kerb can be impossible to surmount if you are pushing a heavy person in a wheelchair and you do not want to wreck your back. In the late 1990s, I used to take my mother in a wheelchair down to the promenade overlooking the sea at Ramsgate. There was one problem. I had to wheel her for quite a distance in the road until we reached a lowered pavement. I wrote to the highways department of Thanet District Council, explained the problem and asked if it would install drops at points which I suggested. It agreed.

Surfaces

Lowered pavements are just one aspect of ensuring that the surface underneath your or your relative's feet is convenient or safe to use. Walk or get somebody to walk your local journeys and make a note of any problems. There may be a stretch of rough, gritty tarmac which needs resurfacing or uneven paving slabs on both of which you might trip. Sometimes unsuitable surfaces, like gravel, seem to have been provided simply because nobody has thought about the choice of material from any aspect other than cost. Do not forget alleys. We are fortunate that far-sighted

Victorian town planners provided this alternative transport system, but many are now woefully neglected, beset by potholes and weeds, not to mention litter and dog-dirt. So you might need to remonstrate with the council about repairing surfaces or controlling littering or dog-fouling more effectively; sometimes you will find yourself lobbying others, such as a church council or a football club.

If you visit a town with which you are unfamiliar on a day out, it is useful to know about any obstacles in advance – fixed features such as steep steps, or temporary obstacles such as the pavement being dug up – which could make life very difficult, particularly if you are relying on a mobility aid or a wheelchair. Try telephoning the Town Centre Manager of the local council. Many town centres, including those in suburbs, employ such people. They patrol their areas frequently and are more likely than anybody else to know of any such difficulties with which you might come face to face.

Seating

Adequate seating is terrifically important for elderly people. A few comfortable seats between the house and the shops can make an enormous difference. Even where plenty of seats are provided in recreation grounds, they are often located with the needs of other groups in mind, such as parents keeping watch over their children on the swings, rather than elderly people who have to cross the park to get to the post office.

Where seating is inadequate in shopping malls, or where what is provided is uncomfortable or lacks supports to enable users to get themselves up and down, it is the property company or the scheme manager to whom you should turn. Keep a watch on any new shopping developments proposed in your or your relative's area: is adequate seating (amongst other facilities) guaranteed? It is often easier to get new facilities at the planning stage, when developers have to offer the council something in return for the vast profits they hope to make.

Public Lavatories

All you can do here is to lobby your local council or councils to provide lavatories (or to ensure that developers provide them in new developments). Where new lavatories have been provided in recent years, they are often only urinals for men to prevent street fouling in popular town centres, or for disabled people only. What is needed is far more lavatories for everybody and ones which older people find easy to use: well lit, with handrails, support and contrasting colours for fittings.

If you have no joy with your council, try your MP: a Parliamentary cross-party committee on public lavatories has been set up, so MPs should be aware that the dearth of public loos is an issue which should be addressed. The British Toilets Association is the main campaigning group and can provide advice, although it does not have local branches.

Parking Bays

A useful facility is a parking bay outside the flat or house of an older person who cannot walk far and has no form of off-street parking to minimize the distance between any vehicle which drops them off or which they drive and their own front door. Councils often do not publicize the fact that they will install personalized parking bays for disabled people if asked to do so, fearing the bay may stay if the disabled person dies or moves away. So if you have serious mobility problems, apply to the council for one. An occupational therapist will normally assess a bay applicant. If approval is given, drop kerbs will be put in and street furniture which is in the way will be moved. Once the bay is installed, however, anyone with a disabled badge can park in it, so you may find your 'spot' occupied by somebody else.

Supermarkets

Today you not only have to cope with greater distances than your parents or grandparents to reach the shops at all, but the supermarket itself can pose difficulties. First comes the challenge of extricating a trolley with the aid of a coin and disentangling it from the others to which it is tethered. Then there is coping with your own shopping trolley while you are going round: very few supermarkets provide lockers and if you hang your trolley on the hook at the rear of the shop's trolley, ten-to-one it will swing around and get in the way. Then there are the distances to be negotiated: there may be seats at the far side of the tills, but supermarkets rarely interrupt aisles with seats. Older people often have difficulty in stretching or bending to reach the items they need and in reading small labels. Then there is the hazard posed by other shoppers to people who cannot get out of the way quickly. There may be slippery floors after a spillage and large toddlers perched in supermarket trolleys or even zipping around on their own scooters.

If you encounter problems such as these, discuss them with the manager. Many supermarkets will provide an assistant to accompany a blind person and ought to do so for a frail person too; indeed, supermarkets which gain the reputation of giving older people adequate help ought to attract more older customers. If the assistance which you consider you need is not forthcoming, threaten to complain or to write to the local paper or talk of raising the matter with the Disability Rights Commission (pages 124–5). Old-style town-centre department stores used to lay on not just plenty of seating but also lavatories, complete with assistants. Today's supermarkets, with the millions of pounds profit they make each year, ought to be able to run to such basic facilities too. Some do, but many do not.

Many town centres offer wheelchairs for hire under a scheme called Shopmobility (page 102).

Action which you or perhaps your son or daughter can take to try to make the urban environment easier to negotiate may sound like a lot of work. It is. There are no lobby groups on the ground (yet) which campaign in this sort of area, so you are breaking new ground. Probably your best ally is your local councillor. Any journey is a sum of its parts and you may find yourself having to negotiate with a number of organizations to effect improvements. But take heart: the action that is necessary – a repaired pavement here, seating at a suburban street corner, additional lighting in an alleyway, a CCTV camera – do not involve massive public works. These are all things for which public organizations have budgets. Action on your part may require only a letter to prompt a bit of spending in a way that had not been planned.

People with Disability
Fortunately, help is at hand in the form of the Disability Discrimination Act, 1998. Many people are under the impression that all this legislation does is help people with very significant

disabilities, such as blind people and people in wheelchairs, to challenge discrimination in the workplace and get ramps and disabled-friendly loos installed in large public buildings. In fact the Act, and in particular a strengthening of its provisions coming into place in October 2004, can help frail people of many types and levels of disability.

The Act defines disability in a very broad way as 'a physical or mental impairment which has a substantial and long-term adverse effect on a person's ability to carry out normal day-to-day activities'. 'Long-term' is defined as having existed for at least 12 months or likely to last for at least 12 months. To come within the scope of the Act, such difficulties have to affect the 'day-to-day activities' on which the impairment impinges. The activities must be:

> normal activities carried out by most people on a regular basis, and must involve one of the following broad categories: mobility – moving from place to place; manual dexterity – for example, use of the hands; physical co-ordination; continence; the ability to lift, carry or move ordinary objects; speech, hearing or eyesight; memory, or ability to concentrate, learn or understand; being able to recognise physical danger.

Help could therefore go to somebody whose arthritic knee has a substantial and long-term effect on their ability to move around, someone with a hearing problem (whether or not he or she uses a hearing aid), someone with lung disease who gets breathless on exertion or someone who cannot handle items easily for example.

The legislation requires that providers of services to the public must consider making changes to physical features on their premises which make it unreasonably difficult for people with disability to use their services. A service provider includes your corner shop, hairdresser, church, estate agent, off-licence, football ground, betting shop and stately home open to the public. The intention is not to put small operators out of business by requiring substantial costly rebuilding: service providers have to make 'reasonable adjustments', which could include not only changes to the physical fabric but also providing extra help or changing the way in which services are provided.

The Disability Rights Commission is a government agency set

up to administer the Act. Service providers and users can contact it for advice on rights and responsibilities through a helpline. The Commission also offers a conciliation service. It can require service providers to make major changes that would benefit all disabled and frail elderly people. If conciliation is unsuccessful, the Commission suggests recourse to the courts – for instance, a claim through the small claims procedure, which in England and Wales does not usually need a solicitor. Further details are provided in free literature from the Commission.

So what are the kinds of 'reasonable' adjustment the Commission might require? It would not expect a small second-hand bookshop accessible up a front step and with only one member of staff to install ramps and lifts, but it would expect handrails by the step, help for people who cannot reach the higher shelves and the installation of stronger lighting to make access easier for visually impaired people. However, if the bookshop were larger and part of a national chain, the Commission would expect much more, such as the installation of a level or well-ramped entrance, improvements to lighting, improvements to signage, lower shelves or the provision of trained staff to help locate books out of reach.[3]

There seems no reason why the Act should not apply to the grounds of a church, parks, seaside promenades and the like: in all these cases somebody is providing a service. Indeed, the Commission's booklet *2004 – What it means to you: a guide for disabled people* makes it clear that the physical features to which service providers might have to make reasonable adjustments are not just buildings or indoor facilities. They include seating in the street or a pub garden, stiles and paths in a country park or fixed signs in a shop or leisure facility (the last of these emphasizing the point that visual disability is just as important as any other).

It will be interesting to see to what extent the Act can force operators to provide additional facilities such as comfortable seating and lavatories. Where public lavatories are already provided, the Commission clearly expects changes, such as the installation of grab-rails, non-slip flooring and a good contrast between the colour of the walls and the fittings. Such changes would not be enough for most wheelchair users, but would help people with a mobility or visual impairment. If no lavatory is provided at all, what then? It is to be hoped that users as well as organizations representing elderly and disabled people will fight test cases to see whether, for instance, supermarkets which fail to provide lavatories could be forced to do so.

This legislation has the potential to provide an enormous amount of improvement if we are all prepared to challenge service providers. Although the duties on physical features do not come into force until October 2004, the Commission expects providers to be considering changes before then, so readers might care to alert their supermarkets, leisure centres, councils which own beaches or city farms, favourite bed and breakfast establishments, pubs and many more to their interest in ensuring that any obstacles to use on account of disability should be removed as soon as possible. Potentially this legislation offers the possibility for physically or mentally frail people as well as those who have a sight or hearing impairment to challenge the unacknowledged assumption that still operates in so many walks of life that once somebody, young or old, develops a disability, the range of activities which they can undertake on a day-by-day basis must be drastically reduced.

Driving

Some people think that older people are barred from driving after a certain age. This is absolutely not the case. But they do have to take the trouble to renew their driving licences. Fifty-six days before your seventieth birthday, the Driving and Vehicle Licensing Agency sends you a form on which you have to declare that you are still sufficiently mentally and physically alert to carry on driving. You have to disclose any new physical disabilities, such as giddiness or worsening eyesight. There is no obligation to get your GP to verify the answers. GPs or consultants who consider that a medical condition is making your driving hazardous, however, have a duty to raise it with you and if necessary inform the DVLA (pages 67–8). If a medical problem has developed, you may have your licence withdrawn, but you may still get it back. I heard of an elderly woman whose driving licence was withdrawn when she developed cataracts. After she had had an operation to remove the cataracts, she reapplied for her licence, got it back and, now 92, is continuing to drive.

Sometimes, however, as people get older they find that driving makes them more tired than it used to, particularly if their eyesight is slightly impaired. This fatigue can be compounded by afflictions of the body, even apparently insignificant ones, which can make driving uncomfortable and even cause accidents. As a group, older drivers are not more dangerous than the young – exuberance and aggression create more hazards than frailty. But when older drivers are involved in road accidents they are more likely than younger people to suffer fatal injuries.[4]

Of course older people can help themselves. Those who find driving more taxing may want to avoid doing so at times and in places which make particular demands. Thus many older people cut down on driving at night, for long distances or on unfamiliar roads.

If you are under pressure to keep motoring, perhaps because you are caring for somebody else, such your partner, try to get somebody else, like a relative, to take on some of the driving.

You may be entitled to help with parking: the Blue Badge scheme essentially enables its holder to park on single and double yellow lines, except where other restrictions operate, for instance in bus lanes and in places where loading is not permitted. Local authorities may in addition provide reserved parking places and may waive charges in their own car parks for badge holders. The scheme was recently extended to Europe and is now known as the European Blue Badge scheme. It is available for disabled people whether they are travelling as drivers or passengers. There is no automatic entitlement on grounds of age, but you are likely to receive a badge if you have considerable difficulty in walking, whether as a result of arthritis or a lung condition, or for many other reasons. The regulations actually say that you must 'have a permanent and substantial disability which means you are unable to walk or have very considerable difficulty in walking'. Your GP will probably be asked to authenticate this.

More straightforward ways to get a badge are by qualifying for the higher rate of the mobility component of the Disability Living Allowance, becoming registered blind or receiving a War Pensioner's Mobility Supplement. To get further details and to apply for a badge, people in England and Wales should contact their local social services department. If you live in Scotland, contact the chief executive or the social work department of your local council; if you live in Northern Ireland, contact the Roads Service of the Department for Regional Development.

If you want to continue to drive for as long as possible, find out about the myriad ways in which cars can be adapted for older and disabled people. The possibilities are enormous: adaptations range from altering hinges so a door opens further, to positioning the seat back further, altering its height and installing a swivel seat (which makes getting into and out of the car easier) and changing the controls. All this information comes in free publications from the charity Ricability. An organization called Motability operates a scheme to help disabled people buy or lease new and second-hand cars. Disabled drivers can get one-to-one advice from the Mobility Information Service and the Mobility Advice and Vehicle Information Service. There are hints on getting in and out of cars on page 215.

Use public transport. You may eventually have to give up driving, but this will be less traumatic if, perhaps after a long period of travelling exclusively by car, you are already used to buses and trains, and especially if you have come to enjoy using them. So collect and use your travel pass and obtain other concessionary tickets, such as a Senior Citizens Railcard. Suggest as a birthday present a Rover ticket providing free travel for a week on local buses or £50 worth of trips by a taxi firm. Get your family to join you on fun days out using buses, trains, trams and steam trains.

Public Transport

Often you come across elderly people who have clocked up long distances driving on holiday in another part of the UK or on the Continent. They may return home exhausted and stressed from driving to and from their destination as well as while they were there, perhaps feeling shaken by some close shave on the roads and needing another holiday. They could of course go on tours, but for those who want the freedom to plan their own excursions, it is a shame that they do not let the train (or the coach) take the strain and use local trains and buses at their destination. Perhaps they imagine that local public transport services, especially in rural areas, barely exist. But this is wrong. There are of course areas where services are thin on the ground, but there are also a great many places where excellent networks of local public transport services still exist, offering terrific holiday and day trip opportunities.

You could base yourself in an attractive market town easily accessible by train, such as Norwich, Berwick-on-Tweed, Ledbury or Hereford and take advantage of local bus services designed to bring people in from villages, but go in the reverse direction. You could take advantage of new public transport services which have been developed over the last ten years with the deliberate intention of enabling people without cars (or car-owners fancying a rest) to get into the depths of the countryside. I am not thinking only of special train services such as steam-train lines: the Countryside Agency and its sister bodies (the Countryside Council for Wales and Scottish Natural Heritage) have been promoting and funding bus services, some running according to a traditional timetable, others round trips, five services a day, on which you buy a ticket for the day and alight and get back on the bus at any place along the route, on a hail-and-ride basis. You will find these newer services in ordinary rural counties as well as in national parks.

Or you could base yourself in an area with a variety of public transport provision and a dense network of services. If you holiday on the Isle of Wight, for example, you will find the main bus station is next to the ferry terminus and there are frequent bus services providing access all over the island, with B and Bs and hotels in glorious settings on the bus route.

Information

The public transport department of your local authority will have details of all public transport services in your area or can tell you whom to contact. In Northern Ireland, you should call Northern Ireland Translink. Tourist offices should also have information on all local public transport services to hand. If you telephone Traveline, you can obtain information on bus, coach and train services throughout the United Kingdom. Train information is of course available from the National Rail Enquiry number.

Tripscope is a particularly useful organization. It provides one-to-one advice for people with some degree of disability who are planning journeys. It will give you up-to-date information on facilities available at train, bus and coach stations, airports and ports as well as general advice on tackling journeys by any transport mode.

Trains

Of all the modes of public transport, the train is probably best for older people. Pluses for train travel include:

- routes away from roads so the journey is more relaxing
- the ability to get up and stretch your legs and so prevent yourself becoming stiff
- the possibility of a table for books, refreshments and so on
- the freedom to buy refreshments on the journey (often)
- the possibility of using the lavatory at any time except on commuter lines; the newer trains have support bars to help you up and down
- the ability to take pets free of charge except in very few circumstances, and space on the floor for the pet to relax
- the possibility of travelling in a wheelchair, with staff helping you on and off with ramps, and on many InterCity trains special places for people in wheelchairs with tables at a comfortable height for them (though you have to telephone ahead to organize these).

The concessionary Senior Railcard is available for people aged 60 and over. It costs £18 and entitles the holder to a reduction of up to one third on all journeys outside the morning peak period for 12 months anywhere in Britain. The Disabled Person's Railcard costs £14 a year and also entitles a companion to travel with the disabled person at up to one third reduction. You can get information on how to apply for these cards at main stations and travel centres or through telephoning the National Rail Enquiry Service. People travelling in their own wheelchair and blind and partially sighted people can obtain discounts on train tickets for themselves and for one travelling companion even if they have not bought the Disabled Person's Railcard. On many trains special space is set aside for wheelchair users and you can place mobility aids in the guard's van.

If you need help at the station transferring yourself and your luggage from one platform to another, or to the taxis or bus stops or down to the Underground, you can usually get help, but you have to give the train operating companies 24 hours' notice.

Disabled people who hold a Disabled Person's Railcard can take advantage of a code of practice which offers people with disabilities a common standard of service. This involves helping people in wheelchairs on and off trains, for instance. You have to give at least 24 hours' notice to the relevant train company. You can find out which company to contact to make the arrangements through the National Rail Enquiries number. A leaflet called *Rail Travel for Disabled Passengers* is available at main stations or by post from the Disabled Persons Railcard Office.

Coaches

Many older people find that coaches open up a whole new world for them. These days, coach travel is very different from what it was a generation ago, with double-decker coaches, often a lavatory on board and refreshments for sale as well as stops to take a breath of fresh air every few hours. The first advantage over rail travel is cost: coach travel tends to be cheaper than rail, especially when you take into account extremely attractive special deals for the over-50s. Then there is the ease of transferring from one service to another in London, since you do not have to make your way from one rail terminus to another as most coaches converge at Victoria Coach Station, which has been rebuilt and is far more comfortable and better organized than it used to be. Many people find themselves delighted at the smooth luxury of today's coaches.

The discount ticket available on all coaches is called Advantage 50 (available to anyone aged 50 and over) and on payment of £9 for a year or £19 for three years it entitles the holder to a reduction of between 20 and 30 per cent on long-distance coach journeys. Travel agents should have details; otherwise you can contact National Express Ltd.

If you are free to choose between train and coach, however, coaches are probably still second best. Although they usually contain lavatories, these tend to be more cramped than those on trains and may be down steep steps. Whereas you can take a pet dog free of charge on the majority of train services, on coaches you can only take a guide dog. National Express does not allow passengers to carry powered vehicles with them and the coach driver has the last word on whether an unpowered vehicle will be permitted; people who use push wheelchairs may decide that they would rather not risk their equipment being damaged in a coach boot and prefer to hire a chair at their destination. Most coaches have several steep steps up to the door and if you need help the coach driver may provide it but does not have to and, particularly if running to a tight schedule, may not. You can telephone the National Express passenger assistance helpline beforehand and a coach station will try to organize assistance, but this cannot be guaranteed.

Finally, there is the question of where you are dropped off. While a train station may have a fleet of taxis outside or a local taxi office next door, coach stations often have no taxi ranks. Many towns do not have coach stations at all. A useful way of checking is through the local tourist information office.

Holiday coach organizers, on the other hand, often provide unrivalled local pick-up facilities. You may find that a coach tour to the Baltic states has a pick-up point just down your road, or even that the organizers lay on taxis to and from a town-centre point. Tripscope keeps details of companies which offer holidays on coaches which are easily accessible for people who move with difficulty or use wheelchairs.

Underground

Subway and tram systems introduced since the 1980s, such as the Tyne and Wear Metro, the Docklands Light Railway and trams in Sheffield, Croydon and Manchester, tend to be pretty good for disabled people. However older underground systems, like those in Glasgow and London, present problems.

Although the London Underground can look a rather unfriendly place, the staff at stations are usually extremely helpful and offer assistance to elderly people if asked. However, for insurance reasons, the Underground does not provide a 100 per cent guarantee that staff will help older people down to platforms and on and off trains, and you need to ask. I have come across many elderly people who have been full of praise for staff. But helping passengers down to the platform is not part of their job, so you cannot guarantee that somebody will help you. One means of finding out whether you can get help is to telephone the management of the particular line or lines (Northern Line, Victoria Line, and so on) on which you are planning to travel. You can get these numbers from Transport for London.

The main problem for elderly people who have mobility problems in using the underground is that except on deep lines and in a few new stations, there are few lifts. This means that if the escalator is out of order there is no alternative to scaling a long flight of steep steps. There are also many short flights of steps which have no escalator alternative. So it is a good idea to telephone ahead of time to check that the escalators or lifts you are going to need are working that day. (See Transport for London's 24-hour travel information number, page 629.) To check on facilities available at stations, buses which serve them and whether maintenance work is underway, you can telephone or look on the interactive tube map provided by Transport for London on their website.

Transport for London also publishes a 200-page book called *Access to the Underground* which lists all stations with details of stairs, lifts, escalators and other facilities. Or you can get a map, *Tube Access Guide*, also from underground travel offices or from the Access and Mobility section of Transport for London. If using the Glasgow Metro, contact Strathclyde Passenger Transport.

Planes and Ships

The larger airports are among the easiest places in which to move around if you are frail. They have plenty of seats, lifts, lavatories and level surfaces. Alert your airport or airline well ahead of time if you would like it to give you additional help. Airlines differ in what they will do: British Airways, for instance, can provide a member of staff to meet you and help with luggage and push you in a wheelchair, if necessary one of their own. If you need to take special medical equipment on board, you must get permission. This applies in particular to potentially dangerous items such as oxygen cylinders.

However much support you get from your airline, certain realities are unavoidable. Lavatories in the airport may be luxurious, but those on planes are cramped, although they may have grab-rails. Don't forget to check with your doctor before flying if you have a serious medical condition. While airports have to comply with the Disability Discrimination Act 1998, airlines have been granted exemption, although there is a code of practice on how people with disability should be helped.[5] Ask for an aisle seat when booking your ticket if you want to be able to move around easily and perhaps have stiff knees which you need to stretch.

A trip on the QE2 should pose few problems, but ferry services to the remoter parts of the United Kingdom may not always be able to offer state-of-the-art support. Check in advance what you might be letting yourself in for.

Buses

Many older people use buses a great deal, but getting on and off can pose problems. However, by 2020, all buses and coaches (apart from holiday coaches) must be low-floor in order to comply with the requirements of the Disability Discrimination Act 1998. Already, more than two-thirds of the current bus fleet in London, for example, (more than 3,500 buses), are low-floor. Low-floor buses are much easier to board: the height of the floor of the old standard bus is 300–400 mm (12–15 inches) off the ground but that of a low-floor bus is 200 mm (7 inches), and the driver can drop it further to 100 mm (less than 4 inches). A ramp can be extended at the second door to bridge the gap between bus and pavement so that a wheelchair can get in easily; there is dedicated space inside the bus for somebody to travel in a wheelchair. Handrails in and outside the bus are non-slip and tactile. The bell-push buttons are all at low-level. To help partially sighted people, the destination and numbers are picked out in yellow and black. There are also priority seats for elderly people at the front.

On any kind of bus, low-floor or traditional, it is important to tell the driver when you get on if you have mobility or balance difficulties, so that he or she can give you time to sit down before moving off.

Concessionary Fares

There is tremendous variation in what you have to pay for a bus ticket in different parts of Britain. For people who live in areas where fares are high, this is bad news. However, recently there have been some very important fare concessions for older people.

Everybody aged 60 and over living anywhere in Scotland is entitled to a pass giving them free travel on local buses. However, you cannot step on a bus in Dundee and travel free to Dunoon: the concession operates only within your own local authority area and not before 9.30 a.m. during the week.

The National Assembly for Wales has introduced a similar

scheme in all 22 local authority areas in the Principality. Unlike the Scottish scheme, there are no time limits or geographical limits, so an older resident of Swansea can travel for free in Bangor, for instance. In neither of these countries are trains, ferries or coaches included in schemes.

Northern Ireland was the first part of the UK to introduce free bus travel for older people. All residents over the age of 65 are entitled to free travel at any time on all scheduled services – bus, rail, coach and ferries. There are no plans to extend the scheme to people from the age of 60. The scheme is administered by the Department for Regional Development of Northern Ireland. Bus passes are issued by Translink.

In England, the only national standard concession for elderly people to which all local authorities have to conform is the provision of a minimum half-fare bus pass system, or its equivalent on local public transport, a requirement in the Transport Act 2000. What this usually means in practice is that you apply to your local council for a free pass, which gives you a 50 per cent reduction on bus fares in its area. Councils may offer more if they choose. In just a handful of areas of England (Merseyside, the West Midlands, Nottingham, Reading, Crawley and Greater London), older people can obtain entirely free journeys on public transport if they apply for a pass which is free or for which the charge is nominal. So Londoners over the age of 60 enjoy free travel on trains, trams, buses and the Underground from Bromley to Harrow or the West End.

Outside these favoured areas, a variety of provision is offered, with some councils much more generous than others. If you are thinking of moving, it is worth finding out what the concessionary public transport deal is in the areas you are considering. Some councils offer tokens as an alternative or in addition to a bus pass, and these can sometimes be used on different forms of transport including ferries, trains, metros and, most commonly, taxis. This system can be particularly useful for people who for reasons of disability are unable to use regular bus services, even low-floor vehicles, and need to take taxis.

Apart from the restriction of bus passes to people who can use buses, the other main disadvantage is their limitation to the administrative area which issues them. In the West Midlands, for instance, the bus pass does not provide a free trip to the Lickey Hills or other areas of attractive countryside on the edge of the conurbation, because these lie in the areas of other local authorities.

If you are thinking of moving to an area to take advantage of free bus travel, it is worth considering one or two other matters before you take the plunge. Free bus travel is terrific if you can use buses, but many older people find they cannot, whether because the bus stop is too far away or their sense of balance is unreliable. Some councils offer dial-a-ride buses, which take people on door-to-door journeys within the area of the local authority on a first-come, first-served basis. These buses are easier to get in and out of than regular vehicles and they can usually accommodate several wheelchairs. However, you may find you take a circuitous route to your destination so that other passengers can be picked up. Also, the services often cannot cope with demand, so you may not be able to make the journey you want without booking well ahead.

Exercise

Exercise has an unfortunate, off-putting image: we think of a 30-something doggedly running miles on a treadmill to train for a marathon, or pushing weights in a gym to enhance body image. Older people can of course do these things, and for the same reasons, but there are far more interesting physical activities which can benefit their health. What you opt for depends on your taste and your level of mobility: it could be walking outdoors, dance (of many different types), *t'ai chi*, seated yoga, gentle exercise in a swimming pool, water basketball and many more. The good news is that the biggest health benefits for older people come to those who have in the past done very little exercise, but start to engage in a moderate amount.[6] But any form of exercise, including stretches and bends conducted from an armchair, helps keep our bodies supple and improves circulation.

Broadly speaking, for a range of health benefits, physical activity five times a week for 30 minutes a day is considered desirable. For older people this can be split into ten-minute blocks. The activity does not have to be formal exercise: it could be digging, it could be housework and it could be swimming. But it does need to involve enough exertion to make you feel warm and slightly breathless: not so breathless that you cannot talk, but sufficiently breathless that you cannot sing. If you are in your nineties and frail, hoovering a room can easily suffice, but some older people will want and be able to engage in far more energetic activity than this.

Most of us, however, young or old, are not sufficiently physically active. In the 45–54 age group, less than 40 per cent of people participate in enough physical activity to benefit their health. By the age of 74, this figure has declined to 14 per cent. Yet two-thirds of people over 70 who are essentially sedentary believe they take part in enough physical activity to keep fit, according to this survey.[7]

Exercise

- Exercise improves health and can be fun.
- Moderate exercise after being sedentary brings the greatest benefits.
- If an exercise causes pain, stop.
- Group exercise brings many advantages.
- Check on instructors' qualifications.
- Expect instructors to monitor progress.
- Dancing can keep you fit and bring new friends.
- Lots of valuable exercises can be performed sitting down.
- Disability like Alzheimer's need not be a bar to physical activity.
- Check which exercises you should avoid: hard running can damage some people.

Why Exercise Matters

Some older people look to exercise because they suffer from a particular medical condition which would benefit from it. They wish to take the exercise their condition requires, and avoid other activities which are not going to help.

Many people think the best form of exercise anybody can take, old or young, is swimming. This certainly exercises a lot of muscles, but it is not what is called 'load-bearing exercise', such as walking, playing table tennis or gambolling with your grandchildren on the beach. It is this load-bearing exercise which helps people who suffer from osteoporosis (thinning of bones), since it imposes force on bones from muscle tendons, rather than only exercising muscles. If you wish to actually increase your bone density, you need to engage in 'high impact' exercise. So walking, for example, should incorporate a jumping action, while targeted activities such as wall press-ups, or standing a short distance from a wall and falling on to it, can strengthen wrist bones (the main fracture sites are hips, spine and wrists). People who are suffering from osteoporosis need to ask their GPs to monitor the condition through bone scans and obtain treatment, which might include hormone replacement therapy, as well as discussing with them movements that might usefully be avoided.

Osteoarthritis, which is also common, affecting about half the population aged 65 years and over, involves inflammation of the joints. Ordinary walking helps keep joints mobile, but exercise which is not load-bearing, such as cycling and swimming, is very helpful in this case because it keeps joints, muscles, tendons and so on working without imposing stress on damaged joints.

You might respond, 'My arthritis may give me terrible pain, but I could not possibly countenance going swimming. Learning to swim was not part of my school curriculum: I have done no more than paddle in the sea for 60 years. The last thing I want to do is do immerse myself in the cold depths of a public swimming bath and have to struggle with slippery steps to take me in.' Think again. Swimming pools and swimming as exercise for older people have undergone a revolution. There could be all sorts of swimming activities out there which could alleviate your arthritis and intro-duce you to new and unimagined pleasures.

Of course you could go swimming on your own or with friends, but many local authorities offer swimming classes specifically for older people. You need to talk to a person in the relevant department (probably Leisure Services) to find a suitable class. Some swimming sessions cater for people who cannot or do not want to swim but wish to move around in warm water, holding on to the side and using floats and engaging in, say, arm exercises. For such people, the water should be chest-high – sufficient to buoy up the body and take weight off knee joints but not deep enough to feel threatening. Some older people relish an almost tropical temperature. Discuss entry to the pool before-hand: look for shelved steps with rails.

Swimming sessions for older people can take other forms, and the instructor ought to be able to respond to whatever participants want to do. Some may want to learn to swim. If the group is quite active they may want to engage in water aerobics or ball games. Blind people who enjoy swimming can find a session which caters for older people valuable because it provides a safer environment than one in which they fear they will collide with younger swimmers.

Another condition which exercise can help is cardiovascular disease. Here, exercise can deliver great preventative health benefits. Coronary heart disease is a common cause of death in old age; people who engage in moderate exercise can see their risk of developing it reduced by as much as 80 per cent compared with people who have inactive lifestyles.[8] More demanding (though not necessarily vigorous) exercise brings down blood pressure; walking 1.8 miles a day results in a substantial reduction in the risk of strokes.[9]

Since exercise involves burning up calories, it helps keep body weight at a healthy level and holds off obesity, which not only puts more demands on the heart but also increases the risk of other conditions, such as diabetes. People who are sedentary or overweight have a higher risk of developing non-insulin-dependent diabetes. Moderate regular exercise improves the body's tolerance to glucose and may help individuals in the early stages of the disease to manage it through diet rather than having to begin insulin injections. Exercise can also benefit people with established diabetes.[10]

An active lifestyle reduces the risk of developing cancer of the colon, probably because it helps food to pass more quickly through the digestive system.[11] Apart from its impact on these particular conditions, physical activity has yet more benefits. It improves strength and stamina. Again, this effect is particularly noticeable in older people who have been sedentary: they only have to exercise for three or four weeks with an appropriate programme (which might be seated exercise) to see some improvement. By strengthening muscles which keep the body upright, activity helps prevent falls (although you are likely to have to follow a specially designed course to improve strength and co-ordination for 12 weeks to see a significant reduction in the risk of falling). Studies have shown that physical activity improves our mood and delivers real psychological benefits through its impact on chemicals which affect the brain.[12] Finally, of course, exercise can also increase our chances of a good night's sleep. Those who sit around during the day cat-napping are often not tired enough to sleep through the night.

Which Exercise?

Your local council's leisure department ought to be able to tell you over the phone what activities it arranges which might suit you. Depending on your physical condition, these might include sport – badminton, bowls, table tennis, bar football, hockey (including sit-down hockey using bean bags and upturned walking sticks) – as well as outdoor walks and exercise classes in the gym. Local authorities will not have information about all registered sports clubs. But Sport England and the Sports Councils of Northern Ireland, Scotland and Wales, which are the governing bodies for sport, will.

You could also telephone your health body, such as the primary care trust, as these often fund exercise programmes. You may see independent instructors' exercise classes advertised locally too, perhaps in a church hall. Private exercise classes in gyms are often expensive, whereas the majority of classes developed by local councils and health bodies are free or cheap.

If you are from an ethnic minority, you may find there are classes aimed at your group. Some authorities have developed classes designed to prevent cardiovascular disease which are targeted at Afro-Caribbean people, who experience particularly high levels of diabetes and heart disease. Others may offer classes specifically for, say, Muslim women.

There may be types of exercise advertised which you have not considered before or perhaps even heard of. *T'ai chi* is not a newfangled fad, but an ancient Chinese practice. A group of people gather together, often in a park, and move very slowly, all together. *T'ai chi* imparts a sense of peace (rather than relaxation) which can have a beneficial effect on blood pressure and internal organs such as kidneys and the liver. It increases strength in the lower body and helps balance. But if it would prove too taxing, you could try seated *t'ai chi*, which strengthens the upper body.

Yoga is largely about breathing, body alignment and relaxation, and older people with a wide range of disabilities can benefit from it. Arthritis sufferers may find seated yoga more suitable. One additional advantage of yoga is that much of it takes place on mats on the floor. Perhaps you have not voluntarily gone down onto the floor for 20 years. If you can become accustomed to being on the floor and getting on your feet again, you can develop confidence to get off the floor in the event of a fall.

A new type of course is coming on-stream to show people how to get off the floor in the event of a fall, how to minimize harm if they have to remain on the floor and to how to help prevent falls through improving balance, muscle strength and co-ordination. This is called 'postural stability training' and trainers have a certificate as postural stability instructors. Whether or not you are at particular risk of falling, it is well worth trying to find out whether such courses exist in your area. Some need referral from a GP, others do not. During the first weeks, exercises are conducted using the back of the chair as a support in order to improve balance and co-ordination. Participants progress to moving off one spot, also doing pulse-raising exercises, stretching and moving from one exercise to another, often to music. After about 24 weeks they start doing exercises on the floor to improve bone density and to practise a safe way of getting up off the floor called backward-chaining (page 152).

Get advice from your doctor before you go ahead with any exercise programme, whether taking part in a group activity or exercising in your own home. If you go out and buy a yoga aerobics video and start exercising at home without advice beforehand, the movements may be too violent for your body. You may wreck a tendon or cause other damage.

Also, get advice from your doctor if you are proposing to continue to engage in vigorous exercise. For example, you can do yourself a lot of damage through high-impact jogging or jumping if you have arthritis or osteoporosis, even if you have been jogging for a long time. The National Osteoporosis Society publishes suggestions for exercises which people with that condition can do safely.[13]

Group Exercising

There are real advantages to group as opposed to solo exercise. It is harder to cop out, and the mere presence of other people increases motivation. You may also make new friends. You are told things that you would not pick up exercising on your own. For example, people exercising often instinctively hold their breath, which is bad because it puts up blood pressure: it is important to breathe in a relaxed way.

A trained instructor can correct more than breathing patterns. Some older people, especially those with arthritis, hold their shoulders tensed up: an instructor would see this and encourage them to bring their shoulders down and relax. Participants can also learn a lot from other participants and spot each other's need to release clenched hands, and so on.

It is very important not to carry on if exercise is causing pain. In the field of exercise and older people, the idea that there is no gain without pain is wrong: if a type of movement hurts, it should be stopped. However, pain should not cause you to give up. Instead, you should adapt the exercise. If exercise performed standing up is putting too much weight on the joints and causing pain, you may be able to perform it sitting down. The main advantage in group activity is the way progress can be made. If you are really going to benefit from exercise in strengthening muscles and bones, it needs to be progressive, so you are demanding just a little bit more from your body each time, whether walking a bit further or a bit faster, or increasing the resistance against which your body must work with weights or rubber bands. In a group, an instructor trained in exercise for older people will be observing how members of the class are coping, asking how they are feeling and cross-checking continuously. Sometimes, as a result, exercises will be modified if they are imposing too much strain on a part of the body. Crucially, monitoring enables the activities to form part of a steady progression which will bring greater benefits in terms of fitness and body strength.

Instructors

If you are planning to take part in a group physical activity, you need to make sure the instructor is qualified. The job is a very responsible one. In some classes for older people, participants will have a range of conditions: say, arthritis, breathing difficulties, heart problems, Parkinson's, MS and *après*-stroke. Some people will want to stand most of the time, some to stand throughout, some will want to sit, and the instructor has to be able to adapt to requirements such as these and to observe participants very closely to see what effect the exercise is having on them. Most important of all, he or she must make sure that participants do not come to harm. But you also want an instructor who is going to make exercise as much fun as possible.

At present, anybody can set up as an exercise instructor. The Fitness Industry Association is beginning to set up a register of instructors, but that has a long way still to go. There are recognized national qualifications. In swimming, look for a qualification as a swimming instructor from the Amateur Swimming Association. The YMCA offers qualifications for already qualified fitness instructors, for instance in 'exercise to music for older persons' and 'fitness training for the older person'. While some health bodies train staff in exercises related to falls, the only national postural stability instructors' course is run by Leicester College of Further Education. Generally, if an exercise class for older people is based in a local authority sports centre, a health centre or a GP's surgery, it will probably be led by instructors with appropriate qualifications.

Fortunately, exercise instruction for older people is not a field which attracts a lot of cowboy operators trying to make a fast buck, but it is important nonetheless to make sure your instructor is suitably qualified and understands some of the medical conditions common in old age. Advertisements for classes in, say, community halls and private leisure centres usually include qualifications under the name of the instructor. The YMCA's courses for exercise for older people include theory (anatomy and physiology) as well as practical instruction.

Be especially careful about enrolling in all-age classes: the instructor may not have any notion of the changing physiology of the older body and may not have received training in monitoring the impact of physical activity on the older body, let alone know how to adapt exercise to suit the myriad forms it takes. A 'Yoga for Everyone' class might be taught by somebody who not only has no knowledge of the ageing body but also has little knowledge of yoga. Yoga's governing body, the British Wheel of Yoga, revealed in 2002 that only half the estimated 10,000 people then teaching yoga were properly qualified. Some had trained for only four weeks before receiving a certificate from one of the plethora of institutions which issue them; the British Wheel says instructors should study for four years before they are fully qualified to teach.[14]

Other Ways

Don't forget that dance is also a valuable and enjoyable form of physical activity and comes in many different forms, from sequence dancing to line dancing (no partner necessary) or Latin American dancing. Some classes for frail people include a seated form of Hawaiian dancing, which is fun. The music which usually accompanies dance not only makes the experience more enjoyable but also encourages movement, so that physical activity seems more natural and less like a task.

In many areas, you will not find as large a range of physical activities on offer as in places where the local authority treats exercise for older people as a priority. At some leisure centres and swimming pools you may nonetheless find qualified staff on hand to help any older people use the facilities. If there are too few, lobby your council or your health body (on which GPs will be strongly represented) to come up with more. Effective and enjoyable exercise instruction is also something for which people can lobby at day centres. It is going to be far more beneficial and probably more fun than sitting still in chairs while an entertainer comes in and plays tunes on an electric organ.

Forward-thinking care home proprietors provide physical activity. If you are going round a care home as a prospective resident and exercise is on offer, it is worth asking particular questions (page 335). Don't ignore such questions just because you or your relative is suffering from a serious chronic condition. Parkinson's disease is a movement disorder, and rhythm, reinforced with counting or music, is known to help sufferers. People with dementia may find physical activity such as dancing, quoits and playing with balls and balloons at least distracting and even rewarding.

Falls

Falling plays a large part in the travails of older people. Falls accounted for 44 per cent of all attendances at Accident and Emergency amongst people aged 65 and over, in one study.[15] Another revealed that more than quarter of admissions to care homes for people over 75 were the direct result of a fall.[16] Older people themselves, their relatives and health professionals can do much to reduce the chances of falling and minimize the disruption caused by a fall. To understand why, we need to know why falls when we are old are different from those when we are young.

Even if older people are not afflicted by any medical condition they are more likely to fall over than younger people. Keeping our balance or staying upright is only achieved through a miracle of physiology. We constantly assess whether we are upright or off-balance through the information fed into our brains from our eyes, the balance mechanisms in our inner ears and touch receptors in our muscles, skin and joints (the joints of the neck are particularly important). Processing all this information occurs in many different areas of the brain. So sophisticated is this system that if one part of it is not working properly, the other parts can

---

Falls

- Falls are often caused at least partly by internal factors.
- A fall can alert you to the presence of a treatable condition.
- Get falls and dizzy spells investigated by a doctor.
- A pendant alarm could save your life.
- Exercise classes can avert falls by increasing body strength.
- Rearranging furniture and other objects in the home can lessen the risk of falling.
- Shoes should fit, the right glasses should be worn and mobility aids should be used correctly.
- Learn how to cope on the floor should you be unable to get up after a fall.
- There are ways to get up safely after a fall.
- Use the *National Service Framework for Older People*'s section on falls to get better treatment.

compensate to a greater or lesser degree. Thus we can usually remain upright and steady with our eyes closed.

As we grow older, however, receptors such as the touch-sensitive mechanisms in the skin and the balance-detecting mechanisms of the inner ear become less sensitive. Meanwhile, the mechanisms which enable us to correct our body position and intercept a fall such as swaying, staggering and putting out an arm to break a fall are less instantaneous in older people. They may indeed come into play, but often not quickly enough.

The gait of older people may also make them more prone to falling. Walking difficulties leave many placing their weight on one leg, or on a leg and a stick, for longer than younger people. Osteoporosis can shift the body's centre of gravity, for example through hunching the back. Osteomalacia, which softens its victims' bones by starving them of calcium, can also cause deformities.

Effects

A fall is much more likely to cause damage to an older body than a younger one. Many older people, men as well as women, suffer from osteoporosis, which makes the insides of their bones far less dense than they should be and thus more liable to break or fracture. So while toddlers tumble and fall all the time without obvious ill-effects, one stumble by an elderly person can result in a broken hip, wrist, nose or whatever.

In fact, most falls in older people do not cause an injury, although they may result in bruising and psychological shock. Forty-nine per cent of people aged 65 and over who said that they had had at least one major fall in a six-month period before they were interviewed reported that the fall had affected their everyday activities for at least a month.[17] For many unlucky elderly people a fall causes serious injury. Treatment may involve surgery, with the associated trauma and the risks of anaesthesia as well as of infection. While in hospital, the elderly person may develop pressure sores and infections in addition to having to cope with pain, sleeplessness and at least temporary loss of independence. And falls sometimes lead people (very often reluctantly) to surrender their independence permanently to live in an institution.

Some older people die as the direct result of a fall, either through the injuries they sustain or because they are not discovered quickly enough. Changes in our temperature regulation mechanisms mean that as we grow older we are more vulnerable to hypothermia. Therefore a person who does not have the physical strength to get up off a draughty floor and is not discovered within a couple of hours, particularly if clad only in flimsy nightwear, may die even though the injuries involved are not that serious.

Falls can also have serious psychological effects. When falls result in older people being confined to the house for two or three months and others doing the cleaning, the shopping and so on for them, they will miss the physical activity which helps them to keep healthy. Nor will they be getting the benefits of mixing with their friends, going out to the cinema or moving generally around the outdoor environment. Some people are so anxious lest they fall again that they suffer a long-term reduction in mobility – once any injuries have healed, they may have lost the confidence to move around freely. They may be so frightened of falling again that they curtail activities outside the home, giving up clubs and voluntary work and avoiding places where they think they might fall, such as buses and trains. Some people become so fearful of falling that they are too frightened to leave what they perceive as the safety of their own home and may develop agoraphobia. Fear of falling can also make people less mobile within their own homes.

If you have a fall, it is important to get medical help. Doctors, whether GPs or hospital physicians, can not only help with the obvious tasks of getting broken bones to knit together and wounds treated appropriately, but they can also initiate a wide range of rehabilitation measures to help the recovery of lost mobility, such as prescribing mobility aids for use at least temporarily, asking a physiotherapist to prescribe exercises and referring the older person to 'postural stability classes' (page 141). The latter are targeted at improving co-ordination and body strength in order to reduce the risk of falling and to help people cope if they should fall.

Causes

Another reason why it is important to get medical attention after a fall is that your fall may be the result of more than an obstruction over which you have tripped. The changing physiology of older people means that they are prone to conditions and illnesses which make falling over much more likely. About one fifth of falls by older people occur without any obvious external cause: in other words, somebody simply falls to the ground without tripping.[18] Many falls are caused by a combination of external obstructions and internal causes. So when you are old, a fall can be a useful – if disconcerting – symptom of some underlying internal problem.

Internal Causes

Blood pressure problems is one of the many possible internal causes of falls. When you are lying down your blood pressure is low, but when you get up suddenly it has to rise quickly. In some elderly people, it takes a little while for this increase to kick in. So if they get out of bed too quickly, for instance first thing in the morning or in the middle of the night, they may feel faint and fall.

A doctor can check for this problem by measuring blood pressure when somebody is lying down, immediately upon standing and two minutes after getting up. People affected by this condition could avoid rising quickly and could sit on the edge of the bed for a few minutes and then stand up slowly. Rather than standing quickly after sitting in an armchair by the fire, they should wiggle their legs before moving.

Blood pressure which is too low can also cause a fall. It may be associated with a small heart attack, or a blood clot in the lungs. Several conditions common in old age, such as ulcers, cancer and diverticular disease can result in internal bleeding which causes blood pressure to fall.

A stroke, in which a tiny blood clot cuts off the blood supply to a part of the brain, often causes loss of consciousness. A phenomenon with a similar cause but whose effects are more temporary, called a trans-ischaemic attack, may cause someone to fall for no obvious external reason. Some people have lots of trans-ischaemic attacks over months or weeks, and these may precede a full-scale stroke. So, alarming as they are, they do offer a useful warning signal.

Sometimes an elderly person feels faint or loses consciousness momentarily as a result of a decrease in the amount of blood arriving at the brain (a condition known as syncope). The heart suddenly stops pumping out blood then spontaneously recovers.

There are many other internal conditions which can increase the risk of falling. These include arthritis, rheumatism, foot problems, vision problems, dementia and Parkinson's disease. Parkinson's is a disorder of movement affecting voluntary muscles. A chemical called dopamine, which is connected with movement, is not secreted in adequate amounts by a part of the brain because of a malfunction. The disease affects individuals differently, but typically can lead to falls for various reasons: a shuffling gait, the fact that the top of the body may move faster than the lower part, and difficulty in starting to move and then in stopping. It is critically important that people with Parkinson's are given their dopamine-replacement drugs at the correct time: if their brains have too high a concentration, they can become very active, hot, agitated and even aggressive – types of behaviour which can easily lead to a fall.

Various types of medication can increase the risk of falling too. For example, many older people take diuretics or water tablets to encourage the kidneys to get rid of water and salts from the blood as treatment for heart failure, high blood pressure or swelling of the ankles and feet. But in lowering blood pressure, these drugs increase the risk of falling. They give rise to another risk too: people taking them need to pass water more often and more urgently, and may fall while hurrying to the lavatory.

People with waterworks problems (page 13) may fall if they rush to get to the lavatory. Diabetes sufferers often need to pass water frequently at night, as thirst is a symptom of diabetes.

While only 2 per cent of the population as a whole have type 2 diabetes, the incidence is nearly 20 per cent among older people. People whose diabetes has not been controlled may develop ulcers and gangrene in their feet, and/or vision defects, which can also increase the risk of falling.

External Causes

An almost limitless number of external forces and objects can trigger a fall, or by their absence increase the likelihood of falling. These include:

- objects to which you must bend down, such as electric sockets at skirting-board level, or stretch up, like overhead cupboards in the kitchen or a light bulb which needs changing

- low-level obstructions, such as side tables, foot-rests and stools, kitchen cupboard doors which do not shut properly
- clutter on the floor (say, magazines around the base of an arm-chair), electric and telephone wires
- too much furniture
- rugs, particularly if they have curled-up corners, fitted carpets with holes, warped flooring
- pets which run freely, items deposited by pets
- wearing the wrong glasses, or glasses which are very dirty, or some bifocals and varifocals which may not enable you to judge the distance of edges accurately
- using mobility aids incorrectly or using the wrong aid – for instance, carrying as opposed to using a Zimmer, using a stick when a Zimmer is called for, or using two sticks which you cannot co-ordinate
- footwear which is poorly fitting so that people shuffle, not done up properly, or inappropriate, such as large slippers in the garden
- lack of equipment such as grab-rails to help those who have difficulty with walking (in care homes and sheltered housing as well as in their own home)
- poor lighting, indoor and out
- kerbs, uneven paving stones, potholed paths and alleys, clutter on pavements like swinging advertisement stands, bicycles propped up outside shops, wet or slippery pavements or flooring.

Action

Fortunately, there are many straightforward steps you can take to prevent yourself falling and to minimize damage to yourself if you do fall.

A Safe Environment

Here are a few ways in which you can make the external environment safer:

- Apply pressure to get pavements and paths repaired and the urban fabric of the locality maintained well, if necessary by complaining to the local council (pages 118–23).

- Ensure that movement around your home and garden is as safe as possible (pages 212–16).
- Make sure your glasses provide the best possible vision and that there are no blind spots, for instance with bifocals.
- Obtain appropriate mobility aids and make sure they are used properly (pages 97–103).
- See a chiropodist regularly.
- Make sure your footwear is comfortable, gives a good grip and fits well.
- Use gadgets as appropriate. Some older people keep long-handled devices for retrieving things off the floor in each room. You might need several different walking aids. Get advice from a qualified occupational therapist or physiotherapist, ideally at a Disabled Living Centre (pages 105–6).
- Obtain a pendant alarm so that you can summon help should you fall. If you don't have one, the effect of a fall, whether the result of some unexpected medical event such as a stroke or internal bleeding or a trip over furniture, could be a lot more serious than it might otherwise have been. After the fall you may never be discovered alive or it may be hours before you can summon help. A fixed alarm, such as a wall button or a hanging cord, does not offer as much protection as a pendant alarm worn round the neck (pages 96–7 and 189–90).

Even if you are wearing a pendant alarm, it is still important to make sure that you and any people who help you minimize the risk of falling. A friend told me of the following incident involving her elderly mother:

> For a time she was supplied with meals-on-wheels, which the delivery person would leave in the kitchen. She had to push them on a trolley to the dining table, transfer herself from trolley to walking sticks or frame and then sit herself down to eat. One of the many strokes she suffered at home occurred when she was in the process of doing this. She grabbed the table, which tipped over, emptying the meal and an opened bottle of tomato sauce all over her. The chair fell backwards and she fell out of it, cracking her head on the marble surround to the fireplace. She tried to pull herself up, grabbing the coal bucket, which also tipped over, and the fireguard, which burnt her hand to blisters.

The alarm she always carried was useless because she was too shocked and confused to think of using it. This could have been avoided if the delivery person had been instructed to put the meal on the table and make sure she was sitting down safely to eat it.

Many suppliers of meals-on-wheels do require that such a safe practice should be adhered to, but this example shows what can happen if care is not taken. It is important to check what the procedure should be.

Safe Behaviour

It is important to know what to do to minimize harm to yourself if you do have a fall. Clearly, a pendant alarm can be enormously useful in summoning assistance quickly. However, you may have to wait some time for help to arrive, you may not be wearing a pendant or you may never have acquired one and be unable to reach a telephone.

When people fall, their instinct is to try to sit up quickly and get off the floor as soon as possible if they have not been injured. Raising the head abruptly and sitting up quickly can mean pulling your back and becoming dizzy because your blood pressure may not yet have realigned from the lying-down position. It is better to use a technique called backward chaining, which is taught at special postural stability training classes which also demonstrate exercises designed to prevent falls (page 141).

What you do is to roll on to your side, bend your legs, stay there for a bit, ease yourself halfway up leaning on an elbow and a hand, stopping again to let your blood pressure readjust, then move on to your hands and knees and (slowly throughout) edge yourself to a firm surface which you can use to support yourself, such as the seat of an armchair. Facing the chair, get yourself into a standing position, then turn and sit down.

It is also very important to know what to do should you fall but be unable to get up or summon help. If you know that somebody will turn up to rescue you in a few hours, you may think the best thing to do is to lie still and even try to sleep. However, if you lie still for several hours you increase your risk of deep vein thrombosis, pressure sores and hypothermia. What you should do is to make lots of noise – in the hope of attracting help – and keep moving, even though you are on the floor. This will help to keep your blood circulating, avoid stiffness in the joints and reduce the likelihood of pressure sores developing through pressure being exerted on one spot for a long time. You may feel you must remain motionless lest you hurt yourself. If a part of your body does hurt, you should not move that part, but move other parts instead, perhaps on the non-injured side of the body. If you have fractured your hip, you can still move your arms, for example.

You should also do what you can to keep warm to reduce the risk of hypothermia, for instance pulling a blanket or rug over yourself. If you are lying in a wet spot, try to edge yourself out of it, as the evaporating liquid will chill the body. Try to get comfortable by placing a cushion or rolled-up clothing under your head.

Medical Attention

If you have a fall, get a friend or relative to help ensure you receive appropriate medical treatment, in hospital or through your GP.

In Hospital

Perhaps the injury people fear most from a fall is a broken hip. In medical terms, this is known as broken neck of the femur. The femur is the long thighbone; at its very top it narrows before widening out into a ball which fits into the hip bone. That neck is the most vulnerable part of the bone and is the part where a break often occurs.

If this bone has been broken, the rough edges cut against internal tissue, causing bleeding and giving rise to often severe (sometimes transferred) pain. An easy indication of a broken neck of femur is the fact that when the two legs are side-by-side, the one which has suffered the break will be slightly shorter than the other and the foot will be pointing outwards. It is important that the person should get to hospital as quickly as possible and be treated to relieve pain, stem the bleeding and get the healing process started. The longer treatment is delayed, the more likely are complications such as dehydration and pressure sores.

It is extremely important that older people to whom this mishap has occurred should have someone they know with them in A and E and later on the ward to provide constant help and reassurance, and if possible two people. The list of challenges with which they must cope is daunting: the pain from their injuries, the trauma of the fall, the trauma of the rush to hospital and the fear of what lies ahead.

Some of the particular medical steps you would expect when an elderly person has fractured a hip include:

1. Sophisticated pain relief as soon as the patient has been examined and before any X-ray.

2. Pressure-relieving equipment should be placed under areas where pressure sores might develop because the patient is leaning on them, for example heels, an elbow or one side of the hip (page 431).

3. An operation should take place as quickly as possible. The *National Service Framework for Older People* recommends: 'Operations for fracture repair should be carried out within 24 hours of admission by experienced staff.'[19] Note: 'experienced staff'.

4. Pain relief should also be provided after an operation, when the patient is being encouraged to move around and walk. The medication needs to be not only effective but effective at the right time, before procedures such as washing, turning and getting out of bed. Your relative will find it particularly difficult to get on her feet again if she is in pain or frightened of pain.

5. If there is a delay in operating, intravenous fluids should be given. Don't let your relative be denied food and water for an unnecessarily long time before surgery. A report by the Audit Commission published in 1995 commented: 'Research has shown that a four-hour period is usually sufficient. But in some hospitals food is withheld by routine; patients scheduled for surgery in the morning are starved from midnight, those scheduled for the afternoon list from 6 a.m. Patients on a morning list may be starved for up to 12 hours. To minimize the risk of dehydration, water and food should be denied for no more than four to six hours, calculated individually for each patient by counting back from the time of operation. If food and drink are withheld for more than eight hours, intravenous fluids should be given.'[20]

6. Help with eating and drinking after the operation should be provided if and when necessary. There is also a range of other

nursing matters to which you could usefully pay attention (pages 427–34).

7. Mobilization after the operation should be encouraged. If an older patient lies still in bed for too long the risk of pressure sores, deep vein thrombosis and pneumonia will rise. Expect to be out of bed as soon as possible after the operation. The *National Service Framework for Older People* says: 'Following surgery, older people with hip fracture repairs should be mobilised within 48 hours where appropriate.'[21]

8. Steps should be taken to reduce the risk that people recovering from operations will fall again. To this end, the Audit Commission report recommends the following features on the post-operation ward (usually an orthopaedic ward):

- beds, chairs and toilets at the appropriate height for individual patients
- non-slip floor surfaces
- handrails
- good lighting
- signposting of doorways, exits, toilets and bathrooms
- easy access to glasses, hearing-aids and walking aids
- easy access to personal belongings

Rehabilitation should be planned and supported by an interdisciplinary team with good lines of communication, including, for example, between physiotherapists and occupational therapists. The *National Service Framework for Older People*'s section on Falls explains:

Rehabilitation strategies should aim to:

- increase the older person's stability during standing, transferring, walking and other functional movement by: balance training; strengthening the muscles around the hip, knee and ankle; increasing the flexibility of the trunk and lower limbs; providing appropriate mobility and safety equipment
- help older people regain their independence and confidence to relearn and practise their previous skills in everyday living, and to cope successfully with increasing threats to their balance and increasingly demanding functional tasks

- improve the safety of the older person's environment by, with their consent, removing, replacing or modifying any hazards
- teach awareness of hazards and how to avoid them
- teach the older person strategies to cope with any further fall and prevent a long lie. If possible the person should be trained how to get up from the floor. Otherwise methods for summoning help, including use of community alarms, should be rehearsed. Strategies for preventing hypothermia and pressure sores should also be discussed.
- establish a network of community support and supervision if this is needed, including the voluntary sector and organizations such as the National Osteoporosis Society, many of whom have befriending services to relieve isolation and support rehabilitation of older people.[22]

If you have not suffered a fracture you should nonetheless expect an assessment of bone mineral density to work out whether osteoporosis is occurring. If the result shows that it is, treatment should be offered. You might care to refer to the report by the Royal College of Physicians entitled *Osteoporosis: Clinical Guidelines for Prevention and Treatment,* available on the Royal College's website.

From a GP

If you fall without external cause, even if this happens only once and there appear to be no ill-effects, your GP should take it seriously because, as we have seen, a fall can serve as a useful (if frightening) symptom of an underlying condition which is treatable, such as diabetes. Even if you save yourself from falling or suddenly find you have to hold on to things in order to keep your balance while walking, it is worth finding out what is wrong. Some elderly people give up activities which they have much enjoyed because they have been frightened by a couple of 'funny turns'. Yet remedies are often available. A trip to the GP could save you from imprisonment at home. It might also result in treatment for a condition which would otherwise pose a greater risk to health.

An example, an older man who already suffers from angina suddenly starts having falls in which for brief periods he loses consciousness. He goes to his doctor, who wires him up to a box which looks a bit like a personal stereo and which takes recordings from his heart over a 24-hour period. The information is fed into a computer, which translates it into data about the rhythm of his heartbeat. This reveals episodes when his heart beats with an abnormal rhythm, pumping less efficiently, so that blood-flow to the brain drops and consciousness is lost. Treatment involves putting in a pacemaker or giving the man a drug that smoothes out the rhythm and thus stops the falls.

Doctors should now be more likely to take an interest in falls because they are singled out for special mention in the *National Service Framework for Older People*. The section on falls recommends that the NHS and local authority social services departments should come together and set up specialist services to help older people who are at high risk of falling. The idea is that GPs should refer patients to such services, which would diagnose the cause of the fall, seek to relate it to the patient's health and environment, establish how the patient and any carers coped with the fall and identify strategies for coping with falls in future. They would also identify any psychological consequences of the fall which might lead to self-imposed restriction of activity, and investigate, and if necessary treat, osteoporosis. Even where specialist falls services have yet to materialize, the Framework's proposals help establish the importance of falls.

If you feel your GP still needs to take a fall more seriously, you could mention an article by Cameron Swift, Professor of Health Care of the Elderly at Guy's, King's and St Thomas's School of Medicine, London, published in the *British Medical Journal* in 2001, which stated: 'Falls are a key syndrome in medical gerontology. They may be the first indicator that all is not well medically, and they should prompt a diagnostic appraisal aimed at early detection and intervention.'[23]

A 'diagnostic appraisal' should not simply be your GP's hunch, but a systematic assessment (various technical falls assessment procedures are available). Separately, but also importantly, the health check which GPs should carry out annually on all patients over the age of 75 should incorporate a falls risk assessment, according to Professor Swift.

If there is a clear medical cause for a fall, the GP should diagnose and treat it. If there is not, you should still expect treatment.

Balance-training exercises guided by a physiotherapist might be called for, or a visit by a professional occupational therapist, who can explain how to make a living environment less hazardous, or postural stability exercises to strengthen particular muscles and improve co-ordination prescribed by an exercise instructor (page 143). In other words, your GP should be tackling a fall in a multi-faceted way, taking into account medical matters, environment and physical fitness

Chapter 7
Where to Live

As people get older they often think about moving. It is not hard to persuade retired people sitting on money tied up in property in the UK to swap a pokey home in this rainy country for a villa with swimming pool in Cyprus or Spain. For others it seems natural to move to smaller accommodation: the children have left home, you need less space, you can save on maintenance, management and heating, and perhaps release some capital. Some people like the idea of moving into 'sheltered' housing, with the reassurance it seems to promise. Others, feeling they would like to see more of their children and grandchildren, may sell up and move into a granny flat, perhaps in another part of the country, perhaps in the expectation that their children will look after them if they become unable to care for themselves. Still others want to move to the place where they grew up or enjoyed holidays or where their friends live, or perhaps to the country cottage for which they have long yearned. All these options and others have advantages, but they also hold pitfalls for the unwary. Staying put, however, raises issues of its own. Could you adapt your surroundings to any disability you may develop and ensure it is always safe and warm?

Moving House

How Big?
Smaller accommodation brings lower running costs – not just council tax bills, but also maintenance and heating. Less maintenance means less bother as well as less cost. However, space can actually be an advantage for older people.

It is obviously easier to have guests to stay if you have extra bedrooms. As my mother grew frailer in her early eighties, her sight beginning to fail and arthritis making walking difficult, I found my family and I were going to see her for long weekends far more frequently than hitherto, to help her make small adjustments to her lifestyle and to provide reassurance and company. The fact that she had a house made a big difference. It was not just a matter of spare bedrooms: the run of a whole house and garden made staying a lot easier and pleasanter than it would have been had she been living in a sheltered flat, where we should have had to book the sheltered scheme's guest room in advance or, if it were not available, perhaps sleep on a sofa-bed in her living room.

Day visitors are also probably more likely to come if you have space for things which will interest them such as a piano, games or equipment for hobbies. These provide a potential focus for interaction, as well as reflecting your own interests. Space for entertaining is also important. Researcher John Percival conducted in-depth interviews with 60 older people on their feelings about their domestic spaces. Some of his interviewees who had moved to sheltered accommodation with small kitchens and dining areas were dismayed not only at the loss of physical space but also of the resulting role of being a host to their families.[1]

You may feel like abandoning your garden once you can no longer keep it in pristine condition, but you may live to regret giving in to this impulse. Grandchildren or great-grandchildren like a bit of wildness to play in, or a paved area in which they can kick a ball. As John Percival put it, 'Of course not all older people want the responsibility of the garden. . . . But for those who value their own plot of land, a future without a garden can be rather bleak.'

Older people usually do not realize that there may come a time when they need quite a lot of additional space for support purposes and that by surrendering that space they may unwittingly surrender the possibility of continuing to live independently in a home of their own. If your legs start to play up, for example, and you feel like investing in an electric-powered scooter, you will have to have somewhere to store it, together with its battery-recharging equipment. A garden shed or a garage with a power supply is ideal. Indoors, wheelchairs and other mobility aids, even Zimmer frames, need space to manoeuvre, as well as to be stored out of the way.

As you get older, you may need human help too. You may

want a friend to come and stay for a while when you come out of hospital. And if you should need a live-in helper for any length of time, whether hired or a relative, you will not be able to have one if your accommodation is too small. One of Mr Percival's interviewees had had to turn the dining room of her sheltered flat into a bed-sitting room for her live-in carer. Even if you just want somebody to come in and help bathe you or do the laundry or some paperwork, you may find it is more difficult to attract staff if they see that working for you would involve moving around in cramped surroundings. So while there is no doubt a case for an older person to move from, say, a five-bedroomed house to a two-bedroomed one, there is also a case for resisting the temptation to move to something smaller still.

Character

It is of course extremely difficult to predict what might prove wrong with a dwelling once you are older, but being forced to move when you are old and frail because your home is no longer suitable is something to be avoided. Try to think ahead as far as you can if you are looking at accommodation. (Internal design is also discussed on pages 194–7.)

Steps

If you are thinking of buying a flat, do not buy one off the ground floor unless there is a lift: countless conditions of old age make climbing steps difficult.

Similarly, if you are buying a house, avoid one which has steps up to the front door, particularly steep ones. It is possible to install a ramp over front steps if there is plenty of space for the slope (which should be no steeper than 1 in 12, so a ramp to replace three steps needs to be 7.2 metres, or 7.8 yards, long) and even possible to install a stair-lift outside; some councils will even help you do so.[2] But of course you cannot guarantee that this will be an easy adaptation or a cheap one.

Stairs inside can also prove a problem, although many people do get stair-lifts installed, with or without financial help from their local council (page 96). And of course some people simply move everything down to the ground floor so they never have to use stairs.

Even single steps can prove a problem. That half-timbered, olde-worlde country cottage in a remote location whose single steps down into every room you hardly noticed when you bought it becomes the most unsuitable place to live once one partner has fallen victim to, say, dementia. People suffering from this condition may fall every time they enter a room because they cannot remember there is a step.

Heating

A house or flat should have a heating system which is capable of keeping the temperature at 21°C (70°F) throughout when the outside temperature is minus 1°C (30°F). So it is important to ensure that this is possible, to work out how much heating is going to cost and to consider whether the insulation is adequate or could be improved. In a compact, well-heated home, condensation can be a problem, so it is also worth ensuring that there is adequate ventilation to keep this at bay. See also page 347.

Windows

Older people tend to spend more time at home than younger people and if they are unwell they may be confined to the house for long periods. So the amount of natural light and the views can be extremely important. You may look round a retirement flat, say, and think the windows will be perfectly adequate because, although the kitchen has no window, the lounge does. In fact, you might find the absence of a kitchen or a bathroom window a blow. If confined to the house more than you used to be you may relish the prospect of another space in which you can sit and eat. What is more, if you can eat in the kitchen you will not have to carry food so far, with the risk of dropping it or tripping.

It is also important to ensure you can open and close windows easily. In a kitchen, the window can be behind the sink and difficult to reach. Arthritis and osteoporosis are among the medical conditions which can result in people feeling dizzy if they bend their head back and reach up.

Plugs, Sockets, Lights

Electricity sockets at waist-height – and a sufficient number – are ideal, although if the property you are contemplating buying has sockets at skirting-board level, you can get them moved.

Changing a light bulb can be very dangerous because you need to stretch up. Even standing on quite a low stool can result in a fall, which may in turn set off a whole host of different problems. So, if you can, choose a property which has at least some of its light leads extending a long way down; the one over the dining table could be one which you can easily reach from a sitting position to change. Long-life bulbs offer the benefit of fewer changes as well as cost-effectiveness.

Doors

It is possible to get doors made wider, but it is obviously a good idea if they are wide enough to take a wheelchair or a mobility aid easily before you move in, just in case you should ever need one. If possible, avoid even a small lip step between French windows and patio.

Bathroom, toilet and kitchen doors should open outwards, to ensure that if somebody falls against the door, help can get to them. Many falls involving older people take place in the bathroom, often at night. If you collapse in the bathroom and the door opens out of the room, somebody can get in and rescue you. But if the door opens inwards and you collapse against the door, they can't.

Bathroom

A walk-in shower is a very useful feature: in other words, it should have no step but be flush with the floor and then drain downwards. If the bath does not have grab-rails, make sure there is sufficient space for them to be put in. If you are buying housing specially designed for older people, you should expect a bath with some kind of ledge at the non-tap end so that you can sit on it and then swing your legs over before lowering yourself down using handles already installed. It should ideally not be a full-length bath (1.7 metres/6 ft), but a short one (1.5 metres/5 ft). You can't have quite such a nice wallow in this, but you will not accidentally slip down and drown or be unable to get out. So when viewing, take your tape measure with you. There are also various specially designed baths with lifting devices as an option.

As far as the lavatory is concerned, you should look for a little more space than usual in case you need to have grab-rails or some support installed and/or people to help you. So if the lavatory is squashed up into a corner, look elsewhere. Older people tend to spend more time in the bathroom and lavatory than younger people and it should be as warm and pleasant an environment as possible.

Where?

Perhaps you have had a life-long dream of living within earshot of cathedral bells and padding along to Evensong as the mood takes you. Perhaps you have always wanted to live within sight of the sea, or in the remote corner of rural Wales from which your forebears were forced to migrate to seek work in the factories of Manchester. Conversely, perhaps you want to move to a town centre so that you can easily walk to the shops and other facilities.

To the Country

People who live in the country often have to be more self-reliant than those who live in urban areas simply because if something goes wrong with the house there may be less chance of finding somebody to fix it at short notice. The lack of people to help may affect you more than you imagine. In the country, the way you keep your garden can play an important part in the way you are perceived. Older people unable to maintain their gardens as well as they used to may feel a greater loss of dignity and self-esteem than they would in town.

Facilities of all types will be scarcer. You may well appreciate that a move to the country will mean less choice of shops, restaurants and adult education centres, for example, but you may not imagine you would ever enter a local sports or leisure centre. But it is these places which often run exercise classes for older people. One way of keeping arthritic joints moving is swimming, but you can hardly go swimming every other day if you live far from a pool. You may need specialist health care which will only be rendered promptly if you pay for it. Physiotherapists and masseuses will cost you a lot more if they have to travel a long way to your charmingly remote home.

Local authorities do of course have the same obligations to older and disabled people in the countryside as they have in towns. However, councils' enthusiasm for fulfilling these obligations varies. A study by Help the Aged in 1996 (entitled *Growing Old in the Countryside*) found that spending on providing human help in the home and aids and adaptations was lower in rural than in urban England.

Whether you get help privately or through a local council, there may be other problems you have not thought about. Bad weather may cause floods which cut you off and stop a care worker reaching you. If power lines are brought down you may lose your electricity. Before you move, you may think you would never step inside a day centre, but if you do become frail or disabled, the prospect of hot, home-cooked food and amenable company close by can become much more appealing.

In the heart of the countryside, transport is a big issue. You may not want to confront the fact, but one day you may no longer be able to drive. Often a husband dies, leaving his wife, who never learned to drive, stranded. So check that your new home would be accessible by public transport. Public transport services in the British countryside are not always as bad as is supposed, particularly if you are flexible about when you travel. Pockets of the countryside have very good bus services into a nearby market town, while nearby areas have nothing, so study the timetables and route maps. The public transport department of the relevant local authority should be able to advise you on the scope of conventional services and also of any self-help transport systems provided by volunteers – community buses, car-lift schemes and so on. These arrangements do anything from giving lifts to people unable to use regular buses to providing community minibus services to supplement the official services, perhaps fitting in with doctors' surgery hours. Wiltshire County Council publishes an exemplary guide to public transport in the county for elderly and disabled people, down to giving details about each railway station: its distance from the nearest bus stop, whether there is level access to the platform, whether it is staffed and whether toilet, telephone, parking and waiting-room facilities exist.

Councils differ widely in the extent to which they subsidize public transport and the range of concessionary tickets they offer to older people (pages 134–6), so check this as well. The state of the taxi service may matter more than the buses. There will always be journeys you cannot make by public transport and

Moving House

- Think twice before downsizing accommodation.
- Homes with steps up to the front door are to be avoided.
- Care workers may be unable to reach people living in remote places in inclement weather.
- Before moving to a retirement area, live there in midwinter for a trial period.
- Before an elderly relative moves in with a family, ground rules should be established.
- Security of tenure is important for people who live with others.
- A young lodger could provide refreshing company.
- Living close to old friends can make it possible to share home helps and care workers.

there may come a time when you are no longer able to get on or off a bus or wait at a bus stop which has no seat.

Do not, however, rule out a move to the country for fear of transport problems. It is perfectly possible to live in some of the most beautiful corners of our countryside and be served by frequent bus services. Elderly friends of mine have recently moved to a static caravan park in a beautiful rural location in Surrey which enjoys hourly bus services to two different towns and is not too far away to make taxis prohibitively expensive.

Once you have moved, do start using public transport even if you continue to use a car on most journeys. You do not want to have to get the hang of where the buses stop, where they go and how to get hold of the timetable once failing eyesight has driven you from the wheel. There are also attractions in avoiding the stress of driving and being able to see over hedges and chatter to your fellow passengers.

To a Town Centre

Some people yearn for the facilities in a town centre rather than the countryside. They relish the thought of pottering in and out of the public library, with a local supermarket or tea shop no more than a few minutes' walk away. This can turn out well, but it does not always. A town centre property may have to be smaller than a suburban one, bringing with it new problems. If you move into a flat, there will be the additional expense of ground rent and possibly high maintenance charges over which you have little control, as well as the possible problems of dealing with other tenants and a ground landlord. A dearth of green space may bother you more than you expect. Furthermore, as demand on town centre space is intense, you could find yourself having to cope with noisy redevelopment work.

You may move to be close to shops, pubs and other facilities only to find that six months after moving in you can no longer manage even the short walk to the shops. Town centre sheltered housing schemes offer few parking places to residents (one for every three flats is not unusual). Living further out and relying on hiring taxis, shared perhaps with a friend, or investing in an electric scooter or buggy, may prove more suitable.

To the Seaside

I heard a familiar tale at a bus stop in Ramsgate recently. An elderly gentleman had moved to the resort five years before from Shepherd's Bush in west London, after enjoying holidays there for many years. He wished he had not moved after all. As he and his wife had not lived in the area when they were working and their children growing up, they lacked the rich tapestry of human links enjoyed by indigenous older people. Though he had deplored the heavy traffic of Shepherd's Bush, he now missed the range of public facilities available at the end of a free underground or bus journey; the concessionary travel tickets were far less generous than those available in London.

It is easy to want to get out of a bustling area only to find that strolls by the sea, particularly in winter, are insufficient compensation for lost human interaction. At the seaside, such facilities as exist may often be seasonal and open only during the tourist months. So do not rely too heavily on recollections of holiday experience when making the decision to move.

Overseas

People who move abroad in their later years usually do so before ageing is advanced. Lured by a warmer climate, cheaper housing, lower living costs and attractive landscapes, many of Britain's older citizens migrate to France and southern Europe. This is a massive step. Anyone seriously considering it should get hold of Age Concern England's free leaflet, *Retiring Abroad: Information for older people planning to leave the UK*. In Spain, for instance, problems may arise if you become frail and disabled. Medical care in hospital can be good, but the sort of home care which you could obtain in Britain independently or through your local authority is another matter – in Spain older people rely heavily on their own families for support and domiciliary care workers are unlikely to speak English. The Attendance Allowance you could claim to help pay for help in the home in Britain would not be available (although you would still receive your British State Retirement Pension). You might not feel comfortable in a Spanish-speaking care home, eating only a small tapas lunch, no tea and your main meal at nine in the evening. As a result, you might be faced with the choice of moving back to the UK or trying for a place at one of the small number of Spain's expensive English-speaking care homes.

Back-up
Whether an area has a neighbourly feel can often be important when you are older, but you can find this present – or absent – anywhere from an urban terrace to a remote Highland glen. Live close to your proposed new home as a trial if you possibly can. Bungalows are often ideal for older people, as they are on the level, but they are not so ideal if located in an area where everybody is out at work all day, there are no public facilities and no public transport. A relatively spacious terraced house close to either a town or neighbourhood centre has a lot going for it – you could summon neighbours easily and security may be better than in a free-standing and isolated property. A choice which might suit many is a location away from a town centre but close to a neighbourhood centre, with little traffic on roads which are easy to cross and offer stress-free driving, and a park or two in a generally pleasant and leafy environment, plus a café, pub or day centre with hot, nutritious and cheap meals and amenable company. Good public transport links to an urban centre, the countryside and seaside might make things even better.

Another matter to consider is public services. Many older

people moving within Britain are struck by the considerable difference in the quality and quantity of public services available and in the attitudes of the organizations which provide them. Some local authority social services departments bend over backwards to help older people live independently in their own home, while others provide them with the minimum of information and support and try to get them to sell their property and move into a care home and therefore out of the council's hair as soon as possible. So it is well worth finding out about the attitude of the local authority into whose area you may move in advance. You could ask the council what concessionary travel arrangements it offers older people and how many day centres it provides or subsidizes to get an inkling of its attitude.

Some of the other factors to bear in mind include:

Immediate Environment
What would it be like walking to the shops, GP's surgery, chemist, bank, post office, library, place of worship, day centre, cafes and pubs? Are they easily reachable? Are any of them threatened with closure? What are the pavements like – well-maintained or cracked and uneven? Are they strewn with litter and leaves on which you might slip? Are there comfortable benches in case you need to sit down for a rest? Are there conveniently situated public lavatories? Is there a network of safe alleyways, paths and relatively wide pavements with dropped kerbs at frequent crossings for scooters and other mobility aids? Is the environment well-lit and would you feel comfortable going out alone in the evening?

Transport
Could you or somebody else park easily outside the property? How close is it to bus stops and the railway station? Are there seats at the bus stops and the station? When and where do the services go? Might they be reduced in the future? How much would it cost to travel around by public transport?

With Whom?
As they grow older, people often think of going to live with one of their children. There are however, many other possibilities.

Do you want to live among people of your own age who may see things your way? Or are you prepared to cope with the stresses but also, perhaps, the greater rewards of sharing your life with younger people? If you want the society of people your own age, how exclusive do you want that society to be?

Relatives

There are a number of options:

- You could live with one relative sharing living accommodation.
- You could live with one relative but in separate living accommodation, such as a granny annex or a separate floor of the house.
- You could live with more than one relative in rotation.

In any of these cases, you may run up against the fear of younger family members that, if they have you, they will have to care for you should a time come when you are unable to look after yourself. I have come across middle-aged people who would love to have a parent come and live with them, but believe it would mean they would have to give up their job and care for the parent should he or she become frail or disabled. Other people would value their parents' company, but are themselves suffering from some chronic condition, such as ME, and so rule out the possibility because they know they could not care for a frail parent.

In fact, however, sharing accommodation with somebody does not oblige you to look after them, even if they are your father, mother, brother, sister or even spouse. In law we are no more our mother's keeper than our brother's. We have a legal obligation to care only for our children. A husband has a legal obligation to maintain his wife financially, but not to care for her should she be unable to care for herself. The legal responsibility to care for somebody unable look after him- or herself falls to the state, through local authority social services departments. Anyone is free to choose to become the main carer of somebody living in the same house, however, and today such 'carers' have legal entitlements (pages 556–69).

Let us consider the situation of people choosing to live in close proximity with an elderly person, but leaving open the question of becoming his or her carer, which is discussed in Part 8.

Family Relationships
When we move in with a relative we bring with us the baggage accumulated through a long relationship history. How will it work out if that person is living under the same roof? Moving in together can enormously enhance our relationship with our loved ones, but it can also cement unhealthy aspects. Also, once an elderly parent is living with his or her child, or perhaps an elderly sister moves in with her brother and his partner, all relationships in the household are likely to change. The dynamics of one relationship will impinge on those of another. It is important to recognize this and to plan for it, otherwise problems may develop which can cause much misery. For instance, would certain members of the household tend to gang up in a disagreement, alienating and isolating others?

There is also the important question of resentment that can be generated by differential support. Let us suppose that an elderly woman moves in with her daughter. Another daughter lives 200 miles away and visits as often as she can. But resentment builds up. Relatives ask why the faraway daughter could not have moved in with her mother, as she is single while her sister has children. She points to her brother, who lives near his mother but rarely visits and yet nobody apart from her is suggesting he should do more. In time, this daughter's visits to her mother, taking place in her limited time off work, become overshadowed by these family tensions. While her mother is alive, they simmer. At her funeral, they erupt.

Resentment may also work the other way. A son or daughter taking a parent into their home can generate jealousy among siblings. Suppressed competition for the parent's love in childhood can resurface. It may take the form of suspicion that the parent is being stripped by the sibling, deprived of assets which would otherwise have been shared out equally in the will. If housing equity is pooled through a move into a bigger home to accommodate the new grouping, siblings may resent the acquisition of parental equity, which may have to occur on the parent's death if the house is not to be sold. You may imagine that such monstrous thoughts could never surface in your family. Wait and see!

Security of Tenure
A scenario not uncommon: an unmarried son gives up his job to devote himself to caring for his elderly mother who has Parkinson's disease, moving back into the large family home where he grew up. His brother and sister, both married, carry on with their own lives. Ten years on, the old lady dies. She has left her estate to be divided equally between her three children, believing this to be fair. The house is sold and the proceeds divided equally. The money comes in handy for the married children, who use it to support their children, but the unmarried son finds himself turned out of his home. His full-time devotion to his mother has lost him his professional position and he is forced to take a job in a field in which he has little interest. His share of his mother's estate is too small to buy him a house in the same locality and his new job pays too little for him to get a sufficiently large mortgage. He has to leave the area in which he grew up and has lived all his life to find new accommodation in another town.

Another scenario, also not unusual: a couple, perhaps in their seventies, move in with their daughter in another part of the country. They sell their house and use the proceeds to extend and improve their daughter's home, though she retains full ownership of it. All goes well for a few years, but then the elderly father develops dementia and his behaviour begins to annoy the daughter, her children and her friends. She asks her parents to leave and things turn acrimonious. Her father goes into a care home; her mother finds herself living alone in rented accommodation in a town in which she has few friends, estranged from her daughter.

Before you move in with younger or older relatives, or indeed with anybody else, it is crucially important to think through all the possible problems that could arise which might leave you, or those with whom you will live, homeless. Don't think it cannot happen to you. It probably can. It is worth talking things over with a legal adviser and if necessary drawing up a legal agreement setting out the ownership and financial arrangements in order to avoid future dispute. Essentially, there are quite different ways of sharing the ownership of a home, with vastly different implications. You need to know which you are choosing and why.

Similarly, if you are becoming, or taking in, a tenant or lodger, you need to know not only the basis on which the arrangement will run, but also the exit routes for all parties.

Living Arrangements

If you go and live with one of your children, you may assume that you will get on much as you did when they really were children. In fact, there are almost certainly bound to be major issues to be sorted out. These include:

- **Room temperature and open windows** This is not just a matter of taste. Elderly people often like and actually need a higher ambient temperature than younger people. Are you going to ensure that temperature can be varied from room to room so that disputes can at least be minimized? Are you sure there will be no resentment when the heating bills come in?
- **Food** Who will do the shopping, cook the meals and decide what is to be to eaten? How often will everyone eat together?
- **Household tasks** A daughter-in-law may feel she is doing more than her fair share by waiting on in-laws who could do more themselves. Or elderly parents can easily find themselves doing more than their fair share of household tasks. They may feel they are bringing fewer resources to the party and so negotiate from assumed weakness rather than strength, doing far more than their fair share of washing up, gardening, cleaning, cooking, mending, babysitting, pet-minding and so on. So pre-existing relationships can make formal arrangements for the allocation of household tasks more rather than less necessary than they would in the case of strangers of the same age embarking on a flat-share, in which equal responsibilities would be automatically assumed to be the rule.
- **Self-esteem** The division of domestic labour is likely to overlap with the creation of boundaries to protect each party's right to pursue his or her own interests. If you are doing much of the menial work while your son-in-law occupies himself with a prestigious job, your self-esteem may well be eroded. You need to feel appreciated for yourself, not just for what

you do. How are members of the household going to feed and enhance each other's self-esteem?

- **Financial matters** Family factors make dividing up the bills harder, not easier. Older people may feel under pressure to contribute more than their fair share of household expenses – or even to give money away. To people in their early twenties, grandparents can seem to be awash with money which they do not need. Older people may feel under pressure to contribute more than their fair share of household expenses or help out with school fees, medical bills or trips to the cinema. This is fine if they really want this role and will not need the money themselves at some point in the future for an electric buggy, a hearing aid or medical treatment.

- **Benefits** Another area of financial concern is the impact on benefits. If you share your home with another adult, such as a grown-up child, you may lose council tax benefit or your single person discount. If you receive the disability benefit Attendance Allowance (page 486), you might lose Severe Disability Premium, an additional amount paid to people receiving Guarantee Credit (page 493). Many cases of fraud involve people receiving Severe Disability Premium and then neglecting to notify their Social Security Office when a grown-up son or daughter moves back home (the benefit is not available to those sharing their household with a 'non-dependent' adult). So get a benefits check from the Citizen's Advice Bureau or other organization (page 500), if you are proposing to share your household with a relative, a friend, a lodger or, of course, a partner. If somebody is going to be your 'carer', that is, provide you with regular and substantial care, he or she ought to be entitled to carer's benefits (pages 568–9).

Rotating Relatives
An elderly lady I know who is unable to look after herself lives in turn with two daughters and one son and their families, spending one month with each in different parts of the country. This has worked well, and does in other cases too. The peripatetic parent can develop a circle of friends and move on when he or she gets fed up with one lot. Disruption to the existing links between a younger husband and wife are much reduced when they know

they will soon get back time to themselves. However, it means more families have to find space in their homes for facilities such as ground-floor lavatories and extra bathrooms, and somebody in all the relevant homes may need to have time to give full-time support. Sometimes older people start to become disorientated moving from place to place, even though they may have spent a lot of time in each house in the past. It may be much more difficult to set up support arrangements such as paid help in the home if these should become necessary, whether or not this is steered by the local authority's social services department.

Strangers
In some continental countries there are schemes which support the integration of older people into living arrangements with people to whom they are not related: the 'familiar welcome' scheme in Portugal provides temporary or permanent integration of an older person within another family.[3] Communes in theory offer older people a great deal but no well-known organizations exist to point them in the right direction.

An older person could of course rent out part of his house to a lodger. But the lodger will not necessarily provide company: he or she may only exchange an occasional greeting at the front door, while often coming and going in the middle of the night, so not even providing the reassurance of another presence in the house at night.

One scheme which aims to enable older people to secure companionship, a presence in the house at night and some practical help in return for accommodation at a much reduced rate is called Homeshare. An elderly householder (or it could be a younger disabled person) makes a monthly payment to the charity of £85 while the sharer, a younger person, pays it £65 per month. No money changes hands between the two parties. In return for his or her own bedroom and shared use of the home's facilities, the sharer provides ten hours per week of practical support and undertakes to be present in the home overnight. Practical support could be shopping, light cleaning or cooking – it depends on what the two parties agree. The requirement that the sharer must be home by midnight means that people who come in from clubbing at three in the morning are ruled out. The sharer can be away from the home on only one weekend a month, and cannot bring partners to stay overnight.

Such conditions might be difficult to insist upon in a one-off situation. The existence of the organization and the fact that both parties signed an agreement puts such a situation on a business-like footing which makes it easier for strictures to stick. Sharers undergo reference checks and interviews. A facilitator from the organization monitors the arrangement, there is provision for notice, and if one arrangement does not work well a new sharer may be found. In 2003 Homeshare operated only in London (it cannot monitor situations too far away for its co-ordinators to visit), but there was growing interest in the system.[4]

Contemporaries
Some people prefer to live among people of their own age, with whom they are likely to have shared experiences, a shared cultural heritage and shared understanding of the realities of ageing. You can choose an environment peopled exclusively by older people, such as sheltered housing, a retirement complex or a care home. Or you can live close to other older people in the wider community.

Buying a property close to people of your own age and interests whom you already know well often works well. One such situation I have come across involves a number of elderly ladies who over the past few years have come to buy flats in the same block in a pleasant residential street in south-west London close to a suburban shopping centre. They already knew each other well as they had lived in the area and attended the same church, but over the years they had separately come to the conclusion that they wished to move into smaller dwellings close to shops and services, often after the death of their husbands. Such a group can easily socialize informally and look out for each other. You have the advantage of independence, your own front door and greater security of tenure than you would have in a care home or in much retirement housing. There is also the possibility of companionship and mutual help, and not just during the day – lots of elderly people do not sleep very well and relish the possibility of somebody to talk to during the long hours of the night.

If people in this situation decide they want to hire help in the home, they can often hire the same person or people. One professional care worker may thus be able to get a full-time wage by working for a small group. The presence of people of other ages nearby also means there is none of the feeling of ghettoization which you can find in housing units accommodating only older people. If you move into, say, retirement housing, you may meet people of similar experiences and cultural heritage, but you run the risk (particularly in an enclosed retirement complex with its own facilities, such as shops) of engaging less and less with the outside world.

Retirement Housing

Some people feel that they would rather live among people of their own age, with whom they are likely to have shared experiences and a shared cultural heritage. Older people will, they feel, be far better able than younger people to understand ageing and thus offer support and helpful advice. For them retirement housing seems the obvious solution.

Retirement housing differs fundamentally from the other main type of accommodation specifically for older people – care homes. In the latter, residents not only get all their meals provided and a roof over their heads in a building in which someone else does the household chores, but also the attention of staff (to help with personal tasks such as washing, dressing and, in a care nursing home, some nursing tasks) at any time of the day or night.

In retirement housing people are expected to be much more independent: retirement housing is essentially housing rather than care. It consists of grouped apartments, rooms or houses for older people which they may lease, rent or occupy under some agreement. Nonetheless, there is a long list of facilities which may be on offer besides shelter.

One form of retirement housing, called sheltered housing, provides grouped accommodation for older people in which alarm systems have been installed and wardens are available. People may come to the building to help individual residents with the day-to-day practical tasks of living, but they will probably come from an organization such as a care agency whose

---

Retirement Housing

- Retirement and sheltered housing differ widely in price, type of location, tenure and security.
- 'Sheltered' can mean many different things.
- No national minimum standards or regulations cover retirement housing.
- Functions and training of wardens and scheme managers vary widely.
- Check that the alarm which will summon help is as accessible as possible.
- Check that building design will accommodate mobility aids or human help in case these become necessary.
- Would you like to spend time sitting in the grounds?
- Check on the scope for increases in charges, including rent.
- In private schemes, check service charges and management fees.
- Stay in the guest flat for a trial period before you commit.

---

ownership is quite separate from that of the housing provider and which is the same type of agency which helps elderly people living in ordinary houses and flats. If personal care is provided, it would put the housing provider within the definition of a care home and thus make the scheme subject to national registration and inspection like a care home. Retirement housing providers who also offer their own in-house personal care if it is needed exist but are scarce. Residents in typical retirement housing needing more help than can be provided through care workers coming into their flats at pre-arranged times usually have to move out, if only because their individual flats are not large enough to accommodate another person who needs to be present day and night. So retirement housing is not always housing for life: some people find they have to move out, usually at the time when they are particularly ill equipped to handle a move. Many retirement housing schemes, particularly sheltered housing schemes, will, however, help residents find somewhere else if this becomes necessary.

Homes for the Fit

There are types of retirement housing which refuse to countenance any practical or personal care for their residents. Here, residents have to move out even if they need only the sort of care which in other settings, such as an owner-occupied house or an ordinary leasehold flat, could be provided by visiting care workers. The providers include clauses in occupancy agreements requiring residents to move on even if they become only slightly disabled.

Such establishments usually charge a monthly fee for meals, cleaning, lighting, heating, use of communal rooms and grounds and perhaps a minibus to take residents into a nearby town if the location is rural. They normally provide no grab-rails, supports by the lavatory or wheelchairs. At one scheme I know, a resident was asked to leave when she appeared downstairs with a Zimmer frame.

If you are brave enough to move into such a place (and these are often glorious buildings in glorious locations for wealthy older people), fine. But you have to appreciate that should you develop difficulty in walking or one of the many afflictions of old age which can limit your ability to look after yourself, you will have to find somewhere else to call home. The situation can be difficult to deal with, particularly if you have, say, suffered a stroke. So scrutinize the occupancy agreement carefully.

Sheltered Housing

Around half a million people over the age of 65 in England alone live in sheltered housing; this is of the same order as the number of people who live in care homes (although they tend to be older). Many people are attracted by the very word 'sheltered', but what does it mean in this context?

If you find the maintenance and management of your own property bothersome, the idea that somebody else will sort out leaking gutters and keep the garden under control seems appealing. You may think sheltered housing will offer you more security against intruders. A feeling of security can arise from the presence of somebody to call on in an emergency or to provide support and care. It is important to distinguish these desires from what people actually get when they move into sheltered housing.

Sheltered housing varies enormously. Unlike other parts of

the eldercare system such as care homes, there is no national definition which sets down what a scheme should contain if it is to go by the name of sheltered housing. There is no set of national standards for sheltered housing, let alone any inspection by a national organization as obtains with care homes. This is not to say that the providers of sheltered housing do not do their own checks, while some have signed up to various often self-enforced codes of good practice. In addition, there are the rules and inspections in fields such as fire, food hygiene and health and safety, as in other kinds of establishment. Also, external controls impinge through state funding – grants to housing associations from the Housing Corporation and through a new system called Supporting People. This provides a grant from central government to local authorities to provide housing support services to local authority and housing association tenants assessed as needing them (pages 291–2). These services could include, for example, the provision of emergency alarms and wardens. In dispensing these funds to individuals, councils should be keeping tabs on aspects of sheltered housing schemes which they are thereby helping to support. However, these checks are unlikely to cover all the aspects of a scheme which affect its residents, while private retirement housing is likely to be unaffected by Supporting People in the early years.

To clear up a potential source of confusion, the private sector is often unwilling to describe housing which has the characteristics of sheltered housing as such, preferring the term 'retirement housing' (although as we saw above, the latter term can also embrace something very different from housing with wardens and alarms).

Whether publicly or privately provided, what you are likely to get in sheltered housing essentially is:

- Your own self-contained accommodation – usually a flat, but in some schemes a bungalow or house. Occasionally there are two bedrooms, often one, but sometimes no separate bedrooms and instead a bedsit lounge. Most will have a separate kitchen and bathroom, and there may also be a balcony. If you are on the ground floor, you may have a tiny garden.
- The maintenance and management of the external fabric of

the building, internal communal areas and the grounds will be carried out by a management organization rather than individual residents.

- A warden (now often called a 'scheme manager' or 'sheltered housing officer') will manage the property day to day and keep an eye on residents, usually by contacting them each morning either through a visit or through an intercom. The warden is expected to summon help in an emergency and to provide friendly chat and help, mainly advice of the sort a good neighbour might proffer. Some wardens lay on social activities, but they are not allowed to provide domestic help or personal care. Some wardens live on the premises, some off-site but are present during office hours. Other schemes rely on a peripatetic warden who travels between a number of schemes.

- There will be an attractive and well-lit hall and communal areas such as corridors, stairs and probably lifts, which are easily accessible to older people.

- A communal lounge which residents can use when they like.

- A laundry room available to everybody.

- A guest room where visitors can stay.

- Easy access on foot or by public transport to shops, places of worship, post offices, banks and other facilities.

- There will probably be some kind of door entry system so that residents feel safe.

- There will be an emergency alarm system in each flat. This often takes the form of a long cord hanging from the ceiling which, when pulled, rings a bell in the warden's office. He or she would then go to the flat in question to find out what was wrong, using a master key if necessary. Sometimes pulling the cord alerts a control centre elsewhere, from which help is summoned, for instance by telephoning a relative, who is then expected to call on the person who first pulled the cord. Since somebody in need of help would often find difficulty in getting to the corner of the room to pull the cord, some additional means of summoning assistance, such as a pendant worn round the neck, may be provided.

Some attention will have been paid to the design of the property with the needs of older and frailer people in mind, such as the provision of waist- or knee-high power sockets. However, sheltered housing is not usually designed as housing for disabled people, so while you could, for instance, probably get a wheelchair through the door, there is unlikely to be plenty of space to manoeuvre it.

Occasionally a large sheltered housing scheme forms part of a retirement complex, which may include a range of facilities including a fitness centre, library, shops and canteen, as well as a care home, which in turn may be divided into a part corresponding to a residential home (for people who need to be able to summon personal care at any time of the day or night) and a nursing home. The idea is that if people in the sheltered housing part come to need the sort of care which would be provided in a care home, they can get it within the complex rather than having to move to a completely unfamiliar environment.

Very Sheltered Housing

A very small proportion of sheltered housing (up to about 5 per cent) has additional facilities and is known as 'very sheltered housing' (or sometimes 'assisted living', or 'close care housing'). This too varies, but you are likely to find a very sheltered housing scheme providing at least one cooked meal a day, together with an environment a little easier to move around in for elderly people, and the guarantee of a resident warden and some other services.

These services vary: sometimes they will include housework and even personal care. Sometimes there will be other facilities such as social activities. The Abbeyfield Society's schemes, for instance, provide at least one and often two main meals a day and a resident housekeeper; efforts are made to help people feel at home and to combat social isolation through the use of volunteers who visit regularly and organize trips and events. Residents are still expected to keep their own rooms clean and tidy and make their own breakfast.

Although very sheltered housing makes up only a small proportion of the total amount of sheltered housing at the moment, it is expected that this proportion will increase over the next few years, both in the private and housing association sector.[5]

Sheltered Housing Providers

In England, 82,000 older people live in sheltered housing provided by the private sector, which they lease or occasionally rent. A development company owns the freehold, sells the individual leases and charges an annual ground rent (usually nominal) and also possibly charges for parking and rent for the warden's office. The developer often passes the ongoing maintenance and management of the property to another company, which levies an annual service charge on the lessees to pay for this. (In Scotland, people buy the freehold of private sheltered housing, not a lease; there were about 5,000 such housing units in 2003, managed by a management company, just as south of the border.)

Private sheltered housing expanded in the 1970s and 1980s after the founder of Britain's largest private sheltered housing developer, John McCarthy of McCarthy and Stone, discovered that local authorities were readier to grant planning permission for retirement housing than for ordinary housing in town centres – they believed that retired people would own fewer cars and generate less traffic. Developers felt able to place more housing units on one site since they could allocate less space for garages and parking.

Housing associations and local authorities provide four-fifths (about 450,000 units) of sheltered housing in England and Wales;[6] a small number of schemes are provided by charities and trade associations. In the 1950s, local authorities starting building small flats for elderly people whose children had left home and often whose partner had also died. These were provided with a communal lounge and a warden who would keep an eye on residents; later more were built to free up large council houses which older people were under-occupying. During the 1970s and 1980s, housing associations (not-for-profit agencies) started to add schemes which provided, for example, guest rooms and a wider level of service from the warden. They now provide sheltered housing to rent and to buy, including leasehold shared equity schemes whereby a person buys a proportion of the equity of the property.

Although private, local authority and housing association sheltered housing have been inspired by different motives, the various types have much in common. You will not necessarily get better sheltered housing in a private scheme than in a housing association one. Either way, you will find that sheltered housing differs from ordinary houses and flats in a number of important ways.

Property Maintenance

Communal Areas

The maintenance of the outside of the property will be the responsibility of the scheme manager – the local authority, private company or housing association. So things such as periodic repainting, cleaning the windows, the repair of roofs and the maintenance of grounds and gardens will not be your problem. Offloading these tasks is of course one of the main reasons why people move into sheltered housing and why relatives often encourage them to do so. However, it is worth considering two points in this area before you sign a lease or tenancy. First, what power would you have or what legal action might you be driven to take if the company or association failed to maintain the property adequately? Clearly, if the grounds are litter-strewn and the paint peeling, the value of your own stake in, say, a lease may go down. So scrutinize the contract carefully with your lawyer and seek to be convinced that there is a legal requirement on the part of the managing agency for maintenance – and that it has set aside sufficient funds for this.

The chances are, however, that you may be more concerned about over-expenditure on management and maintenance than under-expenditure. Repainting, repairs, garden maintenance and so on are paid for out of the annual service charge which is levied on lessees; for those paying rent, it comes out of the rent. Organizations and companies keen to keep the rents or leases at a high level may be inclined to overspend in this area. So find out what control or influence, if any, you would have as a lessee or a tenant. Scrutinize the elements of the service charge to see what is included and how much is being charged in each case. Items to expect are the costs of the warden, alarms, maintenance, cleaning, insurance and gardening. Much the same goes for the communal areas indoors – how much will all this cost you and what control will you have over cost increases?

On the annual management charge per sheltered housing unit, shop around and compare prices. The fees charged vary according to the number of properties in the scheme, how much money has been borrowed to get it off the ground and other factors. A useful figure is this: the Housing Corporation (which gives grants to housing associations) has said that for 2003–4 it does not expect the management charge to exceed £274 (excluding VAT) nor increases to exceed the retail price index + 0.5 per cent.[7] New legislation passed in 2002 has given leaseholders the right to change their managing agents if half of the leaseholders support the change and a company limited by guarantee has been formed to exercise this right. This means that sheltered housing lessees who are unhappy with their management company can appoint another agent.[8]

Individual Flats

Sheltered housing scheme providers are likely to leave the maintenance and management of individual flats or houses to individual lessees and tenants. So you are still by no means completely done with property management and maintenance. Have a look at the inside of a flat you are thinking of taking on and consider just what management and maintenance it would need and whom you would get to do it. Also, are there any rules in the lease or tenancy governing the frequency with which you should redecorate? Would you be happy with this? Some of the new private retirement flats seem very low-maintenance at first glance, but in fact they can soon look shabby if money is not spent on them. For instance, the fitted carpets are often unpatterned and light coloured, say, grey or pink. This is not necessarily practical for people who may develop a shaky hand and often spill their tea or who may become incontinent. You could be recarpeting quite often.

As older people become frailer, they may need adaptations to their flats. They may wish to refit the already fitted kitchen, perhaps because of failing eyesight. They may wish to install grab-rails and poles on which they can lean. If severely disabled, they may even wish to put in a hoist which runs along a track across the ceiling. It is important to check that the lease, tenancy or other occupancy agreement would allow you to do this, or that if you need the permission of the owner of the freehold, it would be likely to be forthcoming.

Conversely, do you have any power of veto if in the case of a rented scheme your landlord plans to upgrade your kitchen when in fact you would prefer to keep it as it is? I remember talking to an old lady in Wimbledon with severe sight impairment and slight dementia who was concerned because her kitchen was about to be restructured by the housing association and she feared it would take her a long time to get used to the new arrangements. Also, she was worried that, after the refitting, her rent would go up. Do not imagine that housing associations never put up their rents to cope with more than increases in maintenance and management costs. Although they are not in the business of making money for owners or shareholders, they do make profits which they plough back into the work of the association, for instance through investing in new schemes.

Finally, who is going to change the light bulb if you cannot reach it? Or unblock the sink? Or fix the blind? Some sheltered housing schemes leave such matters up to residents, others may provide somebody, or the warden may have a list of reliable tradesmen. But you have to be careful: there is a lot of scope here for financial exploitation. You might find it hard not to ask the warden's husband to fix your dripping tap, even though you know he would charge you more than would a plumber from the *Yellow Pages*.

Help and Care

People who enter sheltered housing often feel they are going to receive some kind of unspecific support and care without having to be consigned to a care home with all the loss of freedom that this involves. But sheltered housing schemes do not in general provide anyone to do housework or personal care or any other work in the flats of individual residents. Residents who need human help, perhaps with washing, dressing or doing the cleaning, will almost certainly have to organize that help themselves or through their local social services department, just as they would if they were living in an ordinary house. A few sheltered housing schemes offer some care, through an in-house team or through an outside agency, but these are very much the exception.

Be very careful in the case of elderly relatives who seem to be getting forgetful and need someone to keep an eye on them. If they are developing dementia, sheltered housing will be particularly inappropriate. For one thing, they will not be able to get used to their new environment. For another, sheltered housing is most unlikely to provide the care they need even at an early stage of dementia. Finally, dementia is one of the classic reasons why people have to leave sheltered housing. The lease or tenancy may well provide some means for the housing provider to ease out dementia sufferers for instance by specifying that as one of the conditions of occupancy you must not become a serious nuisance to other people.

Communal Living
Of course, elderly people living in sheltered housing have their own front door, but they are necessarily engaged in communal living, even if they never take part in organized social activities. If you are used to living alone, it can come as quite a shock to see other people almost as soon as you open your front door. It is important to be sure that other residents are the sort of people in whose company you feel comfortable. Also, in any scheme there is bound to be some noise, particularly if you live near the lift, the lounge or the laundry, and there will be rules which cover some aspects of communal living about which you may or may not be happy, for instance that on keeping pets or on smoking in communal areas.

When you visit sheltered housing as a prospective resident, one of the most obvious things to ask is what sort of social activities are laid on. These will be organized either by the warden or by the residents themselves. The range offered by wardens varies enormously, from virtually nothing to a weekly coffee morning to a whole range of excursions and activities. At one housing association scheme I visited in Margate, Kent, the extremely amiable and helpful warden organized crafts one afternoon a week (for instance painting decorations on cups and glasses for sale in aid of a local children's hospice), a weekly coffee morning and weekly sessions of bingo and whist, in addition to numerous outings, suppers, afternoon teas and Christmas lunch. The lounge contained facilities which residents could use at any time: a music centre, television and video, snooker table, darts board, books and board games. Obviously you need to find out whether the activities offered would be to your taste.

There is no doubt much informal getting together by residents but sheltered housing schemes tend not to offer an enormous range of different activities unless they are very large or situated in a retirement complex, simply because there will not be a sufficient number of people sharing any particular interest. One woman in a sheltered flat in Reigate, Surrey, who was becoming increasingly confined to her flat and less able to participate in activities in the town outside, told me that she had thought of trying to organize a reading circle in her scheme, but as there were only 37 flats she did not think she could muster enough people who would be interested.

For men, facilities can seem particularly thin on the ground. Men tend to be heavily outnumbered by women, both because women tend to live longer than men and because supply and demand ensures that elderly men who lose their wives are more likely to remarry than elderly women who lose their husbands. Couples sometimes move into sheltered housing, but are more inclined than single or widowed people to remain in their own homes. So if you are a man on your own, you may find few other people similarly placed and that a scheme may not run to billiards, darts, draught beer or sport on satellite television.

Any sheltered housing scheme has its own complicated social structure of friendships and rivalries, involving countless interactions and sub-groups,[9] and you might find this too close-knit or even intrusive. Like it or not, gossip will probably feature. When people become less mobile they may compensate by taking more interest in the comings and goings of others. The best way of getting some sense of this is to stay in the guest flat of a sheltered housing scheme to find out what it is like living there 24 hours a day.

So, do take stock of the reasons why you feel that sheltered housing would provide an amenable social environment before you take the plunge. Some people move into sheltered housing when they feel particularly socially isolated, such as after the death of their spouse. It is important to be clear what a sheltered housing scheme is likely to provide in such circumstances. When we lose a partner, we lose the practical help that person gave – such as doing the garden – and either we have to reskill and do those tasks ourselves or hire somebody to do them for us. Clearly, if you go into sheltered housing some of the practical tasks your partner may have performed are likely to be taken off your hands. But you are not going to find an automatic substitute for the emotional support your partner once offered.

The Alarm

It is a basic feature of sheltered housing that an alarm should be available for each resident so that assistance can be summoned quickly in the event of, say, a fall, a stroke or getting wedged in the bath. You might imagine that the alarm system in a sheltered housing scheme would be extremely effective and certainly superior to the pendant alarms which many elderly people have had installed in ordinary houses and flats (page 96), but this is by no means always the case.

Alarms in some sheltered housing units fall short of pendant systems in that they are less accessible. They often consist of a long cord hanging in a corner of each room. But if you have a fall in another corner, you would not necessarily be able to reach the cord. Also, since this system requires that you be close to an alarm, you could not summon help from other parts of the building such as the corridor, the laundry or the grounds, unless there were separate alarms placed there and you were able to reach them. Schemes with cord alarm systems may offer you a pendant as well for an additional extra charge. Or you may choose to organize one yourself. Ricability, a charity which publishes guides for older and disabled people about equipment, has a very useful publication on choosing an alarm.

Whatever form the alarm in your sheltered housing flat takes, the warden should come straight to you without delay if he or she is on duty at the time. In this case, you are likely to get help much more quickly than you would if people living outside had to come round. Wardens will summon assistance if necessary by telephoning a relative or contacting the emergency services, though it is not their role to look after you but essentially to pass the problem on to someone else. Some wardens will provide some help, perhaps helping you into a chair or making you a cup of tea, others will not. If you have suffered a heart attack and are unconscious, some will administer artificial resuscitation, but some will not know how to, and others will know how to but decide they would rather not. It is very important to be clear about all these things before you decide to move in. After all, the reassurance provided by an alarm and a warden is probably one of the main reasons why you are deciding to exchange your existing home for sheltered accommodation.

The Warden or On-site Scheme Manager
One important way in which sheltered housing schemes differ is whether they have a resident warden, or a warden on site during office hours Monday to Friday, or only a peripatetic warden who covers a number of schemes. If there is a warden who lives on the premises, he or she may be on call a great deal but is bound to have some time off. In his or her absence, is there a replacement warden, or are alarm calls or enquiries from residents put through to a call centre or to a peripatetic warden? Some schemes have made their full-time warden part-time, or replaced him or her with a peripatetic warden off-site. Also, a housing provider might try to cut costs by replacing a resident warden with a part-time warden, a peripatetic warden or a call centre. Or it might replace a requirement that the warden should visit each flat every day with a call to each flat every day on the intercom. Before you enter a scheme, find out whether such a move is planned and whether residents would have any means of preventing it.

All wardens will be responsible for the maintenance of the building, organizing repairs and redecorating and cleaning. Clearly, these matters are important. But from the point of view of individual residents and their families, the warden's most important task is to offer help to residents in an emergency, to check that they are all right day by day and, if they are not, to do something about it. How is the warden to know? It seems to me the best approach is for the warden to have to knock on the door of each flat at least once a day and have a face-to-face conversation with the occupant. Instead of this, some wardens contact residents each morning on the intercom and ask them if they are all right, but elderly residents who are ill may still say they are OK, either automatically or to put a brave face on things. They might say, 'I'm fine,' while lying on the floor, eager to be no trouble to the warden. Or they may think they are all right but look sufficiently unwell to prompt a warden to follow up with 'Are you sure you're all right?' or to return later to double check.

Good wardens take about two hours each morning to do a round of 30 flats, although wardens getting round more quickly are not necessarily being negligent. If there is no answer to their knock, they ask next-door occupants if they have heard any noise. If they still get no answer, they ask somebody else to accompany them while they enter the flat using their own keys (as a security safeguard, wardens should not be permitted to unlock a flat door on their own). A good warden would also stay with the resident and if necessary help him or her telephone the doctor to make an appointment. Ideally, the warden would make two daily visits, as otherwise somebody could fall just after the early-morning call and lie on the floor all day and night.

In schemes where the policy is morning visits, residents may be offered a waiver form to sign agreeing to forgo these calls. It is important that residents do not feel under any pressure to sign; if they do not want such visits, what are they doing in sheltered housing at all?

In some schemes, rather than visiting or phoning, wardens merely have to satisfy themselves at some point during the day that each lessee or tenant is all right, without necessarily having been seen or spoken to. Wardens may provide such a check by unobtrusive means, such as noticing whether residents have pulled newspapers through their letterboxes. The housing provider may present this method as the more desirable because it is unobtrusive, but it is hardly foolproof. Residents who have pulled their newspaper through their letterbox may actually be extremely unwell. Or somebody else may have taken the newspaper, either intentionally or absent-mindedly.

In one privately-owned scheme I visited which relied on unobtrusive checking, residents were confused about it. When their regular warden went on holiday, a replacement was seen to note down residents' comings and goings, which made them feel uncomfortable, even though surveillance was part of her job. Wardens have to protect the property and the community as a whole against anything, including individual residents who may pose a threat to it. The extent to which people are seen to pose a threat and as a result encouraged to move out of their flats varies greatly, but this side of things makes the warden a policeman as well as a comforter. Not everyone all of the time will fit the preferred image in many private schemes of well-groomed people engaging in polite conversation around the bridge table. Some residents will sometimes get drunk, some will engage in apparently bizarre behaviour as a result of dementia, others will erupt into the occasional outburst, perhaps prompted by the anguish of losing their sight or hearing.

So if you are contemplating moving into a sheltered housing scheme, have a long conversation with the warden to try to work out how potential conflicts like this are resolved. Housing providers may find it difficult to use the law to get rid of residents who they feel are tarnishing the image of their property or posing a real threat to other people living there, but life can be pretty uncomfortable if you feel that the provider or management company would like you to move when you wish to stay.

There are other basic questions to ask wardens. What is the procedure when they are out of the office as far as emergency calls are concerned? Usually they will be able to divert calls to a call centre. Does this happen every weekend? What is the maximum period for which they are permitted to do this? What happens when they go on holiday? What precisely are their duties? Work out how these are defined, as there is tremendous scope for individual variation here. Wardens may be contractually barred from doing housework or personal care in individual flats, but wardens who see themselves as good neighbours could do many other things, such as help get washing out of the machine for people who are finding that difficult. If residents are returning from a holiday or hospital, they could put the heating on before they get back and buy in milk and bread.

It is important to know just what your warden can and cannot do. Has he or she had first-aid training and followed this up with refresher courses? Even if she possesses first-aid skills, would she use them? Precisely what would she do if a resident had collapsed on the floor? If you ask her to give you an idea of the sort of problems with which she is summoned to deal, you could get a sense not only of what she would do in any particular situation, but also of whether the development itself tends to create particular problems. If people are frequently getting stuck in the bath, there may be some flaw in their design.

What sort of details does the warden keep about individual residents? The possession of some medical details – knowing for instance that somebody is diabetic or on a particular type of medication – could be invaluable, particularly in an emergency. On the other hand, you might fear that other medical details could be used to your disadvantage, such as a history of alcoholism. And how confidential is the information the warden holds about you? To whom might it be disclosed?

Finally, what mechanism is available to residents to complain about or even get rid of the warden? Supposing wardens throw frequent, noisy all-night parties, intimidate (or allow their spouses to intimidate) residents, or simply fail to perform adequately the duties laid down in their contracts, to whom do residents complain? Are their complaints likely to have any effect? Is there a residents' council and what powers does it have?

Security of Tenure
Clearly, you want to ensure that your right to occupy your property is as secure as possible. Local authority and housing association sheltered housing is exempted from the right to buy. If you are renting, try to ensure you get an assured tenancy, which gives you much more protection than a licence or an occupancy agreement (the common form of tenure in almshouses and care homes respectively).

Despite the security of tenure which the law permits, the providers of retirement housing can insert any clauses they choose in tenancy agreements. As a result, the lease or tenancy, particularly for private sector provision, may well say that you occupy the accommodation as a person capable of independent living and that you must not be noisy or a nuisance to other residents. This sounds fair enough, but if you develop dementia your behaviour may become disruptive. So look carefully at the wording. If you should become seriously disabled or develop dementia, you may decide to leave, but you obviously do not want to be forced out or feel uncomfortable about your position. Housing tenure law means that a housing provider would usually need to go to court to evict somebody who did not wish to go. However, many tenants and lessees may not be aware of the extent of their legal right to remain and may comply with a request to move on even when they could put up a fight and probably win. If you are in any doubt about a tenancy agreement into which you might enter or about your right to stay put, get advice from the Citizen's Advice Bureau, your lawyer or a housing lobby group such as Shelter or AIMS (the Advice Information and Mediation Service for Retirement Housing) of Age Concern England, which provides specialist advice on the problems which can arise in sheltered housing, both leasehold and rented. A similar organization called INNIS (a Gaelic word meaning to inform), part of Age Concern Scotland, provides a similar service.

Design

Some design features of accommodation for elderly people anywhere (pages 161–64) apply also to sheltered housing. It is well worth checking these out in advance as well as the points listed below, as the suitability of sheltered housing for elderly people is not guaranteed through any national standards, and you can often find features which are not ideal for the frail or disabled.

Individual Flats

Check points such as the amount of space and the design of the kitchen and bathroom. If you had to use a wheelchair, would there be enough space for turning? The kitchen may look top-of-the-range and extremely modern, but could you easily work out how to use it?

Moving into sheltered housing almost always means having to give up possessions because there is no room for them. Some are more important than others in terms of everyday life. Shelves of books may never be read, and anyway you could borrow them from the library, but if music is an important part of your life, a piano may be a different matter. There is unlikely to be space for one in your flat, and in any case playing it might disturb the neighbours. But is there a piano somewhere in the building which you could play? Ideally, are there others in the scheme with whom you could share your interest?

Sheltered flats can undermine the privacy of their occupants unless they are designed quite carefully, particularly if they are essentially bedsits. Ideally somebody standing at the door of the flat should not be able to see the bed. You want a hierarchy of spaces, with an entrance threshold area which has a different feel about it from the public part of the room, where you would entertain visitors, and the private part, where the bed is located. Even in a bedsit it is perfectly possible to maintain this hierarchy, perhaps through a combination of shape of the room (for instance placing the bed in an alcove or one arm of an L-shaped room), a screen behind which the bed is placed, or through the way the furniture is arranged. A number of different sitting areas in the public space is also ideal, even if each one is small – perhaps on a balcony, by a window or two, as well as by the fire, at a dining table and around a coffee table.

Storage Space

Is space provided for the storage of large items such as suitcases, ironing boards, mobility aids, wheelchairs (for frequent or occasional use) and Z-beds? Where could a battery-powered scooter or buggy be stored and where could it be recharged?

Communal Areas

There are two aspects here: ease of movement and safety. It is important that an elderly person should be able to walk easily through the various spaces, so that all the parts of the building are easily accessible. For instance, how easy is it to get down to the laundry? Doors can sometimes present problems, particularly heavy front doors and fire doors. A frail person finding it difficult to get out of the front door might have to wait around in the lounge until somebody else comes along to open it for him or her.

If you observe that many of the internal fire doors are propped open by wedges, this may suggest they are too heavy for residents to open but the building will not be protected from fire at all. The means of escape would fill with smoke in the event of a fire. The best device is a magnetic catch which allows the door to be held open for some of the time to facilitate passage for frail people, though it will automatically swing shut if a fire alarm goes off.

You should be able to get to all parts of the building. Is there a lift? Does it work all right? Does it break down often? When it is being mended or serviced, what arrangements are made for residents who cannot use stairs easily?

It is of course important that the surfaces on which you walk should be safe. Clearly, they should be non-slip and free of any rugs or obstructions on which people might trip. Also, check that floors do not have shiny, reflective surfaces, since older people can easily be dazzled by glare and become disorientated, which may lead to a fall. They can also be temporarily blinded if they are looking directly at a bright light, for example moving down a long dark corridor with a light or a window at one end.

Both in individual flats and communal areas, it is a good idea if important features are picked out in contrasting colours and tones because of the ways in which vision, in particular colour vision, changes as we grow older (we come to see the red, orange and yellow part of the spectrum much better than the blue and green part). So look out for contrast in features such as handrails, stairs and changes in level or gradient. Within flats, contrast can be very helpful for doors, cupboards and the edge of the working surface in the kitchen.

Another matter to consider in both the communal areas and inside individual flats is acoustic quality. Are the lounge and other places where people might converse fairly quiet? Most older people will have some degree of hearing loss, and that loss will probably be in the high registers, so they find it harder to distinguish certain consonants and as a result cannot understand speech as easily as they used to. That understanding will be lessened if there is a lot of background noise. Features which help sound absorbency can make a big difference, as can systems which deliberately enhance hearing, such as loop systems. You would expect a loop system to be present in the lounge.

Safety and Security
What is the procedure in the event of a fire? How often is a fire practice held and how often is the fire alarm tested? If you are hard of hearing, how would you be alerted? (Flashing lights or vibrators under the mattress are devices used.)

Some schemes ask people to remain in their rooms in the event of a fire lest they get lost or stranded in the communal areas, particularly as lifts would not be used. Would you feel happy with this? When I asked one warden for the first question she would ask if she were a prospective sheltered housing resident, she replied: 'How often is the fire alarm tested? What happens in case of a fire? How can one warden get everybody out?'

Insurance companies often offer sheltered housing residents lower premiums for household contents insurance, as they consider sheltered housing less vulnerable to burglary than other types. It is, however, important not to be lulled into a false sense of security. Crime does occur in sheltered housing and burglars do sometimes get in, particularly to ground-floor flats. So check that the security arrangements are adequate, as these vary enormously. Some schemes have no means whatsoever of stopping anybody wandering into them, particularly at night when no warden or residents are likely to be around to question suspicious-looking characters. On the other hand, other schemes have swipe-card entry systems, though it is important to make sure that they are foolproof and that somebody could not get through simply by swiping another card, such as a credit card. Some individual sheltered flats even run to CCTV, so that residents can see who is at their individual front doors before allowing them entry. Consider whether you would need to add security measures of your own, such as a chain on the front door or a burglar alarm.

The warden will have access to each flat or house through his or her own key. Find out what safeguards exist to prevent the abuse of this system. Is there a requirement that the warden can enter an unoccupied flat only if accompanied by somebody else, such as another tenant or lessee? Who has access to the safe in which all the flat keys are kept? There may be provision for the emergency services to be able to get access when the warden is absent. Are you satisfied that this is foolproof?

Guests
Is there a guestroom? Is it available if a relative should wish to stay or if a resident is ill or in hospital? How much would it cost? Can guests stay in individual rooms? Could grandchildren sleep on the sofa?

Pets

The majority of sheltered housing schemes do not allow pets. Some say that if you already have a pet dog you can bring it, but it must always be on a lead on site, never present in any of the public rooms, not exercised in the communal grounds, and if it dies you must not replace it. Cats too, if allowed at all, are usually confined to individual flats. There are of course reasons for this – pets can be a trip hazard and cause allergies – but these rules can seem very severe to elderly people who have a strong attachment to their pets (pages 238–43).

The Garden and Grounds

If you move into sheltered accommodation, you will probably find yourself sitting in the grounds quite often. Sheltered housing is rarely spacious and residents may often want to go and sit out of doors. If you are considering moving into a scheme, sit on the various seats provided in the grounds and ask yourself whether you would enjoy spending time there. Do you like the surroundings? Would they provide interest and attraction all year round? You do not want to find that in a matter of weeks you are regularly filling a flask and going and sitting in a public park because you do not like the grounds you are paying for. Some people are happy amongst the low-growing, low-maintenance evergreen bushes which dominate many communal grounds; others prefer vegetation with more variety, plants from snowdrops to apple trees which reflect the changing seasons, or roses or herbs which are sweet-smelling.

Are the grounds easy to get around for people who have difficulty walking? Are the surfaces OK for people with mobility aids or in wheelchairs? Are the seats easy to get in and out of? What can you do in the grounds? Would you feel happy picnicking out there with your family? Could your grandchildren play there?

Could you do any work in the grounds if you wished? In one scheme I know in Gloucestershire, a retired man, not a resident, tends a very attractive mix of lawns, flowerbeds and vegetable plots. Residents can go and help him if they wish – taking a trowel to the odd flowerbed, pottering around in the greenhouse, perhaps watering the tomatoes. If you are a very keen gardener you could look for a scheme which encourages frailer people to carry on gardening by providing some raised flowerbeds and lightweight tools. However, the housing provider may have a policy of not permitting residents to tend the gardens.

Are you happy with the provision for car parking?

Paying for Sheltered Housing

If you buy a sheltered house or flat provided by a private company, you may be expecting to pay for it out of the proceeds of a house sale with quite a lot left over, but you will not necessarily have much left.[10] On top of the purchase price, you have of course to allocate sufficient funds to pay the ground rent and service charge, which you still have to pay if you are away on holiday or in hospital. Electricity, water and so on, as well as your council tax, are billed separately. Rents, whether for private, housing association or local authority housing would normally cover the maintenance, management, warden, insurance and associated costs covered by the service charge for leasehold property.

Some people can receive help from their local authority (or the Northern Ireland Housing Executive) to pay the whole or part of the rent for sheltered housing through Housing Benefit (page 496). Some tenants may also be eligible for help through a system of funding housing support called Supporting People, which, for sheltered housing, could help pay for the cost of alarm systems and wardens as well as other things.[11] To receive Supporting People money, tenants will have to be assessed by their local authorities as needing the relevant support. This system is described on pages 291–2.

If you are already a tenant on Housing Benefit you should not need to have done anything to get yourself transferred over to Supporting People. If you are not on Housing Benefit but would be eligible, the range of services may make an application well worthwhile. Contact your social services department or your area office of the Northern Ireland Housing Executive.

Finding Sheltered Housing

The most comprehensive source of information on sheltered housing is the database held by the voluntary organization the Elderly Accommodation Council, which has details of sheltered housing both to rent and to buy throughout the United

Kingdom. If you go to their website you can get details of sheltered housing on a geographical basis, with information on ownership and vacancies. If you telephone the Council, further details may be available, for instance on which schemes accept pets.

Conclusion

Retirement housing, whether intended for fit older people or sheltered, needs careful thought. The lure of attractive premises needs to be weighed against the possibility that at a later date support facilities may matter more than the view. Those seeking social contact could be happy in some establishments, but isolated in others. Choose one where you are likely to get on with the other residents and where there is an emphasis on social support. Some people may discover that sheltered housing offers them no great advantage over their current home in terms of room size, facilities or amenities, and that the only advantage will be a visiting warden on occasion. In such cases, they might be best advised to remain where they are, make adaptations and improvements to their home, and secure help with housework and other tasks independently or through social services. Very sheltered housing does usually offer the consumer rather more support than ordinary sheltered housing, in particular a cooked meal and a supportive atmosphere, but you might be able to get as much living in your own home or in an ordinary sheltered housing unit next to a good day centre.

Before a move into retirement housing, try living in the guest flat for two or three weeks. Afterwards, you may find you cannot wait to move in permanently. Or points may have occurred to you which you had not considered, which suggest that on balance you should stay put. I have met people who are very happy in retirement housing, who have formed close friendships with other residents within a vibrant and stimulating community and would not wish to go back to the house in which they used to live, probably alone. But I have also met residents in retirement housing for the fit who worry about what may befall them should they become mentally or physically frail. I have met others who find themselves in small, lack-lustre sheltered housing flats in which the most obvious wall-hanging is the red alarm cord – reassuring, perhaps, but also an ever-present reminder of mortality. Such people may tell you they left a house and garden which they felt they could no longer cope with but you suspect that they would give almost anything to go back.

Sheltered housing can work extremely well as a social environment, and where this is the case it is often down to a particularly warm-hearted warden or to a shared interest among the residents, as when such schemes are provided by a trade association. It can also be lonely and alienating. As with any new accommodation, it will probably take you about five years to settle in. You need to be absolutely sure that it is going to be right for you before you take what is probably an irreversible step.

At Home

Many people decide that, all things considered, they would rather stay put in their own homes. However, as people get older, they often find the maintenance of their house and garden an almost overwhelming task. Should they become unable to mow a once immaculate lawn, they may view tall grass and invasive weeds with mounting trepidation. While shrinking from tackling this problem, they have to worry about keeping their house clean, getting it adequately insured, having the roof fixed or a washer put in the kitchen tap. Small wonder that managing property can seem an increasingly intimidating task, particularly if a recently deceased spouse has normally shouldered much of the burden. Take heart: a surprisingly large amount of help is available. And relatives can do much to help older loved ones who are finding property management increasingly troublesome.

Repairs

Property repairs pose particular problems for older people who would have taken them in their stride when they were younger. One is disruption to their living space while repairs are being carried out. Another is finding reputable workmen. Then there is the cost of repairs.

Disruption may be easiest to help with. Perhaps you could go away while repairs are being carried out and a relative come to stay in the house to oversee the work (together with consequential work such as redecorating). One wealthy old lady I knew had made no improvements to her house for decades, not because she could not afford to do so but because she found the disruption and the dust intolerable. She had great trouble walking, and it was as much as she could do to look after herself and her dog. However, she had to go into hospital, and while she was there, her legal representative organized all the house repairs which had become necessary and the installation of a washing-machine, tumble-drier and new carpets. When this woman returned from hospital she was delighted. The refurbished house now also provides a more attractive environment for the home care workers she hires.

Some older people feel understandably vulnerable when trying to negotiate with workmen with whom they have not previously dealt. Or they may feel obliged to commission sub-standard builders who perhaps live nearby and whom they do not want to offend, and indeed may rely on for occasional lifts or other help. So they may put off indefinitely even important repairs or get defects botched up rather than sorted out. As a result the house is likely to be less effective as a warm, dry shelter. Relatives may also be concerned that when they come to inherit the property, it will be less easy to sell. They can provide much help by tracking down honest traders offering high standards of workmanship, by commissioning and evaluating estimates and then later by chivvying workers, monitoring progress and clearing up afterwards.

There are a number of registers of supposedly reputable workmen. Some voluntary organizations, such as local Age Concern groups, have compiled a 'home services directory'. The one run by Age Concern York gives the name and address of the trader, a description of the work offered and the hourly rate, any call-out charge and whether emergency work is dealt with. Each trader who appears on its list has been evaluated, with references examined and a police check carried out, and has signed an undertaking that he or she will trade fairly and agree to adopt certain working practices, such as quoting prices inclusive of VAT and treating customers' property with care. In this scheme, a free conciliation procedure to resolve disputes is also offered.

If you take names from lists such as these, check on what the compilation of the list has involved, such as whether police checks are included. Such a source of information can be more useful than a recommendation from a friend and much more useful than a tradesman's boasted membership of a specialist trade organization. Such trade organizations mostly represent the interests of their members rather than of customers. It is important to check what the membership means (for instance, whether it offers any special insurance scheme in the case of building work), and also whether the workman you propose to hire is a current member or simply claiming to be one.

An organization called Care and Repair England publishes a useful free booklet called *In Good Repair*, which includes amongst other things suggestions for dealing with tradespeople, such as checking their insurance certificates and taking references from previous customers. It takes readers through the stages of planning and commissioning work, getting it done and then monitoring its completion.[12]

Local home improvement agencies are a good source of reputable builders. These agencies (also called Care and Repair agencies) are local, non-profit-making organizations scattered over the UK which have been set up to help older people, disabled people and those on low incomes to repair, improve or adapt their homes. (In Northern Ireland the Fold Housing Association performs this task throughout the Province.) Caseworkers visit and help people work out what repairs are needed, how to organize the work and how to pay for it. These agencies focus their efforts on the most vulnerable, marshalling grants and workmen and even get furniture rearranged, perhaps getting the bed moved downstairs. They can offer advice to all older people about their accommodation, whether rich or poor. So whatever your circumstances, if your house is in disrepair and you are putting off the hassle of doing anything about it, a Care and Repair agency could be invaluable. If you cannot obtain or do not wish to apply for a grant or loan from your local authority (see below), the agency should be able to help you work out other ways of financing the work, such as home equity release. Eric Laverick, the Midlands regional manager of Care and Repair, explained to me in 2003:

> The agencies are not just grants machines. They focus on need and advise on options, including repair and whether someone should move. They help people to look at the options, assemble finance, for

instance through local authority grants, insurance, trust funds and loans. They advise on welfare rights, which can be a passport to many other facilities and financial benefits. They provide technical advice and support, and they have registers of reliable builders. And they link with other agencies such as social services.

Grants and Loans

Financial help for home repairs and renovations is provided by the housing departments of local authorities. In Northern Ireland the Northern Ireland Housing Executive carries out this function, administering a Home Repairs Assistance Grant, which is means-tested and targeted at elderly people receiving benefits.

In the remainder of the UK, the grants system is changing. In the past, it had been similar to the one which is continuing in Northern Ireland. Thus until July 2003, local authorities in England and Wales administered national grants which were means-tested and helped in particular poor people, young and old, living in damp, unhealthy accommodation. Under new legislation,[13] these specific grants are being replaced with a general allocation of money from central government which local authorities can spend as they see fit. They can give grants which may or may not be means-tested, but they can also give loans, as well as materials and advice. Each local housing authority will describe how it is going to spend its money in a private sector Housing Renewal Policy, which you should be able to obtain from the authority or a public library. This will set out what kind of help is available, whether it is means-tested, the terms of any repayment and any conditions which are attached. The legislation requires authorities to set out in writing the terms and conditions under which help is being given and to ensure that recipients have received appropriate advice and information about the extent and nature of any obligations (including financial) that they will be taking on. Before making a loan or requiring repayment of a loan or grant, the authority must take account of recipients' ability to pay.[14]

It is too early to say what the effect of this change will be, but clearly some councils will now focus their resources on loans rather than grants and this will clearly be bad news for poor elderly people facing costly repairs. At the same time, the change will be good news in some parts of the country for people who would not have been eligible for means-tested help. However, loans might involve legal charges being put on homes so money is returned on death: this will be unpalatable to some. Much will depend on how individual councils decide to use the money.

In Scotland, a similar change from grants only to other forms of assistance is taking place, and this is expected to come into force in April 2004. However, the Scottish Parliament, unwilling to help wealthy homeowners unless they come within the definition of a 'disabled' person given in the next section, has introduced a requirement that all help must be means-tested.[15]

Adaptations

Different from home repairs are home adaptations. If you face disability as a result, say, of serious arthritis, an adaptation to your home might make the difference between being able to continue to live there and moving to a care home. Perhaps you need a ramp outside your front door, or a washbasin in a downstairs room which you use as a bedroom, or grab-rails along the hall, or a more secure banister, or modifications to a dangerous landing. If so, you may be able to get help with the cost from your local authority. However, there are also certain national grant schemes.

The government has announced that as from June 2003, all house adaptations up to a ceiling of £1,000 (covering the cost of buying and fitting) should be provided free of charge in England.[16] This is an entirely new provision and if you live in England and you are not offered it, you should insist that you are. You have to be assessed by your local authority as needing the adaptation before you can receive help towards the cost.

In Wales, the Rapid Response Adaptations Programme, introduced in 2002 and administered by Care and Repair agencies, provides free house adaptations and minor repairs for frail and disabled people, up to a ceiling of £350. The scheme is often used to put in place small adaptations for people coming out of hospital, but it can also be used at other times. In addition, local authorities and health boards in Wales fund for free up to about £250-worth of work to make people's homes safer, such as the installation of handrails, the improvement of stairways and the resurfacing of paths.

The Scottish Executive has decreed that local authorities should not charge for equipment and minor adaptations supplied to frail older people leaving hospital so long as these are fitted within four weeks following or immediately prior to discharge.[17]

Grants for Disabled People

If you have quite a substantial disability and your income falls below certain limits, you ought to be able to get a Disabled Facilities Grant. This may deliver quite a lot of money: the limit is £25,000 in England and £20,000 in Northern Ireland, for example.

The definition of disabled in this context involves a person 'whose sight, hearing or speech is substantially impaired; or they have a mental disorder or mental impairment; or they are physically substantially disabled by illness, injury, impairment present since birth, or otherwise'. Form of tenure is irrelevant, so grants are available to owner-occupiers and all types of tenant – private, council and housing association. This grant is mandatory: if you meet the criteria, you have to get it. [18]

The grants are typically given for improving access in and out of the property, and to the principal living room, bathroom, lavatory and bedroom, facilitating food preparation and improving lighting or heating. They take quite a long time to process, so it is important to lodge an application promptly if you think you might be eligible. The need for assessment by the local authority's occupational therapist often causes delays, so you might ask the council whether it would accept an assessment from a therapist you yourself commission (page 72). In assessing applications a local authority is not allowed to take its own resources into account. It has to pay the grant within 12 months of the date of application, so long as the work has been carried out. However, delays are frequent, partly because the government has not allocated sufficient money to local authorities.

In Chapters 5 and 9 I explain that local authorities have to provide gadgets and human help to old and frail people only if they meet the council's own eligibility criteria. Councils do not have this flexibility when it comes to people meeting the old definition of 'disabled'. Under the Chronically Sick and Disabled Persons Act 1970, local authorities *must* provide services to meet the needs of disabled people, including adaptations to the home, disability aids and equipment and human help. The social services department should be grappling with the needs of disabled people, and it is a good idea to contact it at the same time as you are approaching the housing department with a Disabled Facilities Grant application; there may be additional top-up funding which will be provided if you need it. Indeed, an application for a Disabled Facilities Grant could be instigated by the social services department as a result of a community care assessment.

If you cannot get your grant, or get it quickly, approach your local council's monitoring officer or consider lodging a complaint (pages 578–80). This is an area in which you need to be prepared to assert your legal rights, and disabled people have more rights to services than people who are merely old and frail. If you think publicity would help, contact the local media: a press picture of an elderly disabled person stranded at home because he or she cannot get up and down the front steps could do the trick. You could also contact your local councillor or MP.

Councils can also give discretionary help for adaptations for disabled people either on top of the Disabled Facilities Grant or as an alternative to it; there is no ceiling on the amount. Such help can also be used as a means of enabling a disabled person to move to a more suitable property where that is more cost-effective than adapting his or her current home, even though the new property may need some adaptations.

In Scotland, the situation is slightly different. There are no Disabled Facilities Grants as such. However, when the Part 6 of the Housing (Scotland) Act 2001 comes into force (this is expected to happen in autumn 2003), local authorities will be able to give home improvement grants up to a limit of £20,000. It is likely that disabled people will be among those eligible. Furthermore, home adaptations for disabled people will attract a minimum 50 per cent grant whatever the applicant's income.[19]

Heating
Cold can pose a serious health risk to you when you are older (pages 26–27). You need an ambient temperature of 21°C (or 70°F), day and night. There are ways of keeping warm in winter (pages 27–28), and much can also be done in the home.

Clearly, you need an effective, efficient and safe source of heating, but installing a new heating system is just the sort of disruptive step which many people put off indefinitely. If the house is chilly or difficult to heat, try to attend to this well ahead of winter. You may be able to get a government Warm Front Plus grant to help pay for a system. These grants arise from an initiative to help people considered to be living in 'fuel poverty', that is, on a low income in a home which cannot be kept warm without a large proportion of the occupier's income being spent on heating it. An older person who is receiving the Guarantee Credit element of Pension Credit or a substantial amount of Council Tax Benefit or Housing Benefit can get a maximum Warm Front Plus grant of £2,500, which could go towards not only loft insulation, cavity wall insulation, high-energy light bulbs and a jacket for the hot-water tank, but also the installation of central heating. Wealthier older people who are receiving non-means-tested Attendance Allowance or equivalent disability benefits are eligible for a lower grant, which can help pay for insulation, heating and so on, but not central heating; the maximum grant is £1,500.

The grant figures and arrangements are slightly different in different parts of the UK. In Wales, the grant is called the Home Energy Efficiency Scheme and the Home Energy Efficiency Scheme Plus. In Northern Ireland, there is the Warm Homes Scheme and Warm Homes Scheme Plus, and in Scotland, the schemes are called Warm Deal and the Central Heating Programme.

You can also obtain details of all these grants through the website of the organization which administers them. National government offices may also issue information – the Department of Health, for example, issues a handy leaflet called *Keep Warm, Keep Well*. Also, Age Concern and Age Concern Scotland publish useful factsheets called *Help with Heating*.

Gas fires need to be checked and serviced regularly, and older people can get free safety checks on any gas appliance, including water heaters and boilers. Make sure that rooms which contain gas fires and appliances are ventilated, and never go to sleep with a gas fire left on.

If you have an open fire, think about putting in an enclosed stove, as this can minimize heat loss out of the chimney. If the fire is not used, it is a good idea to get it blocked up, to prevent heat loss up the chimney, leaving a small hole for ventilation. The Solid Fuel Association offers advice on buying new open fires, ensuring, for instance, that they contain air control devices to regulate the rate of burning.

If buying an electric fire, look at different types on the market in terms of efficiency – ordinary bar electric fires are not so good at heating a room as a fan heater. A lot of heat can be lost from the back of radiators. If you hang aluminium foil behind the radiators with the shiny side towards a wall, you can prevent some heat escaping. This is especially useful on external walls. A small shelf above the radiator helps the warm air to circulate. Obviously, if furniture is placed close to radiators, the heat will be blocked. You can get advice on many aspects of energy efficiency from the Energy Efficiency Advice Centre.

Look at the ways available for spreading the cost of fuel. Most gas and electricity companies offer some way of spreading costs evenly over the year. They are not allowed to cut off older people who have not paid their bills between 1 October and 31 March, unless they can clearly afford to pay or there are younger people living in the household who could be expected to do so.

All older people are entitled to a Winter Fuel Payment. This is one of the few non-means tested, non-contributory, non-taxable benefits. It should be paid automatically, but if you do not get one or are uncertain about it, you can telephone the Winter Fuel Payment helpline. Payment is made to households. Every home containing one or more persons aged 60 or over receives £200. A household in which somebody aged 80 or over is living receives an additional £100. People living in care homes who are not receiving help to pay their bills in the form of Income Support should receive £100. A benefit which is separate, less generous and also means-tested, called the Cold Weather Payment, goes to individuals. The sum of £8.50 is paid each week when the average temperature has been recorded as, or is forecast to be, 0°C or below over seven consecutive days. Payment should be automatic to recipients of the Guarantee element of Pension Credit (page 492).

Security

Crime comes in fashions and one of the most common types of crime to affect elderly people at the moment is visits by conmen who knock on their doors, talk their way in and steal money and other valuables. Sometimes such characters claim to come from a public utility such as a water company, or even to be policemen. Some may claim to be collecting for charity. Typically these people ask the residents whether they have some change and, while they are looking for it, rifle through drawers for wallets, purses and bank books.

Simple steps can be taken to improve protection against bur-glary. A spy-hole is very useful because the prospective burglar (or indeed anybody else who might cause concern, such as a door-to-door salesperson) cannot see you looking to check, as he can if you have to use a window. A door chain is useful if you decide to open the door, but it is important not to leave it on per-manently, in case of fire or other emergency. Some of the steps to take if somebody calls are:

- Look to see who is calling through a spy-hole or window. Put the chain on before you open the door.
- Never allow entry without identification. Check the caller's identity card carefully. If in doubt, ask the caller to give you a telephone number so you can check his or her identity. Never leave the door open while you phone: shut it and keep it locked while you do so. Or arrange for the caller to come back later. A genuine caller will understand your concerns and give you time to check. A caller from a utility company ought to be able to quote your account number or a password.
- Open the door only when you are satisfied that the caller is genuine. If in doubt, ask him or her to return later when you have a neighbour or friend with you.
- If you are suspicious, call the police.
- Keep an eye on the caller while he or she is in the house. Even genuine callers may be tempted to thieve, so do not leave money or any other valuables lying around and do not leave the caller alone in a room, for instance while you go to find your purse.

Other aspects of home security will of course be the same as for younger people – window and door locks, participation in Neighbourhood Watch and so on. You may find that a local home improvement agency or Age Concern group, or the police, will offer advice and even put you in touch with somebody who will carry out work. People receiving the top rate of Warm Front Plus grant who live in high-crime areas are eligible for additional grants to improve home security.

Buying from Home

One type of caller who can be particularly troublesome for older people is the door-to-door salesperson. In 2002, a report by the National Association of Citizen's Advice Bureaux on doorstep selling, based on problems and experiences reported to offices, revealed that salespeople trying to persuade householders to switch fuel suppliers was a common source of trouble, but so too was the sale of gadgets and house adaptations to cope with disability. [20]

People who buy such items as wheelchairs, hearing aids, electric scooters and adjustable beds are often unable to shop easily outside the home and disability products can cost a great deal of money. People frequently reported that on thinking the purchase over after the salesperson had left the house, they wanted to cancel but discovered they could not do so.

Doorstep selling does have the advantage of convenience for the purchaser, but there are many possible pitfalls. If you are considering buying, say, a disability gadget or aid from a doorstep salesperson, some of the questions you might care to ask include:

- Does the price include VAT?
- Could I have details of at least two previous customers with whom I can discuss the service and the reliability of the goods and your company?
- Does the company charge extra for delivery and installation?
- How can I get the product repaired? Do I have to use an approved supplier of replacement parts?
- Are there any possible future trade-ins after the product has outlived its use?

You need also to know whether you have the right to cancel, how you can contact the seller again, whether the product is good value, whether you would really use it, whether you can afford it and whether it best suits your needs.

If you are in doubt about your consumer rights, including the right to cancel, contact the Trading Standards Department of your local council. Essentially, if the goods or services cost more than £35 and you did not invite the seller to call, you generally have seven days to change your mind and cancel the contract. But if you responded to an advert or leaflet dropped through the door, that counts as inviting the seller to call.

Complaining about goods which do not work as advertised or in the way that was described by the salesperson and getting a refund or a replacement can be extremely difficult. If the mobility scooter for which you have paid thousands of pounds will not go up a kerb in the way in which the doorstep salesperson told you it would, you may have to spend a lot of energy seeking redress.

Your Trading Standards Department can also give you information about other doorstep transactions, such as the factors to bear in mind if you are considering changing your gas or electricity supplier.

Safety

Environment

One of the calamities which can overtake older people in their own homes is a fall at least partly caused by a feature of the property itself, such as a rug over which they trip or an outdoor step without a handrail. There are countless ways in which houses and flats can be made safer for older people. Some local authorities offer a falls assessment service. If you are at high risk of hurting yourself from a fall, ask your GP or council if an occupational therapist could come round and look at the ways in which this risk could be minimized. Some of the external causes of falls and some of the easy steps which can be taken to avoid them are set out on pages 149–53.

Obstacles

Go round the house and garden and look out for anything over which you or your relative might trip. This could include items of furniture such as low side-tables, cupboard doors which are left permanently open or do not close properly, electric flexes and telephone wires on the floor, clutter, flooring or carpets in need of repair, or rugs with curled-up corners. You might find you need to:

- Tape any cords or wires to the floor or tuck them away.
- Tape down any necessary rugs. Remove any which are not necessary, especially those at the top or bottom of stairs.
- Check that staircarpets are secure. Tape down any tears.
- Go round and see where equipment could be installed, such as grab-rails. Ensure that the property has plenty of grab-rails even if you are only slightly unsteady. They cost little to fix on the wall; social services will often pay for or subsidize installation, although they may take months to do so and it is often much quicker and may be cheaper to do it yourself. Grab-rails provide much safer and firmer support than radiators, the bathroom basin or tables.
- Move low items of furniture out of the way to clear broad paths along which you can move freely.

Lighting

Older people need three times as much light as 20 year olds to see as easily. So make sure lights are especially bright in parts of the house where you are at greatest risk of hurting yourself, such as the landing and staircase. Switch on the lights at night whenever you visit the bathroom (and take a pendant alarm) or keep a commode near the bed.

Make changing light bulbs easier with long lead fittings and use long-life bulbs to reduce the frequency with which bulbs need to be replaced (page 163).

If your sight is not good, mark out the edges of things with white, red or yellow strips (rather than blues and greens, which are less readily distinguished by older eyes). If you are making major changes, such as refitting the kitchen, you can buy kitchen units and working surfaces with highlighted edges (page 93).

Levels

Both bending and stretching can lead to falls. Try to reduce the need to bend or stretch by thinking creatively about whether things have to be on their present level. For example:

- Could you hook a basket behind the letterbox, so mail does not have to be picked up from the floor?
- Could you get an electrician to move electric power points, or at least those in most use, to waist level?
- Could you reorganize furniture so that you do not have to reach across it to draw the curtains? Might a curtain pull-cord be safer?

Washing and Drying

Try to reduce the need to venture outdoors in icy weather to hang out washing. You may have managed perfectly well for years without a washing-machine or tumble-drier, but particularly if you develop continence problems and need to wash sheets every morning, a washing machine can be a real life-saver, along with a tumble-drier to save your having to slither down an icy garden path in winter. Clothes horses in the living room and open oven doors with garments and household linen drying over them create trip and fire hazards.

Behaviour

Here are a few guidelines if you are frail:

- Go up and down stairs sideways, so you can hold on to the banister with both hands for extra support.
- Reduce the need to keep going up and down stairs by performing all your tasks upstairs before coming down in the morning and have duplicates of items you often need on each floor. Small items can be carried around all the time in a shoulder bag.
- Avoid the need to reach up. Things used frequently can be placed on the lower shelves of cupboards or on working surfaces. Avoid the temptation to stand on stools or chairs. A fall from even a small height can fracture a bone. If you must stand on something, non-slip steps with safety features should be used. Avoid looking up for long periods if giddiness is a problem.

- Use high furniture, as it is easier to get in and out of. Armchairs should have a firm seat. When getting out of a chair, don't be tempted to pull on anything in front of you – it may tip over (this includes a Zimmer frame). Instead, slide to the front of the chair and use the armrests to push yourself up. Lean forwards and use your leg muscles to straighten your knees. To get on to a Zimmer frame from a chair, push yourself up using the arms of the chair, stand and get your balance, and only then use the Zimmer. People often fall when they use their Zimmer to try to pull themselves on to their feet. When you want to sit down again, feel the chair with the backs of your legs, remove one arm from the Zimmer and place it on the chair arm, repeat with the other arm, then lower yourself.

- Place your bed higher, say on bricks: this reduces the amount of lowering and raising you need to do. Make sure there are no long bedspreads on which you might trip. Don't get up too quickly from bed, whether in the morning or during the night to go to the lavatory, as your blood pressure may not adjust quickly enough from the lying-down position and this may make you feel dizzy. Rise slowly and carefully, and if you do feel dizzy, take a few deep breaths and wait until the dizziness disappears. Tense your muscles to get them working. As you get up, make sure the bed is behind you so if you lose your balance you will fall on to it. If you wear spectacles, always put them on, even if you are walking only a short distance from your bed.

- If you cannot get out of bed easily, you could try rolling on to your side, dropping your feet over the edge of the bed as you push on your arms to lift your trunk, and then reverse the process to get into bed.

- Consider buying an electrically-driven bath seat. Not only can they help people who, perhaps because of arthritis, find it difficult to get themselves in and out of a bath, but they also reduce the risk of falling by removing the need to lower yourself into the bath or to pull yourself up from it, since you simply sit on the seat and let that lower or raise you.

- Place a plastic bag on the seat before getting in and out of a car; this should enable you to slide in and out of it more easily, particularly if you go in bottom first (while minding your head), and then swing your legs in. Remove the bag when the car drives off or you might slip down. You can buy swivel car seats.

- Use the range of gadgets as appropriate, including a pendant alarm (pages 96–97).

The Garden

When older people become unable to tend their gardens in the way they have in the past, they can get extremely upset. An unruly jungle where once spread immaculate lawns and carefully weeded flowerbeds provides ever-present evidence of a decline in physical abilities. If a garden gets really out of hand, it can identify the house as an older person's and that may make the occupant feel vulnerable to thieves. Some people reluctantly give up their house because they can no longer manage the garden and this is a great shame. What can be done?

You could think about hiring help. If you have trouble finding a gardener, contact a local organization such as Age Concern, which may keep a list of reputable gardeners or even have its own volunteer gardeners or suggest where you might be able to find one. In Scotland, some local authorities offer garden maintenance services for elderly residents, some for council tenants only and others for other tenants and owner-occupiers as well. It is mainly grass cutting and hedge trimming that is involved, although some councils offer weeding. Age Concern Scotland holds a directory of council gardening services.

There are plenty of ways in which a garden can be refashioned so that it requires less work. These include:

- Replacing grass lawns with lawns which do not need mowing, such as thyme or chamomile, which are also sweet smelling.
- Replacing annuals with perennials which will not need planting each year, such as daffodils, tulips, valerian and cranesbills.
- Introducing plants which require little maintenance and crowd out weeds, such as heather.
- Introducing plants for which any management can be done without bending, such as roses. Perhaps you could fence off one area with a trellis and give it over to roses, while paving another area in which you place tubs and hanging baskets (not too high).
- Installing tubs and raised beds to enable a gardener to sit while

working, perhaps from a wheelchair. Raised beds are a fantastic idea and are used widely in gardens specially developed for older and disabled people, as in London's Battersea Park.

The market has responded to the large number of frail people keen to carry on gardening with the development of a range of tools which can make it much easier, such as long-handled trowels, so that you can garden from a sitting position, lightweight tools and even a gadget which will sow rows of seeds through a drill, so you do not need to bend down to the ground. The Arthritis and Rheumatism Council in their free booklet *Gardening with Arthritis* and the Carry on Gardening website offer advice and ideas. Ask your GP or physiotherapist for advice about posture while gardening: he or she might recommend kneeling on thick cushions and bending forwards with your head down, rather than squatting and craning your neck.

At Home

- House repairs, maintenance and management can become daunting
- While major works are in progress, see if a relative would housesit while you go on holiday
- Care and Repair agencies are not well known but can be very helpful
- Many councils, Age Concern groups and Care and Repair agencies have lists of reputable builders, plumbers and electricians
- Substantially disabled people can get grants to adapt their homes
- If your income is low, you may be able to get a grant to install central heating
- Be prepared for bogus callers
- Be careful about buying mobility equipment from door-to-door salespeople
- Install grab-rails, cupboards which do not require bending or stretching and extra lighting on the landing
- If you can no longer weed the flowerbeds, don't move: rethink the garden instead

Chapter 8
Keeping in Touch

In 1982 researchers in the United States conducted in-depth interviews with 2,800 people aged 65 and over, and then re-interviewed them every year for 13 years. After that, they collected information about which of the participants had died and from what cause. The researchers compiled a profile of three types of activity in which their interviewees took part: 'fitness activities' (such as walking, active sports, swimming and exercise), 'social activities' (such as church attendance, playing cards and bingo, visits to the cinema and participation in social groups) and 'productive activities' (voluntary work, preparing meals, paid employment and gardening). Contrary to expectations, 'Social and productive activities were observed to confer equivalent survival advantages compared with fitness activities,' the researchers reported. Indeed, 'Social and productive activities that involve little or no enhancement of fitness lower the risk of all causes of mortality as much as fitness activities do.'[1]

Although participating in clubs, playing games or simply going out and chatting to other people can confer real health benefits (quite apart from making life more interesting), as we grow older we can easily be tempted to disengage from the wider world. Perhaps moving around becomes more difficult and we do not want the bother of involvement. Retreating into a private world of home and garden can seem the thing to do. Indeed, society seems to encourage this – witness free television licences for over-75 year olds. Watching television, gardening and sitting doing nothing are all excellent activities. But, as the American survey suggests, if we cut ourselves off in our later years, we may pay a price.

People who live to their nineties and beyond must have something to tell us about how to live successfully and healthily when we are older. Researchers Michael Bury and Anthea Holme conducted in-depth interviews with more than 200 nonagenarians and centenarians in England in the 1980s. Of all the leisure pursuits their respondents enjoyed – reading, doing crafts, listening to music, listening to the radio, watching TV, talking and chatting were the most popular.[2] You might assume that those most likely to engage in conversation would be those living surrounded by other people. In fact, far fewer of Bury and Holme's interviewees living in care homes reported talking frequently to other people than did those living alone.

You might also assume that people living with relatives are less likely to feel lonely than people who live on their own; again, the evidence points the other way. In Greece, extended families are common and only 5 per cent of people over the age of 65 live alone. Yet in a recent survey one third reported that they were often lonely. In Denmark, in contrast, fewer than 5 per cent said they felt lonely often, yet in that country many older people live alone.[3]

It is thus important not to confuse solitude with loneliness. Many people, old and young, are perfectly content to live alone. Maturity perhaps makes them more interesting company for themselves than they would have been when younger. This is just as well, since today 40 per cent of Britons over the age of 65 live alone – a huge increase from 1950, when the figure was 10 per cent. Today, by the time they are 75, over one third of men and two-thirds of women will be on their own.

Undoubtedly, a sizeable number of older people do nonetheless experience the misery of loneliness. A survey in 2002 revealed that a quarter of elderly Britons reported that they were sometimes lonely, while nearly 10 per cent reported that they were lonely often, very often or all the time.[4] That would mean there are more than one million elderly people living with the unhappiness caused by loneliness. The fact is that while new means have emerged for people who live alone to keep in touch, like e-mail and car travel, if you are lonely when you are old, that loneliness can be crushing, particularly if disability prevents your getting out and about.

If you are old and you feel like informal contact with your fellow human beings, where can you go? In France, you would go to a local bar, not only a place serving alcohol, coffee and food but also one in which people of all ages sit around, chat, discuss, play games and perhaps place bets, while others come and go, on their way to go shopping or to work. In Britain, we do not have quite an equivalent: women often feel uncomfortable entering a pub on their own. So older people often have to look for something slightly more formal, contrived perhaps, to stay in touch. There are plenty of opportunities which you can readily find out about in your local public library – clubs and societies, adult education classes, groups associated with organizations such as the Women's Institute and The Royal British Legion. Later in this chapter I explore some possibilities you may not have fully considered, but first I look at some special difficulties of which you may need to be aware.

Making Friends

Friends and Neighbours

In the past, some degree of companionship was often provided automatically by neighbours. On the street of small terraced houses in Ramsgate, Kent in which I grew up in the 1950s and 1960s, there was much mutual support involving chatting and running errands for older people. Every Thursday one elderly neighbour would spend the whole day in our house: my mother thought she might be lonely. Today, with so many middle-aged women going out to work or seeking self-fulfilment outside the home, entertaining and regularly running errands for older neighbours will probably be crowded out. Yet neighbours, old and young, may still provide valuable help and support, though today elderly people may need to do a bit more to engage their interest.

When you are older it is easy to feel you have little to offer, so no one will want you. This can become self-fulfilling. Concentrate on what you can give. If you are trying to cultivate a friendship with a younger neighbour, there are practical things you could offer alongside the benefits of wisdom and experience. For instance, you could offer the very valuable facility of taking in parcels or deliveries, you could help young children with their reading, or teach them games and skills which their parents may not know or have little time to impart. Older people should not minimize what they have to offer. There is not just the offering of skills: there is also emotional support. One of Bury and Holme's

Making Friends

- Forty per cent of older people live on their own.
- Loneliness is not inevitable: many remedies exist.
- Some voluntary work can be done in your own home.
- Formal befriending schemes can be invaluable, but volunteers should be screened.
- Contact the Elderly offers monthly outings which can provide new friends.
- Hired help can be contracted to sit and chat.
- Paying somebody to visit an older relative can be an effective option.
- The hard of hearing need special help to communicate.
- People with dementia have a particular need for companionship, comfort and love.
- Age should be no bar to romance.

nonagenarians reported: 'I have friends who I know come to me with their problems. Like that I feel I am here for some good.'

However, what many isolated older people crave, especially as bereavement takes its toll, is a real friend. The idea that somebody whose company you will enjoy is going to call, even if only once a week, provides something to look forward to. Even if you are going to be alone for the rest of the time, you will know that you will eventually be able to recount your experiences to someone else. Another person will provide a new angle on things and propose new interests. Conversation is not only a great pleasure, but provides mental stimulation as well. Explaining yourself to a friend enhances your own sense of identity. Visits, with the anticipation, tidying up and other preparation involved, make us all more active and help give shape to our lives.

So how do you find a friend, or how can a son or daughter who lives away and cannot visit often find one for you?

Finding Friends

The good news is that although many of the middle-aged women who would have provided friendship to neighbours 40 years ago are now out at work, there is a large band of people of

all ages and walks of life who voluntarily offer their time for
activities like visiting elderly people.

But embarking on a new friendship is always risky. You do not
want to be enraptured by a new friend, only to find that you
never see him or her again. What are some of the things to look
out for? You want:

- somebody who is honest and reputable
- somebody who is prepared to commit a certain amount of
  time
- somebody who will have something in common with you or
  your relative
- ideally somebody who will take you or your relative out
- someone who is sensitive to any particular difficulties

Formal Befriending Schemes

Two types of scheme have particular advantages. The first is
a formal befriending scheme targeted at older people. Age
Concern York runs the kind of operation that can prove useful.
The scheme has 130 befrienders, each going to the home of a
particular elderly person once a week for one or two hours.
People are referred to the service by GPs, social workers, families
who live away, care workers and sometimes the beneficiaries
themselves. Those benefiting are usually very lonely and often
housebound; some live in care homes. Alas, there is a waiting list
of people wanting befrienders. The volunteers are from all walks
of life and of all ages: they may be people working in commerce
or industry, young mothers, retired people or students, for
instance. Contact may involve no more than chatting or perhaps
playing a game. Befrienders read the local newspaper aloud to
blind people and discuss its contents. Some befrienders take their
companions to the shops, the park or the country. Men often feel
out of place at day centres; befrienders may take them to the pub
to talk about cricket and football.

If you are arranging contact by a volunteer, rigorous background checks are essential. Very occasionally a volunteer may
be on the lookout for somebody from whom to steal money, or
may be well-meaning but have psychological, medical or perhaps
alcohol-related problems that make them less than ideal. It is

therefore best to go through an organization which runs rigorous checks on prospective volunteers and maintains regular contact after the initial introduction.

The York scheme is meticulous about recruitment, not just to avoid abuse but also to ensure that befrienders possess suitable qualities. Two people interview each prospective volunteer, and two and sometimes three references are taken. Volunteers receive a half-day's induction training. The scheme organizer is present at the first meeting between volunteer and elderly person, after having met each separately, and then monitors progress. Volunteers receive a newsletter four times a year and can attend quarterly support group meetings.

Befriending can be tough on the volunteer if the person dies. The York team provides support in such circumstances, holding bereavement group meetings every six months, not to provide formal counselling, but simply to talk about those who have died. Often those who are befriended are themselves recently bereaved. Day centres and clubs are suggested first, but for some these are not enough. The testing time tends to be not immediately after a bereavement but a few months later, when initial support may have waned and real loneliness has set in.

One man, a music enthusiast, was considering suicide after the death of his wife. The scheme matched him with a music student at York University. The student invited him to concerts and in time he was able to go out to clubs and on outings: his life completely turned around.

A new pilot development involving Age Concern York pays people to befriend those for whom it has been impossible to find a volunteer befriender, perhaps because the older person has mental health problems. The paid employees encourage those they visit to get out to day clubs and so on, accompanying them on the bus for the first few times; in time these individuals should not need such intensive help and may perhaps be befriended by a volunteer.

Outing Schemes

The second type of scheme which can be well worth seeking out involves being taken out with a small number of other older people by groups of volunteers on a regular basis. The pioneer in this field is an organization called Contact the Elderly. On one Sunday afternoon each month, groups of eight to ten people are taken out in four or five cars for an outing, perhaps to the countryside, and this is followed by tea at the home of a volunteer Contact hostess. The criterion for being befriended by a Contact group is that you have to be living on your own without much support. You can refer yourself, or perhaps your GP may pass on your name. But one of the enduring pluses is that people who are really quite frail and need an arm to lean on can be involved, in contrast to most day centres, which only take people able to be completely independent. And of course you get out not only into the homes and gardens of other people, but also into the wider environment.

Overall there are more than 200 Contact groups in Great Britain, based in small towns and larger cities; there are groups (often several) in all of the London boroughs. Coverage continues to spread and a Highland Development Officer has been appointed to set up groups in small towns in the Highlands. Because the same elderly people and drivers are involved on each monthly trip, people get to know each other. Contact screens the drivers by taking up references; it does not screen hostesses, each of whom is involved only once a year on a rota basis.

There are similar schemes operating here and there. One which I came across in Surrey made a feature of the organizers not deciding on the destination but asking the older people where they would like to go. This sounds an obvious idea, but often older people are simply taken to places rather than asked where they would like to go. The man who told me about this scheme described sitting next to an old lady on a seat facing the sea at Bognor Regis. She started crying and when he asked her why, she replied, 'I never thought I would see the sea again.' Other destinations were people's birthplaces, a new university, or simply 'to see the children play'.

Other Ideas
More and more formal befriending schemes are being set up, and you should be able to get details from your local public library. Or perhaps a benevolent association or another group with which you are associated, like Jewish Care, for example (page 233) runs a

scheme. There are also many volunteer bureaux which organize volunteers to do all sorts of things, including visiting.

Hiring help in the home can bring regular, informal friendly contact. Hiring a gardener often involves chatting as part of the arrangement, with the gardener coming in for a coffee break. The elderly father of a friend of mine hires two different people, who each come in once a week. One cleans and then chats with him over coffee; the other chats for the first half-hour and then tackles any current task, from mending his pockets to clearing out a cupboard.

It is of course possible to pay somebody to visit. My own mother, who has dementia and lives in an NHS unit for elderly mentally ill people, derives a great deal of benefit from the attentions of such a person, who visits her for two hours each day, talking and responding imaginatively to my mother's often unintelligible speech, or simply sitting and holding her hand.

One advantage of sheltered housing is that it can enable residents to establish neighbourly relations almost like those of a college hall of residence, with neighbours popping in for coffee, scrabble and shared meals. Life in a care home, too, can bring new, cherished friendships. Writing of a shared spiritual journey, Quaker Margaret McNeill wrote, 'And in the experience of living in a Home with others, a deep sense of sharing the darkness and the light can lead to a sense of community not known before.'[5]

Additional Difficulties

Many of the disabilities and ailments to which senior citizens may fall prey can increase the likelihood of social isolation. One in 50 people over the age of 80 contracts Parkinson's disease. Such people not only have to cope with difficulties involving movement, but they are also often unable to smile in the normal way and so their feelings can be misinterpreted. Most sight loss occurs in old age yet our usual image of a blind person is likely to be that of a young adult who can read Braille and has a dog. The young can become members of the blind community, learn a language of their own and remould their identity. But if you lose your sight when you are old, it is harder to adapt.

In terms of numbers of people affected, perhaps the two most significant conditions which cause problems in communication

for older people, and thus in developing and sustaining friendships, are hearing impairment and dementia.

Hearing Impairment

All disabilities affect self-image to some extent, as well as the role
of sufferers and the expectations others have about them.
Whatever the nature of the disability, the person with it has to
come to terms with it, as do partners and close relatives.

When hearing is impaired these issues are accentuated because
deafness or being hard of hearing is necessarily an experience
shared with other people, as it affects interaction with others.

The impact of hearing impairment was examined in depth by
researchers Raymond Hétu, Lesley Jones and Louise Getty in
1993.[6] The team identified several practical elements which make
inter-relating difficult for people with hearing impairment.

First, maintaining attention and concentration when you
cannot hear well takes a good deal of effort: you are trying to
follow a conversation, probably relying to some extent on lip-
reading, having to deal with interruption from background noise
and mis-hearing sounds, so words do not make sense. This has to
be coped with in addition to all the other things we are trying to
do when we engage in conversation, not least making ourselves
understood.

Even a hearing aid will be affected by background noise. But
some people do not wear them. The reason is often psychological. Unlike sight impairment, hearing impairment attracts a
stigma. Because deafness is an invisible affliction and often
results in sufferers not understanding what others are saying to
them, those who are hard of hearing may be thought simple-
minded. Deafness is also associated with ageing: if you are hard
of hearing, you are perceived as being old, and in an ageist
society, these factors add up to undermine the self-image of
people with hearing impairment. It can put them off using a
hearing aid, and it can put them off communicating at all, in case
they reveal their hearing impairment during the course of conversation.

It is easy for people whose hearing is normal to fail to appreciate that there are awkward steps a person who is hard of
hearing is forced to take when trying to engage in conversation,

and that these inevitably disrupt the flow of speech because they often involve the violation of social rules and so prompt negative reactions. These steps include asking people to repeat and asking questions because the deaf person is unable to follow what is being said.

Problems do not end with communicating with acquaintances outside the home. If family members do not understand hearing impairment, they may simply assume it resembles turning down the volume, rather than involving certain frequencies which a person cannot hear. 'How can he hear what she is saying but not what I am saying? He only hears what he want to hear!' people may say.

Dr Hétu and his colleagues identified three sorts of communication breakdown which can happen between couples in which one member is hearing-impaired. First, there are misunderstandings because the hard of hearing may not hear properly, answer or give appropriate responses. Second, frequency of interaction declines, as it is stressful and tiring to communicate. Third, the content of communication becomes restricted. People try to make themselves understood only about important, necessary things, and so the interest and companionship arising from engaging in the ordinary conversation of everyday life is lost. Clearly, all these observations are sweeping generalizations, but they are nonetheless real.

Hearing-impaired people may find they have to strive to retain a normal social identity as they fear that the disability and the association of deafness with stupidity will hamper them in social situations. As a result, they may avoid the social scene, or at least avoid certain social situations, particularly those involving people outside close family with whom they may want to keep up the image of being normal. Or the hard of hearing person may avoid threatening or demanding situations. Another possible result is the control of conversation. The person who cannot hear well may become more assertive and prevents any disturbance of the conversation.

People react in their own individual ways to hearing loss, and their reactions are influenced by their experience of hearing loss in others. As partners, relatives and friends, if we can understand some of the problems those who are hard of hearing face both in communicating with us and in interacting with the social world, we can perhaps begin to offer them better support.

Dementia

Elderly people with dementia are particularly likely to find their needs for love and affection unmet. Although they experience a progressive decline in their cognitive powers and language skills, the parts of the brain which control feeling and intuition are less affected. Yet because the capacity for logical thought, for retaining facts and for communicating with others have degenerated, those around may believe that the whole person has disappeared.

Dementia sufferers are handicapped not only by other people's lack of understanding of their condition, but also by the disdain with which it is often regarded. In part this is an inevitable consequence of the horror associated with degeneration of the mind. Nowadays, however, another factor is the fashionable emphasis on looking after our own health, with the corresponding idea that disease is in some sense the sufferer's fault. A disease in which mental capabilities become progressively impaired can be seen as the result of neglecting to keep the mind agile. In fact, dementia can strike the most intellectually well-used brain. Alzheimer's, which affects men and women equally, is no respecter of class or education level: its incidence is no higher in countries in which the population is poor and uneducated. Furiously playing bridge or learning Shakespeare's sonnets when you are older is not going to stop you getting Alzheimer's: the risk is something you have to live with if you are lucky enough to live a long time.

It is also an unhelpful myth that dementia causes little or even no suffering to its victims. It is a variable condition, which sometimes develops only gradually, goes through stages and in some cases perhaps does not cause that much distress. But in other cases the distress is acute.

Dr Tom Kitwood, who wrote a ground-breaking book called *Dementia Reconsidered: The Person Comes First*, pioneered the development of what he called 'person-centred care' for people with dementia.[7] He argued that their central need is for love. He further argued that this need could best be delivered through focusing on giving five things to them. These are:

- comfort (which provides a kind of warm and strength)
- attachment to other people (to help counteract the difficulty that their memory loss means they continually find themselves in situations which they experience as strange)
- inclusion (human beings like to feel part of a group, and if people with dementia feel socially isolated, their misery is likely to increase still further)
- identity (a challenging task when people with dementia may no longer remember where they used to fit into the world)
- occupation (if people can be occupied, they may be absorbed and their self-esteem may be enhanced; Dr Kitwood argues that the need to be occupied is instinctive).

Dr Kitwood's extremely useful guidance was aimed at close relatives and care workers, but those who understand best how to reach sufferers may be those who have fallen victim to the condition themselves. One example from my own experience: when my mother was in the middle stages of Alzheimer's and also unable to see well, she was cared for in the mental health assessment ward of a hospital. Usually, as soon as I entered the ward on a visit I would hear her melancholy wail as she repeated in confused anxiety over and over again: 'Where am I?' or 'Who am I?' On one occasion I wondered why I could not hear her, but when I saw her sitting quietly, I understood. Each of her hands was laid on the arm of her armchair, but over one was the hand, lightly placed, of another patient. I asked this pleasant-looking elderly man his name. 'I cannot quite remember that,' he replied.

I have been amazed several times by my mother's ability to sense emotions around her despite the massive reduction in her mental powers and in her vision. On another occasion, about 18 months later, when her memory had declined still further, I was sitting beside her weeping silently because a care worker had just reported (out of earshot of my mother) something rather poignant. Although I said nothing of this, my mother stretched out her hand and placed it over mine. At other times I have noticed that although she cannot understand what is said, she picks up the tone and seeks to enter into the spirit of the exchange. So we need to give people with dementia a special sense of warmth and love and also allow them to feel involved in life around them.

Day Centres

A major source of company for older people is day centres. Day centres differ from other clubs and activities in that they are specially designed for elderly people. The thousands of day centres dotted across the UK are not part of a national organization and each has grown up in its own way, with the direction often shaped largely by volunteers.

Farncombe Day Centre, at Farncombe in Surrey, for example, operates from Mondays to Fridays in a refurbished former Victorian school at the heart of this little town near Guildford. Forty people come each day, half arriving in the centre's own minibus. After sitting and chatting over hot drinks and snacks, followed by playing one game of bingo, they eat lunch – a hot, two-course meal, cooked each day on the premises, with baked potatoes, salads, omelettes and sandwiches as alternatives. After lunch, some people make their way to a lounge, where there are magazines, large-print books, games and a computer, on which staff will help attenders use the internet or e-mail. In another lounge, people sit, chat and listen to entertainers, or occasionally engage in gentle exercise.

A hairdresser is present all the time and nurses, opticians, chiropodists and hearing specialists make visits. Staff can help with filling in forms and making appointments to see health professionals. A bathing assistant helps some attenders on a rota basis, using a bathroom in a sheltered housing scheme next door. Once a year staff take attenders on a holiday at the seaside, and there are day trips too. Although sticks and walking frames are used by many attenders at Farncombe, the centre does not have enough staff to help people move around or use the lavatory, so they must be able to look after themselves. My impression was that people appreciated first and foremost the company the centre provided and its hot, nourishing meals. The convenience of getting a bath or seeing a specialist nurse in a place to which you were going anyway also went down well.

The Indian Muslim Federation at Leytonstone, East London operates a lunch club for older people of any race or religion once a week: while Indians predominated on the day I visited in 2002, there were Hindus as well as Muslims and some white people (the food is Asian; mine was superb). But the main activity here is a day-care centre, where staff and volunteers provide a higher level of individual support for 12 elderly people with some degree of disability or dependence than at Farncombe. These people from the Indian subcontinent are collected from their homes and arrive between 10 and 11 a.m., when they are given refreshments. For an hour there is gentle exercise, then lunch, then a rest, followed by English classes, arts and crafts, reminiscence and tea with fresh fruit. At any time people can make use of a prayer room and obtain advice from an outreach worker. There are talks on health-related matters, some visits from health professionals, outings and trips, while all festivals, English as well as Asian, are celebrated. On a small stage, plays are performed. As at Farncombe, attenders cannot come every day, as space is limited, and there is a waiting list.

Other day centres may offer less than these two. Specialist medical services of the type on offer at Farncombe are not that common. Some centres offer more or different activities, such as pottery. More activities would be desirable at day centres, but the organizers cannot afford to pay many teachers, and volunteers are thin on the ground.

There is room for developing possibilities. Participants and their families could be encouraged to a greater extent than is usual to say what they would like to see at their day centre, perhaps backing the suggestions up with offers of fund-raising. Also, if adult education classes in relevant subjects were sometimes held in day centres, older people would find it easier to participate.

Most day centres also have the potential to offer more permanent activities than they do at present, and again there is no reason why attenders themselves and their relatives should not make suggestions and, if necessary, help through fund-raising to buy any equipment. One room might be given over to, say, bar football or snooker, darts, table-tennis or a jukebox, all of which could generate a bit of income.

Valuable though day centres can be, they come with no guarantees. Most get some grant from their local authority, but centres and paid staff have not been brought within the inspection and registration processes of the National Care Standards Commission and the National Social Care Council, or their

Day Centres

- Day centres and lunch clubs can provide a hot meal and more, including exercise classes, entertainment and outings.
- There are no national standards or national inspections of day centres; they vary greatly.
- Waiting lists are to be expected at good day centres, so get your name down.
- To secure a day centre place you may need to be referred by your social services department.
- Lunch clubs, day centres and social clubs may also be provided by local religious organizations or community groups, and you may not need to be a member.
- Venues such as leisure centres also offer facilities and sessions for older people.
- Look for lunch clubs and day centres you might not have thought of, such as those aimed at ethnic groups other than your own.
- Facilities in day centres can be extensive and you can persuade your local centre to include new ones.
- You need to be independent at a day centre: there is no one to help in using the lavatory.
- Day-care centres offer more support than day centres and are often geared to people with dementia.

equivalent bodies outside England, with a register of workers in the field or national minimum standards of service provision and building design (page 53). This does not, though, mean that day centres do not provide much of great value. The social services department of your local council should be able to give you details of day centres in your area. Some centres take people who apply to them direct; others, or often the same place, take people referred to them by social services. If you find a centre which looks promising, show an interest early. Do not wait for referral by social services if you do not have to. If social services are involved, telephone them and ask to be considered for a place.

Some centres are geared to specific disabilities or conditions.

At some of these, the building is simply designed to make it user-friendly for, say, blind or severely disabled people, and activities are geared towards these groups, although you will probably need to look after yourself. Day-care centres at which staff and/or volunteers provide one-to-one help, as at Leytonstone, are far less common. Others specialize in people with particular conditions, such as Alzheimer's disease. If the calamity of dementia should befall one of your loved ones, such a place could prove a godsend during the early stages, not only for the person with the condition but also as time off for his or her carer. But introducing a relative in the early stages of dementia to a new, ordinary day centre could be cruel, as remembering where the lavatory is and socializing with new people may prove distressing.

Day centres and lunch clubs provided by a community group from a particular ethnic minority may also be specially attractive. At Leyton in East London, the Sikh Community Care Project provides volunteers who bring older Sikhs to the centre, where they can obtain a meal and take part in exercise classes and discussions about health matters (South Asian people are particularly prone to diabetes, heart disease and stroke). The situation of older Asian people has become more difficult as more women go out to work, with the result that the traditional practice of families looking after their elderly relatives is less easy to maintain.

Jewish people living in southern England and in particular in London may care to contact the charity Jewish Care. This is an impressive organization providing a comprehensive system of support to Jewish people of all ages, although the majority of the people it helps are elderly. It has day and day-care centres and care homes, runs a helpline called Jewish Direct, and commands its own team of qualified social workers and a large number of volunteers, who provide anything from a befriending service to a handy-person service for small tasks around the home.

The best way of finding out what is available and what might be suitable for you is through directories of local organizations produced by councils, or available in public libraries, or through information kept at local mosques, temples and synagogues.

If you enjoy visiting a day centre but subsequently go into a care home nearby, see whether you could continue to make visits to the centre after entry into the home. Your local authority social services department is unlikely to subsidize the place, but you might decide that the usually small amount you would have to pay is worth spending. Or perhaps a close relative could pay the weekly sum for you.

Faith Groups

In Britain, much existing state support to the weaker members of society grew out of the Christian tradition. A massive range and variety of support still exists, and is not necessarily confined to people who are members of a particular church or even attend any of its services. Much of this support is provided by lay people in the form of pastoral care.

Pastoral Care

In the Christian churches, pastoral care essentially involves a team of lay members of the congregation being allocated a number of church attenders to whom they offer friendship and help, but not spiritual support, which is the role of the minister. Most frequently, pastoral care involves friendship, occasional visits and the guarantee that if somebody needs help, there is somebody to whom they can turn. There is a tendency to restrict such care to people who attend church, but they do not necessarily have to be regular attenders or church members. Even if you are not an attender it is still worth contacting the church if you think it could help you.

Some pastoral care teams organize themselves very systematically, allocating people with particular expertise to those in need of, say, bereavement support or advice on coping with the health and social services care machine, and may even hire paid staff; others are more informally organized.

Social Activities

Churches often provide social clubs to which they welcome outsiders, as well helping church members to socialize. Most Methodist churches, for example, offer once-a-week get-togethers with an outside speaker, discussion and refreshments. Whereas these 'guild' meetings are usually for all age groups, there is frequently at least one weekly meeting especially for older people, again with a speaker and a cup of tea, usually in the afternoons. As these tend to attract women, a meeting especially for older men may also be on offer. These social activities often include outings. There may also be a lunch club, or lunches offered occasionally. Since churches are aware that many of the attenders at these social activities are not church-goers, religious input is usually minimal. If you need a lift to any such meetings you should expect to get one, Christian charity being on call.

Both pastoral care and social activities for older people are by no means confined to the Christian church. Larger synagogues run day clubs and organize outings for elderly members. Mosques often have lay visitors who will visit older people in their own homes; some mosques run social clubs for older members and organize visits and outings, perhaps socializing with similar groups elsewhere. Sikh temples can be extremely useful, since the vast majority provide three meals a day and the chance to socialize. If elderly Sikhs find attendance difficult, local community projects may step into the breach and run day centres, such as the project described above.

Deeper Involvement

For people who want to get involved in the life of their local church or other faith community, the benefits are by no means only a supportive environment to sustain them, perhaps through stressful life changes, a source of practical assistance when needed, and a social world. Involvement in a religious community can provide a philosophy of life, as well as kindred spirits with whom to share and explore it in an atmosphere of acceptance and forgiveness.

There may be even more to it than that. Churches, for example, offer people the opportunity to go on contributing, working and giving. The range of possibilities is very wide – from running raffles or manning stalls to helping at catering events, attending committees and discussion groups, welcoming people to services, and helping in the Sunday school.

If you want to get involved in church activities or are already doing so, do keep on for as long as you wish. Do not be put off by disinclination to make your own way to evening committee meetings, for example. Ask for a lift and encourage other older people without their own transport to do likewise. You could perhaps suggest your own house or flat (and that of other similarly placed people) as a venue for meetings.

Attending Church

People who attend church services can clearly expect more support than those who restrict themselves to the occasional social activity, if only because their presence is more obvious. Socially there can be many benefits. Some people value contact with young children at church services and at the chat over coffee afterwards, others simply the general friendly atmosphere in a church, and perhaps a practice of inviting elderly people who live alone to Sunday lunch in members' homes.

The details of church practice can be extraordinarily important in encouraging or deterring frail elderly people from attending. Is a large-print hymn book offered by a welcoming steward? Is the hearing loop system adequate? Are the lavatories easily accessible? If there are problems in areas such as these, it is worth bringing them to the attention of your or your relative's minister or pastoral visitor or a church steward. If necessary, mention the provisions of the Disability Discrimination Act 1998, which require the providers of any service to the public to ensure that reasonable steps are taken to remove barriers preventing people with any of a broad range of disabilities from using it (pages 123–6).

Ministers of Religion

Ministers of religion should also proffer friendship to all elderly people, whether in their congregations, in the ranks of church-based social clubs or simply living in the community, including in care homes. For people in hospital, there should be a chaplain; you may wish to supplement his or her ministrations with support from a local minister.

Ministers of religion tend to have great freedom of action, since they are contractually obliged to do little more than preach and teach. There is a wide range of action they could take, such as holding services in care homes and retirement housing complexes, visiting those who are housebound including taking communion to them, and discussing spiritual matters one-to-one or with a group of older people.

Faith Groups

- Feed spiritual needs in the widest sense: through music, scenery, works of art, lectures, religious experiences.
- Get your religious institution to take any crisis of belief seriously.
- Churches, chapels, mosques, synagogues and temples often offer social facilities, meetings and outings for older people.
- Places of worship often provide pastoral support organized by lay members.
- Ensure you or your relative can go on contributing to the life of a church, chapel, mosque, synagogue or temple.
- Encourage long-patronized religious institutions to continue to involve you or an elderly relative in their activities.
- If your or your relative's place of worship is not welcoming, lobby the minister or lay committees.
- Be aware that most ministers of religion will have only a passing knowledge of eldercare.

You might find you have to ask as what you would like may be an action he or she had not previously thought of offering. Ian Knox, the author of a book published in 2003 called *Older People and the Church*, which was based on a large number of interviews, commented: 'I found it significant that no church leader or member spoke of helping older people to face their own death'.[8]

Ministers are only a tiny part of the manpower (and womanpower) of any church, and some religious groups, such as the Quakers, do not have ministers at all (within the Society of Friends every member feels responsible for every aspect of life in the meeting house, although some might take on special responsibility for the care of older members and attenders). There is a strong tradition in Judaism and Islam of synagogues and mosques fulfilling a pastoral as well as a religious role, and rabbis and imams are expected to visit local members of the synagogue or mosque, especially when they are sick. The Islamic Foundation, a research and education institute based in Leicester, has launched courses for imams to provide additional information and training for them in their pastoral work. The tradition of pastoral support from the religious leader is not always obtained however, and is less well established in the priesthood of Sikhism.

Animal Magic

As we grow older, we tend to confine thoughts of how to stay healthy to diet and getting treatment for disease. Now, the value of exercise is also becoming widely recognized (pages 138–40). Earlier in this chapter I reported the very good news that engaging in social activity can be as good for you as physical exercise. But if the scientific studies on which that fact is based are little known, so too are others which bring welcome news: pet-keeping can also deliver concrete benefits to health.

Stroking a pet actually causes blood pressure to fall and even the presence of a dog in a room or watching fish swim around seems to have a calming effect.[9] Studies have shown that pet-owners have significantly lower levels of cholesterol in their blood and lower blood pressure than their non-pet-owning counterparts – all factors which are thought to be good for health.[10]

Pets also seem to aid recovery when we do become ill. A study in the United States which compared the survival rates of people who had suffered heart attacks found that pet-owners had a significantly better chance of surviving for more than a year after the attack than others.[11] Elderly pet-owners suffer less from depression and loneliness, feel more secure in their home, and when they go out, take more exercise and talk to others more often – presumably because the presence of the pet facilitates social contact.[12] Also, older people who have pets to look after seem to take better care of themselves, eating more regularly and keeping their homes warmer.[13] Being greeted by a pet when we return home, stroking it by the fireside, watching it play or enjoy its dinner, taking it for a walk and getting into conversation with other pet owners: all of these things may provide at least as much comfort and joy to older people as they do to the young.

Choosing a Pet

The responsibilities and challenges of pet keeping do, however, become more onerous as we grow older. Anybody taking on a pet has to consider the cost of feeding it and paying vets' bills and the difficulty of providing exercise. When you are older, the likely lifespan of the creature becomes a more significant consideration. It can be heartbreaking to see your beloved pet put to sleep because you have to go into hospital or a care home and no one can be found to look after it. On the other hand, it could be devastating if your pet predeceases you and you are unable to replace it. In the United States, a federal law specifically prohibits the managers of state-assisted rented housing for older people from preventing tenants from owning pets. Yet in Britain, many sheltered housing schemes bar tenants or lessees from owning pets, while few care homes allow newcomers to bring pets. Sometimes new residents are allowed to bring pets with them but are not allowed to replace the pet if it should die. So if possible, involve your family or friends when you select a pet, on the understanding that if you are unable to care for it, they will take it on.

Small dogs can be easier for older people to manage, but they tend to live longer than larger ones. Terriers, for example, can live to 18 or even 20. Older people often do not want a very young animal which they will need to house-train and which can cause a lot of work chewing its way through goodness knows what. A reputable rescue centre is one place to acquire an older animal, such as Battersea Dogs' Home, Wood Green Animal Shelters or the Blue Cross, The Royal Society for the Prevention of Cruelty to Animals (with more than 50 rehoming centres), the Scottish Society for the Prevention of Cruelty to Animals and the Irish Society for the Prevention of Cruelty to Animals. Such a centre will ensure that the animal has received health checks and been vaccinated and wormed, and will know the sort of environment it is accustomed to. Such centres try to match temperament and lifestyles; they ought to be able to narrow down your choice so that you can choose between three or four possibilities. If the pet turns out to be unsuitable, a reputable centre will take it back and you can try again.

You could also approach a rescue centre if you are going into retirement housing or a care home which will not accept your pet. Giving advance notice allows the centre more time to try to match your pet to a new owner, such as another older person. It

Animal Magic

- Pets are not just good company: studies point to benefits to health.
- However, pet keeping can be more onerous for older people.
- Involve family and friends when you select a pet, on the understanding that they will take it over if that proves necessary.
- Select the type of pet carefully. Cats are ideal. Some breeds of dog are much more suitable than others.
- Rescue centres can be a good place to find a suitable pet.
- The Blue Cross, the RSPCA and the PDSA provide concessionary medical treatment for the pets of people on low incomes.
- If you go into hospital, look for a pet fostering scheme.
- In hospital, look for a PAT dog or cat visiting scheme.
- Many care homes and retirement housing schemes say they forbid pets; make sure they really mean this, as they sometimes relent.
- If you move, cannot take your pet and have nobody to hand it to, contact a pets rehoming service.

can also cut down the disruption your pet will have to face. On rehoming, the RSPCA's then chief veterinary officer, Chris Laurence, told me in 2002, 'There is far more chance of finding a home for an elderly pet if it has been given a check over by a veterinary surgeon and we have adequate notice of the requirement.'

Cats' relative independence also makes them a very attractive proposition for elderly people. They do not need to be exercised, and older cats are often more than happy to curl up on a lap and so provide psychological support. The head office of Cats Protection can introduce you to a rehoming branch in your area.

Small caged animals such as birds, gerbils and hamsters do not of course have to be taken out for a walk, yet are easily transported to somebody else if you are going on holiday. If your eyesight is poor, you still know where the animal is, although grooming may be difficult, as can retrieving a bird let out of its cage. Fish can be extremely restful and interesting to watch, and although tortoises cannot now be bought new, they are easy to look after and respond to their owners.

However, many people insist on a dog. Though large dogs may have a more manageable lifespan, it is not a good idea to have a dog that could pull you over or which you could not lift when it is unwell. Also, large dogs eat a great deal: will you be able to carry home tins of dog food? Some small dogs, on the other hand, can be very bouncy and easily tripped over, or even sat upon.

Are there particular breeds which suit older people? It is possible to generalize, with the proviso that every dog should be judged as an individual. Frail people should avoid dogs bred for working which need a great deal of physical and mental exercise, such as German shepherds, springer spaniels and border collies. Setters can be extremely affectionate, but they are often difficult to train, highly-strung and need a huge amount of exercise.

Cavalier King Charles spaniels can be attractive pets for older people, although may be prone to particular medical problems. Dachshunds, corgis and terriers can also make good pets, although terriers are bred for ratting, so they are quite active, and may be yappy. Shetland sheepdogs make excellent companions but need a lot of grooming and quite a lot of exercise. Some of the very tiny exotic breeds can also need a lot of grooming, but are of course very light to pick up. Whippets are very gentle, sweet-natured and quiet, and of course have short coats; greyhounds need surprisingly little exercise (although they can be heavy to lift). Although Labrador retrievers are large and highly demanding until about the age of six, an older Labrador can be gentle and extremely companionable. Mongrels, if they combine the good traits of the breeds from which they are derived, can make very satisfactory pets.

Support

If you are concerned about vets' bills, try to find out if there is a People's Dispensary for Sick Animals facility near your home – a Pet Aid hospital or an agreement with a private veterinary practice. To qualify for free PDSA help, you must be in receipt either of Council Tax Benefit or Housing Benefit, so this is an extra reason to apply for these benefits if you are eligible. Blue Cross and the RSPCA also offer subsidized treatment for the pets of people receiving benefits; most local RSPCA branches provide a voucher scheme to help pay vets' bills.

The Cinnamon Trust's volunteers provide practical help when some aspect of petcare poses a problem. They will walk a dog for a housebound owner, and foster a pet whose owner has to go into hospital. The trust is also able to care for some pets at its two sanctuaries (in Devon and Cornwall) when owners have died or moved to a care home. The owner is kept in touch, with visits if possible, or at least regular photographs and letters. Similar schemes are also run by Pet Fostering Services Scotland, Cats Protection and the Animal Welfare Trust.

If you are in hospital, you may want to see if Pets as Therapy (PAT) is operating in your area. This scheme has 4,500 dogs and 50 cats which, with their volunteer owners, visit people in hospitals, prisons, schools and care homes. Only dogs which pass tests covering health, temperament and behaviour can enter the scheme. Volunteers are also assessed and trained. All the dogs must possess current vaccinations, have been wormed, received flea prevention treatment and be washed and groomed. The dogs never visit at mealtimes or enter kitchens or dining rooms, and patients and staff are encouraged to wash their hands well after handling them. All are covered by public liability insurance. Canine Concern Scotland Trust is a similar organization.

It is worth getting hold of and following the PAT procedures if there are no PAT volunteers in your area and you have to look for an animal yourself to visit an elderly relative or friend in hospital regularly. The managers of long-stay NHS units and care homes can be nervous about admitting an unknown pet without certain guarantees about behaviour.

Care Homes and Sheltered Housing

You can get details of care homes and sheltered housing schemes which accept pets from the Elderly Accommodation Council and The Cinnamon Trust. The main sheltered housing provider which allows pets is the Anchor Trust. However, researchers at the University of Warwick found that care homes are often more flexible about taking pets than might appear at first sight; there seems no reason why this should not also be the case for sheltered housing. June McNicholas, Glyn Collis and Ian Morley sent questionnaires and letters to veterinary surgeons, veterinary nurses, animal shelters and nearly 300 care homes in 1993. When they talked to care home managers who took pets or who were persuaded to do so after an initial reluctance or refusal, they found that, contrary to many stereotypical views, many care homes believed that pets benefited residents and that non-pet-owning residents were very tolerant of other residents who wished to own pets. The notion that pets could pose a health risk was dispelled by the fact that many homes allowed visiting pets, such as those belonging to members of staff or those brought in under the PAT Dogs scheme. [14]

So if you have to go into a care home, it is worth asking whether you could bring your pet, even if the policy is supposed to be no pets. Offer suggestions on how your pet could be managed. These suggestions could cover:

- The degree of freedom the pet should have: in which parts of the home, including the grounds, should it be allowed to roam freely and from which banned or taken in only on a lead
- Who is going to buy and pay for food
- Arrangements for summoning vets
- Arrangements for walks – how often? When? Who will take it? What happens in inclement weather?
- Responsibility for breakages
- What happens if the resident is ill? Or if they have to go into hospital?
- What should happen to the pet if the resident should die?
- What happens if the pet does not settle in?

Ideally, staff in a care home need to be able to recognize when a pet is asking to go out or come in or to be fed, or is in need of a vet, and to understand the dangers of animals being outside all night.

For some, a pet is not an option. However, watching wild birds can be enormously enjoyable, and some sheltered housing schemes and care homes will allow you to place a bird table outside your window.

Chapter 9
Professional Helpers

There are two groups of professionals who hold the key to much of the help needed by frail older people – GPs and social workers. Your general practitioner can help determine when you die and how much illness affects your life; social workers have much influence over help in the home, especially if you cannot afford to pay for it yourself. In Chapters 5 and 7 we saw how they can arrange provision (sometimes free) of gadgets, aids and house adaptations. Here we look at the human help social services can arrange. We also look at human help in the home generally and how to hire it privately.

Your GP

As you get older, your doctor becomes a more and more vital part of your life. How do you get the best out of him or her? And if you are moving to a new area or leaving a practice for another reason, how should you choose a new GP?

Choosing a GP

When choosing a GP, consider the practice as a whole. Some practices have a wide range of professional health workers, from continence advisors to occupational therapists, counsellors and palliative nurse specialists, who can play a very important role in the lives of older people (pages 69–74). Smaller practices may not allow such easy access to such people, though the reorganization of the health service, in England for example to form primary care trusts containing 30 or 40 GP practices, should improve matters.

However, many people prefer single practices, cherishing the continuity and certainty that they will see their own doctor, who cannot hide behind other practice members in taking time off or otherwise being unavailable.

Knowledge

The training of older GPs will probably have taken little account of the diseases of old age which are now common, such as osteoarthritis and Parkinson's. Some of them will have taken the trouble to plug gaps in their knowledge and to keep abreast of the latest developments, but others will not. It is therefore well worth trying to find out whether any member of the practice you are considering using has a special interest in geriatric medicine. Specialist knowledge may mean one of the rarer conditions of old age being diagnosed when it might otherwise be missed, and medication for particular conditions being chosen from a wider range.

GPs' knowledge of other parts of the eldercare system also varies widely. Some will interest themselves in what their patients pay for care offered by social services; others will not. If your GP says you should be cared for after, say, a fall, check that the place to which you are being sent is free of charge. People are used to being sent to hospital 'under doctor's orders'. If, however, social services step in and organize your transfer for recuperation to a care home, you may well find that the challenge of convalescence is overshadowed by the challenge of finding the money to pay for your stay.

Diagnosis and Treatment

The power invested in GPs in deciding the root cause of your symptoms is enormous. That cause may be emotional rather than physical, or a side-effect of medication. The GP will decide, prescribe and control your access to the rest of what the health service can offer. Life or death, blindness or vision, immobility or freedom of movement, all these and much more are theirs to determine.

How many times do GPs misdiagnose? How many times do they fail to notice key symptoms? No one has any idea. It is well documented that doctors make a hypothesis on the cause of a patient's symptoms very early on in a consultation, usually in the first 30 seconds. After they have formed their hypothesis – which may of course be absolutely right – their subsequent often rapid-fire questions are usually directed more towards proving that hypothesis than floating new ones.[1] Inevitably, shortage of time pushes GPs in the direction of swift diagnosis.

Other factors often play a part as well. One is the traditional doctor–patient relationship with the doctor beneficent and paternalistic, knowing what is wrong with you and absolutely to be trusted to do whatever is necessary to make you better. This notion does not sit happily with the idea of patients and doctors discussing a condition as equals, with equal access to the information necessary. Doctors' approach originated in the eighteenth century, when their specialism was one among many and they had to compete with other practitioners, such as herbalists, who often produced better results. At some stage, doctors settled upon the ploy of persuading patients they were a kind of super-parent to be trusted absolutely. Naturally, information was not to be shared with the patient – hence, perhaps, doctors' traditionally illegible handwriting. To sustain this attitude, some doctors doubtless feel obliged, probably unconsciously, to declare at an early stage the cause of your problem. The idea of priest-like power is bolstered by rituals such as examination and prescription, together with the trappings of white coats and respectful

---

Your GP

- Get a flu jab.
- Insist on the annual health check available to over-75s.
- Insist on your annual review of medication if you are over 75.
- Take advantage of additional health checks such as breast screening.
- Choose a GP with care and try to keep the same one after entry into a care home.
- Build up your own information base about any serious condition.
- Early diagnosis of many conditions can make all the difference.
- Depression is common among elderly people but it is treatable.
- A wide range of health specialists can help other than hospital consultants.
- Be prepared to badger your doctor for a referral.

receptionists. All of this is further buttressed by the belief, doubtless well-founded, that calm reassurance from an apparently authoritative figure plays an important part in the healing process.

Today, many doctors seem ready to relinquish some of this approach by wearing ordinary clothes in surgery and commissioning tests before diagnosis. It is worth encouraging more open-mindedness on the part of your doctor, even if you find a God-like manner more reassuring. If you are nonetheless stuck with an old-style paternalist, you should try that much harder to keep a day-to-day record of your symptoms and other detailed information in the hope that any speedily confident diagnosis is based on all the facts to hand. And you should also be ready to ask your GP, if necessary in writing, to refer you to specialists such as physiotherapists, palliative care nurses, dieticians and so on if he or she does not offer to do so.

Older people do need a GP who is going to be prepared to diagnose and treat early, if necessary by prompt referring on, in areas in which early diagnosis is very important. Most people would be aware that early diagnosis is important for cancer and coronary heart disease, diabetes and glaucoma. However, for afflictions such as arthritis, osteoporosis, Alzheimer's and cardiovascular disease new discoveries are being made all the time, and often the new drugs which are being developed only affect patients in the early stages.

Imparting Information

Doctors tend to tell you only what you need to know. There is something to be said for this. Often they have to impart really important information about what you should and should not do, and do not want this lost amongst unnecessary details. To take all this in, it is often useful to have somebody with you.

GPs may fail to volunteer advice proactively even when this could be very useful. They are particularly reluctant to offer suggestions to a third party and can justify this on the grounds of patient confidentiality. Yet if, say, somebody is diagnosed as suffering from dementia, it will be extremely helpful if the GP checks that close relatives know just what that means – the sufferer may soon be incapable of taking decisions for him- or herself and so huge decisions about care will shortly confront his or her representatives. A doctor's timely advice could make all the difference, but it may not be forthcoming in a very helpful form. It is not enough for a GP to simply say, 'I think your father may be in the early stages of dementia' and leave it at that. Also, doctors do not always volunteer information about the possible downsides of treatment. Often you have to ask them specific questions – for instance, on the mathematical probability of deleterious side-effects, such as the development of thrush if antibiotics are prescribed, or of wound infections after an operation on an older body.

Carers

Carers, that is, people who look after somebody in their own or their relative's home may face a variety of health hazards, from sleep interruption to back strain, as well as social isolation (pages 553–5). Carers' organizations and the government have set out ways in which GPs and other primary care workers could play a more proactive role in caring for carers. One proposal is that carer status should be recorded on medical notes, so that a doctor or a district nurse, say, is immediately aware of this aspect of a person's life. But a survey in 2001 of GPs and district nurses in Sussex found that while many offered written information for carers in their waiting rooms, fewer than one in four GPs and only a third of district nurses were routinely recording carer status.[2]

Apart from identifying patients who are carers and patients who have a carer, the government has also recommended in its *Carers' Plan* that GPs and other members of primary care teams should:

- check carers' physical and emotional health whenever a suitable opportunity arises, and at least once a year
- routinely tell carers that they can ask social services for an assessment of their own needs
- find out whether there is a carers' support group or a carers' centre in their area, and, if there is, tell carers about these.[3]

The attitude of a GP can make a great deal of difference to a carer looking after someone at home at nights and weekends while going out to work during the day. There is a world of difference between having a doctor who visits regularly once a week and also sends unprompted other specialist health professionals like a continence nurse adviser and a district nurse, and a workaday GP who will only ever make a home visit in an emergency and refuses to sign a sick note for the caring relative so that he or she can occasionally take a few days off work when exhausted from caring.

Health Checks

It is a part of every GP's contract with the NHS that patients over the age of 75 should receive a home visit and a check-up from their GP every year, quite apart from other consultations. This is supposed to occur in the patient's home, if he or she prefers, and to cover not only general and mental health, but also mobility and medication. It does not, however, always happen. A study of 40 GP practices in Nottinghamshire in 1997 found that as many as one in five over-75 year olds were not being offered their annual check.[4] In some practices, a selection process applied: 13 of the practices offered no checks to people living in nursing homes and nine ignored residential homes' patients as well. Yet the Nottinghamshire survey found that a quarter of the checks carried out revealed a problem previously unknown to the patient's doctor. So if you are over 75 and your GP is not offering you your annual check, ask for it.

One of the most blatant examples of ageism in the health service involves screening for breast cancer. Women are sent routine invitations for breast screening from the age of 50 to 65, but after that age they are not, yet 40 per cent of breast cancer cases occur in women over 70. Older women need to ask for such screening themselves.

If you feel you are being pushed to the back of the queue in this or any other area of health care (perhaps there is a service or drug which you think could benefit you, but you are not receiving on grounds of age), then demand it. Quote if necessary Standard 1, 'Rooting out ageism', from the *National Service Framework for Older People*: 'NHS services will be provided, regardless of age, on the basis of clinical need alone.'

Loyalty

Quite apart from the quality of care they themselves deliver to you, GPs have a lot of discretion in the amount of energy with which they push your case upon other related professionals. In a national opinion polls survey in 2000, GPs were asked about the extent to which they believed age rationing occurred in the health service. Sixteen per cent said that they thought that older people had to wait longer for NHS treatment than younger people and one third that older people do not receive the same quality of care in hospital as other people.[5] Your doctor's loyalty to you can make a lot of difference to your fate.

Referring On and Treatment

The readiness with which GPs refer on patients whom they are uncertain how to treat varies a great deal.

Parkinson's disease is a disorder of movement affecting voluntary muscles (page 149). If you develop Parkinson's disease, you should expect a referral from your GP. Guidelines sent out by the NHS in 1999 urged GPs to refer any patients whom they suspect of suffering from Parkinson's to an expert, rather that start to treat this complex condition themselves.

However, a survey two years later found that only 45 per cent of 400 randomly selected GPs were following the guidelines recommending all patients for specialist assessment; many had not read the guidelines.[6] When deciding whether or not to refer, age was a major factor: 44 per cent of the GPs said that they were influenced by it. Ninety-four per cent of the GPs questioned referred all patients aged 50 or under for specialist advice, compared with 58 per cent who always referred patients aged 71 or over. Eleven per cent of GPs said they never referred patients over 81. Many patients treated by GPs receive the drug levadopa. This can be dramatically effective in relieving symptoms, but its effects may begin to wear off after five years, leaving patients with disabling motor fluctuations. Ninety-five per cent of the GPs who initiated treatment were prescribing levadopa, possibly, according to the researchers, unaware that other options are now available for newly diagnosed Parkinson's sufferers.

Other common conditions of old age in which the attitude of a GP can make a lot of difference in both referring on and in the treatment he or she delivers him or herself include age-related macular degeneration (AMD), depression and dementia. For GPs and stroke see pages 442–3, for GPs and falls see pages 156–8.

AMD

You should expect a referral from your GP for age-related macular degeneration, or AMD. In some cases, the length of time it takes to see the specialist can make a big difference to the amount of sight you are left with. AMD is the most common vision impairment among older people, with half a million sufferers in the UK, and while it should not leave those afflicted completely blind, their vision is progressively reduced to the periphery as the cells in the centre of their retinas die. There are two types: 'dry' AMD is by far the most common. It accounts for perhaps 85 per cent of cases and no means have been found of arresting its progress, which takes several, perhaps six, years. However, the 'wet' kind, which develops much more rapidly, sometimes in a matter of days or weeks, and leaves the sufferer with greater central vision loss, can in some cases be slowed down. Only an opthamlogist, to whom you are referred by your GP, can diagnose AMD, ascertain the type and the level to which it has developed and then initiate treatment if appropriate.

A regular eye-check with your High Street optician is very important, but do not wait for such a test if you experience any change in vision: go straight to your GP. The early symptoms of AMD are often hazy or misty vision, or distortion of straight lines so that a window frame or lamppost has a kink in it, or slight colour shifts, so reds appear more brown and blues more green. But as both eyes are not usually affected at the same rates and the brain compensates for defects in one, you may not notice such change unless you close or cover one eye or until you reach a later stage of central vision loss. If an optician thinks you may have AMD, he or she will write to your GP, who should then in turn write to the hospital's ophthalmologist asking for an appointment (although some opticians can refer direct to a hospital). These stages can take a while. If you are really worried, or if you experience sudden change, such as distortion, a black patch or flashing lights, circumvent the whole procedure by going straight to Eye

Casualty at your hospital, where you ought to be able to see an ophthalmologist without a prior appointment.

This is not to say that you do not need your GP's swift action even if you have untreatable AMD, as in this case an ophthalmologist should be able to recommend dietary change which could help slow down the condition's progress. The ophthalmologist ought also to offer reassurance: you should not go completely blind, but many with AMD suffer from hallucinations as the brain adjusts to changes in the eye, and these can be frightening. If you develop AMD in both eyes or you develop another impairment in your second eye, at some stage the GP or the ophthalmologist should refer you to a specialist 'low vision clinic' which will look at the tasks you are having problems with and come up with suggestions to help. They ought also to register you as partially sighted, which will get you automatic access to the disability awareness team in the social services department of your local authority.

You may need to prompt your GP. A survey conducted in 2002 found alarming levels of ignorance among GPs about AMD. Eighty-five per cent of the GPs surveyed had seen patients with the condition during the previous 18 months, yet only 12 per cent considered that their knowledge of AMD was good or very good.[7]

Depression

Between 10 and 15 per cent of people over 65 span suffer from depression.[8] It develops when changes take place in the brain which lead to mood change. It is difficult to disentangle the causes of depression: the roots may be internal or they may be external events, such as bereavement, which set in train changes in the brain. People suffering from clinical depression of the most common type (not bipolar disorder or manic depression, which has different symptoms and patterns) usually feel lower than they would if they had simply been saddened by an external event. But people with depression often experience other symptoms: they may lose their appetite, feel very anxious, have difficulty in concentrating and be unable to summon up energy or motivation for tasks or pleasurable activities. The range of these other symptoms and the fact that many of them are the same as those of other conditions – digestive disorders, diseases of the blood, vitamin deficiencies and so on – means that it is not always easy to diagnose depression. Also, how low does one's mood have to be before it becomes clinical depression, as opposed to a natural response to a depressing event? In the past, symptoms like reduced energy and concentration levels did not always ring alarm bells in GPs' minds as possible indicators of depression. Nowadays, however, GPs are much more on the lookout for depression.[9] This is important because depression is treatable. Of course, many people get better without treatment, but some do not or they take a long time to do so.

David Anderson, a consultant at Mossley Hill Hospital, Liverpool, has pointed to a two- to threefold increased risk of death among depressed elderly people.[10] The reasons are likely to be many and varied. If you are depressed you may not get enough to eat, partly because you may lose your appetite and partly because you may lack the motivation to shop and prepare food. You may have less incentive to get better from or to avoid other illnesses – through getting your flu jab, for example. You are unlikely to feel impelled to take sufficient exercise or to go out and meet your friends. You may even commit suicide.

Suicide, though rare, is slightly more common among older than younger people, although of course some people take their own lives when they are not clinically depressed.[11] 'Every older person with depression should be considered for anti-depressant drug treatment or referral to a specialist in old age psychiatry,' according to Dr Anderson.

The *National Service Framework for Older People* encourages GPs to consider a range of action to treat clinical depression. It recommends treatments not involving drugs as the 'first line of management wherever possible', such as individual counselling and cognitive behaviour therapy (which involves trying to change the way people thinks about their situation rather than focusing on the origins of the problem), so your GP should be referring you to specialists like psychotherapists, community psychiatric nurses, clinical psychologists and counsellors (pages 71–2). If you do not think you are receiving treatment from which you might benefit, then you could suggest some of these possibilities. Expect careful diagnosis (to rule out other possible causes of your symptoms) and, if you receive therapy, the offer of referral to a social worker to help you deal with practical problems. The effects of psychotherapy are comparable to those obtained from drug treatment. Often psychotherapy is combined with treatment with anti-depressant drugs prescribed by a GP or a psychiatrist, and in these cases success rates are even higher (near 80 per cent).[12]

With depression it can be difficult to find the correct drug and dosage the first time. Retired psychiatric nurse Sharon Williams wrote in a letter published in the *British Medical Journal* in 2003, 'People taking any kind of drug, particularly psychoactive drugs, need to be monitored closely and questioned carefully and regularly until the effectiveness of the drug is determined and any adverse side-effects have been evaluated.'[13] Depressed people also need time from their doctor lest he or she misdiagnose or prescribe inappropriate drugs. Nurse Williams again: 'Information gathered on an initial visit is likely to be extremely superficial and inadequate simply because the patients are depressed. They are not thinking clearly and usually forget to tell the doctors the most important things the doctors need to know'.

People with depression may not feel up to monitoring side-effects of drugs; if these are serious, they may wish they were dead. Relatives need to make sure not only that their loved ones receive treatment but that all concerned are sensitive to these issues.

Dementia
While GPs now seem far readier than in the past to diagnose depression, the same is not true of dementia. In carrying out research for their report *Losing Time: Developing Mental Health Services for Older People in Wales*, published in 2002, the Audit Commission in Wales sent a questionnaire to all GPs in the Principality. Of the 42 per cent who responded, only 62 per cent considered that an early diagnosis of dementia was important. This compares with 90 per cent who said that an early diagnosis of depression was desirable.[14]

In the past, GPs may have been reluctant to diagnose dementia because, at least in the case of Alzheimer's disease, they could not offer any medical treatment to slow down, let alone cure the condition. To avoid upsetting patients, they have often refrained from offering a diagnosis until a crisis such as a fall has occurred, even if signs were clearly present. Early diagnosis made in a non-crisis situation, in which the sufferer is simply becoming progressively worse while living at home, enables action to be taken under less pressured conditions which may make life easier and more comfortable later on. But the person with dementia may be injured by a fall and the progress of the dementia possibly accelerated, while decisions about his or her future may then have to be taken in crisis circumstances, perhaps while in hospital. If dementia of some type (pages 5–6), is diagnosed, a son or daughter might ask, 'Can my father remain safely and happily at home with help? If so, for how long? Could he come and live with me or another close relative or friend? What does he want to do? Should he go into a care home?' These are major questions which need plenty of consideration, as each carries with it considerable financial, legal, caring, medical and other implications.

Another benefit to early diagnosis is the possibility of medication. The second most common cause of dementia is vascular or multi-infarct dementia, resulting from the occurrence of many tiny strokes which cut off the blood supply to groups of brain cells and kill them. If vascular dementia is responsible, there is a range of steps which can be taken to reduce the likelihood of further strokes, for example, reducing blood pressure with drugs.

Although the cause of Alzheimer's is unknown, drugs have recently been developed which can delay the development of certain symptoms if administered early enough: they can prevent the breakdown of an enzyme called acetylcholine, a chemical found at lower than normal levels in the brains of Alzheimer's sufferers. These drugs, which include Exelon, Reminyl and Aricept, have no effect on the underlying progress of the disease, but can temporarily delay memory loss and other aspects of cognitive decline in people at the early stages, bringing benefits to both the sufferer and his or her carer. They are effective in about two-thirds of cases: in some people the improvement is impressive for perhaps 12 months; in others there are marginal but noticeable benefits. Side-effects can include nausea and dizziness.

These Alzheimer's drugs usually have to be prescribed by a consultant rather than a GP, so clearly it is important to get moving as soon as possible. Nonetheless, there is a downside to early diagnosis. It can undoubtedly distress the person affected, so a very considered judgement must be made. Is a diagnosis likely to cause so much distress and confusion that it will outweigh the benefits which may result? Could these benefits be secured without the person affected being informed, at least at this stage, of the diagnosis? Or even misled? Or do you consider he or she has a right to know anyway?[15] If the condition is diagnosed, the GP ought to arrange access to a range of specialist helpers, such as community psychiatric nurses, continence advisors, district nurses and social workers. Such specialists can help not only with dementia itself but also with other conditions which become more difficult to handle when dementia is present, such as incontinence or depression.

Whether or not drugs are used, sympathetic care is extremely important. The person with dementia needs people, whether care workers or family carers, who can give him or her expert, patient care and make a real effort to empathise. In addition, various kinds of therapy have been shown to be beneficial and can be tried at home, such as dance, exercise and pet therapy (a grand term for allowing someone to pat and stroke a dog). [16] An intriguing and increasingly popular therapy called 'Snoozelan' involves the provision often in company with other people of a combination of light, sound, touch and smell stimuli; this is becoming increasingly available in day-care centres. Dolls therapy is discussed on pages 355–6. Not all these things will help everyone, since each person's development of dementia varies according to the parts of the brain affected by the plaques and tangles of Alzheimer's or the tiny strokes of multi-infarct dementia (page 6) and their individual responses to such changes.

Be careful with 'reminiscence therapy', which aims to activate long-term memory in group conversation: if not sensitively conducted it could make the person with the condition feel threatened because he or she cannot remember or learn things. The same is true of 'reality orientation', which tries to keep people with dementia in touch with the present-day worlds by reminding them of the time of day, where they are, who everybody is, correcting muddled speech or actions and prompting them to behave appropriately. Neither is likely to deliver any long-term amelioration. [17]

A conscientious GP will also be on the lookout for other conditions. Frequently people who develop dementia also become clinically depressed, but depression is treatable either through drugs or psychotherapy or both. People suffering from dementia are likely to become less and less able to explain other ailments which may arise, but this will not stop them suffering pain. So you need a GP who is aware of the patient's previous conditions and prepared to make a real effort to spot new ones.

You also want the GP to provide access to any new treatments for dementia which could prove helpful, such as Ebixa, a drug launched in the UK in 2002 which is the first to be developed that can slow the progress of symptoms in perhaps 30 per cent of people in the middle and late stages of Alzheimer's disease.

Finally, you also want a GP who will ensure your relative is given good palliative care, through advising carers such as nursing home staff or through referral to a palliative care specialist nurse, or even an Admiral nurse or a hospice, if such is available in your area. Most dementia sufferers die of a chest infection or a stroke rather than Alzheimer's itself, but the nature of their condition means they require particularly sensitive end-of-life care and support.

GPs and Medication

Many people do not realize that medicines can affect older people differently from when they were younger. Yet people who have taken a particular drug for many years may find that its effect on their body changes when they grow older. One of the reasons for this is the ageing of the liver (page 10). This change in the body's response to medication is difficult to predict, as it varies from drug to drug and from person to person. It is affected by the general state of the body, including any diseases which may be present, and the influence of other medicines, since drugs may interact with each other. Drugs often take longer to leave the bodies of older people and so build up in the bloodstream.

The side effects of drugs are particularly dangerous for older people, because some of them can increase the risk of falls (page

149). Studies of hospital admissions have shown that about one in ten elderly people were admitted solely or partly because of the side effects of their medication.[30]

Many older people are taking five or six different drugs, some as many as ten. Making sure you take the right drug, at the correct dosage, at the right time, can be challenging (although useful gadgets are available – see page 93). Some people do not manage very well. One hospital geriatrician told me of patients turning up for admission with a carrier-bag full of drugs, some of them out-of-date and all mixed up together. It is easy to over-dose yourself inadvertently, or not take the medication you need because you mistakenly think you have already taken it. You have to manage any side-effects of the different drugs. Bear in mind that they may interact with drugs you are taking of which your doctor is unaware because you have bought them over the counter.

But all this has to be set against the fact that drugs can bring terrific benefits. There might be drugs from which you could benefit which your GP is failing to prescribe. *Medicines and Older People*, which forms part of the government's *National Service Framework for Older People*, says that the control of pain through medication in people who are dying is not as good as it could be while anti-depressants, preventative treatment for asthma and anti-thrombosis drugs to prevent strokes are underused in older people.[191]

In view of all this, it is important that older people are given only the drugs they really need, at the correct dosage. Patients and doctors should be alert to possible side effects, and doctors should review regularly the drugs they prescribe to older people. One particularly useful recommendation in the *National Service Framework for Older People* is that all people over 75 should have their medication reviewed at least once a year and people taking four or more medicines should have it reviewed at least every six months. The Framework explains that medication reviews should include patients and their carers.

If your GP has not carried out such a review, ask for one. It could produce surprising results. A study of medication reviews for care home residents reported in *Medicines and Older People* revealed that in nearly 50 per cent of cases the recommendation of the reviews was that a drug should be stopped; in an astonishing two-thirds of these cases, there was no stated reason for the medicine being prescribed in the first place.[20]

In the Home

As we get older, help from gadgets and tools (pages 91–115), no matter how sophisticated, is often not quite enough. If you need human assistance in the home and cannot obtain it through friends, family, volunteers or neighbours, paid help may be the answer. If so, the sooner you get the wheels turning, the better. This is because accepting the help of strangers often takes considerable psychological adjustment. If you have long been used to doing everything yourself, the idea of strangers in the house can seem unsettling, especially when you feel frail and anxious about what the future holds. Using paid help early on gets you accustomed to this state of affairs before the tasks involved become too intimate. Without paid help, you can easily find life dominated by the challenge of performing day-to-day tasks. Things which once made life enjoyable, such as getting out and seeing friends, may be squeezed out. There is also the danger of becoming over-reliant on one person, like your spouse or partner. If he or she suddenly becomes ill, a crisis can occur. It is always easier to make arrangements before events force you into action.

Help can be hired for a couple of hours a week or 24 hours a day; it can be hired privately or arranged and/or provided by a local authority social services department. A system called Direct Payments (unrelated to the Direct Payment method of receiving the State Pension) offers the chance of effectively hiring help privately but with the benefit of a subsidy from the council and a support system to help you deal with employment administration. In 1999, 670,000 people in the UK were receiving private help in the home and 610,000 homecare through their local authority, some people being in both categories.[21] Direct Payments affect a tiny number, but they have only recently been introduced, their use is growing and the government is so keen to see them become much more widespread that it is requiring councils to offer this option to individuals.

Whichever route you go down, whether you are rich or poor, you should consider applying for the non-means-tested state benefit Attendance Allowance (pages 485–9). You are free to spend this allowance however you like, although it is intended to help cover the additional cost of frailty and disability and might thus reasonably go towards, for example, taxi fares or hiring somebody to do some housework. To get Attendance Allowance you need to approach the Department for Work and Pensions, although social services will point you in the right direction if you are unsure.

If you live in Scotland, again whatever your financial circumstances, you could take advantage of a state handout called Free Personal Care. The Scottish Executive foots the bill for help your local authority considers necessary with personal attention (washing, dressing, moving, bathing, going to the toilet, getting ready for bed, eating, taking medicine). To access Free Personal Care, you need to approach your local authority's social work department, and we return to this later when we turn to how to secure state support for help in the home (pages 293–4).

Doing your own Hiring

To find paid help, you can ask around or advertise and hire somebody yourself, or you can approach an agency which will find, supervise and pay workers. If you hire somebody yourself, you retain control, but also responsibility. You have to ensure that workers are paid on time, that any National Insurance and tax are deducted, and sickness and holiday pay are provided. In addition, you will want to cover yourself for employers' liability and check that you are already covered by occupiers' liability insurance (page 263; see also page 304).

This may sound daunting, but going it alone ensures flexibility as well as control. You can hire somebody for 2 or 20 hours a week, and decide when he or she comes, for how long and what he or she does. You might want the work to follow the same pattern at every visit, or to vary week by week within agreed limits. For example, you could get somebody to come in for perhaps three hours a week to do any of a range of tasks, depending on what calls for attention in any particular week – sewing on buttons, helping to prepare a couple of meals, one of which could be placed in the fridge, hoovering, clearing out a cupboard, going shopping or accompanying you shopping, accompanying you on an outing, or providing company, which could include anything from chatting over a cup of tea to playing cards. If you do not like the way your helper is polishing your horse brasses or sorting your socks, you simply ask for it to be done differently. You rely on yourself to judge character and ability, and to take up references.

If your worker is unwell or goes on holiday, you will have to do without or find a replacement. Some people get round this by loosely teaming up with two or three others hiring helpers in a similar fashion, on the understanding that if one worker is absent the others will try to fill in. Or you could use an agency to provide workers for the odd occasion such as this.

Over the next few years, people who do personal care work in the home (which means helping with tasks involving the body like washing, dressing and undressing, moving, feeding, going to the loo and taking medication, but not housework, preparing food, visiting, gardening or shopping) should be placing their names on a register compiled by the General Social Care Council in England, the Care Council for Wales, the Scottish Social Services Council or the Northern Ireland Social Care Council. This should provide minimal guarantees about their fitness to work and their commitment to sound principles (pages 54–5).

Whether or not the names of any people you are contemplating hiring appear on such a register, make sure that you take up references, even if you are hiring somebody for only a short period. Happily, model documents seeking references and drawing up terms and conditions of employment have been published in a free document which also outlines the legal background to employing people. The organization which produced this document, the National Centre for Independent Living, supports people who are using Direct Payments; the relevant publication is *Everything you Need to Know about Getting and Using Direct Payments*, which is equally useful for people who are operating entirely independently and have nothing to do with Direct Payments. Local voluntary organizations for disabled people and elderly people which support people using Direct Payments may also produce useful guidance.

You can also get a security check on a prospective employee. Contact the Criminal Records Bureau to find out the name of an

Help in the Home

- Accepting help in the home can keep you independent.
- Apply for Attendance Allowance when you hire help, even if you are well-off.
- Hiring help yourself may be better than using a care agency.
- Find out precisely how agencies recruit and train staff and cover for sickness.
- If you use an agency, obtain a copy of the new national regulations and standards.
- If you use a care agency, get a service user's plan.
- Expect workers to sign up for the Social Care Councils' code of conduct.
- Councils can save you a lot of money by sanctioning help.
- Get a community care assessment even if you hire your own staff.
- Plan in advance how to handle your community care assessment.
- Don't settle for meals-on-wheels if eating out or home-prepared food would be preferable.
- If you live in Scotland, claim free personal care.
- Direct Payments give you control while the council helps pay.
- Your council may keep quiet about the Direct Payments option.
- If you are unreasonably refused Direct Payments, lodge a formal complaint.

organization, called a registered body, which acts on behalf of the CRB in your area. Your prospective employee should apply to that body and say that he or she would like an Enhanced Level Disclosure Check to be carried out. The registered body approaches the CRB, which sends the result to the applicant and to the registered body; you can ask your prospective employee to see the disclosure, which will be dated. The process cost £29 in 2003. But do not set too much store by a CRB check: diligently pursue your own investigations through references as well.

Employees have certain rights, such as the right to be paid the minimum wage, the right to written terms and conditions and the right to maternity, paternity and holiday leave and sick pay. In addition, employers have to consider such matters as tax and insurance. Take heart – a free publication sets everything out, and you may find that much does not apply in your own case. The document is *A Guide to Receiving Direct Payments,* available from the Department of Health and the Scottish Executive.

Insurance

It is important to be covered by insurance in case your employee is harmed while working for you, whether in your house or outside it. The occupiers' liability cover which often comes with house contents insurance protects you against claims from friends or workmen who come into the house and have an accident. Under the 1969 Employers' Liability Compulsory Insurance Act, as an employer you also have to have employers' liability insurance and to display a certificate of insurance on your premises. A firm called Fish Insurance has designed a policy with the needs of personal assistants for older or disabled people specifically in mind, and most local authorities use Fish.

You need to make sure that your house insurance covers damage to your property and its contents by a hired worker. A friend of mine had no such cover; workers she hired to look after her mother while she went out to work accidentally started three fires, one of which caused thousands of pounds worth of damage.

Health and Safety at Work Regulations

Employers have a responsibility to ensure that the working environment they provide is safe. You can get advice on good practice from the Health and Safety Executive. However, health and safety law does not apply to the employment of staff in a private household. If you obtain helpers through a domiciliary care agency, it is worth checking that it has taken this responsibility on board.

National Insurance and Tax

Usually, a worker in your home is considered to be employed by you. This means you are responsible for deducting National

Insurance Class I contributions and tax from his or her salary under PAYE.

If you are paying your personal assistant less than a set amount, the lower earnings limit (£89 in 2003–4), then you do not need to worry about NI. But if you are paying more than this amount, you will have to pay employer contributions, deduct employee contributions from what you pay and send them to the Inland Revenue.

Tax is different, because in deciding whether you need to deduct it, your employee's earnings from all his or her sources of employment are relevant. This does not mean that you need to know her total income. The rule is that if your employee's only job is with you and you are paying less than £89 per week, then no income tax is payable. But if she is also earning money from other people, then she will have to pay tax on her total earnings, once the basic personal allowance has been deducted, and it will be up to you to deduct tax at that rate from her earnings from you and send them to the Inland Revenue.

If you think you need to deduct PAYE tax or pay NI contributions, telephone the New Employers Support Line at the Inland Revenue. You may be able to register for the Simplified Deduction Scheme. The Simplified Deduction Scheme is an easier system to use than the standard one, so when you ring up, ask whether you are eligible and get their Starter Pack. It is also a good idea to get hold of other leaflets, such as those on Statutory Sick Pay and Statutory Maternity Pay.

Your assistant will probably be an employee, but some personal assistants are classed as self-employed. If this is the case, you will not have to make any tax or National Insurance deductions from what you pay. You need to telephone your local Tax Office to determine the status of the worker before you go ahead. Neither you nor your assistant can choose whether he or she is considered self-employed: this is up to the Inland Revenue, applying certain rules.

You may well not have to pay any NI or tax whatsoever, but it is very important to check before you go ahead.

Using an Agency

Rather than hiring your own assistant or assistants direct, you can use a domiciliary care agency which has a contract with you to supply workers on a regular basis (rather than an employment agency, which finds you somebody whom you then hire yourself). You may not get the same worker each time, but you should get somebody, even if your usual person is sick or on holiday. Another advantage of using a domiciliary services agency is that it should deal with tax and National Insurance: you just send the agency a cheque, usually every week. Beware, however, of assuming you have no responsibilities at all. You may still need occupier's liability insurance, for instance.

The agency will of course take a cut of the money you send it. This might be a third, a half or even more of the hourly fee you are paying. So you need to be sure you are getting more for your money than you would if you hired a worker or workers yourself.

Quality of Service

The other and perhaps most important consideration is the quality of the service you get from the agency. This will depend on the type of people it recruits, their qualifications, training, the conditions under which they work and whether the agency has put in place adequate quality-control mechanisms. Monitoring mechanisms like time sheets (which the worker fills in each time and the client signs) and an agency telephoning clients for feedback are important because domiciliary care necessarily takes place in an isolated work environment, with no other professionals around to blow the whistle. If an older person is alert with good sight and hearing, he or she will be able to ensure that care workers perform the tasks expected to a minimum standard. But people with sight or hearing difficulties or dementia are particularly vulnerable to being short-changed.

Help in the home provides work for a large number of people: there are 1.2 million care workers, now sometimes known as 'social care workers', in England alone (some work in care homes, some in both environments). People working for care agencies are many and varied. Often they do not receive a regular salary and count themselves fortunate if their agency gives them guaranteed hours. Some put in as many hours as they possibly can, as they do not know what if any work will be forthcoming in future. Others see their agency work as pin money and rely principally on other income, for instance, their husband's, or a regular job in a supermarket or a care home. Many agency workers are conscientious and kind people, but others are on an agency's books because they are untrained and could not get any other kind of work. They will leave if something better turns up, so turnover is high.

People who have a real commitment to working with older people often try to quit agency work and set up on their own. They may hope to make more money by avoiding the agency's cut, but they will also gain control over which clients they take on and what they have to do for them. Such people tend to call themselves personal assistants, emphasizing the importance of fulfilling the specific requirements of individual clients and helping them do things for themselves, rather than taking over their lives. Such people may well be more inclined to gather qualifications such as National Vocational Qualifications.

Care agencies also vary. Some buy staff uniforms, others do not. Some pay for training, others expect workers to pay for it themselves and undertake it in their own time. Some pay mileage and travel time, others do not. Some ensure their workers are kindly, well-motivated people who have been trained well and are expected to carry out their work in ways recommended by respected organizations, such as the British Association of Domiciliary Care (BADCO), which publishes useful guidelines on best practice, from food hygiene to helping people with dementia. However, other agencies dispatch untrained workers to carry out tasks as cheaply as possible.

In eldercare it is important to be aware that there is an unavoidable conflict between the demands of good care and the imperative to make a profit. Providing well rather than minimally trained staff costs more money. So does paying higher hourly rates and having pay scales in order to attract and keep well-motivated, conscientious and committed workers. So does allowing workers time – not only time to carry out tasks well, but also time to communicate with clients, if this is what the client would like. Studies have demonstrated that having sufficient time and talking as a means of building and maintaining a relationship are key elements in caring for others (pages 550–51).

Controls on Agencies and Organizations

After years without statutory control on whom domiciliary care agencies could send into people's homes and the quality of the service they offered, in 2003 the government introduced regulation of all domiciliary care agencies providing personal care. This control has not been extended to Northern Ireland, but readers there may care to read on to find out what things they should look out for when dealing with agencies.

Registration

Any organization providing personal care has to register with the National Care Standards Commission (NCSC for short, in England), the Scottish Commission for the Regulation of Care or the Care Standards Inspectorate for Wales. In the main, the organizations involved are the commercial agencies which provide the majority of care workers. But the legislation applies to any organization which offers personal care and so also embraces a number of voluntary organizations, local authorities, primary care trusts and housing associations. Any organization which carries out personal care is operating illegally if it has not applied for and been granted registration. So if you are proposing to use an agency for some form of personal care for yourself or a relative, the first thing to check is its certificate of registration. You should be able to do this either with the agency itself or with your local office of the NCSC or its equivalent.

It is the person running the agency who has to have a certificate of registration. Managers have to send the Commission personal information such as a recent photograph, documentary evidence of any relevant qualifications and training and a report by a GP on the basis of which the Commission decides whether they are mentally and physically fit to manage an agency and possess sufficient integrity and good character and so can become the 'registered person' of the agency.

Information about the agency itself must also be sent to the Commission. This information is pretty basic for the most part and includes the nature of the services the agency provides and the scale of charges payable by users of its services.[22] But registration also requires that information about each of the agency's personal care workers has to be provided to the National Care

Standards Commission – his or her identity, two written references, a recent photograph and a full employment history, together with a satisfactory written explanation of any gaps in employment. Workers have to provide information about any qualifications and training they possess and a statement about their physical and mental health. The regulations also require agencies to provide information about any criminal convictions and cautions through a Criminal Records Bureau police check. However, in the past this had been suspended because of a backlog of applications still pending, so you need to check. Also bear in mind that care workers from overseas are not subjected to a criminal records check: the CRB simply sends back forms saying the information is not available. An agency (or a care home) manager may also have difficulty pursuing references abroad. Finally, many people who commit offences are never brought to book anyway.

However, the requirement for registration by no means covers every agency you might be interested in. Only those which provide personal care to people living in their own home will have to be registered. An agency which provides workers to do gardening, cleaning, laundry, food preparation, washing up, shopping or visiting will be outside the system. In the early days there will no doubt be confusion among agencies which deal mainly in non-personal care but also offer some personal care. Also, these controls do not yet operate in Northern Ireland, although health and social services boards carry out their own checks on agencies with which they have block contracts for the provision of homecare services.

Regulations and Standards

The mere fact that domiciliary care agencies now have to be registered and certain checks carried out is certainly useful to the consumer. But that is not all. The government has published regulations (the *Domiciliary Care Agencies Regulations 2001)* which agencies must comply with. If they do not, the Commission can take enforcement action ordering them to remedy deficiencies, and it can even withdraw their registration. The new *National Minimum Standards for Domiciliary Care* fleshes out the regulations in more detail. Inspectors from the NCSC and its sister bodies will take into account the extent to which agencies are meeting such standards when they carry out their inspections, but agencies have to comply with all the regulations if they are to avoid enforcement action or refusal or withdrawal of registration. If you are going to use an agency, it is well worth obtaining a copy of both the regulations and the standards from the NCSC or its equivalent, either by post or on the website and studying them carefully.[23]

On pages 286–89 I highlight some of the regulations and standards which seem to me to be particularly useful. Three short examples here. First, agencies must draw up a 'service user's plan' for each client, setting down their personal care needs and how these are going to be met. This plan has to be prepared after consultation with the client and kept under review. Second, the regulations stipulate that no domiciliary care worker should be supplied by the agency unless he or she has the experience and skills necessary for the work that he or she is to perform and is also physically and mentally fit for the work. Third, the registered person of an agency must ensure that personal care arranged by the agency is provided 'so as to promote the independence of service users', according to the regulations. Number 9 of the *National Minimum Standards for Domiciliary Care*, explains: 'Care and support workers carry out tasks *with* the service user, not *for* them, minimizing the intervention and supporting service users to take risks, as set out in the service user plan, and not endangering health and safety.'

An important question yet to be answered is what impact the new regulatory system is going to have on the operation of domiciliary care agencies on the ground. There is a vast number of such agencies hiring out an even vaster number of workers, and clearly the standards to which they operate and the skills of their workers are not going to be transformed overnight. Furthermore, inspectors may refrain from enforcing the new controls too strictly in the early days lest large numbers of agencies pull out of the sector. This may well happen anyway as agencies decide they do not want the hassle and expense of introducing new working procedures and training workers. The potential for radical improvement nonetheless exists. But much effort will be required. Ninety per cent of the people working as care workers in people's homes in England in 1998 held no formal qualifications in care work.[24]

In the early years, consumers may have to flex their muscles and show that they are aware of and are prepared to use the potential of the regulatory system. Consumers also should be ready to take the agency to task if it fails to meet the regulations and standards and, if necessary, complain to the NCSC or one of its sister bodies.

The range of new controls has limitations, and it is important to be vigilant. You may still want to check on many things, in particular meeting workers whom an agency proposes to send to your or your relative's home in order to form your own assessment of whether they are capable, trustworthy, have a pleasing manner and the right sort of expertise. The new regulations and standards have little to say on the important area of the content of contracts, including the rate it is reasonable for agencies to charge. When I used agencies in the late 1990s, I had no idea how the lengthy contracts with which I was presented compared with what I might be offered by other agencies. Now, fortunately, a model contract has been drawn up between the provider of homecare and the user by an organization called The Continuing Care Conference, a coalition of commercial, charitable and public service organizations with an interest in the care of older people.[25] You can get a copy of this model contract free from the Conference, and it is worth doing so in order to compare clause by clause what an agency offers with the model. That way you will be a lot better placed than I was to shop around or insist on modifications to an agency's contract.

These regulations and national minimum standards apply only to organizations. If you find somebody through an advert in your local newspaper or shop window, their work in your home will not be checked upon in any way because they are not working through an agency. However, there is nothing to stop you telling your own workers that you expect all the standards and regulations which apply to help in the home provided through organizations also to apply in your case. So even if you never go near an agency, get hold of the national minimum standards and the regulations if for no other reason that that they will give you ideas for things to look out for and ways in which things might be done.

Registers for Workers in Social Care
In years to come, however, a separate register will be drawn up for individual care workers who carry out personal care. People whom you find yourself, just like people working through agencies, can submit their names and details for inclusion on this list if they wish (this registration is not compulsory). This second register will be compiled by the General Social Care Council in England, the Care Council for Wales, the Northern Ireland Social Care Council and the Scottish Social Services Council (pages 54–5).

The main purpose of these registers will be to protect the public against people who would be unsuitable for employment in the personal care field. Essentially people will not be accepted on the register of social care workers unless they are of good character (in other words, criminal conviction checks have turned up nothing significant), are physically and mentally fit to perform their work (health checks have been passed) and they have satisfied any training and conduct requirements which the Council may impose. The main register will be open to the public, although it is not yet clear how much of the information on each person will be publicly available.

The registration of care assistants in the UK is not going to happen overnight. The Councils also have to register other types of worker, and social workers and the managers of care homes are among those who will be registered first, in England from 2005. By the time the Councils get round to care workers, perhaps in 2007, the sheer numbers involved will mean that the process will take some time. Registration is not compulsory for any type of care worker, although it may become so.

A second, even more long-term aim of registration by the Social Care Councils is to try to transform care work into a profession. Those care workers on the register will be expected to adhere to a code of practice. All four Social Care Councils in each of the countries of the UK have agreed on one code and some elements of it are useful, for example that care workers should not 'abuse the trust of service users and carers or the access you have to personal information about them or to their property, home or workplace'. Most of the code is couched in very general terms. You can obtain it from any of the Councils,[26] and it is worth having it to hand: it is not unreasonable to expect care workers to comply with the code in the years before registration as 'it is intended to reflect existing good practice'.

At the time of writing, it was not clear what qualifications or level of training the Councils would stipulate. Again, only workers who perform personal care are covered, so anybody who comes into your home to do shopping, cleaning or any other housework, gardening, food preparation or visiting will not be expected to register. Also untouched by this system are volunteers, paid workers who run day centres and the wardens of sheltered housing.

Help from the Council

Approximately as many people who commission private help in the home receive help provided or organized by their local authority. There is probably much overlap, with people hiring some help independently (to do their gardening perhaps) and also accepting help organized by their council (say, attendance at a day centre, or help with having a bath). So how does help come from the local authority? And is it worth having?

At some point, an older person may be asked by the social services department of the local authority if somebody can come and see if everything is OK. This often happens when a GP or district nurse considers that an elderly person has reached a stage at which some of the non-medical facilities and services which a local council can provide might be of use. Their name is then passed to the local authority's social services department. Local authorities provide a gateway to a wide range of what are known as community care services, of which there are four kinds:[27]

1. Outdoor services, such as day centres and luncheon clubs, or being accompanied shopping.
2. Personal domiciliary care services which are provided in your home, such as help to have a bath, to wash and dress, take medication and get ready for bed. (Anything medical, such as an injection or wound dressing change, counts as medical care, and is provided separately for free by the NHS.)
3. Practical domiciliary services, such as housework, bringing in shopping, collecting a pension or prescription, and preparing and serving food.

4. Delivery of meals to your house – in other words, meals-on-wheels.

If you agree to accept council help, a social worker will visit. Perhaps all you need is an answer to a particular enquiry, such as how to get hold of a travel pass. Otherwise, a formal 'community care assessment' of your needs will be made.

The Community Care Assessment
Community care assessment is provided for under the National Health Service and Community Care Act 1990, which says:

> Where it appears to a local authority that any person for whom they may provide or arrange for the provision of community care services may be in need of any such services, the authority –
> (a) shall carry out an assessment of his needs for those services; and
> (b) having regard to the results of that assessment, shall decide whether his needs call for the provision by them of any such services.

An assessment is followed by a 'care plan', setting out what will be provided, usually in the same document.

Instead of waiting for a GP to act, however, an elderly person can take the initiative and make the first contact with social services. Even if they will not provide help themselves, they may offer useful advice about local services you can access independently. Also, they may be able to point out state benefits of which you are not taking advantage, perhaps because you think they are restricted to people on low incomes, such as Attendance Allowance. If you think social services might be able to help you, ask for a Community Care Assessment. You have an absolute right to have one carried out. A council cannot excuse itself by saying that it thinks you are wealthy enough to organize things for yourself, or that you have children who should be able to sort out private homecare for you, or that it has no money left in this year's eldercare budget to subsidize any services.

Quite minor deficiencies can be addressed in an assessment. Perhaps you stay in more than you would like and shop only infrequently when a neighbour takes you because you are unsteady on your feet. An assessment could result in your being taken out to a day centre or luncheon club and the provision of somebody to accompany you on a shopping trip, say, once a week. At least some of this will almost certainly be subsidized by the council, and the net cost to you may well be small. In addition, you might be pointed in the direction of facilities not part of the formal local authority community care system which might be provided free, such as a befriending scheme (page 222).

But the community care assessment is also the only gateway to a wide range of services which, if you need a large amount of them, would be extremely expensive had you to bear the cost entirely yourself. It could result in your receiving hundreds of pounds each week to help cover the cost of enabling you to remain in your own home, or thousands or even tens of thousands of pounds over a number of years. The more help you can get to support you in your own home, the longer you will be able to remain there. If you become one of the many people who have to cope with a number of disabling conditions, then the cost of hiring help independently could soon become overwhelming unless your council can rescue you. Many older people who have never been assessed could benefit enormously from facilities to which assessment could open the way.

Community care assessment also comes into play, and in a very important way, when consideration is being given to discharge from hospital (pages 466–7). The person involved may then be chronically ill or suffering the after-effects of a stroke or an operation. He or she may be desperate to return home, but social services may incline towards nudging him or her into a care home. Insisting on an assessment may save the day, though it could still conclude that entry to a care home is desirable, either on a permanent basis or for a period of respite care.

However generous it is, every local council places a ceiling on the level of spending per elderly person above which it will not normally go. It will also normally demand that the recipient contributes to the cost if he or she can afford to. So you have an interest in ensuring that the result of your community care assessment – your care plan – includes not only the services best suited to you, but the services which will not cost too much.

Assessment: Your Rights

Your absolute right to have your needs assessed by the council in your area is complemented by a legal duty for that council to determine whether or not to provide services to meet those needs. In pursuing these rights, a valuable source of help is guidance which central government has issued: *Care Management and Assessment: A Practitioner's Guide.*[28] A council's failure to comply with this guidance strengthens your position if you complain. Should such a representation fail to spur your council into action, you can threaten a formal complaint and/or take up the matter with your local councillor and/or your MP (pages 577–80).

Parts of the guidance on assessments which may prove especially valuable include:

- You should be able to have somebody with you during the assessment. You could choose a close relative, or an independent 'advocate', for example. There seems no reason why you should not ask for more than one additional person to be present.
- You should be able to choose where the assessment is to take place. A social worker could carry out an assessment over the telephone, but this is hardly ideal, as it is important that the social worker should be able to understand your problems. How can he or she assess whether you are able to cook or clean or whether you feel lonely if he or she does not see you in your everyday surroundings? So if you think a social worker is carrying out what sounds like a community care assessment over the telephone and you are unhappy with that, say so and ask for a home visit.
- Our needs can take many different forms – social, emotional and cultural as well as a physical need to have help with the housework. You may be lucky and have a local authority prepared to provide high-quality support tailored to your particular needs without any hassle. Or you may have a social worker who will want to plug you into a package of existing services which ignore many of your needs, laying on meals-on-wheels, for instance, when you crave social contact as you live alone, have difficulty getting out and your neighbours are out all day, so visits to a luncheon club or a care worker coming to your

home to help you prepare food would be much more desirable. The 1991 guidance made it plain that in trying to help older people remain independent, community care assessments should look at all their needs.[29] What is more, the courts have held on a number of occasions that community care assessments have to investigate all possible needs.[30]

- The social worker should tell you at the assessment that you can have a written copy of the assessment sent to you. You should also be sent a copy of the care plan. This requirement is frequently overlooked. If it is, chase it up. If this does not work, try saying you would like to come in and see your entire social services file. You have a right to do so (page 50), but social services will probably not want this and so may hasten to send you a copy of your assessment and care plan.

It is important that you should have a copy of your assessment and care plan from the moment they are drawn up because you need to be absolutely clear what services will be provided. If you do not know, you cannot tell for sure whether care workers are doing what they are paid to. If you think they should be doing something yet they believe that it is not in their brief, confusion will result, and often bad feeling.

One useful but often overlooked fact is that if asked, a local council has a duty to carry out an assessment even on someone not ordinarily resident in its area. Suppose you are considering having your elderly mother come to live with you but are unsure whether your own local authority would provide plenty of homecare or you would have to do everything yourself. In its eagerness to avoid the burden of an extra elderly person, your council may insist that it can conduct an assessment only when your mother has moved in. You need not take the huge risk which would be involved in waiting until then.

Last but by no means least is a provision which could help the many people whom social services probably think they have assessed but who, at the time that assessment supposedly took place, were unaware that it was happening and were therefore unable to participate in it fully. In a case in 1998 involving Bristol City Council, the judge took the view that somebody who is unaware of being assessed has not been.[31] So if social services tell you that they have carried out an assessment and that comes as news to you, you can demand a new assessment, referring to this case. If you are refused, pursue the matter, if necessary through the complaints procedure of your local authority.

Eligibility for Services

Councils must somehow translate the money which they have allocated for the support of older people into spending on individuals, so they have to decide which needs they will meet and which they will not. The way they do this is by devising eligibility criteria. These ensure that individuals have to be experiencing a threshold level of inconvenience or difficulty before the council will step in and help them. The height of these thresholds reflects the degree of support which particular councils give to older people. Both the type of need to which a council will respond and the level of need may differ from place to place.

One type of need some councils would ignore is a need to look after a pet, crucial though that might be to the happiness of its owner. However, North Lanarkshire Council, for example, includes taking a dog for a short walk among the tasks which care workers are expected to perform for elderly individuals, if the council considers this is necessary to enable a client to maintain a normal lifestyle and there are no significant risks involved. Some councils are reluctant to provide much support with housework, but others, such as North Lanarkshire, provide much help with housework (which it calls 'essential hygiene' or 'home management'). A need which all councils will take seriously is for help with washing and dressing, but they will vary in the degree of difficulty somebody has to be experiencing before they will offer help. Some councils will meet this need only if a person takes hours to perform these tasks; others will do so if any significant difficulty is encountered.

Varying the type and level of support available to older people may be considered a legitimate function of local democracy, but like other 'postcode lotteries', variations strike many people as unfair, and to meet this complaint the government has recently sought to standardize eligibility criteria to some extent. Much variation will nonetheless continue, but in England there will probably be considerable convergence towards the Whitehall model.

In 2002, the Department of Health published a piece of policy guidance on eligibility criteria called *Fair Access to Care Services*.[32] This tells councils to place eligibility criteria in four categories: critical, substantial, moderate and low, according to the extent to which a person's independence will be put at risk if particular problems are not addressed. Any need should be deemed 'critical' if 'significant health problems have developed or are likely to develop' and 'there will be, or could be, little or no choice and control over the immediate environment' if the need goes unmet. A need classed as 'low' may mean that, for instance, 'there is, or could be, some inability to carry out one or two daily routines'.

Do not worry too much about ploughing through the complexities of eligibility criteria. The important thing is to know that they exist and to understand that what will determine whether a need is important enough to be met is the risk which will be run if it is not met. Today, many councils do little more in a community care assessment than correlate a risk assessment with the services they can easily plug you into. Since it is easier to appreciate – and easier to be embarrassed about ignoring – needs for sustenance and cleanliness, these and other needs which might result in serious physical harm if unmet, tend to take priority.

Some councils will not quibble about providing and subsidizing virtually all the services you think you need. But for those which do not, the trick is to demonstrate that you will be at risk if you do not receive what you want, with the result that your independence will be threatened. If you feel the need to keep in close contact with your own cultural or ethnic group, say, but your level of disability threatens your continued ability to do so, you could point out that the impact on your social well-being could put your mental health at risk. You could ask your GP to write a letter to this effect. Social services often find it difficult to ignore such missives, so they can greatly increase your chances of securing, say, a mobility aid or attendance at a day centre specific to your own group.

If your council will only meet a high degree of need, you may have to demonstrate that your needs are exceptional. Despite the existence of criteria, the courts have always held that councils must never apply eligibility in a blanket fashion: they must consider each individual case. So if, say, your council says it never helps with pets, look for reasons why you might be a special case. A council may find it easier to say 'We never do night visits' than to argue about why you should not receive a visit at 6 a.m. when you particularly need one. The more peculiar your reason, the more likely it is to make you special.

Services

When a care manager proposes specific services as a result of an assessment, you need to determine whether these best suit your needs. If your social services department is generous, conscientious and imaginative, this may not be a problem. But many councils rely on off-the-shelf services which may have drawbacks. If some of the services they suggest could be replaced with more effective and cheaper means of meeting your assessed needs, that should leave more money available to be spent on gadgets and other services to help you.

So which services might be suggested and what are the alternatives?

Washing and Dressing

Many care managers like to send in a care worker in the morning to help older people get up, washed, dressed and to cope with their bed, particularly if they suffer from night-time incontinence. For some people, help with at least some of these tasks is essential. Many people find it reassuring to be called on first thing in the morning. But there is a downside with this practice. You have to get up at the time which has been set for the care worker to call: you cannot have a lie-in simply because you feel like it, or because you are feeling slightly off-colour. You have to get up, get washed and get dressed fairly quickly, for the worker will have a schedule to meet. If the care worker is late, you will be left hanging around in your night attire when you may have an appointment to keep. You may not like somebody else helping you wash and dress. You may get a different worker on different days, and you may not wish to explain to a perfect stranger where you keep your underclothes. Washing will normally mean a stand-up wash by the basin – not a shower or bath, which you might prefer.

Instead of a care worker's visit, however, you could find gadgets sufficient and preferable. If a stroke, Parkinson's or arthritis has made movements such as bending painful and difficult, a long handled shoe-horn may help you get your shoes on and another gadget may pull on your socks. Aids are also available for washing, bathing, using the lavatory and working in the kitchen (pages 91-5). Many are provided free of charge (pages 107–9).

If gadgets will not suffice, changing or modifying your clothing may make dressing easier. If your wrist is in plaster, it is pretty well impossible to fasten a bra. So why not invest in bras which fasten at the front? All sorts of clothes exist which are far roomier and easier to get in and out of than ordinary garments; you can see or get information about these at Disabled Living Centres. You could also try stitching panels or wedges of cloth into existing night-gowns, dresses, trousers and so on, to make them easier to slip on and off.

Meals-on-Wheels

Meals-on-wheels is another stock solution offered to older people. It may be that you find it difficult or painful to stand for long; perhaps you cannot easily manipulate tools in the kitchen; perhaps you suffer from tremor and might spill scalding fluid. Nourishing hot food is essential for older people, particularly in winter. So for many social workers, the answer is simply to add you to the list for meals-on-wheels. Perhaps this service evokes in you the vision of a stalwart and friendly lady from the Women's Royal Voluntary Service ladling out generous portions of highly nutritious, piping hot food just like mother made. These days, however, many of the meals-on-wheels are prepared by private companies which have tendered for the work and won the contract by promising to charge least. Arrangements vary, but a portion-controlled meal will generally arrive in a foil container. Usually it will be freshly cooked, but nutrients such as vitamin C are likely to have degraded while the meal is kept hot in the van delivering it to your door (there is normally a maximum of two hours between packing and delivery). Not all meals will be for immediate consumption. Many suppliers do not deliver at weekends or over public holidays, but provide frozen meals instead along with the last hot meal before the break. There may be a vegetarian alternative, but there will often not be any other choice – a severe disadvantage, perhaps, if you are used to Chinese or Afro-Caribbean food. Of course you have to eat the food when it arrives, whether this be at noon or 2 o'clock: if you put it in the fridge and reheat it later, you may reactivate bacteria and give yourself food poisoning.

Alternatives to meals-on-wheels include visiting a luncheon club or a day centre. There you should receive freshly cooked food within minutes of its coming off the stove. The portions may be larger, and there may be the opportunity for seconds. Dishes will look more appetizing by being served on a plate, while eating will involve social contact and, you may at least hope, interesting conversation.

You are more likely to get outside provision if a need for social contact has been written in to your community care assessment. Otherwise your council may prefer meals-on-wheels, which will cost less than arranging your attendance at a centre and perhaps also your transport there. Some people find the idea of a day centre off-putting, but look around: you may find a particular luncheon club or day centre more amenable than you expect (pages 230–34). Or if your council is subsidizing your support under Direct Payments (pages 297–306) you can simply take its money, add some of your own if you wish, and get a hot meal and company wherever you choose.

A further alternative to meals-on-wheels is help with the preparation of food in your own home. As we have seen, there is a wide range of often inexpensive aids available (pages 93–4). If you still cannot manage unaided, the council might send in somebody to help you prepare food, carrying out just those tasks you cannot manage. If such help would not be enough to warrant a care worker making a special trip, perhaps it could be combined with help with other tasks. If you can persuade the council to support you in continuing to cook for yourself, you retain control over the choice of your main meal.

Shopping
For those who have trouble getting around, a council will often propose a shopping service. Care workers, usually from agencies,

used to carry out this function, sometimes accompanying the older person; increasingly, councils are using supermarket home delivery services. The latter are normally their cheapest option, but while it can be convenient to have heavy items brought to your door, life can be bleak if you never get to go round the shops. This is not just a matter of varying your environment, but also of exercising choice informed by seeing what is on offer. So if you need help to go shopping which cannot be provided by some kind of mobility aid, stress your need to get out and about, to continue to participate in the outside world and to retain control over as many areas of your life as you possibly can.

Preparing for the Assessment

Before the community care assessment takes place, there are things you can do to maximize your chances of getting the most out of it.

1. Self-assessment

Think beforehand about what help you need. You could keep a diary over a week and jot down the things which cause you special difficulty. Write down how long it takes you to carry out tasks which you feel justify help. Be prepared to negotiate. If you feel you need help with preparing a midday meal, maybe you could manage the washing up as long as you are promised aid with cooking.

You should be looking for help to help yourself, as the new Domiciliary Care Regulations and Standards make clear (page 267). In the past, social services have often sent in workers who do things in a way which undermines people's morale and self-esteem and probably makes them lose faculties at a greater rate than they otherwise might. Things should be different now. Try to think through the sort of services you would really like to have. If you can get an idea beforehand about the type of solutions to your problems your council favours, so much the better: that will give you time to consider whether you think they are right for you. If your needs are considerable, try to find out the maximum amount social services might subsidize your care at home, so that you have some idea of the boundaries of discussion. Some councils publicize this figure; many are reluctant to broadcast it, so you may have to probe. Often councils subsidise support in the home up to the amount charged by a local care home for low-dependency care, which might be £320 per week.

2. Commissioning Services

As we have seen (pages 260–66), you can of course buy in any services a local authority might provide yourself, if you can afford to do so. Many people do not realise that if you get into bed with your council, you can still commission additional services privately on top of those which your local authority is prepared to support. You actually have a real incentive to do this. The government framework within which councils draw up a formula for charging people for community care requires that when they assess the income of elderly citizens they must disregard any payments those citizens are making to buy services related to their disability.[33] These can include: purchase of disability-related equipment; payment for an alarm system; the costs of special clothing or footwear, or additional wear and tear to clothing and footwear caused by disability; any heating costs above the average levels for the area and housing type; specialist washing powders or laundry; special dietary needs; the costs of a gardener, cleaner or domestic help, if necessitated by the individual's disability and not met by social services; and the costs of any privately arranged care, including respite care. So consider whether you wish to commission or buy any of these things before the assessment, ideally in the light of what you know your council is usually prepared to support.

3. Watch Out

If your council is one of those which is pleased to arrange and pay for sophisticated and generous support in the home, you may find your assessment and care plan go without a hitch. If, however, your council has other priorities, expect to fight. Such councils may underestimate or ignore your needs, put forward inadequate proposals (often too little, too late) or neglect to give you important information. They may also try other dodges.

One is to persuade you to move into sheltered housing, not in order to enhance your life, but to get the benefit of a resident warden, so social services can cut down on community care services. The reality is that the role of wardens or sheltered housing scheme managers is not to provide personal care services or even practical care, but to manage the building, to summon help in an emergency and to provide a friendly presence. However, many wardens are kind-hearted people who do help residents in various ways, collecting a little shopping for them perhaps, or organizing social activities. A social services department may thus calculate that it can cut down on community care services where there is a warden around. There can be advantages in moving to sheltered housing, but you do need to think it through very carefully first (pages 177–201).

Another way in which councils may avoid the cost of care in the home is by getting older people who have capital tied up in their own homes to enter into care homes, even when they could, with help, remain at home, and would prefer to do so. This may seem strange, since life in a care home is likely to cost a great deal more than even a very large amount of care in one's own home. But the money that pays for care-home care is not solely the local authority's: much of it comes from central government and the residents themselves, through their savings and the sale of any property they possess. This is because the local authority steps in to pay for people living in care homes only once those people have got through much of their own assets, until their savings (including the proceeds from the sale of their house or flat) are depleted to about £19,500. [34] However, much more of the money to pay for care in people's own homes comes from the local authority's eldercare budget, even if the recipients have to make some contribution. A local council cannot force you to enter a care home: it cannot evict you from your own home. But by controlling how much money will be spent on enabling you to live in your own home, it can effectively push you out of it.

In Scotland, things are different. The Scottish Parliament has abolished charges for personal care for older people, whether living in their own home or in a care home. This does not obliterate all charges (in care homes residents still have to pay for their accommodation costs and meals, and at home for practical services such as housework and shopping). But this step will certainly do much to remove the perverse pressure to turn elderly people out of their homes. In England, Wales and Northern

Ireland, free personal care is not being introduced in any setting, so the situation remains unchanged.

The Local Authority Route

Once your needs are set down in a community care assessment, the council will come to a decision about those it will meet with human help and set this down in a care plan. Who is going to provide this help and how? If you go to social services where help in the home is concerned, there are three possibilities:

• The in-house team of care workers employed by your local authority
• Care workers hired by an agency with which your local authority has a contract
• Care worker(s) whom you hire independently yourself, using money from the council (under the system known as Direct Payments).

In most cases, Direct Payments are better than the first two alternatives, and certainly much better than the second (pages 297–306). However, it is not always easy to get your council to operate through a Direct Payment and some people may prefer another route.

If you are given a choice between the first two options, try to get your council to send you its own in-house workers. These will almost certainly be better trained than those from a private care agency and their recruitment will have involved more rigorous screening. However, you cannot insist on this course, and some councils, particularly outside Scotland, now have only small teams of in-house workers as a result of privatization in the 1990s.

If social services organize community care for you, and in particular if private agencies are to get the work done, there are a number of things to bear in mind. People who organize services independently of social services but who use agencies might also care to read on.

Monitoring

Make sure that social services and/or the care agency have put in place an adequate system for recording attendance by care workers. A time sheet, with space for each care worker to insert time of arrival and departure and for the care recipient to sign to confirm the times, is essential. Otherwise, no proof that the care worker actually called will be provided. An even better time sheet will also have space for the care worker to add any note or comment for the use of the next health or social care worker who calls – for instance, that the client was not keen to eat breakfast and might be sickening for something. Time sheets which have a space for each task to be ticked off by the client also provide an *aide-mémoire* for scrupulous workers who, provided with an incomplete brief from their agency and rushing to get to the next client, may simply forget.

Time sheets have their downsides. People with a sight impairment or dementia may not be able to sign them reliably. Some people may feel too intimidated to flag up deficiencies and sign off false claims to keep the worker and the agency happy. Many older people worry about signing forms: 'What am I signing?' But time sheets are certainly better than nothing. Because of such difficulties and the importance of monitoring care workers, new devices have become available. One uses the client's telephone or the worker's mobile and a call tracing system which indicates the location of the care worker, another a smart card which is slotted into the mobile phone to show that the worker is in a particular house.

A more effective inducement to monitoring may be through the *National Minimum Standards for Domiciliary Care* (pages 53 and 268–9). Number 16 of the standards published for England, entitled 'Records Kept in the Home', states: 'With the user's consent, care or support workers record on records kept in the home of service users the time and date of every visit to the home, the service provided and any significant occurrence.' The standard insists that clients (whom it calls 'service users') should be informed about what is written on the record and have access to it. It explains that the records should include the time and dose of any medication given on a special chart, any financial transactions undertaken on behalf of the client, any accident (however minor) to the client or the care worker, and details of any changes in the client's circumstances, health, physical condition or care needs.

The Task

Care workers have plenty of opportunity to omit particular tasks or do the minimum only where the care recipients are not in a position to monitor performance themselves. Some care workers deliberately neglect to carry out tasks which they know they are supposed to perform.

Before the first care worker arrives, make sure that you have a copy of your (or your relative's) community care plan and that you also have a copy of the instructions which your local authority is proposing to send to the agency, so that if they are incorrect or are not comprehensive, you can try to get them changed. When my mother's social services department organized agency help for her, she and I were endlessly baffled by agency people turning up incorrectly briefed. When I tried to clarify what they should be doing, especially if I tried to make small amendments in the light of the situation on the ground, the social services care manager became annoyed.

However, consumers now have a golden means of clarifying what care workers should be doing which was not available to me and my mother in the late 1990s: the 'personal service user plan' – a novel concept which translates the community care assessment into a detailed brief for care workers (page 269). Some social services departments are not likely to draw users' attention to this provision, at least in the immediate future, as it would entail considerable extra work for them, so be ready to draw it to their attention if need be. Do not be fobbed off with the line that such plans will be introduced only for new users. If they are right for new users, they are right for old ones. Ask for a plan to be drawn up. If your council and/or the agency is slow to respond, draft one yourself and invite them to comment. If they still do not come up with the goods, complain to the agency, to social services and also complain (or at least threaten to do so) to the National Care Standards Commission or its equivalent.

One other standard of the *Domiciliary Care Regulations* which should be useful in clarifying your arrangement with an agency is Number 4, which entitles each user to a written contract or statement of the terms and conditions under which care is provided. This should specify:

- name, address and telephone number of agency
- contact number for out-of-hours and emergency service
- contact number for the office of regular care workers and their manager
- areas of activity which homecare or support workers will and will not undertake and the degree of flexibility in the provision of personal care
- circumstances in which the service may be cancelled or withdrawn, including temporary cancellation by the service user
- fees payable for the service, and by whom
- rights and responsibilities of both parties (including insurance) and liability if there is a breach of contract or any damage occurring in the home
- arrangements for monitoring and review of needs and for updating the assessment and the individual service user care plan
- process for assuring the quality of the service, monitoring and supervision of staff
- supplies and/or equipment to be made available by the service user and by the agency
- respective responsibilities of the service user and of the agency in relation to health and safety matters
- arrangements to cover holidays and sickness
- keyholding and other arrangements agreed for entering or leaving the home.

Confidentiality, handling money, giving medication, preventing infection and safety in the home are some of the other aspects of care workers' tasks and behaviour which could prove helpful to you. For instance, on safety in the home, Standard 15 stipulates that protocols should be in place covering the action to be taken when a worker is unable to gain entry. This is very important. Some care workers, on ringing the front door bell of an elderly client and receiving no answer, drop their card through the letterbox and drive off, even though clients might be unable to answer the door because they are unwell, and so in greater need of help than usual.

If you have a concern about any aspect of domiciliary care, the chances are that the standards will have something to say about it. So do get hold of those published for your part of the UK (page 53).

Obstructive Rules
Although the social worker or care manager may give you the impression that 'the rules' are set in stone, they may turn out not to be. Two examples. One woman was told by her council that her agency-provided care worker could only shop for her within geographical limits which prevented the worker from taking the bus a few stops to the supermarket which stocked the goods the woman preferred. As a result, the worker was forced to walk to other shops within the approved zone but not served by a direct bus service. This took up much of the allotted time and prevented her from buying the goods which the client wanted. After protest, it emerged that the council's apparently inviolable decree could easily be amended.

The same London borough had arranged for elderly people unable to do their own shopping to have goods delivered weekly from a local supermarket. Orders were phoned in one day and the goods were delivered the next. So far, so good. However, the delivery company insisted that the clients should pay for their shopping by cheque or credit card, although many preferred using cash. As a result of group protest, the procedure was amended and the company now accepts cash, although this costs the council more.

Reassessment
Your needs for community care services may be reassessed at any time and if they are, you want to know that this is happening so you can think beforehand about what you want to say and arrange to have somebody with you if you wish.

Why might you be reassessed? The obvious reason is that your needs have changed: perhaps you have been in hospital and what you can and cannot do for yourself has changed. Perhaps you feel that you need more help because, say, your arthritis has worsened, so you ask the local authority for a reassessment. But beware of a third reason why you may be reassessed: your local authority has decided that it does not want to spend as much money on you as it has up until now. It is not allowed simply to stop or scale down services it is already providing – it can do so only if, after reassessing you, it decides that your needs are not what they were.

Joint Assessments

Joint assessments by the NHS and social services were promised in the *National Service Framework for Older People*. In 2002 the Department of Health issued *Guidance on the Single Assessment Process for Older People* (Health Service Circular 2002/001, Local Authority Circular 2002/1), which is available from the Department of Health. In this circular, the government points out that it expects the different organizations and professionals involved in the support of older people – social services departments, hospitals, GPs and so on – to carry out joint assessments much more often. The purpose of what it calls 'the single assessment process' is essentially to reduce duplication, so that lots of different professionals are not carrying out similar assessments, and to try to get better-informed decision-making through joint working.

Joint assessment is not as straightforward as it sounds; the different professionals often have different approaches and may know little about each other's work. GPs, for instance, may know little about the funding of homecare support, which is currently channelled through social services. The single assessment process does not replace the community care assessment, which is a statutory tool in which consumers have been provided with rights. In a sense, the community care assessment is already a type of joint assessment in that while social services take the lead, other professionals should be involved if their expertise is relevant.

The single assessment process guidance does, however, usefully emphasize the importance of supporting the independence of older people and giving them what they and their carers say they want, rather than imposing off-the-shelf services:

> At all times, older people should expect respect and courtesy from health and social care professionals who are helping them. They should expect assessments of their needs to begin with their perspective, and for their views to be kept to the fore throughout the assessment and subsequent stages of care planning and service

delivery. They should expect assessment to focus not only on their needs, but also on the strengths and abilities they can bring to bear in addressing these needs, and for assessment to help them achieve maximum possible independence. Assessment should take account of support older people receive from family members, relatives, friends and neighbours, and whether these carers have needs in their own right.[35]

The Supporting People Programme

Some older people will be assessed for housing-related support. This arises from a new initiative called Supporting People, introduced in April 2003 throughout the UK, administered by local authority social services departments and area offices of the Northern Ireland Housing Executive. Its basic objective is to enable vulnerable people to live independently but, unlike the community care system, the means of achieving this is by supporting their housing arrangements. However, although the scheme could cover older people living in any form of housing tenure except care homes and long-stay NHS units and may do so in Scotland, in England its benefits have been conferred mainly on council and housing association tenants.

How the system will work will vary across the country with the energy local authorities put into bidding for Supporting People money from central government and the priorities they apply. People renting housing association sheltered housing or council accommodation and already receiving the means-tested Housing Benefit may not notice a re-sourcing of their funding, but they may see an improvement in the services on offer.

These services may not correspond to those often available in sheltered housing. Supporting People has been devised for other groups as well as older people, such as people with learning difficulties (who may have trouble with paperwork) and homeless people who are given a tenancy but are unable to sustain it because they cannot manage their money sufficiently to pay the rent and bills. This means that the services offered are different from those which have usually emerged out of a community care assessment: one from which an older person might benefit is help with paperwork involving paying household bills, which can be very valuable. Help with organizing things is also the sort of thing to look for from Supporting People – say, help to arrange transport to a community centre or for shopping to be brought in, or for your windows to be cleaned. But Supporting People money will not actually pay for the transport, shopping service or window-cleaning.

It is all slightly complicated and, at the moment, uncertain. But watch this space. Your council may be one of those (like, for example, Manchester City, West Dunbartonshire or the London borough of Camden) which is thinking of innovative ways of helping older people through this new route. Or it may be one which will do so in a year or two. The category of older people likely to benefit most in the early years is sheltered housing tenants, simply because the sort of services which Supporting People could help fund will already be in place or could be assembled relatively easily, such as the provision of measures to keep accommodation safe and secure including alarm systems, the provision of social activities by a warden, and help with filling in forms.

Local authorities do not have to charge for Supporting People services, but they probably will. They will carry out a financial assessment to work out what proportion of the cost of a service the recipient should contribute. People who already receive Housing Benefit are unlikely to be charged.

Only those on fairly low incomes are eligible for Housing Benefit, but local authorities use a more generous means-testing system when they are assessing what if anything older people should contribute towards the cost of community care services.

Charging for Community Care Services

Once social services have sorted out which community care services you will receive, they will work out charges for them. Whoever conducted the community care assessment, or a colleague, will calculate what percentage of the actual cost of services they will charge to you, bearing in mind the authority's policy on charging and, in Scotland (see below), a significant new state handout. In arriving at the final figure, the council will probably take into account not only the amount of care you will be receiving and its cost, but also your income and your savings. The council should then write and tell you how much it intends to charge you and how it has calculated that figure. It should not simply start sending you a monthly bill. If it does, protest. Councils know they should not do this, as Department of Health guidance in England clearly states:

> Once a person's care needs have been assessed and a decision has been made about the care to be provided, an assessment of ability to pay charges should be carried out promptly, and written information about any charges assessed as payable, and how they have been calculated, should be communicated promptly. This should normally be done before sending a first bill. Charges should not be made for any period before an assessment of charges has been communicated to the user.[37]

The best councils set out precisely how they calculate charges for services. Unfortunately, many other councils volunteer only very scanty information, but should still produce information on charging if asked. The Department of Health guidance mentioned above states: 'Clear information about charges and how they are assessed should be readily available for users and carers . . . Information should be made available at the time a person's needs for care are assessed.'

If you have trouble getting hold of this information – or understanding it – contact an organization in your locality which is likely to have experience of this subject, such as the Citizen's Advice Bureau, an Age Concern group, a carers' centre or a disability organization. Such bodies may also provide further help if you decide formally to challenge the charge the council is proposing to make.

What you have to pay for homecare varies hugely council by council: this is the ultimate postcode lottery. Somebody receiving personal care in their home might face a charge of more than £100 a week more for the same service than somebody elsewhere in England or Wales in identical personal financial circumstances, according to an Audit Commission report in 1999.[38] Thus in one place you might be charged £20 for a total three hours' home care per week; in another area, £40.

In deciding how to charge for homecare services, councils are making political decisions. The key decision is whether to penalise wealthier citizens or people who need a high level of service. Through a means test, your council may assess your income and such assets as it wishes to take into account, and charge you more the more you have; the result will be that better-off older people using services will be subsidising those worse off. Or your council may impose a series of flat-rate charges, so everyone pays the same, regardless of means, for the same level of service: the more you need, the more you pay, so people of modest means who need a high level of support carry the most onerous financial burden. The Audit Commission found that just over half of councils combine these two approaches, varying their charge to one individual both with the level of services he or she receives and his or her ability to pay.

In Scotland a very significant change to all this was introduced in 2002, when the Scottish Parliament introduced free personal care throughout the country. There has been a misconception that free care for elderly people in Scotland applies only to the residents of care homes. This is not the case. There are certainly changes there too (pages 389–90), but the new provisions also have the potential to alter very substantially the financial position of people receiving care services in their own homes.

Now, every person aged 65 or over living in Scotland who is receiving personal care services after a needs assessment by their local authority should not have to pay for that personal care. Those charges should simply be deducted from the bill before the older person receives it. This provision does not affect entitlement to state benefits such as Attendance Allowance, which people can go on receiving alongside free personal care in their own home. However, people will still be liable to pay for other, non-personal services such as housework, shopping, meals-on-wheels and attendance at day centres. Charges for gadgets and house adaptations are also unaffected by free personal care (although these may be free anyway). The new system is explained in two publications by the Scottish Executive.[39]

Wherever you live in the UK, it is important to be clear from the outset what your local authority proposes to charge you for domiciliary services, for two main reasons. First, the charges may be so high that you decide not to get involved with the council at all, but to operate entirely privately. Second, you may want to dispute the charges. Local authorities are required by law to impose charges on anyone only when these are 'reasonable' and 'practicable for him to pay'.[40] These grounds enable you to challenge the charge, or even ask for it to be waived altogether. But you want to get any disagreement sorted out as soon as possible, lest you find yourself getting into arrears.

If you refuse to pay a community care charges bill, your council cannot withdraw the service. The guidance states: 'Once someone has been assessed as needing a service, that service should not be withdrawn because the user refuses to pay the charge.'[41] However, if you do refuse to pay and it is subsequently confirmed that the council was entitled to what it demanded, you may find yourself running up debts which the council will be entitled to pursue.

The Audit Commission discovered that certain councils in England and Wales were charging so much that some recipients ended up with less money to live on than the amount they would have received on Income Support (or the Guarantee Credit element of Pension Credit, as it is now called in the case of older people, see page 491). This criticism helped prompt the government to issue new guidance to local councils in England in 2002 called *Fairer Charging Policies for Homecare and Other Non-residential Social Services*.[42] This document makes it plain that councils will continue to have substantial discretion in the design of charging policies, but must now ensure that their charges leave all recipients with an income at least 25 per cent above the level of Guarantee Credit to which they would be entitled. Individuals do not have to be receiving Income Support for this protection to apply to them. If charges your council wishes to make would reduce your income below Guarantee Credit plus 25 per cent, then you should ask your council to reduce its charges or even waive them. If you are already at the Guarantee Credit plus 25 per cent level, then you should not expect to have to pay for homecare.

There are several other things worth checking when you receive your notification of charges.

• See whether you are going to receive any subsidy from the council. Better-off people whose councils target support at low-income users may be charged at a rate close to or even substantially above that of private providers. In this case you may decide to go private. Even if you are relatively poor, you may find you are better off staying outside, perhaps because you are receiving a low level of service but are hit by a flat-rate payment level which is relatively high.

- If you would receive no subsidy for homecare services, do not assume that the community care assessment is a waste of time. There may be some non-homecare but still community care services into which your council happens to put a lot of subsidy and charges users relatively little. Day centre attendance and meals-on-wheels are often charged on a different basis from personal and practical services in the home. Some councils put a lot of subsidy into day centres and charge all users relatively little.

- Check that when the council assesses your wealth it is not taking into consideration the capital tied up in your property. The new guidance clearly says that while councils can consider savings, the value of any property should be excluded. It also says that if somebody's savings are being used up by charges for domiciliary care, the council should make provision for those charges to be reviewed.

- Check that the council is deducting the costs you are already incurring on services purchased because of your frailty or disability when it calculates your assessable income. For instance, you may be spending more money than you otherwise would on laundry costs because you suffer from night-time incontinence, or you may have spent a lot of money buying a hearing aid or an electric scooter. Your council may well not ask you whether any of this applies. But it should be deducting costs such as these before it establishes your assessable income.[43] So keep the receipts for any of these services and for any pieces of equipment which you have bought out of your own pocket to cope with any disability or frailty, and make sure the council deducts these as well as any other relevant costs in calculating your assessable income. Councils should have been doing this in the past, but the Audit Commission report (see page 293) found that only a third of councils were doing so. If consumers were unaware of this facility and so did not take it up with their council, they were foregoing a considerable amount of money.

- Check that all your income is assessed net of any income tax, National Insurance contributions as well as housing costs such as council tax you are paying (after receiving any Council Tax Benefit).
- Check that you are not being charged for any health service provision. You should not be paying for any health services, even if they are put in place at the same time as your social care services and as a result of a community care assessment. On page 56 I quote the government statement on the range of health services which should be provided free, such as the care of terminally ill people. 'Intermediate care' which can be provided in a person's home and should also be free is discussed on pages 422–6.

In addition, the Scottish Executive has decreed that all social services authorities north of the border should provide free homecare for up to four weeks for an older person who has been in hospital, even if for no more than one day: the older person does not have to be terminally ill, for example. Most councils outside Scotland will not go this far, but it is worth asking whether special exemptions from community care charging operate if you or your relative is in this situation.

As you can imagine, charging for domiciliary services can be the subject of very bitter struggles between councils and clients. It is one of the main causes of complaints to local councils. Try first of all to resolve any difficulty by talking and writing to social services. If they have deliberately or inadvertently failed to take into account a cost which should have been included in your financial assessment, write and point this out to them: it should result in their adjusting their calculations. If you consider that you cannot afford to pay the charge the council is asking, request a formal review: if you can convince the council that you are too poor to pay the amount they wish to charge, they ought to reduce or waive it.

Direct Payments

If you hire help in the home privately, you keep control of who comes and what they do, but you have to foot the entire bill yourself. If you go through social services, you take advantage of public subsidy, but you can find yourself in a system over which you have little control. But suppose your local council did its community care assessment and drew up its care plan, and rather than organizing the resultant provision it gave you the money it would otherwise have spent and told you to make the arrangements yourself, you would have the advantages of both approaches without the main disadvantages. Good news! Such a system has indeed been devised, and it recently came on to the statute book. It is called Direct Payments.

As with many of the most consumer-friendly parts of the eldercare machine, Direct Payments was the result of campaigning by groups representing disabled adults – people in their thirties or forties, perhaps blind or in wheelchairs, who wished to live as independent and mainstream a life as possible. The last thing such people wanted was for bureaucrats to organize all their homecare support: they wanted as much control and choice as possible in this as in all other areas. Their campaigning bore fruit in the Community Care (Direct Payments) Act 1996, which enabled local authorities in England and Wales to offer a payment to a disabled person instead of a service, and legislation has followed in Scotland and Northern Ireland.

The 1996 Act did not apply to people over the age of 65, even if they came within the definition of 'disabled'. But campaigning by organizations representing older people led to the removal of this restriction in 2000, so that older people assessed as needing community care could receive Direct Payments. The only qualification for older people to receive Direct Payments is that their council must have decided that they should receive community care services to help them live independently and that they must be 'willing' and 'able' to take on Direct Payments, which means they have to consent and have to be capable of exercising choice over who should do what.

How It Works

Under Direct Payments, care recipients take on both the advantages and disadvantages of being in charge of their own staff. They have ultimate responsibility for recruiting people, paying them, sorting out difficulties, getting themselves covered by employers' liability insurance and so on. For a frail older person that can seem daunting. However, the government has said that people receiving Direct Payments should be able to receive as much support as they need to administer them.

The government has made it clear in guidance to local councils that no one should automatically be barred from Direct Payments, perhaps because they are blind or have dementia. Each case must be assessed individually.[44] All that is necessary is that the person should be capable of exercising ultimate choice over who, what and when, since the provision of more choice to consumers is the ultimate objective.

This does not mean that it will necessarily always be easy to get Direct Payments: the 'willing' and 'able' qualifications apply. Some councils are still likely to obstruct older people who wish to have them and neglect to volunteer information about them (although, as we shall see on page 306, local authorities in England and Scotland have recently become obliged by law to offer people the Direct Payments option). Nonetheless readers throughout the UK are still likely to have to challenge councils who say, 'We never/cannot give Direct Payments to elderly people.'

In some parts of the UK, mainly in the larger urban areas, support systems are already in place to help younger disabled adults administer their Direct Payments. Now that elderly people are eligible for Direct Payments, these support schemes are widening their client base and other schemes are being developed by local voluntary organizations for elderly people and by local authorities themselves. What these schemes do varies: some will operate your payroll for you, others will not. Many will, however, help with recruiting staff and giving people all the information they need and much support in the fields already discussed when we looked at hiring staff independently – that is, insurance, health and safety at work, contracts of employment and so on (pages 261–4). If such a system exists in your area, you are likely to find the operation of Direct Payments much easier.

If you have access to the Internet, look on the website of the National Centre for Independent Living. This Centre grew out of a group of disabled people who lobbied for the introduction of Direct Payments, but is now funded by the Department of Health to provide information to local authorities and potential users about the system. It has information about support centres throughout the UK. These are increasing in number all the time.

You can also obtain information through an organization called Direct Payments Scotland.

Under the system in place in Kingston-upon-Thames, for example, the voluntary organization which administers Direct Payments for the council, the Independent Living Scheme (ILS), receives all the money for those in the scheme from the council and allocates it quarterly. The council tells the ILS the number of hours of support which each recipient has been assessed as needing, and this is multiplied by an hourly figure to give the total sum. The funding which the ILS sends to each client also covers additional costs some will have to pay, such as National Insurance and paid holidays. The ILS does not operate a payroll, so clients have to send payments to their employees and to the Inland Revenue themselves and keep accounts, but the ILS is on hand to provide much back-up advice.

It is possible to run a Direct Payments scheme without the help of one of these support structures: it is no different from hiring help yourself, except that a part – possibly a large part – of the bill is paid for you. You simply open a dedicated bank account, pay your cheque from your local council into that account, and make the payments to your care workers or personal assistants from it, together with other relevant payments such as employers' liability insurance. Use the advice earlier in this chapter on hiring help independently, and/or booklets available from organizations such as the National Centre for Independent Living. There will also be some monitoring requirements, such as time sheets and receipts.

Social services departments are supposed to provide as much support as recipients of Direct Payments need, so if there is no support system, your social worker ought to be able to provide some assistance, but he or she cannot take on responsibility for running the system for you. Recipients can appoint somebody else, perhaps a son, daughter or partner, to act on their behalf as an agent, or can set up a trust to administer it involving three or four trustees who could, for instance, include a solicitor.

Advantages
The advantages of going down the Direct Payments route can be summarized as follows:

Choice

Under the social services system, whether care is provided by a local council's in-house workers or through an agency, choice is minimal for the client. Under Direct Payments, however, you choose whom you want to come into your home, how you want them to look after you and what you want them to do. Choice pervades every area. Because you recruit your own staff, you are in a position to choose somebody you consider will be competent, reasonably flexible, reliable, understand your needs, will treat you with respect and with whom you will have a good working relationship.

You choose how the total amount of money is to be spent. If you wish, you can offer a lower hourly rate for less skilled tasks but a higher rate for, say, getting somebody to drive you places or to do paperwork.

Because you choose how the money should be spent, it is a good idea to get the needs which must be met through the Direct Payments as widely drawn as possible, to ensure you have the maximum flexibility. If the care plan states that you need a total of two hours a week to help you prepare a meal at lunchtime, your room for manoeuvre is more limited than if the care plan simply states 'the provision of support to make meals'. Even more ideally, the plan would say 'support to live in his or her own home'. We have already seen that it is a good idea to have a need for social contact or to integrate into the local community set down in your care plan. This would allow you to get your helper to take you out when you wanted to go. You thus enter a completely different world from that in which social services lay on meals-on-wheels day after day for you to consume in isolation.

Clearly, if part of your Direct Payment is to enable you to do your shopping, you decide whether to ask your local supermarket to deliver your groceries, or pay somebody to accompany you to the shops or go out and do the shopping for you, or whether you do one thing one week and another the next. You might be able to save money by getting groceries delivered and then use the money you have saved to get your helper to take you out somewhere different – so long as the trip can be seen to be meeting your assessed needs.

Familiarity

If you hire somebody through Direct Payments (or indeed, of course, hire them privately yourself independently of the council) you get the same person each time, so there is no question of having to explain to yet another stranger how you like something done. Since the care may involve helping with showering or bathing or dressing, it is a good idea to have one person you know and are familiar with, rather than lots of different people.

Independence

Under social services, you are expected to refer back to your care manager if changing circumstances mean you want your helper to do something slightly different or work for a slightly longer period or at a different time, even if it is only for one day. This is time-consuming and can be irritating, particularly if your social worker is out and you want to contact him or her immediately. Under Direct Payments you can do what you like. You decide whether you want chicken Kiev or beans on toast: you are at liberty to set down the tasks you expect care workers to be performing.

Security

It is good to know the background of the person who is coming into your home. Scrupulous agencies should send you honest and reputable people, but you do have that extra sense of security if you have taken out the references and seen up-to-date Criminal Records Bureau reports yourself. You are also in a better position to make it absolutely clear the extent to which you wish your personal situation to be treated as confidential.

Consistency

You enjoy a consistent service, and as a result can begin to forget about completing day-to-day tasks and devote more of your energy to less mundane matters.

Neighbourliness

If your assistant lives locally and the assistants of other people do too, you get an increasing sense of people looking after each other in the same area, which enhances the sense of a mutually supportive community and may in turn lead to improvements to the wider environment, such as to streets and public parks.

Responsibilities

Direct Payments offer much flexibility and choice, but it is clearly important that recipients should use the money for the purposes for which it is being given – to meet the assessed needs written down in their care plan. If they start using the money for some other purpose, the council is entitled to protest, and this may lead to the withdrawal of the Direct Payments facility and a demand for the repayment of the misspent money.

For example, if you are receiving Direct Payments money for help with personal care and you use it to buy aromatherapy, or if you are receiving a payment to commission housework but get the helper to do the decorating, you will be in trouble. Not only will you be misusing public funds, but you will also be missing out on help which you have been assessed as needing. The rules say you cannot pay a partner living with you in the same household or a close relative living nearby under the scheme. However, local authorities are empowered to make an exception for relatives living outside the household – perhaps if you live in a remote rural area where it is difficult to find somebody else to provide help.

Are Direct Payments available to people who are already receiving council-organized community care? The answer is yes. You can come out of the social services system – there is nothing to make you remain there forever. Or you can mix and match, organizing some of your services through Direct Payments but getting social services to organize the remainder. This is a good way of trying out Direct Payments if you are nervous about them. There again, you could use Direct Payments for a discrete period. For instance, suppose you have had some mishap such as a fall and have been assessed as needing to go into a care home to recover. Instead, you could press for a Direct Payment for, say, six weeks in order to hire support. Bear in mind that if Direct Payments do not work for you, you could come back into the social services system as a safety net. If you are in the social services system at the moment and wish to switch to Direct Payments, a good time to do this is when social services reassess your needs, either on their own initiative or as a result of a request from you.

People can also receive Direct Payments to buy services they are assessed as needing which are not provided in the home, such as day care or attendance at a day centre. If you are, say, looking after your mother as a carer and have been the subject of a carer's assessment for the services and equipment you need in this role (pages 556–68), you can opt to receive these things through a Direct Payment too. Also, if you are assessed as needing certain equipment and you wish to make the choice yourself, you can opt for a Direct Payment, in which case you receive a voucher from the local authority for the equipment. You can then, if you wish, top up the voucher to enable you to buy a more expensive wheelchair, mobility aid or whatever.

Disadvantages
There are, however, some disadvantages to Direct Payments. You have the responsibility for recruiting your own staff. No matter how much support you receive, there can be difficulties, particularly in areas of high employment. If you are offering say, 5, 10 or 15 hours work a week, that does not provide anyone with a full-time job. What is more, you may want someone to work at quite a difficult time, such as the early morning or the evening. The sort of people who become personal assistants are sometimes looking after their own children. This means that they will want clients who can be flexible around family arrangements and the needs of young children. Or the personal assistant may be somebody who has three or four elderly or disabled people to work for. So you have to accept that your assistant is also working for somebody else, who may perhaps have sudden problems which will require your assistant to stay with them a little longer than usual. (From the assistant's point of view, the work can be varied and interesting. Indeed, a new class of job is growing up – personal assistant to disabled or elderly people, involving anything from driving to providing home hairdressing, help with paperwork or personal care.)

If you are stuck and cannot find a helper, you could fall back on an agency. There is nothing to stop you using your Direct

Payments to pay a care agency. As the holder of the contract with the agency, you are in a better position than you would be under social services to influence the choice of agency staff you are sent. However, I found that it is quite difficult to do this: you may meet the person whom the agency says it is going to send in to help, but in a world in which there is a high staff turnover and shortage of staff, you may soon find somebody else being sent in instead.

The other main drawback is the responsibility of being an employer. You have to make sure you are keeping accounts books up to date and sending payments to your employee and to the Inland Revenue if necessary, not to speak of computing working families' tax credit. You may also have to deal with employment problems: what are you going to do if your employee is persistently late or not working to the job description? Government guidance says that recipients of Direct Payments should have as much support as required from councils. You may or may not get that, but in any case the final responsibility as an employer is yours. If you sack your worker, it is you, not the council, who could face a suit for unfair dismissal. If you find that you have perhaps unwittingly hired somebody who is seeking but has not been granted asylum, it is you who could be prosecuted.

If you are going to use Direct Payments, it is important to be aware that the new provisions for the registration of care agencies and social care workers and national minimum standards for domiciliary care may not benefit you directly unless you are using workers provided through an agency or another organization covered by the rules. However, there is no reason why you should not say that you expect your workers to conform to the national minimum standards.

One important point: although Direct Payments offer many advantages, they are not suitable for everybody and it is important to realize that you do not have to use this scheme if you do not want to. One disabled younger person I talked to was in a Direct Payments scheme because her council had never told her that an alternative existed. She needed a considerable amount of help, and organizing that help was not easy. She operated through care agencies because she felt too frail to hire staff herself. A friend came round weekly to help sort out the finances. Her council provided no administrative support what-soever, and the woman in question felt that the council was using this scheme as a means of palming off the bother of managing her care staff. Not only had her council never told her that it could organize her care; it had not obtained her consent to Direct Payments, except in so far as she understood that this was the only way to proceed.

Use

Despite the advantages of Direct Payments and the fact that support agencies report that those who receive them are very happy with them, few elderly people currently use them. In 2001, only 537 older people in England were receiving Direct Payments – less than 0.1 per cent of those receiving help in the home organized through their local authority. There is a reason for this. The culture of social care provision in Britain is one of local authorities doing things for people, of taking over and laying on services or accommodation in care homes, rather than only stepping in to help when it is absolutely necessary and allowing people the freedom to do as much as possible for them-selves. Direct Payments represent a challenge to this ethos, which many officials are disinclined to accept. At the same time, Direct Payments can upset councils' links with private and voluntary care agencies. Such agencies are unlikely to be happy to see large numbers of people opting for Direct Payments and hiring staff independently, as this will reduce the amount of work local councils will offer them – the more so if an agency's workers opt to leave *en masse* and set themselves up as personal assistants.

Despite local councils' lack of enthusiasm, central govern-ment is extremely keen on Direct Payments and the personal autonomy they provide. In 2003, the Department of Health published new guidance to local councils on how Direct Payments should operate. This is well worth reading.[45] But the Department of Health is not relying only on guidance to cajole and encourage: new regulations passed in 2003 now place a legal duty on local authorities in England to offer people assessed as needing community care services the Direct Payments option.[46] This move follows the passage of legislation in Scotland which has laid a similar requirement on councils.[47] So if your local council is lukewarm about working with you through Direct Payments, you can now insist that it does if you live in England or Scotland. Councils in Wales and Northern Ireland will be aware that their national governments are keeping an eye on the situation in case they should see fit to introduce a similar stick.

Conclusion

Different systems of organizing help in the home, whether private, through the council or under a Direct Payment, will suit some people but not others. Broadly speaking, if your local authority is energetic in its support of older people and has its own team of homecare workers, you are probably best off allowing it to arrange and provide help for you. If it is not, and if it does not have an in-house team of workers but if it farms out the task to care agencies, you may be better advised to proceed independently, particularly if the hourly rate you would have to pay an agency organized through the council is more than you would pay under a private arrangement. Or, you could take advantage of any public subsidy the council is offering but then organize and hire staff yourself through a Direct Payment.

Income is another factor to bear in mind, as this public subsidy is often means-tested. Rich or poor, if you have some degree of disability you should apply for Attendance Allowance and, in Scotland, free personal care. This will not, however, cover other types of help such as housework or somebody to do your shopping – in that case, you might opt to go entirely private. If all you need is a bit of help in the house and are not frail, wherever you live you probably would not be eligible for council help in any case. But if you are a local authority or housing association tenant, perhaps in sheltered housing, you might be eligible for quite a lot of help through Supporting People (pages 291–2).

If you need a lot of help in the home, it is worth bearing in mind other possible sources of funding. Some organizations like the Civil Service Benevolent Association and The Royal British Legion do sometimes help out – just as they may help top up care home bills with a small weekly payment. They may not provide very much, but it could make all the difference.

Part Four
Care Homes

Chapter 10
Choosing a Home

Basics

In the United Kingdom, 480,000 older people live in 25,000 care homes. This is about as many as live in sheltered housing, although the care home population tends to be older.[1] There are two main types of care home. The first is what used to be called (and often still is) a residential home. This is a place in which elderly people live under one roof, usually spending much of their time in communal sitting rooms, each normally with their own bedroom, though some share. They receive most of their meals in a common dining room, with staff on hand to help attend to personal care (such as washing, dressing, feeding, getting in and out of bed and using the lavatory) when necessary, and domestic services such as cleaning and laundry carried out by the home's staff.

The second main type of home is what used to be called a nursing home. Nursing homes have to employ more staff since residents have a higher level of dependency. Nursing homes also offer some nursing expertise: each shift must include a registered nurse. Nursing is a huge area and there will be some tasks the home's nurses cannot perform – perhaps syringing ears. For these, as for other medical services, people in nursing homes have as much right to free care through the NHS as people living in their own homes (pages 56–7 and 468–9).

The year 2002 saw major changes in state control of 'care homes'. One of these changes is that now residential and nursing homes are all supposed to be called care homes. However, they still vary in the same sorts of ways. The old residential homes are now called Care Home, PC (standing for 'personal care'); a nursing home is known as a Care Home, N (the 'N' denotes 'nursing'). Some homes take both low-dependency residents and those who need regular care from a qualified nurse. The other main category used to be called (and again often still is) EMI homes, standing for 'elderly mentally ill': such places care for people with diagnosed mental conditions, in particular, dementia. Now, the letters DE after a care home denote that it specializes in dementia care, MD stands for 'mental disorder' while PD stands for 'physical disabilities'. As it will take time for this new nomenclature to catch on, I use both types in this chapter, or, wherever possible, simply the generic term 'care home'.

Advantages

There is a tendency to view going into a care home as a wholly negative step. In fact, a lot of people living in care homes are very happy, even though leaving their own home may have been quite a wrench. Many find that once they have settled they are pleased to be free of the responsibilities of running their own home and catering for themselves. No longer do they have to worry about what they are going to eat and drink day by day, let alone whether the roof needs mending. In a care home there should be help on hand to provide personal care or just with moving around. Shunting off tasks such as cooking, shopping and cleaning to others means that care home residents have time to do other things, although physical and mental afflictions often prevent them from taking as much advantage of the time released as they would have done in their younger days. In addition, there will be some organized social activities and probably trips out as well and, of course, company. Many people assume that however difficult life is living in their own home, their quality of life there is bound to be better than if they were living in a care home, but this is not necessarily the case. The companionship and relationships that can develop in good care homes mean that people can have some of the best times of their life in this environment.

Disadvantages

However, there are many reasons why elderly people do not want to enter care homes. They may not wish to leave their own home and the independence as well as the memories it enshrines (pages 29–30). Moving into a care home inevitably involves loss of freedom in terms of many aspects of life which you have previously taken for granted, such as what you are going to eat and with whom you are going to share communal spaces and facilities, from the sitting room to the lavatory. If you need help with bathing and going to the loo, you may have to do these things when the home says you will. As a result of some inevitable timetabling of staff tasks, life in a care home can be quite regimented, although there are plenty of homes which will do their utmost to avoid an institutional atmosphere.

Moving to a care home also usually involves a reduction in personal living space: you may share extensive grounds and large sitting rooms with others, but your own personal space is almost certainly going to be a substantially smaller than you would have enjoyed in an ordinary house and even in a sheltered flat. You may be pleased that you no longer have to work a garden, but you may not be pleased that you no longer have any piece of earth with which you can do as you choose. Also, and importantly, your legal status in the home is less than that of a tenant in rented accommodation: you may in effect be paying the rent plus other costs to the care home proprietor, but you live there only under licence governed by terms set out in a business contract between the home and you, or the person or organization paying the bills. There are likely to be clauses in the contract which specify the grounds on which the home could terminate your contract and thus render you homeless – including not just non-payment of fees but also any circumstance or behaviour which the home's proprietor considers severely detrimental to the home or its residents. The 'behaviour' could in theory be that of members of the residents' families rather than residents themselves.

Ways In
Some people go into a care home temporarily, either for a rest or for rehabilitation after a spell in hospital. There are two main routes in for permanent residents.

Independently
Some elderly people enter care homes by themselves or with the help of children or other close relatives or friends, but independently of the social services departments of local authorities. For instance, a son may consider that his father is not coping well

and needs more support than he is currently receiving in his own home or in sheltered accommodation. He looks around for a care home for his father and persuades him to sell up and move in. Or perhaps an elderly lady, perfectly healthy and in her early eighties, feels she would like a change of living environment after the death of her husband, looks round some homes and then moves into one of them. If the person has enough money to pay care home bills until he or she dies, this approach seems to hold no drawbacks. But beware: it does.

Elderly people entering care homes off their own bat may not realize they could have carried on in their own home with the aid of additional support, such as pendant alarms to summon help in an emergency and visiting care workers. They may thus surrender their independence unnecessarily.

Several studies have revealed that a significant number of care home residents do not need to be there. A study of admissions to nursing homes in six areas of England and Wales in 1995–6 discovered that, were its findings extrapolated to the whole of these two countries, 6,750 of people admitted could have coped in a more independent environment, such as a residential home or in their own home.[2] Another study revealed that fewer than half of the sample of care home residents studied had been receiving any local authority organized home care before going in, which suggests they may not have had any information from social services when evaluating alternative courses of action.[3]

Sometimes it is not the older person, but their adult children who lack vital information about the alternatives, because it is the children who are the prime movers, touring homes on behalf of their parent. These close relatives, well-meaning as they may be, often have no idea of the range of help which could be brought into the elderly person's house, or the range of adaptations which could be made to it, or the gadgets which could be summoned up to solve apparently intractable problems. They may rely for this momentous decision on anecdotal information garnered over the years and the advice of the care home proprietors whose properties they view. Yet proprietors can hardly be expected to give entirely impartial, objective advice, and have a financial reason for playing down, to some extent at least, the downsides of going into a home.

Care Homes

- Many people enter care homes when they do not really need to.
- Don't assume you can find a care home in one weekend.
- Don't trust recommendations from other people when you are choosing.
- Don't assume that the best homes will be those which are most expensive.
- Selecting a care home should involve five stages:
  1. Trawling
  2. Touring the establishment
  3. Sitting and watching
  4. Analysis of the prospectus
  5. A trial stay
- Ask for a Deferred Payments Agreement if you don't want to sell the family home.
- Claim free nursing care (and, in Scotland, free personal care as well), even if you are well-off.
- Make sure your relative has a care plan.
- Arrange for regular meetings with the manager once your relative is a care home resident.
- Agree on a set of changes about which you will be consulted.
- Show appreciation to the staff.
- Team up with other relatives to organize trips out.
- Make sure your relative votes and stays in contact with the world outside.
- Provide maximum support on entry to the home.
- Get teeth, glasses and hearing aids labelled.
- Look out for national regulatcry body inspections.
- Be prepared to complain at any time to the manager, social services if appropriate, and the National Care Standards Commission or its equivalent.

Close relatives may be so concerned about 'dangers' in an elderly person's lifestyle that they pressure them to move to a care home where they will be 'safe'. Inevitably the relatives' idea of the proper balance will be conditioned by their own idea of an acceptable degree of risk, rather than the older person's, and perhaps a concern for their own peace of mind at the expense of the older person's real concerns. So elderly people can be vulnerable not only to their relatives' ignorance, but also to their preconceptions, likes and dislikes and even neuroses.

A daughter, perhaps, might be worried about cleanliness in her elderly father's house. Perhaps he suffers from night-time incontinence, does not move easily and so has trouble doing the laundry and taking a bath or shower. She operates under the misconception that somebody who becomes incontinent has to be looked after in a nursing home. Perhaps she is house-proud and is appalled at what she sees as grubby surroundings, for instance wallpaper discoloured by smoking. In addition, perhaps she finds the demands he makes irksome – pleas for help with household tasks and dealing with minor emergencies. Surely if he were sensible enough to go and live in a private nursing home, both his and her problems would all be solved?

Situations like this need unpicking very carefully before a decision is made to start looking for a care home. It may be the best solution, but the possibility of support in the person's home should be thoroughly investigated first. Talking to a local authority social worker or somebody on the national helpline of voluntary organizations can open relatives' eyes to an Aladdin's Cave of unexpected options. It can be highly productive to get a more informed decision. This is not just because it may reveal that a care home can be avoided. It may also improve your choice of care home if that is indeed the option selected.

Input from a geriatrician, accessed through a GP, can also be invaluable if your relative is suffering from, say, chronic lung disease which requires constant access to oxygen, or osteoporosis which is causing vertebrae to crumble and giving rise to much pain. Many people might assume that such conditions could be managed only in a care home, yet somebody coping with both might well be able to live for many years in their own home, with support.

Elderly people must pay part or all the cost of care home care if their total savings, including the value of any property, amount to more than about £19,500.[4] But when care home costs have brought a resident's resources below this level, their local authority should start chipping in. Once the resident's savings are depleted to about £12,000,[5] the council takes over responsibility for meeting the fees, with the resident contributing only their State Retirement Pension and any state benefits: they keep what remains of their savings. But the council will only contribute in this way, paying care home fees for the remainder of the person's life, if a community care assessment at the stage at which its help is sought indicates that care home provision is a necessity. If the council decides after its assessment that you do not need to be in a care home, you will have to look for alternative accommodation, perhaps private rented property. If the council concedes that you do need care home accommodation, you could be in trouble if the fees are higher that those the council normally pays. It can use its discretion to pay more, but if it does not, either you must persuade the care home proprietor to let you remain but charge what the local council is prepared to pay, or you have to find a benefactor (usually a hard-pressed relative) to pay the difference. The other alternative is you move into a care home which the local council is prepared to countenance, which because it will be cheaper is likely to be inferior and may have to be found quickly rather than after a lengthy search.

If you go into a home independently but have had a community care assessment before entry which indicates that you need care home provision, you will know that if the worst comes to the worst, the council will pay for a care home place. If the home you choose is one which they would not fund, at least you know. Also, you have made contact, so you know where to go and whom to telephone if you need their help.

Involving Social Services

Entry into a care home often comes about not at the initiative of the elderly person but because a community care assessment carried out by social services has concluded that the elderly person has needs (almost certainly mainly personal care) which can only be met in a care home setting. In other words, a social worker has decided that the person can no longer be looked after adequately in his or her own home, even with homecare and other support brought in. This assessment may be carried out while the person is living at home, perhaps after his condition has worsened, or while he is in hospital and awaiting discharge.

Those who pay their own fees because their own savings exceed about £19,500 and their income is relatively high are known as 'self-funders'; they may have two alternatives. Option 1 is to go 'self-funding', which means that they enter a contract with the care home themselves. When their resources have dwindled so that they are approaching the £19,500 threshold, they notify the local authority, so that it will start chipping in. Under Option 2, social services has the contract with the home and the resident pays social services – again until his or her resources are depleted down to the £19,500 threshold. However, not all local authorities offer this option and they are not required to do so.

Some people's assets will be less than £12,000 (or its equivalent figure in Wales and Scotland – see pages 368, 373 and 596) when they enter a care home. If their income is not high, then the local authority will start paying a contribution to care home bills right from the beginning. Some people think that if social services have the contract with the home and have taken on full responsibility for paying the fees then residents have no choice about which care home they enter. This is absolutely not the case. If the elderly person expresses no view, a social worker will simply ring round homes with which his or her local council has a block contract and the person will be sent to one of these. Inevitably, those who do not argue will often go to the places that are least popular and therefore have vacancies. However, you do not have to go to one of the homes to which that local authority regularly sends people. In these circumstances, local authorities are legally obliged to enable an elderly person to live in the care home of his or her choice – which may be in an entirely different part of the country – provided certain conditions are met.[6] These are:

- The home must be capable of providing the care necessary to meet the person's assessed needs.
- The home must provide accommodation which satisfies the authority's usual terms and conditions.
- The preferred accommodation is actually available; if it is not, the authority should be willing to consider accommodating the person temporarily in another home.
- The cost of the home is not more than the local authority

would usually pay to provide for someone with those assessed needs. However, councils have discretion to pay more than their normal rate, for instance if there are particular needs specified in the assessment and care plan which cannot be met elsewhere. These could be provision for a particular disability, or spoken language (if English is not the resident's mother tongue), or location (usually because it is considered important that an elderly person should live close to relatives). And it is possible to go to a more expensive home if some other reliable source can be found to meet the difference (what is usually called 'a top-up'). That source might, for instance, be a son or daughter, or a professional or occupational benevolent fund connected to the person or a local charity.

Owners

Care homes have three main types of owner. A small number are owned by local authorities. Many more used to be, but, particularly outside Scotland, the vast majority have been sold off. A further small number of care homes are owned by organizations which do not exist to make a profit, such as Methodist Homes for the Aged, the Royal Masonic Benevolent Institution, the Church of Scotland and Action for Blind People. However, the bulk of care homes beds, about 80 per cent, are in homes run for profit. Typical of these independent homes are small businesses with a husband and wife running just one home or local businesspeople running a small number of homes, employing a manager in each. Larger companies have been increasing their share of the sector in recent years, particularly in the nursing rather than the residential side; they now control about a third of it. The motives of for-profit providers vary considerably: some people came into the field to provide the best possible care for their own elderly parent or parents, others look only to make a profit and might have moved in from, say, shipping or running a football club.

When choosing a care home, you need to take account of the kind of owner you are dealing with. All homeowners must grapple with the conflict between care and costs. The inspection system described below should ensure that every home provides a basic level of care (at least, when the inspector calls), but much more than this can be delivered. An almost limitless amount of money could be spent on improving the living conditions of elderly people in care homes, and different homes make the judgement on how to balance profit and care in different ways.

The consumer has to look at each case individually and come to a judgement based on as much evidence as can be assembled. For example, you need to be wary of assuming that a not-for-profit home must be better than the alternative, although they often are. Such homes still have a budget to balance and will set fee levels and provide care accordingly. They may levy a 'profit', or surplus, which will not go to shareholders but may be used to further the aims of the organization, perhaps outside the particular establishment in which they are raised.

Just as the type of owner provides no guarantee of the quality of a care home, neither does price. There is an enormous range of fees, but it does not necessarily match the enormous range of quality on the ground. There have been few surveys of care home quality, but Dr Sue Davies of the School of Nursing and Midwifery at the University of Sheffield talked to residents, staff and relatives at three nursing homes in the north of England between 1999 and 2001. The most expensive home had impressive décor and high-quality fittings, but a significant proportion of residents felt that their needs, particularly for social contact and conversation, were not being met. Although attention was given to the education and training of staff, this tended to focus on health and safety and customer care, rather than quality of life. Dr Davies found a more vibrant, friendly social atmosphere at a smaller, less expensive home.[7]

One result of the diversity of ownership is an uneven distribution of care homes across the country. Although the state provides much of the ultimate funding for care homes by paying or subsidizing fees, homes are provided where it suits their owners to provide them. There has been no national planning or co-ordination, so variations in the quality of care homes are compounded by marked variations in availability.

Regulation

Before a care home can operate in the UK the owner must be in possession of a certificate of registration from the National Care

Standards Commission (in England), the Standards Inspectorate for Wales, the Scottish Commission for the Regulation of Care or one of Northern Ireland's four health and social services boards (until the Health and Social Services Registration and Improvement Authority is set up in in the Province in April 2004). If the owner is not responsible for day-to-day running of the home, then its manager must also be registered. The national regulatory body has to satisfy itself that the manager and the provider are mentally and physically fit to manage the home, of integrity and good character and have the necessary qualifications, skills and experience. It also looks at the premises, facilities, staffing and other matters, and if it is satisfied that these are appropriate, issues a certificate of registration which sets out the type of care home the registered person is allowed to provide and the maximum number of people he or she is allowed to accommodate – for instance, nursing care for 30 elderly people, or in another establishment, low-dependency care (equivalent to the old residential care) for 50 elderly people. Thereafter, the Commission will conduct inspections of the home twice a year, in one announced and one unannounced visit, although it has the discretion to make unannounced visits at any time of the day or night if there is the suspicion that something is amiss.

All homes have to abide by regulations which have been drawn up for each part of the United Kingdom, although they arc very similar; in England, these are called the *Care Homes Regulations 2001*. They stipulate that the registered person has to provide various facilities and appropriately trained staff, put in place a complaints procedure, provide appropriate premises, and so on.

One part of the regulations little known to residents and relatives is the requirement that the registered provider must prepare two documents: a 'service user's guide' and a 'statement of purpose'. The former, aimed at current and prospective residents, should describe the accommodation and services provided, the qualifications and experience of the manager and staff, the number of places provided and any special needs catered for, and should contain the home's most recent inspection report, its complaints procedure and an indication of the views of its residents. The 'statement of purpose', written primarily for the inspection organization, can also be illuminating for prospective residents: it identifies the type of client, such as low-dependency, and should explain the ways in which the home will meet their needs.

If a home breaks the regulations, then the inspector from the regulatory body can take enforcement action. The ultimate sanction – closing the home through removing its certificate of registration – is rarely deployed and usually only where serious abuse of residents has been uncovered. But inspectors can also use a range of other enforcement measures, issuing orders which must be complied with. For example, an inspector might find that a home was operating at below the level of staffing required (perhaps after a tip off from a visitor or a resident) and could require that the situation be remedied within a specified number of days, if not immediately.

Apart from checking that a home is meeting all the regulations, inspectors must also examine the extent to which homes are meeting new National Minimum Standards for care homes.[8] These standards, like the regulations, take a very similar form in each country and range through most areas of care home life, from working practices to residents' rights. Unlike the regulations, the standards are not mandatory, but inspectors must bear in mind the extent to which a home is meeting them when they inspect it and thus come to conclusions about whether it should be given a warning notice or even closed down or, more usually, make recommendations for improvements in their reports. Even if not all the standards are being met (and many probably will not be in many homes for some years), their existence signals to care home proprietors in a clearer way than ever before what is expected of them.

It is well worth getting a copy of the regulations and the standards so that you can be absolutely clear what is both required and expected. Those mentioned in this chapter are the ones which have been published for England and were revised in 2003. You can obtain both the regulations and standards from the website of the National Care Standards Commission, Care Standards Inspectorate for Wales and the Scottish Commission for the Regulation of Care, or by post. Those for Northern Ireland can be obtained from the Department of Health, Social

Services and Public Safety. These documents may also be available in other forms – for example, you can buy a booklet which contains both the regulations and the standards for England from Stationery Office bookshops.

If you have a dispute with a home or a query about any part of the arrangements, the chances are that the regulations or, more probably the standards, since these are more detailed, will have something to say on the matter. However, there are also areas in which the standards provide only limited help. They do not attempt to regulate fees, for example, so different people receiving similar treatment in the same home can pay different amounts. Also, the standards do not regulate contracts and suggest no framework timetable for care home life.

Although the arrival of the Commissions and minimum standards is welcome, it is important not to allow them to lull you into a false sense of security. The inspection process is only a snapshot. Inspectors do not go and live in the homes for a week or two or pay older people to do so. For its announced inspection, a home will probably spend several weeks preparing and may well hire additional staff for the actual day or two days. Conversely, on the day of an unannounced visit, the cook may be off sick and the manager have a bad headache, giving an unfavourable impression even though the home is a good one. In any case, inspectors are unlikely to be too pushy about the national standards if it looks as if this would push homes into closure when demand is exceeding supply.

The Vulnerability of Residents

These days, most people do not go and live in a care home until they are quite frail. Such people often need help with many different aspects of personal care. Because so much of what they once did for themselves must now be done for them by others, they often feel at a disadvantage when they get into a care home. This feeling of vulnerability may be compounded by events preceding admission, which may have included a fall or a stroke. Some residents are far more vulnerable than others. Somebody with a combination of severe chronic lung or heart disease which renders her breathless after only a few steps, and osteoporosis which gives her a lot of pain, but who is mentally alert and spends her time reading, listening to tapes, receiving visitors and being taken out on trips is in a far different situation in the vulnerability stakes to someone of the same age with dementia and failing eyesight and/or hearing. The first woman is vulnerable to inadequate care by staff who do not understand her medical needs and who might not provide the nebulizers and so on which she requires to keep her alive. But if they should slip up, she has only to press her alarm button and summon help, and she would expect any complaint she made to be taken seriously so that the mistake was not repeated.

The second woman, by contrast, may be completely dependent on care staff spotting that she needs help and approaching her, because she cannot learn how to operate the alarm system. If a care worker is filching money from her purse, she may not notice because of her failing eyesight. If she does, her dementia may mean that she does not remember that this has occurred; if she manages to report the misdemeanour despite the loss of language skills common in Alzheimer's sufferers, the home owner may not accept her word against that of the miscreant and may say that she did not know how much money was in her purse to start with. It is estimated that about 70 per cent of care home residents have some degree of dementia (this figure includes homes which specialize in the care of dementia sufferers, so in other homes the figure will be lower).[9]

Other afflictions may render people vulnerable in different ways. An elderly man who cannot walk may feel unwell and wish to summon his GP. The manager may tell him she does not think he needs to see the doctor. The man would, of course, be perfectly entitled to telephone the surgery himself, but perhaps the phone is placed just a little bit too far out of his reach, whether deliberately or not. The national minimum standards say that homes have to enable residents to make telephone calls in private,[10] but on the ground, day by day, this requirement is not always going to be observed. The old man knows that if he goes against the manager's wishes there are a thousand ways in which she could, even if not a specially vindictive person, get her own back – from delaying her response to a call for help with going to the lavatory to leaving the television on when she knows this will annoy him.

The resident in a care home is thus in a very different position from somebody staying at a hotel where, if the service rendered is not what we believe it should be, we can leave and demand a reduction in the bill. We have a home to go back to – unlike care home residents, who have moved themselves and their earthly goods to the care home, have lost the independence afforded by having a home of their own to return to, and in any case are probably not in a physical condition to summon a taxi and ask to be taken somewhere else.

All this means you have to select a care home carefully and to make sure you trust the manager. It is just not possible to foresee all the contingencies that might arise when somebody is in a home and therefore all the possible questions you could ask before you sign the contract, however long your interview with manager. There are bound to be many things which will emerge only after you, or your relative, is actually living there or has recently moved in.

The Selection Process

Often the middle-aged children of an older person visit a care home and talk to the manager (who, if female, often calls herself 'Matron', and I shall henceforth use this term[11]). They then tell their parent that it is ideal and that he or she is bound to be very happy and well cared for there. The elderly person signs the contract and the only return visit which is made before entry occurs when, say, a son-in-law returns with a tape measure to work out which furniture will fit into the bedroom allocated. It is very easy to take this approach – and the reassuring attitude taken by Matron, together with the elegant fixtures and fittings and perhaps the name of the establishment (many are called Something-or-Other-Manor, hinting at the well-ordered running of the Edwardian stately home) all lead customers to assume that everything will be tip-top. This expectation is of course compounded by the eagerness of the relatives, perhaps affected by guilt or anxiety, to convince themselves that this will indeed be the case.

However, I recommend approaching the selection of a care home in five separate stages, all to be completed before you sign the contract with the home.

1. Draw up a shortlist of possible homes gleaned from directories, catalogues and suggestions from other people or organizations.
2. Visit each one, talking to the manager or owner and touring the establishment.
3. If you are interested in pursuing the matter further, arrange to return in order to sit and observe what the home is actually like – how staff interact with residents on a minute-to-minute basis, whether residents are happy, what they do all day, whether people with dementia are ignored and so on. Try to visit several times, at different times and on different days of the week.
4. Then consider other matters such as the draft contract and the fees the owner would like to charge.
5. Lastly, encourage your relative to move in for a trial period. If all is well, sign the contract and go ahead.

While I have written this chapter largely from the point of view of a relative doing the groundwork, the person whose fate is in the balance should be involved as much as possible. Older people need to be very careful about who is doing any groundwork for them. It is important that their representatives should see homes through their eyes as prospective residents. Whether the older person really would settle in happily can be tested finally during the trial period, but it is obviously better to gauge this early on if possible.

How can people without a partner or a close relative get someone to view homes for them? As we have seen, if social services are footing the bill, they tend to usher people into homes with which they already deal, which may or may not be suitable. More and more local authorities and voluntary organizations are offering advocacy services, or somebody who will speak out independently on behalf of a particular person (page 82). You can find out whether an advocacy service is available in your area by telephoning local statutory or voluntary organizations such as social services or an Age Concern group or the Older People's Advocacy Alliance. If elderly people have nobody to act for them, social services are legally obliged to find accommodation and make arrangements for them to enter it, but only if they have assessed the person as needing care home care.

Do not feel bullied into entering a care home quickly because you are in hospital and are made to feel guilty at occupying a bed (pages 465–7). You have every right to make a proper choice of what will probably be their home for the rest of their life.

The Trawl

The first thing potential care home residents and their representatives need to know is what sort of home they should look for. That sounds obvious, but I was certainly not aware of the differences between homes (residential, nursing, EMI residential, EMI nursing and so on) when I started my first trawl. The type of home required should be clear from your relative's community care assessment; if he or she has not had one because you are acting entirely independently of social services, go and discuss his or her requirements with his or her GP (obviously, with your relative's consent). Not only do you need to know into which of these broad classes he falls, you also need to know whether there are other medical conditions which are relevant, such as asthma or diabetes, and have a good idea yourself of how such conditions should be managed, so that you can assess whether the homes you visit are up to coping with them.

Each home is constrained by the terms of its registration in the sort of care it can provide, so you will be wasting your time if your mother requires nursing EMI (or DE) care and you start contacting and visiting homes registered only for residential EMI. If your mother enters a residential EMI home and later needs nursing support, the home may keep her, but they will not take her as a new resident. But you do not want to move her initially into a residential home only to find within weeks that she really needs a nursing home.

If your relative is suffering from dementia, even if he or she is in the early stages, you need to be convinced that the home understands the nature of the condition, is sensitive to the needs of sufferers and is keen to keep abreast of developments in the field. All homes should be able to cope well with it, but the fact is that many do not. In view of this, your relative may be better off in a home which specializes in dementia care. Conversely, life can be very isolating and dispiriting for somebody who is mentally fine but, perhaps because of a clutch of medical conditions, needs nursing care and finds that the majority of the other residents have dementia.

Next, you need a list of homes that might be suitable. Most people will start with an assumption about the geographical area in which they are looking. But you do not have to restrict yourself to your own local authority area, even if it will be footing the bill (page 318). If you have a particular geographical area in mind, you can get a list of homes there from the *Yellow Pages*, or, with more details, from the social services department of your local authority (whether you are involving them in the move or not) or from the Elderly Accommodation Council (page 413). If your relative is suffering from a particular condition, such as dementia or blindness, and particularly if there are no overriding reasons why they should stay in a particular geographical area, it is worth contacting the national office of the voluntary organization which specializes in that condition. Such organizations often have their own lists, which may contain further details. There are also still a few homes which take people from particular professions, such as the rag trade, nursing and journalism, as well as homes which specialize in people from the armed forces. These homes should be listed in local directories, but you can always check through a union or trade association; it is also worth contacting organizations such as The Royal British Legion and The Royal Masonic Society if appropriate.

People from ethnic minorities who wish to find a home run and peopled from the same community should contact local community groups before they start searching. It is not always easy to find an ordinary home which can cope with the dietary and religious requirements which, say, a Muslim may seek, or even to find one which serves food your relative likes. I heard of one elderly Chinese man, who, unable to find a home which served Chinese food, had to make do with one where he could obtain meals from a nearby Chinese takeaway twice a week. In addition, it is worth bearing in mind that dementia sufferers frequently lose the ability to speak a second language as the disease progresses, and retain only their first language. Local ethnic community groups may also be able to come up with an advocate for elderly people who cannot get to view homes themselves and have no close relative in the area in which they are looking.

Social workers advising self-funders as well as voluntary organizations which provide lists of homes are wary of recommending individual homes. Clearly such organizations fear that dissatisfied customers would complain to them, but from the consumer's point of view there is a very good reason for not setting too much store by recommendations, even if they are forthcoming. Homes can very easily change over time, what may suit one person may not suit another, and some people may simply be uncritical. So relying on recommendations, whether from individuals or organizations, however tempting, is not a good idea, except perhaps as a very rough guide when you are conducting your initial trawl. It is easy to set too much store by the recommendation of say, a retired GP, and to come a cropper as a result.

There are private organizations which, for a fee, guarantee to find a home or a short list of homes for you, but you do need to be sure that the organization knows your relative well enough to judge how he or she would fare in a particular home and has up-to-date information about the current condition of homes it recommends.

Preparing to Meet Matron

When you have made an initial selection of care homes which look promising, telephone each in turn and ask to speak to the manager. Explain the timescale involved – whether you are looking for a room tomorrow or at some point in the future – and be prepared to give some indication of the sort of care your relative would need. Make an appointment to discuss the possibilities further and to look round.

Before you go for this first visit, have a look if you can at previous inspection reports, both the pre-April 2002 reports by local and health authorities and the later ones by the National Care Standards Commission, the Scottish Commission for the Regulation of Care or the Care Standards Inspectorate for Wales or one of Northern Ireland's health and social services boards. These should be available in your local public library and on the website of the relevant Commission. If you cannot find them, ask your local social services department or the local Commission office. Individual care homes will have their own copies which you could ask to see, but it is a good idea to peruse them before you turn up. Try to look not just at the most recent inspection report but at previous ones as well, to see whether concerns voiced by inspectors have been repeated year after year, such as a need for better staff training, and whether the same facts have been frequently reported, such as high staff turnover. The latter might indicate that the home is rather unsettled and has difficulty keeping staff, perhaps because it pays them very low wages.

Also have a look at the brochure which the home itself produces and which Matron will probably offer to send you. But bear in mind that brochures are sales documents, so they are bound to put a favourable gloss on things, and may well leave out important facts and figures. The national regulatory bodies now require that homes prepare 'service user's guides' with specified contents (pages 321–22), but it will probably be some time before all brochures or guides provide such comprehensive and detailed information for consumers.

Some people maintain that it is a good idea to turn up on the doorstep of the home, claim you are passing and ask to look round there and then, rather than telephone the manager and make an appointment to visit. That way you ensure that whoever shows you round will not have had a chance to prepare. If you are going to take this approach, you might as well turn up at a time of day when the home will be least prepared for visitors – say, 4.45 p.m., after usual visitors have departed. The drawback of this approach is that you could antagonize the proprietor of a home in which you subsequently wish to place your relative and which has a waiting list (homes' waiting lists are infinitely flexible: some people remain forever at the bottom), since he will probably suspect that you were out to catch him napping. A prearranged visit is thus safer.

Meeting Matron

The person with whom you have your initial interview will almost certainly be the proprietor of the home or its manager. As explained on page 325, female managers frequently call themselves 'Matron'. If the home is registered for nursing care, Matron will probably be one of the qualified nurses the home employs.

Matron is in a similar position to the head teacher of the school you might be touring as a prospective parent: she may imbue the establishment with its ethos, but she is very unlikely to have much contact with residents day by day and night by night. If it is a good home that should not matter, as she will have an assistant manager, care managers and a staffing structure that should ensure everything is done properly.

When you go round a home for the first time, it is also useful to bear in mind what the proprietor or manager is looking for as far as you and your relative are concerned. He or she will be working out whether his or her staff could cope with your relative and whether they want to take on somebody with that level of dependency, whether it is high or low: a good home will want to have a mix of high- and low-dependency residents. Matron is also likely to be considering whether your relative would fit in well with other residents and staff and be a pleasant person to have around – unless she is desperate to fill her vacant bed, in which case she will take almost anybody, whatever their needs, and even if her staff lack any sort of training to cope with, for example, somebody suffering from schizophrenia.

Matron will also be sizing you up in ways which will depend on the outlook of the home. If you are a self-funder, what fee could she charge you? (It is common for self-funding residents to be charged higher fees than local authority-funded residents, and the care homes regulations and standards do not control what fees homes charge.) Do you look wealthy enough to stand a hefty top-up if your relative's resources run down to the level at which social services step in (page 318)? What sort of family would you be? A good home will welcome relatives who visit often and wish to get involved in relatives' committees and the life of the home. A bad home will hope you do not visit lest you should spot something untoward and contact the National Care Standards Commission inspector. It will do what it can to minimize the opportunities for relatives talking to each other lest they start comparing the fees each is paying, let alone forming committees which might make formal requests. One home in which a friend of mine placed her mother even forbade relatives to band together to raise funds for additional facilities.

Also bear in mind that the person who is showing you round

is a salesperson. He or she wants to fill a bed and you may buy it – just as an airline operator wants to fill all the seats on all flights. This salesperson will choose where most of your interview is conducted – perhaps at the window of the best and most recently decorated bedroom, which offers a fine view, or in an attractive activities room. Be aware of the impression that you are being invited to take from the place to which you are steered. You may be encouraged to linger in the hall opposite a wall hung with framed certificates. In researching this book, I myself have picked up a file of beautifully inscribed certificates, which would no doubt look impressive on a wall: there are plenty of certificates in the eldercare field which, when actually read, testify simply to attendance at a one-day course rather than passing challenging exams.

Staffing

At your first meeting, Matron will no doubt list for you the number of care staff in her establishment and you will probably scribble down what she tells you. Don't be too easily impressed. The staff will be those she has to have to avoid enforcement action by the NCSC or its equivalent. Homes do not usually employ many more staff than they are obliged to, since staff account for about three-quarters of the day-to-day costs of a home; also, at present, they are in short supply.

Staffing levels are important because effective care requires plenty of person-hours – to bathe people carefully, washing them well and at the same time checking for evidence that something is amiss, from developing pressure sores to a lump in the breast. If staff are rushed off their feet, these basic tasks will not be performed well. Time is needed to take residents for walks, perhaps in a wheelchair, or to help them get dressed. It is especially important for conversation.

Time also gives staff the opportunity to respond sensitively in order to nip potentially serious psychological problems in the bud. Residents in care homes frequently have to cope with a cavalcade of massive problems to which they may react in various ways. Losing your sight, for example, is very difficult to cope with, particularly if you are already deaf. Somebody may have been a mayor, or an accountant or some other kind of high-flyer and suddenly find him- or herself unable to control his or her life. Such people may become sad, angry, aggressive or with-drawn; all these reactions require sensitive handling.

So you need to know whether there will be sufficient staff with sufficient time and energy to care for the home's residents. The majority of the staff will be care workers or care assistants (or social care workers, as they are now sometimes called). But does the staffing structure of the home allow these staff to care for residents for long enough? Are they often helping out in the kitchen because there are too few staff there? Or cleaning, if too few cleaners have been employed? Or loading the washing machine because there are too few laundry assistants? It is prob-ably not too disastrous if a care assistant does a little cleaning or sorting the clean laundry, but you would expect a good number of ancillary staff to be employed in addition to care staff. The important thing is that there should be sufficient care hours built in so that care staff are not hoovering when they should be bathing a resident or chatting to them.

You also need to know how many of the staff on duty at any time are members of the home's payroll staff or are agency workers Matron has had to bring in because of staff shortages. Agency staff may or may not be well trained, but they will be unfamiliar with individual residents. There may also be a short-age of nurses in nursing homes, which means that agency nurses will be brought in. This may not be the fault of the nursing home, but if it is happening frequently, it is not going to be helpful. Also, you need to know who is in charge when Matron is away. Probably the best way of assessing the extent to which the home relies on agency staff and the extent to which care staff have to perform the duties of ancillary staff is to ask to see the staff rota for the last week. Matron should not object to such a request. You are proposing to spend your family's inheritance on the services she claims to be able to provide, and there is no reason why you should not understand how her home is staffed. From the rota you ought to be able to see how many staff were actually on duty day and night and in what capacity. You can also see whether there is a split between domestic and care staff or whether they are muddled up.

Key Workers
Apart from the manager, there are certain other key staff it is very important to meet and assess, both for competence and for the ability to relate successfully to your elderly relative. The concept of the 'key worker' is currently fashionable. Essentially it means that one member of the staff will have special responsibility for particular residents. What the key worker will do will vary, but it might include keeping charge of their residents' clothing, helping them with personal care and perhaps serving them breakfast in their rooms and answering telephone queries from relatives about their condition.

Don't be bowled over by the key worker idea. It sounds mildly impressive, but it has drawbacks, so you need to find out from Matron what steps she takes to minimize them. The first unavoidable drawback is that your relative's key worker will be on duty for only one-third of the time in any average 24-hour period; in addition, he or she will have time off and holidays. So it is really essential that other staff are acquainted with your relative as well as the key worker – knowing not only the type of help he needs and why, but also his background and personality, his likes and dislikes.

The other big potential drawback is incompatibility. Your relative may not like her key worker. What say does a resident have in choosing her key worker? What opportunity is there for changing the key worker? Think of the care with which you select your best friend when you go to school. It is perhaps a measure of ageist attitudes that when people go into care homes it is assumed that the key worker, in effect their best friend, can be chosen for them.

The Activities Organizer
One other person you should definitely try to meet is the activities organizer. Most homes engage somebody to come in on weekday afternoons and organize some kind of activity, be it growing tomato plants, playing bingo, running quizzes, playing music, organizing painting, crafts, sing-songs, dancing, light exercise or birthday parties. These people can be the life and soul of a home. Or they can be damp squibs and, if not warm and responsive to residents and possessed of some basic training in interact-

ing with frail and disabled people, almost worse than nothing. So meet the activities organizer, sit in on her session, observe whether she is sparky and inspiring and interacts well with residents. If she insists on making bingo a major part of her repertoire, then residents who cannot see or hear well are going to feel even more isolated than they otherwise might, unless she or care assistants are helping them on a one-to-one basis. What does the home do when the activities person is on holiday? If it does not run to a replacement, three weeks in August, for example, with no activities organizer can make for a long, drab time.

Forward-thinking care home proprietors will provide exercise sessions led by trained instructors (page 144). If this is the case in the home you are touring, it is worth asking a few questions. What form does the exercise take? Is it seated or standing? Can the instructor adapt exercises for people who need to be seated or standing? How long does it last? At what kind of intensity is it? What equipment will be used? What other opportunities are there to be physically active apart from this? For example, are staff available to accompany residents on a walk around the grounds?

Night Staff
Night staff are terrifically important for the individual resident for the obvious reason that elderly people who wake in the middle of the night, perhaps disorientated or unwell or distressed because the sheets are wet, need somebody who is going to be kind, who will deal with any problem efficiently and help them to get back to sleep quickly. You often find that the same people will stick to night shifts, rather than mixing nights with days. Sometimes night staff are kindness and professional competence personified; sometimes they are people you would prefer not to find yourself confronting when you wake at 2 a.m. So if you possibly can, get to meet the night staff or at least try to build up a picture of what they are like.

Staff Induction, Training and Qualifications
Find out the staff's areas of expertise and see whether they tie in with the particular needs of your own relative. It is all very well to have staff who are expert in tissue viability (preventing skin

tears and sores developing), but such expertise is very different from that needed to cope with depression. Have some members of staff had training in blind and deaf awareness (most residents will have some degree of hearing and/or sight impairment)? If your relative is to have a key worker, does he or she have expertise in your relative's particular afflictions?

The qualification which care assistants work towards is the National (or Scottish) Vocational Qualification (NVQ or SVQ) in Social Care. This is essentially training on the job and perhaps some study at college. So find out from Matron what proportion of her care assistants have achieved NVQs, to what level, and what proportion are currently working towards them. The national minimum standards say that homes should ensure that 50 per cent of their care staff are trained to NVQ level 2 by 2005. In a good home, expect the majority of workers to have received or at least be undergoing training. Also, find out whether the home is paying the NVQ registration fee; although not much, it is a significant amount for low-paid staff, and willingness to pay it indicates some commitment to improving training.

NVQs are not, however, fantastically impressive qualifications: level 2 should give people basic knowledge of safe working practices (such as moving people without straining the back), but will not equip them to respond sensitively to elderly people suffering from dementia or the after-effects of a serious stroke. A study by the King's Fund in 2001 reported of the NVQ system, 'Not all training is of equal value, and the NVQ model appears to be highly variable.'[13]

Eldercare is complex but interesting. A good home will try to inspire staff at all levels to become genuinely interested in the subject – to consider the context of their role and ask questions about the power relationships involved in caring and to understand how individuals with particular afflictions perceive the world. This is education, rather than training. At the purpose-built Abbeyfield home for people with dementia at New Malden, south-west London, the top floor is given over to a room equipped with an overhead projector for staff training days, involving all staff from registered mental nurses to receptionists. At least is there a bookcase of relevant publications designed both to inform and to interest staff? Are there well-thumbed copies of journals such as *Nursing Standard* and the *Journal of Dementia Care* in Matron's office?

The Timetable

Matron will probably go through the daily and weekly timetable. She will explain the hours at which meals are served and any special activities such as church services or social activities, perhaps crafts in the afternoons. She may also explain that your relative will be bathed at least once a week and that she may choose to have her hair done on a particular day by a hairdresser. You need rather more detail than this. You want a good idea of your relative's personal timetable and how much choice she will have in the time at which help is given to her. You don't want general statements, but specific guarantees.

For example, you need to know at what time your mother will be woken and helped to get up in the morning, as well as the hour at which she will go to bed. How much choice will she have over these times? Is there sufficient leeway in the system to allow residents to have a lie-in if they wish?

Some of the most undesirable practices in bad care homes occur during the night. These can include waking incontinent residents every two hours and putting them on the lavatory or the commode, lest they soil the sheets. Very occasionally, a resident might prefer this, but the practice may well be followed to save on laundry costs and staff time in changing sheets and nightwear. Obviously you don't want to condemn your relative never again to enjoy a good night's sleep and if Matron tells you this is the only way of dealing with your relative's incontinence, she is wrong. There are plenty of other steps that could be taken (pages 111–15). Standard 8.6 of the national minimum standards states, 'The registered person ensures that professional advice about the promotion of continence is sought and acted upon and aids and equipment needed are provided.'

Food and Drink

Try to meet the cook and form some impression of whether he or she is reliable, seems to enjoy the work, is likely to turn up most days and understands the nutritional requirements of older people (pages 18–26). Constipation is a common and tedious problem for older people: does the cook recognize this and incorporate sufficient fibre in meals? Does he or she understand which foods your relative should avoid for medical reasons? Is there sufficient choice? If this is a family business, does the family eat exactly the same food as the residents? If it does, that probably bodes well.

The cook will of course be working within a budget set by the home's proprietor or manager according to the relative priority given to good food and maximum profit. One sure-fire indication of this trade-off is the type of tea-bag used. It hardly needs saying that the quality of cups of tea or coffee can be very important to residents. As you tour the home with Matron, you will probably pass through the kitchen: you should ask to see it if she does not offer. When you are there, look around. What brands of tea-bag and coffee are used? If you cannot see, ask. If it is a really cheap kind and the resulting beverage is served highly diluted, then you can be pretty sure that costs are being kept to a minimum in other areas where the comfort or well-being of residents conflicts with profit, from the choice of lavatory paper (soft or hard) to the amount of lighting permitted, the temperature of the individual and communal rooms and whether residents are offered seconds at lunch.

Many care homes give their residents two cooked meals a day, one slightly lighter than the first. Is this enough or will your relative be left hungry? If he is peckish, day or night, what additional food and drink could he obtain? Is tea a proper high tea or simply a sandwich and a piece of cake? Does breakfast consist of porridge, egg on toast and more toast plus drinks, or a couple of thin slices of toast and a piece of Weetabix? Or perhaps no toast at all? If you arrange a visit at which you can just sit and observe what goes on, it is a good idea to include a mealtime (pages 350–51 and 352–3).

Older people very often need help with eating and drinking (page 450). Without help such people will probably lose weight, lack essential nutrients and fluid and lose out on the enjoyment of eating and drinking.

Apart from help at meal and coffee-break times, is drinking water always available where residents can reach it? Do staff offer water or soft drinks frequently to residents who need help with drinking, especially during warm weather? Finally, what about alcohol? Is it allowed whenever residents want it? Not only is alcohol a pleasure that it would be a shame to deny, but it can encourage elderly people whose appetite is waning to eat.

The Tour
After an interview, Matron will show you round. Here are some of the main things you might care to notice.

Design
Care home inspectors tend to take quite a lot of note of fixtures and fittings and whether corridors are wide enough for wheelchairs and other aspects of the internal design of care homes, but here are some points you might care to bear in mind. Those identified on pages 194–9 for the corridors and communal rooms of sheltered housing are also relevant.

Lighting
This should be ample everywhere, from the least visited lavatory to the lounge. An older person needs three times as much light as a 20 year old. But it is important that lighting should not generate glare, as this can disorientate and cause falls. So look for an absence of shiny, reflective surfaces and of single lights shining down dark corridors.

Preventing Falls
Look for non-slip flooring, a lack of clutter and obstacles underfoot and other physical features such as an abundance of grab-rails which can help prevent falls (pages 150–51). Observe whether residents are encouraged to move around in a safe manner (pages 149–50).

Coping with Vision and Hearing Impairment
Get Matron to describe the steps that have been taken to help people with sight and hearing loss. For example:

- Are there loop systems (electronic aids which can enhance hearing through hearing aids) in the lounges?
- Are there free-standing enhanced listening devices, such as the

RNID's Crystal Listener, available? These can be useful aids for people who do not have or cannot cope with a hearing aid.

- Are books and other written material available in large print, Braille or on audiotape? Is a television switched to subtitling?
- Are rooms labelled clearly or otherwise easily recognizable? This is helpful for people with a hearing impairment as it reduces the number of questions they have to ask in orientating themselves. Partially sighted people may be helped to recognize their own room through raised lettering or a raised picture. A good home caring for residents with severe sight impairment will have guide rails along corridor walls to help them.

The Lounge

There should be a variety of sitting rooms, not just one lounge with a television on continuously, so that different activities are possible. Chairs should be positioned to facilitate interaction, not ringing a room. Do the windows of the sitting rooms offer pleasant and interesting views? Views of homely things, such as washing flapping on the line, may be preferable to sterile-looking grounds covered by low-maintenance shrubbery or a gravel drive. Whatever the view, is it one which your relative would find interesting and which would help keep him or her in touch with the outside world, whether that be a city street with plenty of passersby, a seaside promenade or perhaps an area in which people walk their dogs? Or are views screened out by long net curtains?

Are there roomy lavatories easily accessible from the sitting rooms?

Lavatories

A sure-fire way of ascertaining whether a home has been designed with genuine attention to the comfort of its residents is to look in the lavatories. Though these are extraordinarily important in the lives of residents, Matron will probably not linger in them during her tour. If she does not, excuse yourself somewhere near the lounge so that you can inspect one of the lavatories which residents share. Look out for the following points:

- Is it clean? It is easy for urinary tract infections to be spread in care homes, and they are very unpleasant, so you want evidence that the loo itself is cleaned frequently and also that the hand-washing facilities minimize the risk of transmitting infection. Soap should not be in slabs, as bacteria can live in the cracks, but provided through a dispenser with disposable towels.

• How easy is the lavatory to use? Is there sufficient support to take the weight of your elderly relative when she is lowering herself and adjusting her clothing and when she is getting up again? Sometimes you find dreadful wobbly frame contraptions in care-home toilets, which must be a nightmare for a heavier older person to have to rely on for support. Look for a special seat which raises the height of the lavatory seat and ideally has a tilting mechanism to make sitting down and rising easier, together with plenty of firm supporting structures, such as horizontal bars which are fixed to the wall, can be lowered and have a supporting leg at right angles to provide additional firmness.

• Is there enough space for care workers to help?

• Is it a pleasant room? Has it been nicely decorated and does it look homely?

• Is it well lit?

• Is it well ventilated?

• Is it warm? This is very important. If in doubt, get out the thermometer you should be carrying in your handbag when you tour care homes and check the temperature. An owner who scrimps on heating in the loos is one to treat with suspicion.

Other Design Features

Where is Matron's office or the workstation or office from which workers will sally forth on each shift? Is it close to residents' areas, so that workers will easily be able to spot any problems, or is it tucked away down a corridor? Worse still, are most of the staff sitting in it a great deal, chatting over coffee?

How easy is it to move in and out of the building, back and front? If you visit on a warm day, are residents using the garden? Are members of staff walking with residents who have mobility problems?

Even if only one or two of the residents are suffering from dementia and are mobile, the home will need to make sure they cannot get out on to surrounding roads. Look to see how this is done. It is a shame if all residents are confined to the building lest any with dementia should get out into the local neighbourhood and hurt themselves or get lost. There is a home in Bradford specializing in the care of people with dementia which consists of a Victorian house on a large site surrounded by a mature garden in which the only barrier is the surrounding wall and gates through which people can drive out only by operating a keypad. As a result residents can wander freely in and out of the building and around the grounds, benefiting from fresh air, exercise and the stimulation of an open environment.

At Home

Will your relative feel at home? There are three main types of care home building. The majority are conversions of earlier buildings such as large town houses and country mansions. There is a diminishing number of purpose-built care homes constructed by local authorities several decades ago. Thirdly, there are new privately owned purpose-built homes, which are usually large with at least 60 beds; some of these specialize in particular conditions.

As you tour the home, you may be bowled over by the embossed ceilings and elegant furnishings, but what matters is the environment in which the person on whose behalf you are choosing the home will feel comfortable. Would your uncle really feel comfortable here? If he is coming from a modest-sized house which he has not modernized for decades, then a spacious open-plan care home with the feel of a modern hotel might entrance him – or, perhaps once an initially favourable impression has worn off, it might repel him by its unfamiliar appearance. It is very easy when you go round a care home to be impressed by what impresses you rather than what would appeal to the person who might live there.

For people suffering from dementia, even if they are only in the earliest stages, familiarity of surroundings is very important. Clearly, the environment will be unfamiliar to start with, but if individual features within it look familiar and are in familiar places, then sufferers are more likely to be able to negotiate its mysteries. Judith Torrington of the University of Sheffield is conducting research into how different types of care home buildings suit dementia sufferers. Her initial results suggest that some features of traditional buildings are better than purpose-built ones at helping dementia sufferers to orientate themselves.[14] For instance the open-plan forms of many purpose-built homes can separate people from the external environment, making it harder to pick up the clues we absorb without thinking whenever we look out of the window about the time of day, the time of year and the weather. Seeing washing flapping on the line not only tells you what the weather is like, but also provides a familiar sight, which you will not get and may miss if the washing is simply delivered, clean and folded. Also, fireplaces without real fires in them, materials that look like wood but are really plastic and lever taps instead of twist ones can spread confusion in people with dementia. Judith Torrington's initial conclusions are in line with the thinking of Dr John Carr and Professor Mary Marshall of the Dementia Services Development Centre at the University of Stirling, who write, 'Designing a building that makes sense to people with dementia should be the aim of any architect, and for most people with dementia the style most familiar to them will be domestic.'[15]

Your Own Room

As you do your tour, Matron will show you the room she is offering to you or your relative. Under the new care home regulations, the contract between resident and home should specify which room is to be occupied. Make it clear to Matron that you are aware of this and assume that the room she is showing you is the one which will be your relative's permanent private space unless both she and you or your relative agree to a move. It has been the practice in some homes to show prospective residents the best unoccupied room in the establishment, only to move them to an inferior room a week or two after entry.

So what should you look for in the room?

Space

You will probably want a spacious room – in which to sit as well as to sleep and large enough to chat to visitors and for them to visit if you are confined to bed. The original minimum standards for care homes in England specified that from April 2007 single rooms would have to offer at least 10 square metres (12 square yards) of usable floor space, which should exclude any *en-suite* facilities. Shared rooms would have to contain at least 16 square metres (19 square yards) of usable floor space, excluding *en-suite* facilities. However, in 2003 the Secretary of State for Health, responding to continuing objections from the care home industry, modified these standards in England. In a revised edition of the national minimum standards, he laid down that homes already in existence before the Care Standards Act came into force on 1 April 2002 – the vast majority – would no longer be expected to meet these 'environmental' standards. Instead, they would be expected to ensure merely that the relevant dimensions had not declined since 31 March 2002.[16] However, at the time of writing, such changes had not been proposed for other parts of the UK. Also, new-build homes in England are still expected to meet the original environmental standards: there, the minimum is 12 square metres or 14 square yards for single rooms, excluding *en suite* facilities.

Just because these standards have been dropped does not mean that prospective residents of care homes in England should not try to find homes where the standards are actually met. In many homes they are met, sometimes because owners have carried out alterations so that they would be.

There were good reasons for these standards. Ten square metres is not actually a very large area. The figure is based partly on the desirability of having enough space for certain pieces of furniture. Standard 24 of the national minimum standards (and essentially the remaining standards in England stay in force) specifies that as a minimum an individual room must be furnished with a bed with a minimum width of 900 mm (2 feet 9 inches), drawers, an enclosed space for hanging clothes, a table to sit at as well as a bedside table, and comfortable seating for two people; in addition there should be curtains or blinds, a mirror, at least two accessible double electric sockets, overhead and bedside lighting and a wash-hand basin (unless the room is *en suite*).

The other reason for having rooms which are not too small is to allow people to be helped. If two care workers are going to have to attend to a person in bed, space is needed on either side for them to move around. If hoists and wheelchairs are required, then quite a lot of space will be needed. Bear this in mind if your older relative needs help with moving. Also make sure that all parts of the room will be large enough. For instance, it is easy to be impressed by the fact that your mother's room has an *en-suite* lavatory and washbasin. But if she needs help to get to them and the *en suite* is not large enough or its doorway not wide enough, say, for a hoist on wheels, it will stand empty in the middle of the night while she is taken to shared facilities perhaps some distance away, or has to make do with a commode by her bed.

Privacy

One other important change to the environmental standards in England involves room sharing. The original standards stated that from April 2007 all existing homes would have to provide 80 per cent of their places in single rooms. The revision says that such homes should now provide at least the same percentage of places in single rooms as they did on 31 March 2002.

If what you are being offered is a shared room, you will want to consider a number of matters (page 359). Also, the national minimum standards say that if people are sharing a room, there should be a screen 'to ensure privacy for personal care'. This is very important. It is hard to think of anything more likely to erode your dignity than to be washed in front of somebody else.

A Call System

One of the important features in the room will be a call system so that assistance can be summoned during the night. Is it easy to reach from the bed? If there is just one button in the far corner of the room, its occupant will probably be unable to reach it should he or she fall over in the other corner, so what safeguards exist to cope with this eventuality?

There is also the question of whether your relative will be able to work the alarm. People with very shaky hands might not be able to press a small button easily. A strip of Velcro placed over the button can help a partially sighted person find it. Good care homes will come up with imaginative solutions. You need to be convinced that your relative could easily summon assistance or that assistance would come quickly without privacy being unacceptably infringed. This involves discussion about the range of suitable devices, the frequency with which night staff patrol rooms and the particular condition of the individual.

Broadly speaking, people who are perfectly *compos mentis* and can operate an alarm manually only need an alarm which is accessible at all points in the room, adequate night lighting in case they get up on their own and the reassurance of a human being checking them regularly (whether they are asleep or awake). But if they have dementia they might not be able to learn how to use the room's call system. Even if they can, they might get up without summoning assistance. Cot-sides are sometimes used, but these can be dangerous if the resident is capable of trying to climb over them and may trouble the person they seek to protect. A mattress on the floor might be the answer, together with a light left on all night, but staff would need to know if such a person were stirring, so there would need to be a baby alarm or a device placed under the mattress which would sound an alarm on a worker's pager if a resident got out of bed. Mechanisms such as infra-red movement sensors or pressure pads adjacent to the bed will not alert staff until the resident is up.

People with dementia might wake in the night, but instead of attempting to rise they may lie awake in great distress, confused about where they are and perhaps calling out for help. Here again, something like a baby alarm suggests itself, together with frequent patrols by night staff. New inventions are coming on stream all the time in this area.[17] You need a system which will offer your relative as much safety as possible without imposing an unacceptable level of intrusive surveillance. You also want to watch that the home is not using technology as an excuse to reduce regular night-time patrols.

Also...
Some of the other points you might care to consider in the individual bedroom are:

- Is there an individual temperature control? It can be extremely frustrating to be unable to control this aspect of your own environment.
- Can you see out of a window when sitting up in bed? Does it afford a pleasant view?

- Is there a small lounge nearby which residents can use if they cannot sleep at night?
- Are there plenty of grab-rails?
- Is the bedroom quiet? Do not forget that the sleep of older people is often shallow, that they are more easily woken from it and take longer to get back to sleep
- Can your relative bring in her own furniture and hang her own pictures on the walls? This can be extremely important.
- Can she decide on the choice of wallpaper if the room is to be redecorated?
- Are there shelves for ornaments, pictures and books?
- Are there television and telephone sockets? Can residents have their own telephone number?
- Are any special needs catered for adequately? For example, if your relative is hard of hearing, what steps have been or could be taken to ensure that he can be alerted in the event of a fire, such as a flashing light or a vibrating alarm placed under the mattress? Is there sufficient space for any special flashing-light telephones or enhanced hearing systems with handsets or vibrating alarm clocks he or she may need?

The Internal Environment

As you go round the home, how warm or cold does it feel? Judith Torrington, who teaches architecture at the University of Sheffield, has designed care homes herself and has served as a lay care homes inspector, recommends a temperature of 23°C (73–4°F) for virtually all parts of a care home which elderly residents use – slightly higher than the generally recommended ambient temperature for older people of 20–21°C.[18] If you are in any doubt, ask what the temperature is, or use your thermometer.

As you go round the home, notice things which are out of the ordinary, though these will not necessarily be a bad sign. For instance, if the light in a resident's bedroom is lacking a shade, that is not necessarily because the home has failed to provide one. It may be that the resident's sight is very poor and the home is anxious to provide as much light as possible. This is to be commended, and will have to have been explained to the National Care Standards Commission inspector.

Similarly, you may come across residents who are dressed in an idiosyncratic manner. Perhaps somebody used to be a fireman or an army officer and likes to continue to wear the uniform. It is homes who allow, indeed encourage, residents to do their own thing which should be applauded; homes which should make alarm bells ring are those in which everybody looks similar and somehow depersonalized, slumped in chairs round the edge of the lounge in the middle of the morning.

One thing which should concern you is the sight of a resident sitting apart from the others. If he is in his room with the radio blaring out, he has probably chosen to be there, but if he is in his room doing nothing or seems to have been placed alone in one of the communal rooms far from others, it may well be that the home is trying to ignore him. Perhaps he has dementia and has been calling out a great deal. If this is the case, he should be being cared for by a member of staff, not being isolated in a way which will probably only compound his confusion, anxiety and misery.

Staff in good care homes will talk to dementia sufferers in normal human speech, although clearly and not too quickly, about their families and about their daily lives – their sons' football matches, family expeditions, what they are going to buy their children for Christmas. When they perform personal tasks for them they will talk them through what they are doing, even if such tasks have been performed many times before. If they are in really good homes, staff will be enthusiastically incorporating some of the new types of therapy being developed, such as dolls therapy, into the day-to-day life of the establishment (pages 355–6). Bad staff will treat people with dementia as social isolates, sometimes leaving them in a room on their own, never talking to them as normal human beings, chattering between themselves while cold-shouldering the sufferer. As a result, to the wretchedness and confusion imparted by the affliction is added a sense of being ostracized by fellow human beings.

Sitting and Watching

The most important factor in the lives of people living in care homes – the quality of their care – is the most variable. It is far harder for a prospective resident to judge the quality of care than the state of paintwork or the quality of bedroom accommodation. You can best tell whether your relative would be treated sympathetically and proficiently by simply sitting on your own in a care home and observing the behaviour around you. So if you think the home you have visited might suit your relative, ask Matron if you can come and just sit in, say, the lounge for an hour or two and get the feel of the place. No matter how much training staff may (or may not) have received, how high-calibre or how lowly, how many or how few, you need to know how they behave during the normal course of their work. Observe, too, who is doing the caring. A large home may have a number of qualified nurses and many care assistants, some with top-level NVQs, but they may shut themselves away in an office and leave most of the actual work to care assistants with little training. Ideally, qualified staff should be involved in activities such as helping residents to get up in the morning and bathing, as these tasks provide valuable opportunities for committed staff to chat to residents.

Once you are sitting on your own in the lounge, here are some things to look for:

- How are care assistants communicating with residents? Are staff sitting down and initiating conversations with residents and generally taking time to chat?
- Are care assistants taking account of any hearing impairment by bending and speaking distinctly close to the ear, perhaps holding the hand of the elderly person at the same time? If the resident is relying to some degree on lip-reading, are care assistants making sure that the resident can see their face before they speak and that it is well lit? If the person's hearing loss is severe, are care assistants prepared to write things down, or do they make the choices for residents, saving themselves the bother of asking?
- How do residents summon staff? Some residents will not be able to use some call systems – how are they being looked after? Are staff on hand, easily reached and looking out for people who might need help?
- Are residents treated with respect and warmth by staff? Are they all treated equally or is there evidence that staff have favourites? Is a special effort made to include people who might feel excluded, perhaps because they cannot take part in group activities?

- What role does routine play in the life of the home? Does it dominate, or provide an unobtrusive framework?
- What activities are residents actually participating in? It is all very well having an activities co-ordinator, but it is of limited help if her activities are unavailable to some.
- Are residents choosing to spend time in the lounge or in their own bedrooms? If you are visiting in the early evening, say about 6 o'clock, it is probably not a good sign if the lounge is empty and residents are opting to watch television in their own rooms. Conversely, might some be remaining in their rooms because they have not been offered help to move into the lounge?
- How are people helped to move around? Techniques for moving residents should vary according to their disabilities, but you ought to be able to judge whether people are being moved with consideration and skill.
- How do visitors get on in the home? Does it look as if they can approach Matron easily if they wish to? Do they seem to be encouraged to take an active role within the home? If you can get talking to a visitor, find out whether relatives are encouraged to get involved in decisions about residents' care.
- Look at how those residents least likely to complain or speak up for themselves are treated, such as those suffering from dementia or the aftermath of a severe stroke. Even if your relative does not suffer from such a problem, observing how care assistants are treating those who do is a good indication of their underlying motivation.

When you sit and watch you may need to ask for doors to be opened. An example from my own experience. I was interested in placing my mother in a smallish family-run care home which seemed friendly and welcoming and had a rather pleasant informal air, with staff apparently motivated to communicate with residents: I noticed them all discussing the contents of the local newspaper in the lounge during my pre-arranged visit mid-morning. After going away and mulling things over, I asked if I could come back just to sit. Waiting in the lounge while some elderly ladies not far away had their high tea, everything seemed all right, although the atmosphere was far more subdued than on my previous visit: the ladies taking their meal ate in silence and there was no background music or broadcast speech. One thing puzzled me particularly: I had thought the home contained more residents than this group. Where were the others? When I asked the proprietor, she tried to fob me off, but finally admitted that there were other residents; would I really like to see them? I insisted that I should. She led me to a room slightly out of the way with its door shut. On opening it, I beheld two young girls, who could not have been long out of school, attempting unsuccessfully to keep order round a table at which residents, probably all with dementia, were trying to eat. It was complete bedlam.

Hygiene
A good indicator of the quality of care practices is the effort taken to prevent the transmission of infections between residents and between staff and residents. If you are watching in the morning when care workers are scurrying up and down corridors changing the beds, how are they carrying bed linen? Holding it at arm's length indicates that they have received some instruction in good hygiene. If you hold dirty linen to your apron or overall, bacteria can be transferred to it and then on to other linen and indeed people. For the same reason, when workers come off their shifts, they should be changing out of their uniform before they leave the premises. That uniform may have faeces on it, and germs will be transmitted if the worker, say, hugs her children or leans over the delicatessen counter in a supermarket. Care workers who know these things will put their uniform into a bag and take it home with them or wash it on the care home premises.

Infection control is important because older people are often more susceptible than younger people to colds, chest, skin and urinary tract infections. Some will be taking medication, such as anti-cancer drugs, which depress their immune systems artificially. People taking steroids to combat various serious infections are likely to have paper-thin skin which, if broken, can allow in infections. Not only do such infections cause discomfort and distress, but older people often take a very long time to throw them off and antibiotics prescribed may have their own side-effects.

It is often difficult to control the transmission of germs in a care home because residents are unable to get out a tissue quickly enough to catch a sneeze or cough, or they forget to wash their hands after going to the lavatory, thereby perhaps leaving bacteria on door handles.

However, the main means of transferring serious infections in a care home (and hospital) is from the hands. Are care assistants washing their hands when they should? If they are carrying out personal care, they should be using a pair of disposable gloves. If they are going to touch food they should be washing their hands. So are care workers who have been in the lounge and possibly picking up infection through touching the clothing or the hair of a resident washing their hands before they hand out a cup of tea and a biscuit? Are they washing their hands thoroughly before they lay the tables or serve meals? And how are they washing them? Hand washing should be thorough, involve soap from a dispenser and take between 15 and 30 seconds, then make use of soft, disposable towels (page 341). Staff should not be applying hand cream after a wash, as they should have been told that this makes hands sticky and bacteria and dirt are thus more likely to stick. (Any staff who are about to carry out tasks such as dressing wounds or dealing with catheters should first wash with an alcohol skin rub, rubbing their hands for at least 30 seconds.)

Mealtimes

At a mealtime, are things rushed, even chaotic? Do residents get their food hot or is heat lost during transfer because serving is inefficient?

Transferring residents who cannot walk to the dining table takes staff time and effort. Is this available? When residents who need help are being sat at table for a meal, are their chairs eased in gently or are they pushed in roughly so that their feet drag or bump over the floor? Residents who can only be moved with a hoist may be left to eat their meal alone in armchairs because staff cannot be bothered or do not have the time to move them, even though this means they are excluded from the hub of life in the home. Are some of the residents left in wheelchairs at the dining table when they would clearly prefer to be on dining chairs? (A wheelchair will probably be less comfortable and offer less support than a dining chair.)

Is there interaction between residents during meals and between residents and staff? Is there a buzz of conversation or are residents sitting in silence? Are staff taking time not only to serve the food and where necessary help people to eat it, but also to stimulate social interaction? If residents reject food brought to their table, even though they may have asked for it, are requests for a replacement complied with quickly?

Ethos

As you sit and watch or perhaps when you go away afterwards and think about what you have observed, try to come to conclusions about the ethos of the home. You might find it useful to structure these around the following trade-offs which homes have to make, consciously or unconsciously.

Profit versus Care

Don't base your judgement only on spending which is particularly obvious to visitors, such as a newly-decorated lobby with matching carpet and curtains. The amount of money actually spent on heating, lighting, tea-bags, supports in the loo and staff training should enable you to come to a more informed conclusion on this fundamental clash.

Efficiency versus Empathy

Many homes are efficiently administered, beautifully furnished and spotlessly clean with never a hint of an unpleasant smell, and residents may be physically well. But such places can still be cold at heart if the manager is unable or unwilling to empathize with her residents. He or she may be knowledgeable in tissue viability and safe moving and handling, and may not cut corners in terms of expenditure, but may still not exude warmth. He or she may never have sat down for a moment and imagined what it must be like to be a resident, or what residents must think about all day as they sit waiting for the next ministration. You can easily imagine such a manager as a child, with dolls lined up to be washed and dressed in turn, but never really existing as individuals. Thirty years on, such people treat the residents in their care homes in exactly the same way. So when you meet the manager, ask yourself whether behind that capable smile there is a warm-hearted person, not simply an excellent organizer (and organizing a care home is no mean task), but someone with deep human warmth and sufficient imagination and inclination to empathize with her residents.

The cold efficient type often shows little flexibility in what will be countenanced. Pets will probably not be permitted. Partners or close relatives who have been carers and would like to continue to participate, perhaps helping with bathing, may be denied the chance by the inflexibility of the home's arrangements. Workhouse-like rules may prevail – no alcohol, smoking discouraged, idiosyncratic behaviour frowned upon, romantic relationships between residents obstructed, visits by partners in the privacy of a resident's bedroom made difficult. Of course, in these areas there is a balance to be struck between individual freedom and the sensitivities of other residents, but a good home will manage to achieve this in a way which keeps everybody happy without too much trouble.

Helping versus Taking Over
Elderly people going into a care home will still normally be capable of performing a range of tasks – sorting books, DVDs and videos, helping to plan menus, activities and outings and many more (page 34). It is easier for the care home to get staff to do all these things, but residents who engage in such tasks probably benefit in many ways, from the physical and mental exercise to the enhancement of self-esteem which comes from feeling that they are doing something useful and creative. How does the home resolve this conflict? A home which figures out ways in which residents could help if they wish to do so, and without exploiting them, is probably going to be one which shows a greater awareness of the whole person. And of course activities like these provide countless opportunities for interaction between residents and between staff and residents.

Appearance versus Care
Home managers may be tempted to put disproportionate effort and money into the appearance of their homes, as this is the packaging of the product and helps it to sell. But a good home will have its heart in the care of its residents, not in the state of

the paintwork. I remember going round an EMI nursing home in a beautiful listed building set in spectacular grounds with the owner, who had a nursing qualification. We passed many people in need of much assistance. The owner did not respond to them. However, when we passed a tiny patch of dirt on the carpet – left by a workman who had been decorating – she was immediately on her knees with brush and dustpan to sweep it away.

A really good home will be keen to consider new approaches to care. These do not have to be expensive. Merevale House in Warwickshire cares for people with dementia, some of them under 65. It has pioneered the use of dolls therapy. Individual residents are encouraged, if they wish, to have their own doll, which they communicate with and care for (feeding, dressing and washing). Some of them are aware that it is a doll, others refer to it as their baby, or call it by the name of one of their children. David Moore, a psychologist who worked at Merevale House, explained in an article in 2001, 'My previous training had taught me that giving an individual with dementia a doll was childish, patronising and demeaning – the opposite of our aim to treat each individual with the respect they deserved.'[19] But he changed his mind. Residents (men as well as women) with dolls became less agitated, less aggressive and wandered around less. The dolls stimulated interaction, occupied residents' thoughts and channelled their physical energies too: 'Staff and the individual talk about the doll, about what clothes the doll should wear, and help fold the clothes.'

David Moore believes that dolls perform many other useful functions. Residents may transfer their own emotional state on to the doll, claiming that their baby is upset, which staff take as an indication of the individual's own feelings. Dolls may help meet a psychological need for attachment to others by providing a sense of comfort and security. Particularly valuable, in my view, is the notion that dolls can give individuals with dementia a sense of purpose and usefulness. My mother, an Alzheimer's sufferer, would endlessly ask, 'Who am I? What should I do now?' while sitting in a chair from which she did not realize she could no longer rise.

Dolls will not suit everybody, however. Some might instead prefer soft-toy dogs or ducks. Dolls might cause increased agitation in people who might worry that they would not be able to look after their doll properly. And of course many people would not welcome a doll at all. But at Merevale some relatives, too, have entered into the spirit of things, bringing in new dolls, dolls' clothes and even in one case a cot and pram; the dolls have provided a new route to the soul of people with dementia who had otherwise become unreachable.

Other Matters
If you have been through these stages of evaluation and are confident that your relative would be well cared for and happy in a certain home, there are further matters to consider before you commit yourself.

Location
Probably the location of a care home will matter less than the quality of care. However, you might like to be reassured that relatives and friends could visit easily, including elderly friends travelling by public transport. A community of people close by, whether in a town centre, a suburb or a village, increases the chances that other people will pop into the home, visiting, carol-singing, taking in schoolchildren and otherwise involving residents in community projects and community life.

Is the home close to the sort of facilities your relative likes, whether football grounds or art galleries? Are there places to which the home's residents can be taken on short trips either by car or on foot or in a wheelchair? Homes in seaside resorts with promenades affording safe walking or wheeling with views of the sea and shopping centres close by have an undoubted advantage that homes in glorious grounds but in remote countryside may not have: field paths can be impossibly bumpy in a wheelchair, and country lanes dangerous.

Another reason for choosing a home which is not too remote is staffing. Many homes find it difficult enough to find staff even if conveniently located: if they are in out-of-the way and thinly populated areas, they will almost certainly have trouble filling holiday and sickness slots with agency workers. Other human help may also be harder to come by. If your relative wishes to keep his or her existing GP, he or she will need to remain within the practice's catchment area or close by (the boundaries are often a little flexible).

Doctors, Dentists and Opticians

When people move into a care home, they can retain their original GP if the home lies within the geographical catchment area of that GP practice. If it does not, they usually transfer to the practice associated with the home. Care homes usually have a link with a local GPs practice. This may mean no more than most residents are patients on the lists of that practice's GPs. Often, however, homes pay an annual retainer to a doctor or a practice, separately from fees GPs receive from the NHS in respect of all patients on their lists. In return for this retainer, the GP will undertake to take on existing and any new residents at a home who do not already have a doctor, attending them when necessary. He or she may also visit the home at regular intervals, say once a week, and see any residents who need attention. The cost, which is the result of negotiation and varies widely, is passed on to residents through higher care home fees. A survey in 2001 by the Association of Charity Officers found that a third of care homes surveyed were paying retainer fees to GPs. However, it also found that the most active non-retained GPs provided a greater range of services than some of their retained colleagues.[20]

So ask Matron for details of any GP practice associated with the home, and if you wish, go and meet the doctor or doctors involved before you decide on entry. Also find out whether the retainer the home pays the practice delivers any more than a practice should be expected to deliver for free in return for payment from the NHS (pages 56–7 and 468–9). For instance, you should not have to pay for your flu jab.

In a care home you have as much right to choose your own GP as anybody else. Paragraph 13 of the Care Homes Regulations emphasizes the point: 'The registered person shall make arrangements for service users to be registered with a general practitioner of their choice.'

Find out what arrangments the home has made to provide opticians, dentists and chiropodists prepared to visit residents who cannot easily get out. Not only do needs for teeth and glasses change over time: they may get lost and even thrown away by accident. If this happens, you need to be sure that your relative would get replacements as soon as possible.

Contracts

It is extremely important that a care home resident should have a contract. If the place is being provided through a contract between the social services department and the home, residents should still have a statement of the detailed terms and conditions under which they will be living.

Without a contract a resident is at the mercy of the home, which may choose to impose additional charges, cut services, change the regime of care or alter accommodation arrangements, for instance moving your relative out of a single bedroom to share with somebody else. You may feel that the manager of your home would never behave in that way, but supposing she leaves or the ownership of the home changes? It is extremely dangerous to move in without the contract having been finalized and signed. If you do, you are in a very weak position to object to anything, from a hike of the fees or a major change in the pattern of care, to eviction.

Standard 2 of the national minimum standards for care homes provides a useful basis for a contract. It states:

> Each service user is provided with a statement of terms and conditions at the point of moving into the home (or contract if purchasing their care privately).
>
> The statement of terms and conditions includes:

- Rooms to be occupied
- Overall care and services (including food) covered by fee
- Fees payable and by whom (service user, local or health authority, relative or another)
- Additional services (including food and equipment) to be paid for over and above those included in the fees
- Rights and obligations of the service user and registered provider and who is liable if there is a breach of contract
- Terms and conditions of occupancy, including period of notice (eg short/long term intermediate care/respite).

Before you sign the contract, get a solicitor to scrutinize it clause by clause. Also, you might care to compare it with the

Framework Contract between Residential Care Provider and Resident drawn up by a group of commercial, charitable and public service organizations called the Continuing Care Conference which revised its model contract in 2002 to take account of recent legislative changes. This model is extremely useful for showing what could be covered in a contract and also what should not be there. You could also seek advice from a voluntary organization.

Room Sharing

The Care Home Regulations lay down that the contract between resident and home should specify which room is to be occupied. This is an extremely useful provision – if homes comply with it. It has been the practice in some homes to show prospective residents the best unoccupied room, only to move them to an inferior room a week or two after entry, with just a cursory mention that this is about to happen. So check that your contract with the home or that between the home and social services specifies the room you have agreed, and expect to be consulted if management would like to shift you to another room; if they fail to, or if they move your relative without consent, they are breaking the contract.

Suppose you act as your relative's representative but live some distance away, and Matron rings you up to say she would like to move your relative (who perhaps has dementia and is deemed incapable of making such judgements) into a shared room. How should you respond? Matron will doubtless say it is in your relative's best interests, but as you are not present in the home during the night you do not know whether he or she would value company then, as perhaps Matron claims, let alone the company of the particular person proposed. How can you judge?

Don't let yourself be pushed into a quick decision. This is an important matter. There are advantages and disadvantages to sharing, and much depends on what individuals feel comfortable with. If you do not sleep well, nights in a care home can be very long and very lonely, all the more so if you have always shared a bedroom, in childhood with brothers and sisters and later with a spouse. Sharing with a person with whom you get along and who has a similar sleep pattern to your own may be more appealing than the alternative.

However, a home might have its own reasons for putting two residents in the same bedroom. The most obvious incentive is to create more rooms so it can take more residents and make more profit. There may be others. For instance, if two residents demand more attention than others during the night, it is easier to care for them both if they are together. But this might not benefit those residents. Just as one is getting back to sleep, the other might wake up, generating sleep-wrecking commotion as staff minister to him or her. You need to bear such factors in mind, and also of course the character of the room-mate proposed. Would he or she provide welcome company during the dark watches or provoke antagonism?

Complaints

Every home has to establish a procedure for considering complaints made to it by residents or people acting on their behalf. It also has to ensure that any complaint made under this procedure is fully investigated and must inform the person who made the complaint of any action which is to be taken within 28 days of the date on which the complaint was made.

The way in which a home deals with complaints is quite a good indicator of how it is likely to treat residents and their relatives. A home that does no more than comply with the regulations in the most minimal way will probably try its utmost to brush off complaints. It may not see the resident or relative as someone with a valid point to make and may assume that any critical comment implies a lack of understanding of how care homes are run. Such an attitude is not unusual. The people who run care homes, particularly large or medium-sized ones, are essentially managers, and it can be a management objective to manage complaints to minimize the disruption they cause, regardless of the validity of the complaints or the corrective action they demand. I remember well attending a training day for care home managers when we were instructed in various ways in which managers could defuse the annoyance of residents, the assumption always being that they would be misguided, misinformed or petulant, or that frustration at some incurable condition was causing them to make absurd criticisms of the home. In other words, those who complain were to be treated like children – they should be given a sweet to distract them from their absurd preoccupation, leaving staff to manage the home as only they know how.

You need a complaints procedure which implies that complaints may be perfectly valid and will be looked at objectively. There should be a willingness not only to apologize, but also to take action to prevent recurrence if the complaint is justified. Relatives often protest that if they do complain, the home responds with an apology but no action is taken, or if it is, no further steps are taken to ensure that the problem will not recur. So does the procedure contain a guarantee not just of apology but also of action?

You also want evidence that the home understands the unenviable position of a relative or resident who has a concern. Complainants often fear victimization: look in the complaints procedure for reassurance that no resident will be penalized in any way because of complaining.

The procedure should also make it clear to whom a complaint should be addressed and spell out clearly further steps a complainant could take if remaining dissatisfied, such as contact details for the local National Care Standards Commission inspector.

Smoking and Other Considerations

If your relative likes to smoke, you will need to find out in which parts of the premises this is tolerated. If this is just one sitting room and your relative smokes a good deal, the character of that room – its size, furniture, outlook and facilities, such as the presence or absence of a hearing loop system – are going to be very important. If your relative needs help to light up and perhaps supervision while smoking, will that be forthcoming and, crucially, how often? It is heartbreaking to see an older man with dementia asking over and over again if he could please have a cigarette or his pipe when staff control his access to the weed and refuse to let him smoke as often as he would like to.

Other matters you might care to consider include:

- If you have a pet, can you bring it in with you? If you can, how can the pet best be managed (pages 242–3)?
- Does the home encourage young children to visit? Older people often value encounters with children and babies,

whether or not they are related to them. If your older person likes to see and hear infants, does the home actively encourage young children by providing toys and games or perhaps a climbing frame?

- Can visitors appear at any time? Can they stay for meals? Is there any accommodation for them to stay overnight and, if so, what is it like and how much does it cost?
- Are religious services held in the home? Could the home organize reliable transport to enable your relative to attend services nearby? Get a real guarantee if this is important, not just 'Oh, that won't be a problem.' You may find that, contrary to what Matron has led you to expect, Sunday mornings never deliver members of staff who could drive residents to church.
- To what extent do residents participate in the life of the community? Were they taken out to the local town's Golden Jubilee celebrations? Did the majority of residents vote at the most recent elections? Voting can keep care home residents in touch with the outside world and make them feel they are still valued members of society.
- Would a trial stay be welcome and how could it be arranged (page 394)?

Another matter which alas takes longer to consider is the fees and how they can be paid.

Chapter 11
The Cost

Fees

Care home residents fall into two main categories: those paid for largely by the state (a small number by their health body if they have a high level of health care needs, the remainder by the Department for Work and Pensions and their local authority); and those who pay their bills themselves, usually with some contribution from the state.

The vast majority of care homes contain a mixture of residents paying for themselves and others funded by the NHS or their local authority. The care these two groups receive is the same; the main difference, if there is one, is that the people paying for themselves ('self-funders') often have a better choice of room. However, care homes particularly like self-funders because they often pay higher fees than local authorities or the NHS are prepared to stump up (page xxvii). Self-funders do not usually know what these authorities are paying for the same care as they are getting, nor which of their fellow residents are state-funded.

What this means is that if you are paying your own fees, you may well have room to haggle when a care home manager tells you the tariff: he or she may be asking you for a lot more than he or she would receive from the state. If you know when you are bargaining with the manager what rate a home is paid by local and/or health authorities for their residents, you are in a stronger position, so ask the authority beforehand. Then you can ask the manager how he proposes to justify charging you, say, £150 a week more. However, if places in the home you favour are in short supply, you may decide to pay whatever the management demand lest you lose the room.

Once you have agreed the level of fees, you should make sure the home cannot increase them whenever it chooses, by ensuring a limit is set in the contract. You could aim to limit rises to the rate of inflation at a set date once a year. Homes in which residents have entered into care payment plans (page 369) sometimes agree to a limit on increases of 5 per cent a year. You may have difficulty in negotiating a tight limit to fee increases if there is a shortage of care home places. Obviously any institution will try to avoid being tied down when it has no idea what may happen to wage levels and regulatory demands in the future.

Whatever the level of the fees, it is important that you should be clear what they cover. The fee should in any case be broken down into charges for accommodation, food and care. It should state clearly what is included, such as food, cleaning of the bedroom and communal areas, insurance (find out what it covers), an alarm system in the bedroom, the provision of 24-hour care, and therapy and equipment as set out in the care plan (page 394).

If you are receiving nursing care, there should be an element which will be paid by the state, not by you, no matter how wealthy you are – the free nursing care element (page 384). In Scotland, this will embrace personal care as well (page 389). Both these elements should also be set out in the fees statement.

Supplementary chiropody, aromatherapy, transport, hairdressing, clothing, toiletries, stationery, non-prescription medicine, dry-cleaning and telephone calls may be excluded from the fees. If they are, you need to know so that you can budget accordingly.

Third-party Top-ups

We noted in the last chapter that people with low incomes whose savings fall below the upper capital limit (£19,500 in England and Northern Ireland, £18,500 in Scotland or £20,000 in Wales in 2003) can look to their local authority to meet part of their care home fees and councils meet the whole of the fees for people with modest incomes whose savings amount (perhaps after they have been depleted through paying care home bills) to the lower capital limit (£12,000 in England and Northern Ireland, £11,500 in Scotland and £12,250 in Wales in 2003), after these people have contributed items like their State Retirement Pension.

However, people funded in this way do not necessarily have to rely totally on the level of funding which social services is prepared to add to their own contribution and that from the Department for Work and Pensions. They are free to try to secure what is called a 'third-party top-up'. This means getting somebody else to agree to meet the difference between the fee the local authority is prepared to pay and what a chosen home demands. Top-ups therefore enable people to live in care homes which are more expensive than the ones local authorities are prepared to countenance.

The source of the top-up could be a relative, a friend, a charity, trade association, benevolent association, or a combination of these. Residents themselves are not allowed to provide their own top-up, except in two particular circumstances (known as a deferred payments scheme and the 12-week disregard; pages 373 and 376). The argument is that were they to do so, they would be depleting their resources more quickly from the upper to the lower capital limit and thereby beating the system.

If somebody agrees to top-up your relative's fees, it is vital to know whether he or she will continue to do so until your relative leaves the care home or dies (and you could be talking about £100-plus a week indefinitely), otherwise your relative may have to move to a cheaper home. The person also has to be prepared to pay for a share of increases in care home fees; the proportion should be firmed up beforehand with the local authority, but councils often like to make it clear that increases will not necessarily be shared evenly between themselves and third parties paying top-ups.

Before a person or organization agrees to provide a top-up, make sure that the council itself should not be covering the whole of what would be met by the top-up. It is tempting for councils to contribute less than they might if they think they can lean on relatives. Councils are not permitted to say they never pay more than a certain amount to fund a care home place: they have to pay whatever it costs to meet a person's assessed needs, while doing so at the lowest possible cost (pages 318–19).

Paying the Bills

Some people do not need to worry about their bills because these will simply be paid for them. Some of these people are in independent nursing homes and are paid for by the National Health Service through their local health body because it has been decided that they meet the criteria for 'Continuing NHS Care' (pages 469–78). These people eventually lose most of their State Retirement Pension as well as other state benefits such as Attendance Allowance and Income Support, but they are free to keep their occupational or personal pensions as well as their savings. There is thus no question of their having to sell their homes.

Another category of residents have their bills paid in care homes when they are placed there after having been compulsorily detained in hospital under section 117 of the Mental Health Act, 1983. Sometimes local authorities charge people in this situation for their care when they should not; if you think this is happening to your relative, take up the matter with your health body or local council and seek a refund. One local authority found itself having to pay back £60,000 for this reason.[1] A grey area is how long the health authority or the local authority should continue to pay under this provision; dementia sufferers who have been sectioned and then placed in a care home might be able to receive free care thereafter for the rest of their lives. If you are taking action, it is worth contacting one of the major voluntary organizations such as Mind or the Alzheimer's Society. The Local Government Ombudsman issued a useful report in 2003 about the reimbursement of people who have been wrongly charged in this way.[2]

Apart from these categories of people and those who enter care homes only for a temporary or a trial stay (page 394) people moving into care homes are funded in one of several different ways.

Some people will have sufficient income to pay care home fees themselves for the whole of their lives, even though these fees might run to £30,000 every year. In addition to their state pension, they may have occupational or personal pensions, insurance or investments. They may decide to sell any home they own as well, but may not need to do so. Instead, the house may perhaps be rented out or lived in by members of the family. Or it may be sold and the money invested, perhaps in a care homes payment plan, so that while some cash is released to pay current bills, the remainder is invested so that the financial estate regenerates itself.

However wealthy such people may be, they are entitled to access to two non-means-tested state benefits. Attendance Allowance is a benefit payable as a contribution towards the extra costs imposed by disability on people who become severely disabled at the age of 65 or over (pages 485–8). To qualify, individuals must demonstrate that they have a need for care from others. Some people receive Attendance Allowance when they are living in their own homes. There is no requirement to spend it in any particular way. It is neither taxable nor contributory. In 2003 it stood at £38.30 each week, and £57.20 for people with a higher level of disability.

People in a nursing home can also receive a contribution from the state to cover the cost of care by a registered nurse. 'Free nursing care' is available to residents in nursing homes in England, Wales and Northern Ireland. In Scotland, care home residents can receive a contribution to cover both nursing and personal care costs in a care home, whatever their financial circumstances, although they lose their Attendance Allowance when they do so. We return to free nursing and personal care later (pages 384–90).

If people are deemed to have insufficient income to pay their care home fees and their total savings amount to no more than the lower capital limit (£12,000, or £11,500 in Scotland and £12,250 in Wales), the state steps in and helps them out.

Their fees are met from three different sources. They themselves have to contribute their State Retirement Pension and any additional pensions such as an occupational pension. They have to apply to the Department for Work and Pensions (or DWP) for Income Support, which goes to pay part of the fees; finally their local council makes up the remainder.

These people essentially lose their financial independence, having only a small sum (£17.50 each week in 2003) to call their own – an amount of money their local authority has to make sure they receive and which is called the 'personal expenses allowance' (page 380). As we have seen, some of these people are in homes more expensive than those to which their local authority would normally send people because a third party is paying a top-up.

A third group has insufficient income to pay care home fees

week by week, but still has assets (including the value of any home they own) which exceed the upper capital limit (£19,500 or £18,500 in Scotland and £20,000 in Wales). These assets will disqualify them from receiving a local authority contribution to fee payment so they will have to foot the bill themselves, even though this will eat up their savings. If they have a sum between the upper and the lower capital limits (£19,500 and £12,000 or the equivalent figures in Scotland and Wales), the authority will contribute part of the cost because, although they will be expected to contribute their income, they will no longer be expected to make such a large contribution from their capital.

This constitutes a large group of older people entering care homes. These people will be over the capital limits threshold, but not be so well off that they can keep their house while paying care home bills from other sources such as investments. They must make some choices about their home.

When councils assess elderly people for entitlement to a contribution from them to care home bills and the Department for Work and Pensions for entitlement to Income Support to help pay for support in a care home, both take the value of any house or flat into account. Their assumption is that the property will be sold and the proceeds used to pay care home bills until the elderly person's resources are depleted to the upper capital limit threshold (£19,500 or equivalent), at which the local authority begins to contribute, or the £16,000 threshold below which elderly people in care homes are eligible to receive Income Support.

People over the upper capital limit threshold should therefore make sure that they are receiving the non-means-tested payments to which they may be entitled – Attendance Allowance and free nursing and personal care contributions. They also need to prepare to ask their local authority for help if and when their savings approach the upper threshold figure. Social services will not know people are approaching that point unless they are told. Once told, they will not necessarily jump into action. In any case, they will start paying out only when they have carried out a community care assessment and a financial assessment. All this means that you would be well advised to alert them several months before you or your relative will actually be entitled to their help. People often find that funding by the local council is not set up in time, and they have to go on footing the entire care home bill even when they are below the threshold. If this happens to you, ask the council for a refund, quoting if necessary the Minister of State for Health, who stated during the passage of the Health and Social Care Bill in 2001, 'No one should be asked to contribute unfairly, outwith the terms of the means test. If a resident is asked to contribute in that way, it raises the issue of compensating him for the charges that he has been asked to pay.'[3]

Once you have sought financial help from your local authority, that authority will almost certainly tell you to prepare to apply to the DWP, through your local Social Security Office, for Income Support, for which you will be eligible once your savings go down to a (confusingly different) £16,000 threshold.

Finally, this third group too can maximize revenue from the house sale by investing the proceeds while allowing a certain amount to be available to pay current fees. The method of doing this is called a 'care fees payment plan', and you can get details from the Nursing Homes Fees Agency or through the Help the Aged Fees Advisory Service, which works with the NHFA and several different insurance companies, or through Age Concern England, which has links with a scheme run by the Norwich Union. If the circumstances are right, it can mean that financial resources from the house sale generate healthy revenue over the years.

The Fate of the Family Home
What relatives of people in this third group want to know is: can we somehow keep the house rather than surrender it to pay care home fees? In particular, should ownership of the house be passed to, say, a son or daughter ahead of time, so that should care home admission become necessary, the house does not have to be sold?

One of the most agonizing aspects of moving into care can be the prospect of losing the family home. Some people cling to the idea that going into a care home may be a temporary measure. If their house has been sold, they know they can never return to it or the memories it harbours. Other family members may share some sense of bereavement as their childhood environment disappears.

There are certain circumstances in which a local authority is forbidden from taking into account the value of an elderly person's house or flat when carrying out a financial assessment to see what contribution he or she should make to care home bills. If the stay in a care home is only temporary, the value of a dwelling cannot be assessed for care home payments. Some stays are for a rest or recuperation, perhaps as part of a planned programme of temporary, recuperative stays. A trial period stay also counts as temporary.

If the dwelling is being lived in by a spouse or partner, a close relative over the age of 60, or a relative under 60 who is incapacitated, it is also off-limits. Not only can the inhabitant continue to live there, but the owner can retain the deeds.

One group not necessarily covered by this arrangement are middle-aged children who have been living at home and caring for their parent or parents. In that situation, the local council is allowed to take the value of the property into account; it can, however, ignore it if it chooses to exercise a discretion so to do.

A middle-aged friend of mine spent many years looking after her frail elderly mother, who suffered a number of strokes in her own home. My friend went out to work and hired help in the home, at first just a little, later for 24 hours a day as her mother needed far more help than the local council was prepared to part-fund. Eventually, the old lady went into a care home. The council refused to contribute towards the bills on the grounds that there was a property which should be sold, and it chose not to exercise its discretion in my friend's favour. Had the house been sold, my friend would have had to find another home for herself. She did not want to sell the family home, in which she had grown up and which her parents had designed when they got married: it was conveniently located close to the care home, and she liked to bring her mother back there for tea at weekends. So she was forced to take out loans to pay the care home fees herself; five years on, she is continuing to repay these debts, although she herself is now about to retire. In such a situation, all you can do is lobby your council to smile on you, but it may well say it has more pressing claims on its undoubtedly limited resources and you may be left to make arrangements as best you can.

If permanent care home residence is in prospect and no spouse or other qualifying person also lives in the house or flat, defensive measures suggest themselves. By passing ownership of their houses to their children while still living in them, elderly people may hope to mitigate tax as well as cheating the council of an eventual contribution to home-care bills. However, neither the taxman (pages 509–10) nor the council is to be foiled without careful planning.

Care home bills have to be paid by somebody. Why should the resident be spared this burden if the real beneficiary may be an heir perhaps far better off than many of the taxpayers who will otherwise be stumping up? This is at least the logic of the law of England, Wales and Northern Ireland, though Scotland shows more respect for the idea of universal provision of a cradle-to-grave Welfare State.

Why Selling Up Hurts

In practice, elderly people can lose a great deal more from the sale of their house or flat than the ability to pass on what is probably the bulk of their wealth to their children. They lose the chance to return occasionally to, and the very idea of, a home of their own. These considerations can justify relatives' efforts to safeguard the family home, apart from their own self-interest.

The possibility of returning to the family home can do wonders for the well-being of a care home resident. A community care assessment may indicate at some point that care home support is appropriate, but perhaps after a while your relative's health may improve so that independent living becomes possible again. If there is any chance of this, make the most of it when negotiating an assessment with social services, in particular whether residence should be temporary or permanent. The thought of going back home can act as a strong incentive for rehabilitation and give people extra motivation to persevere with, say, exercises prescribed after a stroke or an operation. People who know that staff in a care home will be on hand to serve them all their meals and take charge of the cleaning and laundry for the rest of their lives can be forgiven for giving up.

The possibility of returning home occasionally can also be therapeutic. One of the most satisfactory arrangements I have come across involves an elderly lady living in a care home from Monday until Friday, the bills paid by her local authority as she had handed her own house over to her children several years before she was assessed as needing care home provision. On Friday evenings, her son, who works full-time during the week 70 miles away, drives down and takes his mother back to the family home and cares for her until he returns to his own home and work on Sunday evening. When one of his sisters comes from overseas each summer for a few weeks, she can stay in her old family home and her mother can come back and live there with her. Clearly, this sort of arrangement is not possible unless adaptations have been put in place in the family house beforehand, as people assessed as needing care home support are usually pretty frail and may not, for instance, easily be able to negotiate their own front step. And there needs to be somebody willing and able to care 24 hours a day when the elderly person is staying at home. Family members may feel readier to make such efforts, however, if they know their parent has given them the family home.

Another important reason for passing the house to a close relative is that such a person may otherwise lose out if he or she lives in the house with a parent before the latter moves into a care home; the local council may decline to disregard the value of the property in its calculations, and such relatives would lose their homes, unless they could afford to pay the care home bills themselves.

Saving the family home may help older people feel better, quite apart from its implications for their own lifestyle. Even if they cannot return to it themselves, it may be useful for their children or grandchildren to stay in while visiting. Its continued existence in their minds may help them adjust to the new world in which they find themselves. Having passed on the fruits of their lifetime labours to their children can strengthen their own sense of self-worth, which will face many attacks.

It may be possible for the children to rent out the family home to tenants, generating income which might be used, for example, to pay a top-up, while keeping other options open. The house will no longer be available for family members to live in, but at least the house remains in the ownership of the family.

If a sale is forced and it is carried out by children using a registered enduring power of attorney because their parent has lost the mental capacity to handle his or her own affairs, they sometimes try to keep news of the sale quiet to save their parent distress. This may mean ensuring everyone lies to the elderly person, or is at least non-committal – relatives, friends, care staff. That can place additional stress on already troubled people. Maintaining such a web of deception can be a nightmare.

Borrowed Time

There are ways of avoiding at least some of these horrors. It is important to avoid being pushed into selling the house quickly. This should be easier since the government introduced in 2001 what it calls 'the 12-week disregard'. This ensures that from the start of permanent admission to a care home, local authorities are legally obliged to disregard the value of new residents' property for 12 weeks, and have been given extra funds from central government to do so. After 12 weeks, with a house to sell, you can become totally independent of the council if you wish, as a self-funder, or you can let your council have the contract with the care home while you pay the council, if your council operates that sort of arrangement. During the 12 weeks, you can claim Attendance Allowance and, if your capital is fairly low, Income Support as well.[4]

The 12-week disregard is one of the occasions on which residents in care homes are allowed to top-up out of their own resources. However, they cannot top-up using the value of the property they are going to sell, and topping-up must not bring their savings to below the lower capital limit (£12,000 in England and Northern Ireland, £11,500 in Scotland and £12,250 in Wales).

The disregard allows you more time to select a buyer you believe will be sympathetic to the character and general atmosphere of the house, something which may mitigate the distress caused. When an elderly relative moves into a care home, relatives find themselves with much to do, not least in ensuring that the elderly person is as happy as possible, and so it is tempting to hand the sale over to agents. If you do, and you think you are going to care about who will be living in your family home in years to come, make sure you meet the prospective purchaser. After all, you are not selling the house in order to make money for yourself, but to relieve the state of a financial burden.

Transferring Ownership

The obvious way of preventing the house being sold to pay care home bills is to change the ownership of the house in advance so it cannot be counted as the property of the older person if he or she has to go into care and the council comes to pounce. People have been doing this for a number of years. However, it is not foolproof. Even if somebody has passed property to their children, social services and – separately – the Department for Work and Pensions can still get hold of the money tied up in the property if they consider that the transfer has taken place with the deliberate intention of depleting the resources of the older person. If either body considers that this 'deprivation of assets' has happened, it can require that the amount involved be taken into account: in other words, the children to whom the property may have been passed will have to find the value of the house in cash.

The idea has developed that there is a seven-year statute of limitations – that so long as the property has been transferred to children for at least seven years, neither a council nor the DWP can touch it. This is a myth – there is no such limit and the authorities can look back as far as they like. The confusion has probably arisen because of the seven-year rule which exempts gifts from inheritance tax (pages 509–10). Nonetheless, the council has to take into account the difficulties of proving the motive for the transfer, and the longer-standing the transfer, the more likely you are to get away with it. Don't bother trying to do this within six months of moving into a care home.

Clearly, elderly people must make sure they trust the person or people to whom they transfer the ownership of their property – a transfer which may take place years before they move to a care home, if indeed they ever do. They may feel they can trust their son and daughter, but are they so sure about their son- or daughter-in-law? What if their son or daughter dies and it is the in-law who becomes their new landlord? Supposing the son or daughter remarries and the new spouse fancies moving into the house, with or without the elderly person? Suppose a son or daughter decides to extend the property without the parent's agreement, remortgaging it to do so, only to find subsequently that they cannot meet mortgage repayments so the property is repossessed? Those who transfer property to other people, even their own children, need to discuss possibilities such as this. Most will find it too distasteful and embarrassing to do so. If so, they need to be ready to live with the consequences.

Arrangements must anyway be made to apportion responsibility for maintaining the property. The new owner(s) need to decide when and how it should be decorated and whether the elderly person should pay rent to them (pages 173–4). A transfer may affect an elderly person's eligibility for various grants to help maintain and repair property (pages 203–5). So before you go ahead, think through the possibilities carefully and get legal advice if you are in any doubt.

Those concerned to protect the family home but seeking formal safeguards for a potential care home resident may consider placing the house in trust. A 'life interest' trust could transfer ownership to heirs while guaranteeing the right of the transferor to live in the property during his or her lifetime. In the event of care home entry, the value of the house should be disregarded when assessment of the contribution paid to fees comes to be made. If the donor and the heirs fall out, the former's right to live in the house will be fully protected.

Another kind of trust, the 'discretionary trust', may serve a similar function. However, both kinds of trust need to be tailored to individual circumstances. Be careful about off-the-shelf schemes. Consult a solicitor and make sure you understand exactly what you are letting yourself in for. As with other transfers of ownership, you will need to avoid so far as is possible the risk of the council or the DWP alleging that you are in breach of the deliberate deprivation of assets rule referred to above.

A Ray of (Partial) Hope

Since 2002, it has been possible in some cases for care home residents to retain access to their former homes even if the equity has to be sacrificed. However, this is an option which local authorities are not legally obliged to offer. If you want to take advantage of it and your social worker does not mention it, then you have got to ask for it yourself.

The Deferred Payments Scheme involves coming to an agreement with your local authority to allow someone entering a care home to defer the payment to be made from the sale of their property until after their death (a sort of interest-free loan from the council). So, if your relative cannot meet care home fees from his or her own resources and therefore would have to sell his home and use the proceeds until his savings dropped to the capital threshold, the council will pay the fees for him under the Deferred Payments Scheme on the condition that the money it spends on his accommodation and care in the home is repaid. In other words, your relative may be able to keep the family home until death; but then it will have to be sold and the money repaid to the council (unless you can come up with another source of funds).

Clearly, with this scheme the children lose that part of their inheritance, but at least the elderly person does not have to surrender the house soon after moving into a care home to pay the bills. The house can still be rented out to tenants, to spin out family resources, or used by visiting family members and perhaps occasionally by the care home resident on trips home.

This scheme offers one of the few opportunities for your elderly relative to top-up care home fees herself. If the council is paying the fees, but she would like to be in a more expensive home, she can pay the difference using her own money. This can include the value of the home which the council will get after her death, with the proviso that she must be left with total capital resources to the value of the lower capital limit (page 368). There seems no reason why the top-up should not be generated from rent from your relative's house while he or she is living in a care home.

Participation in the Deferred Payments Scheme does not affect entitlement to free nursing care but it may affect entitlement to Income Support. You can continue to receive Attendance Allowance under a deferred payment scheme so long as you are not receiving Income Support and you pay the local council back in full.

If your council refuses to enter into such an agreement with you, it must provide reasons. You can challenge its decision by means of the authority's complaints procedure. Councils have been allocated a special grant by the Department of Health to spend on Deferred Payments, but in 2002 not all of this was used up, presumably because councils were unenthusiastic about offering the agreements and few care home entrants were aware of its existence. As a result, the Department of Health issued guidance to local authorities in England reminding them that they should have a Deferred Payments Scheme in place and that they could be challenged if they do not use their discretion to offer such payments to individuals.[5] Clearly, the Deferred Payments Scheme has the potential to remove a great deal of the emotional trauma involved in a move into a care home, not only for the entrant but for the family too.

Into Bed with the Council

Self-Funders

Self-funders may have the choice of operating independently with their own contract with the care home or going through their local authority. Some authorities will offer to enter into the contract with the care home, leaving you to pay them even if you have more than the upper capital limit. The main advantage of going down this road is that you will benefit from the discount councils secure on care home fees compared with individuals if such a discount operates in your area and if the care home is prepared to accept you at the local-authority rate. However, residents on local authority contracts cannot claim Attendance Allowance and the local authority may impose an administration charge, which will bring down any fees differential. In any case, it is not always ideal to be paying the lowest fees possible. A self-funder paying a higher rate may have a better choice of room. If the home has a waiting list, you run the risk of losing the room by opting to pay a lower rate.

A major disadvantage of acting independently, on the other hand, is that councils often take no interest whatsoever in self-funding residents, even if they have been heavily involved in supporting them in their own homes and have carried out the community care assessment which led to their entry into a care home. Social services, though, will consider that residents in homes under their contracts are to some extent their responsibility; one advantage not enjoyed by self-funders is that six weeks after entry the social worker holds a review with the home and the resident to check that all is well. In addition, if your relative has problems with a home at any time subsequently, you can ask the social worker to deal with them.

This facility might be of crucial importance should the home try to expel your relative. Contracts often provide that residents can be asked to leave if they disrupt the peaceful environment of the home. If your relative develops a condition such as dementia, alcoholism or even depression, the home may attempt to use it to ask them to leave under this clause. It might be less inclined to try this on if it feared it could annoy a social services department with which it had a block contract.

This assumes, however, that the social worker is energetic, sympathetic to your point of view, possessed of enough time to pursue your concerns and visits that particular home frequently. None of these things may apply. Furthermore, because the council has the contract with the home, it may be more difficult for you to approach the home with your concerns. The home may tell you it is dealing with the council; social services may feel you have gone behind their back. Keeping tabs on the home through regular meetings with Matron as I have proposed (pages 396–7) may become more difficult.

Self-funders with concerns, but hesitant about pursuing them on their own, could seek help from a voluntary group. In addition they could contact the local office of the National Care Standards Commission, the Care Standards Inspectorate for Wales or the Scottish Commission for the Regulation of Care (or in Northern Ireland the local health and social services board, until the equivalent Commission is established in the Province); the home itself should have its own complaints procedure. See also pages 320–23.

The freedom of action you enjoy if you act independently of social services can be particularly valuable if you want to change homes. The council may not want its charges to change homes since that will involve it in extra bother and may upset the manager of a home the council regularly uses. So on top of the problems you are having with the home you want to relocate from, you will be having to get hold of and persuade a local authority care manager to take action. However, a discussion with social services may be useful in sorting out difficulties, so you could decide to stay put after all. If you are still unhappy, some local authorities will be understanding and agree that as the home does not suit you, they must help you move. But at the end of the day, you do not have quite so much autonomy if you are working through social services as if you are on your own.

Effecting a move may take also longer. If you are really keen for your relative to move, the reason is probably serious misgivings which mean you do not want him or her to stay for another day. The question of the notice period, perhaps two or four weeks, whatever is specified in the contract, arises. Social services will want to give the home the required notice; your relative may wish to leave immediately, even if this means you will have to pay fees over the notice period as well as fees in the new home. Residents in contracts with social services who are below the lower capital limit will find great difficulty in getting out of notice periods, as social services will not want to pay double during the overlap period.

People of Modest Means

It is important that people who are funded by their local authority (that is, of course, only part-funded, because they themselves will contribute pensions and/or Income Support from the Department for Work and Pensions) should use their legal rights. About 60 per cent of care home residents receive some state help with their fees. Some of these people will have gone into their homes being paid for wholly or partly by public agencies; others will have gone in as self-funders and turned to the state when their resources were sufficiently depleted. It is easy for people being paid for by public authorities to feel that they do not enjoy the rights that self-funders possess, but they need not feel like this. The national minimum standards and regulations apply to homes and residents across the board.

One field in which the choice of non-self-funders may be slightly restricted is the choice of a home. A local authority cannot, though, say it will pay only a pre-set maximum amount as its contribution to the fees of people whose savings fall below the upper capital limit (£19,500 or its equivalent; page 368): it has to pay whatever is necessary to meet each person's assessed needs. Local authorities have a discretion here, and, as in other areas in which they have discretionary powers, they must not 'fetter their discretion' – a legal term which means they must not say that they will never use the power. So if your local authority says it never pays more than a certain amount for its care home residents, it is fettering its discretion. You should point this out and complain, if necessary to the Local Government Ombudsman, or take legal action. The council must ensure that the needs it has assessed are met, and if this can only be achieved adequately in a home which is more expensive than the homes with which your social services department has existing contracts, then it should send your relative to a more expensive home and meet the full cost.

This is another reason why it is very important to get your relative's needs adequately spelt out in a community care assessment and care plan (pages 273–90). For instance, if there is only one acceptable but expensive home that would allow your relative to retain close contact with friends and relatives, and such a need is set down as one to be met in your relative's assessment, social services should send him or her there. Perhaps few homes can cater adequately and sensitively with cultural or religious needs by, say, providing halal food, links with a mosque or washing facilities; if a community care assessment recognizes such needs as important, they should be met.

The Personal Expenses Allowance
The real drawback of local-authority-funded care home residence is the very small amount of money that will be at the disposal of residents. They cannot have a high income or savings over the lower capital limit (£12,000 or its equivalent; page 373)) in the first place, or they would not be local-authority funded. As mentioned above, social services departments are required by law to provide each resident with a 'personal expenses allowance'; in 2003, this stood at £17.50 per week. Somehow older citizens have to adjust, perhaps after a lifetime of proud financial independence, to losing their home and their independence and having a pittance handed out to them not unlike a

child's pocket money. This allowance, small though it may be, is supposed to be spent as the resident wishes. It should certainly not be used to pay for facilities or services which the home ought to provide under its contract with social services, nor should the home be demanding it to top up fees.

Although those living in a care home will have expenses such as food, heating, laundry and cleaning covered, there are plenty of things they might want to buy for which they will need their personal expenses allowance. That £17.50 will have to cover Christmas and birthday presents, books, tapes, newspapers, clothing, hairdressing, bets, cigarettes, sweets, alcohol, trips out, telephone calls and toiletries amongst other things, as well as any services such as aromatherapy or chiropody on top of what the NHS provides. Because the personal expenses allowance is so tiny, it is worth considering asking whether it could be increased. It is also important that it should be administered properly.

Many care home residents do not realize that local authorities have the discretion to increase personal expense allowances. They are unlikely to do this voluntarily, so you have to ask them. Try to demonstrate that your expenses are higher than those of most people. If you feel the cold more than most, perhaps because you have lived in a warmer clime, you could argue that you need extra money to buy more clothes. Temporary residents in care homes receive only the same allowance as permanent residents, so if there is the possibility that you might return home you could argue that you have to keep up payments such as your phone rental and standing charges for gas and electricity. Or if you are aiming to return to independent living, you might argue that you need extra payments to enable you to go out. If you are hard of hearing, you could argue that you need extra money to purchase more talking books. The possibilities are endless.

If you are not up to handling your money yourself, try to find somebody to do so who is unconnected with the care home. In his book *Managing Residential Care*,[6] John Burton, who has worked in care homes, gave examples of the misappropriation of personal income allowance by home managers (a situation borne out by an Office of Fair Trading report on *Older People in Care Homes* in 1998).[7] Sometimes residents had not been told either by social services or by the home that they had any personal money coming in. The home, to which social services had passed the money along with their contribution to the bill, had saved the allowance money and used it to buy 'presents' for the resident – perhaps new clothes, a special hairdo, a Christmas or birthday gift, which the elderly person had accepted gratefully. In other cases, managers had pooled residents' personal expense allowances, again without their knowledge, and used them to buy facilities which they had chosen, such as a new television.

It is clearly in residents' interests to keep their financial dealings separate from the management of the care home if they can. Many care home managers are of course entirely trustworthy, but separation removes the possibility for any misuse of residents' money. There have been cases of fraud involving staff from care homes – and indeed other people – acting as the agent of an elderly person and misappropriating funds. It is also a good idea if your relative keeps his or her pension book or records of the pension having been paid into his or her bank account, even if all of the pension goes to pay care home bills, if only because this serves as a reminder to your relative and everyone else that he or she is a paying customer via deferred earnings.

People in care homes who are unable to manage their own financial affairs may have people to act for them under a registered enduring power of attorney, or some other vehicle (pages 515–31). Social services themselves are permitted to manage residents' money through what is known as a 'suspense account'.

Location Costs

If you are paying your own care home bills, you can choose a care home wherever you like. If you subsequently become eligible for state help because your savings after the sale of any property go down to the upper capital limit (page 368), the local authority which you should approach is the local authority covering the home's area, not that where you used to live.

However, sometimes councils dispute their responsibility (called disputes over residency), so it is important to make contact with the local authority in your new neck of the woods if you think you might need their financial assistance and to get advice, for instance from a local Citizen's Advice Bureau, if they show reluctance to take you on. The guidance on all this is set out in a Department of Health circular to local councils issued in 1993.[8]

People who are funded right from the start wholly or partly by their local authority are not restricted to the area of that authority (page 318). Indeed, some authorities have contracts with homes outside their areas to which they regularly send people.

Temporary Residents

A temporary stay in a care home is defined as a period of residence with the intention to return home. (So if your relative's home has been let or sub-let, you will find it hard to maintain that his or her care home stay is temporary, should you need to.) A trial-period stay can become permanent or end in a return home: it is undertaken to work out whether the care home in question would suit the potential resident's needs.

Sometimes a temporary stay is completely free of charge to the resident. A new scheme called 'intermediate care' involves spending up to six weeks in a care home for intensive treatment or rehabilitation, often after a stay in hospital. The advantage to the health service is that this enables expensive beds in district hospitals to be released through transfers to cheaper beds in community hospitals or care homes. Intermediate care is paid for by the NHS (pages 76, 412–13, 422–6).

If people go into care homes for trial or temporary stays, they may still not have to pay much, as their council can use its discretion to forego charging them what they would have to pay under the regular means test it would apply to permanent residents. A council can charge temporary residents for up to eight weeks what it is 'reasonable' for them to pay.[9] However, a council might or might not choose to exercise its discretion. So before your relative goes into a care home for a temporary period or a trial stay, it is extremely important to sort out in what capacity he or she will be staying there: a lot of money may be at stake. People unfamiliar with the social services system who get sent to a care home for a temporary stay, perhaps by their GP in a crisis situation, perhaps after a fall which does not call for hospitalization, sometimes assume that any institution to which a GP sends them must be part of the NHS and therefore free. They are in for a rude awakening (as I was in my mother's case).

Temporary stays can take all sorts of forms. People might stay in a care home once every couple of months as a short-term break. This is sometimes known as a respite stay.[10] A temporary stay can last for up to 52 weeks (or longer in exceptional circumstances), but because of the financial implications, it is important to establish with your local authority before a stay begins that it will be considered temporary.

The main reason for this is that care home residents on a trial or otherwise temporary stay do not have the value of their property taken into account when they are assessed for their ability to pay the bill. Many people will have to foot the entire cost themselves, but those whose incomes are low and whose savings fall below a certain level can have all or part of the bill paid for by their local authority.

Also, whether or not a local authority applies its normal means test for the first eight weeks, in assessing someone's ability to pay it must ignore some of their income to take into account their continued liability to pay bills at home such as water rates, insurance and standing charges. It must also ignore any Attendance Allowance, Housing Benefit, Council Tax Benefit or help with housing costs from Income Support which a temporary resident is receiving. However, if a person gets financial help from its local authority towards the cost of a temporary stay, Attendance Allowance stops after four weeks. Social security legislation allows the Department for Work and Pensions to continue to pay any Income Support housing costs and the local council to pay Housing Benefit and Council Tax Benefit for trial stays of up to 13 weeks, and for up to 52 weeks for those staying on a temporary basis.

Free Nursing Care

In 2001, the Westminster government announced, to a blaze of congratulatory publicity, that it was introducing 'free nursing care' in England. The Welsh and Northern Ireland Assemblies have introduced the same thing, although administered slightly differently. All these moves follow the more radical approach taken by the Scottish Parliament.

The introduction of free nursing care is being presented as a generous gift to older people. However, it is really no more than returning to older people something which should never have been taken from them in the first place.

Older people who live in their own homes or in residential homes have always received any care which had to be given or supervised by nurses free – naturally enough, as this is just the sort of service which the National Health Service is supposed to provide. However, older people who went into nursing homes have been in an anomalous position: they have had to pay for their nursing care for no other reason than that nursing homes have to employ a qualified nurse, though of course they were entitled to free nursing care through the NHS like any other citizen if they went into hospital; they also continued to receive free medical care from their GP while in the nursing home. All Westminster and the Welsh and Northern Ireland Assemblies have done is to decree that older people who are living in nursing homes can now have that part of the fees which they pay for nursing covered by the state. They continue to have to pay for everything else in nursing homes – accommodation, meals, personal care and whatever else is included in the fees.

Under the new system the government is now paying for care provided by registered nurses to nursing-home residents. Residents are assessed by a team led by the local health body to determine whether they need nursing care and, if they do, the NHS sends a specified amount direct to the care home in which they are living to cover the cost of the nursing care. Specialist nursing, such as cancer care, continence advice and mental health nursing is unaffected: it continues to be provided free.

The new payments should cover the time spent by a registered nurse in a nursing home in general nursing tasks, not only in carrying out tasks which only nurses can perform, such as giving injections, but also in planning, delegating and supervising nursing care in the home. Care homes should then reassess the fees of residents to take account of the new NHS contribution. As not everybody could be assessed on the date on which the new scheme was introduced, there was provision for backdating to the date of introduction. The dates (for self-funders) are for England 1.10.01, Wales 3.12.01 and Northern Ireland 7.10.02. The majority of people affected should have seen a reduction of about £85 a week in England and £100 in Northern Ireland and Wales on bills of perhaps £450.

The new policy will not affect older people living in any other situation, such as those living in homes registered for residential but not nursing care. Nor will it affect people in their own homes. A case in 2002 highlighted the kind of care still excluded from 'free' nursing care in England. Barbara Pointer was looking after her husband, Malcolm, an Alzheimer's sufferer, with the help of a live-in care assistant paid for under means-tested arrangements through her local social services department. Mr Pointer, then in the advanced stages of the disease, could not wash, dress or feed himself or walk, was doubly incontinent, had no speech and could not understand the speech of others. Mrs Pointer asked the NHS to pay for a carer to replace her one week in five so that she could have a rest. The NHS refused, on the grounds that what she provided was not nursing care and therefore not covered by the rule change. Although the extensive care which Alzheimer's sufferers need is the result of a disease, it does not count as nursing care because most of it can be provided by people other than qualified nurses.[11]

The Scottish Parliament has been a lot more generous. It is paying not only for nursing care but also for personal care. The latter costs more than nursing care in most cases, but in Scotland the state picks up the bill for both, whether people are in nursing, residential or their own homes, so if Mr and Mrs Pointer lived north of the border, a great deal of Mr Pointer's care when Mrs Pointer takes a break would be free. Care home residents in Scotland still have bills to pay, but they are substantially less than they were. However, the Scottish Executive has removed the entitlement of self-funders to Attendance Allowance, so the difference in what you pay for the same home north and south of the border reduced to £50 a week in some cases, once this has been taken into account. It is reduced still further for self-funders nearing the capital limits below which local authorities contribute to care home fees, since these limits are more generous in England, Northern Ireland and Wales than in Scotland.

In England, a decision on how free nursing care should be administered has meant that many self-funders have not benefited as much as might have been expected. The reason is that payments have not been made to the residents or to their representatives so that they could then pay care home bills using the new source of money. Instead, as a result of lobbying from the care homes industry, the government agreed to forward the money direct to care homes. The idea was that homes would then send out revised bills to residents, from which the payment from the government had been deducted. Instead, however, what many of them have done is to put up their fees and then charge residents as much or nearly as much as before. Only residents whose contracts limit the amount by which fees can be increased have been immune from this ploy. Those whose fees have risen after the introduction of free nursing care who then go into hospital can face real difficulties. Once somebody is in hospital, the free nursing care payment from the government stops, and yet residents still have to pay their nursing-home bills if they want to retain their place in the home.

The change has the most noticeable impact on the bills of self-funders. People living in nursing homes whose bills are already met in full by the NHS are not affected. Those paid for by social services should not be aware of any change, although in fact a proportion of their fees which would have been met by their local authority is now sourced by the NHS.

Self-funders should check with their nursing home that payments are coming in from their local health organization. Any nursing home residents, however wealthy, should be credited with this cash. The nursing home should have itemized the payment on its bill. Make sure it has been paid from the correct date. Make sure the amount is right. In Wales and Northern Ireland, everybody who receives nursing in care homes is getting the same payment (£100 a week), but in England, people receive one of three payments according to the amount of nursing they receive. There are thus three bands – a low band of £40 a week, a medium band of £75 a week and a high band of £120 a week.

Which band you fall into is determined through an assessment by a nurse working to the nursing home co-ordinator employed by the health body; this is provided for under the single assessment process (pages 290–1). You may consider your relative has been assessed in the wrong band. If you do, you can appeal against the assessment. Nursing home co-ordinators have only a limited pot of money to spend on free nursing care, and if they are getting through it quickly, they may be tempted to place people in a lower band than they should. The best approach is to find out when the assessment is to take place and ensure your views are heard if you are at all worried, for instance that your relative will not be placed in the middle band when she should be in the highest.[12]

The assessment should be reviewed after three months and again after 12 months. If, however, you think a review is called for, perhaps because your relative's health has deteriorated, you can request a review before those periods are up.

Continence pads for nursing-home residents are free of charge as part of free nursing care. Before 2001, such residents, unlike elderly people in hospitals, residential care homes or their own homes, had to pay for their own pads. If you become incontinent, even if only at night, you will need a lot of pads and they are expensive. So if a nursing home is charging you or your relative for pads, even if for only part of the cost, ask questions immediately.

Somebody (a nurse or continence advisor sent by the health organization) has to go round and allocate the pads after assessing each resident. Since budgets are fixed, there is a danger that some older people may be assessed as requiring lower-strength pads than they actually need. So, if possible, try to be present when your relative is assessed, as there is no effective means of appeal; all you can do if dissatisfied is to make a formal complaint to your health body. To question an assessment effectively, you need to know about the different products on the market. If in difficulty, seek advice from the Continence Foundation.

You can read full instructions about free nursing care (including the provision of free continence pads) in the following places:

- Department of Health booklet *NHS Funded Nursing Care in Nursing Homes: What It Means for You: A Guide for People Living in or Going into Nursing Homes, their Families and their Carers*; more details in Health Service Circular 2001/17, Local Authority Circular (2001) 26, *Guidance on Free Nursing Care in Nursing Homes*

- Welsh Assembly Government booklet *NHS Nursing Care in Nursing Homes in Wales: A Guide for People Going into Care Homes Providing Nursing Care, their Families and their Carers.* The guidance to the administering organizations is contained in National Assembly for Wales Circular 34/01, *Paying for NHS Funded Nursing Care in Nursing Homes.*
- Department of Health, Social Services and Public Safety of Northern Ireland booklet *Paying for Nursing Care in Nursing Homes, Recent Changes – What These Mean for You: Information for People Going into Nursing Homes, their Families and their Carers.* Further details: DHSSPSNI Community Care Directorate *Paying for Nursing Care in Nursing Homes: Guidance on Implementation of HPSS Payments for Nursing in Nursing Care Homes.*

Free Nursing and Personal Care in Scotland

In July 2002, the Scottish Executive introduced free nursing and free personal care for people aged 65 and over. Every such person in Scotland who is assessed as needing nursing care should receive £65 a week, paid direct to the care home in the case of self-funders and to the local authority in the case of people whose fees are met by their local council.

In addition, people assessed as needing personal care are entitled to £145 each week from the Scottish Executive. This applies to people living in their own homes as well as those in any type of care home, whether residential or nursing. However, self-funders who receive the personal care contribution will no longer be eligible for Attendance Allowance if they live in care homes (they retain it in their own homes). People going into care homes north of the border may still find themselves selling their homes to cover the hotel component of care home bills, but clearly their savings from the property sale are going to last longer than those of their counterparts in the rest of the UK.

These changes are set out in a brief leaflet published by the Scottish Executive called *Free personal and nursing care from 1st July 2002: What does it mean for you?* Much more useful guidance is contained in the Executive's document *Free personal and nursing care in Scotland: Guidance for local authorities, the NHS and other service providers*, which is available on the Scottish Executive's website or by post. Age Concern Scotland is able to offer advice on this subject on its enquiry line.

One very important point is that in Scotland, unlike the rest of the kingdom, self-funding residents already living in care homes will not automatically receive the funding to which they are entitled for free nursing and/or personal care. Each resident has to apply for it to his or her local authority. Individual care homes can apply on behalf of residents. So if your relative is already in a care home in Scotland, it is crucial that you ensure that an application has been made for all the free nursing and/or personal care to which he or she is entitled, whether rich or poor. Self-funders already living in homes do not have to undergo an assessment by the local authority before they receive their cash. Those self-funders who enter care homes after 31 March 2002 have to undergo an assessment of need before they become eligible for the payments. This means that any new residents who are operating entirely independently of social services will fail to receive the funding to which they are entitled unless they initiate the process and, in their case, also subject themselves to an assessment. But at £210 every week (2003 figures) for personal and nursing care, this sum is hardly to be sneezed at.

Spouses and Partners

One in ten of people in care homes are married. A further unknown number will be unmarried but in long-term relationships, both heterosexual and homosexual. Increasing frailty prompting admission to a care home rarely affects both members of a couple at the same time. So an admission to a care home often presents partners with dilemmas.

A few may decide to move into the care home with their frail partner. This is fine if they have plenty of money. But supposing a man moves into a care home with his partner as she needs care home support although he does not. Then she dies. Can he stay on? If he needs help from the council because his savings have been depleted to the upper capital limit (page 368), then he will have to meet the council's test that he is sufficiently disabled or frail to need care home support before they will chip in and part-fund him.

If this test is failed, what then? Most local authorities would probably come to some compromise and fund such a surviving partner as a borderline case, even if only residential care was to be funded when both had been living in a nursing home. But it is down to the discretion of the council, and legally a council is within its rights to say that it is not going to fund a surviving partner assessed as not needing whatever care the home provides. He or she will then have to leave. So, in theory, a recently widowed person could have to move out of a care home to live independently in the community, or perhaps move to another cheaper care home which is all social services will pay for.

In 1998, Dr Fay Wright of the Centre for Policy on Ageing carried out a study of the impact of entry into a care home on relationships with those left outside with a sample of 61 families.[13] She found that relationships between the spouses involved frequently deteriorated when one of them moved into a care home, while relationships with children remained the same or might improve. So if your other half moves into a care home while you stay outside, take steps to sustain your relationship as much as possible, for instance, by taking some meals at the home, taking part in some of the home's activities and having private time with your spouse there. When looking for a home, try to establish that the manager is welcoming to you and keen to see your relationship flourish, as well as making sure that your partner's room would be large enough for the two of you to spend time together in it.

An important financial and psychological benefit for married couples where one member goes into a care home is that social services are not then allowed to take into account the value of the matrimonial home when they work out how much of the bills they will pay. It could hardly be otherwise: if they did take it into account and the house had to be sold to pay care home bills, then the partner who did not go into the care home might become homeless. Retaining the matrimonial home means it is available for one of them to continue to live in, for children to come and stay in, for the care home resident to return to sometimes and for the money tied up in it to be conserved.

If a spouse decides to sell the matrimonial home and buy somewhere smaller, national guidance says that the care home resident's share in the home should still be ignored. However, not all local authorities conform to this advice, and may indicate that they require a contribution. Fay Wright revealed that one of the spouses she interviewed, who had moved to a small property because of shortage of money, had been forced to hand half the capital difference to her local authority; other spouses in Dr Wright's study feared their local authorities would take the same line.

If your wife or husband goes into a care home, the financial assessment which social services will carry out to determine what he or she should pay towards the bills has to be based on the entrant's financial resources only. Any savings which are held jointly are deemed to be held 50:50. Social services are not allowed to require that the spouse left at home reveals his or her personal circumstances. So if there is a section on the financial assessment form which social services asks your other half to fill in before he or she goes into the care home, you are perfectly within your rights to leave the spouse's income and savings section blank.

The reason councils often want spouses to divulge their financial circumstances is so they can put together a requirement for a 'liable relatives payment'. Although spouses have no obligation to care for their other halves, they do have a legal obligation to maintain them, under section 42 of the National Assistance Act 1948. This means councils are perfectly within their rights to require the spouse living at home to make a contribution towards care home bills, with the result of course that the council will not have to pay as much. If the financial assessment form which a local council gives an intending care home resident includes a section on the income and savings of a spouse, and if the spouse obligingly fills it in, the council then has some firm data on which to base a request for a liable relatives payment. However, the spouse is not legally obliged to divulge this information: it is local authorities' problem that in extracting such payments they have no power to force spouses to divulge details of their own financial circumstances.

Another extremely valuable weapon you have in haggling with social services over your liable relative's payment is the absence of clear national guidance on the level which it is appropriate for spouses to pay. The council may find bargaining irritating, but that is its problem. You are in a position to horse-trade. If you neglect to, you may help out the manager of budgets in your social services department, but you will do nothing to deliver better care for your spouse. The national guidance from the Department of Health to local authorities in England states:

> If it is worth pursuing the spouse for maintenance, consider in each case what would be 'appropriate' for the spouse to pay by way of maintenance. This will involve discussion and negotiation with the spouse, and will be determined to a large extent by his/her financial circumstances in relation to his/her expenditure and normal standard of living. In the Department's view, it would not be appropriate, for example, to necessarily expect spouses to reduce their resources to income support levels in order to pay maintenance.[14]

The requirement to make a financial contribution does not apply to a long-standing live-in partner, only to a spouse.

A spouse at home might agree to contribute quite a large amount to care bills for a spouse. However, the more of your income you keep, the more you can spend on your spouse in the home. Those paid for by social services have only the paltry personal expenses allowance amount to spend each week (apart from any savings, if they have them, up to the capital limits). As this amounted in 2003 to only £17.50, it will not stretch to a lot of treats, trips out, holidays, birthday and Christmas presents, magazines, jewellery, clothes, and so on.

The benefit rules when one member of a married couple enters a care home are complex. In this area, as in other financial aspects of care home residence, you can obtain useful information from Age Concern factsheets, books such as *Paying for Care Handbook*[15] and by telephoning the national helplines of the organizations described in *Useful Contacts*.

Chapter 12
Going In

A Trial Stay

If you think a particular home looks promising, the next step is to consider a trial stay. This provides an ideal means of ensuring that there is not an unexpected aspect of life there which your relative would find particularly irksome or difficult to handle. In the past, some care home owners may have looked askance at prospective residents who want to move in for a probationary period, but the national minimum standards for care homes recognize the importance of such a trial stay. Standard 5 of the *National Minimum Standards for Care Homes for Older People* states, 'The registered person ensures that prospective service users are invited to visit the home and to move in on a trial basis, before they and/or their representatives make a decision to stay; unplanned admissions are avoided where possible.'[1]

A trial stay, and thus the question of whether the person involved is a temporary or a permanent resident, has financial implications (pages 383–4).

Preparing for Entry

Once your relative has decided that a particular home is one to which he or she would like to move, there are still steps which you can usefully take to ensure as smooth and happy a transition as possible, as well as to reduce the chances of serious problems arising once he or she is living there.

Care Plans

You should expect to see in a care plan or a service user plan all the things which somebody who had no previous knowledge of your relative and had to care for him or her would need to know. It should address all the ways in which the elderly person's assessed needs should be met – just like a care plan if he or she were living in the community (page 273). But in a home, the care plan needs to include not just what medication people are taking or what therapy they should receive, but, particularly in the case of those who cannot easily express their wishes, anything which an agency care worker would need to know, such as where the person likes to sit in the lounge, whether he uses a hearing aid or glasses, how he likes his tea and whether he likes to listen to certain radio programmes.

The national minimum standards for care homes in England went through many drafts, with some points being omitted after lobbying by the care homes industry. An early draft (although not the final document) set out what a care plan should contain, and you might like to have this as it provides a useful checklist. This draft, entitled *Fit for the Future*, stated:

A care plan must be drawn up for each resident detailing:

- personal details – date of birth, next of kin
- general health record relevant to present functioning
- any medical treatment required
- any medication required
- any nursing requirements
- any therapy requirements
- risk assessment for safety
- ability of resident for self-care
- type of assistance required
- dietary requirements based on a nutritional assessment carried out within the first week
- dietary observances and preferences
- cultural and religious needs
- any other special needs.

It must be written and presented in an easily accessible style and available to the resident. The care plan must be reviewed by care staff in the home at least once a month and updated if necessary.[2]

The care plan, or service user plan, should be part of your contract with the home. You should agree to pay the home, or to contribute your pension topped up by social services and the

Department for Work and Pensions, so long as they deliver the care set out in the care plan. So it is important to get the plan right.

In the past, care plans have tended to downplay emotional and psychological matters. In her study of the quality of life in care homes (page 320), Dr Sue Davies mentioned the case of one elderly lady living in an expensive care home who had been cared for by her husband at home after a stroke until he died suddenly. Dr Davies noted that this woman was having great difficulty in coming to terms with the dramatic changes in her life and wept during the interview. Yet when Dr Davies examined the woman's care plan she found nothing in it about the bereavement or the need for support it might entail. The same resident said she would like the care staff to walk with her sometimes so she could regain some use of the limbs affected by the stroke, but there was nothing about this in her care plan. So try to make sure that your relative's entire needs – psychological, social, emotional and spiritual, as well as physical – are covered in the care, or service user's, plan.[3]

Meetings

When somebody goes into a care home, lots of things may crop up which you want to mention to the home without seeming to pick on a particular member of staff. Relatives have a difficult tightrope to walk: they want things done perfectly for their loved ones, but they know they need the staff on their side. Maybe your mother is being addressed by her Christian name when she prefers to be addressed more formally. Perhaps her glasses are not kept as clean as they might be. All these things are perfectly valid concerns, but it can be disturbing to be making an issue out of each one.

You may also want an opportunity to participate in any review of how your relative is faring generally and hear what the staff have to say. An informal chat with Matron and the key worker, or indeed other workers, is almost bound to throw up ways in which care could be improved. Is your father making friends? Are there other residents with whom he might have a hobby or interest in common? Are there social activities in which he has been reluctant to take part but which you could persuade him to try? Would it help him to settle if he could play a part in the day-to-day running of the home? Might it help if he sat in a different place in the dining room? An article in the *Journal of Dementia Care* in 2002 told how one old lady's mealtimes were transformed by positioning her in a different place so that conversation was not impaired by the clang of cutlery being thrown into the drawer nearby and the constant toing and froing of people, and by providing different lighting and more visual contrast so that she could see her plate more clearly.[4]

In the light of all these matters, it is a good idea to get Matron to agree before your relative goes into a home to hold regular meetings with you. These could take the form of a regular care-plan review, or they could be in addition, ideally, perhaps, monthly.

To this suggestion, Matron might counter that rather than make a regular appointment you should come and see her if you have any specific concerns. That has two disadvantages. First, it turns your observations into verbal 'complaints', with the result that they may be met by Matron's 'complaints-managing mode' – providing you with tea and biscuits, soothing you and deflecting your concerns rather than treating you as an equal partner in the struggle to ensure your relative is well looked after. Secondly, denial of regular meetings will prevent you from finding out how your relative is faring in all aspects of her life in the home. You do not need to take up a huge amount of Matron's time, but you want the opportunity to sit down and read the records the home has been keeping on your relative and then talk to key staff about all aspects of her life which may be relevant, from finding lost dentures to weight loss.

If you fail to secure a regular meeting, look at the records anyway. There is no reason why the home should refuse to let you see any records they keep on your relative, including the daily record of her activities and condition, unless this is contrary to your relative's wishes. You may notice something serious staff have overlooked, such as a lack of bowel movements for a week.

Advance Consultation

Quite apart from such regular meetings, it is useful to get the home's agreement, either as an additional clause in the contract or in a formal letter, to notification – or better still, consultation – before various types of action are taken. The relevant circumstances might include any significant change in your relative's care, such as a reduction in the frequency of or changing the times of bathing, or alterations to continence management. Inserting a catheter, for example, can make life easier for staff, but can have grave drawbacks for the resident (pages 427–9). It is also a good idea to ask to be told about any proposed consultation with a health worker, for instance a speech and language therapist, or a visit by a doctor. You probably won't want or manage to get to all of these appointments, but it is a good idea to know ahead before decisions are made which are difficult to reverse. If your relative has a contract which allows termination in the case of hospitalization, be on your guard for visits by local consultants which could result in hospital entry.

Finally, get the home to agree to contact you whenever your relative is at all unwell. This way you ensure that they summon medical help as soon as necessary. If your relative is under a GP associated with the home who calls once a week, Matron may be tempted to delay a consultation until that visit. If she wants to free up the bed, she may be tempted to delay summoning medical assistance if your relative develops a potentially life-threatening condition. A couple of hours' delay could mean your relative never recovers or does so only after becoming more unwell than he or she would have been. In this very important area, you really do need to feel you can trust the home to act in your relative's best interest, but guarantees, particularly if set down on paper, can help.

Appearance

The clothing, jewellery and make-up which we choose to wear and the way we do our hair are part of who we are. People going into a care home should be able to continue to present themselves in the way they choose. It is very easy for people who cannot speak up for themselves to end up dressed in inappropriate clothes. Inefficient laundry sorting may mean that clothing gets mixed up and so residents end up wearing each other's garments. Sometimes care workers choose clothes which are not to residents' tastes. I heard of a former fighter pilot who had throughout his life dressed always in collar and tie and of an elderly lady previously insistent on jewellery and make-up who were dressed by care workers in track-suits on the grounds that these were easy for care assistants to manage and supposedly afford protection in the event of a fall. So provide the home with guidance on the way your relative likes to dress, particularly if he or she has difficulty expressing personal preferences.

Label garments yourself before your relative goes into a home. If you do not, the home may send them away for marking with the result that your relative may be forced to dress from a bank of clothing kept by the home for such eventualities, just when he or she is attempting to fit into a new social situation. You also need to get false teeth, hearing aids and glasses labelled – they can easily get lost and take a lot of effort to replace.

Make absolutely sure that your relative has all the clothes he or she needs. Bear in mind that garments will often be away in the laundry, so he or she may well need more clothes than before. The washing and drying regime of care home laundries can quickly wear out fragile fabrics such as wool or silk.

Briefing

A good home will compile background information about a new resident in advance of entry, usually in an A4 ring-binder in which staff can easily find information but which is also attractive, often with photographs, and serves to interest staff in the person for whom they are caring. This is especially useful for residents who have dementia, because it provides information not only about their preferences (which they may have difficulty making clear) but also about their background: how they have lived their life, what they did for a living, their family and so on. In this way, care workers can be helped to relate to the person behind the affliction. With residents' permission, the ring-binders, or a version of them, can be made available to other residents too, to stimulate their interest in each other. The following details can be useful:

- birthday – as a prompt for a celebration
- names of brothers, sisters, partner, children and other family members, possibly a family tree, updated (it is important to

share family changes with home staff, as they can influence a resident's mood)
- details of employment and past residence
- lifestyle, hobbies, particular memories
- likes and dislikes – for instance:
music
radio and television programmes
dogs and cats (a PAT dog may be about to appear)
conversation topics
flowers, sweets and cigarettes
tea and coffee formats, cold drinks, alcohol
hairstyles
going to bed and getting up times
number of pillows, presence of radio, clock, night-light
used to a post-prandial nap or would find this disconcerting
conversation topics.

The First Few Weeks

In Laurie Lee's semi-autobiographical account of his childhood in rural Gloucestershire at the time of the First World War, *Cider with Rosie*, he tells of an elderly couple, Joseph and Hannah Brown, who lived together, 'absorbed in themselves as lovers, content and self contained', having raised a large family and been married for 50 years. Suddenly, both became very frail and weak. The authorities decided that something needed to be done and they were moved to the workhouse to be looked after, Joseph to the men's wing and Hannah to the women's. They never saw each other again; in a week both had died.

Most of us have probably heard of elderly people who have surrendered their independence by moving into care homes and died soon afterwards. Whether or not infirmity killed them, the shock and immensity of the transition are surely likely to have played a part in their demise.

It is extremely important that before you or your relative signs the contract with a home, you should be convinced it is ready to smooth the passage and enable your relative to adjust to the new environment, both physical and social, as quickly and as easily as possible. New residents have to adjust to entirely new physical surroundings and find their way around them, even though they may have difficulty moving, or seeing, or hearing, or perhaps all three. Newcomers also have to adjust to an entirely new social situation. There will be a bewildering array of staff in various types of uniform. There will be the complicated social structure which the existing residents have created into which your relative now intrudes – a structure of which newcomers know nothing but which has its own friendships and animosities, cliques and gossips, warm-hearted people and tetchy ones, and people with disabilities, some fraught with sensitivities. New residents must face that daunting first appearance in the dining room: to whom can they comfortably sit next? Are they inadvertently sitting in somebody else's favourite place?

You need to be convinced that a home understands something of what it feels like to be a new resident. At the very least, you should expect all staff to be briefed about a newcomer. Everybody who will come into contact with him or her, from the home's odd-job man to the proprietor, should know his name and be aware of the desirability of making him feel welcome, as well as being told of any special difficulties. If someone is nearly blind but the disability is not apparent, staff should know that she is nonetheless partially sighted so that when they pass her, they should greet her and explain who they are and what they are doing, whether they are the gardener or the manager: for example, 'Hello, Mrs Marshall. This is Ruth, one of the care assistants. How are you today? I am just going to tidy up.'

Many homes offer little such briefing. Matron and the key worker may have read the care plan, but elderly people can live in institutions for months, if not years, without key staff realizing that they are nearly blind or deaf. Yet it is crucial that all staff should know of such problems from day one.

When somebody moves into a care home there is an important role for close relatives, friends and partners. During this potentially stressful transition, the firm support of loved ones is crucial. Do not entertain an injunction from Matron when you leave your relative for the first time to stay away and not visit for a few days to make settling in easier. Perhaps some managers really believe that this is kind advice. But others seem to offer it to break the will of the new resident as well as to assert themselves as the new carer. The effect on new residents, as well as

their families, can be terrible. The resident, who will probably
have been told nothing, can feel abandoned while the family
worry about what may be happening. Older people left in this situation often cannot easily reach a telephone: they may have to
ask a member of staff to take them to one. A good home will
want relatives to share their expertise and knowledge with staff
and to proffer as much support as the elderly person needs. It
will provide a room for them to stay overnight at first if this
seems necessary.

Straightforward practical help from the very start is also
extremely important, not just to help the new resident feel
welcome but also to keep them safe and reduce the risk of falls
during the early days when they will be finding their way around.
New residents need to feel confident about getting to the lavatory and to the dining room and so on. A home which has
invested in blind awareness training will have staff who know
how to guide a partially sighted or blind person properly. For
instance, when guiding such a person up a flight of steps, you
should go half a step ahead of them so they can feel from you
when they have got to the top.

Relatives too will have their own emotions to cope with and
their own sense of loss – most obviously if the person moving
into the home is a husband or wife. Perhaps one day the enor-
mity of this change will be recognized and people will be offered
family counselling to help them through. At the moment, you
may well find little more than lip-service paid to the recognition
that a massive change has happened, to which several people
may find difficulty in adjusting.

Life in the Home

Appreciating Staff

Show staff you appreciate their efforts. Some of the tasks they
have to undertake are not the most pleasant and yet many care
assistants and nurses in care homes carry out their work cheer-
fully and with real commitment. Chocolates and Christmas presents are nice, but it is also good if care staff feel that relatives
and residents genuinely appreciate their efforts and take an interest in them and their lives. They often put a lot of effort into

events for relatives and it is really important to try to attend these if you possibly can. For one thing, this gives you an opportunity to meet other relatives.

Do what you can to make caring as easy as possible. Make sure your relative has everything that he or she needs. Staff will get understandably annoyed if you fail to supply enough toiletries and clothing. The more effort you can make in areas such as this, the more likely they are to appreciate your input.

Visiting

When older people move into care homes, visits from friends and family can soon drop off. A survey commissioned by the Department of Health in 2000 of older people in England found that while 81 per cent of elderly people living in their own home were visited at least once a week by friends or family, the figure was 64 per cent for older people in care homes.[5]

One unpalatable fact is that visiting an older person in a care home is simply less interesting than visiting them in their own home, surrounded by all sorts of items of interest and perhaps a garden. You will often have to make a real effort to plan things to do on a visit to a care home. Yet a care home has its own sources of interest as well. One of these is the other residents. It is easy when you visit to focus only on your own relative, but if you do, you deny him or her and yourself possible enjoyment from interacting with others. You also run the risk of making other residents feel hurt and excluded, particularly if they receive few visitors. They may even build up jealousy and resentment towards your relative.

There are clearly countless ways in which you could interact with other residents and their visitors, including joint outings.

One of the difficulties you will face, whether you are trying to relate to other residents or visiting your own loved one, is ensuring that you relate appropriately. You often find that the managers of care homes (and also NHS long-stay wards) decline to offer visitors guidance on how they should communicate with elderly people with long-term health problems. Visiting somebody with dementia is a very different matter from visiting an older person with cancer or osteoporosis. While of course it is important to be sensitive when visiting anybody with an affliction, dementia is different because the person with the condition often cannot tell you how he or she feels, while ignorance means that visitors can unwittingly cause distress.

Residents with Dementia

If your relative has dementia, it is important to brief visitors beforehand about the stage he or she has reached and what can be some of the more helpful and unhelpful things to say and do. People who are introduced to dementia sufferers often do not realize that asking them their names, where they live or the names of their grandchildren or pets can be challenging and distressing. If sufferers cannot remember, they may well sense that they ought to know. So avoid asking direct questions, and speak in a voice which is soft, kind, unhurried and relaxed, in clear, simple sentences and on the same level as the person, so you are face to face. In her useful and inspiring book, *Alzheimer's: A Practical Guide for Carers*, Frena Gray-Davidson explains: 'Sharp voices agitate; hurry causes nervousness and dysfunction; complexity causes intellectual overload, which will bring about a distress response that could be rage, tears, anxiety, or extreme slowness and inability to do tasks.'[6]

It is easy for visitors who visit only infrequently to address the people they once knew, rather than to try to meet them on their own terms by imaginatively entering the private mental universe which they now inhabit. Some relatives and friends respond by saying there is no point in their visiting once they can no longer be distinguished and will be forgotten almost as soon as their visit is over. But visitors still have it in their power to make sufferers' lives happier, or at least less stressful while they are present.

There are many ways in which you can communicate with people with dementia quite apart from speaking. Some are soothed by music, but others find music which once they would have appreciated jarring and unpleasant. You could try going for walks, playing with balls, playing with other toys, gardening, looking at photographs, meeting babies, patting dogs, feeling things such as modelling clay, soil, play-dough or cake-making ingredients. Some of these activities, such as interacting through dolls, are now being discussed as formal approaches to therapy (pages 256 and 355–6).

Because the experience of dementia in different people varies so widely, impinging on different individuals with pre-existing likes, dislikes and experiences, the best I can suggest is to experiment on a trial-and-error basis to find activities and ways of being which enable you to connect with your relative and to sustain him or her. I found that my own mother could be absorbed in news of minor disasters gleaned from the local paper (which I could of course repeat many times). Sometimes I would pretend that I had been attempting unsuccessfully to make jam before my visit so that my mother could offer advice and so feel positive about herself, without challenging her to recall particular occasions when she had done so.

Visitors can also perform a very useful potential role in observing any difficulties and generally keeping staff on their toes. Do make sure that they channel any observations back to the main caring relative. It is extremely irritating for him or her to be told weeks after the event of mishaps and problems which could have been remedied.

Theft

Though there are no firm data, theft in care homes is probably a frequent occurrence. Simply pilfering cash and items from residents, particularly the most vulnerable, is probably the most common form. So take precautions: don't leave spare money or items of any value around where they might be stolen. Bear in mind that bedrooms are not usually locked, and thus may be entered by any prowling visitor, workman, member of staff or resident, as well as by burglars who may simply breeze in. Keep a record of the money in your relative's purse, making sure that the home knows that you are doing this, and keep any valuables in a safe. Clothes can be stolen too. This is less likely, as the home should make a record of all clothes and other items which residents bring when they move in. But if there are attractive garments which might attract workers – perhaps a new dressing gown – check that they are still being used by your relative and ask questions if they seem to disappear.

Home proprietors and managers themselves can do much to control theft. Good ones will encourage whistle-blowing in this area and even lay a trap for anybody whom they suspect of stealing.

One home proprietor laid a trap which led to a nurse she employed being jailed for eight weeks and struck off the professional register of the Nursing and Midwifery Council.[7] An elderly resident had £40 stolen from her purse on two consecutive weekends. After the first, the proprietor photocopied bank notes in that resident's purse. When they went missing, she called the police, who found, neatly folded in the shoe of the suspect, notes which corresponded with the photocopies.

Links with the Outside World

A yawning gap can begin to appear between the life a resident lived outside and the often closeted world of a care home. Of course, many people may not have been out and about very much just before going in, but if they can be encouraged to keep links with the outside world and to develop new ones, their lives may become more interesting.

Homes themselves could do a certain amount in this area, perhaps making local and national newspapers available and tuning in to local as well as national radio stations, but relatives and friends can do much too. It may take quite a lot of effort to ensure that your elderly relative can continue to attend, say, her Tuesday afternoon church club or some other group. However, such activities not only maintain links with old friends, but also simply get people out of the home into the outside world. If your relative happily attended a day centre before going into the care home, try to ensure that such visits continue (page 234). You could also see if Matron would allow a club to hold some of its meetings in the care home. Homes often have under-used communal areas. If you can get, say, a local University of the Third Age group, or radio hams society meeting, or whatever, in the home once in a while, you might find that some of its members would come back and visit your relative as an individual.

Do not assume that once your relative is living in a care home you should not go on looking for new activities in the wider community which might interest him or her. There might be a befriending service in your local area (pages 222–3). You could pay someone to go and visit weekly or daily too (page 225).

Casting a vote is a valuable means of reminding us all that we are equal players in the political process and have continuing value in the wider community. Standard 17 of the national minimum standards states that 'Service users . . . are enabled to . . . participate in the civic process if they wish' and 'Service users' rights to participate in the political process are upheld, for example, by enabling them to vote in elections.'

This could mean very little – perhaps only enabling people to vote in national elections – something which is becoming easier with postal and electronic voting. But it may be worth seeing if there are other elections in which your relative might wish to cast a vote, such as European and local council elections, and including, if appropriate, elections to parish or community councils. If fellow residents are interested, they might want to encourage a local candidate to visit the home. Politicians seeking votes are one group fully prepared to acknowledge the equal status of elderly people. Older people are noted for their high willingness to vote, compared with younger groups, so time spent with them is likely to prove more productive for politicians than simply going door to door.

Moving Out

When you go round a care home the manager will often give the impression that if your relative moves in that it will be his or her home for life. This may, however, turn out not to be the case for reasons outside your control. Your relative's care needs could change in ways which the home says it cannot handle, so it may tell you to find alternative accommodation. Or the home may close down.

Changing Needs

It often happens that an older person enters a home registered for low-dependency care but in time needs help of a different kind, including nursing care, which strictly speaking the home's owner or manager has not been authorized to provide on his or her registration certificate from the National Care Standards Commission or one of its sister bodies.

Your relative might of course be pleased to move somewhere more appropriate, but if not, what then? The answer is: discuss the possibilities with the manager and, if you come to an impasse, go to the local Care Standards Commission inspector. While a home's registration certificate will specify the level of dependency of the residents and the manager might say he or she cannot keep a person whose needs increase because this would break the terms of registration, this is not a black and white situation. A home registered for low-dependency care certainly might baulk at the idea of managing an intravenous drip or oxygen equipment and the inspector might rule this out too, but he or she might be prepared to countenance other types of help. Alzheimer's, for example, may develop very slowly and varies a great deal in the symptoms it provokes: while some people in the middle to late stages exhibit aggressive behaviour, wail noisily or wander a great deal, others are 'pleasantly confused' and could be managed in a home registered for residential care; at the same time, moving the person involved could set him or her back as result of a change from a familiar environment. The home might insist that it cannot keep your relative because it really wants to divest itself of him or her. But, if approached, an inspector might agree to the home keeping your relative because he or she considers that the home could nonetheless provide appropriate care; this agreement might involve the inspector granting a temporary or a substantial variation to the home's registration certificate.

Closure

There has been much publicity about the closure of care homes during the first years of the twenty-first century. But it was always envisaged that many homes would close after the introduction of the national minimum standards. The aim was to upgrade provision and shake out the worst homes in which residents were accommodated in small rooms along narrow corridors broken by sudden steps and without lifts. Bringing such buildings up to the national standards for rooms, corridors and lifts could be very expensive, and the owners of some of the homes which have closed have not wished to do the necessary rebuilding or have been unable to afford it.

Some owners, having entered the market during the growth years of the 1980s, perhaps in their fifties or sixties themselves, with their property occupying a valuable site, decided to call it a day and invest the proceeds of the sale in their own retirement or in some other business. Homes are also closing because of underfunding by social services departments, some of which will not pay them the fees the homes consider they need for their local authority placements. The departments' difficulty in paying reflects the failure of central government to channel them sufficient funds for this purpose.[8]

When you meet the manager you can certainly ask whether there is any chance that the home might close in the near future. You could also ask to see the accounts, though such a request is unlikely to be granted. However, there may be clues to the home's financial viability in inspection reports, as National Care Standards Commission inspectors have a right of access to the books.

It is important to bear in mind that sometimes care home closures can benefit residents, if they are being moved to more spacious surroundings with better facilities and more staff. Unfortunately, if you are unhappy about leaving a private care home which the owner has decided to close, there is not much you can do. The home has to give the national regulatory body three months' notice that it wishes to cancel its registration, and if it does not do this, it can be prosecuted. But it is not up to the National Care Standards Commission and its sister bodies to instruct a home to stay open. Nor does a private home have to find its residents alternative accommodation, although one hopes it will do what it can to help.

Local authority homes, which have also been closing in recent years, are in a different position. First, they are obliged to find residents alternative accommodation. Second, as they are public authorities, they can be taken to task under the terms of the Human Rights Act 1998. This Act makes it possible to bring cases in the United Kingdom courts for breaches of the European Convention on Human Rights, Article 8 of which provides the right for all citizens to respect for their private and family life and their home.

The Act did not come into force until 2000 and the law in this area may change as cases involving home closures come before the courts. Essentially, at the time of writing, the situation was that local authorities need to demonstrate that they have considered care home residents' rights under Article 8 during their decision-making process and furthermore that the benefits of closure outweigh any infringement of individuals' rights under Article 8.

The only significant advance as a result of the challenges to closure which had occurred at the time of writing has been the recognition that local authorities should involve residents and their relatives fully in a decision to close a local-authority-owned home. Specific progress has come out of complaints made about the way in which Plymouth City Council handled the closure of one of its homes. A three-person complaints panel headed by a judge (Sir Jonathan Clarke) drafted recommendations for the procedure all local authorities should follow if they are considering and then implementing the closure of a residential home,[9] and if you are in this situation, you may wish to take your local authority to task if they look like failing to act within these guidelines. They do not of course have a legal duty to do so, but they would be vulnerable in court if you could show they have not taken Article 8 rights into account adequately. If the home which is closing is a private one, there is no reason why you should not try to get the Clarke guidelines followed by suggesting them as good practice.

Sir Jonathan Clarke and his team say that the decision to close must take into account the impact closure will have on each resident individually – physically, emotionally and psychologically:

> From the individual's perspective, the closure of their home may be a major loss, tantamount to bereavement, with many of the emotions associated with this present in this context – such as denial, disbelief, anger, passive acceptance, immobilisation of feelings.

Sir Jonathan recommends that before any decision on closure is taken, each resident should be individually assessed to work out what the impact of closure is likely to be on them and the risk that might be involved if they were to move. In addition, residents and relatives should be consulted:

> This should not be rushed and must be genuine with face-to-face contact explaining the reasons for closure. Residents should be offered an advocacy service (and access to legal advice) in addition to their key worker, throughout the whole decision-making process.

The Clarke team also make useful recommendations on how closure should be implemented: 'Careful consideration should be given as to whether residents wish to move singly or in groups, explicitly thinking how much significance the group has for them.' Residents, relatives and advocates should be given a plan of the move, including the timescales involved. Special consideration should be given to the timing of breaking the news to residents:

> Using the analogy of bereavement, people must be allowed to go through the various stages such as shock, denial, anger and finally acceptance with skilled staff and others on hand to assist individuals through this process. . . . Building in enough time to work through the stages is crucial.

If you decide to fight a care home closure (or if your relative faces an unwelcome threat of eviction from his or her care home), contact one of the organizations listed on pages 413–14 for advice. Age Concern England has published a useful fact-sheet on home closures which is well worth reading.[10]

One important safeguard when your relative moves in to a home is to make sure that his or her money is held in an account completely separate from that of the home. In its report *Older People as Consumers in Care Homes*, the Office of Fair Trading explains:

> The practice of separating residents' private accounts from the home's own accounts is an important safeguard to ensure that, should the home close for any reason, those sums that properly belong to the residents are not jeopardized or lost. Where the money is kept in the home's bank account, it would be taken as part of the home's assets in any insolvency, while the residents would merely be unsecured creditors, which could result in their losing it all. The OFT is aware of one home which went into receivership where all the residents' monies were found to have been kept in a single account.[11]

Respite and Intermediate Care

Sometimes an older person goes into a care home for a limited period so that a carer at home can take a holiday. It is important to bear in mind that you still need to select a home for a respite stay very carefully. You do not want to return from your holiday to find your relative severely dehydrated, starving hungry because staff have not helped him or her to eat, and tired out from sharing a room with a snorer. Does the home have a quiet sitting room with lighting adequate for residents to read or pursue hobbies such as knitting? Can residents choose what they want to see on television or will it be left churning out endless quiz programmes and pop music? Will staff be available to set up a radio, television or CD player in your relative's own room, and to ensure that he or she has the correct glasses? Are the majority of care workers agency staff who are moved around and so will not build up knowledge of your relative's preferences and needs? Can the chef cope with any special dietary needs your relative may have? These are all important questions to be asked even if your relative is only spending a fortnight in a home.

If your local authority assesses your relative as needing short-term care in a care home, one of the ways in which you could secure more choice is to ask for any subsidy from the local authority to take the form of a Direct Payment (pages 297–306). Guidance issued by the Department of Health states that: 'Direct Payments may be made to enable people to purchase for themselves short stays in residential accommodation.'[12] The stays must not total more than four weeks in any 12-month period, although if the two periods are more than four weeks apart, they are not added together. Thus for example, someone might have one week of residential community care every six weeks. Because each week in residential care is more than four weeks apart, they would not be added together. The cumulative total would only be one week and the four-week limit would never be reached.

'Intermediate care' is often provided in a home registered for nursing care (pages 422–26). Check you are happy with the home before you agree to be transferred. Once there, expect the same standards of care as those indicated in the national minimum standards for permanent residents. Amanda Sherlock, the Regional Director, London, of the National Care Standards Commission, told me in an interview in 2003, 'Residents admitted for intermediate care should expect the same overall standards of care as permanent residents and are covered by the regulations; we would expect to see this reflected in care plans.'

As an intermediate-care resident, you should also expect special therapy from visiting professionals to speed your recovery. The national minimum standards for England revised in 2003 include a specific standard for people receiving intermediate care. One paragraph of this states: 'Specialist services from relevant professions including occupational and physiotherapists are provided or secured in sufficient numbers, and with sufficient competence and skills, to meet the assessed needs of service users admitted for rehabilitation.' If you consider the care home's staff are not able or willing to help you regain your mobility, you could point to standard 6.3: 'Staff are qualified and/or are trained and appropriately supervised to use techniques for rehabilitation including treatment and recovery programmes, promotion of mobility, continence and self-care, and outreach programmes to re-establish community living.'

If you encounter problems, approach one or more of the following, if necessary with a formal complaint: the home's manager, your social worker, the Intermediate Care Team Co-ordinator and the National Care Standards Commission or its sister body in your part of the UK.

Advice

Five main organizations offer advice on care homes.

Age Concern England produces useful general factsheets, with modifications issued for Scotland where necessary. Their national helpline offers advice on aspects of care homes and on funding places. Local groups may be able to help with local information. The organization runs a care homes payment scheme linked to the Norwich Union.

Help the Aged also offers a helpline and a fees advisory service. It can put people in touch with a possible payment scheme involving one of four insurance companies.

The Relatives and Residents Association was set up specifically to support residents in care homes and their close relatives. It also offers a helpline run from its headquarters in London and has a network of local groups which provide mutual support and advice on the ground.

The Elderly Accommodation Council provides a database of care homes throughout the UK on a geographical basis or sorted by a particular feature – for instance, whether the care home accepts pets, speaks a particular language, caters for particular religious affiliations or ethnic groups, or for people from particular backgrounds such as the armed services, or with special needs, such as learning disabilities.

Counsel and Care produces factsheets and also publishes very useful reports designed to improve the quality of care in homes. It provides a national helpline and also offers advocacy, taking up individual cases. These organizations are also discussed on pages 78–80.

Part Five
Hospitals

Chapter 13
Treatment

Sixty per cent of hospital beds are occupied by people over the age of 65. There are several reasons why older people are vastly over-represented in hospital. We tend to get most of our most serious illnesses at the end of our lives, and many major threats to health, such as coronary heart disease and cancer, are much more common in older age groups. Older bodies also take longer to recover from illnesses and operations than younger ones. It is quite a different matter for a woman to get over a Caesarean section than for someone aged 80-plus to recover from surgery. An older body takes longer to heal and to get the whole body system back on track, partly because it has less effective healing processes and partly because it has less functional reserve (pages 16–19). Finally, rehabilitation, or making somebody capable of living the kind of life he or she wants to, is a much bigger part of health care for older people than it is for the young.

A hospital may be a district general, mental health, community hospital or a hospice (pages 74–5). Some people are admitted as an emergency, others go in for medical treatment, others for assessment, for instance to mental health or neurological wards so that a consultant can work out how conditions such as dementia or Parkinson's disease can be more effectively dealt with. Some will go into community hospitals, usually as non-emergency admissions, often for recuperation and rehabilitation after an operation, or for palliative care.

Most people assume that admission to hospital is a good thing. A doctor committed to a patient seems to have secured an expensive hospital bed so intensive treatment can be provided. Yet although hospital can provide life-saving treatment and a tremendous amount of excellent care, it holds dangers for older people which apply much less to the young.

One is the risk of infection. Infections acquired in hospitals are common. In Scotland in 1999/2000, there were more than half a million cases of patients of all ages acquiring infections in hospital, according to a study carried out by the University of Glasgow.[1] As a result, older people, a group particularly at risk from hospital-acquired infections, spent an estimated 130,000 additional days in their beds in Scottish hospitals, according to this study. The dramatic change of environment involved in going into hospital can disorientate some older people, so that when they are ready to be discharged they are less able to look after themselves in their own home, particularly if the stay has been a long one. Also, unlike the young, older people often have pre-existing conditions unrelated to their admission which may get better or worse while they are in hospital. An elderly person, perhaps admitted because of cancer, might fall in a rush to get to the lavatory in unfamiliar surroundings and because of pre-existing osteoporosis, he or she might break a bone. Such dangers come on top of those which surround the treatment for which hospitalization has been called for.

So before you or your relative goes into hospital, quiz the doctor about why hospitalization is imperative. Could treatment not be provided at the patient's house or care home? What is likely to be achieved in hospital? Why that particular institution? And why the ward proposed rather than another?

Many of us are reluctant to ask such questions. As passive consumers in hospitals, we tend to do what the doctor recommends. The hospital environment can increase such passivity. In hospital, as in other environments in which care is given, recipients are at the weak end of a power relationship. We need help, and those in a position to give it are highly trained, often committed and respected members of society, laden with superior knowledge, armed with various pieces of impressive technical wizardry and operating in a world which offers few visible challenges to their authority. As we shed our daytime clothes and don night attire, perhaps even the ubiquitous hospital robe, and sit up in bed as the doctor above us dispenses wisdom, it is easy to feel yet more disempowered and depersonalized.

But it is important to be discerning. Not all care provided in hospitals is excellent, particularly where older people are involved. Try to remember first and foremost that you are or have been paying the bills; second, that patients have rights and expectations as set down in *The Patient's Charter, Your Guide to the NHS Guide* and national service frameworks (pages 58–61); and third, that the relationship between the giver and the receiver of medical care is a fluid one. Today, the doctor–patient relationship on the average maternity ward is far more equal than it was 30 years ago. A similar change in ethos and attitude will probably affect the care of elderly people eventually: it is important not to accept medical dictatorship as an unchanging norm.

What should the relatives of older patients expect from hospitals? What should they look out for? And if they cannot get what they think is needed, what can they do?

Ageism

Individuals can do little to mitigate some aspects of the care machine which are fundamentally ageist, such as the wholesale closure of geriatric beds and the subsidization of the welfare state by self-funders in care homes. [2] Other aspects are, however, easier to tackle.

Medical Attention

Whatever your relative's ailment, it can be instructive to find out what medical care is usually meted out to someone in his twenties with the same condition. For instance, if a young man develops pneumonia after a road traffic accident, what treatment is provided in the way of drugs, physiotherapy and other therapy? Does your 85-year-old aunt suffering from pneumonia get the same? If not, do sound medical reasons account for the discrepancy, or is ageism to blame? If you think it is, point to Standard 1 of the *National Service Framework for Older People*: 'Rooting out age discrimination: NHS services will be provided, regardless of age, on the basis of clinical need alone.'

Waiting Lists

Perhaps the main way in which people fear that ageism will affect their treatment is that the year of their birth will secure them low priority on the waiting list for an operation. Doctors are supposed to consider not chronological but functional age when they consider both suitability for and timing of an operation. They should not put people low on waiting lists simply because they are old.

To make sure this does not happen, you should check that your relative's name has actually been entered on the relevant list. You can also keep in touch by phone with the medical secretary in charge of that list to monitor progress.

Alternatively, if you can afford it, you can go private, which will generally secure an operation more quickly than the NHS. However, one problem for older people in going private is that recuperation is likely to take longer. Before taking out private medical insurance, check that adequate recuperation is covered. If it is not, you need to think carefully about what is going to happen after the operation. One possibility is paying to remain in the private hospital, although this is usually very expensive. Another is to pay a nurse to provide care in your or your relative's home to supplement attention from the NHS through the GP practice. A third is to pay for a stay in a private nursing home. In all these cases, it is vital to check that the nurses' qualifications and experience and the equipment to hand will be adequate. You would almost certainly get superior convalescent support on an NHS hospital ward, but your relative cannot simply leave his or her private hospital bed and check into an NHS one after the operation: he or she would normally have to be admitted through Accident and Emergency because a post-operation problem had arisen – not a very attractive prospect.

Avoiding Hospital

No one denies there are risks for anybody going into hospital or that these increase with age. One condition may be successfully treated only for another to develop. If personal and nursing care in the hospital is inadequate, a patient may well return from hospital with pressure sores or a chest, skin or urinary tract infection. Sometimes people with chronic conditions such as dementia or Parkinson's go into hospital so their condition can be assessed, with a view to altering their medication or some other aspect of their treatment; such assessments may take several weeks. It is important to be convinced that hospital is really necessary for such assessments. Could the consultant visit the patient in his or her home or care home instead?

There is also the risk of losing a place in a care home if the stay is longer than a couple of weeks. A clause in the contracts of some homes specifies that once a resident has been in hospital for a fortnight and no date has been set for discharge within the following two weeks, either party can terminate the contract. A fortnight may sound a long time to be in hospital, but in the world of eldercare it is not. Somebody who goes into hospital to be assessed for dementia can remain in hospital for many weeks, if not months.

Different factors come into play when an older person has only a limited time to live and will need considerable nursing care. Health and social services officials may propose a bed in the local community hospital. But the person in question might prefer to remain at home with specialist nursing and equipment, such as a pressure-relieving mattress, perhaps supplemented by a short stay or day care in a hospice, to put in place an optimal level of medication to relieve any pain and establish other components of palliative care. Officials may not explain that this choice is available, but once people are likely to die in the near future (usually interpreted as within the next 12 weeks), the NHS has an obligation to fund their care wherever they wish to live, including their own home, even if this means that specialist equipment and care must be bought in, including of course at weekends (page 57).

Which Hospital?

It is a good idea to assess the quality of care at the various hospitals in your area before going in either in non-emergency circumstances or through A and E. Hospitals vary greatly: one may have dirty wards and too few staff, with those it has demoralized, sitting at desks and ignoring patients' needs. Another hospital close by may be spotlessly clean with all its wards buzzing with committed staff. It is also worth finding out whether particular hospitals around you offer specialized additional facilities – a particularly good orthopaedic ward or a stroke unit (pages 443–4) for instance – before you agree to be treated at a particular institution. Hospitals do receive star-ratings, but these are too broad to give you much detailed guidance, and the system has been criticized.

There is a danger that an elderly person needing medical treatment will not be sent to a district or a specialist hospital at all, but to a community or cottage hospital – a cheaper NHS establishment with a narrower range of expertise and equipment –

because it is far more expensive to accommodate somebody in a district hospital or a hospice than in a community hospital, which is still more expensive than a nursing home. Of course the former often provide more specialist staff and more sophisticated equipment. But bear in mind other factors which can be important: for example, the staff in the district hospital may (or may not) be less expert in nursing older people than in a community hospital; the latter might be closer to home and thus attract more visitors than a large district establishment.

Intermediate Care

The government is keen to avoid admitting older people unnecessarily to expensive hospitals. Fair enough. It is also keen that older people should be spared the disruption of hospital admission when they could receive medical care elsewhere. With these objectives in mind, it introduced in 2001 the concept of 'intermediate care', a vague notion which essentially means that an older person receives intensive medical treatment for free, up to a maximum of six weeks, by spending less time in district hospitals or avoiding them altogether. The Department of Health's circular on the subject states: 'Intermediate care services should generally be provided in community based settings or in the patient/user's home, but may be provided in discreet step-down facilities on acute hospital sites.'[3]

Often, intermediate care involves a transfer to a care home registered for nursing care after a spell in hospital. For instance, an 84-year-old lady, already suffering from a chronic condition but managing well at home with the help of care workers, has a fall and breaks a bone in her knee. She is admitted to hospital, remains there for a month and is then told by her health authority's[4] intermediate care team that she will be transferred to a care home for intermediate care. A physiotherapist will visit twice a day to help her regain her ability to walk. The nursing home will look after her until she is mobile enough to return to her own home.

That sounds fine in theory. Except that chronic conditions from which the old lady is suffering may be quite difficult to manage. Perhaps she has a chronic lung condition, as well as osteoporosis. In her own home, the oxygen she needs constantly is provided by a machine in the hall which extracts oxygen from the air and sends it down a long tube which ends in two tiny tubes in her nostrils. Using long tubing, she can move freely around her bungalow. The machine is quite noisy, but a hole drilled through the wall for the tube enables her to shut her bedroom door at night.

Her son asks the nursing home if he can bring in the oxygen machine. It refuses: it has no holes in any of the bedroom walls and does not want the machine stationed in the corridor. Use oxygen cylinders instead, it says. Now, oxygen cylinders are big heavy things with only a short length of tubing, so his mother would not be able to move far from the cylinder. But the bigger drawback is that they run out and then need to be switched over. Would care staff be able to manage the oxygen supply necessary to sustain this old lady's life?

All of this actually happened in 2002. On her first weekend in the home, the old lady's son arrived to visit his mother after a long journey and found her grey-faced and barely able to lift her head. The cylinder had run out, on a Saturday, and the home said it could not obtain a replacement until Monday. The old lady had been without oxygen for six hours.

Her son took the law into his own hands. He went to his mother's bungalow with a neighbour and brought her oxygen machine into the home. He was allowed to leave it. Yet, two weeks later, almost exactly the same thing happened again. The oxygen machine had had to be replaced, and the technician who installed the replacement did not set it up to provide sufficient oxygen. The son arrived to find his mother extremely unwell again. Once again, the old lady probably almost died.

Although the physiotherapy worked well, the old lady unfortunately did not return home as she developed a chest infection in the nursing home, had a stroke and died. Her few weeks of intermediate care were not very stimulating, despite the best efforts of her visitors to provide her with books, a radio and audiocassettes. Cut off from the hub of life in an out-of-the-way bedroom and denied the help of staff to accompany her downstairs to the lounge (which would have required her to take an oxygen cylinder), she never shared a meal or even a cup of coffee with other residents. The food was basic and, by the time she got it, often cold. She likened the whole experience to being in prison.

There is no reason to suppose that the experience I have just described is not being repeated elsewhere. Nursing homes providing intermediate care beds have no special incentive to make patients or residents feel especially welcome, give them one of the best rooms or integrate them into the life of the home, as they will be staying for a fixed short period. Perhaps the greatest worry is the lack of any medical care, unless it is brought in from outside, apart from the registered nurse required always to be present in homes registered for nursing care.

In theory intermediate care can be a good thing, since district general hospitals are often not where many elderly people would choose to be. But community (or cottage) hospitals and nursing homes may not be either. At least in the large hospital there will be specialists and advice on tap: in a nursing care home or a community hospital, specialist and often also general medical expertise will have to be brought in.

The idea of intermediate care came in for criticism from the moment it was first mooted. The British Geriatrics Society consists of medical practitioners in the field of geriatric medicine. It asked, in 2001:

> Can alternative institutional settings, such as general-practitioner beds, community hospitals or nursing homes, meet the needs of the acutely unwell older patient? Only if access to medical diagnostic facilities and appropriately trained medical, nursing and rehabilitation staff is greatly improved. . . . Currently, in many 'intermediate' settings proposed as alternatives to acute hospitals, 'low-tech' is equivalent to 'no-tech'.[5]

In a more detailed analysis of hospitals and older people the year before, the Society commented:

> The development of the acute district general hospital model of care was a major advance in the healthcare of older people, immeasurably improving access to a wide range of investigation and treatment facilities. The impact of this change in overcoming the previous ageist institutional barriers to care cannot be overestimated . . . Exclusion of older people from acute district hospital facilities, without the provision of proven effective alternatives, will be a return to the institutional ageism of the past and must be resisted.[6]

So if a doctor says that your relative should go into an institution for intermediate care, or simply that he or she needs medical treatment and should be admitted to a setting which can provide it, such as a community hospital or a nursing home, quiz the doctor carefully and do what you can to ensure your relative goes to the institution which can best look after him or her. Prepare your questions. Intermediate care could work to the patient's benefit, providing a means of staying put at home or in a care home and having medical expertise brought in. It could fund short bursts of intensive medical help at regular intervals – for instance, bringing a patient into hospital every few months or weeks for a short time to check his or her various conditions and adjust any treatment as necessary. But the best environment for that sort of valuable maintenance therapy is a top-level geriatric ward in a district hospital, not a private nursing home.

If you are really worried about a transfer under intermediate care, for instance from a district hospital to a particular care home, you could refuse to comply. The NHS cannot forcefully transfer anyone anywhere without their agreement (unless sectioned under the Mental Health Act 1983), and so must to a greater or lesser extent obtain the patient's agreement. If you find yourself in this situation, complain vociferously to the hospital trust (from which the hospital discharge is technically being made), and make identical duplicate complaints to the relevant health authority and social services department (pages 577–80). Make telephone complaints and send letters not only to the key health and social services officials, but also to their bosses, local councillors and your relative's MP. You could alert the media too.

There is no reason why you should not make suggestions about where you consider intermediate care should be provided if not in the care home to which the health body wishes to transfer your relative. 'Intermediate care' can be provided in a range of settings, including a patient's own home. The hundreds of pounds which the NHS pays care homes each week when intermediate care is provided in that setting could instead fund additional visits by health care staff to a person's own home. The personal care which care home staff provide could be supplied by homecare workers organized by the patient him- or herself or by social services, and paid for separately. In many cases, including that of the lady referred to above, homecare visits will have been taking place before entry into hospital and could be resumed. If additional personal care was considered necessary, the intermediate care budget could fund it.

Hospices

If your relative's life is coming to an end, you might want to investigate hospices in your area. These used to be mainly for cancer patients, but now they take people suffering from a wide range of terminal conditions.

Hospices vary, but you will probably find that they provide more of a homely environment than a hospital – smaller than a district hospital and fostering an atmosphere more conducive to feelings of peacefulness. The emphasis is on trying to achieve a good death, rather than letting death be something that just happens. Care is likely to be more sensitive to the patients' emotions, and more holistic, embracing the need for people to come to terms psychologically with their impending demise. Expertise in the medical aspects of palliative care should be more highly developed. There should be support for relatives both before and after the death. Some hospices hold remembrance services to honour all of their patients who have died within the previous 12 months, as well as offering bereavement counselling.

One obvious disadvantage of a hospice is that you and your relative will have to handle the deaths of a high proportion of the other people being cared for. By no means all hospice patients die in the hospice, however. Many come in to have their condition monitored and as far as possible controlled, and then go back home. But do visit, ask questions and spend a little time absorbing the atmosphere before you decide whether to try to get your relative admitted. The National Care Standards Commission and its equivalent bodies should inspect non-NHS hospices, which form the vast majority (pages 53–4), and national minimum standards will be published. Have a look at those already issued for use by the Scottish Commission for the Regulation of Care to get an idea of what to expect.[7]

On the Ward

When a person goes on to the ward of a district general hospital for any reason, it is easy for relatives to imagine that their main concern should be ensuring swift diagnosis and treatment from a doctor. This is of course extremely important, but it is also important to be aware of the care delivered by nurses. Sometimes we are not aware that really important decisions are being taken by nurses about which we ought to be consulted. Perhaps the most important of these concerns catheterization.

Catheterization

Soon after your relative arrives in a ward, somebody (perhaps a doctor, perhaps a nurse) may decide whether he or she should be catheterized (a tube inserted into the patient from which the urine passes into a bag, which is emptied), perhaps after an operation or a stroke. Often relatives are not consulted on whether a catheter should be deployed and they do not know that a decision is being taken until they discover that it has been put into practice.

Temporary incontinence often occurs, for instance after a stroke. Many elderly patients have had to rely to some degree on continence pads before they come into hospital. But neither reason on its own is sufficient for inserting a catheter, whether intended for only a few days or for long-term use (what is known as an in-dwelling catheter). However, busy nurses (and care workers in care homes) often prefer catheters: the alternative may be helping somebody to use the lavatory or a bed pan or changing incontinence pads, all of which take more time than servicing a catheter (done mainly by turning on a tap and draining away the urine).

The practice has various downsides. Insertion of the catheter can be traumatic, particularly for somebody confused after a stroke or suffering from dementia. People who have had catheters in place for more than six weeks have to relearn how to control their urine outflow. If the catheter is not inserted carefully, it can tear delicate internal tissues. Catheters can erode people's self-esteem. They may come to feel helpless because they can no longer go to the lavatory, and it is easy for their dignity to be diminished still further if the catheter bag is visible. Finally, there is a real risk of urinary tract infection, and such infections can be painful, cause people to feel really unwell and require antibiotics to clear them up. The risk is quite high: 40 per cent of hospital-acquired infections are those of the urinary tract, and 70 per cent of these are associated with in-dwelling catheters.

If it is decided that a catheter is necessary, then it is important that the right type is chosen and that only trained staff insert it and oversee its management. Untrained staff changing a catheter because it has become blocked with mineral deposits can cause excruciating pain. Managing the catheter by draining off fluid from the catheter bag also requires sensitive handling if the catheter user is not to be embarrassed.

Catheters can provide real help in certain situations, and many people do use them, some living in their own homes (with help from a district nurse). Dr David Cohen, who heads the stroke unit at Northwick Park Hospital in Harrow, Middlesex, told me in an interview in 2001:

> The issue of catheters is a very important one. In my view, a catheter should never be used except as a last resort to manage incontinence. There are very few reasons to try to put a catheter into somebody, and most of them involve a blockage to the flow of urine. If for some reason the urine is there but it is not flowing out then I would put a catheter in. In almost all other circumstances a catheter carries more hazards than the problems it solves. It should never be put in for convenience: I feel very strongly about that. There are all sorts of ways of managing incontinence from toileting people regularly to making sure they can call a nurse easily or giving them pads. Pads these days are very strong and can soak up large quantities of urine. In the case of somebody who could not speak and therefore not attract a nurse's attention or was unconscious, I would manage their incontinence with pads rather than a catheter, because pads carry no hazard to the patient at all.

The other circumstances when catheterization might be a legitimate last resort involve somebody completely immobile at home but desperate to remain there even though social services can run to only three visits a day, so that after passing urine between visits they would be wet. Dr Cohen again: 'There may be reasons to use a catheter rather than pads here. But that's a long way down the line from the first few hours after a stroke.'

If you are dissatisfied with what the medical staff intend, whatever it is, ask to speak to one or more of the following people: your relative's consultant doctor, his or her named nurse, the ward manager or the continence nurse specialist (most district hospitals these days have such a person). If you are unhappy with the decision to insert a catheter, try to get staff to agree a date at which the decision will be reviewed.

If a relative has temporary or permanent incontinence and has not been catheterized, you will need to make sure that nurses are changing incontinence pads sufficiently frequently, that the pads themselves are of the correct strength, and that your relative is being washed sufficiently often.

Personal Care

It has been well known for a number of years that older people often fail to receive adequate nursing and personal care support when they are staying in hospital. The charity Help the Aged launched a 'Dignity on the Ward' campaign in 1999 to improve the situation, but problems are still regularly reported in the press. Some hospitals are brilliant, but in others you will find that nurses do not see tasks such as helping with feeding, taking patients to the lavatory or helping them wash as integral to nursing care. Yet clearly elderly people will not get better if they are not getting enough to eat and drink, and patients who cannot walk easily may fall if nobody helps them to the lavatory.

To try to understand why many of today's nurses are not paying attention to these matters, the Nursing and Midwifery Advisory Committee, whose members come from professional bodies and which advises health ministers in England and Wales, carried out an inquiry. The findings were published in a report in 2001 called *Caring for Older People: A Nursing Priority*.[8] One of the main reasons the committee highlighted was the education of nurses. Many nurses do not learn much about the complex physiology and physical and psychological needs of older people, although nursing older people is what most nurses will do (page 69). Their education focuses on what are seen as the more glamorous parts of the nurse's job – equipping them to care for young adults with single conditions which require focused, intense action. Specialism in nurses' education has also helped push to one side the education of nurses in the personal care tasks which a few years ago most nurses would have been expected to be able to do. Although nurses would see it as their responsibility to make sure that their patients get food and drink if they need help, many do not see such tasks as central and as a result delegate them to lesser staff or even overlook them.

In her autobiography, published in 2003, Claire Rayner describes the training she was given in her first nursing post, at Epsom Cottage Hospital, in 1945. 'Under Sister's sharp guidance' she learned to carry out personal care tasks with sensitivity, for example, how to 'give blanket baths without making the patient embarrassed' and how to prevent pressure sores. She writes: 'It is a matter of huge pride to Sister that there has not been a bedsore on her ward since 1937, and that one had been due to self-inflicted injury.'[9] Today, elderly people can count themselves lucky if they manage to emerge from a hospital stay without a pressure sore.

Raising Concerns
If you see that your relative is not receiving suitable nursing and personal care, the first thing to do is to raise the matter with your relative's named nurse (pages 76–7). If you get no joy from the named nurse, or if he or she is not available, ask to speak to the ward manager (usually the ward sister or senior charge nurse). Do not assume doctors will not interest themselves in nursing matters. Many feel strongly about issues such as the unnecessary use of urinary catheters. They are also being encouraged to take a more active interest in nutrition: in 2002, the Royal College of Physicians issued a 'wake-up call to the medical profession to take Clinical Nutrition seriously', in the words of its President, Professor Sir George Alberti, who was launching a new Royal College report calling for nutrition to be addressed seriously by everybody in hospital. The report spelt out the ways in which both under- and over-nutrition can affect the health of patients and how improving nutritional care can help them recover more quickly.[10]

If you are still dissatisfied, you could approach the unit general manager responsible for the wards including that in which your relative is staying (page 77). He or she will be responsible and accountable for what goes on in all these wards. It is important not to be put off by the medical hierarchy: sometimes delay can be very important. And sometimes delay is caused not because staff are busy but because a task has been inadvertently overlooked. For example, perhaps your relative has been on the ward for several days and yet not been seen by a consultant. Perhaps you have tried to speak to the ward manager but he or she is away, the deputy has not taken any action and nobody else seems to be ensuring your relative is seen promptly. Take it up with the general manager.

A matron should also have been appointed to respond to patients' concerns (page 77). Each matron should be responsible for a number of wards and you can raise any matter with him or her, such as ward cleanliness, poor nursing or delays in your relative being seen by a consultant. You could also seek help from the hospital's Patients Advice and Liaison Service.

Try not to wait until things go wrong before taking action, but to sense what the difficulties might be. If a relative has a special condition, you may well have to ask the ward manager to explain to his or her staff something about that condition if it is apparent they do not understand it. For example, as Parkinson's disease can affect movement, speech and swallowing, life on a hospital ward can be very difficult for a Parkinson's sufferer if staff do not understand the condition or are too rushed to help. People with Parkinson's often take a very long time to eat and they may choke on their food. If they cannot swallow tablets, they will need to take them in a mousse. They need to take their medication (to top up the level dopamine in the brain – page 149) at specific times, which may well not coincide with the time of the drugs ward round. Difficulty in moving makes them prone to falls. Difficulty in speaking compounds problems still further.

Some of the aspects of nursing and personal care of which you might care to take especial note are as follows:

Prevention of Pressure Sores

Pressure sores (or ulcers) are open wounds which develop on parts of the body on which we normally rest (page 9). They can develop quickly in somebody who is not moving and they are terribly painful. Pain-relief medication can have side-effects such as drowsiness, which make it harder to take exercise for rehabilitation. So people with pressure sores tend to stay in hospital longer.

Clearly, it is best to stop sores developing in the first place. Regular change of position, whether your relative is in a chair, a wheelchair or in bed, is therefore essential. Precautions include frequent turning, taping protective padding to particularly vulnerable areas (including, surprisingly enough, heels) and using pressure-relieving mattresses. These mattresses contain pockets of air which inflate and deflate every few minutes, so that the points of pressure change all the time. Different grades of mattress match different degrees of vulnerability.

If your loved one is immobile in hospital, expect a risk assessment of the likelihood of pressure sores developing and where, and see that appropriate action is taken, such as removal from a trolley in A and E on to a pressure-relieving mattress as soon as possible. Assessment should take place promptly, as pressure sores can develop even in 30 minutes.

If a sore starts developing, pressure should be kept off the affected area. Your relative should be kept as well as possible and well nourished, so that he or she has the nutrients essential for healing (page 19). It can all take a long time. In extreme cases resort is made to plastic surgery.

Infection Control

The usual infections picked up in hospital are wound infections, chest infections such as pneumonia, skin infections as a result of intravenous infusions, and urinary tract infections. Thirty per cent of hospital-acquired infections are unavoidable: they may result from pathogens in the air. The good news for patients is that the remaining 70 per cent are considered preventable. The steps needed to avoid them are often simple.

It is well established that a prime cause of the transmission of infection in hospitals is inadequate handwashing and changing of aprons between treatments. *The Oxford Textbook of Geriatric Medicine* says: 'The practice of glove use and handwashing is pivotal in terms of infection control practices and is crucial for minimising risk in long-term care facilities . . . Handwashing is the most important and least expensive measure for preventing transmission of nosocomial [hospital-acquired] infections.'[11] The authors cite a study in 1997 which found that an astonishing 82 per cent of interactions between staff and patients could have resulted in the transmission of infection because of lax hygiene standards. Handwashing and the changing of disposable aprons between patients are often visible to visitors on a hospital ward. If you see a nurse moving on to the next patient without performing these functions properly, alert someone in authority. Handwashing should be thorough, involving time, soap and often an alcohol scrub (page 352).

Clearly wards which are not cleaned well will be more exposed to the risk of infection. Bacteria need moisture to germinate, so keep a special watch for damp dirt. Dirt can become damp through contact with a patient. If somebody is having a wound dressing changed and dust is dislodged when the curtains round the bed are swept across, it could fall into a moist, uncovered wound and set up an infection.

If you have doubts, ask the ward manager or even the hospital's infection-control nurse, whose job it will be to advise all wards. Be prepared for the fact that some infection control involves taking quite difficult decisions. Research evidence suggests that intravenous infusions should be re-sited at least every 48 hours to minimize the risk of infection. However, a nurse may have trouble getting access in the first place to the often very frail veins of an elderly person. If a vein seems to be working well, they might decide that on balance they will not re-site. Similarly, every time a wound dressing is changed there is a risk of more bacteria invading the wound, so nurses have to strike a balance between changing the dressing frequently enough to keep the wound clean yet not so often that they introduce too many more bacteria.

The infection which people dread perhaps most of all is MRSA, the hospital superbug. Some people recover from it, but others succumb or suffer for a long time. The bacterium in question actually lives on the skin of about a third of us, but a strain has developed which is resistant to antibiotics (MRSA stands for 'methicillin-resistant Staphylococcus aureus'). The danger arises if this bacterium gets into the bloodstream when resistance is low. Entry may be through the eye, a catheter or a wound, and so it is particularly dangerous for health workers to touch an open wound like a pressure sore or a leg ulcer if they have not washed their hands well or are not wearing plastic gloves.

Feeding and Drinking

Patients who cannot feed themselves and receive no help to do so will become malnourished and dehydrated. This is a very serious matter. Wards vary on how much they help with feeding and drinking. In their study for the *Dignity on the Ward* report for Help the Aged, a team from Sheffield University found that some wards ensured that staff did not take breaks at mealtimes so that all hands were on deck to help with eating and drinking.[12]

Your Guide to the NHS Guide singles out help with feeding for special mention, so point to it if you need to: 'Your nutritional needs and dietary requirements will be assessed (for medical, religious or cultural reasons). You will be provided with a variety of good food, and given any help that you need to eat or order your meals.' Also, since all NHS hospitals are now supposed to operate a 24-hour catering service, it should be easier to entice patients to eat who do not wish to have three meals a day at set times.

If you remain worried after discussing your concerns with the ward manager, you could ask whether it is possible for the amount of food your relative eats to be recorded, which should be a simple matter. Also ask for a fluid balance chart to be drawn up to record fluid intake. Staff should already be recording what the patient is eating and drinking if there is any concern that food or fluid intake is less than it should be.

Activities

Essentially, hospitals do not see it as their job to provide entertainment for patients, unlike a care home. Hospitals vary in the provision of facilities such as television, radio and telephones. Some offer these facilities freely: in others you have to pay for them; in others nothing is available. Traditionally this area has been a low priority in hospitals, yet for people who can take a long time to recover, days in hospital can be very long. You cannot insist the hospital provides entertainment facilities, but it ought to help you provide say, a small television with headphones or a cassette recorder if necessary. . There may be a hospital library, probably manned by volunteers. Providing plenty for your relative to do and plenty of visitors can boost morale enormously.

Don't forget to make the most of the hospital's chaplaincy

service (page 39). This can provide a friendly visitor as well as spiritual support for people of all beliefs and none. If you are keen that your relative should benefit, it is worth telephoning the chaplaincy office yourself.

Transport
Older people, of course, expect free transport in an NHS ambulance in an emergency. But free transport should also be available for them more generally. In its circular to health authorities on the care of older people with ongoing healthcare needs, the Department of Health says:

> Ambulances and other specialist transport should be available from the NHS on the basis of patients' needs for transport to and from hospital or hospice, for emergency admission to a nursing home, and for non-emergency travel to and from health care facilities.

The range of elderly people to whom these words apply is very wide: it includes all those who need care 'over an extended period of time, as the result of disability, accident or illness to address both physical and mental health needs'. This provision applies to all adults over the age of 18, 'but is primarily concerned with older people, older people with mental health needs, people with dementia and younger adults requiring continuing NHS healthcare as a result of illness or accidents'.[13]

'Needs' in this context means clinical needs, and ultimately the decision on whether your clinical need is sufficient to justify free NHS transport is made by the consultant. If you are unhappy with a decision, complain (pages 58–3).

In tandem with this system based on clinical need is another providing free transport more widely to those deemed to be hard up. People who are receiving the Guarantee Credit element of Pension Credit automatically get free transport or their fares reimbursed. Other people with low incomes but who do not qualify for Guarantee Credit may also be eligible for help. Ask at the reception desk of the hospital you are visiting, as financial help with travelling costs is paid at the hospital (not at a Social Security Office). The NHS booklet *Are you Entitled to Help with Health Costs?*, HC11, outlines entitlements. Help the Aged's helpline,

Seniorline, which specializes in welfare benefits, is a good source of advice, although it does not pursue individual cases.

Hospitals often operate transport schemes which take people to outpatient appointments and clinics. These can be useful, but you need to be careful here: you might find it better to organize your own transport. The hospital may collect many other people *en route*, perhaps making the journey very long. This could even mean missing appointments.

Rehabilitation and Other Care (Example: Strokes)

Frequently, rehabilitation is a very important component of an older person's stay in hospital. Rehabilitation involves restoring somebody to optimal physical, mental and social abilities consistent with his or her needs and desires and those of his or her family. It involves examining any damage which has been done to an organ or a part of the body, perhaps by an accident or a stroke, the ways this is affecting bodily function (for instance difficulty in washing and dressing) and the ways in which both of these things influence patients' prospects of stepping back into the life they led before. If two people have had half a leg amputated, but beforehand one preferred to spend her time reading and the other gardening, the first will be less severely handicapped by the amputation than the second.

Strokes illustrate particularly well the need for careful consideration of rehabilitation. They also provide an example of some of the main dangers to be wary of when older people are awaiting hospital treatment on a trolley in A and E or on a ward. Also, strokes are one condition in which quick admission to hospital is desirable but relatives may not realize this. Finally, the choice of ward, especially for rehabilitation, can be important.

Background

Strokes differ from many other afflictions in that they occur as an acute condition but also need long-term treatment. A stroke occurs when the brain is damaged by stoppage of its supply of blood. Four out of five strokes are caused by a clot in an artery; the others are the result of a break in a blood vessel, which causes a haemorrhage affecting the brain. It is important to know what the cause is, because the victims of strokes caused by clots could benefit from drugs which disperse clots or reduce the tendency of the blood to clot, but these drugs could worsen the condition of someone suffering from uncontrolled bleeding.

Often people suffer a stroke without realizing it. This may be because the parts of the body controlled by the affected part of the brain are ones of which we are unconscious. Or perhaps the blood vessel involved is tiny, fuelling only a small number of brain cells. Multi-infarct dementia, thought to cause 30 per cent of dementia cases, results from a series of tiny strokes, each of them often imperceptible at the time, which build up to result in progressive loss of cognitive function (page 6).

What seems to be a stroke may not be. 'Transient ischaemic attacks' resemble a stroke in that the sufferer may experience, say, loss of vision or weakness in a limb, but differ in that people recover completely within 24 hours. Although TIAs have only a temporary impact, it is important to see your doctor if you experience one, as it may precede a real stroke. People may also recover quickly from mini or minor strokes, although not as rapidly as from a transient ischaemic attack.

The kind of stroke I want to consider here is the major event which people usually talk of when they say somebody has had a stroke.

One difficulty is actually knowing that you or your relative is actually having a stroke. There are no hard and fast rules, so if you think a stroke may be in progress, it is important to get medical advice quickly. Watch out for the sudden onset of unusual weakness or paralysis in the muscles in an arm, a leg, down one side or in the face, numbness or pins and needles in a part of the body, dizziness, double vision or loss of vision on one side, difficulty in reading and writing, slurred speech, difficulty in finding the right words and in understanding what somebody is saying. Many other symptoms may occur, depending on which part of the brain has been affected and the extent of the damaged area. Sometimes strokes make people drowsy or unconscious. Sometimes they occur during sleep, without the sufferer realizing anything has happened: only on waking is the victim aware that something has changed.

Many people believe that strokes are prompted by stressful events such as a burglary or bereavement, but this is relatively rarely the case. Most occur as a random event in a susceptible person. High blood pressure is the main cause of susceptibility and this has usually been present for many years, often partly because of genetic predisposition. Apart from inheritance, the main factor affecting blood pressure is the amount of salt in your diet (pages 8 and 23). The condition can be treated by salt reduction, drugs such as beta-blockers and ACE inhibitors, and exercise (page 139).

Although strokes most frequently occur as random events, they are sometimes associated with a rise in blood pressure after major stress to the body, such as an operation or a heart attack. As a result, some elderly people who suffer a stroke are already in hospital. But just because you are in hospital does not mean you will receive the best possible treatment for your stroke.

If your relative is in a hospital which contains a specialist stroke unit (pages 443–4), try to get him or her admitted to it. If the stroke occurs outside hospital, try, all other things being equal, to get to hospital as quickly as possible (making sure that the emergency services recognize the stroke as an emergency) and try to get admitted into a specialist stroke unit. However, many stroke units will only admit people after they have been assessed elsewhere in the hospital, confining themselves largely to rehabilitation rather than emergency care. In fact, a general medical ward is usually a perfectly good place to be during or in the first few days after a stroke.

Acute Care

Once an apparent stroke victim has been admitted to hospital, medical staff should work out whether the cause of the stroke is a clot or a haemorrhage, assess the extent of damage to the brain and establish that a different condition is not to blame. Such conditions may include a brain abscess, a brain tumour, some abnormality in the chemical composition of the blood, or even a migraine. There are two main diagnostic techniques available. The CT scan takes a sort of photograph of the brain. Magnetic resonance imaging traces the passage of water through the brain and can give more detailed information. As more hospitals develop specialist stroke units, it is likely that more will be able to offer such services, but at present few general hospitals can offer a CT scan within hours of a stroke and few have any magnetic resonance imaging equipment. However, it is worth asking why these techniques are not being used.

Aspirin is the most common and most effective immediate treatment for strokes – as long as they have not been caused by a haemorrhage. Aspirin dilutes the blood and thus accelerates the dispersal of clots, but it will make a haemorrhage worse. Because of the delay in getting a CT scan, the benefit of the aspirin administered in the aftermath of a stroke will lie in reducing the likelihood of subsequent strokes. This is important, as the high blood pressure which led to one stroke may lead to another. If your relative is not getting a scan and therefore the possibility of aspirin soon after admission, you could mention *National Clinical Guidelines for Stroke*, written by the Inter-Collegiate Working Party for Stroke and published in 2000 by the Royal College of Physicians. They state: 'Aspirin should be given as soon as possible after the onset of stroke symptoms, if the diagnosis of haemorrhage is considered unlikely.'[14]

Clot-busting drugs, or thrombolytics, which cause rapid destruction of a clot, have been developed, but they need to be administered within hours of the stroke in a specialist ward which knows how to handle them. Not all patients, even those whose strokes have been caused by a clot, can benefit from these drugs; they are not available at many places in the UK at present (though they are used more widely in the United States and in parts of mainland Europe), and experts in the UK are divided on their usefulness.

The reason for getting to hospital after or during a stroke is by no means only to get a brain scan and stroke treatment. Another important reason is the reduction of possible complications, which can relate to:

- **Fluid intake** Stroke victims must receive sufficient fluid. If they become dehydrated, the stroke can become more serious, because the blood is more viscous. Patients who cannot take fluid by mouth will be placed on an intravenous drip or they may be given an infusion of fluid under the skin, called a subcutaneous infusion, which has advantages over a drip (pages 456–7).

- **Pressure sores** These can develop quickly in somebody who is not moving, but simple action can be taken to avert them (pages 431–2).
- **Swallowing difficulty** It may be tempting to offer a stroke victim a cup of tea. But this could prove fatal. Strokes frequently reduce the ability to swallow, though usually only temporarily. If swallowing mechanisms have been impaired, liquids such as tea or water may go down the wrong way and end up in the lungs, where they may give rise to a chest infection which could kill. It is crucial that anyone who has suffered a stroke should have his or her ability to swallow assessed very soon afterwards. Nurses can do this, but the specialists in this area are speech and language therapists (page 73). If swallowing has been impaired, a speech and language therapist or a nurse will decree that the patient should be given only liquids which have been specially thickened – a process which will ensure that nothing passes into the respiratory rather than the digestive system.

Once the feeding regime has been established, it is important to ensure it is actually implemented. There must be no mistakes in the delivery of food and drink to the bedside, or its content. Mistakes will be more likely if the patient is unable to speak up, whether as a result of the stroke or of some pre-existing condition such as dementia.

If the patient cannot swallow at all, fluid and nutrient intake can be maintained by way of a naso-gastric tube, which passes through the nose, or through 'PEG' feeding, which requires the insertion of a tube (by a minor surgical procedure) straight into the stomach through the side (page 457). A relative should expect to be consulted on the pros and cons of such procedures, and should expect the chosen method to be reviewed frequently.

To handle issues such as these, relatives of stroke victims particularly those already suffering from difficulties imposed by such conditions as sight or hearing impairment or dementia may wish to remain with the patient as long as possible. When my mother, who was already suffering from Alzheimer's and nearly blind, had a stroke, family members took it in turns to be at her bedside through her waking hours for the first few days. We were keen to make absolutely sure that she did not consume unthickened liquids, took her medication, had sufficient nutrition and fluid, did not fall, did not topple out of bed, did not pull out her intravenous infusion or her urinary catheter and, later, that her continence pads were changed frequently – not to mention the provision of reassurance and company.

When somebody who has had a stroke is in hospital, relatives should also be alert to decisions being taken about the insertion of a urinary catheter, amongst various aspects of nursing and personal care (pages 427–8).

Rehabilitation

Of people who experience a stroke, about a third die, a third recover more or less, while a third are left with significant disability. The extent to which this final third are permanently disabled depends partly on the location and degree of the damage to brain tissue and partly on the extent to which the brain can continue to operate the parts of the body controlled by the damaged cells by side-stepping them and forming new pathways. These new pathways enable parts of the brain that were hit but not permanently damaged, together with other parts that have survived intact, to take on the functions of the damaged parts. This process takes place either spontaneously or through will-power and practice. A major part of rehabilitation after a stroke involves seeking to regain lost functions, usually through repetitive training, and also learning to cope with disabilities which will only slowly or never be overcome.

The most common types of disability after a major stroke are paralysis, muscle weakness, difficulties in swallowing, difficulties in speaking and disruption of balance. It is hard to overstate the difficulty which everyday tasks may pose if the relevant part of the brain has been impaired. Eating can involve slopping food all over the place; going to the lavatory can take a long time; crossing a room can seem next to impossible. These abilities may return quickly or take some time or never fully come back. The major determining factor is the extent of the damage to the brain. But in situations in which it is possible to regain lost ability that does not return of its own accord, practice and forcing yourself to do things which overnight have become impossible are very important.

Of course, such practice can be daunting. People who have suffered a major stroke can feel shocked and overwhelmed by what they fear they have lost. However determinedly they try to feed themselves again and adopt a positive attitude, they do not know whether that faculty can ever return. Some people will find it even more difficult, perhaps impossible to summon up the motivation to relearn old skills, especially if they are suffering from a challenging pre-existing condition. And after a stroke, when somebody is often feeling very tired as well as concerned about the future, depression can easily set in and worsen an already difficult situation. You could be a very intelligent, optimistic, driven person, but if you have lost a large number of brain cells as a result of a stroke, there is nothing you can do about it, in the same way that you cannot will yourself to get better from cancer.

Success will be made more likely by three things:

1. A considered and realistic rehabilitation programme implemented by specialist staff
2. Understanding of the rehabilitation programme by non-specialist staff, as well as family, friends and others who may be providing care
3. Encouragement by everybody.

All these things are needed whether stroke victims are in hospital, living in care homes or in their own homes. Although a stroke calls for emergency hospitalization, many people suffer strokes without going to hospital or, if they go to A and E, without being admitted to a ward. People who are already living in care homes may remain there. But wherever you or your relative is living, it is important to get rehabilitation services. This may mean badgering the manager of your relative's care home and/or his or her GP. Do not allow the care home to tell you that the kindest approach is to allow your relative to sleep continuously after the stroke and that any rehabilitation would be fruitless unless you are absolutely convinced that this is true.

Lots of people regain lost abilities without specialist help, either spontaneously or through repetitively retraining themselves. But GPs have access to various specialists who have a fund of knowledge about the most effective means of restoring lost faculties and may also be invaluable in monitoring progress and coping with anxieties which arise. Apart from the speech and language specialist, the most important is likely to be the physiotherapist, who helps stroke victims regain the ability to move around by getting muscles and joints back up to speed, and also helps people regain their balance when, as often happens, this has been disrupted. Physiotherapists also advise on aids such as sticks or walking frames if it seems unlikely that sufficient muscle strength will return for unaided walking (page 72). Specialist exercise classes, provided by health or local authorities, can be useful (pages 137–44).

A GP can also ask the local hospital to provide rehabilitation, for instance by asking for the patient's name to be placed on a stroke register compiled by the hospital in the first instance. Such registers record the date of the stroke, the patient's date of birth, the level of any disability and the type of rehabilitation the sufferer has been receiving.

If you or your relative find difficulty in securing what you consider to be appropriate rehabilitation through your GP, you could mention the stroke section of the *National Service Framework for Older People.* This states that by April 2004, primary care groups and trusts will have ensured that 'Every general practice can identify people who have had a stroke and are treating them according to protocols agreed with local specialist services.'

Another document may also help your cause: the *National Clinical Guidelines for Stroke* published by the Royal College of Physicians. In this document, a particularly useful guideline states that 'Patients should see a therapist each working day if possible, and they should receive as much therapy as they can be given and find tolerable.'[15]

Stroke Units

In its *National Service Framework for Older People,* the Department of Health urged district general hospitals to set up specialist stroke units by April 2004. It is a good idea to find out which hospitals in your area have stroke units, so should an emergency arise, you already know where to head for. Stroke units are not, however, the only option to think of if you or a relative is suffering a stroke. You don't want to be based at a hospital far from home, because arranging support at home after discharge can be very complicated and you need to be able to exploit links with your local medical services. Also, if you are in hospital for a long period, visiting will be more wearing if the distance is great. If you find a stroke unit, you need to be careful. Is it a good one? There is a danger that some hospital administrators will respond to the exhortation to establish a stroke unit by adding a few facilities to, say, a geriatric ward, and calling it a stroke unit – quite a different matter from designing one from scratch and giving it committed stroke staff.

There is research evidence to show that patients in them end up spending less time in hospital and have a better chance of surviving their strokes and of suffering less long-term disability.[16] Stroke units can be good places to be in the immediate aftermath of a stroke, since staff will be used to diagnosing the cause of stroke or stroke-like symptoms and averting possible complications. But perhaps the units' greatest strength lies in the benefits they can offer during rehabilitation. If you are in hospital, a specialist stroke ward is usually a much better place to be for rehabilitation than a general medical or geriatric ward.

Nurses working on specialist stroke wards should understand far more about rehabilitation in general and specifically rehabilitation after a stroke than general registered nurses. This means they are well equipped to help patients continue with therapy after, say, they have seen the physiotherapist for an hour per day in the gym. Also, since nurses on stroke wards are used to dealing with conditions which frequently arise with strokes, such as temporary speech or continence difficulties, they are better placed than a nurse on an ordinary ward to anticipate such problems. Asking people who are having difficulty talking whether they wish to pass water, rather than waiting for them to ask, may enable them to retain their dignity and regain personhood that much more quickly.

Finally, nurses on stroke wards are more likely to understand and support emotionally people who have lost a significant part of their abilities. While many people survive a stroke without significant impairment, others become preoccupied with loss. Stroke nurses are more likely to be able to help patients make sense of what has happened and provide consolation and support. The nurse on a stroke unit ought to be on the lookout for symptoms of depression so that this condition receives prompt treatment.

Family and Friends

Just as the staff nursing a stroke victim can help recovery or adjustment by providing support and encouragement, so can friends and family. Their ability to do this will be much enhanced if they understand the rehabilitation programme, and in particular its goals and targets. Families need to understand precisely how much, if any, help they should give to a loved one encountering serious difficulties in feeding themselves. So make sure you are involved in devising the rehabilitation programme for your relative, partner or friend. Doctors should involve the patient's family, if only to obtain information about the environment to which the patient will return. Before the stroke, was the patient playing 18 holes of golf a day or unable to scale a flight of stairs? Does she live in a bungalow or in a top-storey flat without a lift?

Keeping spirits up may be challenging, quite apart from encouraging patients to practise skills they don't enjoy practising and in any case find difficult. Go round a stroke unit and you will find it probably shares the major drawback of all hospital environments: there is little with which patients can amuse or occupy themselves, and of course they have none of the tasks to attend to which they would have back home. Friends and relatives can make it easier to dress in normal day clothes by bringing in laundered garments. Ordinary clothes (as opposed to pyjamas or hospital gowns) add to a sense of dignity and foster a sense of normal life. Sitting in your night clothes by your bed in a place where you expect things to be done for you can induce the feeling that you should be taking things easy rather than doing what you can to relearn old skills and regain an interest in the wider world.

Relatives and friends should be alert to any assessments which are taking place, particularly where these will influence when a patient is discharged, where and with what support. A community care assessment should form a key part of the assessment, so you need to know when this is taking place and to prepare for it (pages 273–83). If you plan to act as the person's 'carer', ask for a carer's assessment (pages 556–68). Be alert for somebody, maybe a nurse, saying early on after the stroke, 'He should get his house on to the market because he will need to go into a care home now.' An off-the-cuff assessment is masquerading as a systematic assessment, and may be taking place far too early. A care home may indeed turn out to be the only realistic option, but in the early weeks it is usually best to wait and see.

Dr David Cohen, the director of the stroke unit at Northwick Park Hospital in Harrow, Middlesex, told me in 2001 that, for many people, recovery from a stroke is so variable and so unpredictable that an assessment of future prognosis and thus any modification to a person's living arrangements should not take place until six weeks after the stroke has occurred. He explained that there are some people of whom quite an accurate prognosis can be made before six weeks is up, particularly those who are going to do very well and those who are going to do very badly. It is the middle group of patients, who are making a moderate recovery and showing some progress, who deserve and need time before assessments are conducted and crucial decisions are taken.

You will find your task of supporting and encouraging your relative easier if you seek advice from the Stroke Association, which provides paid workers as well as mutual support groups (page 86). Equivalent organizations outside England and Wales are Chest, Heart and Stroke Scotland and Northern Ireland Chest, Heart and Stroke Association.

Chapter 14
Your Life in their Hands

When we are in hospital we cannot avoid being largely at the mercy of other people. The implications of this have been dramatically highlighted in recent years by the issues surrounding resuscitation (the artificial restarting of the circulation and respiratory systems when they have stopped after a heart attack).

Mrs Jill Baker, aged 67, who suffered from stomach cancer, was admitted to hospital with septicaemia. Unhappy with her care, she discharged herself and demanded to see her hospital notes. She was horrified to discover that a doctor had, unbeknown to her or her husband, written that in view of her cancer, artificial resuscitation should not even be attempted should she suffer a cardiac arrest. Nine months later she was enjoying a good quality of life.

Mrs Baker's story made headlines in 2000, and as a result of publicity over her case and other similar ones, most people are probably now aware that they should try to get any 'do not attempt resuscitation' instructions in their medical notes altered, if these contravene their wishes.[1] However, the ultimate decision still rests with the doctor and there are many factors to consider: resuscitation is a violent act and may cause bruised or broken ribs and soreness in the throat down which a tube will have been passed, amongst other things. There may be likelihood that it will not sustain life anyway or, if it does, that the patient will suffer another heart attack soon afterwards. Awareness of resuscitation is kept alive by its appearance on our television screens in hospital dramas: the heart is kick-started with an electric shock applied through paddles and any change to the heart-beat shown on a monitoring screen to which the patient is wired up. Yet away from the glamour of the TV casualty ward are other patients, often elderly, facing life-or-death dilemmas which may be less dramatic but are equally real. The question of cardio-pulmonary resuscitation arises only if the heart has stopped beating. There are many other medical circumstances in which doctors can choose between sustaining life and letting it fade away.

Withholding and Withdrawing Medical Treatment

Patients and their relatives must navigate very carefully the whole area of the withholding of life-saving treatment, whether or not it involves artificial resuscitation.

The Key Decisions: Obvious and Otherwise

Finding out whether death may be looming is the first challenge: relatives may not realize that life-prolonging treatment is an issue because they do not realize that death is looming. Doctors are sometimes not very good at breaking bad news: they can talk in euphemisms, which people fail to recognize as such, or they may avoid the subject altogether. A doctor telling you that your father's lungs are worn out or that he will probably not get better might mean to tell you he is likely to die within the next 24 hours; you might not realize you are being told this. There is no standard procedure, and approaches vary widely.[2] Relatives and patients should always ask if a gloomy utterance is really a death knell – unless they would genuinely rather not know.

The second challenge is discovering what may be being withheld or not even considered. This is because no lay person can be expected to know of all the life-saving interventions which may be denied.

One example is that of an elderly person suffering from the advanced stages of a serious lung disease who starts going blue in the face and slipping in and out of unconsciousness. You might assume nothing could be done. In fact, this condition is the result of a dramatic rise in blood carbon dioxide which can very often be treated by drugs to bring down the carbon dioxide, and then by the use of a respiratory support machine. This machine can be taken home and it allows breathing to be effective even at night, when it naturally becomes shallower. A medical team in a hospital or a GP called to an elderly person at home might, however, take the view that such treatment would not be worthwhile. The patient might be housebound and living in an extremely weakened state with limited independence. The condition is terminal anyway. Why prolong the agony?

Most relatives would not be aware that any such decision was being made. They would see the patient becoming confused, drifting in and out of consciousness, going bluer and bluer; the doctor might say the lungs were worn out and imply that death was inevitable. Maybe the patient would not wish to go on living. But maybe he or she would. The relatives might be better placed to judge than the doctor. There might be reasons why treatment to reduce carbon dioxide levels would not work or would work only briefly. Otherwise, relatives might well feel it ought to be provided. Some doctors might consult, but not all.

There are so many possible medical interventions of this kind that neither patients nor relatives can hope to find out what they all are. However, relatives can make it clear that they want all reasonable steps to be taken to keep life going if that is what they want, and they can ask to be consulted if there is any doubt about whether any interventions should be offered. Obviously treatment may involve discomfort and may have a low chance of success. You can nonetheless ask that if any choices arise, you should be consulted, and suggest that if there is doubt, a treatment should be tried.

Sometimes, of course, you will be invited to give your view on whether food, water or treatment should be withheld. On one occasion I arrived to visit my mother, then in the middle to late stages of dementia, at the NHS Continuing Care facility where she was being cared for and found her looking extremely unwell. The nurse in charge explained that the GP who had been summoned might suggest that antibiotics should be withheld in view of my mother's generally poorly state and that I should consider what my response would be. This sort of situation is extremely common where elderly people who are suffering from terminal conditions are concerned. The most frequent decisions involve the withholding of antibiotics, food and water. In this case the choice which has to be made is clear to relatives, whether or not they can easily influence its outcome. But in other cases what is really at issue may not be obvious.

A friend of mine reluctantly agreed that her mother's life should not be prolonged with antibiotics when pneumonia developed; the old lady in question had already suffered two major and countless minor strokes, and was very poorly. But what haunts my friend five years on is not the consent she gave to her mother's death, it is the suffering which the untreated pneumonia imposed upon her mother before she died. A fever made her very hot and agitated, and this discomfort and distress were exacerbated still further by her inability to eat or drink as a result of her strokes and the large amount of infected sputum in her throat caused by the pneumonia. My friend's distress was compounded by the galling discovery after her mother's death that this suffering could have been lessened had the nursing home asked the GP for advice on palliative care (the alleviation of troublesome symptoms without curing the condition). The nursing home manager had decided not to do this, but neither the patient nor her daughter had any idea that this was part of the equation.

The Rules

So what are the legal and procedural frameworks within which doctors and staff in hospitals, hospices and care homes should be working? How does the Department of Health recommend that decisions should be taken in this area? When my mother became ill, my views were clearly going to be sought, but would I have had any recourse were they not? If they had been and I had disagreed with the view of the doctor, what then? And could my friend whose mother died after a week-long struggle with pneumonia have done anything if the nursing home had refused to provide palliative care? Would any official guidance have strengthened her hand in urging appropriate palliative care if the home had refused to give it?

The British Medical Association has published a document called *Withholding and Withdrawing Life-prolonging Medical Treatment: Guidance for Decision-making*, which has been endorsed by the Department of Health.[3] Whether or not it represents ideal practice, it provides patients and relatives with something to back up their case when its recommendations are not followed.

The BMA guidance makes a useful distinction between life-prolonging treatment which could be withheld or could be withdrawn after it had started under certain circumstances (such as antibiotics, resuscitation, kidney dialysis, chemotherapy or the administration of nutrients and fluids to people unable to take them by mouth) and basic care which must never be withdrawn unless the patient absolutely resists it. This basic care involves attention to comfort and hygiene and the offering of food and water by mouth (even if this can only be done with a cup, spoon or syringe). Thus patients who can still take food and drink by mouth should never be denied it, even if life-prolonging medical treatment is to be withheld. So the manager of a nursing home who withdraws food or drink because a decision has been taken to withhold antibiotics is in breach of good practice as identified in this document. Paragraph 21.3 says, 'Basic care should always be provided (including the offer of proper nutrition and hydration and any procedure necessary to keep the patient comfortable).'

What constitutes action to 'keep the patient comfortable' is of course up for discussion. But the distress caused by the pneumonia from which my friend's mother was suffering could almost certainly have been alleviated with nothing more complicated than paracetamol and an electric fan to reduce her fever. These days, palliative care is a highly developed branch of medicine, involving the control of troublesome symptoms rather than cure. For instance, you can dry up chest secretions such as sputum with a drug that is not an antibiotic but is a drying agent. Treating fever with paracetamol and a cooling fan may not affect the infection, but can alleviate its symptoms. A patient troubled by infected sputum and unable to take antibiotics by mouth could receive antibiotics by injection into a vein or muscle to make them more comfortable, rather than to effect a cure.

Action to keep my friend's mother comfortable could well also have included administering at least fluids. Fluids which cannot be taken by mouth can be administered not only by drip but also through absorption under the skin. The swallowing mechanism may be impaired by strokes, and pneumonia can make the intake of food and drink by mouth impossible. Yet this does not mean that food and drink must necessarily be abandoned. The guidance says that artificial nutrition and hydration should never be withheld from a patient by the manager of a nursing home acting alone. It makes it plain (in para. 22.1) that such a decision should not only be made by a doctor, but implemented only after the decision has been separately reviewed:

All proposals to withhold or withdraw artificial nutrition and hydration, whether in hospital or in the community, should be subject to formal clinical review by a senior clinician who has experience of the condition from which the patient is suffering and who is not part of the treating team.

This is reinforced by instructions issued by the General Medical Council, in 2002, which tell doctors that they must seek a second opinion in these circumstances.[4]

The 1999 BMA guidance is not so helpful on the role of patients and especially of relatives in decision-making on withholding treatment. As with resuscitation, it makes plain that the final say should lie with the doctor. What is the doctor to take into account? Essentially, the quality of life of the patient, should that life be extended through the successful administration of life-prolonging treatment. Clearly what constitutes quality in the case of a particular individual is something on which patients and relatives might have something to contribute.

As far as people in a position to make decisions on their own behalf are concerned, the guidance says, 'There is a legal presumption that adults have the competence to make decisions unless the contrary is proven' (para. 13.1). However, there is a sting in the tail, because the guidance goes on to say: 'The graver the consequences of the decision, the commensurately greater the level of competence required to take that decision' (para. 13.2). It explains: 'An individual may have the capacity to express preferences, such as about where to live, for example, but not to refuse life-prolonging treatment', and 'A greater level of understanding and competence will be required to refuse life-prolonging treatment than will be necessary, for example, to refuse a flu vaccination.' The guidance advises that patients who have not attained 'the required level' (whatever that required level is: there is no explanation and presumably it is up to doctors to assess) should still where possible be involved in the discussions about treatment, 'even though their views may not be determinative'.

If the doctor is genuinely uncertain whether the patient has the mental capacity to make the decision, what then? Some patients who are unable to express their views will have already declared in advance in a living will or advance directive whether they would choose to accept treatment such as antibiotics or nutrition and hydration to prolong their life artificially if they were not in a position to say yea or nay at the time (page 541). In the past, it has not always been clear what status living wills have, but the GMC guidance tells doctors that they 'must respect any valid and clinically relevant advance refusal of treatment where you have no reason to believe that the patient has changed his/her mind'. There is a caveat: 'In making this assessment, it is necessary to consider whether the patient had foreseen the particular circumstances which have subsequently materialised, or would have been aware of and weighed up any advances in treatment options since their decision was made' (para.53). This reservation is understandable: it is of course notoriously difficult to know ahead of time what medical scenario you might face and whether you might want to change your mind and give treatment a chance.

If a doctor is unsure whether the patient has the ability to come to a decision, he certainly should not proceed simply on the basis of his own gut feeling, but, according to the GMC, carry out 'a thorough test of mental capacity using professional guidelines'. He should then seek a second opinion if he and his health care team have limited experience of the condition from which the patient is suffering or if he has a serious difference of opinion with other members the team or if he is in any doubt about the range of options, or the benefits, drawbacks and risks of a particular option. If these steps are taken and the patient's capacity to decide still remains in question, the GMC instructs doctors to seek legal advice; this may include asking a court to determine mental capacity.

How is the doctor to form a view on whether a patient's life should be artificially prolonged? This view will feed into the decision-making process whatever the views of the patient and his or her relatives; if the patient or the relatives' views are unclear, the doctor's ideas are likely to assume greater importance. The GMC does not go into this area, but the BMA does. On patients unable to express their own wishes, it says:

> The vast majority of people with even very severe physical or mental disabilities are able to experience and gain pleasure from some aspects of their lives. Where, however, the disability is so profound that individuals have no or minimal levels of awareness of their own existence and no hope of recovering awareness, or where they suffer

untreatable pain or other distress, the question arises as to whether continuing to provide treatment aimed at prolonging that life artificially would provide a benefit to them. An important factor which is often considered in making these decisions is whether the person is thought to be aware of his or her environment or own existence as demonstrated by, for example:

• Being able to interact with others
• Being aware of his or her own existence and having an ability to take pleasure in the fact of that existence
• Having the ability to achieve purposeful or self-directed action or to achieve some goal of importance to him or her.

If treatment is unable to recover or maintain any of these abilities, this is likely to indicate that its continued provision will not be a benefit to the patient. If any one of these abilities can be achieved, then life-prolonging treatment may be of benefit and it is important to consider these factors within the context of the individual's own wishes and values, where these are known, in order to assess whether the patient would, or could reasonably be expected to, consider life-prolonging treatment to be beneficial (para. 1.2).

Had this test been applied to my mother when the decision was being made on whether to administer antibiotics described above (page 449), she might well have failed. How does a doctor interpret whether a patient is able to interact with others? My own mother became unable to recognize me, and a doctor might have taken this as proof of failure to interact. In fact, however, she could still interact with me, though not in a mother–daughter way; she could engage in conversation with people who talked with sensitivity to her, although what she said might be unintelligible to them. She certainly remained aware of her own existence; whether she could take pleasure in the fact of that existence I do not know, except to say that sometimes she was clearly happy and at other times deeply distressed.

The Position of Relatives
What is the status of the relatives of patients who are unable to express themselves, whether because of an ongoing condition

such as dementia or a recently developed one such as a stroke or a heart attack? In England, Wales and Northern Ireland, relatives have no power to give or withhold consent for medical treatment for adults who lack the capacity to make decisions themselves. This does not of course mean that treatment is automatically withheld because a patient is deemed by a doctor to lack decision-making capacity: 'Treatment may be provided, without consent, if it is considered by the clinician in charge of the patients' care to be necessary and in the best interests of the patient.'

On the status of relatives' views, the BMA guidance states:

> There is a widely held misperception that the next of kin may give, or withhold, consent on behalf of an adult patient who lacks the capacity to make or communicate decisions. In fact, no such legal power is given to the next of kin or to those with enduring power of attorney. . . . Currently, decisions about whether to provide, withhold or withdraw treatment are the responsibility of the treating doctor with the advice of the rest of the healthcare team and with reference to the courts in particularly contentious, difficult or disputed cases (para. 13.3).

In Scotland, the Adults with Incapacity (Scotland) Act 2000 has introduced the entirely new concept of the 'welfare attorney', allowing a proxy decision-maker to be appointed who is entitled to give consent to the medical treatment of mentally incapacitated patients over the age of 16 (pages 537–9). The guidance states that: 'Where such a proxy is appointed, he or she must be consulted (where reasonable and practicable) about proposed medical treatment' (para. 13.4). Furthermore, if the doctor in charge of the case and the proxy decision-maker disagree, the doctor must ask the Mental Welfare Commission to nominate a doctor to provide a second opinion. If the two doctors agree, they may proceed without the agreement of the proxy. Any person with an interest in the case, including the proxy, has the option of applying to the Scottish Court of Session for a determination on whether the treatment in question should be given or withheld.

In England, Wales and Northern Ireland, relatives have a far lower status than they do in Scotland in this situation. This is not to say of course that doctors do not frequently consult them, but to point out that the law does not oblige them to do so. New legislation which may be passed in 2004 has the potential to change the status of relatives in the medical arena (pages 539–40).

Doctors are not even required by law to inform close relatives as to why they have come to their decision. However, the BMA guidance suggests that it is good practice to do so (para. 23.2). The patient is certainly supposed to be told where this is practicable: 'Every effort should be made to explain to the patient, to the extent that he or she can understand, the decision which has been reached and the reasons for that decision' (paragraph 23.1).

Questions to Ask

In fact most doctors do consult relatives when the patient is unable to express his or her own wishes. When this happens, they need to be ready with the right questions.

The doctor does not have to provide a particular treatment even if a patient or his or her representative requests it. However, if a doctor refuses one you believe to be necessary, you could always ask for a second opinion. The GMC guidance referred to above advises doctors: 'If a specific treatment is requested which, in your considered view, is clinically inappropriate, you are not legally or ethically bound to provide it. However, you should give the patient a clear explanation of the reasons for your view, and respect their request to have a second opinion' (para. 42).

Alternative Treatment

When a doctor says that a treatment cannot practically be offered, always ask if there are alternatives. As we have seen in the case of pneumonia, antibiotics might be ineffective as a cure but of great palliative help. A particularly vital area of debate often concerns administering fluids to patients who can no longer take them by mouth. Most of us are familiar with the administration of fluids (which can include not only water but also nutrients and antibiotics in solution) intravenously through a drip. This procedure does, however, have disadvantages. The needle in the vein is often uncomfortable, if not painful. The location of the needle must be changed every few days, lest the vein is damaged and an infection develops. The risk of infection is quite high. A patient suffering from some confusion might well try to pull out the intravenous drip. It may be difficult to make a satisfactory incision in the vein in patients whose veins are very fragile. Finally, the paraphernalia of the drip immobilizes the patient.

If you feel that your relative should be receiving fluids but are advised that intravenous administration would be inappropriate, ask about an alternative procedure – subcutaneous infusion. This involves the insertion of a needle under the skin, usually in the abdomen or thigh, through which a bagful of fluid passes under the skin and is absorbed. It does not require an incision in a vein, with the associated discomfort and risk of infection. What is more, it does not require a doctor to set it up: a district nurse can pop in an overnight subcutaneous infusion for a patient living at home or in a care home. He or she can then receive perhaps a litre of fluid during the night and might well feel much better the following day; the infusion does not have to be given all the time, and once it has been given, the patient can move around freely. Subcutaneous infusion does sometimes pose problems and it will not bring benefits to everybody: sometimes the fluid is not absorbed and collects under the skin; patients whose legs are very swollen can find their condition worsened as a result of such an infusion. So it is important that the decision is made by a doctor experienced in this area.

For patients who cannot take sufficient amounts of food by mouth, there are two alternatives. The nasogastric tube, in which a narrow plastic tube bypasses the throat, reaching the stomach through the nose, is probably less comfortable than a drip, but it poses less risk of infection and of course requires no incision in a blood vessel.

The second alternative, known as percutaneous endoscopic gastrostomy (PEG) feeding, involves an incision in the abdomen and a tube passing directly into the stomach. Inserting the tube requires a local anaesthetic, but once in, it is not uncomfortable. Food can be given for instance at night when the patient is asleep and he or she can move around for the remainder of the time. Because the tube is passing into the stomach rather than directly into the bloodstream, the procedure involves little risk of infection.

The GMC guidance instructs doctors to discuss the pros and cons of different forms of artificial hydration and nutrition with the patient or his or her representatives and to provide information about how they have arrived at their decision (para. 24). It also instructs doctors to consider subcutaneous infusion, as well as a nasogastric tube, intravenous infusion and PEG where a patient has a problem in taking fluids or food orally.

Trial Treatment

After asking about alternative treatment, you might next ask about the possibility of a temporary trial for a treatment a doctor is resisting. Why not give it a go and withdraw it if there are no beneficial results?

Here you have the doctor on potentially weak ground. There are a great many scenarios in which the doctor cannot be sure whether a treatment might bring some benefit. Doctors may like to speak firmly because they feel they should reassure patients, but the BMA advice lets the cat out of the bag:

> Despite being evidence based, some aspects of medical treatment will always remain uncertain. Death is a certainty for everyone but, except in a small number of cases, diagnosis and prognosis are based on probability and past evidence rather than absolute certainty (para. 5.1).

The guidance makes it clear that it is accepted practice in view of these doubts first to consult other health professionals, but also to give treatment on a trial basis:

> Where there is genuine doubt about the ability of a particular treatment to benefit the patient, that treatment should be provided but may be withdrawn if, on subsequent review, it is found to be inappropriate or not beneficial (para. 5.1).

What is more, the document recognizes that although there is no legal or moral difference between withholding treatment or withdrawing it once it has been commenced, 'This is not to say that emotionally and psychologically the two are equivalent.' In other words, it may reassure relatives to see that the treatment has at least been tried. So doctors may turn out to be readier to accept this sort of compromise than you might expect.

Palliative Care

A third useful question to ask doctors is: 'Should a palliative care specialist be consulted?' Palliative care is the holistic care of patients and their families by a multi-professional team when the patient's disease is no longer responsive to treatment which could cure it.

A patient with palliative care needs could have a condition which cannot be cured either because it is incurable or because the patient is so frail that to try and treat it would kill him or her. Palliative care is usually offered to people who are 'terminally ill' (usually defined as those likely to die within 12 months), but in practice it is probably most often given to people likely to die within a far shorter period. It can be administered alongside curative treatment when it is not clear whether the cure will work so may benefit some patients years before they die.

In practice, even people who are dying may not receive palliative care expertise. Heart failure, for example, is the most common single cause of death in many hospital medical wards. Yet, two consultants (one in palliative medicine, the other in cardiology) wrote in 2003, 'The palliative care needs of these patients have, until recently, been largely ignored.' They continued: 'However, the national service framework for coronary heart disease specifically requires cardiologists and others involved in the management of patients with heart failure to work with palliative care staff to use or adapt palliative care practices for their needs.'[5]

These days, palliative medicine is a huge speciality. If your relative is terminally ill or is dying (or is at a stage when treatment might not work), much can be done to help make him or her more comfortable. Palliative care has expanded its scope enormously in recent years. The modern hospice movement began in the 1960s at a time when medicine took little interest in people it could not cure. At first, the speciality concerned itself pretty exclusively with cancer patients, but the advent of Aids brought a new group of people demanding specialist palliative care for themselves, their partners or relatives. Today it is acknowledged that palliative care can help people with any terminal condition, from pneumonia to kidney failure. But you may need to press for expertise, particularly if your relative does not have cancer.

A GP can deliver palliative care, but there are other people who are expert, many of them associated with hospices, others employed by health bodies. A growing number of health organizations are hiring specialist palliative nurses to go into nursing homes to advise on symptom control. Large district hospitals ought to have palliative medicine specialists. But just because your relative is in hospital (or in a long-stay NHS unit) and likely to die within a fortnight, you should not assume that he or she will automatically receive the wide range of help which palliative care can deliver.

Palliative care involves far more than the relief of pain and other distressing physical symptoms. This is what the World Health Organization considers are the functions of palliative care:

- It affirms life and regards dying as a normal process.
- It neither hastens nor postpones death.
- It provides relief from pain and other distressing symptoms.
- It integrates the psychological and spiritual aspects of care.
- It offers a support system to help patients live as actively as possible until death.
- It offers a support system to help the family cope during the patient's illness and in their own bereavement.[6]

It is important that palliative care should start as soon as the patient can benefit, rather than waiting until he or she is actually dying. Make sure that all the possible expertise which should be available is on hand. For instance, in hospital a chaplaincy team should be able to help with spiritual counselling, and clinical psychologists and other members of the hospital psychiatric team with psychological support if necessary. You may, however, need to prod. Hospital doctors differ widely in the extent to which they refer their patients for palliative care. For a study of patients present in one week in 1999 in an acute UK teaching hospital, doctors and nurses were interviewed separately about which patients they considered to have palliative care needs. As many as 23 per cent of patients were considered by one or other or both groups to need palliative care, a higher figure than that suggested by previous studies. But there was a low level of agreement between the doctors and nurses about which patients were involved. This was explained partly by a lack of awareness as to the role and potential of specialist palliative care and the stage at which it should be offered. About one half of the patients identified with palliative care needs were not suffering from cancer.[7]

The sort of steps you ought to expect if your relative is dying are set out below. Virtually every symptom is usually amenable to treatment, although of course no one can be sure that symptoms will be completely alleviated.

- **Coughing** This is frequently endured by people at the very end of life and it can be irritating and exhausting. Palliative care would aim to lessen and soothe it. The most obvious treatment is a simple syrup linctus; other treatment could take the form of medication (such as bronchodilators, which keep open the tubes of the bronchi, which lead into the lungs), steam inhalations (to help get rid of excess sputum) and drugs to suppress the cough reflex in the brain. Antibiotics can be administered which dry up secretions rather than trying to cure, say, pneumonia.

- **Insomnia** This may be the result of pain or breathlessness, for instance, which could be treated. Expect the cause of the insomnia to be pursued; sleep-inducing drugs are of course a possibility.

- **Loss of appetite** Many very sick people are disinclined to eat, but this may be the result of factors which can be treated, such as constipation, sore gums, nausea, a dirty mouth (treated with a mouthwash and cleaning the teeth with toothpaste) or even food which is not very appetizing or not to the person's taste. The accompaniment of a little alcohol can make food more appetizing.

- **Pain** All sorts of analgesic drugs are available to treat pain and, of course, a wide range of dosage; account must be taken of side-effects such as drowsiness. Psychological support can be important too.

- **Constipation** The majority of patients with terminal illness become constipated. Consultants Mary Baines and Nigel Sykes in *The Oxford Textbook of Geriatric Medicine* advocate: 'Unless the patient is very frail, an attempt should be made to increase activity, add fibre to the diet, and maintain a good fluid intake.

Assistance with mobility should be available so that the patient can use the lavatory rather than a commode or bedpan.[8] However, in practice laxatives are often needed as well.

- **Breathlessness** Mary Baines and Nigel Sykes assert: 'It is important to seek a diagnosis of the cause (or causes) of breathlessness in a terminally ill patient'; those causes might be treatable. Steps which can help include physiotherapy to bring up chest secretions, medication to reduce anxiety (which often exacerbates breathlessness) and additional oxygen.
- **Vomiting** Causes should be investigated. Anti-emetic drugs present one possible treatment and it is possible to administer them by subcutaneous infusion.
- **Pressure sores** Steps should be taken to prevent pressure sores developing; they can be very painful (pages 431–2). Careful nursing with the application of dressings helps sores to heal.
- **Urinary incontinence** Catheterization may be suggested if someone becomes incontinent, but do argue this through carefully, as pads may be better for the patient (pages 427–8).

Many other steps can also be taken. The discomfort of a dry mouth can be alleviated with water administered through a spray or a blunt-ended syringe gel applied to the lips. Helping to keep the mouth moist is a task which relatives may welcome, as this is something they can do for their loved one themselves.

In all this, bear in mind that patients often play down their pain when they are chronically or terminally ill and that, 'The dissatisfied dead cannot noise abroad the negligence they have suffered.'[9]

Chapter 15
Discharge

As soon as anybody goes into hospital, all sorts of people from the ward sister and the consultant to administrators will be thinking about their discharge, not least because it costs a great deal of money to keep somebody in hospital. The situation is more complex for older people. They take longer to recuperate from medical treatment and sometimes their recuperation is complicated by the onset of other conditions. Some people will never be well enough to return home, even with new or enhanced support in place there by way of gadgets and human help. Others will need the high level of support by way of personal care most easily provided in a care home. Still others will need this plus nursing expertise on tap day and night available in a care home registered for nursing care. And others still will require continuing medical care to a level greater than could be provided even in most care homes.

It is important to see hospital discharge as movement from one setting to another, rather than the end of a process. Most older people do not feel tip-top as soon as they get home after a hospital stay, once the euphoria of actually being in their own home again has worn off. So it is important not to allow the hospital to discharge your relative until all the necessary arrangements have been made for any additional help he or she may need.

Wherever your relative is being discharged to, make absolutely sure that his medical notes contain accurate details of diagnosis and treatment before he leaves. Sometimes doctors record underlying conditions such as dementia on discharge notes, but fail to describe the precise medical reason for admission on the particular occasion. For example, it is not very helpful if 'Parkinson's' is written on the notes when in fact the person was admitted for a digestive disorder whose cause (and thus future treatment) has baffled doctors.

Even when people have been in hospital for only a short time and are perfectly well able to look after themselves, the hospital should ensure that they have transport to get home and somebody to accompany them on the journey if necessary. A social worker based at the hospital should be considering whether any support, even short-term, is needed.

The arrival home itself is important. If you cannot be present yourself, try to make sure somebody, perhaps the warden of a sheltered housing scheme if appropriate, buys in bread and milk and welcoming flowers. Some voluntary organizations, such as local Age Concern groups, operate schemes to help people get themselves back on their feet after a stay in hospital.

Pressures

Improvements have been made to the system of hospital discharge for elderly people who are not fighting fit and are not going to feel tip-top after a day or two. These have been prompted largely by the Health Service Ombudsman in his or her reports and recommendations on particular complaints from consumers. A few years ago, hospitals were discharging elderly patients even though they needed complex continuing medical support, and their relatives had no option but to pay for them to be looked after in private nursing homes or care for them at home as best they could. Others not needing quite so much medical care but nonetheless a measure of support might be sent home without transport and without any additional help, either temporary or ongoing, when they got there. As a result, they might become ill and have to be readmitted to hospital, involving expense to the health authority and distress to themselves. (As explained on page 57 I use the term 'health authority' as a generic one to cover the various health organizations which exist in the different parts of the UK.)

It is important that patients and their relatives should know that hospitals should not allow this to happen. Every hospital trust has to draw up protocols and procedures for hospital discharge. Also, it should comply with advice and instructions from national government. For example, the Department of Health has told hospitals to make available to patients and their relatives *on admission to hospital* a copy of its discharge policy (author italics).[1] Non-compliance with advice such as this can be used by patients seeking a review of a discharge decision or making a complaint to the hospital and the health authority, which can get decisions reversed. The problem is, of course, that patients rarely know that they have rights which are being flouted. On the ground, patients and their relatives often face an uphill battle.

When your elderly mother is facing discharge, it is very easy to feel intimidated by the hospital system. She may already feel like a guest who was initially invited but has now out-stayed her welcome and is 'bed-blocking'. The consultant says nothing more can be done and she should go home. The hospital's social worker has asked if everything will be all right. You have arranged to come and look after your mother, even though you have no idea how long it will be before she is back on her feet, and you need to return to other commitments, such as work and children. Your mother is probably desperate to leave hospital and get back to familiar surroundings and a good night's sleep.

Elderly people in England are likely to feel under additional pressure to vacate their hospital beds as quickly as possible. This is because new legislation to come into effect at the beginning of 2004[2] is empowering hospital trusts and similar health care providers to impose a daily fine on social services departments in cases where patients have not been discharged from hospital as expeditiously as possible because of the departments' supposed failings.

Discharge: Your Rights

In this situation it is important to take a deep breath and look realistically at the future: do not be pushed into an unsustainable situation. When a hospital consultant tells a patient he or she can go home, that does not amount to hospital discharge. The lawyer Luke Clements makes it clear in his excellent book *Community Care and the Law*[3] that hospital discharge is not actually the prerogative of the doctor. He or she is simply turning a first key in a process, by declaring that somebody is medically fit to leave his or her ward. The prime responsibility in hospital discharge as far as older people are concerned rests not with the consultant, but with the social services staff attached to the hospital.

Of course you do not have a right to occupy a hospital bed indefinitely if you do not need any more NHS care. However, patients do 'have the right to refuse to be discharged from NHS care into a care home'. This is an important entitlement, and it comes from the pen of the Department of Health in a good-practice document issued to hospital trusts and the like in 2003 called *Discharge from Hospital: Pathway, Process and Practice.*

Unfortunately, this document, lengthy as it is, does not contain many other useful pledges for consumers. One which would have been welcome was contained in an earlier Hospital Discharge booklet, in 1989 (now superseded), which said that each hospital's discharge procedures should ensure that any support, help, equipment required to enable the patient (and carer(s)) to cope at home *is available by the time the patient leaves hospital.*[4] However, the 2003 guidance does say that discharge should be co-ordinated by a single named person, that patients and carers (relatives and others who care voluntarily) should be involved in discharge as 'equal partners' with the official bodies, and indeed that 'patients, with their expertise and understanding of their own needs and their ability to influence how the discharge process works, must be kept integral to the system'. So if these words could not describe your experience, complain and/or raise the matter with the discharge co-ordinator and/or the hospital's matron, the hospital's Patient Advice Liaison Service and seek help from your community health council or its near-equivalent (pages 61–63).

What is not in doubt is that the social services staff employed by local authorities attached to hospitals have not only to prepare patients and any carers for hospital discharge, but also have a clear duty to assess whether support services need to be provided. The important thing to look out for here is that this is being done through a 'community care assessment'. Officials may talk about 'single assessment' (page 290), but what you want as consumer is a community care assessment as part of whatever other assessment the officials wish to carry out: your relative has clear rights in how a community care assessment is carried out and the factors to be borne in mind (pages 272–91). Be prepared to use all your rights in this process. For instance, your relative can choose the location of the assessment. He or she might therefore care to insist that it should take place in his or her home, so that the social worker and any other professionals such as an occupational therapist can see precisely how she would be likely to cope there, rather than relying on a description from a hospital bed.

If the conclusion is reached that somebody is eligible for particular community care services, then the social services department has to provide them. People who are going to act as carers can ask for an assessment for any support they will need in their role (pages 556–68). The outcome of the assessments could be the provision of gadgets and even house adaptations as well as human help. It might be unreasonable to say that you will not budge until all house adaptations have been put in place (unless there are exceptional circumstances or the adaptations are minor) but you would expect all human help you have been assessed as needing to be ready to run and all necessary gadgets and aids to be already provided before you leave the hospital bed. If in doubt, don't leave. The reality of discharge which occurs too soon is that people go home, can't cope, get distressed or even have a fall and injure themselves, then return to hospital in a revolving-door process.

To a Care Home?

The community care assessment might conclude that your relative can be best cared for in a care home. Of course, if you have plenty of money and can buy in as much home care as you wish and would not be eligible for social services funding in a care home, then you can make your own decisions informed by the assessments of the professionals. If your relative is unhappy with the care home decision but is not wealthy and believes he or she could get by in her own home, with support brought in, then somebody should remonstrate with social services (who may be suggesting the care home route as the easiest and cheapest option for them: page 48). It may be necessary to lodge a formal complaint about the way social services have handled the case or to call on a councillor or MP for support. As noted above, hospital patients cannot be forced to move into a care home against their wishes. But your relative should also refuse to go into a second-choice home as a stop-gap measure if it seems unsuitable. After all, you never know how long such an interim arrangement might last.

This is another example of why it is important to get the right sort of information down in your community care assessment of needs (page 273): the Department of Health *Discharge from Hospital* advice referred to above states that such a transitional placement 'must be able to meet the assessed care needs of the patient, who must receive active help to move on to the home of his/her choice when a place is available'.[5]

If your relative goes into a care home, the NHS continues to bear the responsibility for financing and arranging his or her health care (in other words the registered nursing costs plus other specific health-related services), just as when he or she was at home. The services the NHS should provide are set down clearly in a circular called *Continuing Care: NHS and Local Councils' Responsibilities*:

> Health authorities and primary care trusts are responsible for arranging the following services for residents of nursing homes:
>
> - access to GP and other primary care services (including community nursing)
> - the provision of other nursing advice, e.g. continence advice and stoma care
> - physiotherapy, occupational therapy, speech and language therapy, dietetics and podiatry
> - from October 2001, continence pads and other related equipment
> - specialist medical and nursing equipment (e.g. specialist feeding equipment) normally only available through hospitals
> - palliative care
> - access to hospital care, which should also be arranged whenever it is required.
>
> People should not be charged for any of these services . . .
> The range of primary and community services available in residential care should include:
>
> - access to GP and other primary care services (including community nursing)
> - the provision of district nursing and other nursing services e.g. continence advice and stoma care

- physiotherapy, occupational therapy, speech and language therapy, dietetics and podiatry
- continence pads and equipment and nursing aids
- palliative care.

People should not be charged for any of these services.[6] (my emphasis)

NHS Continuing Care

There is one other factor at play in all this. People with quite demanding health care needs could be eligible for free Continuing Care by the NHS, which will cover personal care and accommodation costs, as well as medical and nursing care. These patients are housed in long-stay NHS units or in nursing homes with which the local health authority has a contract, although it is possible for NHS Continuing Care to be provided in a person's own home (page 75).

Continuing NHS Care is much sought after. Twenty years ago elderly NHS patients with continuing medical needs transferred fairly easily into long-stay NHS beds in geriatric wards and long-stay hospitals. Since 1987, however, the number of such beds has been cut by more than 50,000, or nearly two-thirds.[7] Yet the number of people who need them continues to rise, while the alternatives – caring for patients at home or sending them to a private nursing home – have significant drawbacks. Such people may well require round-the-clock care at home, as well as nursing and other medical care brought in at odd times of the day and night. The private nursing care homes to which they might go will often have fewer expert staff and equipment and while an NHS long-stay bed is free, its nursing home equivalent has to be paid for at a cost of perhaps £600 a week, apart from the deduction of about £100 for what is now known as 'free nursing care' and in Scotland an additional deduction for 'free personal care' (pages 389–90). If the patient is moderately wealthy he or she will have to foot the balance (pages 366–8). So there are very significant advantages in terms of care and finance in securing NHS Continuing Care (or Continuing Inpatient Care, as it is known in Scotland).

Who is Eligible?

Health authorities are supposed to allocate beds for Continuing NHS Care on the basis of eligibility criteria each authority draws up. If you do not know of these beds' existence, you could easily find yourself placing your relative in a private care home and using his or her assets to pay the fees, although he or she would actually be eligible for NHS Continuing Care. So get hold of the Continuing Care eligibility criteria of your relative's health authority and see if you consider your relative meets them. Do not expect the criteria to be kicking around in hospital reception: when I telephoned my mother's hospital in 1999, none of the several secretaries I talked to had heard of them. (Eventually they were sent to me, and after many months my mother's hospital trust decide they would grant her Continuing Care.) Now you should go to your PALS (Patient Advice Liaison Service) or equivalent outside England if you have any difficulty (pages 61–64).

The Department of Health has issued guidance which health authorities in England should consider when formulating their eligibility criteria.[8] In this guidance, the department says a person should be eligible for NHS Continuing Care if he or she is likely to die in the near future from a terminal condition. 'In the near future' is usually taken to mean within about six weeks and a maximum of 12 weeks. The guidance makes it absolutely clear that if the patient wishes to return home to die, the NHS has to fund care there, even if that requires a great deal of equipment and medical support. After making it clear that palliative care is free, it says:

> Patients who require palliative care and whose prognosis is that they are likely to die in the near future should be able to choose to remain in NHS funded accommodation (including in a nursing home), or to return home with the appropriate support. Patients may also require episodes of palliative care to deal with complex situations (including respite palliative care). The number of episodes required will be unpredictable and applications of time limits for this care are not appropriate.[9]

For people who are not likely to die in the near future, the government says Continuing Care eligibility criteria should apply when:

the nature or complexity or intensity or unpredictability of the individual's health care needs (and any combination of these needs) requires regular supervision by a member of the NHS multi-disciplinary team, such as the consultant, palliative care, therapy or other NHS member of the team; or the individual's needs require the routine use of specialist healthcare equipment under supervision of NHS staff; or the individual has a rapidly deteriorating or unstable medical, physical or mental health condition and requires regular supervision by a number of the NHS multi-disciplinary team, such as the consultant, palliative care, therapy or other NHS member of the team.[10]

In the past this guidance was often interpreted by health authorities as justifying very restrictive criteria which would minimize the number of people whose Continuing Care they would be liable to fund. It is possible to challenge such criteria in the courts, but you need to be wealthy to do so. Local authorities have however often challenged a health authority's criteria, since it is they who will often be picking up the tab if too many patients are refused. Nonetheless, a few people end up being funded by Continuing Care; these are often extremely lucky or unusually persistent.

Consider whether your relative might qualify. It is not enough that he or she has a long-term chronic condition which requires a great deal of personal care: does he or she have an unstable condition (perhaps in addition to chronic conditions)? Does he or she need the routine use of healthcare equipment under the supervision of NHS staff? If you think he or she might meet the criteria, the first thing to do is to ensure that he or she is going to be assessed for NHS Continuing Care. The Continuing Care Assessor in the health authority ought to be considering the case, but to make sure, ask for an assessment to be carried out and, crucially, try to meet the assessor when (or before) he or she carries out the assessment. Otherwise rejection may occur without all the relevant considerations being taken into account and you may be plunged into a difficult appeal process.

Getting a Review
If you think your relative should have been granted Continuing Care but has not, then formally ask the health body such as the

primary care trust or local health board to review its decision. Your grounds for a review might be that you consider that your relative meets the health body's eligibility criteria and that these criteria have not been applied properly in his or her case. Or you might argue that the health organization has not followed the proper procedures in reaching its decision. Or you might argue that your relative fits the criteria the Department has set out in its guidance even though he or she does not seem to fit those of the health authority. As you do not need to hire a solicitor to do this and the rewards can be great in terms of care given and money saved, there will be little reason in many cases not to ask for a review if it seems as there is a good chance that your relative would fit the criteria. If you are unsuccessful, make a formal complaint to the health body and, failing satisfaction there, approach the Health Service Ombudsman.

There are set procedures for health organizations when they receive a request for a review of a refusal for Continuing NHS Care. Government guidance tells them that they should deal urgently with the request: the patient and his or her family and any carer should expect a response in writing from the authority, with an explanation of the basis of its decision, within two weeks of their request.[11] The health authority is unlikely to hang around, as your relative will be continuing to occupy an NHS bed while the review is being carried out.

In some exceptional circumstances, the subject of the review will not be in hospital at all but in their own home, so it is important that such people know that the Department of Health has said that each health body 'should aim to ensure that the review procedure is completed within two weeks of the request being received. This period starts once any action to resolve the case informally has been completed, and should be extended only in exceptional circumstances.' While the review is being conducted, 'Any existing care package, whether hospital care or community health services, should not be withdrawn under any circumstances until the outcome of the review is known.'[12]

In coming to a decision, health organizations are expected to seek advice from an independent panel. They are required to maintain a standing panel whose job it is to review challenged discharge decisions. The chairman is supposed to be independent of bias towards either party, although he or she is appointed by the health authority; the other members of the three-person team are representatives of the health body and the local authority.

The health authority should provide your relative with an advocate, or a person independent of the authority, who can help her put forward her case if she wishes, or if she is unable to present her own views. The panel should have access to independent medical advice, and these advisers should be able to advise the panel on the original medical judgements and on how these relate to the eligibility criteria. Although the panel's report is advisory, the expectation is that its recommendations will be accepted in all but very exceptional cases.

Getting a Refund

Perhaps you are reading this long after your relative was refused continuing NHS care and as a result had to spend thousands of pounds paying for his or her own care in a private nursing home. Take heart: you may be able to get the money back.

In 2003 the Health Service Ombudsman, Ann Abraham, upheld complaints against four health authorities which had refused NHS Continuing Care. She maintained they had misapplied the government's guidance on eligibility for NHS funding thereby causing injustice and recommended that money should be refunded to the patients affected.[13]

The Department of Health responded swiftly by instructing all strategic health authorities to make sure they meet the criteria set down by the Department and to look for similar cases where decisions might have been flawed.[14]

The four cases Ann Abraham upheld could be the tip of an iceberg. Talking of similar situations, she observed, 'It is impossible for me to estimate how many people might be affected and the potential total cost of making such payments: but I recognise that significant numbers of people and sums of money are likely to be involved'.[15]

If you think you might fall into this category, contact your health body. If you are proposing to do this, to seek a review of a discharge decision or to make a complaint, it is worth seeking advice from one of the voluntary organizations, such as, say, the Alzheimer's Society, and from your local PALS (Patient Advice

Liaison Services). Age Concern publishes factsheets in this as in many other areas, and there are very useful books, such as the one by Luke Clements (page 465).

Living with Continuing Care

If the health authority decides that your relative has NHS Continuing Care needs which it will fund in a long-stay NHS unit or a private nursing home with which it has a contract, then it is easy to think that you are home and dry. That is very far from being the case. Your relative may indeed be looked after well, but this is not guaranteed.

In any case, the decision to provide continuing care can be rescinded. The health authority might come along at some future date and argue that your relative no longer meets its eligibility criteria. Patients with conditions such as Alzheimer's, although they are not getting better, can find that their condition leaves them less agitated with time, and the authority may argue that as a result they no longer need Continuing NHS Care. If this happens, either you or your social services department will have to find your relative alternative accommodation in a care home, or perhaps in your home with you as the carer – both very difficult courses of action when you are dealing with somebody with complex needs.

The potentially temporary nature of continuing care placements has two obvious implications. The first is financial. If you have power of attorney over your relative's finances and they exceed the threshold below which social services fund care home places (£19,500 in England and Northern Ireland, £18,500 in Scotland or £20,000 in Wales), you need to work to conserve your relative's resources just in case they may be called on to meet care home fees. The more money there is to spend, the more choice you are likely to have over where your relative can be cared for.

Since your relative's funds will not be being drained of hundreds of pounds each week in care home fees, you can spend in other ways. There may be aspects of your relative's life in the long-stay unit which you consider could be enhanced with cash. Perhaps your relative would enjoy outings which could be taken by taxi, or you could hire somebody to visit your relative every day, as my brother and I did.

Drawbacks

Though health care in NHS long-stay wards can be much better than care in private nursing homes, there are certain drawbacks to the NHS Continuing Care road, the main one being that patients have no right to choose where they go. If the health authority decides you meet its Continuing Care criteria, it puts you where it wants to.

Long-stay NHS units for older people vary. Some are housed in the wing of a hospital. So a long-stay unit for elderly mentally ill people, for example, might form a ward in a mental hospital complex. If this happens to be a teaching psychiatric hospital, your relative might well benefit from a stream of clinical psychologists, psychiatrists, researchers and all manner of specialists armed with and keen to apply the latest knowledge in how to care for and communicate with, say, dementia sufferers. But if your relative lives in an area where the mental hospital has been sold and patients dispersed, the ward for elderly dementia sufferers might consist of just a small, perhaps 10- or 12-bedded unit, located on its own far from any centre of medical excellence. It might be visited by only one or two mental health consultants, who themselves might not be up to the minute with the latest thinking, and with day-to-day health care and palliative care supplied through a GP. In this sort of isolated situation, the atmosphere, quality of care, sense of mission and of doing an interesting job and blazing a trail in one of the most challenging of medical situations will depend a great deal on the personality, motivation and interest of the ward manager. You might still find very good care, but you might not. Just as in care homes, you can find NHS Continuing Care units in which patients are offered no therapy or distraction whatsoever. So take nothing for granted: you need to be on your toes even to ensure adequate care, but you must try even harder to make your relative's life as happy as possible.

NHS long-stay units are not inspected in the way that care homes are. A new organization, the Commission for Health Improvement, is inspecting the units in England and Wales as part of its rolling programme of inspecting health trusts but is unlikely to focus on particular units unless specifically asked to do so.[16] While this is useful, it is different from the approach taken to the inspection of care homes, which are subject to both announced and unannounced inspections in which inspectors assess not only whether residents are physically well cared for, but also their emotional care and whether they are given the opportunity to lead interesting lives with entertainment and so on. Furthermore, the National Care Standards Commission and its sister bodies can require instant change if they are concerned about what they find, and can even close down a care home. The CHI has no similar powers of enforcement.

However, NHS Continuing Care units have been told in a letter from the Department of Health that they should take note of the national care home standards and themselves review their services to ensure that they meet them.[17] So take advantage of this guidance if you need to.

Partly because of the absence of outside inspection and partly because the consumer is not paying the bills directly, there is far less consumer power in long-stay NHS units. The power relationship between patient or relative and ward manager is also influenced by the threat of termination of residence: the manager of the unit can be influential in determining that a patient no longer meets the continuing care criteria and should be moved out. The result is that relatives can feel under a lot of pressure to be accommodating, even ingratiating. And if information about food, activities, staff training and complaints procedures is not offered, you may not feel you dare ask.

Although patients allocated NHS Continuing Care have no right to choose where they go, there is no reason why they (or probably more realistically, relatives acting on their behalf) should not nevertheless try to do what they can to nudge the system into providing the long-stay setting they consider best. After all, the decision is as important as the choice of a care home. Indeed, some people with NHS Continuing Care will be sent to private nursing homes but will have their bills paid for by the NHS. Dementia sufferers may go to a care home specializing in elderly mentally ill people. Some of these homes have the edge on some long-stay units, because they may offer activities which an NHS unit may not, because they are expected to provide a home rather than merely a setting for medical care.

The problem for a relative trying to exercise choice is not only that the patient has no right to choose, but also that it can be difficult finding out what the possibilities are. Once the health authority tells you that your relative is eligible for Continuing Care, it will probably simply tell you where your relative will go and suggest you meet the manager if you would like to. You could ask around about where people usually go and what various places are like. But you cannot really turn up and ask to view the possible locations in the way that you would if you were looking for a care home. You could try to lurk outside a long-stay NHS ward, even talk to visitors, or try to observe or overhear how staff are relating to patients, but this is extremely unsatisfactory (although better than nothing).

If you find that one long-stay environment is far better than others, it is probably best to petition for it in non-confrontational terms, lest the health authority thinks you are a nuisance and withdraws the offer of Continuing Care altogether on the grounds that your relative has improved and does not need the care. You might suggest, perhaps, that your preferred choice is far more convenient for you and other visitors to reach.

Wherever your relative goes, you will be keen that he or she settles in satisfactorily. This involves the same considerations as in entry into a care home (pages 394–407). You will also want to ensure your relative receives the maximum amount of therapy and other treatment which could help. In the case of people with dementia, for example, this could involve anything from Snoozelan and dolls therapy to aromatherapy and exercise, including dance (pages 144 and 396).

Continuing Care at Home

Sometimes a health authority grants NHS Continuing Care to take place in a person's own home, pehaps in a situation in which a close relative lives in and is available to do some of the caring, to supplement that of care workers, district nurses and so on. If you are in this position, you should expect to be provided with all the equipment – hoists, bath seats, pressure-relieving mattresses and so on – which would be available in a long-stay hospital or nursing home. Find out what your health body would have to pay a nursing home for Continuing Care, so that you know how much you are saving it. Around £500 a week to cover bought-in help, laundry costs and much else sounds a lot, but beware, it might not be enough, particularly if extra help will be needed during the night. Do not let the health authority use you as 'care on the cheap': if it says, for example, that it will not pay for help during the night, ask why not. The reason may simply be that such care costs a lot.

Part Six
Money

Chapter 16
State Benefits

Fundamentals

Once the most obvious problem of old age, money (or rather the lack of it) is now among the least of an elderly person's worries. The wonders of medical science have yet to crack Alzheimer's or osteoporosis, still less halt the process of ageing. Respect for elderly people and the provision for them of a proper role in society are becoming more not less elusive. But in twenty-first century Britain, older people need not fear penury. Plentiful guidance on the many financial complications of old age can be found elsewhere, but the essentials are outlined below.

The Good News

Senior citizens need not starve to death for one simple reason. Once people in Britain reach the age of 60, the state will provide them with a reasonable minimum level of support if they cannot provide this themselves. Many people who have reached this age today will have grown up with the idea that it is the individual's duty to make provision for retirement. Some may have made financial sacrifices to maintain their record of contributions to the National Insurance system to safeguard their entitlement to a state pension and may also have foregone consumption in their hard-pressed younger years to contribute to a private occupational or personal pension. But such apparent responsibility and prudence may well turn out to have been virtually pointless. The government has taken the view that there can be no 'undeserving poor' amongst elderly people and has undertaken to provide a minimum standard of living even for those who have wilfully squandered income which they could have saved for their old age. There is no prospect whatever of any major political party daring to revise this attitude.

The Poverty Line: Not So Bad

The government now provides a guaranteed income for anyone over the age of 60. Until October 2003 this was called the Minimum Income Guarantee; it is now known as Pension Credit. This ensures that a weekly income of £102.10 for an individual and £155.80 for a couple will be made available to all who cannot provide an income of this level for themselves out of their own resources, such as pension entitlements, including the State Retirement Pension, earnings, investment income or the dissolution of savings.

The main element of Pension Credit and the part which replaced the Minimum Income Guarantee exactly is Guarantee Credit. This frequently takes the form of a £25 top-up to the State Retirement Pension (the basic rate of which is only £77.45 a week), although if you have no income you should receive the full £102.10. However, Guarantee Credit does not stop at £102.10. People with some degree of disability may get an extra £42.95 per week; those caring for someone else who has some disability may get an additional £25.10 week. All you have to do is apply, but savings must be below £6,000 to get the full sum (or £10,000 for care home residents).

There is a further element of Pension Credit which had no counterpart in the old Minimum Income Guarantee. Worth at most £14.79 per week or £19.20 for a couple, it is called the Savings Credit element since it provides a modest additional reward to people who have made some additional modest provision for old age through savings or a small private or occupational pension. We turn to Pension Credit in more detail later (pages 491–96).

To establish eligibility for Pension Credit, those who wish to benefit must disclose many pieces of private information which some, particularly perhaps those who have known more reticent times, may be reluctant to provide to bureaucrats. In the past, elderly people have neglected to claim benefits to which they have been entitled out of either shame or a desire to preserve their privacy. As many as two million eligible people are thought to have neglected to claim Minimum Income Guarantee. It is important to overcome such qualms. In spite of past preaching against the various horrors of means tests, Labour has entrenched them so deeply in the life of the nation that avoiding them has become financial suicide for poorer citizens. Pension Credit, just like its precursor, the Minimum Income Guarantee, is indexed to earnings, not prices, so its buying power will grow over the years (assuming the country continues to get richer), unlike the State Retirement Pension based on contributions. It is well worth the form-filling it entails, for all who do not actively prefer the lifestyle of tramp or bag-lady for romantic reasons. It is impossible to buy a private pension as good as Guarantee Credit on the open market, and if it were it would cost a great deal more than £100,000.

The nation's decision to provide a means-tested minimum living standard for elderly people, rather than increasing the level of benefits requiring National Insurance contributions, is rueful news for some. People who have made only modest provision for old age, for example by maintaining their National Insurance contribution records or contributing modestly to the new stake-holder pensions, will find that the income they receive will simply disqualify them from Guarantee Credit. People with slightly more income or savings which would have disqualified them from the Minimum Income Guarantee can claim Savings Credit, though they will still be penalized for their thrift. By the time prudent older people realize they have been suckered, however, there will be nothing they can do about it.

Financial life for those who end up on Pension Credit is in some ways far easier than it is for those struggling to get by on their own financial resources. Receipt of the Guarantee element of Pension Credit opens the way to many other benefits, such as Council Tax Benefit, Housing Benefit, free NHS dental treatment, free NHS dentures, transport to hospital, cold weather payments, grants to install central heating and more besides (although you may qualify for some of these things even if you are not on Guarantee Credit). As long as you can put up with what will still seem a relatively low level of cash income if you have been used to good earnings, you should find that being poor and old is to be relatively carefree financially, in spite of the constant propaganda about the supposed evils of poverty in old age.

Dilemma of the In-betweens

Of course it is still better to be rich than Pension-Credit-reliant, but those with the trickiest course to chart are those who are neither rich nor poor. If you have modest savings and income of your own you need to keep a sharp eye on your position, which may change from month to month. You need to know whether your assets and income are still sufficient to put the state's means-tested benefits out of reach or whether you have at last reached the means-test borderline. It may even make sense to get rid of money or other assets which are keeping you from a better life on the poverty line, where you would enjoy access not just to Guarantee Credit but also its associated goodies. The most obvious dilemma concerns the threat of effective appropriation of the family home by local councils in Britain and health and social services boards in Northern Ireland to pay for care in a care home (pages 366–79). But means tests also affect other areas, such as the provision of services in your own home (pages 292–97).

You have to be careful: you must not deliberately deprive yourself of assets in order to qualify for means-tested help. But if your savings place you above the limit, you might wish to spend them on things you need which would also have the effect of bringing your assets down. The question social services or the Department for Work and Pensions would ask is whether you would have acted in that way if the benefits system did not exist: in other words, were you depleting your resources in order to increase your entitlement to benefits? If you were spending money on much-needed house adaptations, a winter coat, winter boots, or a new washing machine, tumble dryer and even a freezer (so that you do not have to go outside to shop or peg out washing when it is slippery underfoot), they might not consider that unreasonable compared with, say, making large gifts of cash to your children.

Benefits for All

Whether you are rich as Croesus, a pauper or somewhere in between, certain financial privileges will be available without means tests – the so-called 'universal' state benefits. Some of these may seem irritatingly piffling, and some may seem patronizing, but together they add up to a degree of financial advantage it would be rash to ignore.

The State Retirement Pension

This mightiest and most famed of benefits is the alter ego of Guarantee Credit, the difference being that whereas anyone poor enough can have Guarantee Credit, the pension is generally available only to those who have paid National Insurance contributions during their working lives. Those who have paid contributions during only part of their working lifetimes get a more-or-less proportionate pension, though contributions are credited during periods of unemployment or sickness. Those not required to pay their own National Insurance contributions will have had the option of making voluntary payments. When they reach retirement age they may regret not having done so, but this is less likely with the alternative of Guarantee Credit available to all. In 2003, the Basic State Pension was £77.45 for a single person and £123.80 for a married couple. These sums are taxable, and the rates rise with inflation, but (unlike Guarantee Credit) not with earnings, so they will steadily fall still further below the sum available to those who have no contribution-based entitlement. The importance of the Basic State Pension nowadays is thus often as an income component for those who are relying principally on other streams of income, usually from private pensions but increasingly from alternatives such as rented properties.

The Basic Pension is accompanied by a secondary top-up based on earnings levels, for those who have not at some stage opted-out and transferred their rights under this scheme into a private pension arrangement. The character of this Secondary Pension has changed repeatedly over the years, and you need to find out exactly where you stand. A print-out of your entitlement is available at any time from the Pension Service (page 499–500).

Disability Benefits

When you mention 'benefits' to many people, their eyes immediately glaze over. But if there is only one benefit whose name you remember, let it be this one: Attendance Allowance. Attendance Allowance provides anybody – pauper or millionaire – aged 65 or over with a weekly payment of up to £57.20 as long as he or she meets certain disability conditions. To get this benefit you do not have to reveal anything about your financial circumstances. You can use the money however you wish – bank it if you like, or use it to pay for taxis and hiring a bit of help in the house and garden. You do not have to pay tax on Attendance Allowance. It does not count as income if you are applying for means-tested benefits, so you would get it on top of Pension Credit. You do not need to have bought a single National Insurance stamp in the whole of your working life to receive it: it is a non-contributory benefit. You can receive it if you are living in your own home, but if you are living in a care home and paying your own bills, you can get it too. However, if you recover from the disability, you do have to tell the Department for Work and Pensions (usually through your local Social Security Office), and they might withdraw the benefit or pay it at a lower rate; for example, you might receive it while experiencing difficulty moving around, but this difficulty might disappear after a hip replacement operation.

To receive Attendance Allowance, you have to have been present in the UK for 26 out of the previous 52 weeks, to have needed the help described in the application for six months before the claim and to need it for another six months (in other words, there is a time-qualifying condition, to stop people with a short-term temporary disability applying) and to be ordinarily resident in the UK with an unlimited right to reside (so asylum seekers, for example, are ruled out). However, this residence requirement and the requirement to have been here for 26 weeks do not apply if you are terminally ill. If a doctor certifies that you have only six months to live, then your claim is processed more swiftly and Attendance Allowance is automatically awarded without your needing to prove that you meet disability rules.

Attendance Allowance is therefore a terrific benefit. The major problem is that it is quite difficult to get. The form is long and you have to know what information you need to give and who should give it. What you have to demonstrate in your application is that you are no longer able to do certain things without help or supervision. Attendance Allowance is payable at two rates: a lower-rate of £38.30 and a higher rate of £57.20. The more help or supervision you need, particularly if you need it at night as well as during the day, the more likely you are to be awarded the higher rate. The conditions for receiving Attendance Allowance stipulate that either you need frequent help throughout the day with your normal bodily functions, or you need continual supervision. 'Bodily functions' are anything you do in connection with your body, such as going to the lavatory, washing, dressing, walking, eating or communicating. 'Frequent' is usually defined as more than twice, although the more times help is needed the more likely you are to succeed in your application. 'Continual supervision' is different: it is about being kept safe by the presence of a third party equipped to supervise you, and would apply, for instance, to somebody with moderate to severe dementia.

When you fill in the application form, it is a good idea to work out whether you are trying to meet the 'frequent help' or the 'continual supervision' condition, or both. What you have to do is to paint a picture of all the different ways in which you, say, need help with bodily functions. You may well still be carrying out these functions unaided, but you have to explain how and why you find them difficult. For instance, perhaps it takes you a long time to get dressed in the morning because you get breathless, or you cannot bend or see well. Your living arrangements are relevant, so if you have great difficulty in walking and have only one inside lavatory up a flight of stairs, say so. It does not matter that you already receive help with some or all of these tasks from somebody else, such as a partner or a care worker; all that matters is that you need assistance with personal care tasks, or need to be kept safe through supervision. Some older people adapt to disability by avoiding tasks such as bathing or changing their clothes frequently, so it is important to think of all the bodily functions which you would like to perform, even if you do not currently do so.

There is space on the form for corroboration, a statement from somebody else. You need to find somebody to fill in this section who is going to take some time over it, and who knows you well; this could be a home help, carer, partner, relative, a friend, son or daughter, or the district nurse if he or she visits often. People sometimes ask their GP, but this is not necessarily a good idea. In these circumstances, GPs often simply offer a medical opinion of the ailments from which somebody is suffering. What is needed on this form, however, is not a medical opinion, but a description of the help needed in daily life. To be in a position to give this, a GP would need to have a much better idea of a person's daily life than he or she is likely to. The Department for Work and Pensions may send along another doctor to verify that somebody really is suffering from a particular medical condition, but that is a different matter.

I wish I had sought advice before filling in my mother's application form, as her first application failed. You can seek help from the Citizen's Advice Bureau or a voluntary group (page 500) but also from the social services department of your local council. Some departments will visit at home for this purpose – a successful application can enable them to claw back some of the benefit through charges they impose for help in the home, since they are entitled to take Attendance Allowance income into account when they assess people for home-care charges. As we shall see below, Attendance Allowance has the additional advantage that it can qualify people for a particular means-tested benefit from which they had hitherto been excluded.

For people under the age of 65, Disability Living Allowance is the equivalent of Attendance Allowance. The qualifying conditions in fields such as residence and presence in the country are the same as for Attendance Allowance, but the other qualifying conditions are different. When a Disability Living Allowance recipient reaches 65, Attendance Allowance effectively replaces most of Disability Living Allowance, but not quite all of it. So somebody approaching their 65th birthday might do well to apply for Disability Living Allowance, as it can continue after that age for those already receiving it. Thus after the age of 65, you could receive small weekly amounts in respect of certain aspects of Disability Living Allowance on top of Attendance Allowance.

Disability Living Allowance has a 'mobility component'; the lower rate, £15.15 per week, has no equivalent in Attendance Allowance. To qualify, you do not have to cope with a physical mobility problem. The application form states that the rate is payable to people who can show that they are 'able to walk, but are so severely disabled physically or mentally that, disregarding any ability they may have to use routes which are familiar to them on their own, they cannot take advantage of the facility out of doors without guidance or supervision most of the time'. The sort of people who can benefit from this are physically mobile people who need supervision or help if they are in unfamiliar territory – for instance, a partially sighted or blind person, or somebody suffering from Alzheimer's or another form of dementia. Such people might not qualify for Attendance Allowance, but if they are awarded Disability Living Allowance and then pass their 65th birthday, they can continue to receive DLA, which, like Attendance Allowance, is non-taxable, non-contributory, does not count as income for other state benefits and is not means-tested.

Disability Living Allowance also has a care component, payable at three rates. The top two are superseded by and equivalent to Attendance Allowance. But if you qualify for the lower rate (£15.15 in 2003), that is not replaced by Attendance Allowance, so you could continue to receive it after becoming 65. This lowest rate is paid to people who either 'cannot cook a meal for themselves if they have all the ingredients' (this not because they have never learnt to cook, but because they cannot manage the tasks, such as bending to take a dish out of the oven) or 'require in connection with their ordinary bodily functions attention from another person for a significant portion of the day, whether in a single period or a number of periods'. 'A significant portion of the day' has been held to be 60 minutes, not necessarily continuous.

Other Non-means-tested Benefits

Television Licences
For people aged 75 and over, television licences are free. It does not matter if the eligible person is living in a household containing younger people, as long as the licence is in his or her name. The TV licensing service has no automatic means of knowing when licence holders reach 75 – if you do not apply for your free licence, you will not get it. The exemptions cost the Exchequer more than £300 million a year.

Two groups of people under the age of 75 qualify for a reduction in their licence fee. Some people who live in care homes or certain types of sheltered accommodation qualify for a concessionary £5 licence. Registered blind people can receive a 50 per cent reduction in the fee, although they would usually do better to obtain specially adapted television sound receivers which do not need a licence to operate; details of these can be obtained from the British Wireless for the Blind Fund, which also lends out receivers to blind people.

Further information about concessionary and free television licences is available from the TV Licensing Centre.

Winter Fuel Payments
People aged 60 and over living in Great Britain are eligible for winter fuel payments which reflect the additional needs of older people for a warm living environment (page 209).

Travel Concessions
Public transport concessionary fares for older people are available throughout the United Kingdom, although they vary considerably in value from place to place (pages 130–36).

Christmas Bonus
The Christmas Bonus is a small sum (£10) paid automatically to people receiving at least one of a wide range of benefits including Retirement Pension, Widow's Pension, Attendance Allowance, Carers Allowance and Income Support. It should be paid automatically, but if you do not receive it by the end of December, you should inform your local Social Security Office.

Reduced Entrance Fees
These vary considerably across the country, but people over retirement age are often able to obtain lower admission rates at galleries and museums, leisure centres and swimming pools and reduced fees for adult education classes. Sometimes businesses such as cinemas, restaurants and hairdressers offer older people lower rates at certain times of the week.

Health Care
NHS prescriptions are free to people aged 60 and over. Sight tests are free to everyone aged 60 and over. While hearing aids

for older people are free on the NHS, spectacles are not. However, people with serious eye conditions get a reduction in the cost of their glasses above a fixed floor.

A number of gadgets and aids are available for free through the NHS, including wheelchairs (pages 107–9).

Chiropody under the NHS is free. However, there is much variation in the extent of provision and many people find themselves supplementing their visits to NHS chiropodists with private treatment. You should check that any private chiropodist you approach is a member of the Society of Chiropodists and Podiatrists.

Old age does not automatically entitle you to free dental treatment. Older people receive dental treatment free or at a reduced rate under the NHS only if they are on low incomes or receiving the Pension Credit 491–6. The Department of Health publishes a leaflet called *Are You Entitled to Help with Health Costs?*, HC11, which is available in post offices and Social Security Offices or through the Department's Health Literature Line. Applications for help with NHS costs should be made on HC1 forms, which are available from Social Security Offices and dentists and opticians. You cannot qualify for any help if you have savings over £8,000.

Benefits for the Needy

Pension Credit

Pension Credit is essentially older people's version of Income Support, the benefit which bumps up the income of needy people of all ages whom the government considers sufficiently deserving. Older people, however, used to be reluctant to apply for Income Support, a benefit which in previous manifestations such as Supplementary Benefit and before that National Assistance had stigmatized recipients, at least when self-reliance was still considered desirable. People entitled to state benefits were therefore living below what was considered the poverty line and thereby embarrassing caring politicians. To encourage these people to apply, the government increased the amount which an older person could receive, renamed the benefit the Minimum Income Guarantee, tied it to earnings instead of prices so its value would grow, and in 1998 relaunched it with a TV advertising campaign fronted by Thora Hird. In 2003, it decided to rename it Pension Credit. This may have been partly to encourage people still reluctant to apply for anything which smacked of going cap in hand to the state since it gives the impression that the benefit has something to do with the State Retirement Pension (it does not). The name may also have been designed to disguise the government's reluctance to increase the (contribution-based) State Pension.

Guarantee Credit

The element of Pension Credit which approximates most closely to the Minimum Income Guarantee is called Guarantee Credit. It is not that high – £102.10 for a single person in 2003. It is, however, higher for older people who meet certain conditions unrelated to their income. To get more money you have to show not that you are specially poor but that you need more money to live on. If you achieve this, you can qualify for quite substantial additional weekly payments. This is how it all works.

The Guarantee Credit is made up of a personal allowance of £54.65, which is equivalent to what an eligible younger person would receive as Income Support, plus a pensioner premium of £47.45. Guarantee Credit for a couple in 2003 was £155.80, because the personal allowance for a couple was £85.75 and the pensioner couple premium was £70.05.

In calculating how much any particular older person should receive, the Department for Work and Pensions works out their 'appropriate amount', which is the minimum the government guarantees, since it is the amount considered necessary to live on. The appropriate amount is made up of a personal allowance and premiums which take account of circumstances, which may increase living costs.

The way to receive more than £102.10 in Guarantee Credit is to show that you fall into another premium category, since the reasoning is that a premium means you need that much more to live on. For older people, the other possibly relevant premiums are the Carer Premium and the Severe Disability Premium. The personal allowance and any premiums are totalled to give the appropriate amount. This is compared with their income. If a person's income is less than this, the government makes up the difference.

Take a deep breath because what follows is complicated, but worth pursuing. The Carer Premium is only worth £25.10 per week, but it is a much under-claimed benefit. There must be lots of married couples who would be entitled to receive it. The first qualification obviously is a low income, since it is a premium added to Guarantee Credit. If you are caring for somebody for at least 35 hours a week and that person is sufficiently frail or disabled to be receiving Attendance Allowance, you ought to be entitled to Carer Premium. To get it, you need to apply for Carer's Allowance. If you get that, fine, but if you do not you should send the letter of refusal to accompany your application for Guarantee Credit. One reason why you might be refused Carer's Allowance is that you are receiving another overlapping benefit which disqualifies you. So in the case of a married couple entitled to Guarantee Credit who were both receiving Attendance Allowance and caring for each other, the Carer Premium could increase weekly income by more than £50.

Severe Disability Premium has the potential to be especially useful. People who have been awarded Attendance Allowance – which as we saw above is a non-means-tested, non-contributory benefit paid in respect of certain disability conditions – automatically qualify for Severe Disability Premium in Guarantee Credit (they have to apply for it). Of course, many people who receive Attendance Allowance will have far too high an income to qualify for Guarantee Credit, so in that case Severe Disability Premium is not relevant. But the premium, £42.95 for a single person or £85.90 for a couple, both of whom qualify, can be useful in two situations. The first is that of people who qualify for Guarantee Credit: their appropriate amount will not be £102.10 but £102.10 plus £42.95, or £145.05. And of course they will also receive Attendance Allowance of £38.30 or £57.20.

The second category is people who did not qualify for Guarantee Credit because their own income was higher than £102.10; in this category you could find somebody with few or no savings receiving a personal or occupational pension just bringing them over the Guarantee Credit limit. However, a

---

Money

- Even the relatively well-off are entitled to state benefits.
- Attendance Allowance is non-means tested, non-taxable and non-contributory.
- The Guarantee Credit part of Pension Credit ensures no older person need be really poor.
- Recipients of Guarantee Credit are automatically entitled to other benefits.
- Higher rates of Guarantee Credit are available to those who meet certain conditions.
- Don't wait too long to cash in a private pension.
- Private health insurance may not cover long-term problems.
- Care insurance can save your home.
- Value locked up in your home can be equity released to provide income.
- Don't give away your money: you may need it for unexpected contingencies.

---

successful application on the part of such people for Attendance Allowance would not only increase their income by the amount of the Attendance Allowance, but could also make them eligible for Guarantee Credit payments, since their appropriate amount would have increased by £42.95. The new total might well be higher than their existing income.

People who come into that second category should not wait until their application for Attendance Allowance is successful before filing an application for Guarantee Credit. Attendance Allowance applications can take several months to process and, if an appeal is involved, as much as two years. Therefore people in that situation should send in an application for Income Support at the same time as one for Attendance Allowance, with a note to say they are claiming because they are also making a claim for qualifying benefit. They may need to apply for Income Support again once the outcome of their application for Attendance Allowance is known.

The financial rewards of the original application for Attendance

Allowance will not stop there. Guarantee Credit provides an automatic gateway to the highest rates of Housing and Council Tax Benefits, amongst others.

There are restrictions on Severe Disability Premium. Generally speaking, you have to be living alone, no one can be claiming the Carer's Allowance in respect of you, and there must be no 'non-dependants' living in your household, such as a grown-up son or daughter. However, if you live with a partner or somebody else who themselves receives Attendance Allowance or is registered blind, you can receive Severe Disability Premium. But beware: the stipulation about non-dependant adults in a household means there is the potential for inadvertent fraud if you are receiving Severe Disability Premium and an able-bodied adult comes and lives with you as part of your household (page 174).

Savings are also taken into account when income is calculated to work out Guarantee Credit entitlement. Capital below £6,000 is disregarded. Above that, savings are converted into a notional weekly income on a sliding scale. The figure is worked out by assuming £1 of income for every £500 or part of £500 of savings; this is called tariff income, and it is added to your actual income when the calculations are made. For example, if you have savings of £9,000, £3,000 will be converted to a tariff income of £6 per week. You need to look carefully at the elements which could be considered both savings and income for Guarantee Credit purposes. Sometimes it is not clear, and appeals can therefore be lodged.

Income Support also goes to help people in care homes pay their bills; for these people, the capital limit is higher: £10,000. People who use Income Support to pay care home bills are usually also receiving help from their council to pay the bills (pages 367–8).

Savings Credit

Savings Credit is fundamentally different from the Guarantee Credit element of Pension Credit in that the amount that is paid is smaller and it is available only to people who have a minimum income already. The maximum any person can receive under the Savings Credit heading is £14.79 per week if their income is the basic rate for Guarantee Credit (£102.10); the maximum figure for a couple is £19.20. The amount you receive varies in a complicated manner according to where your existing income falls within a certain band. To receive anything under Savings Credit, your income has to be at the level of the State Retirement Pension (£77.45); thereafter it increases until £102.10 and thereafter drops until about £139, after which nothing is payable. The equivalent figures for couples are £123.80 and about £204. However, if you are receiving a higher level of Guarantee Credit than the basic, for instance because you are receiving Carer Premium, then the figures shuffle up accordingly. Savings Credit is very complicated and it is quite difficult for people to work out the amount to which they would be entitled. Some people will qualify for both Guarantee and Savings Credit, some for one and others for the other. While Guarantee Credit is available from the age of 60, you have to wait until you are 65 to receive Savings Credit.

Housing Benefit

Housing Benefit is a means-tested benefit paid by local authorities to people on low incomes with savings of not more than £16,000 who pay rent. For elderly tenants of local authority and housing association property (but not yet that owned by private landlords), a new stream of funding is being added to Housing Benefit; this is called the Supporting People Initiative (page 291).

Entitlement to both Housing Benefit and Council Tax Benefit is reduced if applicants have someone else living with them apart from their partner or a dependent child, a joint tenant or joint owner. Such people are known in benefits-speak as 'non-dependants'; the idea is that grown-up children are usually expected to contribute to housing expenses.

If you are already receiving Guarantee Credit, you will automatically be entitled to Housing and Council Tax Benefits at the maximum rates and you ought to receive it automatically (although this was not the case with the Minimum Income Guarantee and you might care to check that an automatic application has been lodged).

The big nuisance about means-tested benefits is having to reapply and present original documents supporting a claim. If you lose out on benefit because you fail to reapply, you can lose out on a lot of cash. However, bear in mind that Council Tax

Benefit and Housing Benefit can be backdated for up to 52 weeks if there is continuous good cause for a late claim. So if you go into hospital and fail to renew your claim by the due date, put in a bid for back-claiming. If you do not ask for backdating, you will not get it. Ill health is usually considered a good reason for backdating a claim. To be doubly sure, send the claim by recorded delivery or ask somebody to deliver it for you – a claim is not recognized as a claim until it has been received.

Council Tax Benefit

Council Tax Benefit, like Housing Benefit, is paid by local authorities according to national rules. Again, it is available only to people on low incomes with savings of less than £16,000 and what you get depends largely on how much money you have got. Perhaps two million people entitled to claim Council Tax Benefit fail to do so; most of these are thought to be over 60. Aside from any Benefit, property may be placed in a lower band if it has certain features providing for a person with substantial and permanent disability, such as extra space for a wheelchair or a bedroom downstairs.

Other Benefits

Pension Credit provides a very useful gateway to a number of other means-tested benefits. These include:

- Help with the cost of travelling to and from hospital for NHS treatment (see page 435). (It is important to check with the hospital before you travel if you are uncertain about whether it will reimburse, say, taxi fares.) People visiting close relatives in hospital may be able to get a reduction on their fares from the Social Fund (page 498).
- Free dental treatment, check-ups and equipment such as false teeth provided by an NHS dentist. This extremely valuable benefit is also available to the partner of a person receiving Pension Credit. People who are not receiving Pension Credit but whose income and savings are low may be entitled to help with dental costs.
- Free support tights (elastic support stockings are free to all people aged 60 and over), wigs and fabric support aids.

- A voucher towards the cost of spectacles. You can pay an additional top-up yourself if the glasses (or contact lenses) you wish to purchase cost more than the voucher.
- Council Tax Benefit
- Housing Benefit
- Cold weather payments (page 209)
- The top rate of grants to improve insulation and heating (pages 207–9).
- Funeral payments. If you are the partner of a person who has died, or someone else, such as a close relative, for whose funeral it is reasonable to expect you should take responsibility, you can apply for a grant to help cover the costs. The payment covers the cost of the burial or cremation, local authority fees, certain necessary travel expenses and up to £700 for other costs such as a coffin. Any money available from the estate of the person who has died or from insurance policies or pre-paid funeral plans will be taken into account in assessing your application. You do not have to be receiving Pension Credit to obtain a funeral payment – Housing Benefit and Council Tax Benefit are also qualifying benefits.

People receiving Income Support or Pension Credit may also receive certain payments through the Social Fund. These are discretionary payments: in other words, they can be withheld, unlike some other elements of the Social Fund, which are guaranteed for people who qualify for them. Get advice before applying for these discretionary payments – their allocation is widely acknowledged by experts to be unfair; for instance, the time of year when you apply can affect your chance of success. Yet they are available for very important purposes, and if you are below the savings threshold you stand to gain a lot. The benefits in this category are outlined below.

Community Care Grants
These can be paid to people of any age to help cover the following costs:

- Travelling – for instance, to visit a relative who is ill, or to attend a relative's funeral.

- The effects of exceptional pressures on a family, perhaps as a result of disability, chronic sickness or a relationship breakdown.
- Enabling somebody to continue to live at home, perhaps to buy essential furniture or equipment (for instance to replace a cooker which has broken), to carry out minor house repairs or to move furniture to more suitable accommodation.
- Helping somebody move out of an institution, again perhaps help with removal costs, or to buy essential furniture.

However, the savings threshold for Community Care Grants is extremely low: £1,000 (£500 for those under 60). If you have savings of less than this amount, you can in theory receive quite a lot of help, but if your savings are more than £1,000, you are expected to contribute all the amount over that figure.

Budgeting Loans and Crisis Loans
People on Pension Credit may also receive Budgeting Loans (not grants, but interest-free) through the Social Fund. These enable them to spread the cost of one-off expenses, perhaps for furniture, footwear, removal costs or home improvements. Again, any savings over £1,000 (£500 for the under-60s) will reduce the amount of the loan. Budgeting Loans are awarded only if it is considered that the person can repay them. There are also Crisis Loans, which are available to all (not only those people on Income Support) who need something urgently in an emergency, perhaps as a result of fire or flood.

Administration and Advice
In England, Wales and Scotland the administration of benefits is the responsibility of the Department for Work and Pensions. In 2002, this department took over benefits and pensions work from the Department of Social Security, which operated Benefits Agency offices. The local offices of the Department for Work and Pensions are called Social Security Offices and they should be listed in your telephone book. You may be directed to particular parts of the DWP such as the Pension Service, which looks after the State Retirement Pension and the Minimum Income Guarantee, or the Disability and Care Service, which

administers Carers Allowance, Attendance Allowance and Disability Living Allowance.

The DWP publishes a useful guide to pensions and benefits called *Pensioners' Guide: Making the Most of Government Help and Advice*. You can obtain a copy, or the slightly different one for Scotland, over the telephone. Leaflets about benefits as well as advice on claiming them are available at local Social Security Offices and Citizen's Advice Bureaux. Age Concern publishes useful free factsheets on various benefits and also an annually updated book by Sally West called *Your Rights: A Guide to Money Benefits for Older People*. You will find more detailed coverage in a thick tome entitled the *Welfare Benefits Handbook*, which is published every year by the Child Poverty Action Group in London and the Disability Rights Handbook, published annually by Disability Alliance. There is provision for appealing against decisions on all government benefits; you can get details of the various procedures from Social Security Offices or main post offices in a leaflet called *If You Think your Decision is Wrong*, GL24.

The Department for Work and Pensions offers information and advice helplines, as set out in Useful Contacts at the back of this book. Benefits in Northern Ireland are very similar to those on the British mainland. However, they are administered by the Social Security Agency, which is part of the Department of Social Development. People on the DWP helpline will respond to your questions about particular benefits but they do not usually offer suggestions about benefits for which you could usefully apply: they are essentially responsible for the administration of benefits, not benefits advice, although some people from the Pension Service of the DWP visit day centres, for example, and give advice. The people on the helpline may well be trained only in one particular benefit and thus unable to take such an overall view.

A very good place to go for benefits advice is your Citizen's Advice Bureau. Staff there are highly trained at running benefit checks on individuals. If you provide them with basic information, they will advise you on benefits to which you are entitled but not receiving, or are receiving but at a lower rate than you could claim. They may help you fill in the application form. For example, a claimant might have applied for Attendance

Allowance some years ago but has come to experience more severe symptoms of a condition such as Parkinson's Disease and may now be eligible for the higher rate. You can also obtain advice on benefits from non-government organizations such as Help the Aged, Age Concern, Counsel and Care, The Princess Royal Trust for Carers and Carers UK. Many local authorities have welfare rights advice offices. The Legal Services Commission provides information on organizations which give advice in various areas of law, including benefits, as well as lawyers which specialize in this area.

It is a very good idea to go for benefits checks. Say you are living in private retirement housing: you might be eligible for Council Tax Benefit, Attendance Allowance and/or Pension Credit, for example. When in doubt claim, claim early and claim often.

If your application is turned down, consider appealing. Decision-makers in the DWP are often low-grade (students are hired over the summer) and there is provision for appeal (to a tribunal, a commissioner and finally the Court of Appeal). Citizen's Advice Bureau officials as well as advisers in the voluntary bodies and welfare rights advisers in local authorities ought to be able to give you advice on lodging appeals.

It is important to notify the Department for Work and Pensions (usually through your local Social Security Office) or the Social Security Agency in Northern Ireland of any significant change in your circumstances which could affect your entitlement to benefits. This is not necessarily a financial change: as we have seen, allowing an adult not in receipt of Attendance Allowance to come and live in your household disqualifies you for the Severe Disability Premium of Guarantee Credit (page 174). If you go into hospital (and when you come out), benefits, including pensions, are reduced by various amounts after various periods of hospital stays. You or somebody holding registered enduring power of attorney on your behalf could be liable to repay benefits paid in error. The DWP leaflet *Going into Hospital?* (GL12) provides a basic guide. Help the Aged's free leaflet, *Going into Hospital*, is invaluable.

Chapter 17
Self-help

Private Pensions

Most elderly people not wholly dependent on the state for their incomes will be relying mainly on private pensions, either occupational or personal. Most of the crucial decisions relating to this may have been made long before retirement, however unwittingly, and many are irrevocable. However, any that remain to be made should be taken very seriously because of the huge difference they can make to financial standing.

Essentially, the state allows people (and their employers) to contribute to pension funds from their before-tax incomes during their working lives in the hope that this will make them less likely to require means-tested benefits from the state in their old age. In general the fund built up in a pension must therefore be converted sooner or later into an annuity (an income for life which evaporates on death). On the whole, people relying on a pension from employment will simply start receiving this when they retire. Those such as the self-employed with personal pensions who have built up a cash sum rather than an entitlement to a proportion of their income in work are likely to be in a much worse position, as annuity rates have tumbled because of increased life expectancy. They may nonetheless have choices which may be quite difficult to make.

You may have the option of taking a quarter of your fund in cash, tax-free, instead of using all of it to buy an annuity. This is usually a good idea: even if the cash sum is used primarily to supplement annuity income, the remainder remains available for house repairs, private health treatment or a holiday. And once it has gone it ceases to block access to means-tested benefits, which higher annuity income might do. A more difficult choice may be when to cash in a personal pension fund by converting it into an annuity or combination of lump sum and annuity.

Pension holders may have the freedom to convert their pension into an annuity at any age between 50 and 75. If they need the cash, no problem. If they can wait, should they? The longer you wait, the higher the rate, but even a high rate will not do you much good if you cash in at 75 and die at 76. On the other hand, if you die before you cash in, the whole sum in your fund becomes available to your heirs entirely free of inheritance tax, unlike, say, your house. This can be particularly valuable: not only do your life savings not disappear with you, but the money can be used to pay the inheritance tax on your estate. As this tax has to be cleared up before any legacies can be paid out, it can come in very handy.

Not surprisingly, some people therefore delay cashing in their pensions longer than is wise and, equally unsurprisingly, they are sometimes encouraged by their relatives to do so. The issue can be fudged by converting the pension bit by bit, though expert guidance should be taken here, as the schemes are complicated. Once the decision to cash in is made, it is important to shop around for the best annuity rate and not settle for the scheme provided by whoever is managing the pension fund. You can opt to receive a fixed monthly sum, which will of course be eroded by inflation, an inflation-indexed sum or a sum rising each year by a fixed percentage. The latter choices may sound tempting, but of course you pay heavily for asking the provider to take the financial risk you will be avoiding. You can arrange for a pension to be paid for the first five years even if the recipient dies in that time for a modest reduction in the rate. Arranging for a proportion of the pension to go to a surviving spouse will of course drive the rate down further.

Insurance

Health Insurance

Some elderly people will already have taken out health insurance to beat the queues and other deficiencies of the National Health Service. Such schemes obviously look more attractive as you come to appreciate you will need more health care and you hear more about discrimination against older people in the NHS. However, the cost increases sharply with age, for obvious reasons, and the tax relief which used to be provided has now been withdrawn. Should you nonetheless wish to go ahead, the rates and terms of the big providers such as BUPA or PPP can readily be compared. Look out, of course, for what is excluded, such as rehabilitation. Strokes have an acute phase but then often a much longer phase of rehabilitation. Elderly people take longer to recover from operations. You might get a hip replacement more quickly, but then have to fall back on the NHS very soon afterwards because your health insurance did not make adequate provision for recuperation.

Care Insurance

Health insurance, which is now well understood by people of all ages, needs to be distinguished from another form of insurance which may come to loom much larger in the lives of elderly people. In theory, at least, everyone should get adequate health care free from the NHS. Care in a care home is of course provided outside the NHS and though this is also funded by the state for those unable to pay for it themselves, the quality of publicly funded care often leaves much to be desired, although you will not necessarily receive better care in a very pricey establishment (page 320). Those who go into care will, however, have their whole lives utterly and permanently transformed by it. Insurance can mean they get the chance to choose the care home they want rather than the facility their cash-strapped local authority is prepared to fund. Insuring to achieve this may be a more sensible use of limited money than insuring to beat NHS queues.

If you have more money than you need from day to day, it is well worth considering investing in care insurance. Since the first care insurance scheme was introduced in 1991, the number of such policies in force has risen to over 20,000. Maximum benefits payable can be over £30,000 a year and there is no upper age limit for some policies.

As well as giving elderly people a wide choice of care home, insurance can also protect their assets, including their home, from being effectively seized by the state to pay for their care. Long-term care insurance can also give them a wider choice in the provision of support within their own homes. But it does not come cheap. On the whole, you get what you pay for. The healthier you are and the sooner you take out a policy, the lower your premiums will be. The average age at which policies are taken out is around 67.

You can either pay a regular monthly premium, which will vary according to the level of cover and your state of health, or pay one lump sum up front. More complicated arrangements are tied to investment growth. You should think carefully about the impact of premiums on your immediate quality of life before going ahead. Most people, after all, never need to go into a care home. The problem of course is that most of us do not know whether we shall. But do not pay for more cover than you really need. It is only necessary to insure against the costs you anticipate which you could not cover from existing income, such as pensions and investments. Of course, this will mean that those best placed to pay high premiums need pay the lowest, and vice versa. That's life. In the case of a couple, consider insuring only the spouse likely to live longer; perhaps you can rely on the hope that the other will be able to get by on the spouse's care with some paid additional support. Find out what happens if you can no longer afford to pay premiums.

A lot turns on the tests that will have to be met before the scheme pays out. Check these out in the light of your or your relative's likely problems, insofar as you have an idea of what these might turn out to be. The most common disabilities in old age are with mobility and hearing. So how are mobility problems defined? What is said about 'cognitive impairment', as conditions such as Alzheimer's are likely to be classified? Is it worth taking out this insurance for somebody who is already in the first stages of Parkinson's or Alzheimer's? Policies may only pay out half-benefits if debility is ranked as partial. Check for how long benefits will be paid. Tell your GP and your relatives that the policy exists, so that it will be called upon should you become unable to draw attention to it.

Living off Your House

In a country which has chosen to put so much of its wealth into bricks and mortar, many elderly people, after a lifetime spent paying off the mortgage, feel there is something silly about ending up 'asset-rich, income poor'. Especially in the south of

England, it is easy to end your days living in what seems like a gold-mine, disproportionately valuable compared to the meagre lifestyle enjoyed by its inhabitant. With annuity rates tumbling and investment income growing more sparse, homeowners who did not expect to are feeling the pinch. Is there not some way of siphoning off some of the cash locked into that brickwork and spending it while you are still able to enjoy it?

There is. 'Home equity release' schemes enable homeowners to receive cash immediately in return for pledging all or part of their house to a financial institution. These schemes got a bad name in their early days when some of those who took them up found themselves losing their homes as the debts they incurred snowballed beyond the value of their homes. Nowadays, home equity release has been cleaned up, and most schemes guarantee that whatever happens, participants will be able to carry on living in their homes till death. All the same, nothing is for nothing. If you invite a financial institution to take a stake in your house, it will have to make its own profit: you will therefore have to pay for its participation. It may make much better financial sense for you to sell your home and move to a smaller house or flat or even a fixed mobile home, perhaps in a cheaper area, and to pocket the cash that way rather than to involve a middle-man who will take his own cut.

Nonetheless, some elderly people want to stay in the home they have grown used to whatever happens. As long as they do not also want to pass it on to their children, equity release may be the means of providing just the boost to their lifestyle that they want, or indeed of enabling them to pay the maintenance costs of what may be a much larger property than they could other-wise afford to keep up. The money released can also be used to pay for health insurance, long-term care insurance or a specific health treatment, or adaptations to make life possible in the house if they have a disability. There are three main types of home equity release scheme. You usually have to be at least 60 to take up any of them.

'Mortgage roll-ups' are currently the most popular arrange-ment. Essentially, you take out a mortgage against your house and pocket the sum borrowed, but instead of paying off the interest each month, you allow it to 'roll up' into a lump sum.

This is paid back to the bank or building society along with the capital borrowed when the house is sold, on the death of the mortgagee if that is when this occurs. Interest rates can be either fixed or variable, though of course the latter risk more of the property's value being gobbled up than might have been anticipated if rates rise. Do not expect to be able to liberate more than half of the value of the property at most; you may be able to extract only 20 per cent. The older you are, the more you will be able to get out, since the lender will have less cause to fear ending up out of pocket.

Under a 'home reversion plan', you would sell part of your property to a bank or insurance company in return for a lump sum. On death, the portion sold belongs to the financial institution, and the remainder goes into the estate. However, the reversion company will not pay the current market value for a share – it might pay as little as 35 per cent of this figure. It should, however, still be possible to move house, even after such a deal has been entered into.

A 'home income plan' converts your house, or part of it, into an annuity, that is, an income for life, but only for life, while allowing you to carry on living in the house until death. Nothing is left of the value of the house, or that part of it involved, on death.

An organization called Safe Home Income Plans (SHIP) has been created to ensure that problems created with earlier schemes, such as those that led to repossession in some cases, are not repeated. Look for a scheme operating under SHIP rules.

Clearly the choice of scheme and the extent to which it is pursued may be affected by the balance between your desire for cash now and your eagerness to leave as much as possible of the equity involved to heirs. You should, however, also consider your own potential need for the money locked up in the house at some later date before extracting it early on essentially disadvantageous terms. It can also be disastrous to discover after the event that the sum of money neatly tucked into your bank account serves only to disqualify you from means-tested benefits which could have been worth rather more, for money from equity release will be taken into account in means-testing for benefits.

On the other hand, it can look clever to have liquidated equity in a home and lived high on the hog on the proceeds, if you later go into a care home whose fees then have to be paid by the council instead of through a house sale. Watch out here: the council and the Department for Work and Pensions (which would also be part-funding care-home care) can order money to be repaid if they consider it has been shifted to reduce liability for care home bills or provide eligibility to state benefits such as Housing and Council Tax Benefits and Pension Credit. Another effect to consider is that if a large chunk of the value of a house is destined to be claimed in inheritance tax, spending the money during the owner's lifetime in home equity release can cheat the taxman of his booty. You need to try to work out just which of the competing schemes is offering you the fairest, or least unfair, share out of the equity. Beware of complicated charges, such as arrangement fees, and early redemption charges. Make sure negative equity would not prevent you from moving. You may say that you are certain you want to stay where you are till you die. Then a neighbour from hell moves in next door and starts picking on you. Altogether, home equity release is something to think particularly long and hard about before making the leap.

Protecting Inheritance

Younger people are often surprised to find that their elderly relatives turn out to be most concerned about the implications their financial affairs may have for their children or other heirs. You might have assumed that older people would have enough to worry about without thinking of those who will outlive them. Yet throughout history human beings have shown a keen desire to pass on their wealth, perhaps as a means of ensuring they can still influence events after their own death. So some elderly people seem willing to put up with considerable hardship in their own lives for the sake of the beneficiaries of their will. If this is their choice, fair enough. Naturally, some younger relatives are only too happy to go along with this attitude. Surprisingly often, however, they would rather see their older relatives spending their money on themselves. If you find yourself in this position, you might as well make your feelings clear rather than waiting for a legacy you do not need and which is going to be tainted by guilt.

The Tax Spectre

Once safeguarding inheritance has become an issue, the tax problems of achieving this will quickly come into view. Where legacies greater in total than around £255,000 are in prospect (including the value of a house), the taxman will walk away with 40 per cent of the proceeds above that figure in inheritance tax, if nothing is done to stop him. Escaping this tax can develop into something of an obsession, not only for elderly people, but also of course for their relatives. Assuming, however, that heirs have their elderly relatives' best interests rather than their own at heart, everybody involved needs to beware. All is far from straightforward in this field.

King Lear Syndrome

The obvious way to beat the taxman may seem to be for the elderly person to give away his or her assets while still alive. Elderly people are all too likely to find themselves surrounded by others only too ready to drop hints that this would be an extremely good idea. After all, older people don't really need much money, do they? Not in comparison, perhaps, to the burgeoning needs of their nieces and nephews, who will be bullied unless transferred to private schools, or whose lives will be worthless without ponies or ballet lessons. A home made over to a son or daughter may be kept from the council's clutches if its elderly owner has to go into care, and the son or daughter can take over those increasingly burdensome home maintenance problems. Beware, beware.

The Department for Work and Pensions and a local authority can claim the value of the house anyway if it considers ownership has been shifted in order to offload liability for care home bills (page 374). But there are other considerations to bear in mind too.

You may feel certain of the strength and health of family relationships. But like King Lear, you can be mistaken. People change, even close relatives, and the arrival or prospect of wealth is exactly the kind of thing that makes this happen. However much elderly people love their children, they can be shocked by the experience of coming within their power. Those who really care for their elderly relatives need to keep an eye on siblings and in-laws. 'Gold,' said Shelley, 'is the old man's sword. He should be careful before he relinquishes it.'

The most obvious problem is that an elderly person may develop unexpected needs for cash which he or she has prematurely given away. A good digital hearing aid could cost £5,000 and purchase of an electric-powered scooter might cost another £5,000. Kitting out your home with a full range of mobility aids because a major stroke has confined you to a wheelchair might cost a sum undreamt of when you handed over your spare cash to pay your grandchildren's school fees. You could find that your income and savings, although you have offloaded a great deal of them, nonetheless disqualify you from the help your council might have provided.

What is for sure is that relatives who accepted an elderly person's cash years before are not going to be in a position to return it later. As a result, what seemed like an act of spontaneous generosity can sow the seeds of resentment and guilt. Should the donor come to ask the council or the Department for Work and Pensions for help, those organizations might say that the sums given away involved deliberate 'deprivation of assets'; in other words, the step was taken in order to bring down income and savings to get access to state benefits which would not otherwise have been available. They could ask for the money to be repaid before they would step in to help.

Giving money away may not anyway provide a way round inheritance tax. Only £3,000 a year in total may be given away without tax implications. Any gift above that level is only a 'potentially-exempt' transfer, and inheritance tax will be payable on it unless the donor survives for at least seven years after making it. If an elderly person continues to live in a house after giving away the freehold, it will be considered a 'gift with reservation' and inheritance tax will still be payable.

There are better ways to avoid inheritance tax that do not require you to be stripped clean before death. Being married is one. You can leave as much as you like to a spouse without paying a penny in tax, though to get maximum value out of this benefit, it makes sense for the first spouse to die to leave some of his or her estate to the children, so that both spouses' exemptions are used to the full. Otherwise, if you want to escape as much inheritance tax as possible, your best bet is to set up a trust designed to achieve this. This is surprisingly cheap and easy: it will mean giving some control of the assets involved to trustees, but the loss of autonomy involved can be minimized. Independent financial advisors will be only too happy to explain the products involved.

Advice

The Financial Services Authority has statutory powers and reports to Parliament; two of its key objectives are to promote public understanding of the financial system and to secure the appropriate degree of protection of consumers. The Authority regulates annuities and can provide much information about what they are and the rules which govern them. For example, new rules in 2002 provided that people should have clear information about their options when buying an annuity and should not be restricted to buying one from their pension fund manager. The Authority does not regulate equity release or health or care insurance, but it can provide information about these areas. It publishes many booklets. You could telephone its consumer helpline. If you use its website, a particularly useful section is the FSA Handbook. There is even an online consumer help-page which makes often complex matters much clearer.

You need to exercise great caution in choosing an individual financial advisor. Check, for example, whether he or she is working on commission and whether he or she has specialist knowledge in the area in which you are interested. Codes of practice governing the sale of various types of insurance can be useful, but find out what they actually mean and whether your advisor is covered.

Part Seven
Representation

Chapter 18
Legal and Financial

There are several situations in which elderly people need somebody else to represent them in financial and legal matters.

Collecting Pensions and Benefits

Suppose you want somebody to go to the post office and collect your pension because you are temporarily unable to do it yourself. This is very simple. You authorize somebody to collect money for you, but not to spend it, by completing the declaration in your pension book. If you want to keep the agency situation going for a period, you can do so through an agency card. You can find out precisely how this is done through a Social Security Office leaflet called *Helping Hand for Benefits: How somebody with an illness or disability can get help to collect or deal with social security benefits* (GL21).

This procedure sounds simple enough, but it is open to fraud. Signatures can be forged. People can sign their pension book when they think they are signing something else, perhaps because they cannot see well. It is supposed to be impossible for agents to be appointed by people who are unable to understand what they are doing, so when people develop dementia, close relatives cannot lawfully receive their pensions on their behalf unless the pensioners authorized such an arrangement when they were *compos mentis* or granted some other more wide-ranging power such as enduring power of attorney (pages 518–19).

If you cannot or would prefer not to collect your pension, it is safest to get it paid direct into a bank account. Often people who want their pension collected, say, by care workers employed privately or through social services, also ask the collector to spend some of the pension on shopping. Pensioners should then check the money in their purse against the receipt and the amount they receive each week through their pension book. But some will not do this or will be unable to do it with any degree of certainty, perhaps because of sight problems. So, despite the risk of not having sufficient cash available at home, having the pension mandated direct to a bank account is probably the best way to proceed.

The system of paying pensions is in the process of change. By 2005 the government hopes that everyone will receive his or her pension direct into a bank, building society or post office account. This new system is called Direct Payment (not to be confused with the system of receiving money for community care services called Direct Payments). Payment of a pension into a bank or building society account has always been possible. Post office account-holders will get a plastic card and pin number rather than a payment book and swipe their cards. People collecting pensions on behalf of others will need their card and pin number. They will, however, only be able to withdraw one week's pension entitlement, so the risks will be limited. If you wish somebody to collect your pension on your behalf regularly, you can set up a second card for them. Payment under the new system can be restricted to just a part of a week's entitlement, which is an advantage over the old system. There will however be no 24-hour hole-in-the-wall access: money will only be accessible during post office opening hours (this is not the case of course if you opt to have your pension paid direct into your bank or building society account). You will also be able to collect other state benefits through Direct Payment including Attendance Allowance, Carer's Allowance and Bereavement Benefits. Further details are available on the Direct Payment Information Line and in Department for Work and Pensions leaflet DPL 1.

Bank Authorization

You may want to authorize somebody else to carry out various transactions at your bank or building society. In this case, you should contact the bank or building society to ask what form of authorization you will need – perhaps a letter of authority or a form has to be completed. Sometimes you have to fill in a form every time you authorize another person to act on your behalf at the bank, but in other cases a single form suffices. However, if a person with whom you hold a joint account at a bank loses mental capacity, then the person who retains mental capacity cannot lawfully use the account until the bank has received new instructions from a person or persons acting on behalf of the incapacitated person, such as somebody holding a registered enduring power of attorney.

Ordinary Power of Attorney

Sometimes people feel under the weather for a while or are away from home. They feel that they do not want the bother of paying bills and administering other financial transactions, perhaps because they are in hospital for a short period having an operation. Or they might go into hospital or abroad at a crucial time, perhaps when in the middle of buying and selling property. Clearly it would help if they could hand their affairs over temporarily to a trusted representative, but ideally not the family solicitor, who would charge a fee. In this case, the mechanism they could choose is an ordinary power of attorney.

With an ordinary power of attorney, you grant powers to a person, or more than one person, to enable them to act on your behalf. The power of attorney may end on a specified date or you can cancel it before then if you no longer need it. It can be a general power to handle all your financial and legal affairs, or it can be limited to a particular act, for example, buying a house or buying and selling stocks and shares. You can specifically exclude, say, the power to write out cheques above a certain amount or to sell your stocks and shares or any property you own.

You can grant an ordinary power of attorney only if you understand what you are doing. The procedure is quite straightforward. You get a form from a law stationer's or from your solicitor and sign it; some people get their solicitor to draw up the form for them. In any case, it is a good idea to discuss any form of representation which you may be contemplating with a solicitor before you go ahead: he or she can advise you on ways around some of the matters arising.

Once power of attorney has been granted, the donor is still perfectly free to act on his or her behalf, signing cheques and so on. The donor can terminate the power at any time and from that moment the attorneyship becomes null and void. However, if donors lose their mental faculties an ordinary power of attorney ceases to be valid.

Enduring Power of Attorney

Older people can of course become mentally incapable of handling their legal and financial affairs long term because they have developed some degree of dementia. Suppose you are the only close relative of your mother or father, and live 400 miles away, and you find that he or she is writing out lots of cheques which are unusual or that all sorts of bills are piling up. What then?

What happens depends on whether your relative has already granted enduring (or in Scotland continuing) power of attorney. This is the same as ordinary power of attorney in that a person who is *compos mentis* authorizes another or others to act on his or her behalf with or without limitations. It also comes into effect when the attorney is signed, after which the attorney and the donor hold powers concurrently. This means that should an unexpected problem arise – for instance, entry into hospital after a fall – the attorney can keep the show on the road until the donor is back on his or her feet again.

An enduring power differs from an ordinary power of attorney in that if the donor so provides, there can be provision for it only to come into effect should the donor lose his or her mental faculties. It is to make provision for this eventuality that people usually grant enduring power of attorney. If it should happen, the attorney then has complete control and can do anything which the donor could have lawfully done (unless restrictions have been placed, for instance on the sale of property).

This second-stage power operates only when the attorney or attorneys register with the Court of Protection. The Court of Protection is not like a legal court: essentially it is an office in London where officials administer the controls and safeguards in the field of representation. The relevant arm of the court for people living in England and Wales is the Public Guardianship Office. The equivalent institution in Scotland is the Office of the Public Guardian, and in Northern Ireland, the Office of Care and Protection. Legislation likely to be introduced into Parliament in 2004 seeks to replace enduring power of attorney in England and Wales with a new mechanism called 'lasting power of attorney', which will be similar to it but can also cover decisions about health and personal welfare, and to set up a new court to administer existing enduring powers of attorney and new forms of representation (pages 539–40).

Although it might seem dangerous to hand other people *carte blanche* as described above, a wide enduring power of attorney is important because all sorts of things may need to be done. In particular, if the older person needs 24-hour care, those holding attorney will need to sort out the cash to pay for this, which could include liquidating assets.

Receivership

If no power of attorney has been granted, the son or daughter 400 miles away has another possible course of action. He or she can apply to act as the receiver for the parent (a similar tool, outlined on page 522, is available in Scotland). Receivership is very different from attorneyship. As a receiver, you are authorized not to act on behalf of someone else, but on behalf of the Public Guardianship Office. What essentially happens is that the office assumes control of the individual's affairs, but delegates tasks on request to the receiver. A relative may have to apply to act as receiver if he or she would otherwise have had the powers of an attorney but the person involved did not grant them before deterioration of the mind set in. Receivership also has to cover situations in which older people declined to grant attorney because they did not feel they could trust anybody with this power, including the person applying to be the receiver. Finally, it has to embrace people outside the family who become receivers for elderly people, such as solicitors and officials in social services departments.

To apply for receivership, obtain a form from the Public Guardianship Office and send it back together with the fee and a copy of the last will, if that is available, and the name and address of somebody willing to provide a reference as to your fitness to act as receiver. The office will also need medical evidence to satisfy itself that the person involved is incapable of managing his or her own financial affairs because of mental disorder.

Receivers do not have *carte blanche* to manage the estate of the older person. The powers still lie ultimately with the office, which can, with respect to the property and affairs of the older person (who is known as the 'patient'):

... do or secure the doing of all such things as appear necessary or expedient (a) for the maintenance or other benefit of the patient, (b) for the maintenance or other benefit of members of the patient's family, (c) for making provision for other persons or purposes for whom or which the patient might be expected to provide if he were not mentally disordered or (d) otherwise for administering the patient's affairs.[1]

It is the receiver who does all the work on the ground, but unlike an attorney, he or she has to report back to the Public Guardianship Office at regular intervals and seek its say-so for many steps. If the older person's property is in need of major repair, the receiver has to write to the office to get permission to use the money in this way. He or she has to submit estimates to the office and to demonstrate that the resources will not be squandered. The decision on how assets should be invested rests with the office; the receiver makes suggestions to it. If property is going to be sold to pay care home bills, the office will want to see several independent valuations from surveyors. Every year, the receiver must submit accounts with receipts in respect of all financial transactions, and also for any out-of-pocket expenses he or she wishes to claim, with receipts. You cannot be paid for acting as a receiver or an attorney, unless you are doing this as part of your work as a solicitor, an accountant or social services official.

On the face of it, receivership seems to have advantages for parents who feel they cannot trust their sons or daughters absolutely. However, it brings disadvantages too. The Public Guardianship Office does not handle your affairs for free. Fees are levied at every point: when the receivership is first set up, when it is cancelled on death, if a house is sold and every year when the accounts are submitted for approval. Over the years quite a substantial amount of money can be paid to the office and so the older person's estate is depleted that much more rapidly than it would otherwise have been.[2]

Another disadvantage to the older person is that it can be upsetting at the beginning when a receiver is appointed. Suppose an older person is not paying bills or is writing out uncharacteristic cheques. If the son or daughter or indeed anyone else applies to act as receiver, the Public Guardianship Office has to notify the person for whom receivership is being applied, explaining why the application has been made and by whom, unless there is medical evidence to demonstrate that this would cause him or her alarm or distress. Delay is likely as the various checks are made when the office considers the application, although there is provision for an emergency order.

A receiver is not always a relative. A solicitor, a social worker or other professional person can be appointed. There is provision for somebody to apply to act on behalf of somebody else if the person's assets are less than £16,000. This is a simpler procedure than receivership, but you still have to apply to the Public Guardianship Office to obtain it.

Appointeeship

If, however, all that is needed is that somebody should be authorized to collect a state pension or other benefits for an older person who has lost mental capacity, there is a less cumbersome procedure than receivership, called appointeeship. A prospective appointee can apply to the Secretary of State for Work and Pensions. Before granting the power, officials have to satisfy themselves that the older person is unable to handle his or her affairs and that the prospective appointee is a suitable person to do this instead. They usually take the view that a close relative who lives with the older person or visits frequently is the most suitable kind of person.

Sometimes people living in care homes lose mental capacity and have no relative who is prepared to take on appointeeship. In this case the manager of the care home may be authorized to act as the appointee. Clearly, this situation offers the potential for fraud. Officials from the National Care Standards Commission, the Care Standards Inspectorate for Wales, the Scottish Commission for the Regulation of Care and health and social services boards in Northern Ireland should check on appointeeships and any other vehicles in place for handling residents' finances when they inspect care homes.

Scotland

Much of the system of legal and financial representation in Scotland is similar to that south of the border. The system of continuing power of attorney in Scotland operates in a similar fashion to enduring power of attorney south of the border, with attorneys applying to register an attorneyship with the Office of the Public Guardian in Falkirk (if the attorneyship was granted after 2 April 2001). The system of appointeeship is also similar. But in Scotland an additional tool is available which has no equivalent in England: if no attorney or guardian has been appointed, a carer, relative or friend but not a social worker can, with the consent of the Office of the Public Guardian, become a person's 'withdrawer'. This will enable him or her to access funds from one account for specified purposes, such as to pay gas bills or care home bills or to buy clothes. This simple tool has the potential for much beneficial use, for instance if somebody has not granted power of attorney but his bank account contains money which could be used for his benefit for everyday items like a new piece of furniture or extra services.

Since the enactment of the Adults with Incapacity (Scotland) Act 2000, the equivalent of receivership has been a form of 'guardianship'. A potential guardian applies to the local sheriff court to act on behalf of a person whose mental capacity has declined but who has not granted anyone power of attorney. Guardianship can cover welfare as well as legal and financial matters and a narrow or a wide range of powers, so that the equivalent of receivership is guardianship with full financial powers. Another new tool in Scotland, the 'intervention order', empowers an applicant to take an action or decide something for someone else. The court notifies the Office of the Public Guardian when intervention orders or guardianships are granted.

These new tools came into effect in 2002 and further details are available from the Scottish Executive. Alzheimer Scotland has published a very useful explanation entitled *Dementia: Money and Legal Matters: A Guide*.

Granting Enduring Power of Attorney

In view of all this, it is clear that the big decision in the field of legal and financial representation which older people need to make is whether to grant enduring, or in Scotland continuing, power of attorney and, if so, to whom and whether they should impose limitations on the power of the attorney(s). In many cases the power will never have to be used, because the older person will retain mental capacity until death. But all concerned will enjoy the security of knowing it is there if needed.

The advantage of enduring power of attorney is essentially that it has a very wide compass and enables people to act in a wide range of ways. They do not need to refer major decisions to the Public Guardianship Office, with the delays, additional work and payment from the donor's estate which that entails.

There are important psychological benefits to the older person in the attorney, as opposed to the receivership (or in Scotland the guardianship), approach. First, you choose your attorney, but you do not choose your receiver. Second, it cannot be very pleasant to hear that somebody is making a receivership application involving you, particularly if you do not like the person making the application. Third, if somebody has clearly become mentally incapable and yet would be distressed to give up rights and freedoms, things can proceed on a gradually increasing basis until the power is registered. Before registration, the attorneys have some power to act (though less than after registration), and the donor should ensure, if able to do so, that he or she knows whether the attorney is using the power. During an emergency it can be used. However, it could also be used in a joint manner, so as to offload some of the burden of the day-to-day running of financial affairs. So a helpful bank could arrange for the intended attorney to be a counter-signatory for cheques, for example, or the attorney might even take sole charge of the donor's credit or cheque card.

There are plenty of people around out to exploit older people. One example: an elderly lady who does not wish to embarrass herself with her family finds herself in need of a large sum of money. An individual specializing in equity release schemes persuades her to mortgage or transfer 50 per cent of her property to him in return for the sum of money. She does not carry out checks on the company and he directs her to a solicitor of his suggestion. Perhaps the firm and the solicitor are perfectly reputable; on the other hand, perhaps the deal stinks. If somebody with power of attorney's signature was required for such transactions, that would be a safeguard. Relatives should try to take a healthy, yet not intrusive, interest in their older loved one's

---

Representation

- Grant people you can trust enduring power of attorney. It may never need to be used, but can save a lot of time, trouble and money if you lose mental capacity.
- Consider carefully to whom to grant attorney, in what form, and whether you want to impose conditions.
- Enduring power of attorney can help in other fields in which strictly speaking it does not apply, such as medical and social care.
- If your relative loses mental capacity, don't forget to register an enduring power of attorney.
- Be ready to object to an application for registration if you are suspicious of those to whom it has been granted.
- If you are an attorney or a receiver, keep careful accounts and make sure that any state benefits are correct.
- Commission others to manage your relative's estate if necessary.
- If you live in Scotland, appoint welfare attorneys as well as legal attorneys.
- If you don't live in Scotland, consider making a formal declaration of health and social care proxies.
- Increase chances of health professionals respecting your views by demonstrating a deep understanding of your loved one's needs and desires.

---

financial affairs. Elderly people can be very vulnerable to salespeople trying to get one over on them.

As enduring power of attorney represents trust, it can be useful in other fields. For example, if you wish to inspect your relative's records, such as health or social services records, the fact that you were trusted enough to be granted enduring power of attorney is usually recognized as sufficient to ensure you are given a look. This is even though, strictly speaking, power of attorney applies only to financial and legal matters and not to medical or social care.

It can have an even wider effect. Outside Scotland, there is no mechanism recognized in law for proxy decision-making in medicine. Thus, I cannot act as if I were my mother when decisions have to be taken about her medical treatment in the way that I can act as if I were her in dealing with stocks and shares and even giving Christmas presents. Such a law has never been put in place outside Scotland because it might be abused in the field of euthanasia. In the absence of such a mechanism, to be able to say that you hold enduring power of attorney does have an advantage. Because enduring power of attorney represents the maximum means the legal system allows for somebody in effect to demonstrate their trust in somebody else, being able to say that you hold this power carries weight everywhere.

To grant enduring power of attorney, you have to use a special form which you can get from a stationer which supplies legal documents, or a solicitor can draw up a tailor-made document. Your signature on the form has to be witnessed by an independent person, who could be, but does not have to be, a solicitor. Each attorney also has to sign in the presence of a witness and it is advisable to do this as soon as possible after the donor has signed.

It is tempting to limit the power of attorney – to say that a house or stocks and shares cannot be sold, for instance. In fact, those who need an attorney at all need one with the widest possible powers. People who develop severe dementia and have to go into a care home, for example, will need attorneys to be able to do everything possible to generate as much money as they can from the estate to provide the best possible care. For example, suppose an elderly person with dementia is granted NHS Continuing Care and wants to receive that NHS free care at home rather than in a nursing home (pages 577–8). Their health body might say it would cover the cost of all care needed throughout the day but that hiring help during the night would exceed the amount it would have paid to a nursing home. In that case, money from the person's estate might be used to pay somebody to help out during the night. This might make the difference between the person being able to live at home rather than in a nursing home.

Choosing an Attorney

Before you sign, you need to think carefully about who should be your attorney. Obviously you want somebody you can trust. You also need to think about who should step into the breach should that person die, lose his or her own mental capacity or be unwell or abroad for a time. Some people sign two powers of attorney or make provision for a fallback alternative in one power of attorney. Thus they may appoint their partner to be their main attorney and their children in the event that their partner is no longer able to manage their affairs.

If you appoint more than one attorney you have to decide whether they need to get each other's agreement for every decision – in which case it is a 'joint' attorneyship – or whether you will allow them to act separately – known as 'several' power of attorney. If the attorneys are appointed jointly, all their signatures will be required on every cheque and the attorneys cannot reach decisions unless they are in agreement. If one of the attorneys is unable to act, perhaps being out of the country or sick, the attorneyship can have no force.

You could make the attorneyship 'joint and several'. For instance, if you consider you could trust Peter more than Paul and Peter is going to be on hand to do most of the work anyway but you do not want to offend Paul, you could grant a joint and several attorneyship, with specified areas of authority for Peter. Or you could provide for several powers, so that each attorney can do what he or she is good at without constant reference to the other, but you could require that all the attorneys should have to sign for transactions above a certain amount of money. Some people set up completely different attorneyships for different areas of their estate.

Attorneys, like receivers, cannot charge unless they are professional persons such as solicitors or accountants. They are not meant to profit from the role at all, in the same way that members of a family trusteeship are forbidden by law from profiting from that role. But attorneys are not expected to be left out of pocket, so they can claim full reasonable expenses. They can also make gifts of the kind the donor would have made, as long as the terms do not prevent this.

Those choosing an attorney need to consider whether any conflicts could arise between their interests and the interests of the attorneys, particularly if the latter are the main beneficiaries of their will. Clearly, if you need to be looked after in a care home and the money from the estate must be used to pay the bills, then Peter and Paul face a conflict between buying you the best care possible and inheriting as much as possible. It is also very important to consider whether the prospective attorneys would be likely to disagree between themselves. If they would, you could grant the power severally. Or you could find somebody outside the immediate family to act as attorney – though clearly, if you choose a solicitor, this will be expensive.

On the other hand, you want people prepared to take some time and trouble to ensure that your money generates as much income as possible. So you need somebody who can manage money well and is prepared to give some thought to investing it, or is capable of obtaining sound advice and acting on it. If he or she stands to inherit some of that cash at the end of the day, that may provide an additional incentive. For instance, if your estate has to be liquidated to pay care home bills, you want somebody sufficiently at home with money or at least enthusiastic about it to look for an investment scheme, so that the estate regenerates itself as well as delivering a certain amount each year to pay the bills.[3] Attorneys do not need to do this themselves: as in the case of receivership, it is perfectly in order to delegate tasks to stockbrokers, accountants, solicitors, estate agents and so on, even though the estate will have to pay their fees. There again, this may provide a disincentive to offload work on to such professionals if there is the prospect of inheritance at the end of the day.

Registering Attorneyship

The full powers of an attorney come into effect only if and when the donor loses mental capacity. When this happens, the attorney or attorneys must register the fact on a form obtained from the Public Guardianship Office. They do not need to provide medical evidence unless the particular attorneyship says they should. When they register, there is an opportunity for close relatives to object, and the final decision on whether to confirm or refuse the registration lies with the Public Guardianship Office. The donor must also be notified and can object, unless it is considered that giving notice would harm or distress him or her.

It is important that attorneys realize that the onus to register is on them, not on the family solicitor, even if the solicitor witnessed the signing. Many attorneys probably assume that the solicitor will do this – we tend to think that solicitors do anything connected with courts – but they do not have this obligation. Good family solicitors will advise attorneys, or remind them that registration is necessary, and also check that it has been done if property is to be sold, but they do not have to.

The power for the donor or close relatives to object to registration and thus the activation of the attorneys' power can be important. At least three close relatives must be informed. Often prospective attorneys are close relatives; they do not count, so there must be three in addition to them. There is a set order of priority for informing relatives of the applications for registration: first, the husband or wife; second, children (including those adopted but not stepchildren); then the donor's parents; next, their brothers and sisters; the widow or widower of the donor's child; grandchildren; nephews and nieces; aunts and uncles; and finally the donor's first cousins. Those relatives who have been notified have four weeks to object. Objection is dealt with by correspondence, but if this does not enable the Public Guardianship Office to come to a decision to dismiss the objection or to withhold the attorneyship, a hearing in London is held.

The donor or other relatives may object on one or more of the following grounds: that the registration is not valid, that it no longer applies, that the application is premature because the donor is still mentally capable, that the prospective attorney or attorneys have committed fraud or put unnecessary pressure on the donor to make the power of attorney, and finally that the prospective attorneys are unsuitable to hold that role. If the Public Guardianship Office is convinced through evidence (medical evidence in the case of the first three types of objection), it can refuse registration. However, if the potential donor is mentally incapable, an application for receivership will almost certainly then have to be made.

It is not only millionaires whose attorneyship provokes objections. A study found that the average size of the donor's estate in contested cases in 2001 was £150,000 and typically consisted of a property worth £120,000 and savings of £30,000.[4] However, of all the applications to register enduring power of attorney in 2001, less than 1 per cent went to the stage of the attended hearing. Denzil Lush, the Master of the Court of Protection, who carried out this survey, commented:

> Although objections occur in a very small percentage of cases, when they do occur they are time-consuming, stressful and acrimonious for all concerned. They can be expensive too, and usually the donor bears the cost. Many objections could be avoided – or more easily rebutted – if, when the power is made, a little more thought were given to the possibility that someone might object to an application to register the power.[5]

The person granting the power of enduring power of attorney can cancel the power at any time before application is made for registration. However, if the donor wishes to cancel it after registration, he or she has to secure the agreement of the Public Guardianship Office, which has to satisfy itself that the donor is now mentally capable of coming to that decision.

Acting as an Attorney or Receiver

Anybody contemplating acting as an attorney after registration or applying to become a receiver (or in Scotland a guardian) should think about things carefully before going ahead. These forms of representation can involve a lot of work. You will have to use a separate bank account and keep all the money connected with the attorneyship separate from your own. You will need to keep receipts, file them carefully and keep full accounts. A receiver will have to submit annual accounts to the Public Guardianship Office and consult it over many steps. Attorneys will need to cover themselves so that they can show that they did not misappropriate money and that the steps they took were in the donor's best interests: they will have to be able to respond should anybody raise questions about their attorneyship with the Public Guardianship Office. If you are claiming the cost of phone calls made in connection with the attorneyship, you will have to comb through your phone bills to select the relevant items and then total them. You will need to keep separate books of stamps, and so on. This is all on top of work you will have to do which is not strictly speaking part of being an attorney, but certainly is part of caring for a elderly relative whose mental capacities have diminished: ensuring that he or she is well cared for, wherever he or she is living.

Other unforeseen work may arise. If staff have to be hired, you will be responsible not only for paying them but also for ensuring that you do not fall foul of the law on anything from statutory sick pay to National Insurance contributions (pages 263–4). You might have to take legal action on behalf of the donor of the attorney; he or she might have legal action taken against him or her. Donors' property might require considerable attention.

In view of the considerable amount of work involved, it is tempting for attorneys to divide up the tasks. Helen, for example, living hundreds of miles from her father, might suggest that she should look after the financial side of things, so that bank statements are sent to her and she applies for any necessary state benefits; while Jane, holding joint power with her sister but living much closer, should concern herself with actual care, whether in a care home or at home with paid staff. But this approach, logical as it can seem, has dangers.

The reality is that in the field of eldercare, legal and financial matters are inextricably bound up with supervising care. You cannot select a care home without understanding how homes set their fees and how people pay the bills. You cannot work out additional steps you could take to enrich your elderly relatives' lives without understanding their income and their outgoings. Conversely, the person who is supposed to deal with the financial side of things may not realize that steps have to be taken, because her involvement with the caring side of things is too intermittent. For instance, when an older person goes into hospital, the Department for Work and Pensions, usually through a local Social Security Office, has to be informed lest the patient should continue to receive various state benefits which the rules decree must stop when somebody is in hospital for more than a certain minimum period. Helen, far away from the action yet meticulously checking bank statements, may not realise what has happened while Jane, who is busying herself providing her father with the food he likes and keeping up his spirits while he is in hospital may assume that if there are financial matters to consider, Helen will be attending to them. Yet all this is a serious business. If benefits are paid which should not have been, they have to be repaid. Attorneys (as well as other legal representatives like receivers) may be held personally liable if the donor's money is not handled in a responsible manner. Whatever informal arrangements may have been made between attorneys are irrelevant in that situation: both heads are on the block if a mistake has been made.

Of course the reality is that people agree to become attorneys hoping that their relative will remain mentally able and so the attorneyship will never need to be registered and thus brought into full effect. They acknowledge that if they do not become attorneys there is simply nobody else around who would. But the immensity of the responsibility remains the same.

Advice and Further Information

Further details about these legal instruments can be found in free advisory booklets published by the Public Guardianship Office, the Office of the Public Guardian in Scotland and the Office of Care and Protection in Northern Ireland. We have already noted Alzheimer Scotland's useful publication (page 522); other organizations such as the Alzheimer's Society and Age Concern publish factsheets. There are useful textbooks, such as Gordon Ashton's *Elderly People and the Law* (Butterworth/Age Concern) and Aled Griffiths and Gwyneth Roberts' *The Law and Elderly People* (Routledge).

It is a very good idea to discuss matters of representation thoroughly with your solicitor before you go ahead. For instance, if you are proposing to grant enduring or in Scotland continuing power of attorney you may have nagging fears which a solicitor could help you circumvent or tackle, and if you have reservations about a particular relative to whom you might grant attorney, your solicitor ought to be able to suggest ways round the problem.

Chapter 19
Nursing and Other Care

Though throughout the UK there is a well-established system for proxy decision-making for legal and financial decisions, there are no such established arrangements in the fields of day-to-day nursing, medical and personal care, though these may be far more important to elderly people. There is an exception: Scotland, where new legislation which came into effect in 2002 has established representation on behalf of others in the worlds of both medicine and general care through the appointment by individuals of 'welfare attorneys'. Elsewhere, there is still no recognized means in law to speak on behalf of somebody else in these fields. Somebody with registered enduring power of attorney, who can sell a person's house (in theory without even informing him or her, a perhaps justifiable move if the news would be upsetting), has no proxy powers in the care world. Attorneys and other relatives may be consulted by paid workers in these fields, but their status remains that of a consultee only. In *Chapter 14: Your Life in their Hands*, we examined the position of relatives in the the offering or withholding of potentially life-saving treatment (pages 404–6). But the question of medical, nursing and care representation does not arise only in these situations.

If your relative goes into hospital, there are many decisions which are made which do not involve withholding potentially life-saving treatment but are nonetheless significant, such as catheterization (pages 427–8). Were the patient *compos mentis*, he or she would be in a position to grant or withhold consent for steps such as this after hearing the pros and cons from the professionals. In the absence of this possibility, nobody else is automatically asked to give consent for nursing decisions such as this on behalf of the patient, and the patient's consent is often simply assumed. Yet there are countless decisions taken day and night in caring for people who have lost mental capacity in hospitals and long-stay NHS institutions which could be questioned.

This is not to say that relatives' view will necessarily be best or that they will not often be asked for a view, but their lack of any power means that they are not likely even to be consulted in many of these cases and, if they are, their views will not necessarily count for very much. Even in Scotland, appointed welfare attorneys are unlikely to be consulted about every important care decision and may well need to ask to have their views heard.

For example, you turn up at your aunt's long-stay NHS ward and, in the course of conversation, you ask her whether she needs to go to the lavatory. She says she does and you summon a health care assistant. The assistant tells you your aunt was toileted half an hour before you arrived, but as she has apparently asked to use the lavatory then she must be helped to do so. This involves struggling to place a piece of stout cloth under her, hitching the corners of this to a crossbar, winching her up into the air using a hoist, lowering her on to a bed, changing a continence pad if this proves necessary and then winching her back again. As your aunt has severe dementia and the staff do not seek to reassure her by gently and repeatedly explaining what they are doing, this exercise causes her much distress, as she seems to have absolutely no idea what is being done to her. Indeed, every time it takes place when you are visiting, you hear her distressed calls from behind the closed door of her bedroom. So when you hear that she has recently been toileted and knowing that, in view of her dementia, she may think she wants to go to the lavatory when she does not, you say to the health worker, 'In that case, please don't bother.' But the health care assistant insists on going ahead, pointing out that the rules say that if the patient has asked to go to the lavatory this request must be complied with. You may point out that were your aunt *compos mentis* there is no doubt that, on being reminded of this fact, she would immediately reverse her request. But her dementia does not allow her to absorb facts and arguments and reason logically, and you have no power to step in and alter the course of events. As a result in this case the views of the person with advanced dementia carry more weight than those of the person who would like to represent her interests and is *compos mentis*.

Or perhaps your aunt is kept in her own bedroom, with the door wedged open so that staff can see her as they walk past. She is frequently distraught, calling out repeatedly, 'Help!' You feel she needs much one-to-one reassurance and that she is most likely to receive this not isolated in her own room but in the communal lounge. But staff dismiss her frequent calls for help as meaningless repetition and say that being in the lounge troubles her more. You suspect the real reason is they do not relish the bother of providing reassurance and find her calling out irritating. But neither you nor any other relative is in a position to speak for your aunt and insist on choosing the place in which she should spend her days: you can only ask.

Restraint

Another area to consider is restraint. Because of scandals in the past involving people with dementia being strapped down, these days it is very difficult to get the managers of care homes to impose artificial restraint of any kind, even when there is a high chance that this would prevent patients from hurting themselves and, in at least some cases, would be unlikely to make them feel they were being confined. People with dementia are liable to fall over. They therefore tend to hurt themselves, causing bruising, perhaps breaking shoulders, wrists and hips. They will probably not be able to remember that this sequence of events happened the day before or five minutes previously. How do you prevent them getting up and falling again? Were they *compos mentis*, they might plead that something like a car seatbelt should gently restrain them in their armchair, but you are unlikely to find this course of action being countenanced. Instead, the manager might agree to place furniture judiciously in front of their chairs – although this would be more dangerous than a seatbelt since they might fall in an effort to get past it.

Similarly, at night restraining measures such as cot-sides attached to beds are frowned upon because they smack of forcible restraint, even though they could prevent a nasty tumble out of bed. (They have to be used very carefully because the most agile will climb over them and fall further.) Instead, you may find a home suggesting that your relative's mattress should be placed on the floor since this is not seen as restraint, even though the manager will say its purpose is to ensure that if your relative should get up in the night he or she will not have so far to fall. Yet people with dementia could find it extremely confusing and distressing to wake to find themselves sleeping on the floor. If they manage to struggle to their feet, they might fall.

Restraint is a difficult area.[1] Of course no one wants physical restraint being deployed as an alternative to measures which involve no restraint and which might well help – making sure the environment is safer, say, by giving a person a walking frame, encouraging him or her to wear hip and knee pads to reduce the risk of injury, above all having sufficient staff around to help a person who wishes to move around and needs help to do so. Of course the practice of automatically placing a gate across the bedrooms of all mobile residents with any degree of dementia is outrageous (and 'gating' may still occur). But restraint is the sort of matter about which relatives ought to have more of a say, and even be able to speak on behalf of care home residents or patients in long-stay NHS units (pages 345–6). If relatives are consulted about such matters in care homes it is often to ask them to sign a consent form for cot-sides (presumably then rendering the home less liable if the residents should harm themselves in an accident provoked by the restraining device).

Sexual Apartheid

One area of decision-making involving the daily lives of people in long-stay NHS units and in care homes is gender separation. A partner or close relative, even armed with an enduring power of attorney, has no power to override professionals in facilitating contact for a relative without his or her full mental powers with members of the opposite or the same sex, even if convinced this is what the person would like.

Gender separation is seen to be an advance in hospitals, and probably many people would not want to be in a mixed ward if they were in hospital for a short time. But when you are in a care home or long-stay NHS unit, the situation is rather different: these places are your home for the rest of your life. Just because you are old and frail does not mean that you cannot respond romantically, sensually and sexually to others. Almost certainly, however, any physical contact will be countenanced only if it is initiated by a professional, such as a reflexologist, who applies manual pressure to various parts of the soles of the feet on the understanding that this can affect internal organs.

As a result, immobile elderly men and women are often kept sitting in armchairs in separate bedrooms during the day, or contact is discouraged in the lounge if there is any hint that it might involve romance. Patients or residents might benefit much from holding or stroking each other's hands. Clearly, they cannot be let loose on each other without some provision for another person to step in if it is felt that one or other party is unhappy. But that is a different matter from keeping them forever in effective isolation.[2] Were the dementia sufferers themselves able to make a choice, would it be separation? If research has shown that they respond positively to therapy such as patting and stroking dogs, why should they not benefit from sensory stimulation by each other?

What Relatives Can Do

In all these situations there is at present little more that relatives can do than build up a relationship with health and social care professionals which makes it clear that they wish to be involved in decision-making, that the elderly person trusts them (as demonstrated perhaps by the fact that they have been granted enduring power of attorney) and that they have a deep understanding of the individual's wishes and desires.

However, before an older person becomes mentally incapacitated, there seems to me no reason why he should not declare in the presence of witnesses that he would like to appoint a particular person or persons to be treated as his proxy in matters of medical and social care decision-making. Such an arrangement may not at present be recognized in English law (although there is much pressure for change in the law and it is possible that it will be changed in the near future), but the existence of such a declaration could strengthen the hand of a relative.

Declarations could potentially be useful in three types of circumstance: first, when decisions are being made about the withholding of life-sustaining treatment for patients who cannot for whatever reason voice their own wishes (pages 452–4); second, when decisions are made about all other types of medical and nursing treatment but again when older people are unable to speak up for themselves; third, when decisions are made about the lifestyle of older people in care homes and long-stay NHS units whose mental capacity has declined very significantly.

Welfare Power of Attorney

In devising the form this declaration could take, we can look to a new mechanism specially devised to cope with this need enshrined in the first major piece of legislation passed by the Scottish Parliament, the Adults with Incapacity (Scotland) Act, 2000. This Act has introduced a particularly interesting and potentially useful tool entirely unlike anything in England, Wales and Northern Ireland, called 'welfare power of attorney'. People who would like others to take personal decisions on their health and social care if mental incapacity prevents their doing this themselves can appoint proxies called welfare attorneys. The power of the welfare attorney comes into effect only if and when mental capacity is lost (in which case the attorneyship must be registered with the Office of the Public Guardian in Scotland). If a person has appointed a welfare attorney, then a doctor who knows that this is the case must seek the proxy's agreement if it is reasonable and practical to do so before he or she treats the 'granter'. Furthermore, there are procedures for cases in which the attorney or attorneys disagree with the doctor. Therefore the position of the welfare attorney, who will often be the closest relative, is enormously strengthened compared with that of close relatives in the remainder of the UK.

It is integral to the Scottish legislation that those appointed as welfare attorneys should take steps to ascertain the wishes and needs of the granters, consult them frequently and allow them to continue to take as many decisions as possible. The Scottish Executive has drawn up a detailed code of practice in this area which, together with much other material on welfare attorneyship in Scotland, is available by post from the Executive's Civil Law Division or online at www.scotland.gov.uk/justice/incapacity. Attorneys are also expected to ascertain the views of the nearest relative and the primary carer.

Whilst older people outside Scotland cannot appoint welfare attorneys, they can at least adopt some of the procedures being introduced in Scotland in the hope that this will strengthen the hand of their close relatives. They could make a declaration appointing people whom they wish to act on their behalf in the field or medical and social care field, signed in front of a witness such as a solicitor, and the person or people they appointed could also sign in front of witnesses. The declaration itself could include a clause to say that the person involved was not under any undue pressure to sign it, and a certificate could be obtained from a doctor certifying that the signatory had full mental capacity on the day on which it was signed. You could use two documents which have been drawn up by the Scottish Executive: a model certificate granting welfare power of attorney and a model form to be completed by a person certifying that the granter was able to understand the nature and extent of the power he or she was conveying on the date in question. Another very useful source of information is *Dementia: Money and Legal Matters: A Guide*, published and regularly updated by the voluntary organization Alzheimer Scotland.

It is important to point out that such a declaration outside Scotland might well be disregarded. But it might nonetheless strengthen the hand of relatives in some situations, although it is clearly not going to elevate their status fundamentally in the way that seems likely to happen in Scotland with attorneys expressing wishes as if they were the person they represent. It is unlikely to enable proxies to override doctors or care staff, but it should certainly strengthen their hand in arguing about anything from restraint and room sharing to resuscitation and the withholding of life-sustaining medication and nutrients. At the same time, relatives north and south of the border need to work as closely as they can with professionals and to strengthen their position by demonstrating a deep understanding of the older person's needs and desires, based on their own contact, perhaps over a lifetime.

A final situation in which representation in the care world could be beneficial involves people who are *compos mentis*. Your elderly mother goes into hospital. You, her closest relative, are not on hand and you telephone the ward to ask how she is. You may well find you are told very little, even though you know – and you point this out to the ward manager – that your mother would have no objection whatsoever to your learning all the details of her condition. The ward manager says that confidentiality restrictions prevent him releasing more than a minimum amount of information. Similarly, you visit your mother in hospital and she feels too weak to speak up for herself when she sees doctors, nurses and perhaps social workers. It is only she who can explain the nature and severity of her symptoms and how she is feeling in general. But she might well wish she could hand over all other matters of communication to a partner or son or daughter whom she trusts.

In this case, welfare attorneyship cannot be deployed (since it comes into effect only when mental capacity is lost). However, older patients could make their wishes about representation in these circumstances very clear to all concerned.

New Legislation

In 2003, the government invited public comment on draft legislation in England and Wales which would provide representation for people with significant mental incapacity. The Mental Incapacity Bill 2003, which might become law in 2004 or 2005, would introduce for the first time proxy decision-making in the fields of health and personal welfare.

Unlike the situation in Scotland, there would be only one mechanism to cover legal and financial matters and health and personal welfare; people granting attorney could mix and match as they wished, giving whichever powers they liked and to whoever they liked, either jointly (so that they must all join together in any decision) or severally (which means they can act independently all together). This new mechanism would be called 'lasting power of attorney'. It would replace the existing enduring power of attorney.

Not only does the Bill seek to provide for proxy decision-making outside the legal and financial spheres, it also sets down new rules for people holding power of attorney. They would have to operate under a statutory requirement that all steps and decisions must be taken in the best interests of the grantor of attorney. They would have to involve the grantor as far as possible, have regard to his or her past and present wishes and feelings and consult with others to gain views on the past and present wishes and feelings of the grantor and the type of considerations that he or she would have been likely to bring to bear in making a decision. In addition the decision taken should always be the least restrictive one available.

The draft legislation specifically provides that where a lasting power of attorney has enabled decisions to be made about a grantor's personal welfare, an attorney should be able to give or refuse consent to medical treatment being given or continued. In other words, a personal welfare lasting power of attorney would authorise the attorney to make healthcare decisions, although this would be subject to any restrictions that the grantor had included in the lasting power of attorney document.

The legislation proposes to establish a new Court of Protection to administer the new system and to investigate concerns and complaints about attorneyships which have been granted. This court would include judges who would be able to hear cases on the ground in regional offices. A Public Guardian would administer the day-to-day running of the system.

Where someone had not granted a lasting power of attorney, the court would be empowered to appoint a deputy or deputies to act on their behalf if mental capacity deteriorated. These deputies would be authorized to deal with a specified matter or matters, for a specified period of time, subject to review.

Enduring powers of attorney which have already been granted would not be revoked but they would operate under the rules set out in the new legislation, which are very similar to the existing rules. However, once the new legislation was in place, people who had granted enduring power of attorney in the past and still have mental capacity could usefully consider replacing this with a new lasting power of attorney to take in health and personal welfare matters as well as legal and financial ones. Or, they could complement their existing enduring power of attorney with a new lasting power restricted to health and personal welfare.

As with power of attorney in the legal and financial fields, it is of the utmost importance that you should select very carefully to whom to grant powers and how (pages 525–27). If the new legislation is passed as it stands, people will not have much control over their own destiny once they have granted lasting power of enduring covering the care sphere. To be sure, attorneys will have to take decisions in the best interests of those on whose behalf they are acting. But who is going to make sure that they do? You could have quite a fight on your hands if you had granted such rights but later disagreed with what was being done in your name.[3]

Advance Directives

An advance directive or living will is a statement by a mentally competent adult indicating wishes about medical treatment if, at some later stage he or she should lose mental capacity. It can be made in addition to appointing people to act on his or her behalf should he or she lose capacity. Tips on making living wills are given in a useful factsheet produced by the Alzheimer's Society entitled *Future Medical Treatment: Advance Statements and Advance Directives or Living Wills*, which is freely available on the organization's website or by post to members and non-members alike. We noted in *Chapter 14: Your Life in their Hands* that the General Medical Council has told doctors to respect any advance refusal of treatment where it is considered valid in circumstances where it is clinically relevant (page 453). However, this has the status only of guidance. In Scotland, on the other hand, the Adults with Incapacity (Scotland) Act 2000 requires doctors to take into account the past and present wishes of their patients when deciding upon treatment, and living wills are considered to be an indication of past wishes.

The Mental Incapacity Bill 2003 referred to on page 539 seeks to clarify and strengthen advance directives to refuse treatment. If enacted, it will increase the status of such directives so long as they are made appropriately, the person in question has lost mental capacity and the circumstances in which a decision is to be made are applicable.

The term advance directive or living will is usually considered in the medical context. However, there is nothing to stop people expressing their wishes in case they should be unable to do so in other spheres, such as how they would like to be cared for and by whom. Such declarations are often called 'advance statements' and are also explored in the Alzheimer's Society paper mentioned above. They are not covered by the Mental Incapacity Bill 2003.

Part Eight
Carers

Chapter 20
A Vital Role

Context

We all know that care for elderly people in most cultures, and in the past in our own, has normally been provided by their children. Lack of children to perform this function used to mean the horror of the workhouse. The need to guarantee care in old age is credited with the overpopulation of the Developing World. Nowadays, the state has taken it upon itself to fulfil this role in theory, though we all know that the practice is far from perfect, that something of the workhouse may still await those whose nearest and dearest consign them wholly to state care. People still often feel that they have a responsibility of their own towards their older relatives and feel guilty when they seek to evade it. Contrary to popular opinion, a surprising number make no effort to evade it and take the responsibility as natural. Close relatives, friends and spouses care for a larger number of elderly people than do paid care workers.

These close relatives, friends and partners, dubbed 'carers' in the world of eldercare, are in theory best placed to look after those older people who need help since they are more likely to be able to empathize with them and meet their social and emotional needs, as well as being highly motivated to help with physical tasks. They still have to earn a living themselves, of course. You might imagine that much of the public money spent on eldercare would go to help carers. Alas, the opposite is the case. The government talks about 'caring for carers', but has not put its money where its mouth is, as we shall see (page 568) Low-earners who care for more than 35 hours a week are entitled to receive the Carer's Allowance,[1] a miserly £43.15 a week, with an additional £25.10 if they are on Income Support or the Guarantee Credit element of Pension Credit (page 492). Nonetheless, as many as five million elderly people in the UK are looked after by carers. In some cases, the carers are providing a moderate amount of support, but about 1.2 million provide a really significant amount of physical work and personal care for older people. [2] Carers thus provide not only the largest, but also by far the most cost-effective cog of the eldercare machine. If you calculate how much it would cost for the elderly people currently looked after by carers to be supported by paid care workers in their own homes or in care homes, the figure runs into billions of pounds. Carers UK, one of the leading non-government organizations representing the interests of carers, has put the figure at an astonishing £57 billion. [3]

It is useful to distinguish two main types of carer. First there is what I would call the main caring person, that is, somebody, be they a son, daughter, friend, possibly but less usually a partner, who does not live under the same roof as the elderly person in need of support but who has decided to look out for that person in all sorts of ways and to fight his or her corner whenever necessary. There may be more than one such person, and in such cases there may be a division of duties. For instance, in the case of my mother, my brother took on the responsibility of checking bank statements and ensuring that she received her pension and other entitlements, and later overseeing the sale of her house to pay care home fees. I was the person who would accompany her to hospital appointments and other consultations, visit frequently, provide moral and practical help, remain continuously available on the telephone, if necessary respond at short notice, and try to get her all the equipment and support I could muster. I was acknowledged as the main caring relative so that when, for instance, my mother's social worker was proposing to carry out her community care assessment (pages 273–7), I was told that I might like to be present, as is recommended in Department of Health guidance. This says that the views and interests of carers, including those who do not provide a lot of live-in help, should be taken into account when a community care assessment is carried out.

The other main type of carer is a person who usually but not always lives with the cared-for person and provides regular and substantial help. Such people are defined in the first Act of Parliament for carers, the Carers (Recognition and Services) Act of 1995, as 'persons who provide or intend to provide substantial care for a disabled, elderly or ill person on a regular basis'. People who provide care for payment, such as care workers, are excluded from this definition, as are volunteer carers who provide care through a volunteers' agency. To be included in this category, it is not essential to do nothing but look after an older person, or indeed put in a huge number of hours: some people in this situation also have paid employment outside the home, and much of their assistance may be emotional support. The point is that the support is regular and substantial, and that the cared-for person would be at real risk if it ceased. Since 1995, people acting as carers in this second category have received considerable recognition within the health and social services support system and valuable rights of their own as carers.

A Statutory Carer

Becoming the carer of your parents or parent, or indeed your spouse or partner, is a choice: we have no legal obligation to look after those nearest and dearest to us – though we may feel a moral obligation to do so. Many still choose to care for a father, mother, partner or friend in need of help as a result of age and affliction. Fortunately, they now do so in a context in which the state is not only obliged to support elderly and disabled people but also their carers.

As a result, unlike previous times, there is now the opportunity for people who become carers to have themselves viewed by the state not as the thankless providers of 24-hour care who abandon the rest of their lives, but as people opting to give help but maintaining their own jobs and a life of their own. This means that once their caring role is over they have a life to which to return. They are also more likely to find caring fulfilling if they are not doing it single-handedly for 24 hours a day.

Should You Become a Carer?

If you are contemplating becoming the carer of an older person, you still need to weigh up very carefully the pros and cons of such a step. Though you can get support in theory, the practice may be doubtful. It is very easy to drift into becoming a carer without making a conscious decision to do so.

Suppose you are in your late fifties, your partner in his seventies.

He pulls his weight around the house while you go out to work or carry on self-employed work from home. But he goes into hospital and when he comes out is unable to continue shopping and cooking – indeed, now he needs human help to wash, dress and move around, as well as a good deal of emotional support. Automatically you start not only taking on all the household chores which he used to undertake but also helping with personal care, as well as providing emotional and moral support, not least at night during the long hours when he cannot sleep. At first you desperately try to keep up your old life outside your relationship, but you soon find you are too tired even to consider pursuing old hobbies, while the relentless round of work and support also takes its toll on your paid work.

Five years on, your partner dies. In addition to your sadness at his death, you also have to cope with the loss of the contribution to the household budget he once provided. But when you cast around for employment in your own field, you find it is not easy to step back to the position you once occupied. Technological and other changes have passed you by, younger people have taken over positions of authority, and prospective employers hold ageist attitudes which work against you now that you are no longer young yourself. While you may consider that the years of full-time caring enabled you to develop skills and knowledge in many new important areas, your prospective employers feel that such caring was not proper work.

People also drift into becoming carers of their parents. If you asked your father or mother to come and live with you and share your household or live in a granny annex you might feel it was churlish if you did not become his or her carer should the need arise.

Nor do you necessarily have to be living in the same household to be providing regular and substantial care. Many older people themselves become carers not only of their partners but also of friends living close by. They find themselves popping in more and more frequently, day and night, until they can certainly be considered to be providing regular and substantial care. This may well have a deleterious impact on their own social life, perhaps their financial situation and even maybe their mental and physical health.

Carers

- Caring for an elderly relative at home can be enormously rewarding and enriching, but can bring significant draw-backs.
- New legislation throughout the UK has given carers a right to an assessment of their needs.
- Refer yourself to social services and ask for an assessment of your needs as a carer.
- Do research before the assessment so that you can figure out what to secure from social services.
- Insist on maintaining your own employment status and social world while a carer.
- Ensure you get training.
- Plan breaks from caring.
- Alert your GP to your carer status.
- Allocate support roles between family members: don't let yourself take on everything.
- Seek out a local carers' centre for advice, support and contact with similarly placed carers.

Other people make a quite deliberate decision to become somebody's carer. There are infinite variations. One situation with which I am familiar involved a widowed lady in her seventies choosing to become the carer of a man 20 years younger who was suffering from cancer. They had known each other for many years, as they had been members of the same church, and she invited him into her house and cared for him.

Whether we drift into becoming the carer of an older person or we take a decisive step, it is extremely important to weigh up fully beforehand the pros and cons both for ourselves and for the person to be cared for.

Advantages
The first advantage to the older person of having a partner, child or close friend as their carer must be that the caring will probably be better.

Many people seem to imagine that the only qualities necessary in a carer, whether paid or unpaid, are a warm heart and common sense. In my view, important as these qualities are, others are also essential. The first is knowledge. If you do not know the best way to help a frail older person get up from an armchair or car seat, you could cause physical harm, particularly if bones are weakened through osteoporosis. If you are not aware of the danger of pressure sores and fail to take action to avert them, such as ensuring the person cared for sits in different positions or is turned during the night, then however kind and well motivated you may be, you could be unwittingly responsible for painful avoidable injury.

The second essential quality is time. A study by the Health Advisory Service of the care of older people on acute hospital wards in 1999 showed that lack of time and not being available to talk underpinned many difficulties.[4] When older people are staying in hospital, specialist medical procedures take up only a small proportion of the time spent caring for them: most of the care involves help with washing, dressing, feeding, drinking, going to the lavatory and giving tablets, and it is during these times that most opportunities for interaction occur. A team from the School of Nursing and Midwifery of the University of Sheffield, which drew up a guide to good practice in acute hospital care for older people entitled *Dignity on the Ward: Promoting Excellence in Care*, published by Help the Aged in 2001, highlighted this reality.[5] They concluded that 'having sufficient time' and 'talking as a vehicle to building and maintaining relationships' were absolute prerequisites for effective caring.

People who are caring for older people need to take the trouble to talk to them, to explain what they are doing and to reassure when necessary. Anybody suffering from dementia requires explanations which may need to be repeated again and again. Time, and time to talk, require that the care-giver is not under pressure to get on to the next task or the next person and has an incentive to communicate with the cared-for person.

Although professional care workers can in theory offer these things as much as a caring relative, there is less likelihood that they actually will. Many agency workers are under extreme pressure to get on to the next person. In the isolation of somebody's home, will they have the same incentive to talk sensitively that a close relative would have? No survey has been conducted to find out, but what do you think the reality would be?

A third essential quality is empathy. Below I have reproduced the attributes of effective caring which the Sheffield team drew up, based on work by Dr B. Tarlow in the United States. All five of the elements the team identify as determining the quality of caring seem to me to rely on the ability of the person doing the caring to empathize with the cared-for person. If you can truly put yourself in the position of the person for whom you are caring, then you are more likely to be sensitive to their needs, to act in their best interests and to understand how to ensure some element of reciprocity, so the cared-for person feels that he or she is giving something as well as receiving. Here in particular the carer has the edge on the care worker. For it is surely only a person who has developed a relationship with somebody else over a long period of time who can really understand and thus empathize with him or her.

Attributes of effective caring
Prerequisites:
- Having sufficient time
- Being present and prepared to help when needed
- Talking as a vehicle to building and maintaining relationships.

Attributes which largely determine the quality of caring:

- Sensitivity to the needs of others and the ability to 'notice' when situations change
- Acting in the best interests of another
- Caring as feeling, based on concern or affection
- Caring as doing, to act on behalf of another (when judged appropriate)
- Reciprocity, a negotiated but often tacit understanding of the give and take in relationships. [6]

For example, as a son you may understand your father in countless ways. You know how he likes his tea without having to be told or reminded, you know what might interest him and what might distress him. This is not to say that strangers, whether they are paid workers, volunteers or friends, cannot provide very welcome stimulus to an older person in need of care, but it is the close relative or partner who is best endowed to care with understanding and sensitivity, simply through long association.

The related carer's understanding also makes possible empathy with pain or other affliction in a way that no paid or volunteer carer can quite match. You may not know what the pain of your mother's arthritis feels like, but because you know her, you understand what it will mean to her not to be able to do certain things any longer, and what can be done to make her feel better about her situation. And if there are particular psychological problems you are best able to help her through them. Finally and perhaps most importantly, your mother can benefit simply through knowing that her nearest and dearest are prepared to offer day-to-day support.

The cared-for person need not, however, be the only beneficiary of your care. It can help you too. First, you should expect to get satisfaction from doing your best for someone near to you. When he or she dies, you will know you offered the best care you could and that while you were caring he or she would have felt truly valued because of the support elicited from you.

Of course, a son or daughter who lives away and wishes to continue with life as it is can support a relative by phoning and visiting while others do the day-to-day caring and still gain much satisfaction. Everybody has to decide the extent of their caring role. Some people carry on with a job during the week and travel sometimes long distances at weekends when they become a parent's carer.

The caring will not necessarily last a very long time – you can of course generally not know. But if, say, your parent is in the early stages of dementia, seeing him or her through those early stages can be of enormous benefit, and later you will probably feel pleased that you were there when you were needed perhaps more than your parent will have needed anybody at any time since his or her early childhood. Once dementia has reached a point at which your parent is no longer aware of who you are or where or even who he or she is, you may well feel that you can hand over to a care home. But during that period when cognitive faculties are just beginning to deteriorate and insecurity, doubt and worry ravage a personality, a close relative with empathy based on a lifetime's understanding can be especially valuable.

Both carer and cared-for can expect to benefit from the enrichment of their relationship. We are told that the most important phase of the relationship between parents and children occurs when children are very young. But in many cases the relationship can be even closer when the parent is approaching the end of life and needs to receive instead of give care. At that later stage, relationships between parents and children are enriched by the family experiences they have shared and the understanding which has grown up over a lifetime. Relationships with our parents when they are older, whether they need our care or whether they do not, are relationships to look forward to and to cherish. Caring for an ailing parent need no more be seen as an irksome nuisance than our relationships with our young children are viewed in such a light.

Drawbacks

Nonetheless, the drawbacks of caring can be as striking as the benefits. At worst, the relationship can end up in abuse. Isolated at home, an older person can be the victim of slapping, bullying, tormenting and neglect.

In fact abusive behaviour by related carers is not that common. A survey of calls to the helpline of the charity Action on Elder Abuse between 1997 and 1999 found that most calls concerned care workers.[7] Abuse by a related carer accounted for less than 2 per cent of the calls. However, the research revealed quite a lot of abuse, mainly psychological and financial, by relatives and partners not identified as carers. Grandchildren, sons or son-in-laws, daughters or daughters-in-law can be involved in the fraudulent use of bank accounts, the misuse of power of attorney and the appointeeship system for handling state benefits. Probably common, although rarely picked up in surveys, is abuse through over-medication, in which a carer administers just a little bit extra of a drug designed to calm down an elderly person who is perhaps irritatingly demanding so he or she sleeps during the day and the carer gets some peace. So before older people agree to allow somebody to care for them, they should make sure they not only get on well with that person but also trust them.

They should also bear in mind the practical skills of the carer. Does he or she possess as much common sense and practical skill as would a paid care worker in a care home or coming into the home? Is he or she likely to gain an equivalent degree of expertise and training?

The carer faces real health risks, both physical and mental. In a care home or other place of work, health and safety regulations require that two people should share any lifting which may be necessary, and lifting anyway is much discouraged. However, carers at home can find themselves faced with having to move or lift an elderly person on their own. If they do not get appropriate training or equipment, for instance to get somebody in and out of the bath, they can hurt themselves badly and end up with persistent back problems and other afflictions, such as hernias. A study in 1998 for Carers UK revealed that 51 per cent of carers had suffered a physical injury such as a strained back since they had begun to care.[8] The mental stress involved in 24-hour responsibility for another person can also be gruelling. When carers' health does deteriorate, it is not only their problem. The admission of an elderly person to hospital or a care home often occurs as a result of deterioration in health of their main carer.

If you take on a caring role, it may also cost you financially. Your earning capacity, if you are working, will be reduced. The main state benefit for carers, Carers Allowance, is small, and often will not meet a carer's own living costs, let alone the additional care costs of laundry, transport and so on. A lot of carers find they are dipping into their savings. A survey by Carers UK in 2001 found that more than three-quarters of the carers involved said they had become worse off as carers; one in three had trouble paying gas and electricity bills, and one in four had had to ask friends or family for financial help.[9] And if you give up your job to become a carer, you will lose not only the money but also the status you derive from work and the social world that goes with it.

The cared-for person could lose certain state benefits (page 174) although, as we shall see in Chapter 21, the state also provides limited financial rewards for carers.

Becoming a carer is also bound to involve some loss of the freedoms which most of us take for granted. The extent of this will depend a great deal on the condition of the care recipient. If you have returned home to live with an elderly aunt who is suffering from, say, severe arthritis and emphysema but is mentally fine, your life will probably not be overly constrained. You will provide reassurance that another person is in the house should she feel unwell during the night and, while you may well be out at work most days, you can provide general assistance and companionship when you are at home. If, on the other hand, your aunt is in the middle stages of dementia, you may find that you dare not even pop out to post a letter. You cannot just leave somebody who might get up as soon as you have left the house and turn on the gas or fall over, forgetting that because of a previous injury she should be keeping still. In any case, a dementia sufferer can get very distressed simply because she may not understand that you will be returning in a few minutes: she may feel that she has been abandoned. Nor can you easily bundle such a person up and take her with you, as you could a toddler. Change of scene can make a person with dementia worse, while a frail older person could easily catch a chill if taken out.

Another drawback of caring for both parties may be a change in their relationship. Being too much in the presence of a close relative or a spouse may mean that you get on one another's nerves so much so that you resent each other's presence. If a child or a partner starts helping an older person with personal care, such as bathing and going to the lavatory, that may alter their attitudes to each other. If you are contemplating being either a carer or a cared-for person, it is important not to allow the goodwill this signifies to blind you to real difficulties which may arise in your relationship and to consider how to handle these.

If after weighing up the pros and cons, you are inclined to become a carer, the next step is to think through the practicalities. It is important to get as clear an idea as you possibly can of what it would actually be like to be a carer, day by day, minute by minute.

Chapter 21
Practicalities

If you have decided to become a carer or are seriously contemplating becoming so, some of the earlier parts of this book could prove helpful. Find out what aids and adaptations to your home might be useful (pages 205–7), what help in the home you could hire (pages 259–72) and what gadgets might be useful (pages 91–109).

Additionally or alternatively, approach your local council for help: on top of the gadgets and services which your older person might be able to receive through a community care assessment (pages 273–307) and house adaptations the local authority may help fund (pages 108–9 and 205–7), the council may also provide support to you as a carer – in other words helping you to care, after carrying out a carer's assessment.

Carers' Assessments

The right of carers to be assessed for services was set out in the Carers and Disabled Children Act, 2000. This came into force in 2001 and the Department of Health has published no fewer than three pieces of guidance for local authorities on how they should implement it. These are *Policy Guidance*, *Practice Guidance* and *Practitioners' Guidance*, and they are available on the Department of Health website section for carers, or you can obtain them free by post.[1]

Equivalent guidance has been issued in Wales on the 2000 Act and this can be found on the Welsh Assembly website or obtained by post.[2] The guidance referred to below is that for England. Carers' legislation was passed later in Scotland and Northern Ireland. That in Northern Ireland is the Carers' and Direct Payments Act, 2002, which gives equivalent power to the Province's health and social services boards; that for Scotland is the Community Care and Health (Scotland) Act, 2002, which lays equivalent powers on social work departments north of the border. Readers are advised to contact the Belfast or Glasgow office of Carers UK, the Northern Ireland Executive or the Scottish Executive to keep up to date with the developing situation, including the publication of guidance for local councils. Broadly speaking, the approach in all four countries is similar.

Caring about Carers: A National Strategy for Carers, which the government published in 1999, with a foreword by Tony Blair, set out a framework of proposals for services for carers and additional funding throughout the UK. In this document the government explained its aims as follows:

> We want to enhance the quality of life for all carers. This means finding ways to give them:
> • the freedom to have a life of their own
> • time for themselves
> • the opportunity to continue to work, if that is what they want to do
> • control over their life and over the support they need in it
> • better health and well-being
> • integration into the community
> • perhaps most importantly, peace of mind . . .
> Carers care for those in need of care. We need now to care about carers.

Section one of the Carers' and Disabled Children Act, 2000 states that if a person ('the carer') provides or intends to provide a substantial amount of care on a regular basis for another adult and he or she asks a local authority to carry out an assessment of his or her ability to provide and to continue to provide care, the local authority must carry out such an assessment, if it is satisfied that the person cared for is someone for whom it may provide community care services (defined on pages 272–3).

The Act goes on to require the local authority to consider the assessment and decide whether the carer has needs in relation to the care provided, whether those needs could be satisfied wholly or partly by services which it could provide and, if this is the case, whether or not to provide them.

A carer's assessment can thus be the gateway to services ranging from aids and adaptations such as hoists or bath seats to human help with cleaning, shopping or dealing with laundry. The only exception to services provided under the Carers' Act is services of an intimate nature to the cared-for person, such as personal care.

Even if you have no interest in getting services or gadgets at least part funded by your local council, it may still be worth asking for a carer's assessment, since such an assessment can inform your thinking about whether or not to become a carer by providing information on the range of both council and non-council help which may be available. It can also provide the reassurance of knowing how to make contact and ask for help should you decide to later on.

If you have a carer's assessment, you may well find the council will not provide all the facilities which the assessment threw up as potentially useful, so you may wish to pay for additional help yourself or use free or inexpensive facilities provided by other people and organizations, such as voluntary carers' groups, local clubs, churches and local branches of disability or ailment-based organizations. Your local authority ought to be able to put you in touch with these. Or you might decide to avail yourself only of the provision your council makes for breaks for carers, which are funded by a special ring-fenced grant from government (page 567).

One important type of carers' services is the provision of breaks for the carer involving the cared-for person being looked after by somebody else for a limited period, often at a day care centre or through a sitting service; this is called 'respite care'. As with community care services, once the local authority has agreed that a particular service should be provided, it is your legal right to receive that service and it cannot be taken away without a reassessment which shows you no longer require it.

Respite care is slightly complicated in that although it arises out of the carer's assessment, it is not in fact a service delivered to the carer. The carer is assessed as in need of a break from the caring role, which is set down in his or her carer's assessment; the person cared for will then need to be reassessed for the additional support that will enable the carer to take a break, and this will be documented in his or her community care assessment or reassessment. So for instance, if the carer is assessed as needing a break every Tuesday for three hours, the cared-for person is then assessed as needing a sitting service for three hours every

Tuesday. The sitting service is a community care service, not a service under the Carers' Act.

Carers' services do not have to end with provision such as this – a key feature of government thinking on the provision of help to carers is that assessment should not be led by the services which happen to be available, but should centre on the outcomes the carer seeks. *The Practitioners' Guidance* clearly states: 'A carer's assessment should be focused on what the carer identifies as the best possible outcome' (paragraph 22). To achieve this, nothing is ruled out, and indeed the guidance mentions such varied possibilities as the provision of a mobile phone so that a carer could go out but be summoned easily if a problem arose, an alarm system, help with transport through taxi fares or driving lessons, and cleaning, shopping and laundry services. The government explains that it has prepared its *Practice Guidance* 'to illustrate the potential for flexibility, creativity, cost-effectiveness and innovation inherent in local councils' new powers' (paragraph 2).

If you are going to make the most of a carer's assessment it is important to understand that there is this wide range of potential provision and that the purpose of the assessment is twofold: to enable the carer to care effectively, and to maintain the carer's own health and well-being.

However, this does not mean that carers are now being provided with all that they would like. Although councils are required by law to carry out carers' assessments, the Carers' Act only empowers authorities to provide services for carers: it does not oblige them to do so. And they are free to prioritize the very wide range of needs presented by their elderly population through eligibility criteria. Indeed, there are a number of hurdles which you must cross as a carer before you will receive the maximum possible help from the state.

The first involves getting your assessment in the first place. A carer's assessment can only be carried out, legally speaking, if a carer requests one. While the social services department of the local authority can make the first move in assessing the needs of an older person, they can only carry out a carer's assessment in response to a request from the carer. But many carers, both existing and prospective, are completely unaware of this entitlement because social services departments have neglected to publicize it. (The Department of Health publishes a handy leaflet called *Help in looking after someone: a carer's guide to a carer's assessment*.)

So the first thing you need to do is to ask for a carer's assessment. Don't be fobbed off with a few questions over the phone or a form to fill in: just as with a community care assessment, a carer's assessment should take place through a face-to-face interview (*Practice Guidance*, para. 61). Also, bear in mind that you can have someone present with you: 'Carers should be told of their right to have a friend or advocate present if they would wish to do so . . . The role of the advocate is to work for the individual, supporting them in expressing choices, facilitating the communication of this to other parties, and working with the individual so that their choices are respected and acted upon' (*Practice Guidance*, para. 60). The advocate is in addition to an interpreter or signer, one of whom should be provided for carers who have language or hearing difficulties.

Scotland is different. Carers' assessments are initiated more readily, because the Community Care and Health (Scotland) Act, 2002, says that if it appears to a local authority that a person is a carer, then it must offer him an assessment of his needs. However, there is no reason why carers in Scotland should not nonetheless approach their local authority's social work department to ask for an assessment.

Carers are eligible for an assessment only if the elderly person for whom they care or plan to care is someone for whom the council might provide or arrange for the provision of community care services. In other words, if your elderly person is somebody whom you help through the odd bit of shopping or running an errand now and again, assessments are not for you: the elderly person has to be so frail or disabled that community care services might be provided for them. The law also restricts assessments to those carers who are providing or who are intending to provide 'regular and substantial care'. Some councils explain how they interpret this phrase. For instance, the London Borough of Sutton makes it plain in a booklet it gives to carers that to be eligible for an assessment under the Carers' Act, you need to show that your caring responsibilities are having a significant impact and/or that you are caring for at least 15 hours a week on average (that would clearly include someone caring only at weekends or only during the evening and night). Other councils do not publish such an explanation and may require a larger number of hours. As this is a crucial area, but one in which councils have considerable discretion, carers may, alas, find that they have to resort to lodging official complaints and appeals.

You do not actually have to be a carer at the time you get an assessment. This is very important, because the degree of help you might get from the local authority may well inform your decision on whether to become a carer or not. So if you live in an area different from your elderly relative and you are considering inviting him or her to come and live with you so you can act as carer, he or she has a right to an assessment by the social services department in whose area you reside, and you have a right to an assessment of your needs as a prospective carer in that area.

Normally the assessment for the carer would take place at the same time as the care recipient's community care assessment (page 273), so a co-ordinated package of support can be assembled, but if the recipient is not having an assessment – perhaps because of having refused to have one or already having had one – then the carer can have a free-standing assessment. This also applies if the recipient has refused community care services. So if a package of support has already been put in place for an elderly person with whom you decide to go and live to provide additional care, you could ask for an assessment of your own. The social worker might assess you alone or combine your assessment with a reassessment of the elderly person's needs. Both the carer and the cared-for person can insist that their assessment takes place in private, separate from that of the other, if they so wish.

Since carers save the country billions each year, it may seem unfair that they should be charged for services provided to enable them to care, but local councils have the discretionary power to impose charges for such services. Just as with services provided directly to elderly people, the size of any charge is determined by the approach of the particular local authority. Councils have the discretion not to charge for carers' services at all. It is a good idea to find out your council's policy early on, as this may well affect the extent to which you wish to pursue the possibilities with them.

Eligibility

As with community care services, councils decide how to allocate their resources through the use of eligibility criteria. In drawing up these criteria for carers' services, councils are urged by the Department of Health to consider whether a particular caring role is sustainable and how large is the risk of it breaking down. To do this, the *Practice Guidance* recommends that councils should consider four key factors:

- autonomy, which means carers should be free to choose the nature of the tasks they will perform and how much time they will give to them
- health and safety, in other words, the risk to the carer's health of his or her caring
- managing daily routines, which means considering whether carers can look after their own domestic needs and other daily tasks
- involvement: 'to what extent carers have freedom to maintain relationships, employment, interests and other commitments outside their caring responsibilities'.

In other words, if there is a real risk to the continuance of care because you may hurt your back as a result, then the council should take action to avert this threat, for instance through providing lifting aids and training on how to move elderly people. Or, if there is a substantial risk that you will have to give up caring because it is threatening your employment or your ability to earn money as a self-employed person, that too should set alarm bells ringing with the council and prompt them perhaps to arrange for your relative to receive day care in a specialist centre or care home.

Bizarrely, the eligibility framework contains no mention of the quality of the care given, yet one would imagine that a caring situation would be unsustainable if the carer were caring badly, whether because of a lack of enthusiasm or inadequate training.

Once the council has decided which services it will provide to a carer and how much if anything these will cost the carer, the question of service delivery arises. The local authority can either provide the services or organize their provision. A relatively new arrangement whereby elderly people who need community care services can receive subsidy but organize the services themselves is Direct Payments (pages 297–306), provided under the Carers' and Disabled Children Act, 2000, for carers as well as the cared-for. The government's *Policy Guidance* states:

> Direct Payments will offer carers the opportunity to be innovative and flexible in how they arrange the delivery of services to them to meet their assessed needs. A carer might choose to use a Direct Payment to employ someone they know to clean for them rather than making use of a local council arranged service. Subject to any exceptions prescribed in regulations, all carers will be eligible for Direct Payments. (para. 11)

Direct Payments can be enormously useful to carers. Through them you can receive financial help, but yourself select the person you would like to help with chores around the house. You are in a position to recruit workers whom you are confident can be trusted to be left alone with your cared-for person when you go out.

The only grounds on which a local authority can reject a request for a Direct Payment is that it considers the person involved is not able to take the ultimate decisions on what service should be provided by whom and when; it is hard to envisage circumstances in which somebody who is taking on a caring role could not make such decisions. Direct Payments are discussed in detail on pages 297–306.

Some carers will not want Direct Payments even if their council offers; in this case, they should simply refuse, as it is a requirement that a council must obtain the recipient's consent to this scheme. If consent is withheld, it is up to the local authority to organize provision of the help it has assessed the carer as needing.

Preparing for the Assessment

Before your carer's assessment takes place, prepare for it just as a care recipient would prepare for a community care assessment (pages 282–5). If you are already a carer, keep a diary of problems you have faced, such as lack of sleep, frustration and fatigue. List the difficulties you face or anticipate that you will face as a carer, and the things you think you need or anticipate that you will need. Think of the people whom you could ask to support your claim for particular services, such as your GP or a consultant psychiatrist to whom you or your cared-for person has been referred. Think of the things you are going to ask for. For example, if you are going to be caring for somebody with dementia, you might wish to demand forcefully that you be given training on how to cope – both for their benefit and yours, since your own mental health could well suffer if you do not feel confident about coping and caring.

Think about whom you could ask to be present at the assessment. An advocate from your local carers' centre? If you think that your GP could be useful in the assessment, perhaps because you wish special consideration to be given to the impact on your own health, you could ask that he or she should be present. Carers' assessments and carers' care plans are relatively new, and there is not much established practice on what they should contain, since the Carers' and Disabled Children Act did not come into force until 2001. Apart from cash which the government has provided for breaks for carers, which is ring-fenced, provision for carers' services comes out of the same budget as other provision for older people, so in many cases carers will have to fight hard to secure anything substantial. Carers are therefore in effect breaking new ground in carers' provision.

Many will see this and the pressure they will often have to place on councils as a drawback. But at least help is now possible, whereas it was not if you were embarking on a caring role 10 years ago. In theory, at least, gone should be the days in which children struggled without any help whatsoever from the state to care for elderly mothers and fathers at home, without training and without any breaks, while endlessly dipping into their savings.

Here are some of the things you should expect from your carer's assessment:

- First and foremost, that the focus will be on you. It should involve a real recognition of your role, the need to support you and the need to ensure that your health and well-being are not impaired by being a carer. The Department of Health's *Practice Guidance* to councils states clearly:

The carer's assessment should be a carer-centred process, listening to the carer, valuing their experience, focusing on outcomes (not just services) that the carer thinks are important in terms of supporting them in their caring role or maintaining their health and well being. (para. 45)

- Recognition that you will not necessarily wish to go on caring forever (Practitioners' Guidance, para. 20). The idea of the carer as endlessly put upon, endlessly uncomplaining, should be over. This will be a hard attitude to break, and probably never will be completely broken, since social services know that when push comes to shove you are not going to abandon your elderly parent but will just carry on no matter how tough things may get. But they will also know that such a situation can easily end in a crisis when the mental and physical health of the carer breaks down and they will have to step in and pick up the burden.
- Recognition of your right to choose what you do. Decide before the assessment whether you wish to do personal care. If your cared-for person is your husband or wife, you may find that carrying out this sort of help changes your relationship irrevocably, at the expense of its sexual aspect. The guidance points out that it is important that social workers or care managers do not make assumptions about carers' willingness to undertake tasks related to intimate personal care. An older person assessed as needing such help could receive it from a care worker rather than from his or her carer.
- Recognition of your employment needs. The government clearly sees it as a role of local authorities under the Carers Act to help carers to join or rejoin the workforce: 'Carers should be supported to stay in work, or to return to work, where this is what they want to do' (Practice Guidance, para. 35). So if you are already in work, it should be a central function for social services to keep you in work. Before the assessment, think about what you are going to ask for to enable you to carry on working. Somebody coming into the house to give you some completely free time for an hour or two hours a day, if you work from home? Day care on two days a week at a care home which offers day places, or a specialist centre? Or, if

your older person's needs are less, a place at a luncheon club or a day centre? In working out the threat to the sustainability of the caring role, the government recommends that councils should consider that the caring role is at critical risk if the carer's involvement in employment is or will be at risk.

- Recognition of your need to have relationships outside your caring work. Again, the government considers that the sustainability of the caring role runs into critical risk if 'many significant social support systems and relationships are, or will be, at risk' (Practice Guidance, para. 70).

- Recognition of your need for training. This is a very important aspect of caring and one which it seems to me is much underplayed. Eldercare is a sophisticated and complex field and you do need to know at least as much about the care of elderly people as you did about the care of babies and young children if you became a parent.

As mobility problems arising from conditions such as arthritis, osteoporosis and chronic lung disease are extremely common in old age, many cared-for people need help to get out of their chair and to transfer between chairs, to lavatory seats and so on. You cannot just learn how to help them from a book: the way you help your parent to move will depend on his or her physical condition and yours, as well as your relative weights. Ensure that the district nurse or an occupational therapist gives you instruction.

It seems to me that carers deserve a fortnight's intensive training before they take on the role, covering groundwork such as how to avoid pressure sores, infection control, nutrition, psychological matters, and moving and transferring, amongst others. If your relative has a particular condition, be it arthritis, cancer or diabetes (and alas, many older people have several conditions), it is important to receive training in those areas too. The local authority may have in-house training which you could benefit from, or you could be sent on one of the excellent day and half-day courses run by Age Concern. You need appropriate training both for your sake as well as that of your older person. Think how dreadful it must be to find that you have inadvertently injured a loved one because you have not received proper instruction.

- Provision for you to have a break from caring so that you can recharge your batteries and come back to caring with renewed inspiration and energy.

The government's *Caring about Carers: A National Strategy for Carers* lists the following types of breaks for carers: you might care to think about which would be most useful for you before the assessment. They are:

- A short stay for the person being cared for in a residential care home
- Time for the person being cared for in a day centre
- Nightsitting service, to allow the carer to get a full night's sleep
- Someone to take the person being cared for on outings, to give the carer time to him or herself at home
- Sunday sitting service, to allow the carer to go to church or visit family and friends
- Evening sitting service, to allow the carer to go to evening classes, to the cinema or have a meal out
- Day-time sitting, for shopping and other activities
- Holidays for both the carer and the person being cared for, together.[3]

Sometimes breaks are provided by a local authority issuing vouchers to carers so they can buy a break or breaks when they feel they need one. In this case, the voucher enables the carer to purchase care from another party, such as a care home, perhaps one specializing in breaks for carers.

Since 1999, the government has allocated local councils a special pot of ring-fenced money to finance breaks for carers. Even if you do not want to use any other kind of council support, you might try to avail yourself of some of this pot, known as the Carers' Special Grant.

After the assessment, expect to receive a written copy of your carer's care plan and an indication of how it will be monitored and when it will be reviewed – although you can of course request a review or reassessment at any time you think circumstances have changed or will change. Carers looking after people with any mental health problem (which can include not just dementia but also depression) 'should have an assessment of their caring, physical and mental health needs repeated on at least an annual basis', according to the Department of Health's *National Service Framework for Mental Health.*

State Benefits for Carers

If you are deciding whether to become a carer, you will want to work out what impact caring will have on your current income and on your own future pension situation. As each person's financial situation is different and the benefits often changing and complicated, I give here only a brief outline of what is available.

The main state benefit for carers was designed to provide a replacement income for people of working age who were unable to work full-time because they were caring. This payment, called Carer's Allowance, is available to carers under the age of 65 who do not earn more than £77 a week. Such people have to be caring for at least 35 hours a week. In addition, to qualify for Carer's Allowance the person for whom the carer is caring must be sufficiently disabled to be receiving Attendance Allowance.

It was not until October 2002 that the government extended Carer's Allowance to carers over the age of 65. However, as this is a means-tested benefit designed to bring people's income up to a certain level, carers over 65 do not receive it if they are receiving a larger amount in the form of the State Retirement Pension. But people who receive a low State Retirement Pension because of gaps in their National Insurance record benefit by the difference between that pension and Carer's Allowance.

You are entitled to certain holiday weeks under Carer's Allowance: if you have been caring for 22 weeks, you can claim it for four holiday weeks over a 26-week period. However, if the person for whom you are caring loses his or her Attendance Allowance, your Carer's Allowance stops too. This will happen if the cared-for person goes into hospital or enters a care home, say, for intensive care for longer than 28 days, or for two periods shorter than 28 days which are separated by less than 28 days and the local authority is contributing to that cost.

Carer's Allowance can erode your entitlement to your or your cared-for person's entitlement to other benefits. If this might apply to you, I strongly suggest you get hold of the free booklet produced by Carers UK entitled *Benefits: What's Available and How to Get Them*. You can also get leaflets on all the benefits from your local Social Security Office (for the address, look in the telephone directory).

Another benefit, the Carer Premium, provides a little extra money (£25.10 a week) to carers who are already receiving Income Support. The Carer Premium is only paid to carers who receive Carer's Allowance or qualify for it but do not get it because they receive another overlapping benefit. For people over the age of 60, Income Support is now the Guarantee Credit element of Pension Credit and the Carer Premium acts by increasing somebody's applicable amount for Guarantee Credit, or the minimum amount the government thinks they need to live on.

People who receive Carer's Allowance also receive credit towards their basic State Pension. From the financial year starting in 2002, they have been credited with a second- tier pension at a rate equivalent to earnings of £9,000 per year. (This same situation applies to people who receive Home Responsibilities Protection, the system introduced in 1978 to provide National Insurance contributions for people caring for children under the age of 16 or for sick or disabled people.) If you are not receiving Carer's Allowance or Income Support because you are a carer and yet you are caring for more than 35 hours a week, approach the Inland Revenue yourself in order to get pension credits. The Revenue should automatically credit you with credits if you indicate on your tax return that you are receiving Carer's Allowance. The Department of Work and Pensions produced in March 2000 a useful booklet called *State Pensions for Carers and Parents: Your Guide (PM9)*.

Other Calculations

You may be reading this after having been a carer for many years or after having become a carer abruptly, perhaps after an older person has had a stroke. But if you are still considering whether or not to become a carer, you will probably also wish to gain information and advice from other quarters.

Read as widely as you can about any special conditions from which your older person suffers to get an idea of what caring for him or her would actually mean. Talk to people who are already carers or at least to people who have contact with carers, say in the carers' support centres dotted up and down the country. It may be, for instance, that your older person would be very clingy or suffer from insomnia, both factors which might influence your decision.

Find out how much help and support other members of your family and close friends would realistically provide. Would they be able to provide help at the drop of a hat if necessary? How much additional help might you get from voluntary groups? GPs and other members of primary health care teams can do much to support carers. They can provide the gateway to all sorts of specialist health care which could help, from family therapy and counselling to physiotherapy and exercise instruction. GPs have been told by government to find out which people on their lists are carers and to pay special attention to them, so they should be bearing in mind your caring role when they diagnose ailments such as pulled muscles, back problems and hernias which could be connected with caring, and also when they or members of their team carry out health checks (page 249).

Once you have talked to people such as these, you ought to be in a position to figure out precisely how you would manage the days and weekends if you take on caring. Would you be getting enough emotional support to continue? Would you feel contented with your life or would you feel shattered most of the time and guilty that you were not spending more time caring for your children or resentful that you were not pursuing your own interests or earning money? Would you have sufficient private time with your partner once you had become a carer? Would care intrude too much into your relationships? Would you get sufficient sleep? Would you have enough money? What impact would caring make on your finances and would it mean that you would have to cut back, and if so where and by how much? Would you get sufficient breaks from caring? How would caring affect your earning capacity both now and after the caring role had ceased? These are some of the many questions you will need to be considering.

Finally, judge any advice very carefully. Social services departments may well encourage you to be a carer even though they can see you will have a struggle, because your caring will save them money. The shortage of places in care homes provides an additional incentive to social services to foist as much care of older people as possible on to their unpaid relatives, partners and friends. In particular, people can find themselves under enormous pressure to take on a gruelling caring role when an older person is about to be discharged from hospital (pages 463–474). The health body wants the bed freed up; social services want care on the cheap: both cry 'Hip, hip, hurrah!' when a carer takes on the job.

Some prospective carers opt for a few counselling sessions before coming to a decision. It is worth remembering that caring is not obligatory. And although saying no to caring may be difficult, caring for an older person, even your spouse, is not actually your legal responsibility. Some people take on a caring role because they feel it is expected of them and that they will be stigmatized if they allow an older relative to 'go into a home'. In fact, the older person might be more expertly looked after in a care home, enjoy a better social life and be generally happier and healthier.

Voluntary Organizations for Carers

There are three main voluntary groups which support carers and they perform different roles.

The Princess Royal Trust for Carers

On the ground, the most important organization is The Princess Royal Trust for Carers, which was set up in 1991 on the initiative of The Princess Royal, who during her hospital visits had talked to carers and considered they were undervalued. The Princess Royal Trust has set up 115 support centres for carers across the United Kingdom. Each centre has paid staff who offer detailed advice, support, access to counselling and some advocacy, in other words taking up individual cases. So if you are at all perplexed when trying to fill out an application for a benefit associated with caring or indeed some other aspect of the paperwork, ask your local carers' centre for help.

Check with your centre that you are receiving all the state financial assistance available to you: benefits and pension rights for carers are complicated and often change. Such centres may be able to help you in many unexpected ways. For instance,

Marian Radford, the director of The Princess Royal Trust
Carers' Centre at Sutton in London, told me that she regularly
writes job references for carers who wish to re-enter the world of
employment after their caring has ceased. A carers' centre may
also offer training for carers. It may run discussion meetings:
attending even two or three of these has helped many.

Carers UK
The Princess Royal Trust does not offer a national helpline, but
another organization, Carers UK, does. You can get advice on
community care and welfare rights and be referred to specialist
lawyers in the field. Carers UK does have local branches, but they
do not have paid staff and are essentially mutual support groups
involving carers offering advice and support to each other. Carers
UK has offices in each country of the United Kingdom and is
the main lobbying group for carers; it publishes reports and advisory booklets.

Crossroads Association – Caring for Carers
Crossroads Association arose out of the ITV *Crossroads* television soap, when a disability expert wrote in about the mistaken
way in which he felt disability had been depicted in the programme. The *Crossroads* producer persuaded his company to set
up a pilot Crossroads project and it put in £10,000. Nearly 30
years on, Crossroads has 200 branches across England and
Wales, and there are separate organizations in Scotland and
Northern Ireland. It provides breaks for carers: holidays, weekends or evenings off, with a trained support worker being sent
into the home to replace the carer. As with all eldercare voluntary
groups, coverage is uneven: the south east is better served than
the north of England, but even in counties such as Kent, which
have lots of branches, there are still waiting lists. Most
Crossroads provision is free, but some branches provide a
service which people can buy.

The Main Caring Relative
While the needs of people who provide 'regular and substantial
care' are at last receiving some long overdue recognition, this is
far less true of those relatives, close friends, sometimes partners

or ex-partners who are usually not living with the older person yet who act as their main caring relative. And there is an almost limitless spectrum of possibilities. You may be living abroad and performing an extremely worthwhile role in society and hear that your elderly father is dying of cancer. Should you put your life on hold and move back and devote yourself to him for his last remaining months? If you do not, but choose instead to make prolonged visits and in the meantime to keep in constant touch over the telephone, you may very well still provide him with an extraordinarily valuable amount of care and support, and your relationship with him may be much enriched, even though you are not present day to day.

Just because you are not a carer providing 'regular and substantial care' does not mean to say that the problems such people face will not be yours too, at least to some extent. If you have to down tools and travel perhaps 100 or more miles to cope with sudden crises, you may find your work suffers. Regular visiting at weekends, even if only every other or every third weekend but often conducted over several years, will inevitably have an effect on your social and domestic life and your ability to pursue outside interests. These sacrifices on the part of the main caring relative are rarely acknowledged within families, let alone in society outside.

There must be at least as many people performing this role as there are those offering regular and substantial care. They, the invisible carers, have to negotiate a relationship with other members of their families who perhaps do not wish to shoulder any support of the older person. This can set up tensions just as surely as can full-time caring.

Sharing control over an older person's finances through a registered enduring power of attorney provides an added area in which the main caring relative must negotiate carefully lest disagreements build up over how an older person's money should be handled, and perhaps as a result the level of care they should receive.

Just as the main caring relative has to cope with the drawbacks of the role, so he or she could benefit greatly from much of the support which at present is considered appropriate only for people who provide continuous care. The main caring relative needs just as much training and information about the particular condition of his or her older person. You need to know how to move your relative, you need to understand particular medical conditions as you will be playing a major part in the decisions about care, and you will be giving some of it yourself. You too need emotional and moral support, sometimes even more so than the continuous carers, because you may also have to cope with feelings of guilt that you have not made a greater sacrifice.

Conclusion

Necessarily, the subject matter of this book will have been at times dreary, at times humdrum and at times distressing. All of this could lead you to think, as so many people do, that becoming elderly or caring for older people is unadulterated misery. Yet while it is as well to be prepared for difficulties, the final phase of life can also be the best. The elderly, for all their problems, are often happier than the harassed young. Only at this stage do many find time to reflect and to find out who they really are. Even their grimmer experiences, like other apparently undesirable life events, are not without their upside.

The challenges which ageing may bring can stimulate as well as debilitate. Those who have known little adversity before can find the new perspectives forced upon them surprisingly rewarding. Like war or other harsh circumstances, old age can provide opportunities for resourcefulness, heroism, generosity and achievement which would not otherwise have arisen. This can be as true for those who find themselves caring for elderly people as for the elderly themselves, particularly when they are closely related.

We are accustomed, perhaps programmed biologically, to believe that the relationship between parent and child is most significant when the child is very young. But engagement between parents who are old or very old and children who have become their carers can be as rewarding as between parents and young children. It is an experience built on a lifetime's understanding of one person by another and on many shared activities from the past. Only at this stage do many parents, aunts and uncles and grandparents break through the barriers which have kept them from really knowing children, nieces, nephews and grandchildren. Of course, the development of dementia poses a particular challenge. But this can be for many the opportunity to repay in kind the care they themselves received in infancy. Our parents suspended judgement and plunged themselves into our world of make-believe when we were infants. Can we thank them enough? Perhaps we may be called upon to do just that.

The new relationship which elderly people must make with the world around them and those who inhabit it is an adventure for both sides. It is an adventure which can have only one conclusion. But even death, when it comes, as it must, should not be a wholly unhappy event. New qualities discovered in oneself and one's loved ones can be something to celebrate, whatever must also be mourned. So can the knowledge that the final stages of life were handled well by all those with a part to play in them.

Complaints

All public bodies, from local authorities' highways departments to the Public Guardianship Office, have to have a formal complaints procedure. So too do many of the non-government organizations which play an important part in the lives of older people, such as private care homes and GP practices. In many cases, the relevant procedure is described in the relevant section of this book. Complaints procedures for the two types of organization about which readers are particularly likely to wish to complain — social services departments of local authorities and the National Health Service — are sketched out in this Appendix.

Complaining can take a great deal of time and effort. It can also be stressful and it can jeopardise relationships. It is therefore important to consider what you wish to achieve from a complaint right from the start.

Your objective may be to secure financial compensation long after a decision you consider was unfair was made, in which case you will have time to prepare your case carefully and, if you get nowhere, say, with a health authority which refused your relative NHS Continuing Care (pages 75 and 469–74), you will have time and much financial incentive to take your case higher. But if you are dissatisfied with the actions of individuals and organizations in an ongoing situation, your calculations and aims could be quite different. Complaining can work wonders, but it is worth thinking through carefully whom you might offend by so doing and whether this could be avoided. If you raise concerns with your social worker about the treatment of a relative in a care home, is he going to treat that information as confidential – or go straight to the care home manager, who may treat it as a formal complaint and henceforth, if she behaves unprofessionally, take a frosty attitude towards your family? If you do make a formal complaint, how will it be handled? Will you be given sufficient opportunity to make your case? Will you be given an opportunity to defend yourself against any accusations by those about whom you are complaining? Many see the best form of defence as attack, and you could find the care home turning round and accusing you of mistreating your relative. It can all get very nasty.

Organizations which may be able to help you with official complaints are the Citizen's Advice Bureau and the voluntary organizations listed in Chapter 4. They ought to be able to provide you also with information about new ammunition you might be able to use, such as human rights legislation. Official organizations which should be able to help with NHS complaints are described on pages 62–4.

You may decide that rather than using the formal complaints procedure (although you could do that as well) you could seek support from your local councillor and/or your local MP, perhaps after a refusal to finance a package of care at home for yourself or a relative, or to supply a much-needed piece of equipment like a stair-lift. Many local council officials hate to see elected members getting involved and they might cave in at the threat of this. You could also seek to interest the local or national media. The secret is to use these channels to make as much of a fuss as possible. It is often the squeaky wheel which gets the oil.

Complaints about Local Government

The government has directed that the complaints procedures which local authorities have in place should consist of three distinct stages.[1] The first is an informal stage, at which attempts are made to resolve the point at issue by negotiation. The complainant does not even have to set down his or her complaint in writing, but the complaint should nonetheless be taken seriously by the authority. This is an important stage for the complainant, because it enables decisions to be reversed or matters in some other way rectified without getting into a confrontational situation which may lead the local authority to resist change because it may feel it will lose face. It is important at this stage that the authority should understand that you are prepared to take the matter further if necessary, even though that will involve you in effort, probably stress, and an inevitable delay in the resolution of your concern.

The second stage is the formal registration of the complaint. You have to put it in writing and it is forwarded to the designated complaints officer of the local authority. The complainant can go straight to this stage if he or she wishes. One of the advantages of this approach is that it does have a clear time limit: the local authority has only 28 days to consider the complaint and provide a formal response. If it thinks it cannot meet this deadline, it must notify the complainant and explain why extra time is needed and when he or she can expect the decision to be made. That decision must be provided within three months at the absolute maximum.

If you remain dissatisfied, you can request that the matter be considered by a review panel which the local authority must appoint. At least one of the members of this three-person panel, including the chairperson, must be independent of the local authority. The panel holds a hearing at which the complainant or his or her representative and the authority and any other people whom the panel chooses to call make their case. No one is allowed to hire lawyers, so the procedure remains relatively informal. The panel must reach a decision in writing within 24 hours of the hearing. This is not a binding ruling, but a recommendation to the local authority, which then decides whether or not to act upon it. Local authorities are expected to act upon a panel's recommendation but they are not absolutely bound to, so if the director of social services chooses to disagree, he or she can.

If you remain unappeased, you can complain to the Local Government Ombudsman, who has separate offices in London, Edinburgh and Cardiff, or the Northern Ireland Ombudsman (who also covers health service matters). However, by this stage you are not talking about a quick decision reversal. The Ombudsman will take a while to investigate the complaint, which has to be made within 12 months of the incident or of the failure of the local authority's complaints investigation. Although time limits are part of that procedure, things can nonetheless drag on. It is only once the Ombudsman is in action that you can feel sure that a truly independent investigation of the complaint will be made in a searching way which is fair to both sides. This is because the panel which the local authority sets up is not truly independent. Of the three people on the panel, two do not have to be independent at all (they usually consist of the head of the service in question and a councillor); the independent person may or may not be an assertive chairperson when faced with the weight of the local authority representatives.

All of the procedures so far mentioned have the advantage to the complainant of being free. The longer the process draws on, the less likely it will provide an immediate benefit to an older relative, although if you are looking for compensation because of bad decision-making, then the Ombudsman can be useful.

Another possibility is to approach another part of the local authority. Every local council in England and Wales has to have a monitoring officer who has a statutory duty to investigate alleged breaches of the law. Again, approaching the monitoring officer is free, and it tends to be a speedy procedure, since the monitoring officer has just 21 days to prepare a report to the full council once he or she believes there has been a credible allegation that the authority has acted outside the law. While this is taking place, the monitoring officer can put a stay of execution on the matter. For instance, if an elderly person is complaining that the authority has reached a decision without following procedures required by law, and this is causing problems, then the monitoring officer can put the matter on hold, so that the complainant's status quo is preserved. This might arise if, for instance, the local authority has peremptorily cut the number of hours of homecare it provides without following the correct procedure of reassessing the person involved (pages 289–90).

The disadvantage of the monitoring officer procedure is that it can be fairly aggressive. You need to know something of the law to present a coherent argument that the authority has been acting unlawfully, and if the council considers after all that the local authority was acting properly, then you are back to square one. It can, however, provide a speedy if high-profile method of getting a matter resolved in a complainant's favour.

A third form of redress is a review of the local authority's decision in the courts, known as a 'judicial review'. This is confrontational and expensive, unless you are entitled to legal aid. It can produce a dramatic change in a decision, with considerable financial implications. For instance, it could result in a local authority releasing a lot more cash to support an elderly person in his or her own home.

Complaints about the NHS

Every NHS organization, such as a primary care trust or hospital trust, has to make available details of its complaints procedure, and you ought readily to be able to obtain such information in any GP's surgery, district hospital or long-stay NHS unit. Government guidance to health organizations says they should make provision for a first stage called 'local resolution', at which the complaint is investigated by people close to its subject. The second stage is 'independent review', when the complaint may be passed to a panel, the chairperson of which is independent of the NHS. The Health Service Ombudsman (or the Health Service Commissioner) can investigate complaints once the relevant NHS complaint procedures have been exhausted. (In Northern Ireland, the Northern Ireland Ombudsman covers the work of the Health Service Ombudsman and the Local Government Ombudsman in Great Britain.)

For the consumer, local resolution is probably the most important avenue, since you may well be trying to secure an immediate improvement in care, and any decision in your favour by the Ombudsman a couple of years down the road may well come too late. Each health body and GP practice should have a complaints manager who is responsible for ensuring that attempts are made to resolve the complaint and who has access to all the relevant records. The purpose of this early stage is to resolve the complaint to the patient's satisfaction informally as quickly as possible, according to government guidance. Although the emphasis is on informality (the proceedings can be conducted orally), it is important to ensure that your complaint is treated seriously and that you are not fobbed off at this first stage. Particularly in hospitals, England's new Patient Advice and Liaison Service teams (page 62) could be drawn in. These may be good at defusing difficult situations, but it remains to be seen whether they will just aim to soothe rather than getting to the bottom of grievances.

If you want to take a complaint further, you have to ask for a review of your complaint by an independent review panel. You have to do this yourself, and put your request to the complaints convenor in the relevant health body. If the convenor decides to agree to your request, he or she must convene the panel within four weeks of your request and the panel should finish its work within 12 weeks. The process should be informal and not adversarial. Complainants can be accompanied by an advocate or an expert or somebody else of their choosing, but no legal representation is allowed. The panel's report is sent to the chief executive of the health body, who must write to the complainant telling him or her of any action the health body is going to take as a result.

The Health Service Ombudsman can investigate complaints about a patient's treatment in any part of the NHS, from long-stay NHS wards to GP practices. He or she usually takes up cases only if NHS complaints procedures have been exhausted. The Ombudsman can investigate complaints about procedures and maladministration, such as the way in which a health body has handled a complaint, as well as failure to buy or provide a service which a patient is entitled to receive, avoidable delays and rudeness. He can also investigate two other important areas, as long as the matter about which the complaint has been lodged occurred after 31 March 1996: the care and treatment provided by a doctor, nurse or other trained professional; and other complaints about GPs, dentists, pharmacists or opticians providing an NHS service locally.[2]

The lawyer Luke Clements has pointed out in his book *Community Care and the Law* that although the Health Service Ombudsman will not usually consider a complaint until the relevant NHS complaints procedures have been exhausted, the Ombudsman has nonetheless stated:

> If there is evidence of a breakdown of trust between the complainant and the NHS body, or if I believe that further local action would not satisfy the complainant, I may use my discretion to investigate the substance of the complaint when the matter first comes to me, even though it has not gone through all the possible stages of the NHS procedure.[3]

The NHS complaints system is not as user-friendly as that of the social services complaints system, mainly because while a local authority has no choice but to appoint an independent panel to review a complaint if asked to do so by an aggrieved member of the public (though not necessarily to act on its recommenda- tions), a complainant has no automatic right to such an independent review of his or her complaint if it concerns the NHS. The only recourse for an aggrieved party denied an independent review is to approach outsiders such as the Health Service Ombudsman or to seek action through the courts – both steps many people might not readily take and which, perhaps most important of all, will probably take a long time.

However, for people denied NHS Continuing Care there is an established process to question refusal separate from the NHS complaints procedure (pages 471–74). Those who seek such a review but are still unable to achieve satisfaction from their health authority might also try the Ombudsman – and perhaps in the process improve the prospects of other people in the future (page 473).

References

Introduction
1. The Office of National Statistics (2003), *Life Expectancy at Birth by Local Authority in England and Wales, 1991–2001*, London: HMSO
2. 'It is almost as if for each decade we have lived, we have gained an extra 20 per cent free.' Professor Tom Kirkwood in his BBC Reith Lectures on Ageing, published in Kirkwood, T. (2001), *The End of Age*, London: Profile Books
3. The Welsh Assembly Government (2002), *When I'm 64 . . . The Report from the Advisory Group on a Strategy for Older People in Wales*, Cardiff: Welsh Assembly Government
4. Sutherland, S., et al (1999), *With Respect to Old Age: Long Term Care – Rights and Responsibilities, A Report by The Royal Commission on Long Term Care*, Chairman: Professor Stewart Sutherland, London: The Stationery Office, Cmnd 4192–1, 14
5. The Department of Health (2000), *A Quality Strategy for Social Care*, London: The Department of Health, para 2, quoted by Henwood, M. (2001), *Future Imperfect? Report of the King's Fund Care and Support Inquiry*, London: King's Fund Publishing, 34
6. Falaschetti, E., Malbut, K. and Primatesta, P. (2002), 'The general health of older people and their use of health services' in Prior, G., and Primatesta, P. (eds), *Health Survey for England: The Health of the Older People 2000*, Norwich: The Stationery Office, 44, 16
7. However, there is evidence that dietary change can help (page 20). The treatments for wet AMD are laser surgery and photo-dynamic therapy.
8. Society's attitudes towards older people and aspects of ageism are discussed by the author in more detail in *Ageism: The Last Frontier* – speech given at Conway Hall, London on Remembrance Day (November 11), 2003; this is available on her website.
9. Harper, S. (2004), *Ageing Societies*, London: Edward Arnold
10. Jewson, N., Jeffers, S. and Kalra, V. (2003), *In our Blood: Respite Services, Family Care and Asian Communities in Leicester,* The Department of Sociology, University of Leicester

11. The House of Commons Health Committee (2002), *Delayed Discharges: Third Report of Session 2001–02, Vol.I: Report and Proceedings of the Committee*, HC 617–I, 35

12. The figures are £19,500 in England and Northern Ireland, £20,000 in Wales and £18,500 in Scotland.

13. The calculation is not absolutely straightforward because it is necessary to deduct from what the self-funder must find the £57 per week which he or she can claim in Attendance Allowance, but even so the difference is substantial.

14. 'Care home crisis', *Which*, 10 February 2003, 10–13

15. Watson, J. (2003), *Something for Everyone: The Impact of the Human Rights Act and the Need for a Human Rights Commission*, London: British Institute of Human Rights

Chapter 1: The Ageing Body

1. Kirkwood, T. (1999), *Time of our Lives: The Science of Human Ageing*, London: Phoenix Press

2. Selkoe, D. J., 'Ageing brain, ageing mind', *Scientific American*, September 1992, 97–103

3. Many experts consider that Alzheimer's is a disease with readily identifiable clinical stages. However, some people contend that Alzheimer's is not really a disease but inevitable change caused by ageing, since changes to the structure of the brain characteristic of the condition have also been observed in the brains of some people who never displayed any symptoms. If Alzheimer's is a disease, it is probably the result of several different disease processes that have still not been differentiated.

4. See reference 3, and Boeve, B., *et al* (2003), 'Mild cognitive impairment in the oldest old', *Neurology* 60, 477–80, and Woods, R. (1999), *Psychological Problems of Ageing*, Chichester: John Wiley and Sons

5. There is a large body of literature which examines the impact of ageing on the human body, including Coni, N., Davison, W. and Webster, S. (1992), *Ageing: The Facts*, Oxford University Press, and Pathy, M. (1998), *Principles and Practice of Geriatric Medicine*, London: John Wiley and Sons. I have found the *Encyclopaedia of Gerontology: Age, Ageing and the Aged*, edited by James Birren and published by The Academic Press in 1996, although aimed at doctors and consultant geriatricians, is surprisingly readable.

6. George, C. F., Woodhouse, K. W., Denham, M. J. and MacLennan, W. J.(1998) *Drug Therapy in Old Age*, Chichester: John Wiley and Sons, 42

7. Weg, R. B. (1996) 'Sexuality, sensuality and intimacy' in Birren, J.

(ed) *Encyclopaedia of Gerontology: Age, Ageing and the Aged*, London: Academic Press, Vol. II, 485

8. Dr James Le Fanu has some useful tips on maximizing vision while waiting for a cataract operation in *How to Live to 90*, London: Robinson, in collaboration with the *Daily Telegraph*, 1991

Chapter 2: Changing Needs

1. McWhirter, J. P., and Pennington, C. R. (1994), 'Incidence and recognition of malnutrition in hospital', *British Medical Journal* 308, 945–8
2. Chandra, R. K. (1992), 'Effect of vitamin and trace-element supplementation on immune responses and infection in elderly subjects', *Lancet* 340, 1124–6, quoted by Webb, G. P. and Copeman, J. (1996), *The Nutrition of Older Adults*, London: Arnold, 69
3. Lipschitz, D., 'Nutrition and Ageing' in Grimley Evans, J., Franklin Williams, T., Lynn Beattie, B., Michel, J-P. and Wilcock, G. K. (2000), *Oxford Textbook of Geriatric Medicine*, Oxford University Press, 140
4. Daksha, P., Trivedi, P., Doll, R. and Khaw, K. T. (2003), 'Effect of four monthly oral vitamin D3 (cholecaciferol) supplementation on fractures and mortality in men and women living in the community: randomised double blind controlled trial', *British Medical Journal* 326, 27.2.03, 469–72
5. Further details from The Macular Disease Society (2001), *Research Information Sheet 1: Age-related Macular Degeneration and Diet.*
6. Lipschitz, D., see reference 3
7. Avorn, J. (1994), 'Reduction of bacteriuria and pyuria after ingestion of cranberry juice', *Journal of the American Medical Association* 271, 10, 751–4, quoted by McLaren, S. and Crawley, H., see reference 2
8. Finch, S., Doyle, W., Lowe, C. *et al* (1998), *National Diet and Nutrition Survey: People Aged 65 Years and Over*, London: Stationery Office, quoted by McLaren, S. and Crawley, H. (2000), 'Promoting nutritional health in older adults', *Nursing Times* monograph, London: Emap Healthcare Ltd
9. Lipschitz, D., see reference 3
10. Prentice, A. M. (1989), 'Is severe wasting in elderly mental patients caused by an excessive energy requirement?', *Age and Ageing* 18, 158–67, quoted by Webb, G. P. and Copeman, J., see reference 2, 211
11. Lipschitz, D. see reference 3, 145
12. Seymour, D., Cape, R. and Campbell, A. (1980), 'Acute confusional states and dementia in the elderly: the role of hydration, volume depletion, physical illness and age', *Age and Ageing* 9, 137–46, quoted by McLaren, S. and Crawley, H., see reference 8

13. Heath, H. and Schofield, I. (1999), *Healthy Ageing: Nursing Older People*, London: Mosby

14. Ibid., 134

15. Maslow, A. H. (1970), *Motivation and Personality*, New York: Harper and Row, second edition

16. Chivite-Matthews, N. and Maggs, P. (2002), *Crime, Policing and Justice: The experience of older people: Findings from the British crime survey, England and Wales*, London: Home Office Statistical Bulletin

17. The Department of the Environment, Transport and the Regions (1999), *Pedestrian Casualties in Road Accidents: Great Britain 1998*, DETR factsheet

18. Bennett, K. M. (2002), 'Low level social engagement as a precursor of mortality among people in later life', *Age and Ageing* 31, 165–8

19. Lecture by Dr Elaine Crieth on bereavement on 26 February 2002 at Birkbeck College, London

20. Walter, T. (1999), *On Bereavement: The Culture of Grief*, Oxford University Press

21. Prior, G. and Primatesta, P. (2002), *The Health Survey for England: The Health of the Older People 2000*, Norwich: The Stationery Office

22. Countryside Agency *Walking the Way to Health Newsletter*, Issue 13, March 2003, 3. See also Pretty, J. Griffin, M. Sellens, M. and Pretty, C. (2003) Green Exercise: Complementary Roles of Nature, Exercise and Diet in Physical and Emotional Well-being and Implications for Public Health Policy CES Occasional Paper 2003–1, University of Essex

23. Woods, R. (1999), *Psychological Problems of Ageing: Assessment, Treatment and Care*, London: John Wiley and Sons, 52

24. Ibid., 62

25. Jewell, A. (ed.) (2001), *Older People and the Church*, Peterborough: Methodist Publishing House. This is a reference to a survey carried out for a team led by the Reverend Albert Jewell, the then Senior Chaplain, Methodist Homes for the Aged.

26. Such matters are discussed by Ian Knox in his book *Older People and the Church*, 2003, London: T. and T. Clark

Chapter 3: State Support

1. In Scotland the process is known as the 'general allocation of expenditure'.

2. Up until now social services departments in England have been evaluated by the Audit Commission and the Social Services Inspectorate. In the future this will be the responsibility of the proposed Commission for Social Care Inspection. The results of

star ratings have usually been published in mid-November. Look out for these in the national press or seek out information through the Department of Health or the relevant government department in your part of the UK.

3. The upper capital limits are in England and Northern Ireland £19,500, in Wales £20,000 and in Scotland £18,500.

4. The Department of Health, *Local Authority Social Services Letters* (99) 16, as quoted by Clements, L. (2000), *Community Care and the Law*, London: Legal Action Group, 35. The Information Commissioner's Office publishes a useful free document called *The Data Protection Act 1998 – an Introduction*.

5. The Department of Health (2000), *No Secrets: Guidance on Developing and Implementing Multi-agency Policies and Procedures to Protect Vulnerable Adults from Abuse*

6. The Department of Health (2001), *Continuing Care: NHS and Local Councils' Responsibilities*, Health Service Circular 2001/015, Local Authority Circular (2001) 18

7. The Department of Health (1995), *The Patient's Charter*

8. The Department of Health (2001), *Your Guide to the NHS*

9. The Information Commissioner's Office publishes a useful free document called *The Data Protection Act 1998 – an Introduction*. The Patients' Association has published a guide called *Making a Complaint* which includes advice on inspecting health records.

10. The Department of Health (2003), *NHS-funded Nursing Care: Guide to Care Home Managers on GP Services for Residents*

11. The Department of Health (2003), *Nurses' Agencies: National Minimum Standards: Nurses' Agencies Regulations*

12. *Health Service Circular 2001/010: Implementing The NHS Plan – Modern Matrons*

Chapter 5: Adapting Surroundings

1. Hearing aids which can transpose frequencies do exist. However, they are rarely used. Because of the way in which speech patterns work, it is not possible to shift a group of frequencies without greatly impairing if not destroying the intelligibility of speech.

2. Social Services, England, *The Community Care (Delayed Discharges etc.) Act (Qualifying Services) (England) Regulations 2003*

3. The *National Service Framework for Older People* requires that single integrated community equipment services must be in place in England by April 2004.

4. Stoddart, H. *et al*, 'Urinary incontinence in older people in the community: a neglected problem?', *British Journal of General Practice*,

2001, 548–51. A good introduction to the subject is Mandelstam, D. (1989), *Understanding Incontinence*, London: Disabled Living Foundation
5. The Continence Foundation's website, 2002
6. Wilkinson, K. (2001), 'Pakistani and women's perceptions and experiences of incontinence', *Nursing Standard* 6, 5, 33–9
7. Thomas, S. (2001), 'Continence in older people: a priority for primary care', *Nursing Standard* 15, 25, 45–50, quoting Royal College of Physicians (1995), *Incontinence: Causes, Management and Provision of Services*, London: RCP
8. Heath, H. and Schofield, I. (1999), *Healthy Ageing: Nursing Older People*, London: Mosby, 199
9. Bassey, E. J. (2000), 'The benefits of exercise for the health of older people', *Reviews in Clinical Gerontology* 10, 17–31

Chapter 6: Moving Around
1. The Scottish Executive Central Research Unit (2001), *Older People in Scotland: Results from the First Year of the Scottish Household Survey*, as quoted by Age Concern Scotland (2002), *Older People in Scotland: Some Basic Facts*, Factcard 2002–2003, 17
2. The Department of the Environment, Transport and the Regions (Feb. 1999*), Pedestrian Casualties in Road Accidents: Great Britain 1998*, DETR factsheet
3. The Disability Rights Commission (2002), *Making Access to Goods and Services Easier for Disabled Customers: A Practical Guide for Small Businesses and Other Small Service Providers*, Stratford upon Avon: DRC. See also Disability Rights Commission (2002), *2004: What it means to you: a guide for disabled people*.
4. Morris, A., Welsh, R., Frampton, R., Charlton, J. and Fildes, B. (2003), 'Vehicle crashworthiness and the older motorist' *Ageing and Society*, 23, 3395–409
5. The Department for Transport (2001), *Consultation Draft: Code of Practice: Access to Air Travel for Disabled People*; available through the Disability Rights Commission or the Department of Transport in London.
6. Bassey, E. J. (2000), 'The benefits of exercise for the health of older people', *Reviews in Clinical Gerontology* 10, 17–31
7. Skelton, D. A., Young, A., Walker, A. and Hoinville, E. (1999), *Physical Activity in Later Life: Further Analysis of the Allied Dunbar National Fitness Survey and the Health Education Authority Survey of Activity and Health*, London: Health Education Authority
8. See reference 6.

9. Ibid.
10. Ibid.
11. Ibid.
12. Ibid.
13. For example, *Exercise and Osteoporosis*, a free booklet published in 2000 by the National Osteoporosis Society.
14. Campbell, D., 'Bend it like the stars and risk wrecking your health', *Observer*, 18 September 2002
15. Burns, E., 'Older people in accident and emergency departments', *Age and Ageing* 30, 2001, 3–6, 30–3
16. Scuffham, P., Chaplin, S. and Legood, R. (2003), Incidence and costs of unintentional falls in older people in the United Kingdom', *Journal of Epidemiology and Community Health*, 57, 740–4
17. The Office for National Statistics (2003) *Health Survey for England 2001*, London: The Stationery Office
18. Downton, J. H. (1993), *Falls in the Elderly*, London: Edward Arnold
19. Department of Health (2001), *National Service Framework for Older People, Standard Six: Falls*, 76–85
20. Audit Commission (1995), *Co-ordinating Care for Elderly Patients with Hip Fracture*, London: Audit Commission, 29
21. See reference 19, 83
22. Ibid., 84–5
23. Swift, C. G., 'Falls in late life and their consequences: implementing effective services', *British Medical Journal* 322, 7 April 2001, 855–7

Chapter 7: Where to Live

1. Percival, J. (2002), 'Domestic spaces: uses and meanings in the daily lives of older people', *Ageing and Society* 22, 729–49
2. Outside stair-lifts are easier to obtain if a person meets the definition of 'disabled' in the National Assistance Act 1948, section 29, that is: 'Persons aged 18 or over who are blind, deaf or dumb or who suffer from mental disorder of any description, and other persons aged 18 or over who are substantially and permanently handicapped by illness, injury, or congenital deformity or such other disabilities as may be prescribed by the Minister.'
3. Walker, A. and Maltby, T. (1997), *Ageing Europe*, Buckingham: Open University Press, 35
4. Help the Aged was planning a national forum on homesharing to take place in London in December, 2003. It believes that schemes are needed outside the capital.
5. Christine Oldman evaluates some very sheltered housing schemes in York, C. (2000), *Blurring the Boundaries: A Fresh Look at Housing*

and Care Provision for Older People, Brighton: Pavilion Publishing.

6. The Audit Commission (1998), *Home Alone: The Role of Housing in Community Care*, London: Audit Commission, 24

7. *Leasehold Schemes for the Elderly: Management Charge Limits 2003/2004*, Housing Corporation Regulatory Circular no. 04/03, available free

8. In England and Wales the legislation is the Commonhold and Leasehold Reform Act 2002, in Scotland the Title Conditions Act (Scotland) 2002.

9. See Percival, J. (2000), 'Gossip in sheltered housing: its cultural importance and social implications', *Ageing and Society* 20, 303–25

10. Price is discussed in Dalley, G. (2001), Gaining Independence in Retirement: The Role and Benefits of Private Sheltered Housing for Older People, London: Centre for Policy on Ageing, 37

11. Supporting People is being organized by the Northern Ireland Housing Executive, in Scotland and Wales by the housing divisions of the Executive and the Assembly, and in England by the Office of the Deputy Prime Minister. Free literature is available.

12. This booklet is available from Foundations, the national co-ordinating body for home improvement agencies in England.

13. The Regulatory Reform (Housing Assistance) (England and Wales) Order 2002 of the Department of Transport, Local Government and the Regions

14. Ibid.

15. The relevant legislation is Part 6 of the Housing (Scotland) Act, 2001. The question of means-testing produced so much disagreement that this part of the Act did not get through the Scottish Parliament until February 2003.

16. *Community Care (Delayed Discharges etc) Act* (Qualifying Services) (England) Regulations

17. Scottish Executive Health Department, Community Care Division Circular CCD2/2001: *Free home care for older people leaving hospital*

18. For further details of disabled facilities grants, see Clements, L. (2000), *Community Care and the Law*, London: Legal Action Group. Carers UK publishes a useful booklet called *Getting Help to Adapt your Home.*

19. The system of grants for disabled people in Scotland is complex, but there is a very clear, detailed, free report available from the Scottish Executive entitled *Using the Law to Develop and Improve Equipment and Adaptation Provision*, Michael Mandelstam for the Strategy Forum: Equipment and Adaptations, June 2003.

20. The National Association of Citizen's Advice Bureaux (2002), *Door to Door: CAB Clients' Experience of Doorstep Selling*, London: NACAB

Chapter 8: Keeping in Touch
1. Glass, T., de Leon, C., Marottoli, R. and Berkman, L. (1999), 'Population based study of social and productive activities as predictors of survival among elderly Americans', *British Medical Journal* 319, 478–83
2. Bury, M. and Holme, A. (1991), *Life after Ninety*, London: Routledge
3. Walker, A. and Maltby, T. (1997), *Ageing Europe*, Buckingham: Open University Press, 26
4. Victor, C., Scambler S., Shah, S., Cook, D., Harris, T., Rink, E. and De Wilde, S. (2002), 'Has loneliness amongst older people increased? An investigation into variations between cohorts', *Ageing and Society* 22, 585–97
5. *Quaker Faith and Practice*, London: Yearly Meeting of the Religious Society of Friends, chapter 22, extract 6 (1995 edition)
6. Hétu, R., Jones, L. and Getty, L. (1993), 'The impact of acquired hearing impairment on intimate relationships: implications for rehabilitation', *Audiology* 32, 363–81
7. Kitwood, T. (1997), *Dementia Reconsidered: The Person Comes First*, Buckingham: Open University Press
8. Knox, I. (2003), *Older People and the Church*, London: T. and T. Clark. See also Jewell, A. (ed.) (2001), *Older People and the Church*, Peterborough: Methodist Publishing House
9. Katcher, A. H. (1981), 'Interaction between people and their pets: form and function' in Fogle, B. (ed.), *Interactions between People and their Pets*, as quoted by *Pets*, a booklet published jointly by the Society for Companion Animal Studies and Age Concern, 1993
10. Anderson, W. (1992), 'Pet ownership and risk factors for cardiovascular disease', *Medical Journal of Australia*, as quoted by *Pets*, ibid.
11. Friedmann, E. *et al* (1980), 'Animal companions and one-year survival of patients after discharge from a coronary care unit', *Public Health Reports* 95, 307–12, as quoted by McNicholas, J., Collis, G. and Morley, I., *Pets and People in Residential Care: Towards a Model of Good Practice*, available from the Department of Psychology, University of Warwick
12. McNicholas, J., see reference 11.
13. Ormerod, E. (1989), 'Pets and the elderly in the USA', *Journal of the Society for Companion Animal Studies* 1, 4, as quoted by McNicholas, J. *et al*, ibid.
14. McNicholas, J. *et al*, ibid.

Chapter 9: Professional Helpers
1. Tate, P. (2001), *The Doctor's Communication Handbook*, Oxford: Radcliffe Medical Press
2. Simon, C. and Kendrick, T., 'Informal carers: the role of general practitioners and district nurses', *British Journal of General Practice*, August 2001
3. Department of Health (1999), *Caring about Carers: A National Strategy for Carers* (1999), 57
4. Brown, K., Boot, D., Groom, L. and Williams, E. I., 'Problems found in the over-75s by the annual health check', *British Journal of General Practice*, January 1997
5. Drury, M. and Neuberger, J., 'Ageing Britain: changes and opportunities for general practice', *British Journal of General Practice*, January 2001
6. Parkinson's Disease Society (2001), *Working Together: Improving Primary Care for People with Parkinson's Disease*
7. AMD Alliance UK, *GPs in the Dark about Leading Cause of Sight Loss*, press release, 24.9.02. The Alliance is made up of the RNIB, Age Concern England, the Macular Disease Society, NALSVI, Fight for Sight and the Wales Council for the Blind.
8. Department of Health (2001), *National Service Framework for Older People*, 93
9. Audit Commission in Wales (2002), *Losing Time: Developing Mental Health Services for Older People in Wales*, London: Audit Commission for Local Authorities and the National Health Service in England and Wales. Evidence for the extent to which GPs failed to recognize depression in the past can be obtained from MacDonald, A. (1986), 'Do general practitioners "miss" depression in elderly patients?' *British Medical Journal*, 292, 1,365–7, quoted by Anderson, D. (2001), 'Treating depression in old age: the reasons to be positive', *Age and Ageing* 30, 13–17
10. Anderson, D., ibid.
11. Baldwin, R. (2001), 'Suicide in older people – can it be prevented?', *Reviews in Clinical Gerontology* 11, 107–8
12. Birren, J. (ed.) (1996), *Encyclopaedia of Gerontology: Age, Ageing and the Aged*, London: Academic Press, Vol. I, 4
13. Williams, S., 'Depressed patients need more than drugs and psychiatrists', *British Medical Journal* 326, 8.2.03, 338
14. Audit Commission in Wales, see reference 9
15. Some of the ethical questions which dementia can bring are explored in Laski, M. (2000), 'Would you like to know what is wrong with you? On telling the truth to patients with dementia',

Journal of Medical Ethics 26, 108–13, and Jones, J. G. (2001), 'Ethical and legal issues in the care of people with dementia', *Reviews in Clinical Gerontology* 11, 245–68.

16. Powell, J. A. (2000), 'Communication interventions in dementia', *Reviews in Clinical Gerontology* 10, 161–8

17. Ibid. and Zanetti, O., *et al* (2002), 'Predictors of cognitive improvement after reality orientation in Alzheimer's disease', *Age and Ageing* 31, 193–6

18. Department of Health (2001), *National Service Framework for Older People: Medicines and Older People*, 1.

19. Ibid.

20. Ibid.

21. Sutherland, S., et al (1999), *With Respect to Old Age: Long Term Care – Rights and Responsibilities, A Report by The Royal Commission on Long Term Care*, Chairman: Professor Stewart Sutherland, London: The Stationery Office, Cmnd 4192–1, 9

22. Agencies and other organizations also have to provide for the Commission a statement about their arrangements for providing services when a care worker is off sick, their requirements in relation to time sheets, their procedures to safeguard clients' property and for the administration of medication and for handling complaints.

23. These two documents are available from the National Care Standards Commission. Similar regulations and standards can be obtained from the Scottish Commission for the Regulation of Care and the Care Standards Inspectorate for Wales.

24. Henwood, M. (2001), *Future Imperfect? Report of the King's Fund Inquiry*, London: King's Fund Publishing, 89

25. The Continuing Care Conference (1998), *Framework Contract between Domiciliary Care Provider and Service User*, London: The Continuing Care Conference.

26. This can be obtained from any of the four regulatory Social Care Councils in each of the countries in the UK by post or on the Internet. It is called *Code of Practice for Social Care Workers and Code of Practice for Employers of Social Care Workers*.

27. Care provided in a care home is also sometimes known as a community care service. Care home support is the subject of Part Four.

28. The Department of Health has published two forms of guidance on community care assessments: 'policy guidance' and 'practice guidance'. The courts expect councils always to comply with policy guidance: in effect, it has the power of law. Practice guidance, on the other hand, explains how a council should go about a task; in courts a council would simply have to explain why it had not fol-

lowed practice guidance. The relevant documents in this case are *Community Care in the Next Decade and Beyond: The Policy Guidance*, London: HMSO, November 1990, and *Care Management and Assessment: a Practitioner's Guide*, London: HMSO, 1991

29. Department of Health (1991), *Care Management and Assessment: A Practitioner's Guide*, London: HMSO

30. For instance, in 1998 the London Borough of Haringey was taken to court because it had considered only the personal care needs (help with washing, dressing and the like) of an older person in its area and was challenged; the court held that this restriction was unlawful and that the community care assessment had to investigate all possible needs. (Haringey, London Borough Council ex p Norton, as quoted by Clements, L. (2000), *Community Care and the Law*, London: Legal Action Group, 56)

31. R v Bristol City Council ex p Penfold, as quoted by Clements, L. (2000), *Community Care and the Law*, London: Legal Action Group, 55

32. The Department of Health (2002), *Fair Access to Care Services (Policy Guidance)*, Local Authority Circular (2002), 13; the Department also published *Practice Guidance* in 2002.

33. Department of Health (2001), *Fairer Charging Policies for Homecare and other Non-Residential Social Services*, paragraph 41

34. The figures are £19,500 in England and Northern Ireland, £20,000 in Wales and £18,500 in Scotland.

35. The Department of Health (2002), *Guidance on the Single Assessment Process for Older People,* Health Service Circular 2002/001, Local Authority Circular 2002/1

36. Supporting People is being organized by the Northern Ireland Housing Executive, in Scotland by Housing Division 3 of the Executive, in Wales by the Assembly's Housing Directorate and in England by the Office of the Deputy Prime Minister. Free literature is available.

37. The guidance goes on to say 'although this may be unavoidable where the user has not co-operated with the assessment. A first bill for a charge for a lengthy past period can cause needless anxiety. Any increase in charges should also be notified and no increased charge made for a period before the notification.' The Department of Health (2001), *Fairer Charging Policies for Homecare and other Non-Residential Social Services*, paragraph 90

38. Audit Commission (1999) *Charging with Care: how Councils Charge for Homecare*

39. Scottish Executive, *Free personal and nursing care in Scotland from 1 July*

2002: frequently asked questions; more details are contained in Scottish Executive, *Circular No. CCD 4/2002: Free Personal and Nursing Care in Scotland: Guidance for Local Authorities, the NHS and other Service Providers.*

40. The Health and Social Services and Social Security Adjudications Act 1983. For further explanation of this point see Clements, L. (reference 43), 339
41. Department of Health (2001), see reference 33, paragraph 91
42. See reference 33.
43. Ibid.
44. Department of Health (2003), *Direct Payments Guidance: Community Care, Services for Carers and Children's Services (Direct Payments) Guidance England 2003*
45. Ibid.
46. Community Care, Services for Carers and Children's Services (Direct Payments) (England) Regulations 2003
47. Community Care and Health (Scotland) Act 2002

Chapter 10: Choosing a Home

1. Thus, while only 4 per cent of the entire population of England over the age of 65 live in care homes, the proportion is 30 per cent for those aged 90 and over. Bajekal, M. (2002), 'Care homes and their residents', in Prior, G. and Primatesta, P. (eds), *Health Survey for England 2000*, Norwich: The Stationery Office, 11
2. Victor, C., *et al* (2001), 'The inappropriate placement of older people in nursing homes in England and Wales: a national audit', *Quality in Ageing: Policy, Practice and Research* 2, 1, 16–25
3. Netten, A. and Darton, R., 'Formal and informal support prior to admission: are self-funders being admitted to care homes unnecessarily?' *British Society of Gerontology Annual Conference 2001: Report*
4. The upper capital limit is £19,500 in England and Northern Ireland but £18,500 in Scotland and £20,000 in Wales.
5. The lower capital limit is £12,000 in England and Northern Ireland, £11,500 in Scotland and £12,250 in Wales.
6. The Department of Health (1992), *The National Assistance Act (Choice of Accommodation) Directions, Local Authority Circular (2) 27*. This instruction, often called the 'Direction on Choice', is referred to in the very useful book by Margaret Richards (2001), *Long-term Care for Older People: Law and Financial Planning*, Bristol: Jordan Publishing
7. Davies, S. (2001), 'Relatives' Experiences of Nursing Home Entry: A Constructivist Inquiry', unpublished PhD thesis, University of

Sheffield. See also Gregg, E. (1977), 'An Ethnographic Study of Life in a Nursing Home and the Provision of Care to the Elderly Mentally Infirm', unpublished MSc thesis, the Department of Human Sciences, Brunel University

8. The regulations and standards for England are as follows: *Social Care, England: Children and Young Persons, England: The Care Homes Regulations, Statutory Instrument No. 3965* (2001), The Stationery Office and the Department of Health (2001), *National Minimum Standards for Care Homes for Older People*, London: The Stationery Office

9. This figure of 70 per cent is frequently used by people in the world of dementia research but it is not derived from any single piece of work. However, a survey by the Personal Social Services Research Unit in 1999 found that 54 per cent of people in residential homes had mild and 25 per cent severe cognitive impairment, while in nursing homes the figures were 38 per cent and 46 per cent respectively (The Office of National Statistics, *Social Focus on Older People*, London: Stationery Office, quoted by the Alzheimer's Society in 2002 in *Is Free Nursing Care 'Unfair and Unworkable'?*)

10. The standards also say that the registered person of a care home must 'provide telephone facilities which are suitable for the needs of service users'. So if you are hard of hearing, a specially adapted phone should be made available (page 92).

11. See the discussion on caring on pages 550–57.

12. The term 'matron' in the care home setting does not imply equivalent status to a hospital matron and denotes no special paper qualifications. Some managers call themselves 'care managers'; again, this term too is used in another context: social workers are often called care managers.

13. Henwood, M. (2001), *Future Imperfect? Report of the King's Fund Care and Support Inquiry*, London: King's Fund Publishing, 124

14. Barnes, S., McKee, K. J., Morgan, K., Parker, C. J., Torrington, J. and Tregenza, P. R. (2001), 'The design in caring environments study', *Proceedings of the British Society of Gerontology Annual Conference*, Birmingham: BSG

15. Carr, J. S. and Marshall, M. (1993), 'Innovations in long-stay care for people with dementia', *Reviews in Clinical Gerontology* 3, 157–67

16. These environmental standards which have been amended also cover the dimensions of doorways and communal spaces, the proportion of single as opposed to shared bedrooms and the numbers of passenger lifts, assisted baths and shared toilets).

17. See Clarke, A. with Bright, L. (2002), *Showing Restraint: Challenging*

the Use of Restraint in Care Homes, London: Counsel and Care; and *With Respect to Old Age: Long Term Care – Rights and Responsibilities, A Report by The Royal Commission on Long Term Care,* Chairman: Professor Stewart Sutherland (1999), The Stationery Office, Cmnd 4192–1, Research Volume 2, 'Chapter 6: The Models: Assisted Technology'

18. Torrington J. (1996), *Care Homes for Older People: A Briefing and Design Guide,* London: Spon

19. Moore, D., 'It's like a gold medal and its mine – dolls in dementia care', *Journal of Dementia Care,* November/December 2001

20. The Association of Charity Officers (2001), Fees Paid to GPs for Services Provided to Residents of Care Accommodation for Older People 2000–2001, Potters Bar: The Association of Charity Officers

Chapter 11: The Cost

1. The authority was Wiltshire County Council and the case is referred to in Thompson, P., Winfield, H., Simmons, D. and Linney, J. (2003), *Paying for Care Handbook,* London: Child Poverty Action Group, 266.

2. Commission for Local Administration in England (2003) *The Local Government Ombudmen's Special Report: Advice and Guidance on the Funding of Aftercare under Section of the Mental Health Act 1983*

3. House of Commons, *Hansard: Proceedings of Standing Committee E, Health and Social Care Bill,* 8 February 2001, col. 533, as quoted by Thompson, P., 'Charges for residential and nursing homes – keeping abreast of the changes', *Elderly Client Adviser,* March/April 2001

4. The rules on eligibility for Income Support are complex. For details, contact the Department of Work and Pensions helpline or the helpline of Help the Aged, Age Concern or Counsel and Care; for greater detail, consult Thompson, P., *et al* (reference 3).

5. Department of Health, *Charges for Residential Accommodation: CRAG Amendment No. 15,* Local Authority Circular (2001) 25; the Department of Health, *Charges for Residential Accommodation: CRAG Amendment No. 16,* Local Authority Circular (2001) 29; and the Department of Health, *Charges for Residential Accommodation: Deferred Payments Scheme,* Local Authority Circular (2002) 12

6. Burton, J. (1998), *Managing Residential Care,* London: Routledge

7. The Office of Fair Trading (1998), *Older People as Consumers in Care Homes: a Report by the Office of Fair Trading,* London: OFT

8. Department of Health (1993), *Ordinary Residence,* Local Authority Circular (1993), 7

9. The arrangements for state support for temporary residents are complex. They are explained in Age Concern (2003) Factsheet 10, *Local Authority Charging Procedures for Care Homes*.

10. Respite care can sometimes be provided free on the NHS.

11. 'Carer seeks ruling from NHS Ombudsman', *National Newsletter of the Alzheimer's Society*, May 2002

12. If you are trying to influence an assessment in England (there is only one rate paid outside England), acquaint yourself with the tool which nurse assessors are supposed to use when determining in which band to place residents. This tool, developed by the Department of Health, is available at www.doh.gov.uk/jointunit/freenursingcare.

13. Wright, F. (1998), *Findings: The Effect on Carers of a Frail Older Person's Admission to a Care Home*, York: The Joseph Rowntree Foundation

14. This extract was quoted by Clements, L. (2000), *Community Care and the Law*, London: Legal Action Group, 335. For further details of the liable relatives charge see the Department of Health, *Charging for Residential Accommodation Guide (CRAG)*, section 11. It is also explained by Thompson, P. *et al*, see reference 3.

15. Thompson, P. et al., ibid.

Chapter 12: Going In

1. The national minimum standards referred to in this chapter are the revised standards published for England in 2003 – see page 344.

2. The Department of Health (1999), *Fit for the Future? National Required Standards for Residential and Nursing Homes for Older People: Consultation Draft*, 34

3. Davies, S. (2001), 'Relatives' Experiences of Nursing Home Entry: A Constructivist Inquiry', unpublished PhD thesis, University of Sheffield. The care plan is provided for in the national minimum standards for care homes.

4. Calkins, M. and Brush, J., 'Designing for dining: the secret of happier mealtimes', *Journal of Dementia Care*, March/April 2002

5. Bajekal, M. (2002), 'Care homes and their residents' in Prior, G. and Primatesta, P. (eds), *Health Survey for England: The Health of the Older People 2000*, Norwich: The Stationery Office, 30

6. Gray-Davidson, F. (1998), *Alzheimer's: A Practical Guide for Carers*, London: Piatkus

7. 'Nurse stole £80 from 93-year-old', *Dorking Advertiser*, Dorking, 27 June 2002

8. The reasons for care home closures are explored in a report by the Personal Social Services Research Unit of the University of Kent

at Canterbury entitled *Care Home Closures: The Provider Perspective* (PSSRU discussion paper 1753/2) which was published in 2002.

9. His Honour Sir Jonathan Clarke, Mrs Annie Stevenson and Mr Brian Parrott, *Report and Findings of the Extraordinary Complaints Panel, Closure of Granby Way Residential Care Home for Older People, Plymouth*, 4.11.02
10. Age Concern (2002), *Care Home Closures: Factsheet 47*
11. The Office of Fair Trading (1998), *Older People as Consumers in Care Homes: A Report by the Office of Fair Trading*, London: OFT
12. Department of Health (2003), *Direct Payments Guidance: Community Care, Services for Carers and Children's Services (Direct Payments) Guidance England 2003*, paragraph 74

Chapter 13: Treatment

1. Walker, A. (2002), *Hospital-acquired Infection and Bed Use in NHS Scotland*, Robinson Centre for Biostatistics, University of Glasgow
2. These matters are explored in *Ageism: The Last Frontier* – see Introduction, reference 8.
3. The Department of Health, *Intermediate Care*, Health Service Circular 2001/01 and Local Authority Circular (2001) 1
4. As explained on page 57, I use the term 'health authority' as a generic one to cover the various health organizations which exist in the different parts of the UK.
5. British Geriatrics Society (2001), 'Commentary: Can we manage more acutely ill elderly patients in the community?', *Age and Ageing* 30, 441–3
6. British Geriatrics Society (2000), *Shaping the Future NHS: Long-term Planning for Hospitals and Related Services: The Society's Response to the Department of Health Consultation Document on the Findings of the National Beds Inquiry*, London: BGS
7. *National Minimum Standards on Hospice Care*, available from the Scottish Commission for the Regulation of Care.
8. The Department of Health, Standing Nursing and Midwifery Advisory Committee (2001), *Caring for Older People: A Nursing Priority*
9. Rayner, C. (2003), *How Did I Get Here from There?* Virago
10. *Patients' Nutritional Needs Forgotten*, Royal College of Physicians, press notice, 9 July 2002. For further information, see *Nutrition and Patients: A Doctor's Responsibility – Report of a Working Party of the Royal College of Physicians*, published in 2002.
11. Michel, J.-P., Lutters, M., Vogt, N. and Krause, K. H. (2002), 'Infection Control' in (eds) Grimley-Evans, J. *et al*, *The Oxford Textbook of Geriatric Medicine*, Oxford University Press, 64–5

12. Davies, S., Nolan, M., Brown, J., and Wilson, F. (2001), *Dignity on the Ward: Promoting Excellence in Care: Good Practice in Acute Hospital Care for Older People*, Sheffield: University of Sheffield, School of Nursing and Midwifery

13. The Department of Health, *Continuing Care: NHS and Local Councils' Responsibilities* Health Service Circular 2001/015, Local Authority Circular (2001) 18, paragraphs 24, 5 and 8

14. This report is available from the Royal College of Physicians by post or on the web at www.rpclondon.ac.uk/ceeu-stroke.home.htm

15. Ibid.

16. Care in a designated stroke unit, staffed by specialist stroke consultants and nurses, cuts the death rate from stroke by 19 per cent and reduces the combined death and long-term disability rate by 29 per cent, according to the report of the Working Party on Stroke of the Royal College of Physicians published in July 2002 (see Boseley, S., 'Specialist stroke units could save 6,000 lives every year', *Guardian*, 24 July 2002, or the report itself on the RCP's website).

Chapter 14: Your Life in their Hands

1. Readers interested in pursuing resuscitation in more detail may care to refer to material on the author's website.

2. See for instance, Ellershaw, J., and Ward, C. (2003), 'Care of the dying patient: the last hours or days of life', *British Medical Journal*, 4.1.02

3. The British Medical Association (2001), *Withholding and Withdrawing Life-prolonging Medical Treatment: Guidance for Decision-making*

4. The General Medical Council (2002), *Withholding and Withdrawing Life-prolonging Treatments: Good Practice in Decision-making*

5. Hanratty, B., *et al*, 'Doctors' perceptions of palliative care for heart failure: focus group study', *British Medical Journal* 325, 14.9.02, 581–5

6. World Health Organization (1990), *Cancer Pain Relief and Palliative Care*, Geneva: WHO, as quoted by Baines, M. and Sykes, N. P. (2000), 'Symptom Management and Palliative Care' in (eds) Grimley Evans, J., *et al*, *Oxford Textbook of Geriatric Medicine*, Oxford University Press, 1113

7. Gott, C. M., Ahmedzai, S, H. and Wood, C. (2001), 'How many inpatients at an acute hospital have palliative care needs? Comparing the perspectives of medical and nursing staff', *Palliative Medicine* 15, 451–60

8. Baines, M. and Sykes, N. P., see reference 6. For further information about palliative care, see Doyle, D., Hanks, G. W. C. and

MacDonald, N. (2003) *Oxford Textbook of Palliative Medicine*, Oxford University Press 9. Mary Baines and Nigel Sykes urge, 'Believe the patient's complaint. In chronic or terminal illness, patients often minimise their symptoms.'

9. Hinton, J. (1967), *Dying*, Harmondsworth: Penguin, as quoted by Baines and Sykes, ibid.

Chapter 15: Discharge

1. Health and Social Care Joint Unit and Health and Social Care Change Agent Team, the Department of Health (2003), *Discharge from Hospital: A Good Practice Checklist*, para 1.3.2
2. The Community Care (Delayed Discharges Etc.) Act, 2003
3. Clements, L. (2000), *Community Care and the Law*, London: Legal Action Group
4. The Department of Health (1989), *Discharge of Patients from Hospital*
5. Department of Health (2003) *Discharge from Hospital: Pathway, Process and Practice*, para.7.6
6. The Department of Health (2001), *Continuing Care: NHS and Local Councils' Responsibilities*, Health Service Circular 2001/015; Local Authority Circular 2001/18
7. The House of Commons Health Committee (2002), *Delayed Discharges: Third Report of Session 2001–02, Vol. I: Report and Proceedings of the Committee*, HC 617–I, 35
8. See reference 5.
9. Ibid.
10. Ibid.
11. See reference 5.
12. Ibid.
13. *NHS Funding for Long Term Care: Report of the Health Service Ombudsman, 2nd Report, Session 2002–03*, HC 399
14. The Department of Health (2003), *Department of Health Directions: Continuing Care Policy*
15. See reference 13.
16. For example, the Commission for Health Improvement published a report in 2003 on Rowan Ward of Manchester Mental Health and Social Care Trust, which provides mental health services for elderly people.
17. Letter from the Chief Inspector, Social Services Inspectorate, the Department of Health, London, concerning the *Care Standards Act 2000: National Minimum Standards – Care Homes for Older People*, CI (2001) 4, March 2001. The letter states: 'Local authorities and inde-

pendent providers of care homes and any NHS trusts which provide residential care homes should take note of these standards and review their services so that they are prepared to meet these standards when they are implemented.'

Chapter 18: Legal and Financial

1. As quoted by Ashton, G. R. (1995), *Elderly People and the Law*, London: Butterworths and Age Concern, 315
2. Administering an enduring power of attorney also attracts fees, for example if and when the attorneyship is registered, but usually fewer payments need to be made to the Public Guardianship Office than under a receivership.
3. Help the Aged issues a useful free booklet entitled *Managing a Lump Sum*.
4. Lush, D., 'Objections to the registration of enduring powers of attorney: a graphic account', *Elder Law and Finance*, May 2001, 4–9
5. Ibid., 9

Chapter 19: Nursing and Other Care

1. Some of these matters are explored in Clarke, A., with Bright, L. (2002), *Showing Restraint: Challenging the Use of Restraint in Care Homes*, London: Counsel and Care. See also page 000.
2. A useful publication is Clarke, A., Bright, L. and Greenwood, C. (2003), *Sex and Relationships*, London: Counsel and Care, which is one of a series of examinations into aspects of care home life published by Counsel and Care.
3. Collins, J. 'Bill of no rights', *Community Care*, 3 September 2003, 32–33

Chapter 20: A Vital Role

1. Until April 2003, this benefit was known as Invalid Care Allowance.
2. Figures from *With Respect to Old Age: Long Term Care: Rights and Responsibilities, A Report by The Royal Commission on Long Term Care*, Chairman: Professor Stewart Sutherland (1999), London: The Stationery Office, Cmnd 4192–1, Research Volume 3, 20.
3. Carers UK (2002), *Without Us*, London: Carers UK
4. The Health Advisory Service (2000), *Not Because They Are Old: An Independent Inquiry into the Care of Older People on Acute Wards in General Hospitals*, London: Health Advisory Service, quoted by Davies, S., Nolan, M., Brown, J., and Wilson, F. (2001), *Dignity on the Ward: Promoting Excellence in Care: Good Practice in Acute Hospital*

Care for Older People, Sheffield: University of Sheffield, School of Nursing and Midwifery, 52

5. Davies, S. *et al* – see Chapter 13, reference 11.
6. Tarlow, B., 'Caring: a negotiated process that varies' in Gordon, S., Bener, P. and Noddings, N. (eds.) (1996), *Care Giving: Readings in Knowledge, Practice, Ethics and Politics*, Pennsylvania: University of Pennsylvania Press, 56–82, quoted in Davies, S., *et al*, see reference 5, 53.
7. Action on Elder Abuse (2000), *Listening is Not Enough*, London: Action on Elder Abuse
8. Henwood, M. (1998), *Ignored and Invisible? Carers' Experience of the NHS*, London: Carers UK
9. Holzhausen, E. and Pearlman, V. (2001), *Caring on the Breadline: The Financial Implications of Caring*, London: Carers UK

Chapter 21: Practicalities

1. The Department of Health (2001), *Carers and People with Parental Responsibility for Disabled Children: Policy Guidance*; the Department of Health (2001), *Carers and People with Parental Responsibility for Disabled Children: Practice Guidance* and the Department of Health (2001), *Carers' and Disabled Children Act 2000: A Practitioner's Guide to Carers' Assessments*
2. The Welsh Assembly (2001), *Carers' and Disabled Children Act Guidance* and the Welsh Assembly (2001), *Practitioners' Guide to Carer's Assessment*. Publication of these documents fulfils a commitment given in the National Assembly's *Carers' Strategy in Wales: Implementation Plan*, published in 2000.
3. *Caring about Carers: A National Strategy for Carers* (1999), no author or government department given; the Prime Minister has contributed a foreword; copies available from the Department of Health, 56.

Appendix: Complaints

1. The Department of Health, *The Complaints Procedure Directions 1990*. For further details of the requirements for complaints procedures, see Clements, L. (2000), *Community Care and the Law*, London: Legal Action Group, 408–25.
2. The guidance says that the primary objective of the first stage of the complaints procedure 'is to provide the fullest possible opportunity for investigation and resolution of the complaint, as quickly as is sensible in the circumstances, aiming to satisfy the patient, while being scrupulously fair to staff' – The Department of Health

(1996), *Directions to NHS Trusts, Health Authorities and Special Health Authorities for Special Hospitals on Hospital Complaints Procedures,* as quoted by Clements, L., ibid., 263.

3. The Health Service Commissioner, *Annual Report 1997/98*, Chapter 3, as quoted by Clements, L., ibid., 269. The Health Service Ombudsman produces a useful free leaflet about his work entitled *Do You Have a Complaint about the Service You Have Received from the NHS? How the Health Service Ombudsman Can Help You.*

Useful Contacts

Abuse

If you fear imminent or have just experienced abuse at any time of the day or night, telephone the main social services or social work department number of your local authority number or, if out of office hours, for example during the night or on a bank holiday, its social services emergency duty team; the numbers should be in your telephone directory. Social services may make an immediate visit, with or without the police. Or you could make your first call to the police: they and social services should be working closely together in this field, so whoever you phone, your concerns should get through to the appropriate person or organization. Also, the charity Action on Elder Abuse operates a helpline during office hours.

Action on Elder Abuse

Astral House
1,268 London Road
London SW16 4ER
Tel: 020 876 5 7000
Helpline: 0808 808 8141
www.elderabuse.org.uk

Age Concern Cymru

4th Floor
1 Cathedral Road
Cardiff CF11 9SD
Tel: 029 2037 1566
www.accymru.org.uk

Age Concern England

Astral House
1,268 London Road
London SW16 4ER
Tel: 020 8679 8000
Helpline: 0800 009966
www.ace.org.uk

Age Concern Northern Ireland

3 Lower Crescent
Belfast BT7 1NR
Tel: 028 9024 5729
Helpline: 028 9032 5055
www.ageconcernni.org.uk

Age Concern Scotland

113 Rose Street
Edinburgh EH2 3DT
Helpline: 0800 009966
Tel: 0131 220 3345
www.ageconcernscotland.org.uk

AIMS

Astral House
1,268 London Road
London SW16 4ER
Tel: 0845 600 2001
www.ageconcern.org.uk/aims

The Almshouse Association
Billingbear Lodge
Carters Hill
Wokingham
Berks.
RG40 5RU
Tel: 01344 452922
www.almshouses.org

Alzheimer Scotland
22 Drumsheugh Gardens
Edinburgh EH3 7RN
Tel: 0131 243 1453
www.alzscot.org.uk

The Alzheimer's Society, England
Gordon House
10 Greencoat Place
London SW1P 1PH
Tel: 020 7306 0606
Helpline: 0845 300 0336
www.alzheimers.org.uk

The Alzheimer's Society, Northern Ireland
86 Eglantine Avenue
Belfast BT9 6EU
Tel: 028 9066 4100
Helpline: 0845 300 0336
www.alzheimers.org.uk

The Alzheimer's Society, Wales
4th Floor
Baltic House
Mount Stuart Square
Cardiff CF1O 5FH
Tel: 029 2043 1990
www.alzheimers.org.uk

The Amateur Swimming Association
Harold Fern House
Derby Square
Loughborough
Leics.
LE11 5AL
Tel: 01589 618700
www.britishswimming.org

The Animal Welfare Trust
Tyler's Way
Watford Bypass
Watford
Herts.
WD25 8WT
Tel: 020 8950 8215
www.nawt.org.uk

Arthritis Care
18 Stephenson Way
London NW1 2HD
Tel: 020 7380 6500
www.arthritiscare.org.uk

The Arthritis and Rheumatism Council
Copeman House
St Mary's Court
St Mary's Gate
Chesterfield
Derbyshire
S41 7TD
Tel: 01246 558007
www.ukcosa.org.uk

The Association of Charity Officers
Beechwood House
Wyllotts Close
Potters Bar
Herts.
EN6 2HN
Tel: 01707 651777
www.aco.uk.net

The Association of Independent Care Advisers
6 Westmount Close
Southwick
Brighton
East Sussex
BN42 4SR
Tel: 01483 203066
www.aica.org.uk

The Association of Welsh Community Health Councils
Ground Floor
Park House
Greyfriars Road
Cardiff CF10 3AF
Tel: 029 2023 5558
www.patienthelp.wales.nhs.uk

The Audit Commission for England and Wales
1 Vincent Square
London SW1P 2PN
Tel: 020 7828 1212
www.audit-commission.gov.uk

Audit Scotland
110 George Street
Edinburgh EH2 4LH
Tel: 0131 477 1234
www.audit-scotland.gov.uk

Battersea Dogs Home
4 Battersea Park Road
London SW8 4AA
Tel: 0207 622 3626
www.dogshome.org

Better Government for Older People
207–221 Pentonville Road
London N1 9UZ
Tel: 020 7843 1582
www.bettergovernmentforolder
people.gov.uk

The Blue Cross
Field Centre
Shilton Road
Burford
Oxon.
OX18 4PF
Tel: 01993 822651
www.bluecross.org.uk

Breast Cancer Care
Kiln House
210 New King's Road
London SW6 4NZ
Tel: 020 7384 2984
Helpline: 0808 800 600
Textphone: 0808 800 601
www.breastcancercare.org.uk

The British Association for Counselling and Psychotherapy
1 Regent Place
Rugby
Warks.
CV21 2PJ
Tel: 0980 443 5252
www.bacp.co.uk

The British Association of Domiciliary Care (BADCO)
6 Meadow Rise
Winnersh
Wokingham
Berkshire
RG41 5PD
Tel: 0118 977 2878
www.badco.org/

The British Association of Psychotherapists
37 Mapesbury Road
London NW2 4HJ
Tel: 020 8452 9823
Helpline: 020 8452 9823
www.bap-psychotherapy.org

The British Association of Social Workers
16 Kent Street
Birmingham
B5 6RD
Tel: 0121 622 3911
www.basw.co.uk

The British Council of Disabled People
Litchurch Plaza
Litchurch Lane
Derby
DE24 8AA
Tel: 01332 295551
Helpline: 01332 298288
www.bcodp.org.uk

The British Geriatrics Society
Marjory Warren House
31 St John's Square
London EC1M 4DN
Tel: 020 7608 1369
www.bgs.org.uk

The British Heart Foundation
14 Fitzhardinge Street
London W1H 6DH
Tel: 020 7935 0185
www.bhf.org.uk

The British Institute of Human Rights
King's College London
8th Floor
75–79 York Road
London SE1 7AW
Tel: 020 7401 2712
www.bihr.org/

The British Lung Foundation
78 Hatton Garden
London EC1N 8LD
Tel: 020 7831 5831
www.lunguk.org

The British Medical Association
BMA House
Tavistock Square
London WC1H 9JP
Tel: 020 7387 4499
www.bma.org.uk

The British Psychological Society
48 Princess Road East
Leicester
Tel: 0116 254 9568
www.bps.org.uk/index.cfm

The British Red Cross Society
9 Grosvenor Crescent
London SW1X 7EJ
Tel: 020 7235 5454
www.redcross.org.uk

The British Society of Gerontology
Secretary: Susan Tester
The Department of Applied
Social Science
University of Stirling
Stirling
FK9 4LA
www.britishgerontology.org.uk

The British Tinnitus Association
4th Floor
White Building
Fitzalan Square
Sheffield
S1 2AZ
Tel: 0114 279 6600
www.tinnitus.org.uk

The British Wheel of Yoga
25 Jermyn Street
Sleaford
Lincs.
NG34 7RU
Tel: 01529 306851
www.bwy.org.uk

The British Wireless for the Blind Fund
Gabriel House
34 New Road
Chatham
Kent
ME4 4QR
Tel: 01634 832501
www.blind.org.uk

The BT Age and Disability Team
Tel: 0800 919 591
Textphone: 0800 243 123

Care and Repair Cymru
Norbury House
Norbury Road
Cardiff CF5 3AS
Tel: 029 2057 6286
www.careandrepair.org.uk

Care and Repair England
Bridgford House
Pavilion Road
West Bridgford
Nottingham
NG2 5GJ
Tel: 0115 982 1527
www.careandrepair-england.org.uk

Care and Repair Scotland
5 Finnieston Quay
Glasgow G3 8HN
Tel: 0141 221 9879
www.careandrepair-scot.org.uk

The Care Council for Wales
6th Floor
West Wing
South Gate House
Wood Street
Cardiff CF10 1EW
Tel: 029 2022 6257
www.ccwales.org.uk

Care Direct
Tel: 0800 444 000
www.doh.gov/caredirect

**The Care Standards
Inspectorate for Wales**
Heol Billingley
Parc Nantgarw
Nanatgarw
CF15 7QZ
Tel: 01443 848450
www.wales.gov.uk/
subisocial/policycarestandards

**The Carers Christian
Fellowship**
14 Cavie Close
Nine Elms
Swindon
SN5 5XD
Tel: 01793 887068
www.carerschristianfellowship.
org

Carers of the Elderly
(provides dementia care training)
Latimer House
40 Hanson Street
London W1W 6UL
Tel: 0207 380 9188
www.dementiarelief.org.uk

Carers Northern Ireland
11 Lower Crescent
Belfast BT7 1NR
Tel: 028 9043 9843
www.carersni.org

Carers Scotland
91 Mitchell Street,
Glasgow G1 3LN
Tel: 0141 221 9141
www.carersonline.org.uk

Carers UK
Ruth Pitter House
20–25 Glasshouse Yard
London EC1A 4JT
Tel: 020 7490 8818
Helpline: 0808 808 7777
www.carers.demon.co.uk

Carers Wales
River House
Ynysbridge Court
Gwaelood-y-Garth
Cardiff CF15 9SS
Tel: 029 2081 1370
www.carcrsonline.org.uk

Caring Matters
132 Gloucester Place
London NW1 6DT
Tel: 020 7402 2702
www.caring-matters.org.uk

Cats Protection
17 King's Road
Horsham
West Sussex
RH13 5PN
Tel: 01403 221900
Helpline: 01403 221919
www.cats.org.uk

**The Centre for Policy on
Ageing**
19–23 Ironmonger Row
London EC1V 3QP
Tel: 020 7553 6500
www.cpa.org.uk

The Centre for Sheltered Housing Studies
First Floor
Elgar House
Shrub Hill Road
Worcester
WR4 9EE
Tel: 01905 21155
www.cshs.co.uk

The Chartered Society of Physiotherapy
14 Bedford Row
London WC1
Tel: 020 7306 6666
www.csp.org

Chest, Heart and Stroke Scotland
65 North Castle Street
Edinburgh EH2 3LT
Tel: 0131 225 6963
Helpline: 0845 077 6000
www.chss.org.uk

The Child Poverty Action Group
94 White Lion Street
London N1 9PF
Tel: 020 7837 7979
www.cpag.org.uk

The Christian Council on Ageing
Epworth House
Stuart Street
Derby
DEl 2EQ
Tel: 01803 722415

The Cinnamon Trust
Foundry House
Foundry Square
Hayle
Cornwall
TR27 4HE
Tel: 01736 757900
www.cinnamon.org.uk

The Citizen's Advice Bureaux Northern Ireland
Regional Office
11 Upper Crescent
Belfast BT7 1NT
Tel: 028 9023 1120
www.niacab.org.uk/web/index.html

The College of Occupational Therapists
106–114 Borough High Street
London SE1
Tel: 020 7357 6480
www.cot.org

The Commission for Health Improvement
Finsbury Tower
103–105 Bunhill Row
London EC1Y 8TG
Tel: 020 7448 9200
www.chi.nhs.uk

The Commission for Local Administration in England
See Local Government Ombudsman

The Consumers' Association
2 Marylebone Road
London NWI 4DF
Tel: 020 7830 6000
www.which.net

Contact the Elderly
15 Henrietta Street
London WC2E 8QH
Tel: 020 7240 0630
www.contact-the-elderly.org

The Continence Foundation
307 Hatton Square
16 Baldwin Gardens
London EC1N 7RJ
Tel: 020 7404 6875
Helpline: 020 7831 9831
www.continence-foundation.
org.uk

The Continuing Care Conference
1 Millbank
London SW1P 3JZ
Tel: 020 7222 1265

Counsel and Care
Twyman House
16 Bonny Street
London NW1 9PG
Tel: 020 7241 8555
Helpline: 0845 300 7585
www.counselandcare.org

The Countryside Agency
John Dower House
Crescent Place
Cheltenham
Glos.
GL50 3RA
Tel: 01242 521381
www.countryside.gov.uk

The Countryside Council for Wales
Maes y Ffynnon
Ffordd
Penrhos
Bangor
Gwynedd
LL57 2DN
Tel: 01248 385500
Information line: 0845 1306 229
www.ccw.gov.uk

The Court of Protection: *see*
The Office of Care and
Protection (for Northern Ireland)
The Office of the Public
Guardian (for Scotland)
The Public Guardianship Office
(for England and Wales)

The Criminal Records Bureau
Information line: 0870 90 90 811
www.crb.gov.uk

The Criminal Records Bureau for Scotland
Tel: 0141 585 8325

Crossroads Association
10 Regent Place
Rugby
Warwickshire
CV21 2PN
Tel: 01788 573653
www.crossroads.org.uk

Crossroads Scotland
24 George Square
Glasgow G2 1EG
Tel: 0141 226 3793

Cruse Bereavement Care
Cruse House
126 Sheen Road
Richmond-upon-Thames
Surrey
TW9 1UR
Tel: 020 8939 9530
Helpline: 0870 167 1677
www.crusebereavementcare.
org.uk

**Cruse Bereavement Care,
Scotland**
Riverview House
Friarton Road
Perth
PH2 8HT
Tel: 01738 444178
www.info@crusescotland.org.uk

The Dementia Care Trust
Kingsley House
Greenbank Road
Bristol BS5 6HE
Tel: 0117 952 5325
www.dct.org.uk

**The Dementia Services
Development Centre**
The University of Stirling
Stirling
FK9 4LA
Tel: 01786 467740
www.stir.ac.uk/dsdc

**The Department for Regional
Development**
Road Service
Western Division
Castle Barracks
Wellington Place
Enniskillen
BT74 7HN
Tel: 028 6634 3700

**The Department for
Transport, Local Government
and the Regions**
Eland House
Bressenden Place
London SW1 E 5DU
Tel: 020 7944 3000
www.dtlr.gov.uk

**The Department for Work and
Pensions (Benefits)**
Quarry House
Quarry Hill
Leeds
LS2 7UA
Tel: 0113 232 4000
Benefits Helplines:
Pensions: 0845 731 3233
State Retirement Pension: 0845
301 3011
Textphone: 0845 301 3012
Carers and Disability Benefits:
0845 712 34 56
Textphone: 0845 722 44 33
Disability Benefits: 0800 88 22 00
Textphone: 0800 24 33 55
Pension Credit: 0800 99 1234
Benefits Advice in Northern
Ireland: 0800 22 06 74
Health charges Advice Line: 0800
587 8982
Health Charges Advice Line in
Northern Ireland: 028 9053 2973
Winter Fuel Payments Helpline:
0845 9 15 15 15
www.dwp.gov.uk

The Department of Health
Wellington House
133–135 Waterloo Road
London SE1 8UG
Tel: 020 7972 2000
Information linc: 020 7210 4850
www.doh.gov.uk

The Department of Health Publications
P O Box 777
London SE1 6XH
Literature line: 0800 555 777

The Department of Health, Social Services and Public Safety, Northern Ireland Executive
Castle Buildings
Stormont
Belfast BT4 3SJ
Tel: 028 9052 0500
www.dhsspsni.gov.uk

The Department of Trade and Industry
1 Victoria Street
London SW1H OET
Tel: 020 7215 0378
www.consumer.gov.uk

Depression Alliance
35 Westminster Bridge Road
London SE1 7JB
Tel: 020 7633 0557
www.depressionalliance.org

Diabetes UK
10 Queen Anne Street
London W1M 9LH
Tel: 020 7323 1531
Helpline: 020 7636 6112
www.diabetes.org.uk

DIAL UK (Disabled Information and Advice Line)
St Catherine's
Tickhill Road
Doncaster
DN4 8QN
Tel: 01302 310123
www.members.aol.com/dialuk

Dial-a-Law Scotland
Tel: 0990 455 554
www.lawscot.org.uk

Direct Payment Information Line:
0800 107 2000

Direct Payments Scotland
27 Beaverhall Road
Edinburgh EH7 4JE
Tel: 0131 558 3450
www.dpscotland.org.uk

Disability Action Northern Ireland
Portside Business Park
189 Airport Road West
Belfast BT3 9ED
Tcl: 028 90 297 880
www.disabilityaction.org

Disability Alliance
Universal House
88–94 Wentworth Street
London E1 7SA
Tel: 020 7247 8776
www.disabilityalliance.org

The Disability Law Service
39–45 Cavell Street
London E1 2BP
Tel: 020 7791 9800
Minicom: 020 7791 9801
www.abilityonline.org.uk

The Disability Rights Commission
Freepost MID 02164
Stratford-upon-Avon
CV37 9BR
Tel: 08457 622 633
Textphone: 08457 622644
www.drc-gb.org

Disability Scotland
5 Shandwood Place
Edinburgh EH2 5RG
Tel: 0131 229 8632

Disability Wales
Wernddu Court
Caerphilly Business Park
Van Road
Caerphilly
CF83 1XL
Tel: 029 2088 7325
Helpline: 0800 731 6282

The Disabled Drivers' Motor Club
Cottingham Way
Thrapston
Northants
NN14 4PL
Tel: 01832 734724
www.ddmc.org.uk

The Disabled Living Centres Council
Redbank House
4 St Chad's Street
Manchester M8 8QA
Tel: 0161 834 1044
www.dlcc.org.uk

The Disabled Living Foundation
380–384 Harrow Road
London W9 2HU
Tel: 020 7289 6111
Helpline: 0845 130 9177
Textphone: 0207 432 8009
www.dlf.org.uk

The Disabled Motorists' Federation
c/o Chester-le-Street CVS
Volunteers' Centre
Clarence Terrace
Chester-le-Street
County Durham
DH3 3DQ
Tel: 0191 4163172

The Disabled Persons' Railcard Office
PO Box 1YT
Newcastle-upon-Tyne NE99 1YT
Tel: 0191 269 0303
Textphone: 0191 269 0304

DVLA (Drivers and Vehicles Licensing Authority)
Medical Branch
Longview Road
Morriston
Swansea
SA99 1WA
Tel: 0870 240 0009/0010
www.dvla.gov.uk

**The Elderly Accommodation
Council**
3rd Floor
89 Albert Embankment
London SE1 7TP
Tel: 020 7820 1343
www.housingcare.org

**The Energy Action Grants
Agency (EAGA)**
Freepost
PO Box 130
Newcastle-upon-Tyne NE99 2RP
Tel: 0191 230 1830
www.eaga.co.uk

**The Energy Efficiency Advice
Centre**
Tel: 0800 512 012

**The Financial Services
Authority**
25 The North Colonnade
Canary Wharf
London E14 5 HS
Tel: 020 7676 1000
Helpline: 0845 606 1234
www.fsa.gov.uk

Fish Insurance
3–4 Riversway Business Village
Navigation Way
Preston
PR2 2BR
Tel: 0500 4321 41

The Fold Housing Association
(for home improvement services
in Northern Ireland)
3 Redburn Square
Hollywood
County Down
BT18 9HZ
Tel: 028 9042 8314
www.foldgroup.co.uk

Foundations
(national co-ordinating body for
home improvement agencies in
England)
Bleaklow House
Howard Town Mill
Glossop
Derbyshire
SK13 8HT
Tel: 01457 891909
www.foundations.uk.com

Friends of the Elderly
40–42 Ebury Street
London SW1W 0LZ
Tel: 020 7730 8263

**The Funeral Ombudsman
Scheme**
Richmond House
156 Sandyford Road
Jesmond
Newcastle-upon-Tyne NE2 1XG
Tel: 0191 230 5554
www.funeralombudsman.org.uk

Gatwick Travel-care
Tel: 01293 504 283

The General Dental Council
37 Wimpole Street
London W1G 8DQ
Tel: 020 7887 3800
www.gdc-uk.org

The General Medical Council
178 Great Portland Street
London W1N 6JE
Tel: 020 7 580 7642
www.gmc-uk.org

The General Social Care Council
Goldings House
2 Hay's Lane
London SE1 2HB
Tel: 020 7397 5100
Information: 020 7397 5800
www.gscc.org.uk

Grandparents Association
Moot House
The Stow
Harlow
Essex
CM20 3AG
Tel: 01279 428040
Helpline: 01279 444964
www.grandparents-federation.org.uk

The Health and Safety Executive
Helpline: 08701 545500
or contact a local office
www.hse.gov.uk

Health and Social Services Councils in Northern Ireland
(the equivalent of community health councils in England and Wales; there is no national association):

Eastern Health and Social Services Council
19 Bedford Street
Belfast BT2 7EJ
Tel: 028 9032 1230

Northern Health and Social Services Council
8 Broadway Avenue
Ballymena
BT43 7AA
Tel: 028 2565 5777

Southern Health and Social Services Council
Quaker Buildings
High Street
Lurgan
BT66 8BB
Tel: 028 3834 9900

Western Health and Social Services Council
Hilltop
Tyrone and Fermanagh Hospital
Omagh
BT79 0NS
Tel: 028 8225 2555

The Health Professions Council
184 Kennington Park Road
London SE11 4BU
Tel: 020 7582 0866
www.hpcuk.org

The Health Service Ombudsman, England
Millbank Tower
London SW1P 4QP
Helpline: 0845 015 4033
www.ombudsman.org.uk

The Health Service Ombudsman, Scotland
28 Thistle Street
Edinburgh EH2 1EN
Helpline: 0845 601 0456
www.ombudsman.org.uk

The Health Service Ombudsman, Wales
5th Floor
Capital Tower
Greyfriars Road
Cardiff CF10 3AG
Helpline: 0845 601 0987
www.ombudsman.org.uk

Heathrow Travel-care
Tel: 020 8745 7495

Help the Aged
207–221 Pentonville Road
London NI 9UZ
Tel: 020 7278 1114
Northern Ireland: 0808 808 7575
Seniorline Helpline: 0808 800 6565
Care Fees Advisory Service: 0500 76 74 76
Textphone: 0800 26 96 26
www.helptheaged.org.uk

Help the Hospices
34–44 Britannia Street
London WC1X 9JG
Tel: 020 7520 8200
www.helpthehospices.org.uk

Holiday Care
2nd Floor
Imperial Buildings
Victoria Road
Horley
Surrey
RH6 7PZ
Tel: 01293 771500
Helpline: 01293 774535
www.holidaycare.org.uk

Homeshare
155a King's Road
London SW3 5TX
Tel: 020 7376 4558
www.callne-tuk.com/home/homeshare

Homeshare International
Tel: 020 7349 0444
www.homeshare.org

The Hospice Information Service
St. Christopher's Hospice
51–59 Lawrie Park Road
London SE26 6DZ
Tel: 020 8778 9252 extensions 262 and 263
www.hospiceinformation.co.uk

The Independent Healthcare Association
Westminster Tower
3 Albert Embankment
London SE1 7RS
Tel: 020 7793 4620
www.iha.org.uk

The Indian Muslim Federation
Trinity Close
London E11 4RP
Tel: 020 8588 6399
www.indianmuslim.org.uk

The Information Commissioner's Office
Wycliffe House
Water Lane
Wilmslow
Cheshire
SK9 5AF
Tel: 01625 545700
Information line: 01625 545745
www.dataprotection.gov.uk

The Inland Revenue
New Employer's Support Line
Tel: 0845 60 70 143
www.inlandrevenue.gov.uk

INNIS
Age Concern Scotland
113 Rose Street
Edinburgh EH2 3DT
Tel: 0131 220 6347

The International Glaucoma Association
108c Warner Road
London SE5 9HQ
Tel: 020 7737 3265
www.iga.org.uk/iga

Jewish Care
221 Golders Green Road
London NW11 9DQ
Tel: 020 8922 2000
Helpline: 020 8922 2222
www.jewishcare.org

The King's Fund
11–13 Cavendish Square
London W1G 0AN
Tel: 020 7307 2400
www.kingsfund.org.uk

The Law Society of England and Wales
113 Chancery Lane
London WC2A 1PL
Tel: 020 7242 1222
www.lawsociety.org.uk

The Law Society of Northern Ireland
Law Society House
Victoria Street
Belfast BT1 3JZ
Tel: 028 9023 1614
www.lawsoc-ni.org

The Law Society of Scotland
26 Drumsheugh Gardens
Edinburgh EH3 7YR
Tel: 0131 226 7411
www.lawscot.org.uk

The Legal Services Commission
85 Gray's Inn Road
London WC1X 8AA
Tel: 020 7759 0000
Helpline: 0845 608 1122
www.legalservices.gov.uk

The Local Government Ombudsman, England
Millbank Tower
Millbank
London SW1P 4QP
www.lgo.org.uk

The Local Government Ombudsman, Scotland
23 Walker Street
Edinburgh EH3 7HX
Tel: 0131 225 5300
www.ombudslgscot.org.uk

The Local Government Ombudsman, Wales
Derwen House
Court Road
Bridgend
CF31 1BN
Tel: 01656 661325
www.ombudsman-wales.org

The Long-term Medical Conditions Alliance
Unit 212
6 Baldwin's Gardens,
London EC1N 7RJ
Tel: 020 7813 3637
www.lmca.demon.co.uk

Macmillan Cancer Relief
13th Floor
89 Albert Embankment
London SE1 7UQ
Tel: 020 7840 7840
Helpline: 0845 6016161
www.macmillan.org.uk

The Macular Disease Society
PO Box 16
Denbigh
LL16 5ZA
Tel: 0800 328 2849
www.maculardisease.org

Marie Curie Cancer Care
89 Albert Embankment
London SE1 7TP
Tel: 020 7599 7777
www.mariecurie.org.uk

Mencap
(The Royal Society for Mentally Handicapped Children and Adults)
Centre House
4 Chapel Bar
Nottingham
NG1 6JQ
Tel: 0115 956 1130
www.mencap.org.uk

Methodist Homes for the Aged
(now **MHA Care Group**)
Epworth House
Stuart Street
Derby
DE1 2EQ
Tel: 01332 296200
www.methodisthomes.org.uk

MIND
(The National Association for Mental Health)
Granta House
15–19 Broadway
London E15 4BQ
Tel: 020 8519 2122
Helplines: 020 8522 1728 and 0845 766 0163
www.mind.org.uk

The Mobility Advice and Vehicle Information Service
O Wing
Macadam Avenue
Old Wokingham Road
Crowthorne
Berks.
RG45 6XD
Tel: 01344 661000
www.mobility-unit.dft.giv.uk

The Mobility Information Service
The National Mobility Centre
Unit B1
Greenwood Court
Cartmel Drive
Shrewsbury
SU1 3TB
Tel: 01743 463072
www.mis.org.uk

Motability
Goodman House
Station Approach
Harlow
Essex
CM20 2ET
Tel: 01279 635 999
www.motability.co.uk

The National Association for Providers of Activities for Older People
5 Tavistock Place
London WC1H 9SN
Tel: 020 7383 5757

The National Association of Citizen's Advice Bureaux
Myddelton House
115–123 Pentonville Road
London N1 9LZ
Tel: 020 7833 2181
www.nacab.org.uk

The National Association of Councils for Voluntary Service
3rd Floor
Arundel Court
177 Arundel Street
Sheffield
S1 2NU
Tel: 0114 278 6636
www.nacvs.org.uk

The National Care Homes Association
54–59 Leather Lane
London EC1N 7TJ
Tel: 020 7831 7090
www.ncha.gb.com

The National Care Standards Commission
St. Nicholas Building
St. Nicholas Street
Newcastle-upon-Tyne NE1 1NB
Tel: 0191 233 3600
Information: 0191 233 3556
www.carestandards.org.uk

The National Centre for Independent Living
250 Kennington Lane
London SE11 5RD
Tel: 020 75871663
www.ncil.org.uk

The National Council for Hospice and Specialist Palliative Care Services
1st Floor
343–344 Britannia Street
London WC1X 9JG
Tel: 020 7520 8299
www.hospice-spc-council.org.uk

The National Council for Voluntary Organizations
Regent's Wharf
8 All Saints' Street
London N1 9RL
Tel: 020 7713 6161
www.ncvo-vol.org.uk

National Express Ltd
Ensign Court
4 Vicarage Road
Edgbaston
Birmingham B15 3ES
Tel: 0121 625 1122
Travel information: 08705 80 80 80
Passengers with special needs:
0121 454 8759
www.GoByCoach.com

The National Federation of Bus Users
PO Box 320
Portsmouth
PO5 3SD
Tel: 023 92814493
www.nfbu.org

The National Federation of Shopmobility UK
85 High Street
Worcester
WR1 2ET
Tel: 01905 617761
www.justmobility.co.uk/shop

The National Federation of Women's Institutes
104 New King's Road
London SW6 4LY
Tel: 020 7371 9300

The National Housing Federation
175 Gray's Inn Road
London WC1X 8UP
Tel: 020 7278 6571
www.housing.org.uk

The National Institute for Social Work
5 Tavistock Place
London WC1H 9SN
Tel: 020 7387 9681
www.nisw.org.uk

The National Osteoporosis Society
Camerton
Bath
Avon
BA2 0PJ
Tel: 01761 471771
Helpline: 01761 472721
www.nos.org.uk

The National Pensioners' Convention
9 Arkwright Road
London NW3 6AB
Tel: 020 7431 9820
www.natpencon.org.uk

The National Rail Enquiry Service
Tel: 08457 48 49 50
Textphone: 0845 605 0600

The National Social Care Commission
St. Nicholas Building
St. Nicholas Street
Newcastle-upon-Tyne NE1 1NB
Tel: 0191 233 3556
www.carestandards.org.uk

NHS Direct
Freephone: 0845 4647
Health costs advice line: 0800 917 7711
www.nhsdirect.nhs.uk

NHS Direct Wales
Tel: 0845 46 47

NHS Helpline Scotland
Tel: 0800 22 44 88

**NHS Quality Improvement
Scotland**
Elliott House
4th Floor
8–10 Hillside Crescent
Edinburgh EH7 5EA
Tel: 0131 623 4300
www.nhshealthquality.org

**The Northern Ireland
Association for Mental Health**
80 University Street
Belfast BT7 1HE
Tel: 028 9032 8474
www.charities.com

**The Northern Ireland Chest,
Heart and Stroke Association**
21 Dublin Road
Belfast BT2 7HB
Tel: 028 9032 0184

**The Northern Ireland
Ombudsman**
33 Wellington Place
Belfast BT1 6HN
Tel: 028 9023 3821
www.ni-ombudsman.org.uk

**The Northern Ireland Social
Care Council**
7th Floor
Millennium House
Great Victoria Street
Belfast BT2 7AQ
Tel: 028 9041 7600
www.dhsspsni.gov.uk/hss/
niscc/_index.html

**The Nursing and Midwifery
Council**
23 Portland Place
London W1N 3AF
Tel: 020 7637 7181
www.nmc-uk.org

**The Office of Care and
Protection**
The Royal Courts of Justice
Chichester Street
Belfast BT1 3JF
Tel: 028 9023 5111
www.caringmat-
ters.dial.pipex.com

**The Office of the Deputy
Prime Minister**
26 Whitehall
London SW1A 2WH
Tel: 020 7944 4400
www.odpm.gov.uk
Free publications: 0870 122 6236
Supporting People website:
www.spkweb.org.uk
Supporting People helpline:
01457 851046

The Office of Fair Trading
Fleetbank House
2–6 Salisbury Square
London EC4Y 8JX
Tel: 020 7211 8000
www.oft.gov.uk

The Office of the Public Guardian
Hadrian House
Callendar Business Park
Callendar Road
Falkirk
FK1 1XR
Tel: 01324678300
www.publicguardian-scotland.gov.uk

The Older People's Advocacy Alliance UK
c/o Parkfield House
Princes Road
Hartshill
Stoke-on-Trent
ST4 7JL
Tel: 01782 844036
www.opaal.co.uk

The Parkinson's Disease Society UK
215 Vauxhall Bridge Road
London SW1V 1EJ
Tel: 020 7931 8080
Helpline: 0808 800 0303
www.parkinsons.org.uk

The Patients' Association
PO Box 935
Harrow
Middlesex
HA1 3YJ
Tel: 020 8423 9111
Helpline: 020 8423 8999
www.patients-association.com

The Pensions Advisory Service
11 Belgrave Road
London SW1V 2RB
Helpline: 0845 601 29223
www.opas.org.uk

The Pensions Ombudsman
11 Belgrave Road
London SW1V 1RB
Tel: 020 7834 9144
www.pensions-ombudsman.org.uk

The People's Dispensary for Sick Animals
Whitechapel Way
Priorslee
Telford
Shropshire
TF2 9PQ
Tel: 01952 290999
www.pdsa.org.uk

The Pet Fostering Service Scotland
PO Box 6
Callander
FK17 8ZU
Tel: 01877 331496
www.globalideasbank.org

The Pre-Retirement Association
9 Chesham Road
Guildford
Surrey
GU1 3LS
Tel: 01483 301170
www.pra.uk.com

The Policy Research Institute on Ageing and Ethnicity
31–32 Park Row
Leeds
LS1 5JD
Tel: 0113 285 5990
www.priae.org.uk

The Princess Royal Trust for Carers
142 Minories
London EC3N 1LB
Tel: 020 7480 7788
www.carers.org

The Princess Royal Trust for Carers, Scotland
Campbell House
215 West Campbell Street
Glasgow G2 4TT
Tel: 0141 221 5066

The Public Guardianship Office
Stewart House
24 Kingsway
London WC2B 6JX
Tel: 020 7664 7300
www.guardianship.gov.uk

The Public Law Project
14 Bloomsbury Square
London WC1A 2LP
Tel: 020 7269 0570
www.nacab.org.uk

The Registered Nursing Homes Association
15 Highfield Road
Edgbaston
Birmingham B15 3DU
Tel: 0121 454 2511

The Relatives and Residents Association
24 The Ivories
6–18 Northampton Street
London N1 2HY
Tel: 020 7359 8148
Helpline: 020 7359 8136

The Relatives Association Scotland
Leslie House
Leslie
Fife
KY6 3EP
Tel: 01877 339242

Ricability
30 Angel Gate
City Road
London EC1V 2PT
Tel: 020 7427 2460
Textphone: 020 7427 2469
www.ricability.org.uk

RightsNet
(laws and policies on benefits)
www.rightsnet.org.uk

The Royal Association for Disability and Rehabilitation (RADAR)
12 City Forum
250 City Road
London ECIV 8AF
Tel: 020 7250 3222
Minicom: 020 7250 4119
www.radar.org.uk

The Royal British Legion
48 Pall Mall
London SW1Y 5JY
Tel: 020 7973 7200
Helpline: 08457 725 725
www.britishlegion.org.uk

The Royal British Legion, Women's Section
48 Pall Mall
London SW1Y 5JY
Tel: 020 7973 7214
www.britishlegion.org.uk

The Royal College of General Practitioners
14 Princes' Gate
London SW7 1PU
Tel: 020 7581 3232
www.rcgp.org.uk

The Royal College of Nursing
20 Cavendish Square
London W1
Tel: 020 7409 3333
www.rcn.org.uk

The Royal College of Physicians
11 St Andrew's Place
Regent's Park
London NW1 4LE
Tel: 020 7935 1174
www.rcplondon.ac.uk

The Royal College of Speech and Language Therapists
2 White Hart Yard
London SE1 1NX
Tel: 020 7378 1200
www.rcslt.org

The Royal National Institute for Deaf People
19–23 Featherstone Street
London EC1Y 8SL
Tel: 020 7296 8119
Helpline: 0808 808 0123
Textphone: 0808 808 9000
www.rnid.org.uk

The Royal National Institute of the Blind
224 Great Portland Street
London W1W 5AA
Tel: 020 7388 1266
Helpline: 0845 766 9999
www.rnib.org.uk

The Royal Society for the Prevention of Cruelty to Animals
Wilberforce Way
Southwater
Horsham
West Sussex
RH13 7WN
Tel: 0870 0101 181
Helpline: 08705 555999
www.rspca.org.uk

Safe Home Income Plans
Tel: 0870 241 6060

SAGA Group Ltd
SAGA Building
Middelburg Square
Folkestone
Kent
Tel: 01303 771111
Enquiries: 0800 505 606
www.saga.co.uk

The Scotland Patients' Association
Gartincaber
West Plean
Stirling
FL7 8BA
Tel: 01786 818008
www.scotlandpatients
association.org.uk

The Scottish Association of Health Councils
18 Alva Street
Edinburgh EH2 4QG
Tel: 0131 220 4101
www.show.scot.nhs.uk

The Scottish Commission for the Regulation of Care
Compass House
11 Riverside Drive
Dundee
DD1 2NY
Tel: 01382 207100
www.carecommission.com

The Scottish Executive
Community Care Division
James Craig Walk
Edinburgh EH1 3BA
Tel: 0131 244 3635
Information: 08457 741 741
Information line on free personal and nursing care: 0800 224488
www.scotland.gov.uk

Scottish Health on the Web
www.showscot.nhs.uk

Scottish Intercollegiate Guidelines Network
www.sign.ac.uk

Scottish Natural Heritage
12 Hope Terrace
Edinburgh EH9 2AS
Tel: 0131 447 4784
www.snh.org.uk

The Scottish Social Services Council
Compass House
11 Riverside Drive
Dundee
DD1 2NY
Tel: 01382 207100
www.sssc.uk.com

The Scottish Society for the Prevention of Cruelty to Animals
Braehead Mains
603 Queensferry Road
Edinburgh EH4 6EA
Tel: 0131 339 0222
www.scottishspca.org

Shoard, Marion
PO Box 403
Dorking
Surrey
RH4 1SA
www.marionshoard.co.uk

Shopmobility
See your telephone book for a local office.
www.justmobility.co.uk

The Social Care Institute for Excellence
1st Floor
Goldings House
2 Hay's Lane
London SE1 2HB
Tel: 020 7089 6840
www.scie.org.uk

The Society of Chiropodists and Podiatrists
53 Welbeck Street
London W1M 7HE
Tel: 020 7486 3381

Solicitors for the Elderly
PO Box 9
Peterborough
PE4 9WN
Tel: 01733 326 769
www.solicitorsfortheelderly.com

The Solid Fuel Association
Information line: 0800 600 000
Or: 0845 6014406

Sport England
16 Upper Woburn Place
London WC1H 0QP
Tel: 020 7273 1500
english.sports.gov.uk

Sport Scotland
Caledonia House
South Gyle
Edinburgh EH12 9DQ
0131 317 7200
www.sportscotland.org.uk

**The Sports Council for
Northern Ireland**
The House of Sport
Upper Malone Road
Belfast BT9 5LA
Tel: 028 9038 1222

The Sports Council for Wales
Sophia Gardens
Cardiff CF11 9SW
Tel: 029 2030 0500
www.sports-council-wales.co.uk

**The Standing Nursing and
Midwifery Advisory
Committee**
Ann Towner
Secretary to SNMAC
Room 527
Richmond House
79 Whitehall
London SW1A 2NL
Tel: 020 7210 4868
www.doh.gov.uk/snmac

The Stationery Office
HMSO
St Clement's House
2–16 Colegate
Norwich
NR3 1BQ
Tel: 0870 600 5522
www.hmso.gov.uk/docs

**Strathclyde Passenger
Transport**
Consort House
12 West George Street
Glasgow
G2 1HN
Tel: 0141 332 6811
Traveline: 0870 608 2 608

The Stroke Association
Stroke House
123–127 Whitecross Street
London EC1Y 8JJ
Tel: 020 7566 0300
Helpline: 0845 303 3100
www.stroke.org.uk

Sue Ryder Care
2nd Floor
114–118 Southampton Row
London WC1B 5AA
Tel: 020 7400 0440
suerydercare.org

**Telephone Counselling
Careline**
Tel: 020 8514 1177

Translink (Northern Ireland)
Central Station
Belfast BT1 3PB
Tel: 028 9033 3000
Textphone: 028 9035 4007

Transport for London
Access and Mobility Section
Windsor House
42–50 Victoria Street
London SW1H 0TL
Tel/ textphone: 020 7941 4600
24-hour travel information
number: 020 7222 1234
www.transportforlondon.gov.uk

Traveline
Helpline: 0870 608 2 608
www.traveline.org.uk

Tripscope
The Vassall Centre
Gill Avenue
Bristol BS16 2QQ
Tel: 0117 939 7783
Helpline: 08457 58 56 41
www.tripscope.org.uk

**The United Kingdom Council
for Psychotherapy**
167–169 Great Portland Street
London W1W 5PF
Tel: 020 7436 3002
www.psychotherapy.org.uk

**The United Kingdom Home
Care Association**
42b Banstead Road
Carshalton
Surrey
SM5 3NW
Tel: 020 8288 1551
www.ukhca.co.uk

**The University of the Third
Age**
26 Harrison Street
London WC1H 8JW
Tel: 020 7837 8838
www.u3a.org.uk

Update
27 Beaverhall Road
Edinburgh EH7
Tel: 0131 558 5200
www.update.org.uk

**The Wales Council for
Voluntary Action**
Baltic House
Mount Stuart Square
Cardiff Bay
Tel: 029 2043 1700
www.wcva.org.uk

**The Welsh Assembly
Government
The National Assembly for
Wales**
Cardiff Bay
Cardiff CF99 1NA
Tel: 029 2089 8200
Information: 029 2082 5111
www.wales.gov.uk

Wood Green Animal Shelters
King's Bush Farm
London Road
Godmanchester
Cambs.
PE29 2NH
Tel: 01480 830014
www.woodgreen.org.uk

**The Young Men's Christian
Association (YMCA)**
640 Forest Road
London E17 3BZ
Tel: 020 8520 5599
www.ymca.net

Index

A

Abbeyfield Society 182, 336
Abraham, Ann 473
abroad, moving 167–8
abuse 51–3, 553, 606
Adults with Incapacity (Scotland) Act
    2000 455, 537
Action on Elder Abuse 81, 553
advance directives 541
Advantage 50 Card 131
advocacy 63, 80, 82–3, 275, 326, 564,
    571
affection 30–1
    see also friendship
Age Concern England 78–80, 168,
    194, 211, 413, 531
Age Concern Scotland 79, 194
Age Concern Sheffield 79
Age Concern York 202, 222–3
ageing
    attitudes xxv–xxvi
    challenges xix–xxv
    human body xx–xxi, 3–17
    theories 3
    types 3–4
    variation 3, 4, 17
ageism xxvi–xxvii, 60, 419–434
age-related macular degeneration
    (AMD) 15, 20, 85, 251–2
air travel 133
alarms
    care homes 345–6
    pendant 96–7, 151, 152, 213
    sheltered housing 181, 189–90
Alberti, George 430
Alzheimer's disease, *see* dementia
Alzheimer Scotland 531, 538

Alzheimer's Society 86, 87, 233, 531,
    541
Anchor Trust 242
Animal Welfare Trust 242
annuities 502–3
appetite loss *see* nutrition
appointeeship 521, 553
arthritis *see* osteoarthritis
Arthritis and Rheumatism Council
    217
assets, deprivation of 374, 375, 508,
    509
Ashton, Hilda 37–8
assisted living *see* sheltered housing,
    very sheltered housing
Association of Charity Officers 357
Association of Retired and Persons
    over 50 82
Attendance Allowance 168, 174, 260,
    273, 294, 485–8
attorney, power of
    enduring 518–9, 522–31, 540
    registering 527–9
    lasting 539–40
    ordinary 517–8
    welfare (Scotland) 537–9
audiologists 103–4
Audit Commission for England and
    Wales 293, 294

B

Baines, Mary 461–2
Baker, Jill 447
balance 15, 98, 99, 145–6
Bassey, Joan 112
bathrooms 95, 163–4, 215
bed-blocking 465

bedding 27, 95, 107, 113–5, 432
bedrooms 95–6, 159–60, 215, 343–5
beds 95–6, 215
bedsores, *see* pressure sores
befriending schemes 222–4
benevolent associations 307, 319, 365
Bennett, Kate Mary 30
bereavement 31, 33, 38, 188–9, 396
Better Government for Older People 81
Blair, Tony 58, 557
blood pressure 8, 223, 142, 148, 149
Blue Cross 239, 241–2
Blue Badge scheme 127
brain 4–7
breast cancer screening 249
British Association of Domiciliary Care 266
British Association of Counselling and Psychotherapy 71
British Council of Disabled People 84
British Geriatrics Society 424
British Institute of Human Rights xxvii
British Medical Association 66, 450–8
British Psychological Society 71
British Red Cross Society 102
Brookner, Anita 7
Brooks, Mary 36
Budgeting Loans 499
burglary *see* security
Burton, John 381–2
Bury, Michael 218–21
bus travel 117, 129, 134–6

C
cancer 64, 70, 139, 247, 459
Canine Concern Scotland 242
cars
  disability 128
  getting in 216–7
  ownership 118
  parking 122

travel 126–9
  see also driving
cardiovascular system 7–8
Care and Repair agencies 203–4
Care Council for Wales 54–5, 261, 271–2
care, difference between health and social xxvi, 43, 383, 386
care homes 23, 24, 144, 225,
  activities organizers 334–5
  advantages 312
  advice and information 413–4
  bedrooms 343–5
  care 312, 332–9, 346–56, 400–2
  care plans (service user plans) 394–5
  choosing 311–23; social services residents 318
  closures 408–11
  communal living 361–2, 400–1
  complaints 360–1, 397, 577
  continence management 120, 352, 411
  contracts 313, 420–1
  definitions 311–2, 327
  design features 14–5, 339–47
  disadvantages 312–3
  entry 313–9, 401–2
  ethos 320, 353–6
  exercise 335
  gender separation 33, 535–6
  health professionals outside 311, 324, 357–8
  health services, rights to 56–7, 107, 468–9
  infection control 341, 351–2
  inspection and regulation 53, 319, 320–3, 329
  key workers 334
  lavatories 340–1
  leaving 407–11
  location 356
  managers 321, 325
  money, handling 521

national regulations and standards 53–5, 267–8, 321–3, 343–5, 358, 394, 395
nights 335, 337
owners 319–20
pets 239, 242–3, 354
psychological aspects 29, 30, 34, 312–3, 410–1
relatives 313, 314–5, 325, 396–9, 404–5
restraint 534–5
room sharing 344, 359
security of tenure 313, 358, 420–1
service user's guides 321, 330
social services 317–8, 329, 364–8, 373–84, 392–3, 409
spouses and partners 390–3
staff 332–7, 402–3, 406–7
trial and temporary stays 394
types 311–2, 319–20
visitors 403–6
waiting lists 320
Winter Fuel Payments 209
see also dementia, fees (care homes), hearing impairment, infection control, intermediate care, respite care, temperature
care plans 273, 276, 279–89, 394–6
Care Standards Inspectorate for Wales 53–4, 267–8
care workers, domiciliary 265, 285–8
confidentiality 288
handling clients' money 265, 288
monitoring 285–6
registration 53–5, 271–2
training 55, 270–2
see also domiciliary care agencies, care homes, infection control, personal assistants
carers 172, 354,
advantages and drawbacks 549–5
assessments 556–68
benefits, state financial 545, 568–9
definition 84, 546–7

eligibility for services 560, 562–3
financial issues 554
GPs 248–9
health issues 554
main caring relative 546–7, 572–3
respite care 558
sitting services 572
training 570
types 546–7
voluntary organizations 84, 571–2
Carers UK 546, 554, 572
Caring for Carers 557, 567
Caring Matters 87
caring, theoretical aspects 353–4, 550–1
Carer Premium 569
Carr, John 343
Cartland, Barbara 7
catheters, urinary 427–9
cats 238–43
Cats Protection 240
chairs 91–2, 215
see also seating in public places
chaplaincy services 39–40, 434
Chartered Society of Physiotherapists 72
charging for
care home residence 284, 318–9, 363–92
community care services 284, 292–7
gadgets and equipment 107–9, 114, 296, 388
home adaptations 205–7
intermediate care 412–3, 422–6
respite care 56–7
Christianity 37–40, 234–7
Christmas Bonus 490
Churchill, Winston 14
Citizen's Advice Bureaux 293, 382, 488, 500
clinical psychologists 31, 71
Cinnamon Trust 242
Clarke, Jonathan 410–1
Clements, Luke 465, 582
clocks 93, 105

clothing 27, 28, 106, 133–5, 280, 398–9
coach travel 131–2
Cohen, David 428, 446
cold weather *see* temperature, body
Cold Weather Payments 209
College of Occupational Therapists 72
Collis, Glyn 243
Commission for Health
    Improvement 63–4
Commission for Social Care
    Inspection 54
communication difficulties 225–9
community care assessment 273–7,
    289–90, 317, 327
  carers 558–61
  joint assessments 290–1
  reassessment 290–1
Community Care Grants 498–9
community care services
  charges for 292–7
  eligibility criteria 277–9
  see also Direct Payments system,
    domiciliary care, meals-on-
    wheels
community health councils 61–2
companionship, *see* friendship
complaints 207, 577–8
  care homes 360–1
  GPs 68–9
  NHS 63, 581–3
  social services 49–50, 578–80
concessionary public transport
    130–1, 134–6, 165, 167
confusion 24
consent, medical 64–5
Consumers' Association xxvii
Contact the Elderly 224
Continence Foundation 113
Continuing Care Conference 270, 421
contracts 270, 287–8, 358
Copsey, Nigel 37
Cookson, Catherine 7
Council for the Regulation of Health
    Care Professionals 66

Council Tax Benefit 241, 483, 497
Counsel and Care 80, 414
counsellors 71–2
Court of Protection 518–29
countryside
  moving to 165–6
  visiting 32
Crieth, Elaine 31
crime 197, 210–1, 405–6
Criminal Records Bureau 261–2, 302
Crossroads Association 572
Crisis Loans 499

D
dance 144
Data Protection Act 1998 50, 61
Davies, Sue xiii, 320, 396, 550–1
day centres 222, 223, 230–4, 272, 274
day care centres 233
death 447, 448, 462, 576
  see also bereavement, withholding
    medical treatment
dehydration 16, 24, 25
  see also fluid intake
dementia 70, 172, 192
  Alzheimer's disease 5
  care 5, 22, 70, 81, 229, 233, 237,
    348, 361, 399, 408, 505, 550
  care homes 22, 324, 342–3, 346,
    361, 399, 404–5, 407, 408
  causes 5–6
  communication 5–6, 403–5
  day centres 233
  decisions 255, 256
  diagnosis 254–5
  emotions 5, 39, 229
  external environment 342–3
  falls 149
  incidence 6, 324
  language skills 403–5
  medication 255, 257
  multi-infarct 6, 8, 255
  palliative care 70, 257
  person-centred care 228–9, 427

retirement housing 193
symptoms 5–6, 229, 324, 408, 533
therapies 256, 355–6
treatment 255–7
types 6
visitors 403–5
voluntary organizations 86, 87
weight loss 22
see also Shoard, Gladys
demographic change xxvii–iii
Denmark 219
dental care 10, 357, 399, 491, 497
  free treatment 497
Department for Work and Pensions
  499–501
Department of Health 445, 57–61
Department of Health guidance and
  instructions 56, 594–5
  access to homecare services 277–8
  carers' services 556–66
  charging for domiciliary care
    292–5
  choice of care home 318, 383
  community care assessment 275–6
  direct payments 306
  domiciliary care services 278
  liable relative's payment 393
  NHS Continuing Care 472, 473
  single assessment process 290–1
Department of Health, Social
    Services and Public Safety of
    Northern Ireland 45
depression 86, 252–4
diabetes 23, 86, 139, 149, 247
dieticians 73
digestive system 10, 139
Direct Payment (method of paying
    pension) 259, 281, 412, 516
Direct Payments system 259, 297–306
  carers 303, 563
  duty to offer
disability 32–3
  benefits 206–7, 485–9
  definitions 84, 206–7

drivers 122, 128
incidence xxi, xxii–xxiii, 32
psychological aspects xxii–xxiii,
    32–3, 107
voluntary organizations 84, 85
see also Disabled Facilities Grants
Disability Discrimination Act, 1998
    117, 123–6, 133, 236
Disability Living Allowance 488–9
Disability Rights Commission 123,
    124–6
Disabled Living Centres 105–6, 280
Disabled Facilities Grants 96, 109,
    206–7
disabled people xxvii, 206–7, 297–8
Disabled Person's Railcard 130
diversity among elderly people 17
doctors *see* GPs, hospitals personnel
    psychiatrists
dogs 238–43
dolls therapy 355–6
domiciliary care 259–307
  agencies 265–70, 285–8, 304
  hiring your own help 177, 260–72,
    300–5
  local authority provision 272–307
  national regulations and standards
    53–4, 268–70, 282, 286, 287–8
  sheltered housing 283–4
  see also care workers, community
    care assessment, Direct
    Payments system, housework,
    personal care
driving 67–8, 126–8
drugs *see* medication

E
Earnshaw, Estelle 40
education and training
  care homes 335–7
  care workers 80, 270, 332, 335–7
  carers 570
  general population xix–xxi
  see also GPs, nurses, social workers

Elderly Accommodation Council
199–200, 242, 328, 413
ethnic minority elderly people xix, 81,
233, 278, 281, 380
care homes 328
day centres 230–1
organizations 81, 230–1, 233
entrance charges 490
equity release 203, 506–8, 511, 523
exercise 3, 11, 28, 136–44
instructors 142–4
eyesight see vision

F
falls 29, 139, 141, 145–58, 196, 214–5,
339
family
care home entry 390–1, 401–2
inheritance issues 171, 509–11
living together 169–75
relationships xxiv–xxv, 35, 390–1,
552, 553, 555, 565, 573–4, 575–6
see also carers
Farncombe Day Centre 230–1
fees (care homes)
capital threshold limits 316, 317,
318, 368, 373
care fees payment plans 369
deferred payments scheme 376–7
items covered 363–4
liable relative's payment 393
personal expenses allowance 380–1
self-funders xxvi–xxvii, 284,
366–9, 377–9
spouses and partners 390–3
temporary residents 383–4
third-party top-up 364–5
top-ups 319, 331
fibre 20
financial issues see money
Financial Services Authority 511
fire danger 195, 196, 214
fires (for heating) 208–9
Flanders, Claudia and Michael 85

flu jab 246, 357
fluid charts 26
fluid intake 24–6, 39, 450–1, 456–8,
462
food see nutrition
foot problems 106, 149
footcare 73, 491
footwear 116, 118, 150, 151
free nursing care 384–9
free personal care (Scotland) 260,
293–4, 296, 390
friendship 218–25
functional reserve 4, 10, 16,
Funeral Payments 498

G
gadgets and aids 91–109, 114–5
see also cars, hoists, wheelchairs,
Zimmer frames
gardens 94–5, 160, 198–9, 201, 216–7,
225
General Dental Council 66
General Medical Council 66, 67, 68,
452–7, 541
General Social Care Council 45, 54–5,
261, 271–2
general practitioners (GPs) xxv, 27,
102, 103–4, 147, 153, 222, 224,
244–59, 324, 357
Attendance Allowance 487–8
carers 248–9, 570
check-ups 70, 157
choosing 244–50
complaints procedure 68
depression 252–4
doctor/patient relationship 246–7
falls 147, 156–8
imparting information 247–8, 448–9
knowledge 245
medication 257–9
organizations 66
practices 65–6
social services 374
training 66

see also care homes, consent,
   dementia,
geriatric medicine 17
Getty, Louise 226–7
glasses 150, 399, 491
Gray-Davidson, Frena 404
Greece 219
guardianship 522

H
hair 8–9, 398–9
hand-washing 352, 432
handy-person services 79, 202, 239
Harper, Sarah xxiv
hats 9, 27, 28
Health, Department of *see*
   Department of Health
Health Professions Council 73
health and social services boards and
   trusts 45, 54, 321
Health and Safety Executive 263
health, private care 64, 504
Health Service Ombudsman 473, 581,
   583
hearing aids
   personal 92–3, 100–5, 107, 196,
      226, 339–40, 399, 491
   other devices 196, 339–40
hearing impairment 15, 107, 226–8
   care homes 339–40, 347, 349
heart attacks 447
heart failure 8, 23
heart disease, coronary 20, 86, 139,
      247, 459
heating 28, 207–9
   see also temperature, Warm Front
      Plus grants, Winter Fuel
      Payments
Heath, Hazel 112
Help the Aged 80, 165, 413, 501, 550
help in the home *see* domiciliary care
Hétu, Raymond 226–7
highways departments of local
   authorities 119–20

Hinduism 38–9
hip fractures 153–6
hoists 107, 185, 344, 533, 557, 566
Holme, Anthea 218–221
home, older person's
   adaptations 205–7
   heating 207–9
   ownership transfer 371–5
   psychological aspects 29–30, 34–5,
      369–72
   repairs 201–5
   security 209–11
   shared living arrangements 169–76
   see also care homes, help in the
      home, equity release, moving
      house, retirement housing,
      trusts
home care *see* domiciliary care
home improvement agencies 203–4
Homeshare 175–6
hospices 75, 417, 422, 426
hospitals 88–91, 424–92
   assessment wards 74, 417
   avoidance, reasons for 417
   chaplaincy service 39, 434
   community or cottage hospitals 74,
      417, 421, 424
   continence management 427–9,
      444
   Continuing NHS Care xxvi, 75,
      469–78
   discharge 75, 274, 317, 425, 463–78
   district general hospitals 74, 417,
      422
   entertainment facilities 423, 434,
      445
   fluid intake 434, 439, 450–1, 456–8,
      462
   infection 417–8
   infection control 432–3
   nursing and personal care 420,
      427–34, 439–41
   nutrition 430, 434, 439–40, 450–1,
      457–8

hospitals (*continued*)
  orthopaedic facilities 74, 154–6
  patient disorientation 30
  personnel 76–7
  pressure sores 431–2
  rehabilitation 417, 436–46
  resuscitation 447
  stroke patients 436–46
  transport schemes 435, 497
  waiting lists 419
  withholding and withdrawing
    treatment 447–62
housework *see* domiciliary care
Housing Benefit 241, 483, 496–7
Human Rights Act 1998 xxvii, 409
hygiene *see* infection control
hypothermia 9, 147, 152, 153

I
immune system 16, 18–9
Income Support 368, 369, 374, 379,
    384, 491
incontinence 25, 70, 109–15, 124, 296,
    316, 337, 533
  catheters 427–9
  management régime, care homes
    120, 352, 411
Indian Muslim Federation day centre
    230–1
Independent Advocacy Services 63
infection 9, 16, 19, 21, 64, 341, 351–2,
    417–8
  see also care homes, hospitals
inheritance 508–10, 527
inheritance tax 510–1
INNIS (retirement housing advice
    service in Scotland) 194
insurance
  care 504–5, 511
  employers' liability 263
  health 420, 503–4, 511
  National Insurance 263–4
  occupiers liability 263
intellectual stimulation 36

intermediate care 76, 412–3, 422–6
Islam 39, 111, 237

J
Jewell, Albert 38
Jewish Care 224, 233
Jewish Direct 233
joint assessments 290–1
joints *see* osteoarthritis
Jones, Lesley 226–7
Judaism 237

K
kidneys 13, 24
King's Fund 594
Kirkwood, Tom 33
kitchens 93–4, 149–50, 215, 338
Kitwood, Tom 228–9
Knox, Ian 237

L
laundry 296, 554, 557
Laurence, Chris 240
lavatories
  care homes 340–1
  design features 95, 163–4, 340–1
  public conveniences xxiv, 116–7,
    121–2
Laverick, Eric 203–4
Le Fanu, James 586
learning disabilities, people with 45
Lee, Laurie 400
leisure and sports centres 144, 164
leisure departments of local
    authorities 144
life expectancy xviii–xix
light bulbs 163, 213
lighting 150, 213, 339, 397
liver 10, 16, 257
living wills 541
local authorities *see* highways
    departments, leisure
    departments, social
    services departments

Local Government Ombudsman 49, 366
loneliness 31, 219–29, 403
longevity xvii–xviii
long-stay NHS units 75
   see also NHS Continuing Care
luncheon clubs 230–3, 274, 275
lung disease xxiii, 316, 422–3
Lush, Denzil 529

M

macular degeneration, *see* age-related
   macular degeneration
Macular Disease Society 85
Major, John 58
Marshall, Mary 343
Maslow, Abraham 28–30, 33, 35–6
matrons 77, 325, 597
mattresses *see* bedding, pressure sores
McCarthy and Stone 183
McNicholas, June 243
McNeill, Margaret 225
meals-on-wheels 21, 24, 35, 151–2,
   273, 275, 280–1, 301
medical check-ups 249
medication 10, 16, 21, 257–9
   reviews 258
   see also dementia, depression,
   Parkinson's disease, strokes
Medicines and Older People 60, 258
menopause 13
Mental Health Act 1983 366
mental health services 71, 253–4
Mental Incapacity Bill 2003 539–41
Methodism 234–5, 319
Minimum Income Guarantee 482,
   283, 492
ministers of religion 38–9, 236–8
   see also chaplaincy services
money xx, 481–511
   see also benefits, care homes, charging,
   fees (care homes), inheritance tax,
   insurance, pensions
Moore, David 355–6
Morley, Ian 243

moving, help with 324, 340, 347, 396,
   402, 566
   see also hoists, wheelchairs
moving house 159–76
   see also retirement housing
MRSA 433
muscles 11–12
   see also exercise
Muslims *see* Islam

N

National Association of Citizens
   Advice Bureaux 211
National Care Standards Commission
   53–5, 70, 267–8, 320–3
National Centre for Independent
   Living 299
National Health Service (NHS)
   age discrimination xxvi
   complaints 61–3, 581–3
   history xxvi 43
   inspections and reviews 63–4
   rights to free health care 272, 296
     care home residents 56–7, 107,
     468–9
   community, in the 67, 357
   Patient's Charter, The 58–9, 419
   Your Guide to the NHS 59–60, 419
   See also clinical psychologists,
   consent, counsellors, dieticians,
   GPs, hospices, hospitals,
   intermediate care, NHS
   Continuing Care, nurses, mental
   health services, occupational
   therapists, physiotherapists,
   psychiatrists, psychologists,
   psychotherapists, records,
   respite care, speech and language
   therapists
National Osteoporosis Society 141, 156
National Pensioners' Convention 82
*National Service Framework for Older
   People* 60, 84, 154, 155, 157, 249,
   258, 419

national service frameworks (other)
60–1, 459
National Social Care Commission
NHS Continuing Care xxvi, 61, 75,
469–78
North Lanarkshire Council 277
Northern Ireland 54–5, 261, 271–2
care homes capital limits 368, 373
Chest, Heart and Stroke
Association 446
Commission for Care Services 54
Commission for Health
Improvement 64
concessionary public transport
fares 135
free nursing care 385
Health and Social Services
Registration and Improvement
Authority 321
Health and Social Services
Registration and Improvement
Authority 321
heating grants 208
Housing Executive 204, 595
Social Care Council 54
see also health and social services
boards and trusts
nurses
employing your own 420
hospital 76–7
training 69–70, 429
types 70–1
nursing homes *see* care homes
Nursing and Midwifery Council 69
nutrition 28
artificial nutrition and hydration
450–8
dietary needs 18–24, 280
eating difficulties 10, 338
enjoyment of food 14, 23–4,
280–1, 301, 338
feeding, help with 430, 434,
439–40, 450, 457–8
malnutrition 10, 18

obesity 23
taste and smell 14–5
see also care homes, dental problems,
dieticians, digestive system, fluid
intake, meals-on-wheels

O
occupational therapists 105, 108, 112,
113
Office of Care and Protection 518
Office of Fair Trading 411
Office of the Public Guardian 518,
522
Older People's Advocacy Alliance 83,
326
older people's champions 83–4
osteoarthritis 12, 23, 93, 94, 98, 138,
141, 142, 149, 217
osteomalacia 19, 146
osteoporosis 13, 19, 86, 138, 141, 146,
156, 157
outings, organized 223–4, 403
Oxford Textbook of Geriatric Medicine 19,
22, 24, 461–2

P
pain 142, 258
palliative care 57, 451, 459–61
parking, *see* cars
Parkinson's disease 86, 94, 144, 149,
250, 417, 431
Parkinson's Disease Society 86
partners, *see* spouses and partners
Patient Advice Liaison Services
(PALS) 62
Patients' Association 69
pavements 120–1, 123, 169
pension, private 502–3
pension, state retirement 168, 483,
485, 515–7
carers 569
collecting 516–7
Pension Credit xx, 294–5, 482–3,
491–6, 497, 498

Pension Service 499–500
People's Dispensary for Sick Animals (PDSA) 241
Percival, John 160–1
personal assistants 304
personal care xxvi, 272, 279, 311, 317–33
  see also free personal care (Scotland)
personal expenses allowance 380–1
Pet Fostering Services Scotland 242
pets 130, 150, 198, 238–243, 277
Pets as Therapy (PAT) 242, 243
physiotherapists 97, 112, 113
Picasso, Pablo 7
Pointer, Barbara and Malcolm 386
police checks see Criminal Records Bureau
Policy Research Institute on Ethnicity and Ageing 81
postcode lotteries 277, 293
pressure sores 9, 70, 102, 152–3, 154, 550
Princess Royal Trust for Carers 571–2
prostate gland 13, 110
psychiatrists 71, 253–4
psychological aspects of ageing xii–xiii, xv, 28–40
psychologists 31, 71
psychotherapists 73
Public Guardianship Office 518–29
public transport 128–36, 165, 169

R
RADAR (Royal Association for Disability and Rehabilitation) 84
Rayner, Claire 430
reassessment 289–90
records 50–1, 61, 524
receivership 519–21, 526, 529–31
rehabilitation 155–6, 417, 436–46
Relatives and Residents Association 413
representation
  legal and financial 515–31

medical and other care 453, 454–6, 532–41
in Scotland 528, 455, 537–8
  see also appointeeship, attorney, guardianship, receivership
residential homes see care homes
respite services 411–2, 558, 567
restraint 534–5
resuscitation 61, 447
retirement x, 21
retirement complexes 182, 188
retirement housing 159, 160, 161, 177–201, 311
  advice and information 194, 199–200
  alarm systems 181, 189–90
  care and support 181
  costs 184–6, 199
  design features 194–9
  managers, scheme see wardens
  paying for 199; see also Supporting People
  pets 239, 2242–3
  private sector
  property maintenance 184–6
  providers 183
  safety and security 181, 196–7
  tenure 187
  social activities 187–8
  wardens 181, 190–3, 197, 272;
    see also Supporting People
Ricability 102, 106
romance 33, 536
Royal British Legion 307, 328
Royal College of General Practitioners 66
Royal College of Nursing 69
Royal College of Physicians 111, 156, 430
Royal College of Speech and Language Therapists 73
Royal Masonic Society 328
Royal National Institute for Deaf People 85, 104, 105, 340

Royal National Institute of the Blind 85
Royal Society for the Prevention of
    Cruelty to Animals 239, 240, 242

S
safety 29
    home and garden 148–52, 214–7
    road 29, 119–20
SAGA Group Ltd 82
Schofield, Irene 112
scooters and buggies 100–1, 167, 195,
    212
Scotland xvi
    care homes capital limits 364
    carers' assessments 560
    concessionary fares 134
    direct payments 298, 306
    free home care 296
    free nursing care 389–90
    free personal care
        care homes 386, 389–90
        in the home 293–4
    gadgets, charging 108
    gardening services 216
    heating grants 208
    house adaptations 206
    see also representation, Scottish
        Commission for the Regulation
        of Care, Scottish Social Services
        Council, Update
Scottish Commission for the
    Regulation of Care 53–5, 267–8
Scottish Social Services Council 54–5,
    261, 271–2
sea travel 134
seaside
    moving to 167
    visiting 224
seating in public places 117, 121, 123,
    125
self-esteem 33, 173–4
self-fulfilment 35–6
self-funders (in care homes)
    xxvi–xxvii, 284, 366–9, 377–9

senile dementia *see* dementia
Senior Railcard 130
Severe Disability Premium 174
sexual needs and activity 11, 33, 96,
    109, 535–6, 565
sheltered housing 34, 159–61,
    179–201, 225
    very sheltered housing 182
    see also retirement housing,
        Supporting People
Sherlock, Amanda 412
Shoard, Gladys xxii, xxiv, 102, 120,
    220, 225, 229, 287, 355, 405,
    440–1, 449, 450, 454, 470, 546
Shoard, Harold xxiii
Shoard, John xxiv, 440–1, 546
Shoard, Marion xvi, xxiv, 120, 220,
    229, 230, 270, 287, 327, 350–1,
    405, 440–1, 449, 450, 454, 470,
    546
Shopmobility 102, 123
shopping 21, 97, 118, 121, 122–3, 124,
    126, 272, 2281–2, 289, 301
Sikh Community Care Project 233
Sikhism 38–9, 235–8
single assessment process 290–1
sleep 13, 14
social activity, value of 30–4, 218
social and demographic change
    xvii–iii
social care workers *see* care workers
Social Fund 498
social services departments of local
    authorities 44–53
    abuse 51–3, 606
    advice 232, 274, 316
    care homes 317–8, 329, 364–8,
        373–84, 392–3, 409
    community care responsibilities
        272–307
    complaints and appeals 49, 579–80
    dealing with 48–9
    eligibility criteria 206
    equipment in the home 108, 109

history 43
home adaptations 204–7
hospital discharge 465–7
performance indicators 47
perverse incentive to encourage
    care home entry 284
records, inspecting 50–1
sensory support teams 105
spending on eldercare 47–8, 274,
    284
Social Security Offices 499–501
Social Services Inspectorate 54
social workers (care managers)
    xxv–xxvi, 45–6, 275
qualifications 46–7
registration 54–5
see also Social Services departments
    of local authorities
Society of Friends (Quakers) 36, 239
Spain 168
speech and language therapists 73,
    440
spiritual needs 36–40, 234–9
spouses and partners 547–9
legal responsibilities 170, 547
sport 140
stairs 161–2, 214
stair-lifts 96
benefits, state financial 481–501
administration and advice
    499–501
for carers 568–9
disability 485–9
see also under name of benefit
Standing Nursing and Midwifery
    Advisory Committee 429
Stockport Metropolitan Borough
    Council 119–20
Strategic Rail Authority 117
strokes 4, 8, 20, 23, 24, 86, 94, 111,
    148, 151
acute care 438–441
causes 8, 436–7
exercise 139

hospital 421, 436–46
medication 258
multi-infarct dementia 8
rehabilitation 441–6
symptoms 437
voluntary organizations and self-
    help groups 86, 446
see also blood pressure, trans-
    ischaemic attacks
Stroke Association 86, 446
subcutaneous infusion 457
suicide 253
supported housing 176–7, 291
Supporting People 180, 199, 291–2
swallowing difficulties 26, 431, 440
sweating 9, 26
Swift, Cameron 157
swimming 138–9, 164
Sykes, Nigel 461–2
syncope 148

T
t'ai chi 140
Tarlow, B. 551
tax, income 264
taxis 135, 165, 166, 167
telephones and textphones 92–3
television licences 489–90
teeth 10, 20–1
see also dental care
temperature
body 9, 147, 207
room 10, 162, 173, 346, 347
terminal illness
definition 459
right to choose place of care 57
see also hospices, palliative care
Thatcher, Margaret 14, 285
time-sheets 286
Torrington, Judith 342–3, 347
touch sensation 15, 146, 149
town centres, living in 166–7
train travel 117, 128–31
trans-ischaemic attacks 148

Transport for London 132–3
Tripscope 85, 129, 132
trusts
    discretionary 375
    life interest 375

U
Underground 132–3
United States of America 6, 218, 239
University of the Third Age 36, 406
Update 84
urban environment xiii–xiv, 116–26, 150, 166–7, 169
urinary system 13
    see also incontinence

V
Vaughan Williams, Ralph 7
vision impairment 93, 94, 100, 105, 124, 125, 126, 196, 213, 225, 286, 340, 490
    aids 92, 93, 100
    see also age-related macular degeneration, lighting
vitamins
    degradation by cooking 21, 280
    needs 18–22
voluntary organizations 78–87
    see also under name of organization
volunteers 272, 547
voting 362, 406–7

W
Wales xvi
    Cabinet Committee on the Needs of Older People 45
    care homes capital limits 364

concessionary fares 135
direct payments 306
free nursing care 385
heating grants 208
house adaptations and repairs grants 205
National Older People's Forum 45
War Pensioner's Mobility Supplement 127
Warm Front Plus grants 208, 211
warmth *see* temperature
water *see* nutrition, fluids
websites 87
weight 22–3
welfare power of attorney (Scotland) 473, 535–6
West Midlands 135–6
wheelchairs 102–3, 107
Williams, Sharon 254
wills *see* inheritance
Wiltshire County Council 165
Winter Fuel Payments 209, 490
withholding and withdrawing life-prolonging treatment 447–58, 536
withdrawership 523
Women's Institutes 220
Women's Royal Voluntary Service 280
World Health Organization 27, 460
wound healing 9, 19
Wright, Fay 391–2

Y
yoga 141, 143–4
YMCA 143

Z
Zimmer walking frames 15, 99, 107